Taxes For Canadians For Dummies®, 2001 Edition

Ten Answers to the Most Commonly Asked Tax Questions

1. **Where do I file?**

   The address where you send your tax return depends on where you live. The Canada Customs and Revenue Agency (CCRA) sends you mailing labels in your tax package each year, but if you've misplaced them you can visit the CCRA Web site at `www.ccra-adrc.gc.ca/tax/individuals/faq/t1filingaddress-e.html` to obtain the address of the tax office where you should send your return. You can also call 1-800-959-8281 to find out this information.

2. **When is my return due?**

   Your 2000 income tax return is due on Monday, April 30, 2001 (or June 30, 2001, if you or your spouse ran a business in 2000). If you owe taxes, make sure that your return is postmarked *before* midnight Monday to avoid late filing penalties and interest.

3. **What happens if I file late?**

   If you file your return late and you owe taxes, you'll automatically be charged a penalty of 5 percent of your balance owing. On top of that, you'll face a penalty of 1 percent of the balance owing for each month your return remains outstanding, to a maximum of 12 months. And don't forget the interest; the CCRA charges interest, compounded daily, on outstanding balances and penalties. Currently the interest rate on overdue taxes is 10 percent!

4. **Can I adjust my return if I find a mistake?**

   Yes, you can file a T1 Adjustment using form T1-ADJ (T1 Adjustment Request) to amend your return for any mistakes you may find after the fact.

5. **How do I answer the foreign reporting question on page 1?**

   You're required to report any foreign property you own if the total cost exceeds $100,000. Form T1135 (Foreign Income Verification Statement) should be used to report this to the CCRA. If you fail to answer this question and don't file the form, you'll be charged a basic penalty of $25 per day, with a minimum of $100 and a maximum of $2,500.

6. **How do I get a social insurance number (SIN)?**

   If you need a social insurance number, be sure to download an application form from Human Resources Development Canada's Web site at `www.hrdc-drhc.gc.ca`. You can also visit an office in your area.

7. **Do I have to mail in my return?**

   With the boom in recent technology, you have many options in terms of how to file your return. You can telefile using your home phone, netfile using your computer, or e-file using an approved e-filer.

8. **I have foreign income to report. What exchange rate do I use?**

   The CCRA posts on its Web site a link to the monthly and annual average exchange rates from the Bank of Canada. There you'll find every exchange rate for every currency you might need.

9. **Where can I get missing forms?**

   The majority of the CCRA forms are available on the CCRA Web site. To order forms by phone, call 1-800-959-2221. If you're missing the package and guide sent to you by the CCRA, you can pick up a copy at your local post office.

10. **When will I hear back from the CCRA?**

    Unfortunately, this is hard to predict. It depends a lot on when and how you file your return. If you file electronically, either by e-file or netfile in March or early April, you should hear back sooner than if you paper file on April 30. Whatever your method, if you haven't heard anything back in six to eight weeks, you should call your local CCRA office.

Taxes For Canadians For Dummies®, 2001 Edition

Savvy Tax Tips for Making the Most of Your Return

Ensure that you have completed all the required information in the identification section on page 1 of your return.

Make sure your name and address are spelled correctly, and that your social insurance number is correct. Also ensure that you've entered your birth date and marital status.

Enter your province or territory of residence as of December 31.

This will determine how much provincial or territorial tax you will pay, as well as what provincial or territorial tax credits you are entitled to.

Apply for the GST/HST credit.

Check the box on page 1 of your return, which asks if you are applying for GST/HST credits. Make sure you fill in your spouse's income and the number of children, if applicable.

Compare this year's return to last year's.

If for no obvious reason your income for this year is significantly lower than that for last year, you may be missing some reporting slips. Alternatively, you may have forgotten to claim some deductions or credits that you claimed last year.

Double-check all calculations.

Particularly if you've prepared your tax return by hand, ensure that you've added and deducted numbers properly, and entered the totals on the correct line.

Make sure you've claimed all the credits and deductions to which you're entitled.

Some of the most common deductions and credits people forget to claim include provincial credits, equivalent-to-spouse amounts, child care deductions, and tuition and education amounts. Believe it or not, some people even forget to claim the basic personal amount.

Double-check that you've accurately entered the income tax withheld at source.

Making a mistake on this number means a dollar-for-dollar error in the amount of tax you'll either pay or receive back.

And last but not least, if you're mailing in your return, make sure you sign it!

The CCRA may just assess your return without a signature, but there is the risk that they will send it back asking for a signature. You don't want to risk this kind of unnecessary delay.

Where Do I Turn for Help?

The CCRA doesn't want you wandering aimlessly in the dark in search of answers to your tax questions. It's here to help. Here's some ways you can make contact.

- CCRA Web site? `www.ccra-adrc.gc.ca`
- Need forms? Call 1-800-959-2221
- Have an income tax question? Call 1-800-959-8281
- Wondering where your refund is? Call 1-800-959-1956
- Waiting for your GST credit? Call 1-800-959-1953
- Waiting for your child tax benefit? Call 1-800-387-1193
- TIPS automated service 1-800-267-6999
- Teletypewriter Enquire service 1-800-665-0354

2000 Federal Tax Brackets

Taxable Income	*Tax on Lower Limit*	*Tax on Excess*
$0 to $30,004	0	17%
$30,005–$60,009	$5,101	25%
$60,010 and above	$12,602	29%

2000 Top Marginal Tax Rates

	Interest	*Dividends*	*Capital Gains*
British Columbia	51.3	34.6	34.2
Alberta	43.7	29.8	29.1
Saskatchewan	49.7	34.7	33.1
Manitoba	48.1	34.8	32.0
Ontario	47.9	32.3	31.9
Quebec	50.7	35.0	33.8
New Brunswick	48.8	32.9	32.5
Nova Scotia	48.8	32.9	32.5
Prince Edward Island	48.8	32.9	32.5
Newfoundland	51.3	34.6	34.2
Yukon	45.4	30.6	30.2
Nunavat/N.W.T.	43.5	29.4	29.0

Cheat Sheet $2.95 value. Item 3-20-2.
For more information about CDG Books Canada, call 1-877-963-8830.

TM

References for the Rest of Us!™

BESTSELLING BOOK SERIES

Do you find that traditional reference books are overloaded with technical details and advice you'll never use? Do you postpone important life decisions because you just don't want to deal with them? Then our *...For Dummies®* business and general reference book series is for you.

...For Dummies business and general reference books are written for those frustrated and hard-working souls who know they aren't dumb, but find that the myriad of personal and business issues and the accompanying horror stories make them feel helpless. *...For Dummies* books use a lighthearted approach, a down-to-earth style, and even cartoons and humorous icons to dispel fears and build confidence. Lighthearted but not lightweight, these books are perfect survival guides to solve your everyday personal and business problems.

"...Dummies books consistently live up to their brand-name promise to transform 'can't into can.' "
— Ottawa Citizen

"...set up in bits and bites that are easy to digest, full of no-nonsense advice."
— The Calgary Herald

"...clear, straightforward information laced with a touch of humour."
— The Toronto Star

Already, millions of satisfied readers agree. They have made *...For Dummies* the #1 introductory level computer book series and a best-selling business book series. They have written asking for more. So, if you're looking for the best and easiest way to learn about business and other general reference topics, look to *...For Dummies* to give you a helping hand.

8/99

Taxes For Canadians FOR DUMMIES®

Taxes For Canadians FOR DUMMIES®

by Christie Henderson, CA, CFP;
Brian Quinlan, CA, CFP;
Chris Saunders, CA;
Suzanne Schultz, CA, CFP;
Leigh Vyn, CA, CFP

CDG Books Canada, Inc.

◆ Toronto, ON ◆

Taxes For Canadians For Dummies®

Published by
CDG Books Canada, Inc.
99 Yorkville Avenue
Suite 400
Toronto, ON M5R 3K5
www.cdgbooks.com (CDG Books Canada Web Site)
www.idgbooks.com (IDG Books Worldwide Web Site)
www.dummies.com (Dummies Press Web Site)

Canadian Cataloguing in Publication Data

Taxes for Canadians for dummies

Includes index.
ISBN: 1-894413-20-2

1. Income tax — Law and legislation — Canada — Popular works. 2. Tax planning — Canada — Popular works. I. Henderson, Christie.

KE5682.T39 2000 343.7105'2 C00-931652-3

Printed in Canada

1 2 3 4 5 VI 04 03 02 01 00

Distributed in Canada by CDG Books Canada, Inc.

For general information on CDG Books, including all IDG Books Worldwide publications, please call our distribution center: HarperCollins Canada at 1-800-387-0117. For reseller information, including discounts and premium sales, please call our Sales department at 1-877-963-8830.

This book is available at special discounts for bulk purchases by your group or organization for resale, premiums, fundraising and seminars. For details, contact CDG Books Canada, Special Sales Department, 99 Yorkville Avenue, Suite 400, Toronto, ON, M5K 3K5; Tel: 416-963-8830; Email: spmarkets@cdgbooks.com.

For press review copies, author interviews, or other publicity information, please contact our Marketing department at 416-963-8830, fax 416-923-4821, or e-mail publicity@cdgbooks.com.

About the Authors

Christie Henderson, CA, CFP, is a partner with Henderson Partners LLP. She has spent over six years in public practice, specializing in financial and tax planning. Christie's undergraduate degree is from Dalhousie University. Christie qualified for the CA designation with Ernst & Young, Toronto, in 1998, and has completed the CICA's in-depth tax course. Christie's clientele consists largely of entrepreneurial owner-managers, executives, and their families. She provides comprehensive financial planning, including retirement planning, investment planning, insurance needs, estate planning, stock option planning, and business succession planning.

Brian Quinlan, CA, CFP, is a partner with Campbell Lawless LLP, in Toronto. He works with individuals and owner-managed businesses to minimize their tax so they can maximize their cash! Brian is a contributing editor at *Canadian MoneySaver Magazine*. His tax planning articles have also been published in a number of other publications. Brian has been a guest on TVOntario's *Money Talks* and Rogers Cable TV's *The Prosperity Show*. He has instructed tax courses for the Institute of Chartered Accountants of Ontario and at Ryerson Polytechnic University, and is a frequent speaker at tax and financial planning seminars. Brian has two income-splitting vehicles: Andrew, ten and Tara, seven.

Chris Saunders, CA, is a graduate of McMaster University, in Hamilton, Ontario, where he holds both Bachelor of Commerce and Master of Business Administration degrees. He obtained his designation as a CA in 1994 and is currently a member of the Institutes of Chartered Accountants of Ontario and British Columbia. In 1997, Chris completed the CICA's in-depth tax course. In addition to this book, Chris has writing credits on several other tax books, including *A Declaration of Taxpayer's Rights*, *R+D Taxation*, and *Winning the Tax Game.* Over the past five years, he and colleague Tim Cestnick have worked on several projects that aimed to educate the average Canadian taxpayer about the opportunities and pitfalls inherent in the Canadian tax system. Chris is currently a technical advisor and tax group manager for a large Canadian institution.

Suzanne Schultz, CA, CFP, is a senior tax manager at The WaterStreet Group, where she provides tax consulting services to a wide range of clients. She has authored courses on corporate taxes and trusts for CCH Canadian Limited, written columns for *The Globe and Mail's* Report on Business section, and has appeared on the television shows such as *The Prosperity Show* and *Investment Television.* Before joining The WaterStreet Group, Suzanne was a tax manager for KPMG. Suzanne received her Bachelor of Commerce. from Dalhousie University and then went on to obtain her CA designation, earning a place on the Ontario Honour Role (14th out of 1,200 writers). Suzanne has also completed the CICA's in-depth tax course, and is a member of the Canadian Tax Foundation.

Leigh Vyn, CA, CFP, is a Tax Manager at The WaterStreet Group, where she provides tax consulting services to clients that include high net worth individuals and owner-managers. She has written articles for CI Mutual Funds, is a regular columnist for *Canadian Shareowner Magazine,* and has co-written articles for *The Globe and Mail*'s Net Worth section. She has co-authored courses for CCH Canadian Limited and assisted with updating the bestseller, *Winning The Tax Game*. Leigh received her Honours Bachelor of Commerce at McMaster University, in Hamilton, Ontario, and then began her accounting career at KPMG. She obtained her CA designation in 1997, and completed the CICA's in-depth tax course. Leigh is a member of the Canadian Tax Foundation.

The WaterStreet Group Inc. is a tax education and consulting firm based in Burlington, Ontario. The firm is affiliated exclusively with the Berkshire Group of Companies. You can contact the WaterStreet Group Inc. at (905) 331-3805 or by e-mail at `www.group@waterstreet.ca`.

ABOUT CDG BOOKS CANADA, INC. AND IDG BOOKS WORLDWIDE, INC.

Welcome to the world of IDG Books Worldwide and CDG Books Canada.

IDG Books Worldwide, Inc., is a subsidiary of International Data Group, Inc., the world's largest publisher of computer-related information and the leading global provider of information services on information technology. IDG was founded more than 30 years ago and now employs more than 9,000 people worldwide. IDG publishes more than 295 computer publications in over 75 countries (see listing below). More than 90 million people read one or more IDG publications each month.

Launched in 1990, IDG Books Worldwide is today the #1 publisher of best-selling computer books in North America. IDG Books Worldwide is proud to be the recipient of eight awards from the Computer Press Association in recognition of editorial excellence and three from *Computer Currents'* First Annual Readers' Choice Awards. Our best-selling *...For Dummies®* series has more than 55 million copies in print with translations in 31 languages. In record time, IDG Books Worldwide has become the first choice for millions of readers around the world who want to learn how to better manage their businesses.

In 1998, IDG Books Worldwide formally partnered with Macmillan Canada, a subsidiary of Canada Publishing Corporation, to create CDG Books Canada, a dynamic new Canadian publishing company. CDG Books Canada is now Canada's fastest growing publisher, bringing valuable information to Canadians from coast to coast through the introduction of Canadian *...For Dummies®* and *CliffsNotes™* titles.

Every one of our books is designed to bring extra value and skill-building instructions to the reader. Our books are written by experts who understand and care about our readers. The knowledge base of our editorial staff comes from years of experience in publishing, education, and journalism — experience we use to produce books to carry us into the new millennium. In short, we care about books, so we attract the best people. We devote special attention to details such as audience, interior design, use of icons, and illustrations. And because we use an efficient process of authoring, editing, and desktop publishing our books electronically, we can spend more time ensuring superior content and spend less time on the technicalities of making books.

You can count on our commitment to deliver high-quality books at competitive prices on topics you want to read about. At IDG Books Worldwide and CDG Books Canada, we continue in the IDG tradition of delivering quality for more than 30 years. You can learn more about IDG Books Worldwide and CDG Books Canada by visiting `www.idgbooks.com`, `www.dummies.com`, and `www.cdgbooks.com`.

Eighth Annual Computer Press Awards 1992

Ninth Annual Computer Press Awards 1993

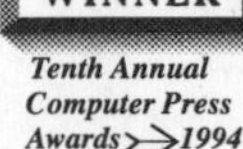

Tenth Annual Computer Press Awards 1994

Eleventh Annual Computer Press Awards 1995

IDG is the world's leading IT media, research and exposition company. Founded in 1964, IDG had 1997 revenues of $2.05 billion and has more than 9,000 employees worldwide. IDG offers the widest range of media options that reach IT buyers in 75 countries representing 95% of worldwide IT spending. IDG's diverse product and services portfolio spans six key areas including print publishing, online publishing, expositions and conferences, market research, education and training, and global marketing services. More than 90 million people read one or more of IDG's 290 magazines and newspapers, including IDG's leading global brands — Computerworld, PC World, Network World, Macworld and the Channel World family of publications. IDG Books Worldwide is one of the fastest-growing computer book publishers in the world, with more than 700 titles in 36 languages. The "...For Dummies®" series alone has more than 50 million copies in print. IDG offers online users the largest network of technology-specific Web sites around the world through IDG.net (http://www.idg.net), which comprises more than 225 targeted Web sites in 55 countries worldwide. International Data Corporation (IDC) is the world's largest provider of information technology data, analysis and consulting, with research centers in over 41 countries and more than 400 research analysts worldwide. IDG World Expo is a leading producer of more than 168 globally branded conferences and expositions in 35 countries including E3 (Electronic Entertainment Expo), Macworld Expo, ComNet, Windows World Expo, ICE (Internet Commerce Expo), Agenda, DEMO, and Spotlight. IDG's training subsidiary, ExecuTrain, is the world's largest computer training company, with more than 230 locations worldwide and 785 training courses. IDG Marketing Services helps industry-leading IT companies build international brand recognition by developing global integrated marketing programs via IDG's print, online and exposition products worldwide. Further information about the company can be found at www.idg.com.

8/24/99

Authors' Acknowledgements

With five authors contributing to this book, we'd like to recognize the following people for their assistance: A special thanks to Tim Cestnick, CA, CFP, TEP, president of The WaterStreet Group Inc., who worked closely with us to complete and edit each chapter. Thanks also to Sandra Lansing of Campbell Lawless LLP for her hard work in formatting the chapters, and to Karen Ellis of The WaterStreet Group Inc., who ensured that all of our deadlines were met.

A sincere thanks to our editor, Joan Whitman, and the staff at CDG Books Inc. for having so much confidence in us to write the first edition of *Taxes for Canadians for Dummies*. We'd also like to thank them for helping us transform what is normally a very dry subject into one that is fun to read and easy to understand.

Thanks to Denyse Becker, at Public Works and Government Services Canada, and Hélène Gauthier, Paul McGregor, and Norm Schroeder, all at Canada Customs and Revenue Agency, for granting permission to reproduce the many tax forms in this book, and for helping secure the 2000 versions.

And finally, we'd all like to thank our families for their patience and support while we wrote this book.

Publisher's Acknowledgements

We're proud of this book; please register your comments through our IDG Books Worldwide Online Registration Form located at `http://my2cents.dummies.com`.

Some of the people who helped bring this book to market include the following:

Acquisitions and Editorial

Editorial Director: Joan Whitman

Associate Editor: Melanie Rutledge

Copy Editor: Allyson Latta

Editorial Assistant: Stella Partheniou

Production

Director of Production: Donna Brown

Production Editor: Rebecca Conolly

Layout and Graphics: Kim Monteforte, Heidy Lawrance Associates

Proofreader: Pamela Erlichman

Indexer: Liba Berry

Special Help

Amy Black, Michael Kelly

General and Administrative

IDG Books Worldwide, Inc.: John Kilcullen, CEO; William Barry, President

CDG Books Canada, Inc.: Ron Besse, Chairman; Tom Best, President; Robert Harris, Vice President and Publisher

IDG Books Technology Publishing Group: Richard Swadley, Senior Vice President and Publisher; Walter Bruce III, Vice President and Associate Publisher; Mary Bednarek, Branded Product Development Director; Mary Corder, Editorial Director

IDG Books Consumer Publishing Group: Roland Elgey, Senior Vice President and Publisher; Kathleen A. Welton, Vice President and Publisher; Kevin Thornton, Acquisitions Manager; Kristin A. Cocks, Editorial Director

IDG Books Internet Publishing Group: Brenda McLaughlin, Senior Vice President and Publisher; Diane Graves Steele, Vice President and Associate Publisher; Sofia Marchant, Online Marketing Manager

IDG Books Production for Dummies Press: Michael R. Britton, Vice President of Production; Debbie Stailey, Associate Director of Production; Cindy L. Phipps, Manager of Project Coordination, Production Proofreading, and Indexing; Tony Augsburger, Manager of Prepress, Reprints, and Systems; Laura Carpenter, Production Control Manager; Shelley Lea, Supervisor of Graphics and Design; Debbie J. Gates, Production Systems Specialist; Robert Springer, Supervisor of Proofreading; Kathie Schutte, Production Supervisor

Dummies Packaging and Book Design: Patty Page, Manager, Promotions Marketing

◆

The publisher would like to give special thanks to Patrick J. McGovern, without whom this book would not have been possible.

◆

Contents at a Glance

Introduction *1*

Part I: Getting Ready to File *7*

Chapter 1: Canada's Tax System and Rates 9
Chapter 2: Who Pays Taxes in Canada? 17
Chapter 3: Filing Non-Tax Returns 29
Chapter 4: Special Taxation Situations 43
Chapter 5: Getting and Staying Organized 55
Chapter 6: Dealing with Those Taxing Administrative Matters 63
Chapter 7: Going Over Your Preparation Options 73
Chapter 8: Different Forms for Different Folks: Choosing the Right One for You 83

Part II: Types of Income in Canada *95*

Chapter 9: Understanding Employment- Related Income 97
Chapter 10: Pension Income and Your Taxes 105
Chapter 11: Dealing with Other Types of Income 121
Chapter 12: Interest and Other Investment Income 139
Chapter 13: Capital Gains and Losses 155
Chapter 14: Reporting Other Income on Your Return 173
Chapter 15: Dealing with Self-Employment Income and Taxes 179

Part III: Tax Deductions and Credits *209*

Chapter 16: Calculating Your Net Income 211
Chapter 17: Calculating Your Taxable Income 239
Chapter 18: Non-Refundable Tax Credits 259

Part IV: Calculation of Federal and Provincial Taxes and Credits ... *273*

Chapter 19: Figuring Out Your Federal Tax 275
Chapter 20: Looking at Provincial and Territorial Taxes and Credits (Line 428) 285
Chapter 21: Other Items: Questions and Opportunities for Taxpayers 311

Part V: After You've Filed *319*

Chapter 22: CCRA Administration 321
Chapter 23: Dealing with Canada Customs and Revenue Agency 333

Part VI: Tax Planning Tips *343*

Chapter 24: Income Splitting with Your Family 345
Chapter 25: Taxes and Estate Planning 353
Chapter 26: Tax Breaks for Employees 365
Chapter 27: Tax Planning for Your Small Business 383
Chapter 28: Strategies for Retirement 401
Chapter 29: Using Investments to Manage Your Taxes 409

Part VII: The Part of Tens *419*
Chapter 30: Ten Ways to Reduce the Risk of an Audit 421
Chapter 31: Top Ten Tax Filing Tips 425
Chapter 32: Top Ten Tax Changes for 2000 429

Appendix A: Tax Forms 433

Index *579*

Cartoons at a Glance

By Rich Tennant

"Leveling, grading and terracing the land IS a deductable expense—for FARMERS Mr. Daniels, not for people with putting greens in their backyards."

page 7

"I set up everything for you to do your taxes. I put out your calculator, plenty of pencils, and a large morphine drip."

page 343

"Here's what I think happened—He was wounded by Schedule 4. Then he was hit by Schedule 3; this brings him to his knees. Then, as he's crawling to reach his calculator, he gets it square in the pocketbook by Schedule 1, and that's what did him in."

page 209

"You know that mail order company that promised to show you how to avoid a tax audit? Well, their package just arrived."

page 95

"Here's the tricky part: pillage is not taxed if derived out of the country. However, it is considered part of your overall plunder done locally."

page 419

"I put an extension on my tax return like you suggested, but I still don't think it's going to get there on time."

page 273

page 319

Fax: 978-546-7747
E-mail: richtennant@the5thwave.com
World Wide Web: www.the5thwave.com
Fax: 978-546-7747 • E-mail: the5wave@tiac.net

Table of Contents

Introduction 1

Why Buy This Tax Book? 1
How to Use This Book 2
Your Tax Road Map 2
Part I: Getting Ready to File 2
Part II: Types of Income in Canada 3
Part III: Tax Deductions and Credits 3
Part IV: Calculation of Federal and Provincial Taxes and Credits 3
Part V: After You've Filed 3
Part VI: Tax Planning Tips 3
Part VII: The Part of Tens 4
Appendixes 4
Icons Used in This Book 4

Part I: Getting Ready to File 7

Chapter 1: Canada's Tax System and Rates 9

Taking the Mystery Out of Canada's Tax System 9
Tax legislation — administration and enforcement 10
Tax planning: A continual process 11
You have the right to pay less tax! 11
What you don't know can hurt your finances 12
The Provincial and Territorial Tax Systems 12
Tax-on-tax systems 12
Tax-on-income systems 13
Taxes in Quebec 13
My Taxes Are How High? 14
Tallying up your effective tax rate 15
Calculating your marginal tax rate 16

Chapter 2: Who Pays Taxes in Canada? 17

Who Is a Canadian Resident? 17
Factors in determining Canadian residency 17
Deemed residents 19
Part-year residents 19
Non-residents 20
Do You Have to File a Tax Return? 21
Filing: Not Just By Invitation Only 22
You disposed of property or claimed a capital gains reserve 22
You received Old Age Security benefits 23
You received Employment Insurance benefits 23
You had funds "clawed back" from you 23
You made a withdrawal from your RRSP under the Home Buyer's Plan or the Lifelong Learning Plan 23
You contributed to the Canada Pension Plan 24
When You May Want to File a Tax Return 24
You've paid too much tax in the year 24
You are entitled to a GST/HST credit 25

You want to receive, or continue to receive, the Child Tax Benefit 25
You are entitled to provincial or territorial tax credits 25
You want to maximize your RRSP contribution room for future years 26
You've paid too much in CPP or EI premiums in the year 27
You have deductions or credits to carry forward to future years 27
You will have a non-capital loss this year 28

Chapter 3: Filing Non-Tax Returns 29

What Is an Information Return? 29
Partnership Income 29
How do I know if I have to file a Partnership Information Return? 30
Partnerships that do not have to file a Partnership Information Return 30
Practical considerations 30
Non-residents of Canada 34
Transactions with non-residents 34
Other Foreign Reporting Requirements 39
Transfer Pricing 39
Information Return of Non–arm's Length Transactions with Non-residents 40
When to file 40
Where to file 41

Chapter 4: Special Taxation Situations 43

Status Indians 43
Leaving Canada 44
Departure tax 44
Filing requirements 46
Newcomers, Welcome to Canada 47
Deemed acquisition rules 48
Filing requirements 48
The Sure Things: Death and Taxes 49
Minimizing your estate taxes 49
Filing requirements at time of death 50
Bankruptcy 51
The bankruptcy rules 51
Special trustee's return 53
Discharge from bankruptcy 53
Absolute versus conditional discharges from bankruptcy 53

Chapter 5: Getting and Staying Organized 55

Keeping Good Books and Records 55
Setting up your record-keeping system 56
Your friend the computer 56
Valuable record-keeping tips 57
Record-keeping timebombs 57
How Long Should I Keep My Tax Records? 57
Missing Information Slips and Receipts 58
Giving the CCRA your best estimate 58
Missing receipts 59
What to Do if the Dog Really Did Eat Your Tax Records 59
Reconstructing missing or damaged tax records 59
Giving them the business: Tips for recreating your records 60
The Cohan Rule 60

Chapter 6: Dealing with Those Taxing Administrative Matters 63

Administration of Tax Law in Canada 63
Declaration of Taxpayer's Rights 64

Social Insurance Numbers 64
- Getting a social insurance number 65
- If you file a return with no SIN 65

When Is My T1 Return Due? 65
- If you are self-employed 65
- Deceased persons 66

Where Should I Send My Completed Tax Return? 66
Withholding Tax 67
- How is the amount withheld determined? 67
- Can I reduce the amount of tax withheld at source? 67
- Can I have my withholdings increased? 67
- Payments to non-residents 68
- Income not subject to withholdings 68

When Is My Tax Payment Due? 68
When Am I Subject to Instalments? 69
- Calculating your instalments 69
- Interest and penalties 70

Technical Interpretations 71
Advance Tax Rulings 71

Chapter 7: Going Over Your Preparation Options 73

Get Out Your Pen and Paper: Calling All Do-It-Yourselfers 73
Using Your Computer to Tally Up Your Taxes 74
- The perks and perils of going the techno route 74
- Shopping for tax software 74

Surfing Your Way to Tax Help 75
When to Get Help from the Tax Collector 75
- The TIPS service 76
- Visiting your local Tax Services Office 76
- Enquiring by phone 76

Making the Most of Tax Pros 77
- Hiring a preparer 77
- Hiring an accountant 78
- Where to find a bean counter 78
- Questions to ask your tax professional 78

E-Filing Versus Paper Filing 79
- What are the benefits of e-filing? 80
- Who can e-file? 80
- Are my chances of audit lower if I e-file? 80

Tele-filing 80
Net-filing 81
Where to Get Forms and Other Information 81

Chapter 8: Different Forms for Different Folks: Choosing the Right One for You 83

The T1 General 83
- Taking apart the T1 83
- One T1 for all of Canada? 84

The T1 Special 85
- The short story on short forms 85
- T1S-Special 86
- Not so fast tax filer: When the short route doesn't work 86
- T1S-A Pensioners 87
- T1S-B Wage and Salary Earners 87
- T1S-C Tax Credit 87
- T1S-D Native Canadians 87

Returns for the Deceased 88
- Understanding the prior period return 88

Filing a final return 88
The Return for Rights and Things 89
Return for a Partner or a Proprietor 90
Return for income from a testamentary trust 90
T3 Trust Income Tax and Information Return 90
Returns that Deal with Bankruptcy 91
Pre-bankruptcy 91
Pre-bankruptcy Return 92
Post-bankruptcy 92
Trustee Return 93
Dealing with bankruptcies that straddle a calendar year-end 93

Part II: Types of Income in Canada 95

Chapter 9: Understanding Employment-Related Income 97
What Is Employment Income? 97
Employee Versus Self-Employed 97
Taxable Benefits and Non-Taxable Benefits 99
Taxable benefits 99
Non-taxable benefits 102
Other Employment Income 103

Chapter 10: Pension Income and Your Taxes 105
First Things First — What Isn't Pension Income? 105
Canada's Income Security Programs (ISPs) 105
OAS Pension 106
Non-resident recipients of OAS 106
OAS eligibility criteria 106
Guaranteed Income Supplement (GIS) 108
Applying for the GIS and yearly renewal 108
Is the GIS taxable? 108
Spouse's Allowance 108
Widowed Spouse's Allowance 108
Old Age Security repayment 109
Lose all your OAS! 110
OAS overpayments 111
Income from the Canada Pension Plan (CPP) and Quebec Pension Plan (QPP) (Line 114) 111
Reporting your CPP/QPP income on your tax return 112
Lump sum CPP or QPP benefit 112
CPP versus QPP 112
Canada Pension Plan retirement pension 112
Reduction in CPP retirement pension 113
Increasing your CPP retirement pension 114
How do you decide when to start taking your CPP retirement pension? 114
Other benefits offered by the Canada Pension Plan 114
CPP retirement pension sharing or CPP splitting 116
CPP and marriage breakdown — splitting CPP credits 117
CPP or QPP overpayments 117
Other Pensions and Superannuation (Line 115) 117
Types of pension income 118
Foreign pension income 118
Non-Taxable Pension Income 119
Pension credit 120
Transferring Pension Income 120

Chapter 11: Dealing with Other Types of Income 121

Line 119: Employment Insurance Benefits (EI) 121
- EI clawback 121
- EI premiums 122

Line 122: Limited and Non-Active Partnership Income 122
- At-risk amount 122
- The T5013 122

Line 126: Rental Income 123
- Reasonable expectation of profit 123
- Types of rental income 124
- Undeveloped land 124
- Real estate rentals — deductible expenses 125
- Rental of your own residence 127
- Capital versus current expenditures 127
- Capital cost allowance 128
- Foreign rental income 130
- Restrictions on rental losses 131

Line 128: Support Payments 131
- Old rules (pre-May 1, 1997) 132
- New rules (post-April 30, 1997) 132
- Specific purpose payments 132

Line 129: RRSP and RRIF Income 133
- Withdrawals from an RRSP 134
- Withdrawals of unused or over- contributions to an RRSP 135
- Home purchase loans 136
- Lifelong Learning Plan 136
- Spousal RRSPs 136

Line 144: Workers' Compensation Benefits (WCB) 138

Line 145: Social Assistance 138

Chapter 12: Interest and Other Investment Income 139

Line 120 Dividends 139
- Canadian source dividends 139
- Stock dividends 141
- Foreign dividends 141
- Claiming dividends received by your spouse 143
- Non-taxable dividends 143

Line 121: Interest and Other Investment Income 144
- How to report interest income 144
- Types of interest income 144
- Methods of reporting interest income 145
- Special reporting methods for certain investments 145
- Interest on foreign source income 147
- Shareholder and employee loans 147
- What is a trust or estate? 149
- Why use a trust? 150
- Income of a trust 150
- Taxation of a trust 150

Registered Education Savings Plan Income (RESP) 151
- Distribution from an RESP 151

Other Investment Income 152
- Mutual funds 152
- Stripped bonds and clipped coupons 153
- Royalties 153
- Annuities 153
- Labour-sponsored venture capital corporations 153
- Exempt life insurance contracts 153

Chapter 13: Capital Gains and Losses 155

Capital Gains Versus Ordinary Income 155
Types of Capital Property 156
Real estate 156
Mutual fund units and shares 157
Bonds, debentures, promissory notes, and other properties 157
Treasury bills (T-bills) and stripped bonds 158
Mortgage foreclosures and conditional sale repossessions 158
Personal-use property 159
Listed personal property 160
Foreign currencies 161
Depreciable property 161
Recapture of CCA and terminal losses 162
Eligible capital property 163
When Does a Disposition Occur? 163
How to Calculate a Taxable Capital Gain or Loss 164
Calculation of adjusted cost base 164
Proceeds of disposition 165
Selling costs 165
Calculation of taxable capital gains 165
Calculation of allowable capital losses 165
Sale of a Principal Residence 166
What is your principal residence? 166
Can you have more than one principal residence? 167
Disposition of your principal residence 167
Sale of Qualified Small Business Shares 168
Sale of Qualified Farm Property 169
The Lifetime Capital Gains Exemption 170
Cumulative Net Investment Loss 170
The Capital Gains Reserve 170
How to calculate and report a reserve 171

Chapter 14: Reporting Other Income on Your Return 173

Retiring Allowances 173
Eligible allowance 173
Ineligible allowance 175
What is not a retiring allowance? 175
Scholarships, Bursaries, and Research Grants 175
What are scholarships and bursaries? 176
What is a fellowship? 176
What is a prize in my field of endeavour? 176
What is a research grant? 176
Death Benefits 177
Legal Awards 177
Foreign Income 178
More Other Income 178

Chapter 15: Dealing with Self-Employment Income and Taxes 179

The Tax Implications of Being Self-Employed 179
How does self-employment save taxes? 180
Choosing a taxation year-end for your business 180
The Accrual Method of Accounting 180
The Cash Method of Accounting 181
The Goods and Services Tax (7 percent GST)/ Harmonized Sales Tax (15 percent HST) 181
GST/HST — a consumer tax, not a business tax 182
Who can register for the GST/HST? 183
Who cannot register for GST/HST? 183

Reporting Your Self-Employment Income and Expenses on Your Tax Return 183
Lines 135 and 162: Business income 183
Lines 139 and 166: Commission income 184
Lines 137 and 164: Professional income 184
Farming income and fishing income 184
Form T2124 "Statement of Business Activities" 184
Organizing your business by the book 186
Some of the expenses you can deduct 187
Capital Cost Allowance (CCA) 192
CCA is an optional tax deduction 192
Eligibility to claim CCA 193
Calculating CCA — the declining balance method 193
Capital cost 194
Common CCA classes and rates 194
A CCA example 195
The impact on the CCA of a short taxation year 195
Undepreciated capital cost (UCC) 196
Sale of capital assets 196
Recapture and terminal loss 196
Exceptions to the declining balance method 198
Restriction on the maximum capital cost of a class 10.1 automobile 198
Eligible Capital Property (ECP) 200
Lines 137 and 164: Reporting Professional Income 201
Form T2032 "Statement of Professional Activities" 201
Work-in-progress (WIP) 201
Lines 141 and 168: Farming Income 202
Method of accounting 203
Form T2032 "Statement of Farming Activities" 203
What if you have a loss from your farming business? 204
Lines 143 and 170: Fishing Income 206
T2121 "Statement of Fishing Activities" 206

Part III: Tax Deductions and Credits 209

Chapter 16: Calculating Your Net Income..............211

Line 206: Pension Adjustment 212
Pension adjustment reversal (PAR) 212
How did the understatement of your RRSP deduction limit occur? 213
Line 207: Registered Pension Plan Deduction 213
Contributions for current service and past service for 1990 and later years 213
Past service contributions for years before 1990 214
Line 208: Registered Retirement Savings Plan (RRSP) Deduction 214
What is a registered retirement savings plan? 214
Tax savings provided by RRSPs 214
Setting up an RRSP 215
What investments are "RRSP eligible"? 215
How much can you contribute to your RRSP? 216
Spousal RRSPs 219
The RRSP Home Buyer's Plan (HBP) 219
The RRSP and Lifelong Learning Plan (LLP) 220
Transferring a severance or retirement allowance into your RRSP 220
Line 209: Saskatchewan Pension Plan (SPP) Deduction 221
Line 212: Deduction for Annual Union, Professional, or Like Dues 221
Deductions for Children and Special Care 222
Line 214: Deduction for child care expenses 222
Line 215: Deduction for attendant care expenses 225
Lines 217 and 226: Deduction for a Business Investment Loss (BIL) 226
Rules in calculating the deductible portion of the BIL 226
Further restrictions in calculating the deductible portion of a BIL 227

Line 219: Deduction for Moving Expenses 227
When can you deduct moving expenses? 227
What moving expenses are eligible? 228
Employer paid or reimbursed moving expenses 229
Coming to or leaving Canada? 229
How do you claim moving expenses on your tax return? 229
Lines 220 and 230: Deduction for Support Payments 230
Spousal support 230
Child support 230
Support payments to third parties 231
Line 221: Deduction for Carrying Charges and Interest Expense for Investments 232
More on interest that can be deducted 232
Line 224: Deduction for Exploration and Development Expenses 232
How to claim exploration and development expenses 233
Line 229: Deduction for Employment Expenses 234
Line 231: Deduction for Cleric's Residence 235
Line 232: Other Deductions 235
Legal fees 235
Repayments of OAS, CPP, QPP, and EI benefits 236
Other deductions 236
Line 234: Net Income Before Adjustments 236
Line 235: Social Benefits Repayment (OAS and EI Clawbacks) 237
Old age security (OAS) clawback 237
Employment Insurance (EI) clawback 238

Chapter 17: Calculating Your Taxable Income 239

Ordering of Deductions in Computing Taxable Income 239
Line 248: Employee Home Relocation Loans 240
Line 249: Stock Option and Shares Deductions 241
Public company shares 242
Canadian-controlled private corporations 242
Stock option deductions 242
Line 250: Other Payments Deductions 244
Lines 251 to 253: Loss Carryovers 244
Limited partnership losses 245
Non-capital losses 246
Net capital losses 248
Line 254: Capital Gains Deduction 249
Qualified small business corporation shares 250
Qualified farm property 251
The CNIL problem 252
Line 255: Northern Residents Deductions 253
Residency deduction 253
Travel benefit deductions 255
Line 256: Additional Deductions 256
Income exempt under a tax treaty 257
Vow of perpetual poverty 257
Employment with a prescribed international organization 257

Chapter 18: Non-Refundable Tax Credits 259

Line 300: Your Basic Personal Credit 259
Part-year residents 259
Non-residents 259
Line 301: Age Amount 260
Line 303: Spousal Amount 260
Line 305: Equivalent-to-Spouse Amount 261
Line 306: Amount for Infirm Dependants 261

Lines 308 to 310: Canada Pension Plan/Quebec Pension Plan Premiums 262
Canada or Quebec Pension Plan contributions payable on self-employment and other earnings 262
How to calculate your allowable contributions for CPP or QPP 263
Making additional CPP contributions 263
Line 312: Employment Insurance Premiums 263
Line 314: Pension Income Amount 264
Line 315: Caregiver Amount 264
Claims made by more than one person 265
Line 316: Disability Amount for Yourself 265
Line 318: Disability Amount Transferred from a Dependant Other Than Your Spouse 266
Line 319: Student Loan Interest 266
Line 323: Tuition and Education Amounts for Yourself 267
Tuition amount 267
Education amount 267
Transferring and carrying forward amounts 268
Line 324: Tuition and Education Amounts Transferred from a Child 269
Line 326: Amounts Transferred from Your Spouse 269
Lines 330 and 331: Medical Expenses 269
Checklist of allowable medical expenses 270
Items you cannot claim as medical expenses 270
How to calculate your medical expenses claim 271
The medical expense adjustment 271
Line 349: Donations and Gifts 271
Allowable charitable donations and government gifts 271
Cultural and ecological gifts 272
Donations of publicly traded securities 272
Donations to U.S. charities 272

Part IV: Calculation of Federal and Provincial Taxes and Credits...273

Chapter 19: Figuring Out Your Federal Tax 275

Schedule 1: Federal Tax Calculation 275
Federal tax rates 276
Alternative Minimum Taxes 276
Line 425: Federal dividend tax credit 277
Lines 431 and 433: Federal foreign tax credit 277
How to claim the federal foreign tax credit 278
Line 429: Overseas employment credit 278
Lines 409 and 410: Federal political tax credit 279
Line 412: Investment tax credit 279
Lines 413 and 414: Labour-sponsored funds tax credit 280
Line 418: Additional tax on RESP accumulated income payments 280
Line 419: Federal surtax 281
Line 421: Canada Pension Plan contributions on self-employment earnings 281
Canada Pension Plan and Employment Insurance Overpayment 281
Line 448: CPP overpayment 282
Line 448: EI overpayment 282
Line 422: Social benefits repayment 282
Line 452: Medical expense supplement 283
Line 457: Goods and Services Tax rebate 283

Chapter 20: Looking at Provincial and Territorial Taxes and Credits (Line 428) 285

Provincial and Territorial Tax Rates 285
Tax Calculation for Multiple Jurisdictions 288
 What is a permanent establishment? 288
 Completing form T2203 288
Provincial Foreign Tax Credits 289
British Columbia 290
 British Columbia tax credits 290
Alberta 291
Saskatchewan 292
 Saskatchewan tax credits 293
Manitoba 293
 Manitoba tax credits 294
Ontario 295
 Calculating Ontario taxes 295
 Ontario tax credits 297
Quebec 299
 Differences between your federal tax return and your Quebec tax return 299
 Medical expenses and refundable medical tax credit 300
Newfoundland 303
New Brunswick 304
Nova Scotia 304
Prince Edward Island 305
Yukon 306
 Yukon tax credits 306
Northwest Territories 307
 Northwest Territories tax credits 308
Nunavut 308
 Nunavut tax credits 308

Chapter 21: Other Items: Questions and Opportunities for Taxpayers 311

Elections Canada 311
Foreign Income Reporting 312
Checking Out the Goods and Services Tax Credit 313
 Who can apply? 313
 How much can I get? 314
The Child Tax Benefit 315
 Who can receive the CCTB? 315
 If I'm eligible, how do I receive the credit? 315
 How much will I receive? 316

Part V: After You've Filed 319

Chapter 22: CCRA Administration....321

Understanding Your Notice of Assessment 321
Help! I've Been Reassessed 322
Dealing with Objections 323
 When can I file a Notice of Objection? 323
 If I file an objection, should I pay the disputed amount? 324
 Will collection actions start against me while my case is under appeal? 324
 How long does it take for my appeal to be heard? 324
 What if I lose the appeal but still think I'm right? 324
 How long after I originally file my return can I be reassessed? 325
 Reassessment outside the three-year limit 325
 Waivers 326

Requests for Additional Information 327
Fixing Your Mistakes on a Return You've Sent 328
What if you discover an error several years back that would have resulted in a refund had you filed correctly the first time? 328
Late-filed elections 329
Refunds: Show Me the Money! 329
The real scoop on refunds 329
Interest on refunds 330
Direct deposit 330
Refunded interest as income 330
Balances Owing 330
Interest on balance due 331
Instalments 331
Nondeductible interest 331
Penalties and Interest 331
Late-filing penalty 331
Repeated failure to report income 332
Failure to provide complete information 332
Failure to file information returns 332
Tax evasion, gross negligence, false statements, or false credit returns 332
Criminal prosecutions 332
Waiving of interest and penalties 332

Chapter 23: Dealing with Canada Customs and Revenue Agency 333

Avoiding the Dreaded Audit 334
Types of audits 334
Avoiding an Audit 336
Scoring your return 337
Here Comes the Judge 340
Informal division hearings 340
General division hearings 341
Making an Application for Fairness 341
Voluntary Disclosures 341
Tax Evasion 342
Tax Avoidance 342
Tax Planning 342

Part VI: Tax Planning Tips 343

Chapter 24: Income Splitting with Your Family 345

Income Splitting in Action 345
Every Game Has Its Rules 345
Transfers to a spouse 346
Transfers to minor children 346
Transfer to an adult child 346
Ideas for Splitting Income 346
Lend money or investments to a family member 347
Split tax on CPP payments 347
Pay salary or wages to family 348
Transfer money for business purposes 348
Pay an allowance to a working child 349
Higher-income spouse should pay the household expenses 349
Invest Child Tax Benefits in the child's name 349
Contribute to a spousal RRSP 350
Contribute to an RESP 350

Chapter 25: Taxes and Estate Planning 353

The Big Wide World of Estate Planning 353
Do I need to plan my estate? 353
The importance of having a will 354
Death and Your Tax Bill 354
Probate fees 356
Minimizing the Taxes You Pay on Death 357
Giving your assets away today 357
Leaving them to your spouse 357
Leaving your RRSP or RRIF to a dependent child 359
Making a final RRSP contribution 360
Donating to charity after death 360
Set up a testamentary trust in your will 362

Chapter 26: Tax Breaks for Employees 365

Taking a Look at Non-Taxable Benefits 365
Tax Deductions Available to Employees 367
Employment Expenses 367
Who is eligible to deduct employment expenses? 368
Form T777 "Statement of Employment Expenses" 368
What's Deductible and What's Not? 368
Automobile Expenses 370
Capital cost allowance (CCA) when an automobile is owned rather than leased 371
Restrictions on certain automobile expenses 373
Home Office Expenses 374
A tale of two tests 374
Restrictions on deducting home office expenses 374
Deductible home office expenses 374
How to calculate the deductible costs of your home office 375
Additional Deductions 376
Transport employees 376
Musician's instruments 377
Artist's expenses 377
Cleric's residence deduction 378
Goods and Services Tax (GST)/ Harmonized Sales Tax (HST) Rebate 379
Assessing your eligibility for GST/HST rebate 379
Expenses that qualify for the GST/HST rebate 379
Expenses that do not qualify for the GST/HST rebate 380
How to calculate and claim your GST/HST rebate 380

Chapter 27: Tax Planning for Your Small Business 383

Choosing the Right Business Ownership Structure 383
Sole proprietorships 384
Partnerships 386
Corporations 388
Tax Planning Opportunities for Small Business Owners 394
Incorporate! 394
Split your income 394
Timing is everything: Asset purchases and asset disposals 395
What Expenses are Tax Deductible? 396
Home office expenses — operating your business through a sole proprietorship or partnership 396
Home office expenses — operating your business through a corporation 397
What Expenses Are Partially Deductible or Not Deductible? 397
Meals and entertainment expenses 397

Club dues and fees 398
Prepaid expenses 398
Life insurance premiums 398
Automobile expenses 398
Advertising in non-Canadian publications 399

Chapter 28: Strategies for Retirement 401

Making the Most of Your RRSP 401
Borrowing to contribute 402
Starting a Preauthorized Contribution (PAC) Plan 403
Assessing employer-direct RRSP contributions 403
Make a contribution in kind 404
Choosing a Self-directed RRSP or RRIF 405
The sky's the limit 405
Organized system 405
Diversification 405
Deciding When to Claim Your RRSP Contribution 406
Avoiding RRSP Withdrawals 406
Understanding the impact of making early withdrawals 407
Making withdrawals in no or low-income periods 407

Chapter 29: Using Investments to Manage Your Taxes 409

What Is Investment Earning and How Is It Taxed? 409
Flow-Through Shares 410
Real Estate Investment Trusts and Royalty Trusts 412
Real Estate Investment Trusts (REITs) 412
Royalty trusts 413
Labour-Sponsored Funds 413
Exempt Life Insurance 414
Temporary or term life insurance 414
Permanent life insurance 414
Using insurance for investment purposes 415
Film Limited partnerships 415
The Once-Popular Art Donation Scheme 416

Part VII: The Part of Tens 419

Chapter 30: Ten Ways to Reduce the Risk of an Audit 421

Audit Your Own Return 421
Report All Your Income 421
Have a Reasonable Expectation of Profit 421
File Your Tax Return 422
Be Consistent with Your Expenses 422
Don't Cheat 422
Think Twice about Taking Cash under the Table 422
Learn from Your Mistakes 423
Don't Give the Taxman Something to Audit 423
Keep Your Fingers Crossed 423

Chapter 31: Top Ten Tax Filing Tips 425

Have Your Kids File a Tax Return 425
Deduct All Interest Possible 425
Remember 1994 Elections 425
Track Reinvested Distributions 426
Consider Transferring Dividends 426

Claim Allowable Business Investment Losses 426
Defer Deductions 426
Avoid Recurring Losses 426
Claim All Donations on One Return 427
Claim Medical Expenses on the Lower-income Return 427

Chapter 32: Top Ten Tax Changes for 2000 429

Reinstating Full Indexation 429
Middle Tax Rate 429
Five-percent Surtax 429
Capital Gains Inclusion Rate 429
Tax on Income System 430
Family Care 430
Employee Stock Options 430
Foreign Property Rules 430
Donating RRSPs, RRIFs, and Life Insurance 431
Mini-Budget 431

Appendix A: Tax Forms 433

Index 579

INCOME/ ***Tax deductions make the cost of moving for a new job or to start a new school much less expensive***

A move less taxing

Taking care of
BUSINESS
Dorothy E.
BROWN

Most people are aware that moving expenses can be deducted on your tax return, but did you also know that if a full-time student moves to a new location and earns income from a summer job there, even if he/she is just moving home, the costs of moving can be claimed against the income earned? A student receiving scholarship or bursary income can also claim the costs of moving to school against that income. Even if the student would not otherwise be taxable, claiming moving expenses may be beneficial if by doing so his/her income is reduced enough that all or part of the tuition and education credit can be transferred to a parent.

Whether or not you are a student, in order to be eligible to claim moving expenses, you must be moving to earn income at a new location, and your new residence must be at least 40 kilometres closer to the new location than your old residence. Your deduction is limited to your income earned at the new location, but if your expenses are greater than this you may carry the excess forward and deduct it the following year.

Eligible expenses include: travel for family members, including meals and lodging en route; up to 15 days temporary board and lodging near your new or previous residence; transport and storage of furniture and belongings; lease cancellation costs; costs of selling your old home, including advertising and legal fees; costs of purchasing a new home if you sold your old one, including property purchase tax (but not GST) and legal fees; costs of revising legal documents, replacing drivers' licences and connecting/disconnecting utilities.

If you drive to your new location, you may choose to keep detailed records and claim the actual amount of gas used plus a percentage of the insurance and maintenance based on the distance driven for the move compared to the total distance driven during the year. Alternatively, you can claim a per kilometre deduction using Canada Customs and Revenue Agency's prescribed rates, which is 42 cents per kilometre in B.C.

Similarly, you can claim the actual amount paid for meals while travelling, or claim a flat rate of $11 per meal up to three meals per day for each person.

If your employer pays all or part of your moving expenses, these payments may be included in your income on your T4 slip. If they are not included in income, they must be deducted from your expenses, and you can only claim the amount which was not reimbursed.

Although you are not required to submit form T1M or your receipts with your return, you should keep all receipts and records to support your claim in case CCRA asks to see them.

Dorothy E. Brown is a manager with KNV, Chartered Accountants.

ACHIEVEMENT/*Thornley Advertising honoured at annual m*

Company wins coveted a

Surrey's Thornley Advertising Services Ltd. has been recognized by the Marketing Association of Credit Unions for its outstanding work on behalf of Van Tel/Safeway Credit Union.

The annual AIME Awards (Achievement in Marketing Excellence) represent the industry's best marketing and advertising achievements. Chris Thornley, the president of Thornley Advertising, is very proud to receive such recognition.

"I am extremely proud of our creative team and especially our art director, Laura Baratta. We won five certificates of excellence at last year's awards and to follow that up with two first-place awards and a certificate of excellence this year is remarkable. I'm also very pleased for our client Van Tel/Safeway because they have worked very hard with us to develop a strong marketing and communications program."

Since 1989, Thornley Advertising has been a full-service advertising agency specializing in graphic design, corporate identity and strategic plan- ...

Thornley Advertising president Chris Thornley and art director Laura Baratta are proud of their company's performance at the Achievement in Marketing Excellence Awards.

been providing marketing and advertising services in the Fraser Valley for more than 10 years. The amalgamation of creative talent means Thornley is now the largest creative design house in the Fraser Valley.

Chris Thornley is president of Thornley Advertising while Bruce Hayne, former president of emc, was appointed the company's vice-president.

Introduction

Okay, we know what you're thinking. This is a tax book. How fun a read can it be? How can it possibly keep my attention? How will I ever get through enough of this tome to learn what I need to prepare my tax return accurately and on time? We're pretty good mind readers, aren't we? But you're only right on one account: this is a tax book. You'll be pleasantly surprised, though (amazed and astounded, really), to find that this book does hold your attention, and you don't have to pore over it from start to finish to get out of it what you need to do your taxes. As for the fun part, well . . . we've tried our best, but this is a tax book, after all!

Canadians have several options when tax time rolls around each year:

- **Option 1:** Wait around 'til you receive your tax forms in the mail, then conveniently bury the bulky package under a pile of clothes. When April 29th arrives, breathlessly dig out the package, tear it open and proceed to work yourself into a mild frenzy attempting to fill everything out on time. Wait a minute, do you even *know* how to fill this thing out correctly?

  Doing your tax return this way is hazardous to your health and your wallet. Returns submitted late are charged a penalty fee.

- **Option 2:** Pay an accountant to do your taxes. Pull together every financial record you think you'll need and send it off. You're more annoyed than surprised when your accountant phones and tells you she's missing a whole bunch of receipts. Where *did* you put that invoice from the moving company? Pull more records together and send them off. Soon, you're in constant contact with your accountant. You become phone buddies. You offer to buy her lunch because she's had to do so much extra work on your tax return.

  Doing your tax return this way is also hazardous to your health (your cholesterol shoots up with all those lunches) and your wallet (accountants' hourly rates are mind-boggling).

- **Option 3:** Use *Taxes For Canadians For Dummies* as a guide to filling out your return. This book answers your tax-preparation and tax-planning questions. It helps you make sense of the newest tax laws and guidelines, reduce your taxes, and get through your tax return with a minimum of discomfort. Imagine yourself leisurely sipping a cup of coffee as you fill out your return with the help of this book. Then imagine yourself sauntering down to the mailbox and dropping your completed return in — ahead of the deadline. Poof. Good-bye.

  Doing your tax return this way is positively great for your health and easy on your wallet.

  We're pleased that since you're reading this introduction, you've obviously made the wise choice of going with Option 3. Thank you for buying this book!

Why Buy This Tax Book?

Like most *...For Dummies* books, this one is easy to read. And reading from cover to cover isn't necessary. In fact, a good way to use this book is to simply dive in to the particular topic you need help with — that's what the Table of Contents and the Index are for, Dummy. Sorry,

er rival. D8

Stelco would fail without court protection, Hap Stephen says. D8

ar.com

Nasdaq	Dollar	Gold (U.S.$)	Oil (New York)
17.54 to 2,022.98 +0.87%	0.35¢ U.S. to 74.89¢ $1 U.S.= $1.3353 Cdn.	$8.70 to $395.80 $529.00 Cdn.	$1.10 U.S. a barrel to $35.68

criminal probe

ent Michael Watson said in an terview.

During the course of our investigation, we came across me information which we ought was more appropriate-dealt with by criminal law aurities."

oyal Group said it was co-opating with the investigation.

The company established a ecial committee of the board directors in late December, 2003, to deal with those matters, consisting solely of independent directors who have retained independent legal counsel and forensic accountants," the building products company said.

"The company will continue to co-operate fully with the OSC."

It's the latest controversy for De Zen, who owns about 80.5 per cent of Royal Group's stock and is the company's non-executive chairman.

Last year, Royal Group shareholders forced the company to make changes to its governance practices and to roll back some of the bonuses received by De Zen and his top executive in 2002.

De Zen's bonus was cut by $1.8 million, leaving him with $3.8 million.

➤ Please see **Probe, D4**

by calling for cuts to social security benefits

we won't make that assumption about you. The truth is, very intelligent people like you all across Canada are reading this very same book, as you read this. We understand. Taxes are a tough topic, and you should feel no shame about needing help in preparing your return!

This is the 2001 version of *Taxes For Canadians For Dummies,* and it also happens to be the inaugural edition. We're sure you'll find that the book lives up to the *...For Dummies* reputation. This book is full of expert advice tipped off with a little humour. Very little humour, actually. But hey, some is better than none. This book also helps if you're in hot water with the tax collector — Canada Customs and Revenue Agency (CCRA). We show you how to avoid tax audits and how to handle one if you're one of the chosen few. You also learn about the newest tax law changes and what they mean for you and your family.

Excuse us while we give ourselves a collective pat on the back, but we really couldn't have assembled a better team of authors to put this book together. Each author is a chartered accountant with considerable expertise in tax matters. Their combined years of experience span more decades than an accountant can count. Each author contributed hours of work to this project. Trust us, at the hourly rates these folks charge, this book is a deal. The bottom line? You can't beat the advice you get in this book, and the value is outstanding.

How to Use This Book

Canadians have two general concerns about their taxes: filling out their forms properly, and keeping more of their hard-earned money each year. *Taxes For Canadians For Dummies* addresses both of these concerns.

Use this book as a reference, or as a textbook. Either way, you'll find answers to your tax questions. As a reference, it's a very handy companion tool while you prepare your tax return — either perched beside you on the table, or resting next to you as you sit in front of a warm fire. (The more studious among you will prefer the first example; those of you who are bon vivants, the latter.) As you come up with questions about your tax preparation, check out the Index or Table of Contents and flip right to the section you need.

As a textbook, this book makes great reading from cover to cover. Really! You're sure to receive a first-rate education on Canadian taxes by taking this approach (we tried to include interesting tips and anecdotes in every chapter). Make reading this book a family affair! Story time was never so educational. Your kids will love the tax lessons (okay, we don't expect miracles).

Your Tax Road Map

By now you've probably had a glance at the Table of Contents. If so, you'll notice that the book has been divided into seven parts:

Part I: Getting Ready to File

This part of the book helps you understand Canada's tax system, including our tax rates, who is taxable in Canada, and who has got to file a tax return in this country. We also talk about other returns (non-tax returns) that you may have to file, special situations that you might find yourself in, how to organize your receipts and other tax information, and the various ways to file your return (no it's not good enough to simply dump your receipts in an envelope and mail them to the tax collector!).

Part II: Types of Income in Canada

What type of income do you earn? Believe it or not, it can make a huge difference in how much tax you pay each year. Perhaps you're an employee receiving salary or wages, or maybe you're retired and receive pension income or income from your registered retirement savings plan (RRSP). What other types of income are there? Retiring allowances, scholarships, business or farming income, alimony, employment insurance benefits, worker's compensation benefits, social assistance payments, and much, much more. And let's not forget about investment income. Your investments can generate interest, dividends, rents, royalties, capital gains — or losses. In this part, we look at how the various types of income are taxed, and how to report them on your tax return.

Part III: Tax Deductions and Credits

Here's the real reason you bought this book, right? You'd like to know about all the tax deductions and credits you're entitled to. Part III covers in detail the many types of deductions and credits available. Chances are that a number of the tax deductions and credits don't apply to your situation — but you'll want to make sure that you claim those that do, and take advantage of the tax relief you're rightfully entitled to.

Part IV: Calculation of Federal and Provincial Taxes and Credits

Unless you're living in Quebec, you're used to filling out just one tax return each year. The reason? The federal government has always administered the collection of taxes for each of the other provinces. That's about to change. Beginning in 2000, some provinces have introduced a tax-on-income system whereby the provinces administer their own tax collection. This means more forms for you to fill out (what do you know?), and a new set of tax credits to wrap your head around. By the time you file your 2001 return, most provinces will have adopted this system. Part IV helps you sort through the maze of federal and provincial tax calculations. We highlight some of the tax credits specific to different provinces, and introduce some other credits available at the federal level.

Part V: After You've Filed

After you've filed your tax return, what's next? You sit and wait to hear from the tax collector to see whether you've bypassed the long arm of the tax auditors one more time, right? Not quite. In Part V we talk about your notice of assessment, filing objections to your assessment, and fixing any mistakes after you've filed. We also discuss dealing with the CCRA.

Part VI: Tax Planning Tips

Tax preparation happens once each year, just in time to interfere with the opening of baseball season in April. *Tax planning*, however — a completely different concept — should take place all year long. In this part, we cover off a variety of tax planning tips sure to save you money. Some of the strategies involve income splitting with family members, planning for your estate, tax breaks for employees (yes, there are some), small business tax planning, planning for retirement, and using investments to help with your tax bill. This is the part of the book you should look at all year long. Keep it on your bedside table. It's okay to take a break from the book for a few days in July, but be sure to come back to it again!

Part VII: The Part of Tens

Every book should have a place for a top ten list. Enter The Part of Tens — Part VII. You will find invaluable tidbits of useful information in this favourite part of *...For Dummies* books. Specifically, we cover the ten major tax changes that have taken place since 1999, the top ten ways to reduce your risk of an audit, and the top ten last-minute tax filing tips. We also wanted to include the top ten chocolate chip cookie recipes we've stumbled across, and the top ten verbal insults for 2000, but the publisher thought these lists would best belong in other books. So, we focussed solely on tax issues.

Appendix

You're going to enjoy the appendix in this book. It's not that it's particularly funny or nice to look at — but it's very practical. We include copies of many of the key tax forms discussed in this book, and some information on tax rates. We should let you know that we've included the most recent forms available from Canada Customs and Revenue Agency (CCRA) at the time of writing. Some forms were only available in their 1999 format. But, in most cases, these forms don't change much from year to year, so you'll benefit from a glance at these as well.

Icons Used in This Book

This nerdy guy appears beside discussions that aren't critical if you just want to know the basic concepts and get answers to your tax questions — that is, if you're using the book as a quick reference days before your return is due (you wouldn't do that, now, would you?). However, actually reading these little gems of information can deepen and enhance your tax knowledge. You'll be the tax-savviest person around the office water cooler.

The bull's eye marks the spot for smart shortcuts and timesavers to help you get your tax return done quickly and with a minimum amount of pain. This is definitely the icon to look for if you're pulling an all-nighter on April 29th.

This is a friendly reminder of stuff we discuss elsewhere in the book or of points we really want you to remember.

Don't make these common, costly mistakes with your taxes! Aren't we nice folks to point them out?

Part I
Getting Ready to File

In this part . . .

This is the beginning, so sit down and get comfortable! You'll be glad to know that in these first few chapters, there are very few numbers and complicated calculations. Instead, we're going to ease you in gently: Have you ever wanted to know how Canada's tax system works? Who is or who is not taxable in Canada? And how, in the midst of all the paper, you figure out what forms to fill out? If so, you've come to the right place. We'll also give you some handy pointers on how to stay organized, or for all you procrastinators out there, how to become organized in the first place. And for those of you who are not do-it-yourselfers, we'll let you know when it's okay to throw in the towel and call for help!

"Isn't it appropriate that the month of the tax begins with April Fool's Day and ends with the cries of 'May Day!'"

—Robert Knauerhase

Chapter 1

Canada's Tax System and Rates

In This Chapter

- Understanding Canada's tax system
- Taking a look at provincial and territorial tax systems
- Investigating the tax structure in Quebec
- Figuring out how high your taxes are
- Knowing your effective and marginal tax rate

Raise your hand if you think you're paying too much every year in taxes. If you're sitting there with your hand waving in the air, you're far from alone. Many Canadians, not only resent sharing their hard-earned cash with our government, but also find our income tax system to be confusing, unfair, and illogical. By understanding the "whys" of our tax system and de-mystifying many of those crazy tax rules we will help you in preparing your 2000 tax return. We also hope you will take some of our suggestions on ways to minimize the income taxes you and your family pay. In this chapter you'll find all the basics, from how Canada's tax system is structured, to a primer on how the federal government and the provinces work together at tax time. Stay tuned and we guarantee that together, we will find some pretty innovative and legal ways to lessen your stress when the tax collector comes calling.

Taking the Mystery Out of Canada's Tax System

Though it might seem confusing at times, Canada's income tax system has two pretty straightforward purposes. One, of which we are all quite aware, is to obtain dollars to finance government expenditures. A second purpose, which is not as obvious as the first, is to encourage certain expenditures by Canadians. That's right, our government cuts you a tax break when you spend money in ways that they approve of. In other words, income tax legislation acts as a tool for the government's desired fiscal policies.

Let's look at a few examples. The government wants to do the following:

- **Encourage you to save for retirement.** There are favourable tax rules for registered retirement savings plans (RRSPs). For much more on these tax-friendly plans see Chapter 16, line 208).
- **Encourage you to go to post-secondary school.** Tuition fees are eligible for a tax credit (Chapter 18, line 323), as is interest incurred on student loans (Chapter 18, line 319). Don't forget that an education credit (Chapter 18, line 323) is allowed to both full-time and part-time students.
- **Encourage you to work.** If you have kids to take care of, a deduction is available for child-care expenses (Chapter 16, line 214).

- **Encourage you to invest in shares.** Dividends from Canadian corporations are taxed at a favourable rate (see Chapter 19), and only two-thirds of the capital gain (see Chapter 13) on a sale of shares is subject to tax. Moreover, if you borrow to invest, the interest you incur is generally tax deductible (Chapter 16, line 221). (It is proposed that the two-thirds portion of a capital gain subject to tax be reduced to one-half on capital gains incurred after October 17, 2000.)
- **Encourage you to invest in small growing Canadian companies.** If you invest in certain Canadian companies, you're protected from tax on the first $500,000 of capital gains by the capital gains deduction (Chapter 13, line 254). If you invest in your employer, there are special rules to minimize the tax on shares purchased through stock options (check out Chapter 9). If your investments don't work out as planned, there are again special rules to let you take a tax deduction for at least two-thirds of your loss (Chapter 16, lines 217 and 228). (Keep an eye on this deduction though — it is proposed that the two-thirds be reduced to one-half for losses incurred after October 17, 2000.)
- **Encourage investments in exploration and development activities in Canada.** Favourable tax deductions are available to investors in exploration and development ventures (Chapter 16, line 224).

The government also recognizes that some of us incur additional costs to earn income, due to disabilities, illness, and living in remote locations. Therefore, the income tax rules include tax savings provided by the following:

- The disability tax credit (Chapter 18, line 316)
- The medical expense tax credit (Chapter 18, line 330)
- The northern residents tax deduction (Chapter 17, line 255)

The government wants you to give to charities — hence, the charitable tax credit (Chapter 18, line 349).

And finally, you can get a federal tax break by contributing to your favourite federal politician or party. Read about the political tax credit (Chapter 19, lines 409 and 410). Tax breaks are also available for contributions to provincial and territorial politicians and parties (Chapter 20). We agree with you — the political tax credit seems to be a little self-serving for the politicians.

Tax legislation — administration and enforcement

The House of Commons in Ottawa must pass changes to federal tax rules. The *Canada Customs and Revenue Agency (CCRA, formerly Revenue Canada)* does not create tax laws. It is our elected government officials who are responsible for suggested changes becoming law. So now you know who to blame!

As indicated by its full name CCRA, in addition to its "revenue" work (that is, income tax collection), it also has responsibility for trade (that is, the goods and services tax), and border crossings (that is, customs). CCRA's mission statement is:

> *Our mission is to promote tax compliance with Canada's tax, trade, and border legislation and regulations through education, quality service, and responsible enforcement, thereby contributing to the economic and social well-being of Canadians.*

Want to know more on what CCRA is all about? Go to their Web site at `www.ccra-adrc.gc.ca`.

Most changes to tax laws are announced in the annual federal budget, usually made public in late February. The minister of finance stands up in the House of Commons and details the economic and financial goals of the government and the changes necessary to reach these goals. Many of the changes will affect the tax rules. Tax rules may change to increase or decrease rates, or to encourage you to spend or save in certain ways.

The Department of Finance writes tax legislation. Once legislation becomes law it is part of the *Income Tax Act.* The enforcement and administration of the *Income Tax Act* falls on the shoulders of the CCRA. Often the CCRA will publish its interpretation of various tax rules. It is important to remember, however, that these are only interpretations and are *not* law. Furthermore, the CCRA does not always follow its own published interpretations in assessing taxpayers. Though this seems unfair, you do have the right to challenge the CCRA. (Refer to Chapter 22, CCRA administration.)

Tax planning: A continual process

With the ever-changing economy and tax legislation, and the investment vehicles available in the market, planning to minimize your taxes is a continual process. There are many opportunities for tax planning when there is significant change in your life — a new job, a new child or grandchild, a new marriage or the end of one, a relocation, a business start-up, a business sale, retirement, death of a family member, and so on.

While preparing your income tax return, you may be frustrated because often *at that time* little can be done to minimize your tax — it is simply too late! The year is over. Tax savings can only arise when you implement a plan ahead of time. Therefore, although many of the tips in this book will help you with your 2000 tax return, the biggest benefit is the ideas we'll offer that you can put into practice *now* to minimize the tax you and your family will pay in 2001!

You have the right to pay less tax!

You have the right to arrange your affairs to minimize the tax you pay. A U.S. federal judge, Learned Hand (1872–1961), is often quoted:

> *There is nothing sinister in so arranging one's affairs as to keep taxes as low as possible. Everybody does so, rich or poor, and all do right. Nobody owes any public duty to pay more than the law demands.*

Canada's tax system is based on self-assessment. Each of us has the responsibility for ensuring our tax return includes all necessary information for reporting income, claiming tax deductions and tax credits and, finally, calculating our tax liability. In complying with the tax laws, we all have the right to pay as little tax as is *legally* possible. We stress *legally*. Planning to minimize your tax is legal. Tax evasion is not! Throughout this book we offer many tips on how to minimize the tax you will pay. All these tips are legal of course — all work within the tax law — not against it. We stand behind the tips we offer, based on the tax law and the currently proposed changes. Remember, however, that as tax laws change, some tips will no longer be valid — and new tips will apply.

Tax evasion occurs when you purposely understate the amount of income tax you should pay. This can occur when you don't report all your income, or when you overstate tax deductions and credits to which you are entitled. At worst, tax evasion can result in a charge being laid under the *Criminal Code*. This is scary!

What you don't know can hurt your finances

As noted above, our tax system is self-assessing. You, and only you, have the responsibility for ensuring your tax return is done right. As detailed in Chapter 7, there are a number of ways you can go about completing your return — you can do it yourself, you can purchase a book to assist you in doing it (hey, you've done this already!), you can purchase tax return preparation software, or you can get your Uncle Stan to do it, hire a tax return preparation firm, or find an accountant.

In many cases, any of the above options will produce a correct tax return. However, the question is not whether your return has been prepared *correctly* but whether it has been prepared *optimally*. Does your return result in a tax liability that is the lowest legally available to you? Does your return reflect all the available deductions and credits to which you are entitled? If you are not aware of tax deductions and credits available to you, don't expect the CCRA to point them out. Under our self-assessing system, it is up to you!

The cost to you of not preparing your tax return optimally is simply that you pay more tax than you need to. Surely you can find other uses for money that are far preferable to paying tax! How about big-ticket items such as vacations, retirement savings, your children's or grandchildren's education, or a pool in the backyard. Small tax savings could pay for a dinner out with your spouse (with or without the kids!) or an extra birthday gift for a child. Goodness knows, for most of us there are no limitations on where we'd rather spend our cash.

Over your lifetime, income tax is probably the largest expense you will incur — perhaps even more than the cost of a home. Oddly, many people will dicker over the price of goods, negotiate aggressively in purchasing or leasing a car and the like, yet spend little time seeking ways to minimize their tax bill. We agree that the tax is complex, confusing, and intimidating. The purpose of this book is to take away some of the complexity, confusion, and intimidation!

The Provincial and Territorial Tax Systems

To make taxes a little more confusing we all have more than one tax collector to deal with. Canada's constitution gives income taxing powers to both the federal and provincial governments. (Somehow the territories get covered in there too.) In Canada, taxpayers are liable for both federal and provincial/territorial taxes. With the exception of taxpayers in Quebec, individuals need to deal with one tax collector — the CCRA. CCRA administers the tax system for our federal government and all the provinces/territories — except Quebec. Taxpayers in Quebec need to deal with both CCRA (for federal taxes) and the Ministère du Revenu du Quebec (for Quebec taxes).

Beginning in 2000 there is a shift being made by many of the provinces from a tax-on-tax system to a tax-on-income system as a way of calculating provincial taxes. With a tax-on-tax system provincial taxes are computed as a percentage of the federal tax. With a tax-on-income the provincial taxes are calculated as a percentage of taxable income.

Tax-on-tax systems

With the exception of Quebec (discussed below, and in detail in Chapter 20), taxpayers in Canada complete only one tax return — a federal tax return. However, whether or not you notice it, the return you prepare is for both federal tax *and* tax for the province or territory you lived in on December 31. In 1999 all the provinces (again, except Quebec) and territories worked on a tax-on-tax system. The provincial or territorial portion of your total tax bill was calculated as a percentage of the federal tax. In other words, your provincial or territorial tax was a tax-on-a-tax. Let's look at an example of how this worked.

Joseph lived in Hamilton, Ontario, on December 31, 1999. When he completed his 1999 personal tax return he calculated his taxable income at $27,000. Joseph correctly calculated his federal tax at $3,435. The calculation of his 1999 Ontario tax is detailed below.

1999 federal tax	$3,435
1999 Ontario tax calculation =	
1999 federal tax (as above) $3,435 multiplied by	
Ontario income tax rate in 1999: 39.5%	$1,357
Total 1999 combined federal and Ontario income tax	$4,792

You can see that the calculation of Joseph's Ontario income tax was fairly straightforward. It was simply 39.5 percent of his federal tax.

In a tax-on-tax system, the provincial and territorial taxes are calculated as a percentage of basic federal tax. This is the figure on line 33 of schedule 1 of your tax return. It does not include the reduction in federal tax for any foreign tax credit you may have claimed on line 36, nor does it include any federal surtax to which you may be subject.

Tax-on-income systems

The example above dealt with Joseph's 1999 tax return — not his 2000 return. This is because in 2000, Ontario, like all other provinces except PEI, decided it would like to have its own tax system rather than piggybacking on the federal system. A *tax-on-income* system gives the province greater flexibility in setting its own tax rates and implementing tax policy.

For the 2000 tax returns, each province (except PEI), will have its own set of tax rates, tax brackets, and tax credits. A separate tax return will *not* be required (except for Quebec). Only the federal return will need to be completed. This return will include specific schedules pertaining to the calculation of provincial taxes and credits. The CCRA will continue to administer the provincial tax on behalf of the provincial governments.

Chapter 20 provides a detailed look at the new tax-on-income system for the various provinces and territories.

Taxes in Quebec

Unlike the other provinces and the territories, Quebec has its own tax return — form TP.1-D-V. Residents of Quebec on December 31, 2000, must separately file a 2000 federal tax return and a 2000 Quebec tax return. The Ministère du Revenu du Québec administers the Quebec tax system. Their Web site is `www.revenu.gouv.qc.ca` and offers service in English and French.

Many of the federal tax rules discussed in this book also apply to the Quebec return. However, Quebec does have some of its own unique rules and calculations. So, if you need to complete a Quebec return this year, you have a little more work ahead of you than those of us who can get by with simply completing the federal return. (We expect the other provinces were a little envious of Quebec being able to have its own tax rules. Perhaps it was this envy that led some provinces to push for the tax-on-income system rather than the tax-on-tax system.) See Chapter 20 for more information on Quebec's income tax.

My Taxes Are How High?

There's no doubt about it — Canada is a high tax nation — all the more reason to ensure the taxes paid by you and your family are minimized. Take advantage of the tax saving tips in this book plus ensure you take advantage of all the tax deductions and credits available to you. Canada's income tax system is a *progressive tax rate system*. The percentage of your income that goes to fund your tax liability increases as your income increases. This is easily illustrated. Take a look at the three federal tax brackets in Table 1-1.

Table 1-1 2000 Federal Income Tax Brackets and Rates (Provincial and Territorial Taxes Not Included)

Tax Brackets	*Tax Rate*
$0 to $30,004	17%
$30,004 to $60,009	25%
$60,009 and above	29%

As you can see, the greater your taxable income through the three federal tax brackets, the greater the percentage of tax that is applied to that income. Let's consider the case of two sisters — Vivian and Diana. After taking advantage of all the tax deductions available to them, Vivian's taxable income is $35,000 and Diana's is $75,000.

Vivian's federal tax

Tax on first:	**Tax Rate**	**Tax Payable**
$30,004	17%	$5,101
$30,005 to $35,000	25%	$1,249
Total federal tax		$6,350
Tax as a percentage of income		18.14

Diana's federal tax:

Tax on first:	**Tax Rate**	**Tax Payable**
$30,004	17%	$5,101
$30,005 to $60,009	25%	$7,501
$60,009 to $75,000	29%	$4,347
Total federal tax		$16,949
Tax as a percentage of income		22.60

As Vivian's and Diana's taxable income "breaks through" a tax bracket, they each pay a greater tax rate on the taxable income subject to tax in the higher bracket. Since Vivian's taxable income is below $60,009, she has no taxable income subject to tax at the 29 percent federal rate. However, Diana does. The effect of this is that Diana's tax as a percentage of her taxable income is 22.6 percent — higher than Vivian's 18.1 percent.

The higher a taxpayer's income rises above the last threshold of $60,009, the higher the tax as a percentage of taxable income.

The tax rates in Table 1-1 are only the federal tax rates, and do not include the federal surtax (see Chapter 19) or provincial/territorial income taxes (see Chapter 20). When your taxable income falls into the top federal tax bracket (that is, greater than $60,009), your combined federal (including the federal surtax) and provincial/territorial tax rate on the portion of your taxable income in the top tax bracket can be as high as the tax rates summarized in Table 1-2 below. However, the tax rates in the charts shown are *before* the tax credits available to individuals like Vivian and Diana. These tax credits are discussed in Chapter 18. Your tax liability is based on your taxable income. Once the liability is calculated, it is reduced by tax credits available to you.

Table 1-2 — 2000 Top Tax Rates (Federal and Provincial/Territorial Taxes Combined)

Province	*Salary & Interest*	*Dividends*	*Capital Gains*
British Columbia	51.3	34.6	34.2
Alberta	43.7	29.8	29.1
Saskatchewan	50.3	35.4	33.6
Manitoba	48.1	34.8	32.0
Ontario	47.9	32.3	31.9
Quebec	51.7	36.3	34.4
New Brunswick	49.2	33.2	32.8
Nova Scotia	48.8	32.9	32.5
Prince Edward Island	49.1	33.2	32.7
Newfoundland	51.3	34.6	34.2
Yukon	45.4	30.6	30.2
N.W.T./Nunavut	43.5	29.4	29.0

Note: All figures are prior to proposals announced on October 18, 2000

As the above table indicates, if you are in the top tax bracket, *capital gains* (the excess of sale proceeds over the cost of an asset) are the most tax-efficient sources of income because they are taxed at the lowest rate. Dividends come in a close second.

With the October 18, 2000, proposals, capital gains become *even more* tax efficient as only one-half of the gain is to be taxed — down from two-thirds! At the beginning of this chapter we commented that one of the purposes of our tax system was to encourage certain expenditures by Canadians. The government wants us all to invest and to reward us for doing so — hence, the preferential tax treatment given to dividends and capital gains. We discuss these preferential treatments in detail in Chapters 13 and 19.

Tallying up your effective tax rate

Your effective tax rate is the percentage your tax is of your total taxable income. It is easy to calculate. It is simply your tax liability (after you have taken all the tax credits you are entitled to) over your taxable income.

$$\frac{\text{Tax liability}}{\text{Taxable income}} = \text{Effective tax rate}$$

Take a look at Micha's 2000 tax return. Micha lives in Thompson, Manitoba. Her taxable income is $53,000. She calculates the tax on the $53,000 and then reduces the amounts for any tax credits she is entitled to. After these credits are deducted, her federal/Manitoba tax liability is $14,000. Her effective tax rate is then 26.42 percent ($14,000/$53,000).

The calculation of your effective tax rate takes into account that portions of your income are taxed in different tax brackets. The effective tax rate calculation "averages" the rates of tax paid in these brackets. The more income you have taxed in the highest tax bracket (taxable income in excess of $60,009), the higher your effective tax rate.

Calculating your marginal tax rate

When tax geeks talk about marginal tax rates, they are talking about the tax rate that applies to your next dollar of taxable income.

Assume your taxable income is $90,000. You are clearly in the top tax bracket. Further assume you live in Alberta. If you were to earn $1 of additional interest income, you would pay 43.7¢ in tax on this. In other words, your marginal tax rate is 43.7 percent (see Table 1-2 on page 15 of this chapter). On an after-tax basis, that extra dollar of income leaves you with only 56.30¢, or 56.3 percent. This is referred to as your after-tax rate of return. It can be calculated as:

1 – Your marginal tax rate = Your after-tax rate of return

The calculation of your marginal tax rate ignores that portions of your income were taxed in different tax brackets and subject to different tax rates. The marginal tax rate is focused on your *next* dollar of taxable income — not your overall taxable income.

The marginal tax rate is an easy way to assess the impact of a raise. With a marginal tax rate of 43.7 percent, you know that if you receive a $10,000 raise you will only be taking home an additional $5,630. When looking at investment returns from alternative investment opportunities, ensure you compare *after-tax* rate of returns.

A marginal tax rate can also be used to calculate the tax savings a tax deduction will provide. Again assume your taxable income is $90,000 and you live in Alberta. You are wondering what the impact would have been if you had contributed $5,000 to your RRSP and taken a deduction on your 2000 return. Your taxable income would have been reduced to $85,000 by the $5,000 RRSP deduction. You know your marginal tax rate is 43.7 percent. The tax saving you would have enjoyed if you were able to deduct the $5,000 RRSP contribution is $2,185 ($5,000 multiplied by 43.7 percent)! You can clearly see why there is so much talk about the tax-saving qualities of RRSP contributions!

Chapter 2

Who Pays Taxes in Canada?

In This Chapter

- Understanding who's taxable in Canada
- Investigating who must file a tax return
- Looking at possible benefits of filing a tax return

There's no doubt about it. The Canadian tax system can be confusing. And figuring out whether you're even taxable in Canada is half the battle. You see, Canada levies taxes based on residency, not on citizenship the way some other countries do. This means that virtually everyone who lives in Canada, whether a Canadian resident or a deemed resident, is liable for Canadian tax. And to make matters worse, once you are a Canadian resident for tax purposes, you could still be liable for Canadian tax even if you no longer live in Canada.

Who Is a Canadian Resident?

If you are a resident of Canada, all your worldwide income is taxable in Canada. But what makes you a Canadian resident?

In general, anyone who lives primarily in Canada is a factual resident of Canada, and is therefore subject to Canadian taxation. Sometimes it's hard to tell whether you live primarily in Canada. For example, it's possible for you to live in both Canada *and* another country. Think of a movie star that has homes around the world. You may still be a factual resident of Canada even though you live in another country for part of the year.

There are a number of factors you must consider when deciding whether you are a resident of Canada. And make no mistake about it: these factors can have a huge impact on how much tax you pay in the year. You see, if you are a Canadian resident you will be taxed in Canada on all your worldwide income. And if these factors determine that you are no longer a Canadian resident, you will be charged a departure tax when you leave Canada. This means that, depending on your personal circumstances, you may want to remain a Canadian resident (to avoid the potentially damaging departure tax) or to cease residency (to avoid the potentially damaging high rates of Canadian income tax).

Don't be too hasty in giving up Canadian residency purely for income tax reasons. Canada will impose a departure tax on the fair market value of most of your assets when you leave the country.

Factors in determining Canadian residency

So, what factors will the CCRA consider when deciding whether you are a factual Canadian resident? Well, it basically wants to see the extent of your ties with Canada. The four factors are the following:

- Permanence and purpose of stay abroad
- Residential ties within Canada
- Residential ties elsewhere
- Regularity and length of visits to Canada.

No single factor of these four determine that you've maintained residency in Canada. All four factors must be considered.

Permanence and purpose of stay abroad

Generally, when an individual leaves Canada for more than two years, he or she is presumed to have given up Canadian residency. This is not a guarantee, however, that the CCRA will consider the individual to be a non-resident. The permanence of the leave and the purpose of the stay abroad will also be considered. If the facts show that the individual has every intention of returning to Canada, he or she may still be considered to be Canadian for tax purposes, even when the stay has exceeded two years.

Residential ties within Canada

The CCRA will consider all an individual's personal ties with Canada to determine residency status. For example, if only one spouse leaves Canada but the remaining spouse and any children under the age of 18 remain here, the individual will probably be considered a resident in Canada for tax purposes due to the strong personal ties.

If you are moving from Canada and want to ensure you will not have residential ties within Canada and therefore not be subject to Canadian taxes, there are some steps you should take before departing. For example, you should cancel provincial driver's licences, provincial health insurance, Canadian credit cards and memberships. In addition, all members of the family should take part in the move.

One of your main residential ties to Canada is your home. Normally it is recommended that you sell the home before leaving the country. However, the principal residence could be converted to a rental property prior to leaving without giving rise to residential ties, but only if you would be unable to reoccupy the residence after your return on less than three months' notice.

Residential ties elsewhere

You may be able to prove that your residential ties within Canada have been broken. However, keep in mind that you still must be a resident of some other country.

You have to be a resident somewhere. If you want to create residential ties in another country, there are steps you can take there — essentially the reverse of your steps to break ties in Canada — including buying a home or entering into a long-term lease on an apartment, opening bank accounts, obtaining a new driver's licence and purchasing memberships. Without strong residency ties in the new country of residence, you will find it difficult to prove that you have given up Canadian residency.

Regularity and length of visits to Canada

Even when all other factors indicate that a person has given up residency in Canada, if the person is present in Canada for 183 days or more in a year, he or she is deemed to be a Canadian resident for tax purposes. We'll get into the rules on deemed residents below.

Even if a person who wishes to cease Canadian residency visits for fewer than 183 days, there is still the risk that the CCRA will not consider the individual to have given up Canadian residency. The CCRA will look at the frequency and length of visits to Canada. If you spend significant time in Canada at each visit, and return often, you could still be considered resident here. It's not an option to avoid departure tax and Canadian income tax at the same time, so you may want to visit a tax pro if you're deciding to live abroad. See Chapter 4 for more information on leaving Canada.

Deemed residents

So perhaps you ruled yourself out as a Canadian resident and have breathed a sigh of relief — you're not a factual resident of Canada. Does that mean you'll escape Canadian taxation? Not necessarily. There are more rules to consider, namely the deemed resident rules.

If you are a deemed resident of Canada, you are taxable on your worldwide income for the whole year even though you don't live in Canada on a full-time basis. So if you spend any time at all in Canada during the year, read this section carefully to ensure you meet your Canadian tax filing requirements. If you visit Canada during the year, you could be a deemed resident of Canada. The rule is this: If you visit Canada for periods totaling 183 days or more in a calendar year, you are deemed to be a Canadian resident for that whole year. It doesn't matter whether you have a home in Canada, or meet any of the other tests for a factual Canadian resident — if you set foot on Canadian soil for more than 183 days in a year, you are taxable here.

You could be taxable in Canada if you spend more than 183 days here during one calendar year. The 183-day calculation includes each day or part of a day you stayed in Canada, including days you attended a Canadian college or university, days you worked here, and days or weekends you vacationed there.

There are some instances when you normally would be considered a deemed resident of Canada (since you've been here for more than 183 days in total this year), but because of a tax treaty Canada has with the other country, you are considered a resident of that country. If you think this could apply to you, contact the International Tax Services Office at the CCRA.

If you sojourned ("visited," to us common folk) in Canada for more than 183 days in 2000, you must file a Canadian tax return for the whole year. Use the special tax return called the T1 General for Non-Residents and Deemed Residents.

If you're deemed to be a resident in Canada and also pay tax elsewhere, don't forget to claim a foreign tax credit for the taxes paid in the other country. This will help prevent "double taxation."

Part-year residents

If you move to Canada to live during the year, you end up being a factual resident of Canada. It doesn't matter if you meet the 183 test to be deemed a resident; since you've moved to Canada with the intention of staying, welcome to the wonderful world of Canadian tax.

You may be wondering if it is fair that you are subject to Canadian taxes even if you've only lived in Canada for part of the year, and maybe even less than 183 days. Well, you're in luck. As opposed to factual residents who've lived in Canada for the whole year, and deemed residents who are each taxed on their worldwide income for the entire year, special rules apply to part-year residents. In fact, before you arrive in Canada you are free from reporting any income to the Canadian authorities and paying tax on that income. Here are the specifics:

Taxes and government employees posted abroad

Certain government agency employees posted abroad, along with their dependants, are also deemed residents of Canada. Here are some examples:

- A member of the Canadian armed forces
- An ambassador, minister, high commissioner, officer, or servant of Canada who was a resident in Canada immediately prior to his or her appointment, was employed by Canada, or received representation allowances in the year
- An agent-general, officer, or servant of a province if you were a resident in Canada immediately prior to appointment or employment by the province, or received representation allowances in the year
- An individual working abroad under a prescribed international development assistance program of the Government of Canada and a resident in Canada at any time in the three-month period before being posted abroad
- A member of the overseas Canadian Forces school staff
- A child and dependant of any of the above individuals and your income does not exceed $500 and the basic personal tax credit
- A family member of an individual resident in Canada and entitled to an exemption from income taxes in the foreign country under a tax treaty

- If you earn Canadian source income at any time in the year (even before you are a Canadian resident), you must pay tax on that income. Don't worry, this is the same rule that applies to any "non-resident" of Canada.
- As of the day you become a Canadian resident for tax purposes (that is, the day you come to live here), you are liable for tax on your worldwide income. For example, say you moved from India to Canada on June 4, 2000. You will have to file a Canadian tax return for June 4 to December 31 that year. In 2001, you will be a resident in Canada for the whole year and will be taxed on your worldwide income for the year.
- If you leave Canada permanently during the year, you will also be a part-year resident of Canada. Before you leave you will be taxed on all your income from all sources.

Non-residents

Even if you're not caught under any of the resident rules, there is still one last case in which you could be taxable in Canada. If you've earned any Canadian source income in the year, this income will be subject to Canadian taxes. The good news is that this doesn't necessarily mean you have to file a tax return in Canada. You see, many payments of Canadian source income made to a non-resident are already subject to withholding tax. In other words, the CCRA will receive its share of your taxes up front. However, there are some circumstances under which you have to file a tax return, or may *want* to file a tax return to get a refund of some or all of these withholding taxes.

The taxation rules for non-residents depend on the type of Canadian source income earned. If you've earned any of the following types of income, you are taxable in Canada and may have to file a tax return.

- Income from employment in Canada
- Income from a business carried on in Canada
- Canadian scholarships, fellowships, bursaries, and research grants
- Taxable capital gains from disposing of taxable Canadian property (for example, Canadian real estate or business property)

You may have had withholding tax already withheld from the payments noted above. Once you file a tax return and claim any deductions allowed, you may be eligible for a refund of some or all of these withholding taxes paid.

There are some other types of Canadian source income that never have to be reported on a Canadian tax return. *Withholding taxes* are required to be taken at source on these items so the CCRA gets its tax revenues up front. These items include the following:

- Interest
- Dividends
- Rental income
- Pension payments, including Old Age Security, and Canada Pension Plan and Quebec Pension Plan benefits
- Retiring allowances
- Registered retirement savings plan and registered retirement income fund payments.

If you're receiving Canadian source rental income, you may opt to file a Canadian tax return even though your tax obligation to the Canadian authorities has already been satisfied via withholding taxes. You see, withholding taxes must be taken off the gross income earned in the year. However, if you incur significant expenses to earn that income, you would be better off filing a Canadian tax return, claiming those expenses, and paying tax on your net rental income. Filing this special tax return is called Electing Under Section 216.

Do You Have to File a Tax Return?

You're now clear on whether you could be taxable in Canada. But, of course, there are more complications. You see, just because you could be liable for Canadian tax does not mean you *have* to file a Canadian tax return.

Confused? Take Bill for example. Bill is 17 years old and just started his first part-time job at a local deli. Bill will earn less than the basic personal amount in 2000, so even if he does prepare a tax return he won't have any taxes payable. Does Bill have to file a tax return? Well, we know that he is a Canadian resident and he's earned some income in the year. This would lead us to believe he must file a tax return. But guess what? Since Bill will not have any taxes owing in the year, he does not *have* to file. Of course, he may choose to file anyway, for reasons we'll discuss later.

Here are the rules. You have to file a Canadian tax return if you are considered "taxable" in Canada (that's what we covered in the first part of this chapter) and any of the following apply to you:

- You will have a balance owing to the CCRA during the year. In other words, you owe taxes!
- The CCRA sent you a request to file a return. You see, sometimes a taxpayer will conveniently "forget" to file a tax return, or will claim he or she didn't have to file. This may be fine and dandy. However, if the CCRA asks to see a tax return, you must provide one. It doesn't matter whether you think you don't owe taxes — they want to see proof.

Pay close attention if the CCRA asks you to file a tax return. If you don't follow its instructions you could wind up with a huge tax bill! This is because the CCRA can assess you on a "net worth" basis. Basically, all of your assets and liabilities will be looked at for both the end of the tax year it is interested in, and the end of the last tax year for which you filed a return. If your net worth (that is, assets less liabilities) has increased between these two periods, the CCRA will assume it is because you had unclaimed taxable income in those years. This means you will have a tax bill for the increase in your net worth.

What is capital property?

O.K. We won't make you wait for Chapter 13 for all the details on capital gains. The rules on capital property and capital gains can be quite complex at times. This aside, there are some common scenarios in which you will sell a capital property in the year. These include dispositions of the following:

- Shares, both private and public; Canadian and foreign
- Farm property
- Mutual fund units
- An interest or share of a flow-through entity
- Real estate
- Depreciable property
- Bonds, debentures, or promissory notes
- Mortgage foreclosures and conditional sales repossessions
- Personal use property (for example, a cottage or a boat, but not a principal residence)
- Works of art
- Jewelry
- Coins, rare folios, manuscripts, or rare books

In some cases this will catch those who are simply not abiding by the rules and are trying to avoid taxes. But keep in mind that there are other reasons that your net worth could increase over the years — and not all of these reasons would normally lead to a tax bill. For example, you could have received an inheritance or won the lottery! The moral of the story? If you are asked to prepare a tax return, do it!

Filing: Not Just By Invitation Only

Just because the CCRA doesn't ask you to file a return doesn't mean that you shouldn't. The appropriateness of to file or not to file has everything to do with what you've been up to, financially and otherwise, for the past year. If you're a rare art collector, get out your pen and paper, and if you were out of work and collected Employment Insurance, you'll need to rev up your calculator. These are just a few of the circumstances that mean it's filing time for you, my friend.

You disposed of property or claimed a capital gains reserve

You have disposed of capital property in the year or you claimed a capital gains reserve on your prior year's tax return. (You'll have to hang on until Chapter 13 for all the gory details. The suspense must be killing you.) In fact, it doesn't even matter if this disposal will result in a tax bill for you. The rule is simple: If you've disposed of capital property, have a taxable capital gain, or claimed a capital gains reserve in the prior year, you must file a tax return.

You received Old Age Security benefits

If you received Old Age Security benefits in the year and have taxable income in excess of $53,960, you will be subject to a clawback of some or all of your benefits in 2000. In addition, you must file a tax return. This threshold will increase each year based on inflation.

You received Employment Insurance benefits

If you've received Employment Insurance benefits in the year, you may have to pay back some of your benefits as well. If you've claimed less than 21 weeks of benefits in the past five years, the clawback will take effect if you earn more than $48,750 in the year. If you've received more than 21 weeks of benefits over the past five years, the clawback will apply after you earn $39,000 of taxable income. And again, if this clawback applies to you, you must file a tax return.

You had funds "clawed back" from you

If you've received Old Age Security or Employment Insurance benefits in the year and you're subject to a clawback of any of these amounts. A clawback is basically a requirement to pay back all or a portion of the government benefits you received in the year because you made too much money from other sources. Of course, the fact that you have income from other sources probably means that you have to file a tax return anyway, since this income will more than likely lead to a tax liability on its own.

You made a withdrawal from your RRSP under the Home Buyer's Plan or the Lifelong Learning Plan

The *Home Buyer's Plan (HBP)* and *Lifelong Learning* Plans *(LLP)* are special programs set up by the government to allow individuals to withdraw funds from their RRSPs to be used toward a home purchase or to attend school. Normally withdrawals from an RRSP are fully taxable in the year of withdrawal. However, with these special programs the withdrawal is not taxable as long as the funds are repaid into the RRSP over a 15-year period. When you've withdrawn money from your RRSP under the HBP or LLP, you need to complete some special forms to let CCRA know you've withdrawn the funds under these programs. To complete these forms, you need to file a personal tax return. This applies only if you have not yet repaid all the amounts withdrawn.

In the years when a repayment under the HBP or LLP is required, two things can happen. First, you will make an RRSP contribution to repay part (or all) of your RRSP withdrawal. Usually an RRSP contribution becomes a tax deduction on your tax return. However, when you must make a repayment under the HBP or LLP, the portion of the RRSP repayment relating to your repayment reduces the RRSP deduction.

Here's an example: Hans withdrew $15,000 from his RRSP in 1995 to purchase a new home. Under the Home Buyer's Plan, he is required to repay at least $1,000 per year for 15 years commencing in 1997. In 2000, he contributed $5,000 to his RRSP. Since $1,000 of this contribution must be used to repay his HBP, he will only be allowed to deduct $4,000 on his 2000 tax return.

The second scenario that may arise is that Hans does not make an RRSP contribution at all in 2000. In this case, the $1,000 required repayment under the HBP will simply be added to his 2000 income and become taxable.

Tax returns must be filed when repayments are required under the HBP or LLP, since this is the mechanism used to track whether RRSP deductions have been reduced or an income inclusion has been made in the year. Even if the taxpayer is otherwise nontaxable, a tax return must be filed to ensure the proper repayments are being made.

You contributed to the Canada Pension Plan

You are required to contribute to the *Canada Pension Plan (CPP).* If you are over the age of 18 but under age 70, and you earn a salary or self-employment income of more than $3,500, this means you. CPP is not optional. If you earn a salary or wages, your employer will normally withhold CPP on your employment earnings. In fact, your employer has to make CPP payments to the CCRA as well, on your behalf. However, if you are self-employed you are both the employee *and* the employer, and this means you must pay both portions of the CPP on your earnings. This CPP is calculated as part of your tax return, which is why — under these circumstances — you are required to file a tax return.

For example, Andrea runs a small hairstyling business out of her house. In 2000, she earned $5,000 (net income) from this business. Because she can earn up to $7,231 tax-free in the year (due to the basic personal tax credit) she doesn't want the hassle of filing a tax return. However, even though she won't owe income taxes, she *will* owe CPP because she earned more than $3,500 in the year. In other words, she must file a tax return.

The maximum CPP a person must pay in 2000 is $1,329.90 as an employee and $2,659.80 if you are self-employed. If you have both employment and self-employment earnings, you can take into account the CPP paid as an employee when calculating the CPP payable on your self-employment earnings. That is, the absolute maximum CPP you will have to pay in 2000 is $2,659.80; CPP payments made while you were an employee will be taken into account when calculating the CPP on self-employment earnings.

When You May Want to File a Tax Return

Even though you may not be *required* to file a tax return this year, you may want to file. You see, tax returns are not always a bad thing. There are a lot of benefits to be gained from filing a tax return. And these benefits will often far outweigh the time and frustration spent preparing your return.

You've paid too much tax in the year

If you've earned employment income in the year, you should receive a T4 slip from your employer. And you will note (in box 22, to be exact) whether taxes were deducted from your pay. Now, these taxes were deducted based on a lot of assumptions, which may or may not reflect your tax reality at the end of the year. Depending on your personal circumstances, these taxes may be too high, which means you are entitled to a tax refund. And you guessed it — the only way to claim a tax refund is to file a tax return.

Any time you've paid taxes in the year, it's a good idea to file a tax return just in case you're entitled to a refund. Take a look at your various "T-slips," such as T4s, T4RSPs or T4As, to see if taxes were deducted. Also consider any instalment payments you made to the government in the year, to help maximize your refund.

You are entitled to a GST/HST credit

Did you know that you might be entitled to a quarterly cheque from the government for the *Goods and Services Tax (GST)* or the *Harmonized Sales Tax (HST)*? That's right, some of these dreaded sales taxes may actually be refunded to you via a tax credit. Not everyone is eligible for the GST/HST credit. However, if you are eligible, you can only receive the GST/HST credit if you apply for it each year, even if you received it in the previous year. What's involved in applying for this credit? Well, it's easy. All you have to do is complete a tax return and check the box that says you want to apply for this credit. The CCRA will do the calculations and let you know if you qualify.

You may be eligible for quarterly GST/HST payments from the government. However, you, and your spouse if you have one, must file a tax return to receive these payments. This is because the actual credit you receive will be based on information provided on your tax return, such as your net income, the net income of your spouse, and the number of children under the age of 18 who live with you. If you have a spouse, only one of you will receive the credit. However, if you have children ages 19 or older who live with you, each of these children can receive a credit all their own. They must file a tax return as well.

You want to receive, or continue to receive, the Child Tax Benefit

If you are responsible for the care of a child who is under 18, you might be eligible to claim the Canada Child Tax Benefit (CCTB) for that child. This benefit was introduced in 1993 to replace the old "baby bonus" child tax credit and tax credit for minor dependants. The new CCTB is paid to certain custodians, based on income figures from the parents' tax returns. Since the actual amount of CCTB paid is based on income figures, a tax return must be filed in order for you to receive, or continue to receive, this benefit. And this means a tax return for both yourself and your spouse (if applicable). It doesn't matter whether you're taxable in the year — when you are entitled to the CCTB, a tax return is a good thing.

If you'd like to make an application for the Canada Child Tax Benefit, you should file form RC66 with the government. This application can be made as soon as your child is born, when a child comes to live with you, or, if you are a landed immigrant or refugee, as soon as you and your child arrive in Canada. Remember to file a tax return each year to continue to receive your benefits!

You are entitled to provincial or territorial tax credits

Many provinces and territories in Canada offer special tax credits to their residents. However, these credits do not come to you automatically. You must apply for them on your personal tax return. We think you're getting the picture. Filing a tax return can be to your benefit. The tax credits offered vary by province and territory. Some of the more significant credits are summarized in Table 2-1.

Table 2-1 Provincial and Territorial Tax Credits

Province/Territory	*Some Tax Credits Offered*	*Form to Fill Out*
British Columbia	Sales tax credit	T1C (B.C.)
	Political contribution tax credit	
	Venture capital tax credit	
Alberta	Political contribution tax credit	T1C (Alta.)
Manitoba	Cost-of-living credit	T1C (Man.)
	Property tax credit	
	Learning tax credit	
Ontario	Property tax credit	T1C (Ont.)
	Sales tax credit	
	Tax credits for self-employed individuals	
New Brunswick	Political contribution tax credit	T1C (N.B.)
	Stock savings plan tax credit	
Nova Scotia	Stock savings plan tax credit	T1C (N.S.)
	Equity tax credit	
	Home ownership savings plan credit	
Prince Edward Island	Political contribution tax credit	T1C (P.E.I.)
Newfoundland	Political contribution tax credit	T1C (Nfld)
Yukon	Low-income family credit	T1C (Yukon)
	Small business investment tax credit	
	First Nations income tax credit	
Northwest Territories	Cost-of-living credit	T1C (N.W.T.)
	Risk capital investment tax credits	
	Political contribution tax credit	
Nunavut	Cost-of-living tax credit	T1C (Nun.)
	Political contribution tax credit	
	Risk capital investment tax credits	

You want to maximize your RRSP contribution room for future years

You are allowed to make RRSP contributions each year based on your RRSP contribution room. This room is calculated using your earned income from prior years. In years when you have little income, you may not see the benefit in filing a tax return. However, down the road when you find yourself independently wealthy, you will appreciate having filed a tax return in past years.

Here's why. Unused RRSP contribution room never expires. So, even though you may not plan on making RRSP contributions in the next few years, in years to come you can still use this room to maximize your tax deductions and minimize your tax bill.

Take Lisa, for example. Lisa is currently 16 years old and works for her father's lawn care company in the summer. She only earned $6,000 this summer so she technically doesn't have to file a tax return since she'll have no taxes owing. However, Lisa is a bright girl and is planning on going to university after she finishes high school. By filing a tax return now, she'll be creating earned income and RRSP contribution room. And when she begins working after university, she'll be able to use that room to make RRSP contributions and save taxes.

You've paid too much in CPP or EI premiums in the year

Canada Pension Plan (CPP) and *Employment Insurance (EI)* premiums aren't actually income taxes; they're technically payroll taxes. Regardless of what they're called, they're deducted from your pay and reported on your personal tax return. If you've worked at only one job in the year, it's unlikely that your CPP or EI premiums were drastically wrong. However, if you had more than one employer in the year, each employer was required to deduct CPP and EI based on your earnings at that job alone. And because of this added complexity, your total CPP and EI for the year may have been miscalculated or overstated. This often has nothing to do with your employer's payroll skills; it's because of the way the calculation is done.

If you think you've paid too much in CPP or EI premiums in the year, don't fret. If you file a tax return you can claim a refund for the excess premiums paid.

You have deductions or credits to carry forward to future years

You may have incurred some costs in 2000 that would normally be a tax deduction or credit, but which, due to your income level in the year, are of no use to you. That is, claiming these deductions or credits will not increase your tax refund or lower your payable tax (probably because you don't have any taxes payable in the first place!).

Don't despair. Certain tax deductions and credits will not be lost forever if not claimed on your current year's tax return. On the other hand, these items should still be reported this year, but then carried forward to be used in future. You see, the CCRA wants to know about these deductions and credits in the year that they occurred. So, to avoid problems later and to minimize future tax bills, file a tax return when you have any of the following items:

- Tuition and education amounts
- RRSP contributions
- Moving expenses.

If you have deductions or credits you want to carry forward to use in future years, fill in all the details on your current year's tax return, and attach slips if necessary. However, ensure you're not claiming the deduction or credit in the current year. For example, if you have tuition and education amounts to carry forward, ensure you do not claim a credit for these amounts on line 323 of your current year's tax return. Instead, show the amount as an unused amount to be carried forward, on Schedule 11 of your tax return.

You will have a non-capital loss this year

So 2000 wasn't so great for you. Your business lost money and you're in the hole. Let's face it, you don't want to add misery to your life by filing a tax return. But all is not lost. You now have what's known as a *non-capital loss* and the good news is that this loss can be carried back for three years or forward for seven years to offset taxable income in those years. This means that you will be able to use this loss to reduce your taxes in the future, or even claim a tax refund for back taxes paid!

Of course, there's a catch. To recognize a non-capital loss, you have to file a tax return. This means giving the CCRA all the details of your income and expenses for the years so your loss can be assessed. If you don't file a tax return, there is no proof on file that you ever incurred the loss.

Use form T1A, "Request for Loss Carry Back," to calculate your non-capital loss for the year and to carry losses back to any of the previous three tax years.

Chapter 3

Filing Non-Tax Returns

In This Chapter

- Understanding information returns
- Looking at partnership returns
- Examining transactions with non-residents
- Reviewing foreign reporting requirements
- Comprehending transfer pricing

In Chapter 1 and Chapter 2 we explain Canada's tax system and rates and review who is taxable in Canada. Now we're going to get into some of the fun stuff! O.K. fun may be pushing it but this is where things start getting interesting. In this chapter we will discuss information returns, for reporting transactions relating to partnerships, non-residents and transfer pricing, and their filing requirements.

What Is an Information Return?

Information returns are non-tax returns that the CCRA requires to be filed to provide them with information such as the amount of interest, dividends, or royalties paid to a taxpayer in a particular year. The CCRA uses these information returns to keep tabs on whether people are reporting all their worldwide income.

An information return is not used for calculating tax payable on income but rather provides the CCRA with information to ensure that certain tax information is being properly calculated and reported. In other words, they are "non-tax returns." In the following sections we will go through the circumstances in which you are required to help out the CCRA.

Partnership Income

A *partnership* is an unincorporated business entity with more than one owner. Each owner is called a partner. The partners carry on business or trade in common with the intention of making a profit.

The partnership itself is not a taxable entity; that is, it does not have to file its own tax return. Instead, you, as a partner, are taxable on your share of the business's net profits (revenues minus expenses) and you are required to report your share of the profits or losses from the partnership on your personal income tax return.

How do I know if I have to file a Partnership Information Return?

Where a partnership that carries on business in Canada, or a Canadian partnership with Canadian or foreign operations or investments has

- six partners or more at any time during a fiscal year or
- a partner that is itself a partnership

it must file a T5013 — information return — annually with the CCRA. The T5013 Summary reports the partnership's results for the year and the amounts allocated out to the partners. The partnership must also provide each partner with specified information on a T5013 Supplementary — also an information return — that details what partners should report on their personal income tax return.

Partnerships that do not have to file a Partnership Information Return

There are some partnerships that are exempt from filing T5013s. They are as follows:

- Investment clubs that file a T3 return, for years ending before 1991.
- Where none of the income allocated from the partnership to the partners is taxable to the partner because the income is tax exempt.
- Partnerships with five or fewer members throughout the year where no member is another partnership.

So, take for example Jeff and Sarah, who decide to operate their carpentry business as a partnership. Since Jeff and Sarah are (obviously) individuals, and there are only two of them, they do not have to file a T5013. Instead, they simply need to calculate the net income from the partnership and claim one-half of the income on their personal tax returns. By the way, the income from their partnership is calculated like that of any other business (although some special rules apply). See Chapter 15 for the details. If you have determined that you need to file an information return for your partnership the following section explains how to file.

Practical considerations

Here are some basic, and valuable, tips to consider when filing.

- For simplicity, one partner should be put in charge of filing the T5013 Summary on behalf of all the partners. Note however that the CCRA will still hold each partner responsible for making sure a return is filed for each fiscal period — so if you have delegated the job, make sure it gets done!
- The return should be filed with the District Taxation Centre for the area where the partnership's head office or principal place of business is located. The CCRA's Web site lists all the offices.

Partnership Identification Number

Once you've determined that you have to file a partnership return, your partnership needs a Partnership Identification Number (PIN). You do not need to apply for a PIN. The CCRA will automatically assign you one when you file your first return. The PIN you are given should be used on the next information return you file.

Due dates for filing the information return

If all members of the partnership are individuals (that is, a physical person as opposed to a corporation, trust, or another partnership) you have to file your T5013 information return on or before March 31 following the calendar year in which the fiscal period of the partnership ended. Generally the CCRA requires a partnership to use the calendar year as its fiscal period. Simply stated, partnerships must generally have a December 31 year end, so for the December 31, 2000 year end, the T5013 must be filed before March 31, 2001.

The CCRA considers the return to be filed on the date the envelope is postmarked, if mailed, or on the date the return is hand delivered to your Tax Services office (they will date stamp it for you). If the due date for a return falls on a Saturday, Sunday, or statutory holiday, the CCRA considers the return to be filed on time if it is delivered or mailed on the first working day after the due date. The T5013 slips must be sent to the individual partners on or before the day you have to file the T5013 information return.

The T5013 must be filed by March 31 of the year following the year for which the partnership is reporting income. If you file it late, the CCRA may assess you penalties.

What if I file the return and subsequently find an error?

If you discover an error in your information return after you file it, simply send a letter to your tax centre explaining the error and including the necessary supporting documentation. Don't adjust your current year's return for errors made in a previous year. If the error affects the net income or loss of the partnership, amend the previous year's documents and issue new T5013 slips to the partners. The partners will also need to ask the CCRA to amend their personal income tax returns for that year. We'll tell you how to do this in Chapter 22.

Penalties for failing to file

Be aware that there are two ways you can be penalized if you fail to file:

- Late filing penalties may apply! The penalties are $25 per day, with a $100 minimum and a $2,500 maximum. The partnership pays this penalty.
- The CCRA can also assess the partnership for simply failing to file an information return (applies to all "non-tax return"). This will cost each partner up to $100 multiplied by the number of months or part months, up to a maximum of 24 months, that which the information return is not filed.

The CCRA means business! If no member of the partnership files an information return as required under the *Income Tax Act* the partners may be guilty of an offence. In addition to the penalties described above, the partners could be liable if convicted to a fine from a minimum $1,000 to a maximum of $25,000, or a fine and imprisonment for a maximum of 12 months.

How to deal with errors on T5013 slips

Amended slips — If you need to change some of the data on a slip for a certain partner, make your changes on a new slip and print the word "Amended" at the top of the revised slip. Two copies of the amended receipt should be sent to the recipient.

Additional slips — If you need to prepare an additional slip for a partner print the word "Additional" at the top of the new slip and send two copies of the slip to the recipient.

Canceled slips — If you issue a slip by mistake and you want to cancel it, send the CCRA another slip with the same data on it as the original with the word "Canceled" at the top. Send two copies of the canceled slip to the recipient.

Duplicate slips — If you issue a second T5013 to replace one that has been lost or destroyed, send the CCRA the replacement slip with the word "Duplicate"at the top and send two copies of the slip to the recipient.

Changes to the T5013 Summary

If you prepare amended, additional, canceled, or duplicate T5013 slips for individual partners and you are also changing the information on the T5013 Summary, you have to file an amended summary. Clearly print the word "Amended" at the top of the summary. You should also provide a written explanation of the changes you have made.

If you are not changing the information on the T5013 Summary, you do not need to file an amended summary just because the individual slips have changed. Simply send the changed copies of the slips to the CCRA with a covering note.

Determining the net income or loss of the partnership and partners

The T5013 Summary is an overview of the partnership's results for the fiscal period. The T5013 Supplementary (or "slip") is a condensed report of the details from the partnership's financial statements, adjusted for tax purposes and allocated to each partner. A partnership can have income or losses from more than one source, such as business, professional, commission, farming, fishing, rentals, and investments. If you do have more than one source of income, you will need to calculate the income or loss from each source separately because the sources may be taxed differently.

There are some expenses you cannot deduct from the partnership's income for tax purposes, either because the government doesn't allow them or because the individual partners must claim them and no sharing is allowed. There are also certain items that shouldn't be included in income because they are not taxable, although there are probably not as many of these as you'd like! When you have nondeductible expenses or nontaxable income, you will need to prepare a reconciliation of the partnership's net income or loss for tax purposes. We discuss the details of calculating partnership income in Chapter 15.

Who gets what? Where to submit your forms

Send the following to the CCRA:

- The original copy of the T5013 Summary
- Copy 1 of all related T5013 slips
- One copy of the financial statements for the year
- One copy of the reconciliation of the partnership's net income or loss for tax purposes.

You do not have to send in official receipts with an information return, but you must keep them, along with the partnership's other books and records, in case the CCRA wants to review them.

Send the following to the partners:

- Copies 2 and 3 of the T5013 slip

Keep the following for the partnership's records:

- Copy 4 of the T5013 slips
- One copy of the T5013 Summary
- One copy of all other attachments sent to the CCRA along with the information return.

How to complete the T5013 forms

General considerations:

- Ensure the information entered on the return is legible.
- Record all amounts in Canadian currency with dollars and cents.
- If no entry is required in a box, leave it blank; that is, do not put in zeros.

Area A — Identification

Enter the four-digit year as well as the month and day, in that order, from the start to the end of the fiscal period for which you are filing the information return; that is, 2000 01 01 to 2000 12 31 represents January 1, 2000, to December 31, 2000.

Enter your partnership's filer Identification Number. Remember, if this is the first time you're filing, leave this space blank and the CCRA will assign you a number.

Enter the partnership's name, exactly as shown on previous partnership information returns, if any.

Enter the complete address of the head office of the partnership.

Place a tick mark in the appropriate box indicating whether you have previously filed a return.

Enter the complete address where the partnership's books and records are located.

Enter the name of the partner in charge of handling correspondence with the CCRA.

Next, go through lines 51 to 57 and answer each question. Don't worry, they're not too tricky!

Area B — Certification

On lines 58 and 59, print the name and telephone number of a person familiar with the records and books of account, and the partnership's financial operations. Someone will need to take responsibility for this! The partner who is in charge of filing the information return for all members of the partnership has to complete and sign this area.

Area C — Summary of partnership's income or loss

Area C breaks down the sources of income and losses into various categories. This is important because different types of income may be subject to different tax rates. The amounts you show on lines 180 to 291 are the totals of amounts you will allocate to the partners in boxes 18 to 29 on the T5013 slips.

On lines 170 to 201, 290, and 291, fill in gross and net income for your partnership's specific type of activities. For example, if you are a partner in a law firm you earn professional income, so fill in lines 172 and 173.

Include amounts from both Canadian and foreign sources. Convert all income into Canadian currency.

On lines 170, 172, 174, 176, 178, 180, 200, and 290,

these amounts are the gross income for accounting purposes from the financial statements.

On lines 171, 173, 175, 177, 179,181, 201, and 291,

these amounts are the net income or losses adjusted for income tax purposes.

On line 220, enter the amount of capital cost allowance you included in arriving at the amount reported in box 291.

On lines 230, 231, and 232,

you will have to enter capital gains or losses from the year in this area. To determine capital gain or loss amounts, do the following:

- Add any reserves allocated in the previous year.
- Do not deduct any allowable reserves.
- Do not convert capital gains to taxable capital gains or capital losses to allowable capital losses.
- Do not include business investment losses.

On Lines 240, 241, and 242,

enter capital gains reserves from dispositions of real estate on line 240 and capital gains reserves from dispositions of all other property on line 241.

We fully explain the ins and outs of capital gains in Chapter 13.

On line 250,

enter the total amount of dividends from taxable Canadian corporations paid or considered paid during the fiscal period.

On line 260,

enter the total interest received from Canadian sources that was included in the partnership's income this year.

On line 270,

enter the total dividend and interest income from foreign sources received during the fiscal period.

On line 280,

enter the total business investment loss of the partnership.

Area D — Selected information from the partnership's financials

Copy the appropriate amounts from the financial statements to the appropriate lines.

Area E — Miscellaneous information

Answer each question by placing a tick in the appropriate box.

If you answer yes to a question, give the appropriate additional information requested.

Non-residents of Canada

You many think that just because a person doesn't live in Canada, that person can escape Canadian taxes. But don't worry — the long reach of the CCRA doesn't end at the border. You see, non-residents are subject to Canadian tax on most Canadian source income paid to them unless all or part of the income is specifically exempt under a tax treaty. This means that non-residents, just like you and I, can be subject to Canadian tax.

The taxation of non-residents is one area where the CCRA can't do it alone. Administratively, it would be very difficult to effectively track taxable Canadian source income paid to non-residents and to collect the taxes owing, so they made you — the individual paying the amounts to non-residents — responsible for collecting the tax and reporting the transactions. This means filing some non-tax returns with the CCRA. And make no mistake about it, not following the rules can cost you.

Transactions with non-residents

There are three different situations in which you are required to file information returns detailing your transactions with non-residents.

- When you pay a non-resident salary, wages, or director's fees for services they performed in Canada in an employment situation, you have to withhold income tax as you would for a Canadian employee.
- When you pay pensions, annuities, investment income, gross rents, royalties, retirement compensation arrangement payments, and estate or trust income to a non-resident, you have to withhold tax and complete information returns called a NR4 slip and a NR4 Summary.
- When you pay other fees or commissions to non-residents for services performed in Canada, other than in an employment situation, you have to withhold tax and complete information returns called a T4A-NR Summary and a T4A-NR slip.

NR4 returns

You have to file an NR4 return if you are a payer or an agent who is responsible for withholding and reporting Part XIII tax.

You are responsible for withholding Part XIII tax if you are one of the following:

- A Canadian resident who pays or credits Part XIII amounts to a non-resident;
- An agent or another person who receives Part XIII amounts, on behalf of a non-resident, from which tax was not withheld;
- Any other payer (including a non-resident) who pays or credits amounts that are subject to Part XIII tax.

So, if you run a business and employ non-residents to work for you, be aware of your filing requirements.

What is Part XIII tax?

Part XIII tax is the tax CCRA requires to be withheld and remitted on the following types of income if paid to non-resident individuals (including trusts) or corporations.

- Pensions and annuities
- Investment income (items like interest and dividends)

- Gross rents and royalties
- Estate or trust income
- Retirement compensation arrangement payments

The withholding rate is generally 25 percent on taxable amounts, unless reduced to a lesser rate in accordance with the provisions of a tax treaty with the non-resident's country of residence.

For example, Mr. Wilson pays rent on a business property to Ms. Wright, who lives in the U.S. The rent paid is $1,000 per month. Mr. Wilson must withhold Part XIII tax from this $1,000 and submit only the remainder to Ms. Wright.

The NR4 return

Once you've determined that you have to withhold Part XIII tax to the CCRA, you will want to know about your filing requirements. These requirements include filing an NR4 return with the CCRA. The NR4 return consists of two forms: the NR4 slip and the NR4 Summary.

The NR4 slip

You have to complete an NR4 slip for every non-resident person you paid or credited the above noted items to in the year. You have to complete an NR4 slip even if you did not withhold tax on these amounts, or you were not required to withhold tax due to an exemption under the *Income Tax Act.* Because of these withholding requirements, the CCRA can be assured that it knows of all non-residents who should have paid Canadian taxes in the year.

The NR4 Summary

The NR4 Summary records the totals of amounts that you report on NR4 slips.

The NR4 segment

If you file more than 300 NR4 slips, you have to divide them into bundles of 300 slips, with an NR4 segment attached to each bundle.

Reporting limits

Not all amounts paid to a non-resident must be reported on an NR4 slip. In general, you only have to report amounts on an NR4 slip if the gross income paid or credited during the year is $10 or more. See Table 3-1 for full details.

Table 3-1 Amounts Required to Be Reported on an NR4 Form

Total Income Paid or Credited	*Tax Withheld?*	*Report Amounts on NR4 Slip?*
Less than $10	Yes	Yes
Less than $10	No	No
$10 or more	Yes or No	Yes

Filing deadline

If you have to file an NR4, it should be done no later than March 31 of the year following the taxation year for which you are reporting. For example, an NR4 for the 2000 taxation year would be due March 31, 2001.

Rates of Part XIII tax

Non-residents have to pay a Part XIII tax of 25 percent on taxable amounts. This amount can be reduced to a lower rate under the provisions of a bilateral tax treaty if you pay or credit amounts subject to Part XIII tax to persons in countries that have tax treaties with Canada. For examples, see Table 3-2.

Table 3-2 Examples of Withholding Tax Rates with Treaty Countries

Treaty Country	*Withholding Tax Rate on Dividend Income*
Spain	15%
Italy	15%
United Kingdom	15%

Any taxable amounts you paid or credited to payees in non-treaty countries will be subject to the 25-percent Part XIII withholding tax. Additional applicable current tax rates may be obtained by contacting the CCRA by mail at this address:

International Tax Services Office
Canada Customs and Revenue Agency
2204 Walkley Road
Ottawa, Ontario
K1A 1A8

Or by phone at 1-800-267-3395.

As the payer or agent, you are responsible for withholding and remitting Part XIII tax at the correct rate. If you withhold too little, you will be on the hook personally for the tax liability.

Reduction in the amount of non-resident tax required to be withheld

A non-resident of Canada who intends to file an income tax return in Canada can apply to the CCRA for a reduction in the non-resident tax that you, as the payer or agent, have to withhold. To do this, the non-resident should use form NR5, "Application by a Non-Resident of Canada for a Reduction in the Amount of Non-Resident Tax Required to be Withheld." When the NR5 is processed, the CCRA will send a letter both to you as the payer and to the non-resident indicating any payments to which a tax reduction applies.

Don't apply a tax reduction unless you receive written permission from the CCRA because if you withhold too little you will be on the hook personally for the tax liability.

Amending, replacing, or canceling NR4 summaries and slips

Amended slips — If you need to change some of the data on a slip for a certain individual, you can change the required entries and print the word "Amended" at the top of the revised slip. Two copies of the amended receipt should be sent to the recipient.

Rental income from real property in Canada

A non-resident who receives rental income from property in Canada can ask that payers or agents be allowed to deduct tax on the net amount instead of the gross amount of rent. In order to do this, the non-resident has to complete form NR6 — Undertaking to File an Income Tax Return by a Non-resident Receiving Rent From Real Property. The non-resident has to file this form on or before January 1 of the tax year for which the request applies, or on or before the date the first rental payment is due.

The CCRA does in practice accept late filed NR6 forms. However, the effective date for withholding the net amount will be the first day of the month in which they receive the form. You will have to withhold tax on any gross rental income paid or credited to the non-resident before that date.

Regardless, when form NR6 is filed, you still must report the gross amount of rental income for the entire year on an NR4 slip.

Additional slips — If you need to prepare an additional slip for an individual print the word "Additional" at the top of the new slip and send two copies of the slip to the recipient.

Canceled slips — If you issue a slip by mistake and you want to cancel it, send the CCRA another slip with the same data on it as the original with the word "Canceled" at the top. Send two copies of the canceled slip to the recipient.

Duplicate slips — If you issue a second slip to replace one that has been lost or destroyed, send the CCRA the replacement slip with the word "Duplicate" at the top and send two copies of the slip to the recipient.

Changes to the NR4 Summary: If you prepare amended, additional, canceled, or duplicate NR4 slips and you are also changing the information on the NR4 Summary, you have to file an amended summary. Clearly print the word "Amended" at the top of the summary. You should also provide a written explanation of the changes you have made.

If you are not changing the information on the NR4 Summary, you do not need to file an amended summary. Simply send the changed copies of the slips to the CCRA with a covering note.

When to remit non-resident deductions

You should remit your non-resident tax deductions so that they are received by the CCRA on or before the 15th of the month following the month you withheld the tax.

The CCRA considers a payment to have been received on the date the payment is received by your Canadian financial institution or the date it is received at the CCRA. The payment being postmarked on the 15th does not mean it was received on time. If the 15th of the month is a Saturday, Sunday, or statutory holiday, however, the CCRA must receive your remittance on the next business day.

How to remit deductions

To make your payment directly to the CCRA, simply detach and return your completed non-resident tax remittance form from either form NR75, "Non-resident Tax Remitter Registration Form" or form NR76, "Non-resident Tax Statement of Account," with your cheque or money order made payable to the Receiver General for Canada. The payment should be mailed to the following address:

Canada Customs and Revenue Agency
875 Heron Road
Ottawa Ontario
K1A 1B1

If it is easier to make your payment at your bank, complete the remittance form, as noted above, and present the completed form to the teller with your payment. The teller should keep the remittance portion and return the top portion to you as your receipt.

You should write your non-resident account number on the back of your cheque or money order to help make sure your payment is processed correctly.

Missing or lost remittance form: If you lose or misplace your remittance form, you must still make your payment by the due date. You can send your cheque or money order to the Receiver General as described previously and include a short note that gives your name, address, non-resident account number, and the year and month covered by the payment.

Notice of Assessment, Notice of Reassessment or Collection Letter for non-resident tax

If you receive form NR81, "Non-resident Notice of Assessment" *or* form NR82, "Non-resident Notice of Reassessment" *or* form NR83, "Non-resident Collection Letter," use only the remittance portion attached to these forms to make your payment for a balance owing.

Late-remitting penalty: The CCRA will apply a late-remitting penalty if it does not receive your payment on time. Failure to deduct or remit tax: You will have to pay the tax yourself if you did not do the following:

- deduct income tax;
- withhold the correct amount of tax; or
- remit the amounts of tax you withheld.

In addition to the tax, you may have to pay a penalty, interest on the penalty, and interest on any amount that you originally should have deducted or remitted. Don't be tempted to ignore the rules — the CCRA means business!

Applying for a refund of tax overpayment

To get a refund of excess or incorrectly withheld Part XIII tax, the non-resident, payer, or disbursing agent has to complete form NR7-R, "Application for Refund of Non-resident Tax Withheld." This must be filed no later than two years from the end of the calendar year in which the tax was sent to the CCRA.

T4A-NR returns

You have to file a T4A-NR return if you make payments to non-residents of Canada for services performed in Canada other than in employment situations.

As the payer you must withhold 15 percent from fees, commissions, or other amounts being paid to non-resident individuals.

The T4A-NR return

The T4A-NR return consists of two forms: the T4A-NR slip and the T4A-NR Summary.

The T4A-NR slip

You have to complete a T4A-NR slip for every non-resident to whom you paid an amount for services they performed in Canada.

The T4A-NR Summary

The T4A-NR Summary return records the totals of all the amounts that you reported on the T4A-NR slips.

Filing deadline

If you have to file a T4A-NR, the CCRA must receive it on or before the last day of February following the calendar year in which you paid the amounts. The non-resident must be sent copies 3 and 4 of the slip also by the last day of February.

Reduction or waiver of the amount of non-resident tax required to be withheld

A non-resident of Canada can apply to the CCRA for a reduction or waiver of withholding tax if the non-resident can demonstrate to the CCRA that the withholding is more than their Canadian tax liability.

Don't apply a tax reduction unless you receive written permission from the CCRA because, once again, if you withhold too little you will be on the hook personally for the tax liability.

Amending, replacing or canceling T4A-NR summaries and slips

The procedures for amending, replacing, and canceling summaries and slips are the same as those for the NR4.

When to remit non-resident deductions

You should remit your non-resident tax deductions so that they are received by the CCRA on or before the 15th of the month following the month you withheld the tax.

How to remit deductions

The procedures for remitting deductions are the same as those for the NR4.

Other Foreign Reporting Requirements

Effective in 1998, the government introduced new rules requiring Canadian residents to report to the CCRA information on certain offshore investments using an information return.

Here are the information return requirements:

- If you transfer or lend money to a non-resident trust, you have to file form T1141 or T1142 each year.
- If you own property with an adjusted cost base of $100,000 or more, you will be required to file form T1135. See Chapter 21 for more information on how to complete this form.
- If you or your business has foreign affiliates (that is, you have a greater than 10-percent interest in a foreign company), you will be required to file form T1134.

Think twice before ignoring the foreign reporting rules. The penalties for failing to file the required information can be painful.

Generally, forms T1135, T1134, and T1141 carry maximum penalties of $12,000 ($500 per month for up to 24 months) plus 10 percent of the foreign property beyond 24 months. Form T1142 carries a maximum penalty of $2,500 ($25 a day for up to 100 days).

Transfer Pricing

The pricing at which services, tangible property, and intangible property are traded across international borders between related parties is called *transfer pricing.* The transfer prices adopted by non–arm's length entities directly affect the profits to be reported by each of those entities in their respective countries. Canada's transfer pricing legislation attempts to stop entities from setting transfer pricing policies that allow them to essentially move profits out of Canada to a country where those profits would enjoy a more favourable tax rate.

This is accomplished by legislation that requires, for tax purposes, that the terms and conditions agreed to between non–arm's length parties in their commercial or financial relations be the same as those that would be expected if the parties were dealing with each other at arm's length. The goal of this legislation is that the entities report substantially the same amount of income as they would have if they had been dealing with each other at arm's length. In order to help the CCRA monitor your transfer pricing policies, it requires you to complete an information return with the details of all your transactions with non–arm's length non-residents.

Information Return of Non–Arm's Length Transactions with Non-Residents

The T106 Summary and Supplementary are annual information returns that the CCRA requires that you file to report certain transactions between you and non-residents. Only some transactions are considered by the CCRA to be reportable on the T106. Reportable transactions include the following:

- Relate to your line of business; for example, if you are a turkey farmer and you sell a cottage to a non-resident, the transaction does not relate to your business. However if you sell 10,000 turkeys at cost to your brother in the United States, the transaction does.
- Exceed $1,000,000 in total dollar value; that is, all your transactions with non–arm's length non-residents.
- Are between non–arm's length parties, that is, the non-resident is your descendant, brother or sister, spouse, or controlled corporation.

These transactions may include the following:

- Sale of raw or finished goods
- Rents, royalties, licence or franchise fees
- Managerial, financial, administrative, engineering services, and the like
- Interest, dividends, insurance
- Reimbursement of expenses.

It is unlikely that as an individual you will be required to file T106 documentation, but if your business operations do meet the criteria for reportable transactions the T106 Summary requires that you do the following:

- Complete the identification areas.
- Report the total transaction amounts reported on the T106 slips in Canadian dollars.
- State your main business activities.
- Provide contact person information.

The T106 Supplementary requires that you do the following:

- Complete the identification areas.
- Report in Canadian dollars the transactions between you and the non-resident by category.
- Indicate the transfer pricing method used.

Note: You must complete a separate T106 Supplementary for each different non-resident.

When to file

The T106 documentation must be filed by April 30 after the end of each calendar year. If you are self-employed, the due date is extended to June 15. Possible penalties are as follows:

- A late-filing penalty or multiple late-filing penalties may be assessed.
- There are additional penalties possible where an individual fails to file a return or to comply with the CCRA's requests for additional information.
- There may be a $24,000 penalty assessed for false statements or omissions.

Where to file

The T106 documentation has to be mailed to the following address:

Ottawa Tax Centre
Employer Services Division
Other Programs Unit
875 Heron Road
Ottawa, Ontario
K1A 1A2

Remember, do not attach the T106 documentation to your income tax return.

Chapter 4

Special Taxation Situations

In This Chapter

- Understanding the tax implications for Status Indians
- Leaving Canada
- Newcomers to Canada
- Death and Taxes
- Bankruptcy

Not all taxpayers are created equal. Sometimes your special situation opens up a whole new world of tax rules for you. You may be surprised what the taxman has in store. In this chapter we will walk you through some unique tax situations and give you all the information you need to prepare your return if they apply to you.

Status Indians

It's a common misunderstanding that Status Indians in Canada are exempt from tax. It is true that personal property of a Status Indian or an Indian Band situated on a reserve is exempt from taxation. This exemption is found in Section 87 of the *Indian Act.* In fact, the *Indian Act* outlines a variety of unique tax treatments that apply to Status Indians. However, it's important to note that income earned off a reserve is generally subject to taxation. Therefore, if you are a Status Indian, it's important for you to know what is taxable and what is not, so you stay out of trouble with the tax authorities. In addition, you should be aware of any tax-planning strategies that can help ensure your income continues to be tax-exempt.

The terms *Indian* and *Indian Band* are very important when determining your tax status. These terms are defined in the *Indian Act.* An Indian is a person who is registered as an Indian or is entitled to be registered as an Indian. So, if you are or were a member of a recognized Indian Band, you may be registered as an Indian. Indian status is passed down through generations, so if you have at least one parent who was entitled to be registered as an Indian, you can also register as an Indian. A band is a group of Indians who share the use and benefit of reserve lands, who share funds held by the Department of Indian Affairs, or who have been declared to be a band by the Governor in Council.

Only Indians and Indian Bands, as defined in the *Indian Act* are exempt from tax.

Just because you are a Status Indian, you are not necessarily exempt from tax in Canada. You see, only certain types of income are exempt. Under the *Indian Act,* "personal property" of an Indian or Band is exempt from tax. But don't worry. Personal property covers a wide range of items. In fact, personal property is generally defined to include everything except real estate, including any buildings and land. This means that most other income items are considered to be personal property for the purposes of the *Indian Act.* The types of income covered in personal property include the following:

- Wages; which includes salary earned from an employer.
- Business income, which includes all income earned from a sole proprietorship or partnership.
- Interest, which includes income earned on investments such as bonds, or GICs, as well as amounts received from lending others money.
- Dividends, which are really just your portion of the profits a company wishes to distribute to its shareholders. Generally, dividend income is earned on stocks and mutual funds.
- Rent. If you rent out any portion of a home or building to tenants, you earn rental income.
- Pensions. Pension income most commonly includes private pension income paid out under a life annuity. Often this is income paid out under a company pension where the former employee receives a fixed amount until death. For those over age 65, it also includes annuity payments out of an RRSP, and RRIF payments. Pension income does not include CPP or OAS payments.

Employment insurance benefits, retiring allowances, and pensions (including CPP and QPP) are also exempt from tax when the employment income that gave you the right to earn these amounts was exempt from tax.

Location is key. Personal property of a Status Indian must be situated on a reserve to be exempt from tax. It's not enough for you to simply live on a reserve. For example, you do not have to pay federal income tax on employment income that you earn while working on certain settlements. Your employer must withhold income tax from your income unless the employment income is for work on a reserve or both you and your employer are resident on a reserve (even if you perform your duties off the reserve). In addition, even if you live off a reserve, some of your income may be exempt from tax. For example, if your employer resides on a reserve and you perform your duties on a reserve, that salary may be exempt from tax. Sometimes whether your income is exempt is a grey area, and all factors must be considered before determining your tax status.

Leaving Canada

We hear almost daily about the brain drain in Canada. Due to a booming economy in various areas of the world (especially the United States), many Canadians are leaving their homeland to work elsewhere. In addition, many retired Canadians are moving south permanently to enjoy the pleasant weather we so often long for in Canada.

Whatever the motivation, the decision to leave Canada should not be taken lightly. You see, depending on your personal situation, the tax implications of the decision could be costly. There are steps that can be taken before you leave, to soften the tax blow. A visit to a tax pro is a must.

Many people leave Canada thinking they're now free from Canadian taxation. This isn't necessarily true. Read Chapter 2 to find out if you are in fact exempt from Canadian tax. Just because you think you're giving up residency does not mean that the CCRA will agree.

Departure tax

When you leave Canada permanently, you are deemed to sell most of your assets for fair market value on the date of departure. The resulting tax is referred to as *departure tax.* And tax proposals released by the Department of Finance on December 23, 1998, have broadened the application of these deemed disposition rules.

Deemed disposition rules

The deemed disposition rules work to tax any accrued gains on property owned by a Canadian resident prior to his or her departure to another country. By imposing a departure tax, Canada is assured to receive its share of tax on the net gains that accrued on property while it was owned by the Canadian resident. On the day of departure, the difference between the fair market value of the assets and their adjusted cost base becomes a capital gain or loss subject to Canadian taxation.

Be aware of the deemed disposition rules before you decide to leave Canada. If you own assets that have appreciated in value since you bought them, you will find yourself with a huge tax bill when you file your Canadian tax return. And since you are only deemed to have sold the assets (you haven't *actually* sold them), you won't have proceeds to pay your tax bill. This means you may have to liquidate some of your assets to pay your bill!

Under the new deemed disposition rules, you are deemed to dispose of almost all your assets, at their fair market values, when you leave Canada. Under the new rules even some items that are taxable Canadian property, including shares in private Canadian corporations, will be subject to departure tax.

Deferring tax:

Clearly, the decision to cease Canadian residency can be costly for many individuals. Because of the large potential tax liabilities on departure, but no corresponding cash inflow (since the assets have not actually been sold), the CCRA will allow you to defer your tax payments until the property is actually sold. This deferral is only available if you post acceptable security for the tax liability. For example, a letter of credit, a mortgage, a bank guarantee, or even the assets subject to the deemed sale could be considered acceptable security. The security will be returned and the departure tax is due when the property is actually sold.

When security is posted, no interest or penalties will be charged on the outstanding tax liability. However, if the value of the assets posted as security declines and the tax bill is no longer covered, the individual will have 90 days, after being notified by the CCRA, to make up the deficiency. If the deficiency is not covered, this portion of the tax liability will be subject to interest and penalty charges.

The deemed disposition rules: The new versus the old

Prior to October 2, 1996, the deemed disposition rules did not apply to taxable Canadian property since this property was taxed when actually sold by the non-resident. For example, Canadian real estate and shares of private Canadian corporations were considered taxable Canadian property, and therefore escaped departure tax. However, due to new and changing tax treaties, Canada was not always able to levy tax on taxable Canadian property when it was sold by a non-resident. Therefore, the Canadian government was not able to collect the portion of the tax revenues relating to the individual's residency in Canada.

On December 23, 1998, the Department of Finance announced new rules with respect to the deemed disposition of assets. This proposed legislation will help ensure that Canada retains the right to tax all gains on property prior to a Canadian resident's departure. These rules apply retroactively to October 2, 1996. Under these new rules, all assets held by a Canadian resident are deemed to be disposed of at the time of departure, except the following:

- Direct holdings of real or resource properties in Canada (such as land)
- Pensions and retirement savings plans (including RRSPs and RRIFs)
- Trust interests acquired for no consideration
- Unexercised employee stock option rights (but not shares acquired under a stock option agreement)
- Property used in a business carried on in Canada
- Life insurance policies (not including segregated funds)
- Assets owned at the time of immigration to Canada. This exception only applies if you've lived in Canada for less than five years.

You can defer the tax on the first $25,000 of departure taxes without posting security. This tax is still only due when the assets are actually sold.

Reporting requirements

Under the new rules, a person emigrating from Canada in 1996 or later and owning property worth $25,000 or more, must file a special information return on departure. This form, called T1161, requires the individual to list all significant assets. However, cash, RRSPs, private company pension plans, RRIFs, retirement compensation arrangements, employee benefit plans, deferred profit-sharing plans, and personal use property with a fair market value of less than $10,000 do not have to be included in the $25,000 total.

Filing requirements

So you've left our land of maple syrup and Mounties for greener pastures. Here are some loose ends you'll have to tie up so you won't get yourself into hot water:

- You have to file a tax return in the year you depart Canada. This return will report all your worldwide income earned before your date of departure, plus any deemed dispositions of your assets. Any income earned outside Canada, after your date of departure, should not be reported on your Canadian tax return. It will be taxed in your new country of residence. On page 1 of the tax return, you must enter your date of departure. This tax return is due on April 30 (or June 15 if you're self-employed).

Treatment of RRSPs for those leaving Canada

RRSPs are one of the few assets that escape departure tax. And since RRSPs are usually one of the largest assets you may own, it's important that you are aware of some tax-planning strategies for your RRSPs before you leave Canada.

First, you should generally leave your RRSPs intact when you give up Canadian residency. Collapsing an RRSP while resident in Canada will mean an income inclusion of the full value of the RRSP. And this means that the value of your RRSP will be taxed at your marginal tax rate. Depending on the value of the RRSP and your other sources of income in the year, this may result in almost half of the RRSP's value being paid in tax! On the other hand, if you determine you need your RRSP funds after giving up Canadian residency, the full value of the funds could be withdrawn and would be subject to a withholding tax of just 25 percent in Canada, which could mean up to 25 percent in tax savings! In addition, if you're moving to the United States. the withholding rate could be reduced to just 15 percent of the withdrawal if you meet certain conditions.

U.S. residents receiving money from a Canadian RRSP will be eligible to withdraw, tax-free, a portion of their RRSP while resident in the United States. The portion that may be withdrawn on a tax-free basis is equal to the book value of the plan on the date that the individual becomes resident in the United States. This means that Canadian residents should ensure that the book value of their RRSP is as high as possible before moving to the U.S. This can be done by selling all the RRSP assets that have appreciated in value and then reinvesting the proceeds. Since the gain is in a registered account there will be no tax implications, but you will manage to have a higher book value to draw from in the U.S. These steps should be taken before you give up Canadian residency.

You should also try to top up your RRSPs before emigrating. This is most beneficial if you are in the highest tax bracket, because, as a Canadian resident, the RRSP contribution is deductible for tax purposes. If you are in the highest tax bracket, this could mean a tax saving of about 50 percent. The money can then be withdrawn when you are a resident in another country, with only 25 percent (or even 15 percent) being withheld for taxes. Therefore, whenever you will pay more than a 25 percent combined federal and provincial Canadian tax in the year you leave Canada, you will save tax if you make an RRSP contribution before leaving the country.

If you continue to earn certain types of Canadian source income after you leave Canada, you must also report this on a Canadian tax return. For example, if you have any Canadian employment income, Canadian source grants, scholarship prizes for achievement or RESP payments in the year, carried on a business in Canada, or disposed of taxable Canadian property, this income must be reported on a Canadian tax return. It does not matter if you are still a Canadian resident for tax purposes when you receive this income.

- You may claim most deductions from your income in the year you cease residency, as long as the deductions apply to the part of the year you were a resident in Canada. You may also claim nonrefundable tax credits; however, some of these tax credits must be prorated for your period of residency in Canada. For example, if you cease Canadian residency on January 29, 2000, you can only claim 29/366ths (or 8 percent) of certain nonrefundable tax credits. (No, we're not crazy — 2000 really did have 366 days!)

Nonrefundable tax credits subject to proration include the basic personal amount, the age amount, the spousal amount, the equivalent to spouse amount, the caregiver amount, the disability amount, disability amount transferred to a relative, unused credits transferred from your spouse, and unused tuition and education amounts transferred from your child. All other nonrefundable tax credits, such as the pension credit, tuition amounts for yourself, charitable donations and medical expenses, do not have to be prorated. However, you must only include on your tax return the expenditures incurred while you are taxable in Canada. For example, if you left Canada on June 15, 2000, and had no taxable income to report in Canada after that date, you would not be allowed to claim on your Canadian tax return any medical expenses incurred on June 30, 2000.

- If you leave Canada owning assets with a fair market value of more than $25,000, you also have to fill out form T1161. This form is due on the date your regular tax return is due.
- You may still be required to file a Canadian tax when you're a non-resident, depending on the types of income you earn. Many types of Canadian-source income must still be reported, and taxed, in Canada. If you will continue to earn any Canadian source income, read Chapter 2 to see if you have to file a tax return.

Newcomers, Welcome to Canada

If you're new to our country you have some major homework to do. Canada has one of the most complicated tax systems in the world. But don't let that deter you from learning about the Canadian tax system and maybe even trying to do your own return. Your own return may not actually be all that complicated. And having at least a general knowledge of tax can help you to structure your affairs to take advantage of our tax rules. Besides, tax can be a fascinating topic (O.K., we may be exaggerating a bit).

Once you are a resident in Canada, the government levies taxes on all your worldwide income. Basically what this means is that you don't have to report on your Canadian return any income you earned before you came to Canada. However, after you arrive in Canada you are taxed on all income earned in Canada as well as any income you earn in other countries. All this income must be reported on your Canadian tax return.

In the year you become a Canadian resident, enter the date you became resident on page 1 of your tax return.

Becoming a Canadian citizen is not the same as becoming a Canadian resident for tax purposes. As soon as you set foot in Canada and establish residential ties here (that is, you are coming to live here), you are taxable in Canada. It does not matter whether you are a citizen of Canada. Even if you are a refugee, have applied for or received landed immigrant status, or have received "approval in principle" from Citizenship and Immigration Canada to stay in Canada, you must file a tax return and report all your worldwide income in Canada.

Once you come to Canada you should apply for a Social Insurance Number. This is a personal identification number used for income tax and benefits purposes. You can apply for a SIN through any Human Resources Centre of Canada. If you don't have a SIN by the time you must file your tax return, you're not off the hook for filing. You should still file your return and attach a note stating you've applied for, but have not yet received, your SIN.

Deemed acquisition rules

Similar to the deemed disposition rules for people leaving Canada, when you come to Canada you are deemed to reacquire all your assets at their fair market value at the time of your arrival. You see, when you sell the assets, the difference between your proceeds of disposition and the adjusted cost base of the asset is taxable in Canada. However, since part of the gain may have been attributable to the period when you were not a Canadian resident, it's not fair for Canada to tax that portion of your gain. Under the deemed acquisition rules, you will bump up the cost base of your assets so the Canadian tax authorities will not tax you on gains attributable to your period of non-residency.

If you're a newcomer to Canada, make a listing of all your assets on the date you came to Canada, along with their fair market values. As you sell the assets in the future, refer to this list to ensure you are maximizing the adjusted cost base of your assets and minimizing your tax bill.

Filing requirements

Once you have determined that you're taxable in Canada, you'll be required to file a tax return. This is the same tax return that is filed by all Canadians, and all the tax rules outlined in this book will now apply to you. To complete your return, you should use forms for the province or territory where you lived on December 31, 2000.

You can get the forms you need to prepare your tax return at your local tax services office, in any postal outlet, or on the Internet.

Your tax return is due on April 30, 2001 — unless you or your spouse carried on a business in 2000, in which case your return is due before June 15, 2001. It does not matter what date during 2000 you became a resident of Canada; your tax return due date will not change.

In addition, in the first year you become Canadian there are some special considerations:

- You are only liable to pay tax on your worldwide income after you become resident in Canada. Any income earned in other countries *before* this date does not have to be reported on your Canadian tax return.
- If you earned Canadian source income before you became a Canadian resident, this income will also have to be reported on a Canadian tax return. This includes income from employment in Canada or from a business carried on in Canada, taxable capital gains from disposing of taxable Canadian property, and the taxable portion of scholarships, fellowships, bursaries, and research grants you received from Canadian sources. Of course, if any of this income is exempt from tax in Canada due to a tax treaty Canada has with your former country of residence, it does not have to be reported. If you don't know your income is treaty exempt, contact the CCRA.
- Your nonrefundable tax credits must be prorated for the number of days you were resident in Canada this year. For example, if you came to Canada on July 3, 2000, you can claim only 185/365 or 50.7 percent of certain nonrefundable tax credits. This is identical to the rule for individuals leaving Canada in the year, so you may want to take a look at the section on Leaving Canada in this chapter for further information.

- There are some deductions on the Canadian tax return that you may not be entitled to this year. For example, you cannot claim moving expenses for your move to Canada unless you are a full-time student at a qualifying post-secondary institution and you received a scholarship, bursary, fellowship, or research grant in the year. Also, you can only claim RRSP contributions once you have RRSP deduction room. See Chapter 16 for details.

Once you are considered to be resident in Canada, you must file a Canadian tax return. Noncompliance can mean penalties and interest. And our tax authorities mean business. They will not leave you alone until your tax obligations are met. But on the other hand, a tax return can be a good thing. By filing a Canadian tax return you may be eligible to take advantage of many credit and benefit programs our government has to offer, such as the Canada Child Tax Benefit and the GST/HST Credit program.

The Sure Things: Death and Taxes

When a loved one dies, the last thing you want to think about is tax. Nevertheless, in the year of death there are many special tax rules that you must be aware of. Some of these rules may seem to kick you while you're down, while others help to soften the blow. Either way, there are a lot of unique rules on death, so don't think that just because you can prepare your own tax return, you can necessarily prepare a date-of-death tax return. Without knowledge of these special rules you may end up losing more money than you should to the taxman, or find yourself in trouble with the tax authorities. It's not that these rules are necessarily difficult, they're just different. Read on, and we'll tell you more.

Minimizing your estate taxes

The first and most important tax rule on death is that you are deemed to dispose of all your assets at their fair market value. Did you get that? You are deemed to dispose of your assets, but you haven't actually sold anything. The implications of this are obvious. You will be

What is an estate?

You may have heard that on death your assets become part of your estate. It is this estate that can be passed on to your heirs. But what are the tax implications?

You already know that when you die you are deemed to dispose of all your assets at their fair market value (unless you leave them to your spouse). As of the date of death, a final personal tax return must be completed for the deceased, reporting all income and gains earned up to the date of death. In addition, as discussed in Chapter 8, there are some supplementary personal tax returns that can also be filed on death, depending on your personal situation.

After death, and after your personal tax filings are complete, your estate is left with your assets. These assets will be distributed to your heirs according to directions in your will, or, if you die intestate (without a will), according to the court's direction. There is often a lag between the time of death and the time the assets are distributed. During this lag the executor of your estate is responsible for taking care of these assets. And during this time income and gains could be earned on those assets. What does this mean for tax purposes? You guessed it, another tax return.

Income and gains earned after the date of death (and before the assets are distributed to heirs) are taxed in your estate. This means filing a T3 return. Basically, your estate becomes a testamentary trust, and a trust must file a tax return just the way a person does. The trust will have to file a tax return for each year until the assets in the trust are distributed to the beneficiaries of the estate. This should usually occur within one year of death.

triggering a tax bill but you will have no cash available. This means that some of the deceased's assets may have to be liquidated to pay this bill. Here's an example: Bart died on October 11, 2000. At the time of his death he owned shares with a fair market value of $100,000. He had originally purchased these shares for $10,000. On his terminal tax return (also known as his final tax return or date-of-death tax return), he will be deemed to have disposed of these shares. Therefore, on Schedule 3 of his return, he will show a capital gain of $90,000 ($100,000 less $10,000). He will be taxed on the taxable portion of this gain in the year of death, even though he didn't actually sell the shares prior to his death.

Estate planning can help minimize taxes on death. We cover various estate planning techniques in Chapter 25.

There is one way to avoid the deemed disposition on death. Leave your assets to your spouse or to a spousal trust. When assets are transferred between spouses, including upon death, the transfer takes place at adjusted cost base, and not fair market value. This means that any tax bill is deferred until the death of the second spouse.

Filing requirements at time of death

There are some special filing requirements and tax rules in the year of death. These include the following:

- The due date of a person's final tax return may not be April 30, as it is for other taxpayers. The due date in the year of death is the later of two dates: April 30 of the year following death, or six months following the date of death. For example, if a person dies in February 2000, the final tax return is due on April 30, 2001. However, if a person dies on November 9, 2000, the final tax return is not due until May 9, 2001. This gives the executor a little extra time to tie up loose ends and ensure he or she has all the information required to file the tax return.

  It is the responsibility of the executor of an estate to file the final tax return of the deceased. If you are the executor and do not feel you have the knowledge required to fulfill this duty, you are allowed to pass this responsibility off to someone else, such as an accountant. However, you are still ultimately responsible for ensuring the return is complete and filed on time.

- All amounts received or earned up to the date of death must be reported on a final return. This includes amounts that were payable but had not been received prior to the date of death. For example, if a person died on April 30, 2000, and earned dividends on April 29, 2000, these dividends must be reported on a final return even if the person did not receive the dividends until after death.

- There is an opportunity to save tax by filing more than one tax return in the year of death. One of the most common extra returns is called the Rights or Things return. This is a regular tax return; however, it will report only certain types of income earned but not received by the taxpayer prior to death. This means that there are opportunities to double up on certain nonrefundable tax credits and take advantage of low rates of tax more than once during the same tax year. We will cover these special returns in Chapter 8.

- Full personal amounts, including the basic personal amount, spousal credit, age amount, disability amount and all other nonrefundable tax credits can be claimed on the final tax return. These credits are not prorated to the date of death. Therefore, even if a person dies on January 1, 2000, a full year's worth of nonrefundable tax credits can be claimed.

  If the spousal credit is being claimed in the year of death, you must take into account the spouse's net income for the entire year, not just the income to the date of death.

- Some special rules apply to certain nonrefundable tax credits that are claimed on the deceased's final tax return. First, when a person dies, medical expenses can be claimed for any 24-month period that includes the date of death (to the extent that they exceed 3 percent of net income, or $1,614, whichever is less). Normally medical expenses can only be claimed for a 12-month period ending in a year. Next, charitable donations of up to 100 percent of the deceased's net income can be claimed on the final tax return. Normally donations of up to 75 percent of net income are allowed.

If a person states in her will that a portion of her assets are to be donated to a registered charity on death, ensure the amount donated is included as a charitable donation of her final personal tax return. Even if the gift will be received sometime down the road, the CCRA will allow the donation credit on the final tax return if you attach a copy of the will, a letter from the estate to the charity advising the charity of the gift and its value, and a letter from the charity acknowledging the gift and stating it will accept the gift.

If donations in the year of death exceed 100 percent of the deceased's net income, consider carrying the donation credits back to the previous year. This will offset taxes paid in prior years, resulting in a tax refund!

- If a death benefit was received, the benefit is income of either the estate (that is, reported on a T3 return) or in the hands of the beneficiary who received the benefit. It should not be reported on the deceased's final personal tax return.

All CPP or QPP death benefits received in a year are taxable. Up to $10,000 of other death benefits received on behalf of a person's employment can be received tax-free.

- If a non-capital loss occurs in the year of death, the normal loss carry-back rules apply, so the loss can be carried back to offset taxable income of any of the prior three taxation years. However, if net capital losses occur in the year of death, special rules apply. Normally, net capital losses can only be used to offset taxable capital gains. In the year of death, these rules change slightly. You see, in addition to offsetting capital gains in any of the prior three years, these losses may also be used to reduce other forms of income in the year of death, and the year preceding death.

If the deceased had net capital losses carried forward from previous years, these losses can be used to offset income from any source in the year of death, as well as in the year preceding death.

Bankruptcy

If you're thinking of declaring bankruptcy, add income taxes to your list of concerns. You see, in the year you declare bankruptcy, there are special tax rules that will apply to you. The good news is that your trustee will help you with some of these tax filings, but an understanding of the rules and of your responsibilities is vital.

The bankruptcy rules

In the year you declare bankruptcy, your year is actually broken up into two taxation years. The first taxation year runs from January 1 to the day before bankruptcy is declared. This is called the pre-bankruptcy period. The next taxation year, which is called the post-bankruptcy period, begins on the day you declared bankruptcy and ends on December 31.

The income tax returns for both your pre-bankruptcy and post-bankruptcy periods are due on April 30 of the following year. You are responsible for filing these two tax returns.

On your pre-bankruptcy tax return you must report income, gains, and losses from all sources, just as you would on any tax return. Of course, only transactions that took place prior to the date you declared bankruptcy must be reported. Your post-bankruptcy return only reports income you earned subsequent to your bankruptcy, and only reports items for which you are responsible. You see, when you declare bankruptcy, a trustee in bankruptcy takes all your assets into management in order to discharge your debts and provide you with some support. You no longer control how these assets are used. Therefore, any income on your assets, including any realized gains or losses, is not reported on your post-bankruptcy return.

In fact, there is a third return, called a trustee's return, that will report income, gains, and losses on assets held by your trustee. This return is not your responsibility. Instead it will be filed by your trustee. This means that your post-bankruptcy return will probably only include any employment income earned directly by you or any types of income you received directly during the post-bankruptcy period. There are special tax rules that apply to both your pre- and post-bankruptcy periods. These include the following:

- You must prorate certain of your personal credits between your pre- and post-bankruptcy periods based on the number of days in each period. In other words, you cannot claim more than one full year's worth of credits between the two periods. For example, if you declare bankruptcy on February 21, 2000, you may claim 52/366 of your basic personal amount, age credit, disability credit, and any transfer of credits from other individuals on the pre-bankruptcy return. The other 314/366 worth of credits is claimed on the post-bankruptcy return.
- If you are eligible for the pension credit, your credit will be apportioned between the pre- and post-bankruptcy periods based on your income level in each period. For example, if you earn $2,000 of pension income in the pre-bankruptcy period and $3,000 in the post-bankruptcy period, your pension credit in the first period will be $400 ($2,000 divided by $5,000 times $1,000 maximum credit), and $600 in the second period.
- If you are eligible for the CPP/EI credit, tuition and education credit, student loan interest credit, or medical expense credit, your nonrefundable tax credits will be apportioned between the pre- and post-bankruptcy periods based on when the actual expenditure took place. So, if you worked during your pre-bankruptcy period and paid CPP and EI premiums only during that period, you will only receive a nonrefundable tax credit for the premiums paid during the pre-bankruptcy period. On the other hand, if you incurred medical expenses throughout the year, you should claim all expenses incurred in the pre-bankruptcy period on the pre-bankruptcy return, and all expenses in the post-bankruptcy period on the post-bankruptcy return.

If you cannot use all your tuition and education credits on your pre-bankruptcy return, you cannot carry forward the excess to use on your post-bankruptcy return. In this case, inform your trustee in bankruptcy of the carryforward for possible use on the special trustee's tax return.

- Charitable donations made in the pre-bankruptcy period must be claimed on the pre-bankruptcy return. Donations made after this period must be reported to the trustee and reported on the special tax return filed by the trustee — not on the post-bankruptcy return.
- Loss carryovers cannot be claimed on the post-bankruptcy return. If there are any non-capital or net-capital loss carryovers from previous taxation years, these losses must be used by the trustee on the special trustee's return.

Special trustee's return

When you declare bankruptcy, a trustee oversees all your affairs. This trustee is responsible for dealing with your assets, including any businesses you own, from this point until you are discharged from bankruptcy. And the trustee is also responsible for filing a special tax return that will report the net income from your assets and businesses managed by the trustee during your post-bankruptcy period. This tax return is due on March 31 and covers your entire period of bankruptcy in the previous calendar year.

The trustee's return is like a regular personal tax return except that no personal tax credits, such as the basic personal amount, are allowed. However, if there are unused tuition and education amounts, or charitable donations made in the post-bankruptcy period, these amounts may be claimed on the trustee's return.

Discharge from bankruptcy

Special tax rules also apply in the year you are discharged from bankruptcy. First, before the discharge is granted, the trustee is still managing your property and business. Therefore, this trustee must file a trustee's return for that period outlining the net income from any transactions made on your behalf during this time.

You also have a tax filing responsibility in the year you are discharged from bankruptcy. You must file a tax return for that entire year. Of course, in the period before you are discharged, you only have to report any income (such as employment income) received directly by you. This is identical to the types of income you reported in the post-bankruptcy period in the year you declared bankruptcy. In addition, your tax return will have to report income from all sources for the period after you are discharged from bankruptcy.

Absolute versus conditional discharges from bankruptcy

There are two different types of discharges from bankruptcy, and depending on the type of discharge, the tax implications will be different. If you receive an absolute discharge from bankruptcy, all your debts up until the time you declared bankruptcy will be erased. This includes any debts owing to the CCRA.

If you've received an absolute discharge from bankruptcy, your ability to carry forward tax credits and deductions will be limited. For example, if you have unused tax losses from prior years, you will not be allowed to apply these losses after your absolute discharge; they are deemed to be nil. In addition, if you have alternative minimum tax (AMT) carryovers, charitable donation credits, investment tax credits, or unused education and tuition amounts, these credits are also deemed to be nil, so you will lose any tax advantages of these credits.

Sometimes you are discharged from bankruptcy but are not absolved of all your debts. For example, you could still be required to pay amounts to certain creditors, one of which could be the CCRA. This is called a *conditional discharge*. If you receive a conditional discharge, any past tax credits and losses remain intact, so you can use them to offset future income and taxes payable.

Chapter 5

Getting and Staying Organized

In This Chapter

- Understanding the necessity of keeping good books and records
- Knowing how long to keep your records
- Dealing with the loss of information slips and receipts
- Taking a look at The Cohan Rule

Do you want to know the secret to making sure you claim every deduction you're entitled to? To saving money when you have a tax preparer do your tax return? To surviving a CCRA audit unscathed? We'll tell you . . . keep good records!

That is all there is to it, really! In this chapter we give you our tried-and-true methods of keeping things organized — methods that will save you time and money down the road.

If you are one of those people with good intentions and a box full of paper in which you might just as easily find your grade 4 spelling test as your tax receipts, don't give up hope. You may have left getting organized a little late — but better late than never. Read on and take heart.

Did you know that when dealing with the CCRA, the burden of proof is on you to provide support for the deductions you have claimed? The CCRA is considered by law to be correct unless you can prove otherwise. This is one case in which you are guilty until proven innocent.

Keeping Good Books and Records

You may think that by filing a tax return for the year you've absolved yourself from any further CCRA requirements. Unfortunately that's not true. You see, the CCRA requires every person who is required to pay or collect taxes, or who is carrying on a business in Canada, to keep books and records. The requirement means you have to keep information pertaining to your taxes in case the CCRA asks to see this information in the future. If reviewed by the CCRA, the books and records must enable the CCRA to determine your taxes payable for the year and must be supported by source documents to verify the amounts reported.

Make sure you keep all source documents pertaining to your tax return. These include such documents as the following:

- Sales invoices
- Purchase invoices
- Cash register receipts
- Formal written contracts
- Credit card receipts

- Delivery slips
- Deposit slips
- Cheques
- Bank statements
- General correspondence.

When deciding what type of source document to keep, consider this: What type of document will best verify your tax records? The stronger the evidence, the less likely it is that your tax records will be rejected by the CCRA. Let's face it. Keeping good books and records is always a good idea because it makes doing your taxes less of a chore. Now that you have two good reasons for keeping proper records, here's how to do it!

Setting up your record-keeping system

In our experience, the number one reason people end up paying more tax than they have to is because they keep lousy records. We know that taming the paper tiger is no mean feat. There are books written on that subject alone. What follows are our best suggestions to make your tax organization and preparation tasks much easier.

Our favourite method of organizing tax information is in an accordion file. You can pick up one of these at any office supply store. Label each section by expense category. Use the categories listed on the tax form you will be completing; for example, office supplies, parking, advertising. As you collect receipts throughout the year, periodically sort them into the proper category. When it comes time to file your tax return, all you have to do is take out the receipts, add them up and enter the total on the tax form.

An alternative way of achieving the same result (if you've had a traumatic experience with an accordion in the past) is by using file folders or envelopes. Label each file or envelope by category, and, again, sort the receipts into the proper folder or envelope on a regular basis. Save all receipts and records that you feel you might be able to use. It is much more difficult to recover receipts that have been thrown away than it is to ceremoniously toss out whatever unnecessary paper you have left after your tax return is complete.

You may want to consider organizing your tax information by the tax schedules you have to file; that is, Statement of Real Estate Rentals, Capital Gains and Losses, Statement of Business Income and Expense. If your tax return is uncomplicated, it might be sufficient to have one file for each year; as you receive your tax information throughout the year, just put it into the file. This will save you from tearing your house apart looking for that investment statement or charitable receipt you were using as a bookmark last June. Keep a copy of the tax return you filed for that year and your Notice of Assessment, once received, in the same file folder.

Even if you end up hiring a tax accountant to prepare your tax return for you, you will save money if you sort and organize your tax information before you hand it over.

Your friend the computer

Your computer can be a huge help in tracking your tax information each year. There are a number of software packages available that do an excellent job. There are many software packages out there, each with its own merits. Speak with a knowledgeable software salesperson before purchasing to make sure you get only what you need. There is no sense in buying an expensive, state-of-the-art accounting package if you are only going to use one or two components.

We recommend the software packages Quicken and Microsoft Money for tracking personal and small business expenses and Quickbooks for tracking the expenses of larger businesses. These packages will help you do everything from tracking your investment portfolio to balancing your chequebook to monitoring payroll. Using a software package to enter your data means more of a time commitment up front, but when you need the records for tax time, the figures will be added up and ready to go.

Valuable record-keeping tips

Keep detailed proof of any expenses you claim. This proof can consist of many things, but the original bill is best. The CCRA will not always accept canceled cheques and credit card statements as authentication of an expense, so if you're one of the unfortunate Canadians who are audited each year, your deductions may be disallowed!

If you do use a computer to do all your record keeping or if you have other valuable papers, it makes sense to store a recent backup of your computer files and those valuable papers, or copies of them, off-site. That way if you suffer a fire or other disaster, all will not be lost.

To support claims for child care expenses, you will need original receipts from the camp or program your child(ren) attended. If a nanny or baby-sitter looks after your children, you must report that person's social insurance number on your tax return.

Record-keeping timebombs

Look out for these special situations:

- **Automobile expenses:** If you are claiming automobile expenses for a vehicle used for both business and personal purposes, you must keep a log to support the vehicle's business use, detailing dates, number of kilometres driven and destinations. You see, you can only deduct the portion of your automobile that you used for business purposes. If you do not have a log, the CCRA may deny some or all of the expenses you deducted in respect of that vehicle.
- **Charitable receipts:** A charitable receipt from a registered charity is the only support accepted by the CCRA for a charitable donation. Canceled cheques and ticket stubs will not be accepted. And if you want to claim a tax credit, ensure you are donating to a registered charity — ask to see a registration number if you're not sure.

How Long Should I Keep My Tax Records?

One of the questions we are most frequently asked is "How long do I have to keep my records and receipts?" The answer according to the CCRA is six years. The books and records must be kept in Canada at your residence or place of business. Remember, these books and records must be made available to the CCRA should they ask to see them.

You may ask for special permission from the CCRA to dispose of your records early; that is, when your apartment is 400 square metres and your tax records are taking up 300 of them. Make sure the CCRA has approved your request before you invite all the neighbours for a bonfire.

Even though after six years the CCRA can't go back and audit your tax return — unless fraud is suspected, in which case all tax years are free game — you will need to keep purchase receipts and investment statements for assets you still own. You may need those records as proof of ownership if you ever have to make an insurance claim or if you sell the asset. And you may need proof of its cost in the future if the gain or loss must be reported on your tax return.

If a particular tax year is under objection or appeal, you should keep your books and records on hand until the objection or appeal has been disposed of and the time for filing a further appeal has expired. It would be a shame to throw out your books and records, only to have legitimate tax deductions denied down the road.

Missing Information Slips and Receipts

Employers and other issuers of information slips are generally required to send you your slips by no later than the last day of February in the year following the year in which you received the payment. This includes slips such as T4s, T5s, and slips from the government. However, T3 slips are often not available until after March 31.

Making sure your employer and financial institution have your most recent address is one way of making certain you get your slips on time. If by mid-March you haven't received an information slip you were expecting (other than a T3 slip), you should contact the issuer of the slip directly.

Giving the CCRA your best estimate

If, after you've made a reasonable attempt to obtain your slip, you are still "slipless," you should estimate your income and related deductions (that is, CPP, EI, income tax, union dues), and report them on your tax return. Attach a note to your return stating you were unable to obtain your slip and summarize the estimated amounts. You should also give the name and address of the person or organization that should have issued the slip.

- If it is a T4 you are missing, attach a photocopy of your pay stubs as proof of your pay and deductions.
- If it is a T5 you are missing, it may be that you were not issued one by your financial institution. They are not required to issue one if the total amount paid to you in the year was less than $50. Unfortunately…you still have to report the income, so you'll have to look back on your meticulous tax records to calculate the amount to be reported. That said, many financial institutions still issue slips for less than $50.
- Foreign income and related taxes should be reported on your tax return in Canadian dollars, even though the slips themselves will probably report the amounts in foreign currency. The CCRA will provide average annual foreign exchange rates for your use. If you've paid taxes to a foreign tax authority, attach to your Canadian tax return proof of the taxes paid, to ensure you will get credit for these taxes in Canada.

You must still file your tax return before the April 30 filing deadline even if you know information is missing. Attach a note to your return explaining what is missing, detail any estimated amounts, and get it in on time! This is especially important if you owe money, since you will be charged a late filing penalty as well as interest if your balance owing is not paid by April 30.

Missing receipts

Receipts for some deductions, such as RRSP contributions, charitable donations, and medical expenses must be attached to your tax return when it is filed (assuming you are paper-filing your return). If these receipts do not accompany your return, processing will probably be delayed and your deductions may be disallowed. Remember, the onus is on you to prove all your income and deductions!

If your receipts are missing, call the person or organization responsible for issuing them to obtain another copy. If you cannot get another copy before the April 30 tax return filing deadline, you should still file your return on time. You can forward the slip to the CCRA when it does finally arrive. Alternatively, you can simply leave the deduction off your tax return and file an adjustment to your tax return once you receive the receipt.

Some other types of receipts don't have to be attached to your tax return. For example, if you have claims for union dues, tuition fees, or child care expenses, the receipts aren't attached to your return when it is filed. However, be aware that the CCRA does regular "reviews" of these types of credits and deductions, so you should still ensure you have the proper documentation on hand should the CCRA ask to see it in the future.

What to Do if the Dog Really Did Eat Your Tax Records

Your worst nightmare has come to life — you're being audited! And to top it off, Sparky has eaten some of your tax receipts. Does this mean you'll lose out on all your legitimate tax deductions? Not necessarily. The CCRA does understand that these situations can occur, and will give you the benefit of the doubt (sometimes) if you can show them reasonable proof of your income and deductions.

Reconstructing missing or damaged tax records

If the CCRA does come calling, and you simply don't have the tax records you need to support your tax deductions, all is not lost. There are other ways of proving your claims were legitimate. It may take you some time to reconstruct records, but when you consider the alternatives (additional tax, interest, and penalties on disallowed deductions from an audit), the time you spend will be well worth it. The simplest way to reconstruct missing tax records is to ask for new ones. For example, if you know you bought a number of prescriptions this year but can't find your receipts, go back to your local pharmacy and ask them for a printout of your expenditures for the year. You will be surprised at how many deductions you will be able to reconstruct simply by asking for duplicate receipts.

Of course, there will be some cases where it seems impossible to reconstruct your tax records. Here are some ideas to consider:

- To determine whether or not you made money when disposing of an asset, you have to know what it cost you and what you were paid for it. If you do not have a record of an asset's original cost, either because you lost the relevant documents or because the asset was a gift, there are several ways to establish a cost figure.
- Look in newspapers from the year you purchased or were given an asset to determine what similar assets were selling for. Your local library should have old newspapers on file or on microfiche.

- If trying to find information on a property, consult with the local real estate board. They usually keep historical data on property in the area. You could also go to the property tax collector's office in your municipality. Their assessed values for the property might be of use.
- If you are trying to establish the price of a publicly traded stock, bond, or other security, try to remember as best you can the date you acquired the security. When you have established the date of purchase, check back issues of a newspaper for prices, or use the securities pricing service of the Securities Exchange on which the security traded. Keep in mind that there may be a fee associated with using a securities pricing service.
- If you inherited an asset, the easiest way to establish its tax cost to you is to check the deceased's final tax return to see at what price they were deemed to have disposed of the property. This disposal price is the same as your tax cost.
- Check your 1994 tax return to see if you elected to increase the cost base of your asset that year. The year 1994 was the last year of the $100,000 capital gains election, and many taxpayers made an election in that year; that means the original cost of their asset is no longer relevant.
- Call your financial advisor for help. Your advisor will keep back records of your financial affairs and may be able to help you find the cost of your shares, mutual funds, or other assets managed by her.

Giving them the business: Tips for re-creating your records

If it is your business records that have been lost or destroyed, you can re-create many of your expenses using the following tactics:

- Get copies of your phone, utility, credit card, rent, and other bills from the companies that issued the bills. It shouldn't be too difficult to get an annual statement from a major vendor.
- It is possible to obtain duplicate bank statements from your bank (all for a small fee, of course!) that will help you to establish income for the year and some of your expenses.
- Automobile expenses may be reconstructed based on a reasonable estimation of what it would cost to run your type of vehicle. The dealer from whom you bought your car might be helpful in estimating these costs.
- Look at your previous years' tax returns to establish your expenses in prior years and also your profit margins. If you have lost those too, you can obtain copies of previous years' returns by request from the CCRA.

The Cohan Rule

Our discussion would not be complete if we didn't relate the story of George Cohan and the Cohan Rule. Mr. Cohan, a taxpayer in the United States, deducted $55,000 in business-related entertainment expenses in 1921 and 1922. The IRS (the U.S.'s equivalent of the CCRA) disallowed his deduction of these expenses on the grounds that Mr. Cohan had no receipts to support his claim and that it was therefore impossible to tell how much he had actually spent.

Mr. Cohan appealed his case and won. The court established the rule of approximation (a.k.a. the Cohan Rule) and instructed the IRS to "make as close an approximation as it can, bearing heavily, if it chooses, on the taxpayer whose inexactitude is of his own making." ("Inexactitude" being a fancy way of saying "no records.") For many years the Cohan Rule allowed taxpayers to deduct travel and entertainment expenses without really having to substantiate what they spent. Taxpayers only had to establish that it was reasonable they should have spent the amounts they claimed.

The U.S. Congress changed the law in the early 1960s to make sure taxpayers could no longer deduct expenses without backup, although there are still some deductions that are allowed based on estimates. These include taxi fares, tips, and petty cash expenses. Of course, Canadian courts do not use U.S. court cases or law to make their legal pronouncements, so the Cohan rule doesn't really apply to us. However, there was recently a useful quote in a Canadian court case (*Merchant* v. *The Queen*) that considered the situation in which a lawyer attempted to deduct certain expenses for which he had no receipts. The judge in this case made the following statement:

"It is my view that there is no requirement in law that expenses be supported by receipts or other corroboration if such expenses can be supported by credible viva voce testimony and the amounts can be identified with a reasonable degree of specificity (quoted from *Weinberger* v. *M.N.R.*, 64 DTC 5060*). Failure to keep books and records carries its own sanction but had Parliament intended that sanction to include non-deductibility of expenses, it would have been quite capable of saying so."*

Are we saying that you no longer have to keep receipts to support your tax deductions? Of course not! However, keep Mr. Cohan and Mr. Merchant in mind if ever you are under the watchful eye of the CCRA and have no receipts to prove your expenses. As they've shown us, if you can otherwise corroborate your deductions, you may be entitled to tax deductions even if you have no traditional receipts. But be prepared for a fight.

Chapter 6

Dealing with Those Taxing Administrative Matters

In This Chapter

- Understanding the administration of tax laws in Canada
- Taking a look at the Declaration of Taxpayer's Rights
- Getting a handle on social insurance numbers
- Submitting your return — the basics
- Withholding taxes
- Understanding Technical Interpretations
- Applying Advanced Tax Rulings

Before going too deeply into the technical rules of completing a tax return, let's stop and take a look at the big picture. This chapter will examine the structure of the Canadian tax system and how the laws are made and administered. In addition, we will discuss the rules of filing tax returns and the services available to assist you in meeting your obligations.

Administration of Tax Law in Canada

While sitting in front of a warm fire on a snowy winter's eve, the question of who administers the tax law in Canada naturally comes to mind. The answer is that the tax law in Canada is administered by the *Canada Customs and Revenue Agency* — the *CCRA* (you may know it by its former name, Revenue Canada). As of November 1, 1999, the Canada Customs and Revenue Agency became responsible for the administration of tax law in Canada. Though the CCRA runs the tax system, it does not make the tax laws. Tax laws are actually formulated by the Department of Finance in Ottawa. The tax legislation is passed into law by Parliament and interpreted by the courts. Revenue Canada is then responsible for using these laws to assess and collect federal tax. Federal tax includes personal and corporate tax, as well as GST and excise tax. The CCRA also collects provincial and territorial personal tax (except in the province of Quebec) and passes the money on to these jurisdictions.

To assist in the administration of the *Income Tax Act,* the CCRA publishes numerous bulletins and articles to help the public understand its position on issues. These documents are called Interpretation Bulletins, Information Circulars, Advance Tax Rulings, taxation guides and Technical Interpretations. The recent replacement of what most Canadians knew as Revenue Canada by the CCRA represented a major change in philosophy for this institution. CCRA moved from a department of the government controlled by the Minister of National Revenue to an autonomous self-governing agency that reports to the Minister. Big deal, right? Well, surprisingly enough this *was* a big deal. The agency now has its own board of directors made up of former ministry staff, provincial and business representatives, as well as other appointed government types. Through this change, Ottawa hopes to reduce the political influences affecting the CCRA, as well as giving business and the provinces a voice in the administration of the tax system. The eventual plan sees the provinces and territories merging their ministries of finance with the agency to create a "super tax-collecting machine." The main selling point of this super agency would be the elimination of the overlap and duplication of services between the federal and provincial governments. The vision of the one-tax authority is unlikely to become reality in the near future, however, since several provinces have already indicated they have no interest in participating.

Declaration of Taxpayer's Rights

Most people believe the only right they have when dealing with the CCRA is the right to pay tax or go to jail. To change this negative perception, the CCRA has established "*A Declaration of Taxpayer's Rights*." It is an attempt to define the rights and responsibilities each taxpayer should enjoy.

Look on the back page of the T1 General Income Guide for a reproduction of the Declaration and you'll find that the policy states that your rights include the following:

- The right to be treated with courtesy and consideration by all the CCRA employees
- The right to privacy and confidentiality
- The right to an independent and impartial review
- The right to bilingual service
- The right to withhold amounts that are in dispute
- The right to be presumed honest *(believe it or not!)*
- The right to complete, accurate information about the *Income Tax Act.*

Most important, the declaration gives you the right to arrange your affairs to pay the least amount of tax that the law allows. Note the phrase "that the law allows." The declaration states that the CCRA will be firm with those who are guilty of tax evasion. Along with these rights the declaration also imposes an important obligation on taxpayers. The declaration says that you are entitled to accurate information about the *Income Tax Act.* The CCRA interprets this to mean that since all the rules are available, you are obliged to follow them. In other words, ignorance of the Act is never an acceptable reason for misstatement on your tax return. These rights are unfortunately not legally binding on the CCRA and cannot be used in court.

If you believe that you have been treated in a manner that violates the word or spirit of this declaration, contact the Disputes Resolution Officer in your local Tax Services Office. This person's job is to resolve problems between taxpayers and the CCRA.

Social Insurance Numbers

Social insurance numbers (SINs) are the glue that holds the entire tax system together. Every individual who works in Canada is required to have a SIN. This SIN must be included on all tax returns and correspondence with the CCRA. The SINs of your spouse or common-law spouse must also be disclosed on your tax return to ensure that credits (child tax credit, GST) and deductions (child care expenses, spousal RRSP) are correctly calculated. Children usually do not require a SIN until they file a tax return or until you open a registered education savings plan (RESP) for them.

Getting a social insurance number

To obtain a SIN for you or your children, you must visit an office of Human Resources Development Canada. These offices are usually located in your local federal government building. To get a SIN you will need to prove your citizenship and verify your current address. Proof of identification such as a birth certificate, driver's licence, or citizenship card will be required. All this information is needed to ensure that the government is not issuing SINs to fictitious or non-existent individuals.

If you file a return with no SIN

If you file a return with no SIN, or the SIN is wrong, you could be fined $100 by the CCRA for failure to provide complete information. If the CCRA cannot identify your return, you will also be assessed a late-filing penalty of 5 percent of the amount owing and 1 percent per month for each month the return is late up to a maximum of 12 months. The CCRA will make an honest attempt to identify your return, but if they are unable to do so, it will be filed with the other unidentified returns and eventually lost. When you discover that your return was never received or identified by the CCRA, you will have to hope that it can be found in the pile of unidentified returns. If it is not found, you will have to re-file your return. Always double-check and photocopy your return before you send it to the CCRA.

If your children have SINs, always include these numbers in the dependent area of your return and that of your spouse.

When Is My T1 Return Due?

Your completed T1 is generally due on or before April 30 of the year following the taxation year in question. For example, your 2000 tax return is due April 30, 2001. If April 30 falls on a weekend, then your return is due the following Monday. There are some notable exceptions though — stay tuned!

If you are self-employed

If you or your spouse carry on a business, then both your returns are not due until June 15 of the year following the tax year in question. If June 15 is on a weekend, then the return is due the following Monday. For example, Ms. A is married to Mr. A. In the year 2000, Ms. A runs a computer business that reports income on her T1 return. As a result, both Mr. A and Ms. A do not have to file their T1 tax returns until June 15, 2001.

Unfortunately, even though the return is due June 15, any balance owing on this return must be paid on or before April 30 of the same year. If you are not filing your return until June 15, you'll need to estimate your balance owing and send payment to the taxman by April 30. If your estimate of your balance owing is too low, you will owe interest on the short payment.

The CCRA suggests that along with your tax payment on April 30, you include a letter outlining your social insurance number, what the payment is for and where it should be applied. This will ensure that the money is not put in the wrong account (that is, your next year's instalment account). If your only business income is from a tax shelter, then the filing extension to June 15 is not available to you, and you must file your return and pay your tax by April 30.

Deceased persons

As we will discuss in greater depth in Chapter 8, tax returns must also be filed for the recently departed. The return must be filed and the tax paid on or before the later of the following dates:

- April 30 of the following year (June 15 of the following year if the deceased or their spouse had business income)
- Six months after the date of death.

The guideline is that if a person dies before November 1, their tax return is due on April 30. If the person dies in November or December, their return is due six months after the date of death. For example, Mr. E dies August 15, 2000. His T1 tax return for the period January 1, 2000, until his tragic and untimely death on August 15, 2000, is due April 30, 2001 (June 15, 2001 if Mr. E or his spouse have business income). If income is received after death, several optional tax returns can be filed. As will be detailed in Chapter 8, each of these returns has specific due dates depending on when the income is received and what kind of income it is. See Chapter 22 for a discussion of penalties and interest on late-filed returns and deficient payments.

Where Should I Send My Completed Tax Return?

T1 or personal tax returns are no longer sent to Ottawa for processing. The Ottawa T1 processing unit was closed in 1990, and the responsibility for processing returns was allocated to the regional Taxation Centres. Based on your postal code, the CCRA decides which centre will service you. If you are unsure which centre to send your return to, you can do one of several things:

- Use the pre-addressed mailing stickers the CCRA sent you in the mail (hopefully you received them). These stickers will tell you where your return is headed. Make a note of the centre for future reference.
- You can also find out which centre to send your return to by calling your local Tax Services Office. They have a master postal code list that will tell them where your return is going.

Even in the worst case scenario, you send your return to the wrong centre, don't worry. This office will take on the awesome and solemn responsibility of processing your return and sending out your assessment. Remember where you sent your return. If you have any questions about your return or the assessment, or if you need to send in additional information, this office will be responsible for handling these requests. You can still go to your local Tax Services Office and make the enquiry, but it will take time for your return to be sent from the assessing office.

Tax Services Offices (TSOs) and Tax Centres are different things. TSOs are responsible for auditing returns, collecting outstanding balances, and providing information and client service to the public, as well as hearing appeals of prior assessments. Tax Centres process and store tax returns for individuals, corporations, and trusts, plus respond to clients requests for information on their returns. A list of all the TSOs and Tax Centres can be found by visiting CCRA's Web site `www.ccra-adrc.gc.ca/contact/tso-e.html`.

Withholding Tax

The CCRA requires that persons paying salary, wages, or any other form of remuneration withhold amounts from the employee and remit these amounts to the federal government on a regular basis. This section goes through the whole process — from how they come up with the dollar amount to withold onto to what you can do to control this process for maximum financial benefit!

How is the amount withheld determined?

The whole process begins when you complete a TD-1 form (Employee's Personal Tax Credit Return) at the commencement of your employment. This form asks questions that seek to determine which personal tax credits and other deductions you are entitled to. Based on the information you provide, a calculation of how much to withhold from your paycheque is determined by estimating your tax liability at year-end and dividing by the number of pay periods. If the credits you are claiming exceed the basic personal credit, then it's a good idea to file this form, since it will reduce the amount of tax withheld.

If your income will not exceed the personal credit, your employer is not required to withhold tax. This is the situation of many students and part-time workers. Why let the government hold your money — when you could?

Can I reduce the amount of tax withheld at source?

The answer is yes! Under certain circumstances there is a process in place that will allow you to request a reduction of tax withheld a source. Section 153(1.1) of the *Income Tax Act* will allow you to request a reduction if the calculated withholdings would cause "undue hardship." An application for a reduction in withholdings should be made to your local Tax Services Office — client service division. The application should be supported by complete documentary evidence, including estimates of income and deductions, plus proof of the amount of tax withheld. You should also include evidence of the deductions that are causing the hardship.

For example, a taxpayer earning a salary will have an amount withheld from each payment. However, if he/she becomes obliged to pay a substantial portion of the remainder of each payment as an alimony or maintenance payment, he/she may be able to establish that the amount of tax otherwise required to be deducted is excessive and results in a cash shortage to the taxpayer, causing him/her undue hardship. The most common reasons cited when requesting this reduction are child support or spousal payments, exercising of stock options, and RRSP contributions at source. You should consider using this section if the tax withheld by your employer consistently causes large refunds at year-end.

The CCRA will follow up and contact your employer to confirm the information supplied in the application.

Can I have my withholdings increased?

Believe it or not . . . Yes! The same process as above can be used to request an increase in withholding tax. Along with the written request you send to the Tax Services Office (TSO), you should also include a completed TD-3 form (available at the TSO). Common reasons to request an increase in withholdings include the following: the receipt of a large sum of money upon which no withholdings were taken (that is, interest or dividends) and to avoid having to pay instalments in future years.

Payments to non-residents

To the surprise of many taxpayers, including large corporations, Canadians paying fees or commissions for services rendered in Canada by a non-resident are required to withhold 15 percent of the payment and remit it to the CCRA.

If you are audited by the CCRA, and they find one of these payments with no withholdings, **you** pay the tax, not the person you paid! Payments to non-residents may not require withholdings if the non-resident receiver has applied for and received from the CCRA a waiver of the withholding tax. If in doubt, call the CCRA International Tax Office in Ottawa and ask if the company has a waiver. Payments to non-residents for rent, royalties, and dividends also require withholdings by the payer. These withholdings can be as high as 25 percent, depending on the country involved. If you find yourself in this situation, it is best to get professional advice.

Income not subject to withholdings

Income received that is not by virtue of employment is not subject to withholdings. This income includes rent, capital gains, dividends, interest, business income, and royalties. Notable exceptions to this rule are amounts withdrawn from an RRSP, pension benefits, old age security payments, and unemployment insurance benefits. That said, remember, in Canada only lottery winnings are truly tax-free. If you receive income, tax will eventually have to be paid. Either put some aside or resist the temptation to spend it all.

The fourth protocol to the Canada–U.S. tax treaty (that is, the most recent update) provides that U.S. residents only pay U.S. tax on receipt of Canadian OAS/CPP/QPP payments. Canada will no longer withhold on these amounts. Conversely, Canadian residents receiving U.S. social security will only pay tax in Canada.

When Is My Tax Payment Due?

The general rule is that any tax owing must be paid on or before April 30 of the year following the taxation year in question. For example, your 2000 tax payments must be made by April 30, 2001. Even if your return is not due until June 15 because you or your spouse has business income, the tax payment must still be made on or before April 30. If an individual dies during the year, the estate must file a terminal return and pay the tax. If the date of death is between January 1 and October 31, then the return and the tax are due by the usual April 30 deadline (June 15 fillers must still pay by April 30). If, on the other hand, the date of death is between November 1 and December 31, the CCRA will give you six months to file the return and pay the tax.

If a taxpayer dies between January 1 and April 30 and they have not yet filed their previous year's return, the CCRA will give the estate six months from the date of death to file and pay the tax owing (if any). For example, Mr. C died March 1, 2000, before filing his 1999 tax return. The CCRA will give the estate until August 31, 2000, to file the 1999 return and pay any tax owing. Mr. C's date-of-death return and tax payment for the period January 1, 2000 to March 1, 2000 will not be due until April 30, 2001.

When Am I Subject to Instalments?

Instalments are quarterly prepayments of tax. You will have to pay instalments if the difference between your total tax payable (that is, both provincial and federal taxes) and the amounts withheld at source is $2,000 or more in the current year and either of the two previous years. In Quebec, if you owe $1,200 or more in federal tax in the current year and any of the two previous years, federal instalments will be due. Instalments are due on the 15th of March, June, September, and December.

For example, suppose Bill paid $2,500 on the filing of his 1998 tax return. The primary reason for this tax liability was that Bill had sold some stocks and had realized a capital gain. There were no withholdings on this gain; therefore tax was due at year-end. In 1999, Bill had no payable or refund on the filing of his return, since the withholdings on his employment income were done correctly by his employer. In 2000, Bill had a large interest income inclusion. Since withholdings are not required on interest income, Bill had to pay tax at year-end. Unfortunately for Bill, he owed $2,001 upon filing his return. The CCRA noticed that Bill owed more than $2,000 on his current tax return and had paid more than $2,000 in one of his prior two returns (1998). The nasty CCRA computer concluded that Bill should have paid instalments.

To determine if you should pay instalments for the current year, ask yourself this question: "Will my tax liability for the current year exceed $2,000?" If you answer yes, then ask yourself, "Was my tax liability last year or the year before greater than $2,000?" If you answer yes again, you need to make instalment payments for the current year. Since the formulae for calculating instalments takes into account the current year plus the two prior years, individuals that have a one-time windfall of income that requires them to pay $2,000 at year-end are usually not caught. Rather, the instalment rules are designed to catch taxpayers who repeatedly earn income from sources that are not subject to withholdings (that is, interest, dividends, capital gains, business, or rental income).

It is the net tax owing at line 485 of your tax return that the computer looks at to determine if instalments are owing. This line includes both federal and provincial tax for all provinces except Quebec.

Since residents of Quebec file a separate provincial return in addition to the federal return, the normal instalment amounts do not apply. For residents of Quebec, if $1,200 of federal tax is payable in the current year and either of the two prior year-ends, then federal instalments must be made.The requirement to pay instalments can only be determined in the current year. This means that if you are reassessed in the future or if losses are carried back, these changes cannot result in instalments either being due or being eliminated for that year.

Calculating your instalments

There are three possible ways to calculate your instalment payments.

Method 1: The first method is to take last year's tax liability and divide by four. The resulting amount should be paid on the 15th of March, June, September, and December of the current year. Method 1 works best if you anticipate the same liability this year as you had last.

Method 2: The second method is to estimate your current tax payable and divide by four. The resulting amount should be paid on the same dates as those in method 1. This method is more difficult than method 1, since it requires you to guess at your year-end liability.

The problem with methods 1 and 2 is that if you incorrectly estimate your year-end liability, you either give the CCRA a no-interest loan or you get hit with interest and penalties on insufficient instalment payments.

Method 3: To solve the above problem, a third option was devised by the CCRA. This method uses a combination of your actual taxes payable in the previous two years. The March and June instalments are calculated as one-quarter of your total tax payable for the year before last. The September and December instalments when added to the instalments already made must equal your total tax payable in the prior year. If you are going to pay more tax this year than last, your instalments must at least equal to your total tax payable in the prior year. This will avoid any penalties or interest. This third option is the method used by the CCRA when it calculates the instalment it is expecting to receive from you. If you follow the CCRA instalment request, you *cannot* be charged interest or penalties, even if you owe more at year-end.

Let's assume that your total tax payable in 1998 was $10,000. Also, assume that your total tax payable in 1999 was $20,000. In the year 2000, you expect that your total tax payable will be $25,000. You decide to use method 3 to calculate your instalments. On March 15, 2000 and June 15, 2000 you will owe one-quarter of your total 1998 tax payable ($10,000 divided by 4 equals $2,500). Now for the tricky part! You know that your total tax payable in 1999 was $20,000. You also know that your total instalments for 2000 must at least equal your total tax payable for 1999, namely $20,000. Finally, you know that you have already made two payments of $2,500 toward your 2000 instalments. What's next? You deduct the payments you've already made from your 1999 total payable and then divide by two ($20,000 minus $2,500 plus $2,500) divided by 2 equals $7,500. On September 15, 2000 and December 15, 2000, instalment payments of $7,500 need to be made. If you were correct in your estimate of tax payable at year-end ($25,000), then at April 30, 2001, you would owe $5,000 when you filed your return. No interest or penalties would be payable since you met the requirement of paying instalments equal to your 1999 payable tax, and the payments made would have been the same as the CCRA instalment requests.

Use form T1033WS "Worksheet for Calculating Instalment Payments." This is available at your local CCRA Tax services office. CCRA will send you quarterly reminders that tell you when the instalments are due, and how much they are.

Interest and penalties

The *Income Tax Act* allows the CCRA to charge interest on late or deficient instalments from the date the instalment was due right up until the filing deadline of April 30. The interest charged is at the prescribed high rate. This rate is approximately 4 points above the Bank of Canada quarterly rate. Interest on late or deficient instalments is not deductible for tax purposes. Interest will be charged from the date the instalment was due until it is paid or April 30 arrives.

Can I reduce or eliminate the interest on late or deficient instalments?

Yes! The CCRA has introduced an interest-offset policy that allows individuals who have incurred interest on their late or deficient instalments to reduce or eliminate it all together. The offset allows a taxpayer to earn interest on early or overpaid instalments and apply it against the interest owing on late or deficient instalments. This earned interest is nonrefundable and can only be used to offset interest owing.

Since the government credits you offset interest at the same high rate that it charges, this offset mechanism is a real and viable method to eliminate interest charges. For example, suppose you miss the March 15 instalment due date. According to your CCRA instalment request, you should have paid $10,000. Interest will begin accumulating against you on March 15. To eliminate this interest, you need to either pay your next instalment early or pay more than is required on the following three instalment dates. One option is to pay $30,000 on June 15. The CCRA will view this payment as the deficient March payment, the correct June payment, and an early September payment. This early payment will begin accumulating the offset interest. Interest on deficient or late payments for $25 or less are waived by the CCRA.

Penalty, interest and payment procedures

In special circumstances, the CCRA will charge a penalty against late or deficient instalment payments. If the interest owing is greater than $1,000, it will charge a penalty of 50 percent of the greater of $1,000 or 25 percent of the instalment interest, calculated as if no instalment payments had been made for the year. Instalments can be paid at any CCRA office, banks, trust companies, credit unions, or *caisses populaire.* Include with your payment the instalment remittance form sent to you by the CCRA. If you do not have the instalment remittance form, use form T7DR or T7B-RF, available from the CCRA. Instalments are considered paid when stamped by the receiving person at the CCRA or the financial institution. A payment is also considered received the day you mail it, if you use first-class mail or a courier.

Technical Interpretations

Technical Interpretations are a service provided by the CCRA free of charge. The CCRA will respond in writing to requests for their interpretation of the tax law. This service is usually used by taxpayers who have a complicated tax issue that requires an interpretation of ambiguous or complex tax law. An Interpretation is a general explanation of how the law should apply. A Technical Interpretation addresses specific issues and is not binding on the government. Interpretations are made available to the public, and can be obtained from private databases or by contacting the Rulings and Interpretations directorate in Ottawa. If you request an Interpretation, be prepared to grow much older waiting. It can take several months to a few years to receive a response to your request.

Always consult a professional tax person for advice before seeking an interpretation. In all likelihood, your question has already been asked by others, and the answer is readily available.

Advance Tax Rulings

Advance Tax Rulings are generally reserved for the biggest and most complex transactions. For a fee, the CCRA is prepared to analyze and rule on proposed transactions. A ruling is binding on the CCRA, and gives the individuals involved the confidence that the transaction is correct from a tax point of view. Situations that normally call for rulings include bank mergers, insurance company takeovers, and corporate reorganizations involving public companies. Information Circular 70-6R3 outlines the policies and rules related to advance tax rulings, as follows:

- Advance Tax Rulings will only be given if a transaction has not taken place. For a completed transaction, no ruling will be given.
- The CCRA will only bind itself in specific circumstances:
- The taxpayer has disclosed all information about the proposed transaction. Any misrepresentation or omission will render the ruling null and void.
- The courts do not alter or change the law that the ruling is based on. If the law changes, then the ruling is no longer applicable.
- The transaction is complete within the time limits specified in the original request. In other words, the ruling does not last forever.
- The transaction must be completed as agreed in the ruling. Any departure from the plan will render the ruling null and void.

Unless the transaction involves lots of money, and the issues are highly technical, rulings are generally not required. And you should know that a ruling is not cheap. The CCRA charges $90 an hour plus GST. The initial deposit before any work begins is $481.50. You should definitely consult a tax professional before you seek a ruling or Technical Interpretation. If you ask for a ruling, disclose all information and follow the ruling to a tee. If you do not, the CCRA will walk away from the ruling.

If you really want a ruling, or if you have enough time to wait for a Technical Interpretation, you can contact the rulings directorate at the following address:

CCRA Rulings and Interpretation Directorate
The Albion Tower
25 Nicholas Street
Ottawa, Ontario
K1A 0L5

Chapter 7

Going Over Your Preparation Options

In This Chapter

- Preparing your own return
- Using preparation software
- Making use of tax help on the Web
- Getting help from the tax collector
- Assessing tax pros
- Evaluating E-filing versus paper filing
- Taking a look at Tele-filing
- Locating forms and other information

Chances are, if you're reading this chapter you've already determined that yes, you need to file a tax return, and yes, you need to do it now. So, now what? Do you prepare your return yourself, or do you throw in the towel and hire someone to do it for you? This chapter gives you some handy advice on when to file your own return, and when you should seek help. We will also discuss various options for filing your return.

Get Out Your Pen and Paper: Calling All Do-It-Yourselfers

Come February, some people anxiously await the arrival of mail from the CCRA containing the forms necessary to prepare their income tax return. Now not everyone gets excited about the thought of preparing their own return, but for many it makes sense. After all, some people are just natural do-it-yourselfers. Preparing your own return is by far the cheapest way to get your return done. This, of course, assumes that you do everything right, and that you don't receive a nasty reassessment in the mail from our friends at the CCRA. Doing it yourself makes sense particularly if your tax situation doesn't change drastically from year to year. This way you can simply see which lines you used last year, and update them with the current year's figures. Obviously the problem with doing this is that you may miss claiming something year after year. One advantage to preparing your own return is that it gives you the opportunity to think about some tax planning. While preparing your return, you'll see where all the numbers come from — which ones are good and which ones lead to more tax. You may even come up with some ways to reduce your tax. After all, you know your situation better than anyone else.

Be sure that you read through this book if you do decide to prepare your return yourself. Not only does it provide you with some handy hints and tips so that you don't make any mistakes, but also it may give you some ideas about deductions and credits you might not know are available.

Using Your Computer to Tally Up Your Taxes

Do you have a home computer? If so, you're not alone. In 1998 about 5.3 million households, or 45 percent, had a home computer. Eight years ago, only 20 percent of households had one. Now, of those of you who own a computer, how many actually use it for something useful? By useful, we're not referring to how many spaceships you can shoot from the sky, or how long it takes you to save the beautiful princess. What we mean is, have you ever thought of preparing your tax return using your computer? Think about it. No more adding machines, or the dreaded smell of liquid paper. No more tearing through the forms when you've erased the amount on line 150 one too many times. Tax preparation software makes sense for those of you who have already dived into the world of preparing your own return. And even for those of you still sitting on the deck, tax preparation software may be the answer to your phobia.

The perks and perils of going the techno route

There are a number of advantages to using software to prepare your tax return. The favourite, of course, is automatic recalculation. When one number on your return changes, the program updates all relevant forms and recalculates your final tax bill. Another advantage is that most software packages are dummy-proof. Do you know which line dividend income is reported on? Do you care? Well, if you answered no, don't worry. Most programs are set up so all you need to do is find the window that corresponds to the particular slip you have, be it a T4, T3, or T5, and fill it in based on what appears in your boxes. The program sees to it that the numbers end up in the right place. Remember that not all computer programs are created equal. Some offer more on-line help than others, including warning diagnostics, helpful suggestions to save you some tax and filing reminders. Often these programs are more expensive, but are generally worth the extra bucks. Make sure you shop around.

Computers aren't people. They can't look at numbers to determine if they're reasonable, or if they're correct. No computer will tell you to think again before deducting as a business expense your all-inclusive trip for two to Jamaica.

Shopping for tax software

There are several programs available to help taxpayers deal with the headaches that April so often brings. Some programs are available on disk or CD, while others are available for downloading from the Internet. Preparation software generally targets two separate markets: single-users (retail) or professionals. Some of the more popular retail packages include:

- **QuickTax:** Gather up your receipts and answer the simple questions posed by QuickTax. The program then puts the information on the forms where it belongs. QuickTax will review your return when you're finished and even alerts you of any missed deductions or credits. QuickTax has extra features such as "what if" scenarios, an auto lease vs. buy analyzer, and RRSP planners.

  For all the non-tax experts out there looking to complete their tax return using a computer program this year, we recommend QuickTax. It's a simple, user-friendly program that makes preparing your tax return fun (well, almost fun). The additional dollars you'll spend on this program, you'll make up for in time savings, as well as tax savings, thanks to the built-in review process.

- **TaxWiz:** Like QuickTax, this program is comprehensive and easy to use. Although not as user-friendly in some aspects, it does offer extra features such as RRSP, RRIF, and mortgage calculators, GST and child tax benefit calculators, and on-screen review. TaxWiz lacks some aspects of QuickTax when it comes to preparing returns for business owners. Some deductions, such as capital cost allowance on vehicles, and business use of home office are not calculated automatically.

- **CoolTax:** CoolTax is a "freeware" program available for downloading from the Internet. It is essentially identical to TaxByte, a professional software package. Since it mirrors the professional package you may find it more difficult to navigate around, and doesn't do the "hand-holding" like the other programs. It also has a diagnostics feature to alert you to possible errors. Although not as user-friendly, it gets the job done — and it's free!

Surfing Your Way to Tax Help

So it's 11 p.m. on April 30, and you need help. What do you do? Well, if you're lucky, you may find the answers to some of your questions via the Internet. There are several Web sites available that provide handy, up-to-the-minute tax tips. As a starter, most of the big accounting firms have tax information available on their Web sites. For example, Ernst & Young Canada has a Tax Mailbag, which on a weekly basis posts answers to questions from readers. KPMG, one of Canada's largest accounting firms, also has a section devoted to tax, where they post a daily Tax Tip of the Day relating to current issues in both personal and corporate tax. Deloitte and Touche has a similar feature called Daily Tax Highlights. If the big accounting firms aren't enough, you may want to visit the Ministry of Finance Web site. For some, reading through the material found here will not be, shall we say, fun, but it is where the most current information can be found. There are a number of Internet and other resources available to answer your tax questions. Let's take a look at our top picks.

- The WaterStreet Group Inc., `www.waterstreet.ca`. Visit this Web site to find the latest information on tax changes, calculate your 2000 tax liability, or participate in the tax forum — a discussion group where you can pose your tax questions. There is also a mailbag where you can "ask the experts" any of your burning tax questions.
- Ernst & Young, `www.eycan.com`. This Web site provides you the latest tax changes, as well as tax calculators, and a mailbag where the experts will help answer your questions. Be sure to visit their new taxweb section. Here you can sign up for a fee to receive e-mails so you can be one of the first to know about any tax changes effecting you. For the more adventurous, you can also subscribe to TaxQuest which will help you with all your tax research.
- Deloitte & Touche, `www.deloitte.ca`. The daily tax highlights provided on this Web site will ensure you don't miss any of the tax changes. Be sure to keep your eye open for TaxBreaks, Deloitte and Touche's bi-monthly newsletter on personal and corporate tax.
- KPMG, `www.kpmg.ca`. You'll find out all the latest tax changes by visiting KPMG's site, and reading their tax publications including the *Canadian Tax Letter* — an easy to read newsletter on current developments in corporate and personal taxation.
- PricewaterhouseCoopers, `www.pwcglobal.com`. Visit the Tax News Network area of the site, to find all the latest tax information. You can also subscribe to receive more comprehensive tax information related to specific industries.
- The Department of Finance, `www.fin.gc.ca`. This is where you go to get the information straight from the horse's mouth — so to speak. All the tax changes, and updates start here. So if you want the changes the minute they happen, go to this site. Be aware that you'll find a lot of technical information here. So you may want to wait until any of the other sites interprets the changes for you.

When to Get Help from the Tax Collector

For some, asking the CCRA for help seems like fraternizing with the enemy. After all, is the CCRA going to help you save taxes, when their mandate is to collect taxes? Well, they're certainly not going to tell you about loopholes in the system, but they are an excellent source of general information. So if you have questions of a general nature, such as "Where do I file my taxes?" or "What form do I complete to claim the disability tax credit?" the best place to start (besides this book, of course) is the CCRA Web site at `www.ccra-adrc.gc.ca`. This site is an ideal place to get information on filing your individual return. You can download a copy of the income tax package, which gives you some information about the most common lines found on your return. The package doesn't go into a lot of detail, but it's a good starting point. There are also a number of additional forms you may need to complete your taxes, many of them including detailed instructions on how to complete them and when they apply. You'll also find answers to some of the most frequently asked questions. Chances are, if you have a burning question, you're probably not the first to think of it, so make sure you check this spot out.

The CCRA's Web site also contains a variety of technical publications that are written for specific taxpayer situations. For example, there are guides and pamphlets on everything from Newcomers to Canada to Students and Income Tax. You'll also find Interpretation Bulletins (also known as ITs) on this Web site. These ITs give the CCRA's administrative position on a variety of specific subjects. They are very technical and make reference to relevant sections of the *Income Tax Act*. These ITs may be intimidating to the average taxpayer, but if you need some bedtime reading, they'll provide you with more information than you can imagine on many complex tax situations.

The TIPS service

If your question relates to your personal tax situation, the CCRA has set up an automated service called Tax Information Phone Service (TIPS). TIPS offers the following services:

- **Telerefund:** This function tells you the status of your income tax refund.
- **Goods and Services Tax/Harmonized Sales Tax credit:** Select this and you'll find out if you are eligible to receive the credit, and when you can expect to receive your payment.
- **Canada Child Tax Benefit:** This service tells you if you are eligible to receive the benefit and when you can expect to receive your payment.
- **RRSP deduction limit:** Want to know your RRSP contribution limit for the year? TIPS has your answer.

If you require any of this information, simply call 1-800-267-6999. It is entirely automated, so you will need to use your touch-tone phone to punch in your social insurance number, date of birth, and the amount you entered on line 150 of your prior year's income tax return. TIPS also provides recorded messages on recent tax and benefit information, as well as general information about particular lines on your tax return. TIPS is available 24 hours a day.

Visiting your local Tax Services Office

If you can't find the information you need on the Web site or through TIPS, you should try contacting your local Tax Services Office in person or by phone. The TSOs are open Monday to Friday (except holidays, of course), 8:15 a.m. to 4:30 p.m. To find the location of your nearest TSO, visit the CCRA's Web site, and click "Contact us" at the main menu.

Enquiring by phone

Agents are also available to answer your questions by phone Monday to Friday (except holidays), 8:15 a.m. to 5:00 p.m. To accommodate the flood of calls during tax season, these hours are extended until 10:00 p.m. weekdays, and include weekends from 9:00 a.m. to 1:00

p.m. from late February to April 30. Contact the CCRA by phone at 1-800-959-8281. To ensure that you are who you say you are, and not someone else pretending to be who you say you are (get it?), the CCRA will ask for your social insurance number, your date of birth, and the amount you entered on line 150 of your prior year's return. Be sure to have this information handy before placing the call. Nothing is worse than waiting for service, only to be denied the information!

If you would like someone else to call the CCRA on your behalf, be sure that you've completed and mailed form T1013 (consent form) to the CCRA. This form gives the CCRA permission to discuss your tax affairs with someone other than you.

Making the Most of Tax Pros

If your plumbing is broken, do you immediately call the plumber, or do you try to fix it yourself? For some, calling for help is the last resort — they wait until the living room is flooding. Some people feel the same way about preparing their own tax return. Sometimes, however, it's a good idea to admit defeat and hire someone before you get yourself into trouble. For instance, if you've just started up your own business and have no idea what kind of deductions you can take, you are probably best to hire someone — for the first year, at least. This will give you an idea of what deductions you're entitled to (and can get away with). As well, if you've recently come to Canada, have retired during the year, or have sold some property, you may want to seek some help.

Be sure you have accumulated all the information necessary before sending it to your preparer. If you have a business, your best bet is to summarize all your revenue and expenses ahead of time. This is one way to cut down your fee and ensure no relevant information is omitted.

Hiring someone may also be a good idea if you need some tax planning advice. Sometimes the additional fees you pay may actually be recovered in saved taxes! Now that's a good investment. Be careful whom you hire for tax planning, since some individuals are more competent than others. We discuss this issue in more detail below. The next question becomes, who do you hire? Basically there are two groups: income tax preparers and accountants.

Hiring a preparer

Income tax preparers are just that: preparers. Since it is quite simple to open up your own shop preparing tax returns, most often these people have the least amount of training compared to other tax practitioners. So if you're looking for tax planning and advice, we don't recommend stopping here. For those of you who despise doing taxes, have simple tax situations, and want your return completed quickly for a small fee, visiting a preparer may be the way to go. Although most preparers who work for large preparation companies complete training before working with clients, you may still end up with a preparer who knows less than you do! As a rule of thumb, if your situation is more complicated than entering the information slips you received from the CCRA, you are probably better off visiting an accountant.

Most preparation companies will charge a percentage of your refund in addition to a fixed fee, if you want your refund immediately. Think twice about signing up for this deal if your return is quite simple, or you may end up forfeiting a portion of your refund for 10 minutes of preparation time.

Hiring an accountant

Generally people should be looking to hire an accountant if their tax situation is complex, or different from that of the previous year. For example, if you run your own business, sold rental property or sold property for a gain, and you're not sure how to report it, chances are you need to pay a visit to an accountant. In Canada there are two types of accountants that may be able to prepare your return. These are Chartered Accountants (CAs), and Certified General Accountants (CGAs). We say "may be able" to prepare your return, because not all accountants specialize in tax. All accountants are required to take tax courses, but some may not be keeping up to date on the latest tax changes if they don't practise tax as part of their day-to-day routine. If you believe your situation is complicated, make sure you ask whether the accountant specializes in tax. If you have your own business, you may already have an accountant who does your bookkeeping and prepares your financial statements. Most likely, this person will also prepare your tax return. If you have any questions that he or she can't answer, be sure to seek help from someone who practises tax daily.

If you decide to hire an accountant, be prepared to pay. Although the fees range significantly from one accountant to the next (and in different areas of Canada), you're probably looking at paying at least $150 per hour of service. But remember, with these fees come experience, education, and specialization.

Where to find a bean counter

Before you go hunting through Yellow Pages looking for an accountant, you should first ask your friends and family who they use. Be sure to find out if they are happy with the service they are getting, and whether they feel the fees are reasonable. Beyond that, you could turn to the Big Five firms in Canada: Arthur Andersen, Deloitte and Touche, Ernst & Young, KPMG, and PricewaterhouseCoopers. All of the accounting firms have a specialized tax department, where you can be sure to get answers to all your questions.

If you're looking for more personalized service, you may want to try a smaller accounting firm. Look through the Yellow Pages to find one located near you. The majority of these firms specialize in smaller owner-managed businesses, and would be happy to help you gather information, prepare your financial statements, and complete your return. If you only require your tax return done, these firms can do it for you. In fact, for many firms, taxes are their bread and butter.

Questions to ask your tax professional

You'll see when you look in the Yellow Pages that there are dozens of pages of accounting firms and businesses that specialize in tax. Finding a reputable tax professional is kind of like finding a mechanic — you've got to be careful. As we've mentioned, some businesses will lead you to believe they are tax professionals, but in reality they're students filling out forms with no idea what they're doing. In your initial meeting, the tax professional should ask a lot of questions about your situation. This means he or she is thinking about your situation to ensure that all the facts are understood and that costly mistakes that may lead to an audit are avoided. Beware of "professionals" who only enter the information you give them without probing a little deeper into the details. To keep you safe from disaster, here's a list of questions to ask your "tax professional" to ensure they can handle your situation.

- **What services do you offer?** Some tax professionals only prepare tax returns, while others will help you with other matters such as retirement planning or estate planning. Some firms will assist you in preparing financial statements for your small business; others won't.

- **Have you worked in this area before?** If you have your own business, or are an avid investor, make sure your professional has worked with similar situations before. Many firms have specialists in particular areas, while some may be used to working with employees who only have a T4 and RRSP slips. Choose a professional who is best suited to help in your situation.
- **Who will prepare my return?** Unless you're dealing with a sole practitioner, the person you're speaking to will not necessarily prepare your return. In many cases, it may be given to a staff member to prepare. If this is the case, find out the qualifications of the staff member, and ask whether the person in charge will be reviewing your return before it's finalized.

Don't be alarmed if you have a junior staff member prepare your return — this is common practice and can actually save you preparation fees. However, ensure that your advisor reviews it for errors.

- **What is your fee structure?** Most tax professionals charge by the hour, so make sure you ask up front for the hourly fee, as well for an estimate of the time your project will take to complete. Also ask what this fee covers and whether or not you'll be charged additional amounts for follow-up questions.
- **What qualifications do you have?** Many tax professionals are Chartered Accountants, and many are also Certified Financial Planners. Those specializing in tax should also have completed a two-year in-depth tax course offered by the Canadian Institute of Chartered Accountants.
- **What experience have you had with audits?** In addition to selecting high-risk returns, the CCRA also audits returns at random. Be wary of a tax professional who claims that none of his clients have ever been audited. This may mean he has prepared very few returns, he's ultraconservative, or he's lying. If he replies that some of his clients have been audited, find out why returns were selected for audit, whether the audits were full-blown audits or specifically targeted one area, and what the outcome was.

E-Filing Versus Paper Filing

You're now at the point where your tax return is complete. Now what? If you've hired someone to prepare it for you, you have the option of e-filing your return. E-file is an automated system that allows approved electronic filers to electronically deliver individual income tax return information to the CCRA. In 1999, more than 5.4 million people electronically transmitted their returns. This represents more than 26 percent of all the returns filed.

You can't e-file your tax return yourself. You must first have your return prepared by an approved electronic filer. Most businesses that offer tax preparation services are registered to e-file returns. Some e-file service providers may be willing to accept a return you've prepared on suitable computer software, but you may have to shop around.

Six signs you should find another accountant

- They haven't filed their own tax return for the past three years.
- Their system of filing receipts is shoving everything in a shoebox kept under their bed.
- They hire someone to prepare *their* tax return.
- They are currently involved in a CCRA tax audit.
- They complete all their clients' tax returns by hand (all 10 of them!).
- They have the number of the head honcho of the CCRA audit department on speed-dial.

What are the benefits of e-filing?

In this fast-paced world, nothing is good unless it's quick. (Except, of course, for some fast-food meals.) Most people like e-filing their return because they get their assessment and refunds faster. In fact, the wait is cut to two weeks from the usual four to six if you're a procrastinator and file towards the end of April. If you're one of those who file in the middle of March, you may actually see your refund in just over a week! As well, since electronically transmitting your return saves the CCRA from having to manually input your data, it reduces the likelihood of data entry errors. Last but not least, e-filing saves you a stamp.

Who can e-file?

The majority of Canadian taxpayers can electronically transmit their return. People who *can't* e-file include non-residents, people who came to Canada during the year, people who have declared bankruptcy, and people who have to pay income tax to more than one province or territory.

Before your return can be e-filed, you must sign form T183, which basically gives the firm preparing your return authorization to e-file. There's no need to worry about getting the form yourself — your preparer will provide it for you.

Are my chances of audit lower if I e-file?

No. E-filed returns are selected for review using the same criteria as paper-filed returns. So if you're worried about an audit, don't think you can reduce your odds by e-filing your return. And if you don't like having any contact with the CCRA after you file your return other than a report card called the Notice of Assessment, then we don't suggest you e-file. You see, since no supporting documentation is sent to the CCRA when you e-file, the taxman may contact you asking for backup information for some of your claims. The most common requests are for medical and donation receipts. The CCRA tries to select only returns for which they think there is a higher probability of noncompliance, but this is not always the case. Don't panic, however, if you receive a request to send more information. It doesn't mean you're being audited.

Tele-filing

Tele-file is another way that returns can be electronically filed. With tele-file, you don't need to have someone else prepare and file your return. You can electronically file your own return without even leaving the comforts of home. All you need is a touch-tone phone. Tele-filing is a lot like getting into the Grammies. Why? Well, for both you need an invitation. You see, only people with simple or basic returns are eligible for tele-file. By simple returns, we mean the T1S instead of the longer T1 tax return form. The system accepts income tax information such as employment income, pension income, interest income, RRSP contributions, and charitable donations. The more complex returns would take more telephone time, and in any case often the CCRA needs to see supporting documentation in order to process more complex returns.

The T1 Special or T1S is only available from the CCRA through direct mail. It is sent to individuals who are wage and salary earners only, students, seniors, and filers who file only to obtain tax credits. The CCRA decides who can file a T1S based on the types of income reported on their return. When individuals eligible to use tele-filing receive their tax package from the CCRA, they will also receive a special invitation, along with an access code and instructions on how to use the system.

To use the tele-file service, you must first prepare your income tax return. Then call the toll-free tele-file number. You'll be prompted by an automated telephone message to enter your tax data using your telephone keypad. After you've given all the information, you'll be asked to confirm that you want to file that information as your income tax return. The CCRA will immediately give you a confirmation number and begin processing your return. In about two weeks, you should receive an Assessment Notice and a refund, if applicable. If you have a balance owing, you must ensure that it is paid in full by April 30 to avoid interest and penalties. To make your payment, complete the remittance form sent with your income tax package, and mail it to the CCRA or pay at your bank.

Complete your remittance form in full, including your name, address, and social insurance number, to ensure that the CCRA applies the payment directly to your account. You don't want to end up paying someone else's tax bill instead of your own! If you tele-file, make sure you keep all your supporting documentation in case the CCRA asks to see it.

Net-filing

Now more than ever, Canadians are doing everything from banking to buying cars to planning the family vacation over the Internet. So why not file your income tax return over the Internet? Net-file is the CCRA's newest filing option — one that allows eligible individuals to file their income tax returns through the Internet. It was introduced in 2000, which gave a selected group of taxpayers the ability to file their 1999 returns using the new method.

Net-file was introduced by the CCRA as a response to the high demand by taxpayers for a paper-less method of filing. Prior to this, individuals could only send their tax returns to the CCRA electronically by paying a fee to an e-file transmitter. Net-file is a free service that provides the same benefits as e-file: faster, more accurate processing. Only individuals who received invitations were able to net-file their 1999 returns. Approximately 3.8 million invitations were distributed. Eligibility was based on types of income reported in an individual's 1998 income tax return. The CCRA plans to make net-file an option for all taxpayers commencing with the 2000 tax-filing season. As with e-filing and tele-filing, your risk of being audited does not increase if you net-file. You may be asked to provide supporting documentation, though, so make sure you keep all your tax information slips in a handy location, in case the taxman wants to see them. In fact, the CCRA says that you must keep all receipts for six years after you file your return, so rent storage space if you must.

The CCRA has set up a Web site for people eligible to net-file. This Web site provides step-by-step details on how to net-file, as well as the requirements that must be met. Be sure to visit it at `www.netfile.gc.ca`.

Before you can net-file your return to the CCRA, you must first prepare your return using certified tax preparation software. Basically, all this means is that the software will save your return in a format that the CCRA can read. A listing of approved software is available on the CCRA's Web site at `www.netfile.gc.ca/software-e.html`.

Where to Get Forms and Other Information

The package that's sent by the CCRA in mid-February contains only the most commonly used forms. If you didn't receive a package or need additional ones, you can pick one up at the post office or the CCRA tax centre nearest you. If you find that you need a form not contained in your package, getting the forms has never been easier!

You have three options. You can visit your local TSO and pick up the form there, download the form from the CCRA's Web site, or request to have the printed forms mailed to you.The CCRA has also introduced on-line "fillable" forms. With most forms you'll need to print out the form, complete it by hand or using a typewriter, and then mail it to the CCRA. The new fillable forms let you enter the information on-line. You'll still need to print out the form and mail it to the CCRA, but at least it eliminates the need for a typewriter (what's that?). The CCRA's Web site also provides access to various tax publications, such as Interpretation Bulletins and Information Circulars, as well as other written reports. So if you find yourself with insomnia one night, try turning to this site for some light reading. For most CCRA forms and publications, the first place to look is CCRA's Web site at `www.ccra-adrc.gc.ca`. If you can't find what you want there, you may need to get in touch with a tax professional who can help you locate the information you need.

Chapter 8

Different Forms for Different Folks: Choosing the Right One for You

In This Chapter

- Completing the T1 General
- Completing a T1 Special
- Preparing a return for the deceased
- Preparing a return after bankruptcy

Now that you have decided to file a tax return, you have another decision to make — what type of return to file? There are several different types of tax returns available to Canadians. These returns were designed for special situations, and if used correctly can offer taxpayers substantial savings in both time and money. Let's start with the return most people are familiar with, the T1 General.

The T1 General

All government forms have a number. Believe it or not, even the telephone message pads have a number (T2003, if you care to know). The number given to the personal tax return is T1.

The T1 General is the catch-all tax return for Canadians. On this form and its supporting schedules is every kind of income and expense that can be reported by a resident of Canada. As we see later in this chapter, the CCRA is attempting to simplify the tax system by providing certain taxpayers with shortened versions of this form that eliminate sections they are unlikely to use.

Taking apart the T1

The T1 General is a four-page document that begins with the words "T1 General 2000" printed boldly in the top right-hand corner. The form is then divided into the following sections:

- **Identification.** This is where you identify yourself and your spouse. This section also asks several questions, such as, Are you applying for a GST credit? Can the CCRA pass on your personal information to Elections Canada? and Do you own any foreign property?
- **Total income.** This section is where you include all your sources of income.
- **Net income.** In this section you reduce your total income with deductible expenses. These expenses are 100-percent deductible against your total income. The most common of these expenses are your RRSP deductions, union dues, child care expenses, moving expenses, registered pension plan, support payments carrying charges, and interest expenses. Chapter 16 delves into net income calculation in more detail.

- **Taxable income.** This section takes your net income and applies capital and non-capital losses, limited partnership losses, stock option deductions, capital gains deductions, Northern residents deductions, and home relocation loan deductions. Make sure you don't pass over Chapter 17 — that's where we show you how taxable income is calculated.
- **Nonrefundable tax credits.** The taxable income is further reduced by nonrefundable credits. Credits are different from deductions in that you only get 17 percent of the expense as a deduction against your taxable income. The most common of these credits are your basic personal amount, age amount, spousal amount, CPP premiums, UIC premiums, tuition, and charitable donations. The reason they are nonrefundable is that these credits can only be used to bring your income to $0 and not below, and thus create a refund. Chapter 18 tells you all you'll want to know about these nonrefundable tax credits.
- **Refund or balance.** And now the reason why this book was written — the line everyone wants to know about. The last section calculates the tax you owe and applies the payments you have made against it. The bottom line indicates tax payable or refund owed.

Along with the T1 General comes 11 pages of supporting schedules:

- Schedule 1 — Federal Tax Calculation
- Schedule 2 — Amounts Transferred from your Spouse
- Schedule 3 — Capital Gains (Losses)
- Schedule 4 — Statement of Investment Income
- Schedule 5 — Details of Dependants
- Schedule 7 — RRSP Unused Contributions, Transfers, and HBP or LLP Activities
- Schedule 8 — Canada Pension Plan (Quebec Pension Plan) contributions on Self-employment and Other Earnings
- Schedule 9 — Donations and Gifts
- Schedule 10 — Refundable Medical Expense Supplement
- Schedule 11 — Tuition and Education Amounts
- Schedule 13 — Personal Amount Supplement

These schedules are available for your use and, if used, must be submitted with your return. In addition to the above schedules, other elections or forms may be required to be submitted with your return. Here are some examples:

- A separate financial statement may be included with your return if you operate a business.
- Form T2200 must be filed if you wish to claim travel expenses in connection with employment.

One T1 for all of Canada?

The T1 General is not a single uniform document. Four slightly different versions are produced across the country:

- The first version is produced for all provinces and territories except Ontario and the Yukon.
- The second version, created only for Ontario, has a box allowing you to donate your refund to the province for deficit reduction. It also omits certain sections pertaining specifically to Quebec withholding tax.

- A third version is printed for the Yukon. This version also omits the Quebec section, and includes sections that identify filers as residents of First Nations settlement lands and charges Yukon First Nations Tax on these residents.
- The fourth version is for non-resident individuals who must pay Canadian tax. This version applies only to non-residents or deemed residents who have earned income other than employment or business income from a permanent Canadian establishment. If you are *only* reporting this other Canadian income, then this package is the one you will need. Examples of this other income include scholarships, fellowships, bursaries, research grants, and capital gains from disposing of taxable Canadian property. This version of the T1 General also includes additional schedules A and B that calculate the tax credits on the non-resident income.

Each T1 General package also carries provincial forms. Each package is customized to carry only the forms required for your province of residence.

You only need the provincial forms for the province you were resident in on December 31. This is deemed to be your province of residence for the entire year.

If you become non-resident during the year, use the forms for your last province of residence.

The T1 General can be used by everyone. As mentioned above, it is the catch-all return. In fact, if you have various sources of income and deductions, you will be forced to use the T1 General because the short or special returns will lack sufficient detail for your purposes. When in doubt, use the T1 General.

The T1 Special

The T1 Specials are smaller, simplified version of the T1 General. The CCRA has developed these special returns to assist individuals by eliminating parts of the T1 General that specific filers are unlikely to use or have not used for several years. In prior years the T1 Specials were referred to as the T1 Short. The original name was replaced by the term T1 Special, when the original T1 Short was modified to create five distinct and special tax returns.

The T1 Specials cannot be obtained from your local Tax Services Office (TSO). These returns are sent directly from the CCRA to individuals it has identified as eligible. The eligibility is based on an examination of your prior returns to determine if you meet the criteria. Even though you believe you meet the criteria for filing a special return, you must file the T1 General until the CCRA determines you meet the criteria and sends you the package. Even if you receive a T1 Special, this does not necessarily mean that you meet all requirements to file this return. You must still examine the accompanying guide to see if you meet the required criteria. If you don't, then you *must* file the T1 General.

The short story on short forms

The CCRA has created five short specialized tax forms to meet the needs of certain groups of taxpayers. These returns are the following:

- T1S-Special — for short, simplified tax returns
- T1S-A — for seniors receiving pension income
- T1S-B — for wage earners
- T1S-C — for individuals with no tax payable
- T1S-D — for registered Native Canadians

T1S-Special

The general or basic T1 Special was originally designed to be used by individuals whose only sources of income were wages, pensions, and interest, and who were only claiming the standard deductions and credits (for example, personal amount, RRSP, child care expenses). The T1S-Special is a scaled-down version of the T1 General, with the same line numbers and organization. The T1S-Special package sent to you by the CCRA contains the same supporting schedules as the T1 General, plus a modified page 3.

Even if the CCRA sends you a T1 Special, you might not be eligible to use it. You must consult the guide that accompanies the return to determine your eligibility.

Not so fast tax filer: When the short route doesn't work

The following list outlines situations where it is **not** appropriate to use the T1S - Special:

- You cannot use the T1S-Special if you have any of the following types of income:
- Business income or losses
- Rental income or losses
- Capital gains or losses
- Limited partnership gains or losses
- Ineligible deductions or tax credits
- Stock options
- Losses carried forward from other years
- You cannot use the T1S-Special if you want to claim a deduction for any of the following:
- Automobile expenses
- Home office expenses
- Any other employment-related expenses
- Expenses related to attendant care or infirm dependants
- Disability credits transferred from a dependant
- Political contribution credits
- Foreign tax credits
- Bankruptcy-related expenses or credits

A good guide as to whether you are eligible to use the T1S-Special is the form itself. If there is no space on the form for your particular income, deduction, or credit, it is safe to assume that the T1 Special is not for you. As time passed and the world slowly cooled, the CCRA decided that it could improve on the T1S-Special by further refining it to meet the needs of more specific groups.

T1S-A Pensioners

This return is targeted at individuals ages 65 years or older who are receiving only pension income. The pension income could be CPP, QPP, OAS, RRSP, RRIF, retirement compensation agreements, interest income, death benefits, social assistance payments, or any other kind of pension income. This return has eliminated all areas of the T1 General except for the ones relating to pensioners. As was the case with the T1S-Special, any income or deduction slightly out of the ordinary will throw you off and force you to use either the T1S-Special or the T1 General.

The T1S-A is accompanied by a special large-print guide, and gives pensioners the option of completing the return themselves or simply providing their information and letting the CCRA do the calculations.

This no-calculation option can be handy but also comes with a downside. The main problems with allowing the CCRA to do the work are as follows:

- It takes a long time for the CCRA to complete your return. This becomes a problem if you owe money, since interest will still be charged on the outstanding amount from April 30 until your return is complete and you pay the amount owing.
- The CCRA sometimes forgets to complete the provincial return. The result is that seniors are denied important tax credits that will reduce their provincial tax.

Any form of dividend or business income will make you ineligible to use the T1S-A. You will be forced to use the T1 General.

T1S-B Wage and Salary Earners

Like the other special returns, this one is aimed at a very specific group. The members of this group are individuals with employment income, EI benefits and interest income totaling less than $50,000 per year. This return is almost identical to the Pensioners return, including the no-calculation option. The only major differences would be the inclusion of the wage- and EI-specific lines on the T1S-B, and the omission of the pension lines. If your income and deductions do not fit on the form, you will have to use the T1S-Special or the T1 General.

Avoid using the no-calculation option. If you owe money, you will be charged interest from April 30 until the return is complete and you have paid the balance. Also, the provincial return might not be done by the Feds.

T1S-C Tax Credit

This return is for people who do not pay tax but must file a return to be eligible for tax credits or other government programs. Typically, this group includes non-working spouses or people on social assistance. The credits and programs generally applied for include child tax benefits, provincial tax credits, and the GST tax credits. The same rules and cautions that apply to the other special returns, apply to this return.

Anyone over the age of 19 is eligible for the GST credit, and you must file a tax return in order to receive it — even if you're not taxable! As well, depending on which province you live it, it may be worthwhile to file a tax return in order to receive some provincial credits.

T1S-D Native Canadians

This is a special return for Native Canadians. These returns are sent directly to the Bands for distribution to registered Status Native Canadians. Refer back to Chapter 4 for more details on how to report income if you are a Status Indian.

Returns for the Deceased

Unfortunately, death is something we all have to face during our lives, or shortly thereafter. The old saying that you cannot avoid death or taxes rings particularly true if you die *and* owe taxes. Surprisingly, death is a rather complicated undertaking in a taxation sense, that is. When a person dies there are potentially six different tax returns that could be filed on their behalf. Knowing the types of returns and the circumstances in which it is appropriate to file them could provide you with a significant opportunity for tax savings. The basic advantage gained by using these multiple returns is to spread the deceased's income over as many returns as you can, and to use the deductions available.

Understanding the prior period return

If a person dies after December 31 and before April 30 of the following year, and has not filed their return for the previous year, the executor of the estate is responsible for ensuring that this return is filed. The CCRA is prepared to give you six months from the date of death to file the previous year's return and pay the associated tax (if any). Example: You die February 2, 2000, and you have not filed your 1999 tax return. The CCRA will give the estate until August 1, 2000, to file the return and pay any tax owing.

If the deceased's will establishes a spousal trust, then the deadline is extended to 18 months after death.

Filing a final return

The final return is the return for the period January 1 of the year of death to the actual day of death. On this return you will report all the deceased's earned income, received regularly or accrued daily during this period. The following list outlines incomes that should be included and excluded from this final return. Include income such as salary, wages, interest, rents, royalties, and most annuities. Do not include amounts not payable to the deceased on or before the date of death, and annuity contracts deemed to be disposed of at the date of death. Income that is not included on this final return will be reported on other returns that we will discuss shortly. On this final return you will be able to claim all the deductions and all the nonrefundable tax credits available to any resident of Canada. The fact that this return is for a deceased person has no impact on the deductions or credits.

The CCRA's IT - 210 "Income of a Deceased Person" and the tax guide "Preparing Returns for Deceased Persons" are excellent sources of information and are available at your local Tax Services Office.

When filing the final return, print the words "Estate of the late ____________." in front of the person's name. This will ensure that the return is identified by the processing person and sent to the correct unit within the CCRA. Table 8-1 shows when a final return should be completed on the T1 General form and when it is due.

Table 8-1 Due Date if Deceased Was Not Self-employed

Period When Death Occurred	*Due Date for Return*
January 1 to October 31	April 30 the following year
November 1 to December 31	6 months after the date of death

Table 8-2 lists the dates that apply when a deceased or their spouse operated a business, for the final returns.

Table 8-2 Due Date if Deceased Was Self-employed

Period When Death Occurred	*Due Date for Return*
January 1 to December 15	June 15 of the following year
December 16 to December 31	6 months after the date of death

Remember, even though the return is not due until June 15, any balance owing must still be paid by the time shown in the chart for individuals who are not self-employed.

What happens if you just don't meet these dates? The same rules as usual apply to late-filed returns (see Chapter 6). There is a 5-percent late-filing penalty that increases by 1 percent per month, up to a maximum of 12 months, while the return is outstanding. If the late filing was due to circumstances beyond the control of the executor, a waiver of penalties and interest can be requested. See Information Circular 92-2 "Guidelines for the Cancellation and Waiver of Interest and Penalties" for details of the process.

The Return for Rights and Things

The third return that can be filed on behalf of the deceased is given the odd name of a Return for Rights and Things. This is an optional return that allows you to take some of the income that normally would have appeared on the final return and put it on a separate return. The advantage of using two returns is that you get to use the full personal nonrefundable tax credits twice: once on the final return and again on the "rights and things" return. Now that I piqued your interest, you must be wondering, What is a right or thing? Well, funny you should ask — a right or thing is income that was owed to the deceased at the time of death but had not yet been paid. A Return for Rights or Things is a great way to reduce the tax liability of a deceased person by doubling up on the deduction of the nonrefundable tax credits. Examples of rights or things include salary earned but not paid, commissions, vacation pay, matured but unclipped bond coupons, bond interest owed but not paid, declared dividends, farm crops, and professional work in progress.

Get the CCRA Interpretive Bulletin IT-212 "Income of Deceased Persons." This will give you detailed information concerning the multiple returns that can be filed on behalf of deceased individuals. Important exceptions to rights and things include accrued interest that is not payable at the time of death, and RRSP income.

Make sure you do not put ineligible income on the Return for Rights and Things. If you do, both the rights and things return and the final return will be reassessed, and interest will be charged on amounts owing.

Here are some basics on how to file a Return for Rights and Things

- Use the T1 General return.
- Print the number "70(2)" in the top right-hand corner of page 1.
- File the return and pay the tax by the later of:
  - 90 days after you receive the assessment notice for the final return
  - One year from the date of death.

Return for a Partner or a Proprietor

If the deceased was a partner or proprietor in a business, and this business did not have a calendar year-end (that is, the year-end of the business did not end on December 31), then a fourth type of tax return can be filed on behalf of the deceased individual — the Return for a Partner or Proprietor. This return, like the Return for Rights and Things, is an optional return that if used correctly can generate substantial tax savings.

To understand the full advantage of the Return for a Partner or Proprietor, you have to remember that income earned by either of these business structures is included in the partner or proprietor's income at the year-end of the business. This return allows you to extract some of the income earned in the business and recognize it on a separate return. On this separate return you are once again allowed to use your personal tax credits to reduce your tax payable.

Let's look at an example. Alain owns a successful business that he operates as a sole proprietorship. This business has a July 31 year-end. Unexpectedly, Alain dies on September 30, 2001. Since Alain has a business with a non-calendar year-end, he is eligible to use the Return for a Partner and Proprietor. Alain's estate will report the business income from August 1, 2001 to September 30, 2001 on the Return for a Partner and Proprietor. The business income from August 1, 2000 to July 31, 2001 will be included in the final return. By splitting the income this way, the estate is able to use the personal tax credits on both the final return and on the Return for a Partner and Proprietor. You can include all the income on the final return, but by doing this you will forgo the ability to claim the tax credits available on Return for a Partner and Proprietor against this income.

To file this type of return you will need to use the T1 General and print "150(4)" in the top right-hand corner of page 1. Make sure it is clearly printed and easy to see. This return, and any tax payable, is due on the same date as the final return.

Return for income from a testamentary trust

If a deceased individual is receiving income from a testamentary trust, and the trust has a non-calendar year-end, then the estate can file a fifth return, for income from the trust. If a person dies on September 21, 2001, and this person is receiving income from a testamentary trust with a July 31, 2001 year-end, the income earned from the trust for the year ended July 31, 2001 will be included in the final return. The income earned from the trust for the period August 1, 2001 to September 21, 2001 can be included in the optional, income from a Testamentary Trust Return. By splitting the income between these returns, you can take advantage of the personal tax credits available on both returns to reduce the total tax payable.

To file this return, use the T1 General and print "104(23)(d)" in the top right-hand corner of page 1. The return must be filed and payments made (if necessary) by the later of April 30 of the following year or six months after the date of death.

T3 Trust Income Tax and Information Return

This is the sixth and final return that can be filed on behalf of the deceased, and will capture all income earned after the date of death. These amounts will include the following:

- Salary or wages paid for a period after the date of death. This normally occurs where an individual's salary is paid to the end of the month of death.
- Severance pay received after death.
- Refund of pension contributions.

- Deferred profit sharing payment.
- CPP or QPP death benefit, if not reported by the recipient.

The CCRA publishes a Tax Guide "T3 Guide and Trust Returns" and an Information Bulletin IT-305 "Testamentary Spousal Trusts" to help you complete these returns.

As we've seen, the primary advantage of filing these optional returns is that they give you the ability to repeatedly claim the personal deductions you normally only get to claim once per year. Let's look more closely at the credits and how they are claimed on these individual returns. Here are the credits that can be claimed on both the final return and the optional returns:

- Basic personal amounts
- Age amounts
- Spousal amounts
- Equivalent to spouse amount
- Amount for infirm dependant age 18 or older
- Personal amount supplement.

Here are the credits that must be split between the final return and the optional returns:

- Tuition credits
- Disability credit
- Charitable donation
- Medical expenses.

Splitting the credits means that the full amount of the credit is split or allocated between the returns. You cannot double these credits by using the optional returns. For example, Cassandra dies April 1, 2001. She has incurred $15,000 in medical expenses. Her income for the year is $25,000. The estate is able to include $15,000 of income on her final return and the remaining $10,000 on an option return. To take maximum advantage of the credits, the estate could put $9,000 in medical expenses on the final return and $6,000 on the optional returns. The total amount claimed cannot exceed the $15,000 in actual expenditures.

Returns That Deal with Bankruptcy

A bankrupt individual will usually need to file three returns in the year of bankruptcy (see also Chapter 4). A Pre-bankruptcy Return, a Trustee Return, and a Post-bankruptcy Return. Let's look at each of these returns in more detail and also run through what you report when and where. Don't kid yourself — bankruptcy tax becomes complicated in the allocation of your income, deductions, loss carryforwards, and personal credits among the various returns. The following section boasts not only handy definitions but also outlines the allocation of income, deductions, and credits on these returns. Assume a taxpayer goes bankrupt April 1, 2001, and emerges from bankruptcy December 31, 2001.

Pre-bankruptcy

The Pre-bankruptcy Return covers the period from January 1 of the year of bankruptcy to the actual date of bankruptcy. As we will discuss later, this return is like a normal yearly return, except that the personal credit will be allocated between this and the later return. This return, just like a normal return, must be filed by April 30 of the following year.

Pre-bankruptcy Return

On the Pre-bankruptcy Return, you should do the following:

- Report all income or losses, as well as deductions, for the period January 1, 2001 to March 31, 2001.
- Prorate the following yearly deductions and credits for the period January 1, 2001 to March 31, 2001 (that is, 90/365 days):
  - Capital cost allowance
  - Personal credit
  - Age credit
  - Disability credit
  - Transfer credits from spouse or children
- Claim the following amounts only to the extent actually paid in the period prior to bankruptcy:
  - Pension credits
  - CPP/UIC
  - Medical expenses
  - Tuition
  - Education amount
  - Charitable donations

Post-bankruptcy

The Post-bankruptcy Return covers the period from when you enter bankruptcy to the end of the calendar year. This return also needs to be filed before April 30 of the following year. On the Post-bankruptcy Return, do the following:

- Report all income or deductions not included in the trustee return. Basically, this means employment income.
- Prorate the following deductions for the period April 1, 2001 to December 31, 2001 (periods of 275/365 days):
  - Personal credit
  - Age credit
  - Disability credit
  - Transfer credits from spouse or children
- The following amounts can be claimed only to the extent actually paid in the period from entering bankruptcy until the calendar year-end (that is, April 1, 2001, to December 31, 2001):
  - Pension credits
  - CPP/UIC
  - Medical expenses
  - Tuition
  - Education amount

Trustee Return

When an individual goes bankrupt, a trustee in bankruptcy is appointed by the court to take over the administration of your property and business. Since the trustee controls these parts of your life, he or she must also file a tax return on your behalf. This return will cover the period from when you entered bankruptcy to either the end of bankruptcy or the calendar year-end, whichever comes first. If your bankruptcy straddles December 31, a second Trustee Return will be filed that runs from January 1 of the next year until you come out of bankruptcy. On the Trustee Return report the following:

- All business and property income and losses for the period between the beginning of bankruptcy, April 1, to the end of bankruptcy, December 31, 2001.
- All loss carryforwards from previous years.
- All charitable donations made while in bankruptcy.
- All unused educational tuition credits.
- All alternative minimum tax carryover.

By year-end, the total of all credits claimed on both the Pre- and Post-bankruptcy Returns must equal the total credit that would have been claimed on a normal single return.

When calculating the RRSP deduction as well as the GST and child tax credit, the CCRA considers both the Pre- and Post-bankruptcy Returns. Both returns are added together to determine the RRSP deduction room and the amount of GST and child tax credit. The RRSP contributions made throughout the year will be deducted on the Pre-bankruptcy Return. If a contribution is made in the first 60 days of the following year, the deduction will be made on the Post-bankruptcy Return.

Dealing with bankruptcies that straddle a calendar year-end

If, in our example, the taxpayer were not discharged from bankruptcy until January 31, 2002, the bankruptcy would be straddling two calendar years. Everything would stay the same as in the previous example, except that two additional returns would be filed during the bankruptcy. These returns would be a second Trustee Return and your regular T1 Return for 2002. The second Trustee Return would be filed for the period January 1, 2002 to January 31, 2002. This return would continue to pick up the business and property income from the beginning of the calendar year until the individual is discharged from bankruptcy. The second return you will file will be your regular T1 Return for the period January 1, 2002 until December 31, 2002.

Be sure to exclude the income and deductions already picked up on the second Trustee Return (January 1, 2002 to January 31, 2002) from the T1 Return for the year January 1, 2002 to December 31, 2002.

The CCRA will often refuse to allow an individual out of bankruptcy until the debt owing to them is reestablished. This is called a *conditional discharge.* In the case of the Home Buyer's RRSP withdrawal, the CCRA consistently requires this obligation to be reestablished before it will allow an individual out of bankruptcy.

Part II

Types of Income in Canada

"You know that mail order company that promised to show you how to avoid a tax audit? Well, their package just arrived."

In this part . . .

Here's where we get into the good stuff. Contrary to popular opinion, every type of income you earn belongs somewhere on your tax return. Unfortunately, it doesn't all belong on one line. Here's where all the various schedules and forms come into play, and where the confusion may begin. That's why we always say: Start with the identification section, ease into the rest of the return, and be thankful you only have to complete your T1 return once a year.

This part walks you through the various forms and schedules that affect the majority of taxpayers. In the traditional ... For Dummies format, we've managed to make this as simple and painless as possible. So whether you're an employee, a business-owner, an investor, or retired, this part's for you!

"The hardest thing in the world to understand is income tax!"

— Albert Einstein

Chapter 9

Understanding Employment-Related Income

In This Chapter

- Defining employment income
- Establishing the difference between employee and self-employed
- Using T4 slips
- Understanding taxable and non-taxable benefits
- Dealing with other employment income

For many Canadians much of their time is spent at work. Of course there are farmers and bankers and teachers and bus drivers among us, plus professions that many of us have yet to imagine. But the one thing that we all have in common is that we go to work to get paid so that we have income to enjoy the rest of our lives. And, much to the chagrin of many Canadians, employment income is where we pay the bulk of our taxes. But don't despair, with some planning and a better understanding of how the CCRA views employment income, we just might be able to help you end up with a few more dollars in your pocket after all is said and done. In this chapter we will discuss what CCRA considers to be employment income and take a close look at how that income is treated for tax purposes.

What Is Employment Income?

Employment income is income earned from an office or employment and includes all amounts received in a year as salary, wages, commissions, director's fees, bonuses, tips, gratuities, and honoraria. You should report all these items — which have been reported by your employer on your T4 slip in box 14 — on line 101 of your personal T1 return. This includes commission income, which is reported again on line 102. You should record any income on the list above that is not reported on your T4, but was received by you, on line 104 "Other employment income" of your T1.

Employee Versus Self-Employed

You may be employed on a commission basis, work out of your home part of the time or all of the time, or work at your employer's place of business. You may consider yourself to be self-employed, but the taxman may think differently. You see, the CCRA makes the distinction between self-employed and employed based on several factors or tests. The distinction can make a huge difference in your taxable income. If you are an employee, the *Income Tax Act* restricts the expenses that can be deducted from your employment income. If a deduction is not specifically mentioned in the Act, the answer's simple — it's not deductible. Self-employed individuals do not have these same restrictions.

If possible, in most situations it's advantageous to arrange your business relationship so that you are an independent contractor rather than an employee. Independent contractors are entitled to claim deductions for many expenses not deductible by an employee. Self-employment is one of the last great tax shelters. Table 9-1 illustrates the factors that the CCRA considers in its determination of whether you are an employee or an independent contractor.

Table 9-1 Factors Determining Employee vs. Independent Contractor Status

Employee	*Criteria*	*Independent Contractor*
Employee is under the direction and control of the employer. Control may not necessarily be exercised but right to do so is.	Supervision or Control	No direct control or supervision exists.
Employee complies with instruction about when, where, and how work is to be performed.	Instructions	Works his own schedule and does the job his own way.
The individual continues to work for the same person/company year after year.	Relationships	Hired to do one job. No continuous relationship.
Hours and days are set by the employer.	Hours	Individual is master of his own time.
Must devote full time to employer's business. Restricted from doing other work.	Exclusivity	Free to work when, and for whom he chooses.
Paid in regular amounts at stated intervals.	Payment	Paid by the job on a straight predetermined basis.
Usually employer furnishes tools.	Materials	Furnishes his own tools.
Cannot realize a profit or loss by making good or bad decisions.	Profit or Loss	Can realize a profit or loss as a result of his services.
Can end his relationship with employer at any time.	Termination	Agree to complete a specific job. Is responsible for satisfactory completion or is legally obligated to make good.
Employed as a part of business; services are an indispensable, integral part of that business.	Integration	Person may perform work that is integral.

These tests may not necessarily yield automatic answers, but they do provide the framework for the taxman's assessments. If you find you pay for a significant number of expenses that you are not being reimbursed for, and you can structure your work so that you qualify as an independent contractor, then you're off to the races.

Self-employment is not for everyone, since it comes with its own pitfalls. As a self-employed person, you'll be responsible for paying the employer's share of CPP, which will effectively double your payments. As well, before leaping at the opportunity to become your own boss, remember, if the company turns sour, there will be no EI or severance waiting for you. Make sure you assess the company's long-term outlook before you agree to become a contractor over an employee.

If the CCRA reviews your status and decides you are, in fact, an employee, the result may be assessment of penalties and interest to both you and your employer. The consequences of being incorrectly treated as a self-employed individual will be reassessment of your T1 return, denying ineligible expenses. Under such circumstances, your employer will be charged with the following:

- Failure to deduct or withhold income taxes.
- Failure to remit or pay income taxes.
- Late or deficient remittances of CPP, EI, and income taxes.
- Failure to prepare T4s and related information slips.

Since the issue of self-employed versus employed is not always clear, you may request a ruling on form CPT-1 "Request for a Ruling as to the Status of a Worker under the Canada Pension Plan or *Employment Insurance Act*."

The CCRA published a Tax Guide called "Employee or Self-Employed," which identifies the factors they look at to determine your employment status. This guide contains a checklist of "yes" and "no" answers to various questions. You can use these questions as a guide, but never send your responses to the CCRA. It may keep this on file, and use your responses to reassess you later.

Taxable Benefits and Non-Taxable Benefits

An employer will sometimes provide other benefits for your work in addition to your paycheque. The majority of the benefits you receive from your employer are considered to be taxable income. A benefit can be received in cash (for example, certain automobile allowances), or in kind, like an all-expense-paid holiday.

Taxable benefits

The following section details some of the more common benefits considered to be taxable. Review these carefully and determine if they apply to your individual tax situation. They will influence your final tax calculations significantly.

Forgiveness of employee debt

Forgiveness of employee debt occurs when your employer settles your debt for less than the amount owed, or completely eliminates your debt altogether. You should include in income the value of the forgiven amount.

Interest on interest-free or low-interest loans to employees

Next time you need a loan, try hitting up your employer for the cash instead of heading to the bank. You'll save interest costs if the loan from your employer is at a lower interest rate than that of the bank. Of course, you'll have to include a taxable benefit in your income as the difference between the CCRA's prescribed rate and the actual rate of interest you pay.

If you received a loan from your employer to enable you to relocate and purchase a home at least 40 kilometres closer to a new work location, the interest benefit on the first $25,000 of the loan is tax deductible for up to five years.

Club dues

If your employer pays your membership dues for a recreational, sporting, or dining club, the taxman views the amount as taxable to you unless the membership is primarily to your employer's advantage.

Automobile standby charge

If your employer provides you with a company car and you have custody and control of that car, there is a deemed taxable benefit to you whether or not you have used it personally. The formula used to calculate the benefit is as follows:

- 2 percent of the number of months of automobile use times the cost of the vehicle; or
- Two-thirds of the number of months times the monthly lease cost including taxes and insurance.

You'll be able to reduce this standby charge if two conditions exist. First, if you use the automobile at least 90 percent for business, and second, if personal use of the automobile was less than 12,000 kilometres for the year.

Think twice before accepting a company car as part of your compensation. You see, you'll be required to pay tax on two separate benefits: the standby charge and an operating benefit. The standby charge will likely be as high as 24 percent of the cost of your car each year! Even though the value of your car is reduced as soon as you drive it off the lot, your standby charge stays the same each year. Thanks but no thanks!

Personal operating costs of an automobile

If your employer pays for operating costs relating to your company car (for example, gasoline, tires, insurance, repairs, and maintenance), you'll be required to include an operating benefit in your income. The benefit for 2000 is calculated as 15 cents per kilometre for each kilometre driven for personal use. If your business use of the car is greater than 50 percent, there is another method you may use to calculate your operating benefit. You have the option of simply reporting your operating benefit as 50 percent of your standby charge. You'll prefer this method if the cost of your car is low, and if your personal kilometres are close to the 50-percent limit.

To use this alternative calculation for your operating benefit, you must notify your employer in writing prior to December 31.

Personal use of an employer's aircraft would also be a taxable benefit.

Your share of a profit-sharing plan

You should include in income amounts allocated to you under the plan each year. These will include amounts received by the plan from the employer, income earned in the plan during the year, capital gains and losses realized by the plan, and amounts previously allocated to other employees who are no longer eligible to receive payments from the plan. When a distribution is actually made by the plan to you, the distribution will generally be tax-free, because you already will have paid tax on the amount received.

Periodic employment insurance

You should include in income payments made to you in respect of loss of income under a sickness, accident or disability, or income maintenance plan if your employer has contributed to that plan. If you pay the premiums, any benefits you receive under the plan will not be included in your income. Make sure your plan at work is set up in such a way that disability payments will be tax-free if you ever have to collect.

Group term life insurance premiums

Group term life insurance premiums paid by your employer should be included in your income.

Reimbursements and awards

Reimbursements and awards received due to your employment; for example, paid holidays or incentive awards from employer-related contests should be included in your income.

There's no harm in extending your business trip to include a personal vacation. Since the initial trip was for business purposes, the costs paid by your employer will be tax-free benefits. Of course, this is provided you pick up all the additional costs, other than the trip home, from your extended trip.

Rent-free or low-rent housing

The monetary difference between rent-free or low-rent housing provided to you by your employer and the fair market rent for an equivalent accommodation should be included in your income. An exception to this rule exists for board and lodging received by an employee whose duties are performed at a remote location or, in some circumstances, at a special work site. See Chapter 17 for further information.

Spouse's traveling expenses

Sorry to say, but if your spouse joins you on a business trip, you'll probably have a taxable benefit equal to the traveling expenses of your spouse paid for by your employer. You won't have to report a benefit, however, if your spouse was primarily engaged in business activities on behalf of your employer.

Gifts from your employer

Gifts received from your employer, in cash or in kind, unless they were a Christmas or wedding gift worth $100 or less, should be included in your income. In the case of a gift, the fair market value of the gift must be included in income.

Gifts that have been personalized with your name or corporate logo will have a reduced fair market value. When the award is a plaque, trophy, or other memento for which there is no market, there is no need to include the value of the gift in income.

Relocation expenses

If your employer compensates you for the diminished value or loss on the sale of a residence necessary to relocate, these benefits are taxable to you. The taxable amount will be half of amounts over $15,000.

Frequent flyer programs

Have you been saving up all your frequent flyer points earned from business trips, to take you and your spouse to Hawaii for your twenty-fifth wedding anniversary? Well, the good news is there's nothing that prevents you from using these points (unless your employer prohibits it). The bad news? You guessed it, you'll have to report a taxable benefit for the fair market value of the points used for personal use. Still confused about whether you have to report a taxable benefit? Don't worry, the value of most of these amounts will be calculated for you and reported on your T4 or T4A slips.

Generally, if you receive a benefit by virtue of employment and it increases your net worth, it will be taxable.

A taxable benefit will usually be more financially advantageous than if you had to pay for the benefit yourself, even if you are in the highest tax bracket. For example, if your employer pays group term life insurance premiums of $4,000 for you annually, and you are taxed on the amount at 50 percent, you will only pay tax of $2,000 — that's much less expensive than your having to pay this amount out of your after-tax income.

Non-taxable benefits

And now for the fun stuff — non-taxable benefits! The following are benefits you may enjoy tax-free from your employer. Keep these benefits in mind if you're negotiating your way into a new job. You should load up on these perks if they are available, they have no negative affect on your tax situation.

Transportation to the job

Some employers provide their employees with transportation to and from work, for security or some other reason. Whatever the reason, there will be no inclusion for the value of the benefit in the employee's income. So now you can sit back and enjoy the ride, without worrying about any tax hit. The same can't be said if you receive an allowance or reimbursement for travel costs to and from work. Unfortunately these types of payments are considered taxable benefits.

Employer's contributions to group pension plans

Employer contributions to registered pension plans, deferred profit-sharing plans, group accident, sickness and health, and supplementary unemployment plans are not taxable benefits.

Private health services plans

Employers may set up a private health services plan (PHSP) to cover costs not covered by public health insurance, such as prescription drugs, dental costs, and hospital charges. Contributions made to a PHSP are non-taxable benefits to the employees.

Food and lodging

Food and lodging will not be taxable benefits if you were required to work at a temporary site for more than 36 hours consecutively. To qualify, the temporary site must be in a remote place or be farther away than a reasonable daily commute from your residence, and you must keep your usual residence.

Personal counseling

Not many people know this, but your employer can pay for counseling related to the mental or physical health of you or someone related to you, and you won't have to report a taxable benefit. This may include counseling related to tobacco, drug or alcohol abuse, stress management, job placement, or retirement. Be sure to negotiate these payments with your employer if you find yourself or someone related to you in need of these services.

Reasonable allowances

Reasonable allowances for travel expenses received by employees involved in negotiating contracts or selling property on behalf of their employer are not taxable. An allowance is generally considered reasonable if it's based on actual kilometres driven for work. This means that a payment of a fixed amount per month won't qualify as reasonable.

If the allowance you received for travel expenses was unreasonably low, you can add the whole amount of the allowance you received to your income and deduct your actual expenses.

Merchandise discounts

Does your company allow you to buy their merchandise at a discounted price? It's a great deal if your company sells chocolate — not so good if it sells cardboard boxes. Whatever it is your company sells, any discounts offered by an employer to its employees will generally be a non-taxable benefit, provided these discounts are extended to all employees.

Subsidized meals

Subsidized meals provided to all employees will not be a taxable benefit to you, provided you are required to pay a reasonable charge for those meals.

Uniforms

If your employer requires you to wear special clothing on the job, you'll be glad to know that the cost of the uniform, as well as its cleaning, will not result in a taxable benefit to you. Unfortunately, we've yet to find a company that provides business suits to all its employees.

Recreational facilities

There's no excuse for not exercising when your employer provides in-house recreational and fitness facilities. And what's more, the benefit, whether you use the facilities or not, is tax-free.

Death benefits

If you pass away and your employer pays a death benefit to your family, the first $10,000 of that benefit can be received tax-free.

Day-care services

If your employer provides in-house day-care services, this benefit will be tax-free. Keep in mind that this is not the same as your employer paying for day-care provided by a third party, in which case the benefit is taxable to you.

Education costs

In 1998, the CCRA changed its policy on education benefits, making the rules much more clear. There are two types of education your employer can pay for that won't result in a taxable benefit to you. The first is specific employment-related training. This means education relating directly to the skills used at work. For example, an employer may send an administrative assistant to a course on Excel because she uses the program every day in her job. This would be a tax-free benefit. The second type of education is general employment-related training. These are courses that don't relate specifically to your required work, but are generally relevant, and may include stress management, first aid, or language skills. There would be no taxable benefit if your employer paid for these types of courses. The third type of training *would* result in a taxable benefit, and it arises when employers pay for personal interest courses that have nothing to do with your work. So, if your employer kindly agrees to pay for your bird-house carpentry course, be prepared for a taxable benefit!

Working with your employer to maximize your non-taxable income is one of the few ways you, as an employee, can get some tax relief.

Other Employment Income

The CCRA asks for certain items to be reported on line 104 "Other Employment Income" that are not technically employment income.

These items include the following:

- Royalties from a work or invention
- GST rebate from a prior year (You'll have to wait until Chapter 26 for more details.)
- Research grants net of expenses
- Amounts received from a supplementary unemployment benefit plan
- The taxable portion of an income maintenance insurance plan
- Director's fees
- Signing bonuses
- Some termination payments and damages for loss of office or employment
- Executor's fees received for administering an estate.

Some of these items, like royalties, may in some circumstances be business income rather than employment income, and would therefore be reported on line 135.

Pension and retirement benefits and allowances, unemployment insurance benefits, and death benefits are not income from an office or employment. These amounts are addressed in chapters 10 and 11.

Chapter 10

Pension Income and Your Taxes

In This Chapter

- Understanding Canada's income security programs
- Making the most of the Old Age Security (OAS) Program
- Preparing for the OAS "clawback"
- Sorting out the Canada Pension Plan (CPP) and the Quebec Pension Plan (QPP)
- Understanding other pensions and superannuation
- Handling foreign pension income

If you're like most Canadians under 65 years of age, you're probably asking yourself whether you need to bother with this chapter. We suggest you take the time to read it — you might be surprised by all the ways pension income can be part of your tax picture, even if you are a spring chicken. True, only three lines of the tax return relate to pension income. And reporting OAS, CPP, and other pension income is usually straightforward. In most cases you will be issued an information slip detailing the amounts to be included in line 113 (Old Age Security), line 114 (Canada Pension Plan) and line 115 (other pensions and superannuation). If we simply went over this, the chapter would be about four pages. So why is this chapter so long? Well, we decided to go further, discussing the various sources of OAS and CPP, and offering you tips on whether you qualify for these payments, how to go about receiving them, and how to pay the least tax on the amounts received. We also delve into the "OAS clawback" and offer you some pension and tax-planning ideas.

First Things First — What Isn't Pension Income?

So let's be clear right off the bat about what this chapter deals with and what it doesn't. Income from a registered retirement pension plan (RRSP) is not considered pension income — we could probably come up with a detailed reason why, but it would add little value to this book. Since RRSP income is not considered to be pension income, we will not go into how RRSP withdrawals are taxed here. (Well, maybe we have space for just a little info — the amount withdrawn is noted on a T4RSP information slip and the amount is included on line 129 of your tax return. Any tax withheld by the RRSP trustee is included on line 437. Much more on taxes and your RRSP can be found in Chapter 11.) RRIF income is considered pension income. RRIF income is dealt with later in this chapter under the heading "Other Pensions and Superannuation."

Canada's Income Security Programs (ISPs)

Human Resources Development Canada (HRDC) is the branch of the federal government that administers Canada's income security programs. These programs include the Old Age Security (OAS) program and the Canada Pension Plan (CPP). Quebec administers it own pension plan (the Quebec Pension Plan or QPP) for residents of Quebec.

OAS Pension

OAS pension is a monthly pension payment. It is available to most Canadians aged 65 and over — even if they no longer live in Canada. The amount is adjusted quarterly for increases in the cost of living. The maximum monthly OAS pension payment for the fourth quarter of 2000, was $428.79. The maximum yearly amount for 2000 was $5,079.51. Payments made to taxpayers under OAS programs are paid from general tax revenues collected. There are no taxpayer contributions required nor is there a separate fund set up to provide for the payments. This is quite different from the Canada Pension Plan, which requires funding from both employees and employers.

Non-resident recipients of OAS

Payments can be made to addresses outside Canada. If you are not a resident of Canada, however, HRDC may withhold "non-resident tax" from your payment of OAS. The tax amount withheld depends on the country in which you reside, and whether Canada has a social security treaty with that country. The maximum withholding is 25 percent. HRDC will not withhold any non-resident tax on payments of OAS if you are a resident of the United States or the United Kingdom.

You can have HRDC deposit your OAS payment directly to any bank account in Canada or the United States. All you need to do is advise HRDC and send them a cheque with "VOID" across it. If you have your payments go to a U.S. Bank, HRDC will send you a form to complete.

OAS eligibility criteria

Eligibility for an OAS pension is based on two issues: age and years resident in Canada. Two categories of people are eligible for OAS:

- **People living in Canada who are**
  - 65 or older,
  - a Canadian citizen or legal immigrant, and
  - have lived in Canada for at least 10 years while an adult.
- **People living outside Canada who are**
  - 65 or older,
  - a Canadian citizen or a legal immigrant, and
  - have lived in Canada for at least 20 years as an adult.

If you do not fall into these categories you still may be eligible to receive OAS. Canada has a number of reciprocal social security agreements with other countries. If you lived in one of these countries or contributed to its social security system, you may qualify for a pension from that country, Canada, or both. Need more information to determine whether you qualify? Contact Human Resources Development Canada (HRDC) at 1-800-277-9914, 1-800-277-9915 (French), or 1-800-255-4786 (TTY/TDD). HRDC'S Web site at `www.hrdc-drhc.gc.ca/isp` or `www.hrdc-drhc.gc.ca/psr` (French) contains a wealth of information.

Ceasing to qualify for OAS

You will cease to qualify for OAS on your death. Also, if you did not live in Canada for at least 20 years after turning 18, the OAS will be stopped if you leave the country for more than six months.

Are you entitled to a full or partial OAS?

The main criteria in determining whether you're entitled to a full or partial OAS pension is the length of time you've been in Canada. You should qualify for full OAS if the following apply to you

- Lived in Canada for at least 40 years after age 18
- Were born on July 1, 1952, or earlier
- Between your 18th birthday and July 1, 1977, you lived in Canada for some period of time
- You lived in Canada for 10 years prior to your OAS application being approved.

Do you not qualify because you haven't lived in Canada for the past 10 years? Don't fret! You should still qualify for full OAS if

- You lived in Canada for the year immediately before your application was approved
- Prior to those past 10 years, you lived in Canada as an adult at least three times, for the same length of time as the total of your absences during the past 10 years. (Go ahead, be confident, do the math!)

If you do not qualify for a full OAS, a partial OAS pension may be available to you. An HRDC office can advise you on the amount to which you may be entitled.

Is my OAS pension taxable?

You bet. The reporting of OAS on your tax return, however, is very simple. If you received OAS payments in 2000, HRDC will send you a T4A(OAS) information slip summarizing the amount paid. You should expect this slip to arrive in February 2001. The amount noted in box 18 is to be included on line 113 of your tax return. HRDC may have held back some tax on the OAS pension payment to you. If so, this amount will be noted in box 22 of the T4A(OAS). Be sure to include the withheld tax on line 437 of your return.

If you want to reduce the amount of taxes that come due on April 30 each year, you can request that HRDC withhold more in taxes from your OAS payments.

If you are a non-resident of Canada and are not filing a regular Canadian tax return, you must file the Old Age Security Return of Income form each year by April 30. If you do not file, your OAS will be stopped in July.

Applying for OAS

To ensure your OAS payments start on time, you should apply six months before your 65th birthday. (You can apply as early as 12 months before you turn 65.) A registration kit is available from any HRDC office, or you can call 1-800-277-9914, 1-800-277-9915 (French) or 1-800-255-4786 (TTY/TDD). The kit (ISP 3503) can also be downloaded from the Web site of HRDC `www.hrdc-drhc.gc.ca/isp` or `www.hrdc-drhc.gc.ca/psr` (French). You cannot apply on-line. You need to download the form (ISP 3000), complete it, and send it to the address noted on the Web site. To view and download the form, you will need Acrobat Reader. If you apply late, you are entitled to a back payment for the past 12 months of OAS that you would have been entitled to if you had applied on time. If you apply more than one year late to receive your OAS pension, you could lose some of the payments to which you're entitled. Don't delay!

Guaranteed Income Supplement (GIS)

The GIS program provides low-income Canadians with benefits in addition to the regular OAS pension. In fact, to qualify for the GIS, the recipient must be in receipt of the regular OAS. The government determines GIS based on the taxpayer's income and marital status. The maximum monthly GIS as of October 1, 2000, is $509.59 for a single person and $331.93 for an individual married to an OAS recipient. The GIS payment is included in the monthly OAS cheque.

Applying for the GIS and yearly renewal

As with OAS pension, you must apply for GIS. The form is available on the HRDC Web site or at an HRDC office. The GIS is renewed annually, since it is based on your income from the previous year. You do not need to reapply each year — just ensure that you file an income tax return each year.

Is the GIS taxable?

No, but the amount must be reported on your tax return. The T4A(OAS) slip will note the amount of GIS you received in box 21. This is first included in your income in box 146 and then deducted on line 250.

Why the inclusion and deduction from income? Though the GIS is not taxable, it may reduce the amount of tax credits you qualify for — such as the Goods and Services Tax/Harmonized Sales Tax (GST/HST) credit. This is because most tax credit restrictions or reductions are calculated based on the "net income" reported on line 236, not on "taxable income" reported on line 260. A GIS recipient will always have a net income higher than his or her taxable income because the GIS is included in the calculation of the former but not the latter. A second reason for the inclusion and deduction is to reduce tax credits claimed by others in respect of you. For example, if you have very low income, your spouse may be claiming a "marital tax credit" (see Chapter 18). The amount of this credit is determined by your net income, not your taxable income.

Spouse's Allowance

This is an additional benefit paid to low-income seniors with a spouse who receives the OAS and GIS. It is like an early OAS pension. The recipient must be 60 to 64 years of age and meet some residency tests. Like OAS and the GIS, HRDC can deposit the funds right into your bank account. If you are receiving a spouse's allowance, you will receive an annual T4A(OAS) slip. The amount received will be noted in box 21. The amount is not taxable but must be reported on your tax return in the same fashion as the GIS. You apply for the Spouse's Allowance using the same form as for the regular OAS – form ISP 3000.

Widowed Spouse's Allowance

This is another "early OAS pension." The benefit is paid to low-income seniors ages 60 to 64, if their spouse has died and they meet residency requirements. HRDC can directly deposit the amount to your bank account. Like those receiving the spouse's allowance, recipients of the widowed spouse's allowance will receive an annual T4A (OAS) slip. Again, the amount received will be noted in box 21 and is not taxable, although it is still reported on your tax return. Again, form ISP 3000 is used to apply for the Widowed Spouse's Allowance.

To continue receiving the GIS, the spouse's allowance, or the widowed spouse's allowance, ensure you file a tax return by April 30 each year. See Table 10-1 for a summary of the tax implications of these items.

Table 10-1 The Taxation of Old Age Security (Line 113)

Type of Receipt	*Taxable?*
Old Age Security (OAS) pension	Yes — and it can be taxed up to 100 percent. (See comments below on the "OAS Clawback.")
Guaranteed Income Supplement (GIS)	No — but it must be reported on your tax return.
Spouse's Allowance	No — but it must be reported on your tax return.
Widowed Spouse's Allowance	No — but it must be reported on your tax return.

Old Age Security repayment

The government giveth, the government taketh! Much to the chagrin of seniors, our government believes those with income in excess of $53,960 do not deserve to receive a full OAS pension. (In other words, our government wants seniors to foot more of the government's expenditures.) Where a taxpayer has received OAS higher than his or her calculated maximum OAS entitlement, the excess amount must be repaid.

When the OAS repayment program began (1990, for those interested) the government continued to pay taxpayers their full share of the OAS without considering whether all or a portion of the OAS would have to be repaid at tax time. The amount to be repaid was not calculated until the taxpayer completed a tax return, and was then added to the individual's tax liability. This often came as a shock to seniors, some of whom had already spent all their OAS pension! Since the government gave the funds and then asked for them back, the OAS repayment became known as the *OAS clawback*. (Picture an eagle's talons grabbing money from your purse or wallet the second you complete your tax return.) In mid-1996 the program was amended so that monthly OAS payments were reduced to take into account an individual's expected OAS repayment. High-income individuals do not receive any OAS at all. The withholding of an expected OAS clawback adds complexity to tax return preparation. This is discussed below.

After you make an OAS repayment, the CCRA tattles on you. They tell HRDC, which then adjusts your future monthly OAS payments. Assuming you file your 2000 tax return by April 30, 2001, the CCRA should assess you by the end of June 2001. Based on the assessment of your income on your 2000 return, HRDC will adjust your next 12 OAS monthly payments beginning with the July 2001 payment. (Your July 2001 payment may be significantly different from your June 2001 payment.) The adjustment to your monthly OAS payments is made under the assumption that your 2001 net income will be about the same as your 2000 net income. In other words, HRDC expects that you will have to repay all or a portion of your 2001 OAS in an amount that is approximately what you had to repay in respect of the 2000 OAS. Rather than paying you the OAS and then waiting for you to repay OAS as part of your 2001 tax return, HRDC simply reduces the amount of your monthly OAS cheque.

What if your 2001 net income is lower than your 2000 net income to the extent that you did not receive 2001 OAS in the amount you were entitled to? The deficiency is paid to you by decreasing your tax liability (or increasing your tax refund) on your 2001 tax return. Confused? Just remember that the determination of your OAS payments is six months after the tax year for which you just filed a tax return.

Another tax! The actual term for the OAS repayment or clawback is "tax on Old Age Security benefits." For high-income earners, the tax can be 100 percent of OAS received.

Calculation of OAS repayment

Let's work through an illustration of how the OAS repayment (or clawback) is calculated.

Jim turned 65 on January 1, 2000. He applied for OAS six months before his 65th birthday. We have purposely made Jim's income exceed $53,960 to detail the calculation and impact of the OAS repayment on his tax return and tax liability.

Old Age Security (OAS) pension	$5,079.51
Other pension income	$60,000.00
Interest income	$2,000.00
Deduction for support payments made to former spouse	($5,000.00)
Net income before deduction for OAS repayment	$62,079.51

Calculation of OAS repayment

Net income before deduction for OAS repayment (as above)	$62,079.51
Less base amount	$53,960.00
Excess net income	$8,119.51
Net income before deduction for OAS repayment	$62,079.51
Less repayment — 15% on excess net income (line 235 on tax return)	$1,217.93
Net income after OAS repayment (line 236 on tax return)	$60,861.58

The amount of repayment owing is included in determining your total tax liability or refund. It is included on line 422 of the tax return as part of the calculation of your total tax liability for the year. Depending on your tax position, the OAS repayment may increase your tax owing at April 30, 2001 — or decrease your refund!

Lose all your OAS!

Assuming the 2000 maximum yearly OAS entitlement is $5,079.51, the mathematically inclined should be able to calculate that once your net income is $87,823.40, all your OAS will be repaid or "clawed back."

Reporting your OAS on your tax return — even when you are subject to a full OAS clawback!

HRDC reduces your monthly OAS payment after they are informed your income is above the base amount. Many high-income taxpayers find they will receive no OAS payments at all. Let's assume you are a fortunate high-income taxpayer. In these cases you would expect that HRDC would not send you a T4A(OAS) slip. Right? Wrong. Well, if they send out a slip, you would expect the amount of OAS reported on the slip would be $0. Wrong again! What happens is this. The slip is sent out indicating you received the maximum OAS for the year — as noted above, this is $5,079.51 for 2000. This is reported in box 18 of the T4A(OAS) slip, and you are required to include this on your tax return on line 113 of your return — just as you would do if you had received the amount. (I know what you are thinking. *Why should I report income I didn't receive?* Bear with us — it's going to kind of make sense in a minute.) The T4A(OAS) slip will have the $5,079.51 reported in box 22 under "income tax deducted." This will be included in the amount you report on line 437 of your return under "total income tax deducted (from all information slips)." All this means that you are considered to have received the full amount of OAS and to have repaid it in full. You have already been subject to the OAS repayment.

As you are considered to have met your OAS repayment obligation, you'll want to ensure the amount is not taxed again. Remember, you included the $5,079.51 in your income on line 113 of your return. You then go through the OAS repayment calculation (see above) and find that your repayment is — surprise! — $5,079.51. This amount is deducted from your calculation of net income on line 235, and the repayment obligation is noted on line 422. So the $5,079.51 appears four times on your tax return.

Calculation of Income Subject to Tax

Old Age Security pension	Line 113	$5,079.51
Deduction for social benefits repayment	Line 235	($5,079.51)
Amount subject to further tax		$0

Calculation of Tax Liability

Social benefits repayment obligation	Line 422	$5,079.51
Income tax deducted	Line 437	($5,079.51)
Additional tax liability		$0

This means you will not be double-taxed and will not be subject to the OAS repayment twice in the same year. (Trust us!) It also means that if HRDC withheld too much from your OAS pension payment — that is, they overestimated what your clawback would be — the excess will be paid to you by decreasing your tax liability/increasing your tax refund. When you prepare your return manually, you may handle the confusing T4A(OAS) slips and the tax return reporting of the figures incorrectly. Tax return computer software will handle the reporting correctly, assuming you can get by the question "Why am I reporting income I did not receive?"

OAS overpayments

You may have received OAS payments in error during 2000 and previous years. Repayments of these amounts are noted in box 20 of the T4A(OAS) slip. (Note that OAS repayments differ from the "clawback.") Repayments are claimed as a deduction on line 232 of your return to the extent that the amount was included in your income in 2000 and prior years.

Income from the Canada Pension Plan (CPP) and Quebec Pension Plan (QPP) (Line 114)

Table 10-2 lists the variety of amounts that you can receive from the CPP and the QPP:

Table 10-2 Summary of Amounts You Can Receive from the CPP and QPP

Type of Receipt	*Taxable?*
CPP/QPP lump sum benefit	Yes — but a portion may be taxed in a prior year.
CPP/QPP retirement pension	Yes
CPP/QPP disability pension	Yes
CPP/QPP child disability benefit	Yes — but taxed in tax return of child.

(continued)

Table 10-2 (continued)

Type of Receipt	*Taxable?*
CPP/QPP survivor benefit	Yes
CPP/QPP child survivor benefit	Yes — but taxed in tax return of child.
CPP/QPP death benefit	Yes — but taxed in estate.

Reporting your CPP/QPP income on your tax return

Each January, HRDC will send CPP recipients a T4A(P). The amount noted in box 20 is to be put on line 114 of your tax return. Figures in the other boxes provide a breakdown of your sources of CPP. None of these figures needs to be reported on your tax return, with the exception of box 16 — your CPP or QPP disability amount. This is to be noted in box 152, which is just to the left of box 114. Do not add box 152 when calculating your total income; the amount is already included in box 114.

Lump sum CPP or QPP benefit

If you received a lump sum benefit in 2000, all or part of it may be in respect of a prior year. The amount needs to be reported in your 2000 tax return. However, you may qualify for preferential tax treatment. Where the amount related to a previous year is $300 or more, you can have that portion taxed in the year to which it relates. This is beneficial if the tax in the relevant year would be lower than your 2000 tax would be if the amount were included in your 2000 return. This would be the case if you had been in a lower tax bracket in that previous year. The CCRA, based on information from HRDC, will reassess your 2000 return and that of the other year, and advise you of the results on a Notice of Re-assessment.

CPP versus QPP

The Quebec government administers the QPP on behalf of the people of Quebec. HRDC administers the CPP for the remaining nine provinces and three territories. With respect to most issues, the two plans operate in a similar fashion. For simplicity and conciseness, the rest of this chapter deals mostly with CPP issues.

Canada Pension Plan retirement pension

The CPP is a monthly pension paid to individuals who have contributed to one of the following:

- the CPP
- both the CPP and Quebec Pension Plan (QPP), if you live outside Quebec.

The retirement pension is designed to be paid starting when an individual turns 65. However, you have the option of taking a discounted payment at any time between the ages of 60 and 64. If you defer your pension until you are 66 to 70, your monthly payment will be increased. (We discuss the discounted and increased payments below.) If you decide to take the pension when you are 60 to 64, you must have "substantially or completely" stopped working. HRDC considers you to have substantially ceased working if you are earning less than the maximum CPP retirement pension — about 25 percent of the average wage in Canada. In 1999 this was just over $9,000.

CPP child-rearing dropout provision

Your CPP retirement pension is based on your contributions to the plan as well as on your contributory period — any time after you turned 18 until you turn 70. Due to your leaving the workforce or choosing self-employment to raise children, you could be penalized for contributory years when your CPP contributions were low or zero. To prevent this penalty, the child-rearing dropout provision helps to increase your CPP retirement pension. The provision permits you to calculate your CPP retirement pension to exclude your periods of low or zero earnings. To qualify, your children must have been born in 1959 or later. If you request this provision, months of low or non-existent CPP contributions during the first seven years of a child's life will not have an impact on your entitlement to a CPP retirement pension. You must request to have this provision applied to you by completing form ISP-1640. This form is available from HRDC offices or via their Web site.

To find out how much CPP you are entitled to at different start dates, you can contact HRDC. Simply fill out form ISP-1003, "Estimate Request for Canada Pension Plan (CPP) Retirement Pension," with alternative start dates. HRDC advises that the closer you are to the date you want your pension to begin, the more accurate the estimate will be. The form is available at any HRDC office or via the Web sites noted above in the section dealing with Old Age Security.

As with the OAS, you may qualify for a CPP retirement pension that is calculated based not only on contributions you have made to the plan, but also on contributions you have made to another country's social security system. Canada has a number of reciprocal social security agreements that provide for this. This is good news if you were only in Canada for a short while before you retired but had previously worked and paid social security taxes to a country with which Canada has such an agreement.

Reduction in CPP retirement pension

If you decide to start your CPP retirement pension before you are 65 years of age, the payments are reduced by 6 percent for each year that you are under 65.

The CPP reduction calculation is actually done on a monthly basis. For each month you are under 65 your CPP retirement pension is reduced by .5 percent (.5 percent times 12 months equals 6 percent for a whole year). If a CPP retirement pension is started on your 60th birthday, you will be subject to a 30-percent reduction in your monthly payment (five years early @ 6 percent per year equals 30 percent).

Let's take James's situation. James will turn 62 in the coming year. He is wondering whether to begin his CPP retirement pension on his 62nd birthday or wait until he is 64. Based on the current maximum monthly CPP retirement pension of $762.92, his payments would be as follows:

	Start on 62nd birthday	***Start on 64th birthday***
Maximum monthly pension	$762.92	$762.92
Discount:		
3 years @ 6% = 18%	$137.32	
1 year @ 6% = 6%		$45.78
Reduced monthly pension	$625.60	$717.14

James's CPP retirement pension payments are reduced, but he will receive the monthly payment longer than if he waited until he was 65 to receive the payment.

Increasing your CPP retirement pension

If you elect to start receiving your CPP retirement pension after you are 65 years of age, you are entitled to an increased amount — again, 6 percent per year (actually .5 percent per month). If you wait until your 70th, your entitlement increases by 30 percent!

How do you decide when to start taking your CPP retirement pension?

HRDC suggests that in making your decision, you consider the following:

- Whether you are still working and contributing to the plan
- How long you have contributed
- How much your earnings were
- What your other sources of retirement income are
- How your health is
- What your retirement plans are, including desired lifestyle.

The decision is yours, says the HRDC. Don't forget, once you have decided to start taking your CPP retirement pension, you must apply for it!

If you decide too late that you should have applied earlier, you may be out of luck. Back payments cannot always be made. On the other hand, if you change your mind and wish that you had applied *later,* you can request your payments be stopped. You must do this within six months after the payments began — and all benefits you received to that point must be paid back. All of this involves a lot of red tape. You are better off considering in advance all the issues that might influence you when you want to begin your payments.

Other benefits offered by the Canada Pension Plan

In addition to the retirement pension, the CPP also provides the following:

- CPP disability benefits
- CPP survivor benefits.

Applying for your CPP retirement pension

HRDC suggests you apply six months before you want your retirement pension to begin. (You can apply up to 12 months early.) A registration kit is available from any HRDC office, or you can call 1-800-277-9914, 1-800-277-9915 (French), or 1-800-255-4786 (TTY/TDD). You can also download the kit from Herd's Web sites — `www.hrdc-drhc.gc.ca/isp` or `www.hrdc-drhc.gc.ca/psr` (French). You cannot apply on-line. You need to download the form (form ISP-1000), complete it, and send it to the address noted on the Web site. To view and download the form, you will need Acrobat Reader.

CPP disability benefits

The CPP will provide you with a monthly pension if you have been a CPP contributor and are considered mentally or physically disabled under the CPP guidelines. Payments can also be made to dependent children. Your disability must be "severe and prolonged." HRDC considers "severe" to mean that you cannot work regularly at any job, and "prolonged" to mean that your condition is long term or may lead to death. The amount paid comprises a flat amount plus a second amount based on the number of years you have contributed to the CPP. The maximum monthly disability benefit in 2000 was $917.43.

Eligibility for CPP disability benefits

To be eligible you must have contributed to the CPP in four of the past 10 years and have earned at least 10 percent of each Year's Maximum Personable Earnings (YMPE). (The YMPE changes each year.) For 2000, the amount is $37,600. If you have not contributed long enough, you might still qualify under other criteria. Contact the HRDC office to find out. The government will cease payments when you are no longer considered disabled, when your regular CPP retirement pension begins (at age 65, or earlier if you so choose), or upon your death.

Children's benefit

If you become disabled, your child under 18 can qualify for a benefit. Even if your "child" is between ages 18 and 25, he or she will still qualify if enrolled in what HRDC considers a recognized institution — usually a school providing post-secondary education. The maximum amount paid in 2000 was $174.07 per month per child. Benefits are adjusted each January to reflect cost-of-living increases.

You must apply for both CPP disability benefits — the regular benefit and the children's benefit. Application forms are available from HRDC offices or from HRDC's Web site. You should apply as soon as you consider yourself to have a long-term disability that prevents you from working at any job. The government will require you to provide a medical report from your doctor.

CPP survivor benefits

CPP survivor benefits are paid to your estate, surviving spouse, and dependent children. There are three types of survivor benefits.

Death benefit

The death benefit is a one-time payment to your estate. The maximum amount for this benefit is $2,500.

Surviving spouse's pension

Your surviving spouse can receive a monthly pension. The amount of the payment depends on how long you paid in to the CPP, your spouse's age when you die, and whether your spouse is receiving a CPP retirement or disability pension. The calculation is based on what your CPP retirement pension would have been if you had been 65 at the time of death. This amount is then adjusted to take into account the age of your spouse. The maximum amount that can be received is 65 percent of what your retirement pension would have been. To receive this, your spouse must be age 65 or over at the time of your death. Where your spouse is younger, the payments are lower. If your surviving spouse is under 35 and is not disabled or raising your dependent child, the amount is deferred until he or she is 65 or becomes disabled. The surviving spouse will continue to receive the pension even if he or she remarries.

Prior to a change in the rules in 1987, a surviving spouse who remarried would lose the pension. If this happened to you, contact HRDC to find out whether you are now eligible.

Children's benefit

The children's benefit is a monthly payment to a deceased contributor's dependent children. At the time of the contributor's death, the child must be under 18, or between the ages of 18 and 25 and enrolled full time in a recognized institution. The maximum monthly amount in 2000 was $174.07. At least one of the child's parents must have been a contributor to the CPP. A child may get two benefits if both parents are deceased or disabled. Payments will cease under any of the following circumstances:

- The child is 18 to 25 and not in full-time attendance in a recognized institution
- The child turns 25
- The child dies.

You must apply for CPP survivor benefits. Applications are available at HRDC offices and on the HRDC Web site noted above. HRDC can directly deposit survivor benefits to a bank account.

CPP retirement pension sharing or CPP splitting

You and your spouse can apply to receive an equal share of the CPP retirement pension you both earned during the years you were together. You must both be at least 60 years of age, and must request that your CPP be shared or "split" at the time you apply for CPP. CPP sharing or splitting is also referred to as an assignment of a retirement pension. Splitting your CPP does not increase or decrease the overall retirement pension to which you and your spouse are entitled.

Why would you split?

The main reason for CPP splitting is to reduce the combined tax you and your spouse pay. This can be done when you and your spouse are in different income tax brackets. Let's take a look at an example to make this a little clearer. Assume your income, before your CPP retirement pension, is about $80,000. This puts you into the top tax bracket in Canada. The actual tax you pay will be based on the province or territory you live in. Let's say you live in a province or territory where the top tax rate is 45 percent. Let's further assume that your spouse makes $10,000, excluding his or her CPP retirement pension. At this level of income, the tax rate is about 25 percent. Your CPP retirement pension is $5,000 and your spouse's is $2,000. As illustrated in the following table, you and your spouse will pay an aggregate of $2,750 in income tax on your combined CPP retirement pension.

	You	*Spouse*	*Total*
CPP retirement pension	$5,000	$2,000	$7,000
Tax rate	45%	25%	
Tax	$2,250	$500	$2,750

Let's improve the situation. You and your spouse agree to split your CPP retirement pension. You can see that the tax is reduced to $2,450 — a $300 saving in tax, just by filling out a form!

	You	*Spouse*	*Total*
CPP retirement pension	$3,500	$3,500	$7,000
Tax rate	45%	25%	
Tax	$1,575	$875	$2,450

This result is optimal when one spouse is in the highest tax bracket (taxable income in excess of $60,009) and the other spouse is in the lowest tax bracket (taxable income of less than $30,000). The saving is enhanced further when the high-income-earning spouse also receives a CPP retirement pension significantly higher than that received by the lower-income spouse.

CPP and marriage breakdown — splitting CPP credits

CPP credits are used to determine the amount of your entitlement to a CPP retirement pension. Since spouses build up credits during a marriage or common-law relationship, both can share in the CPP entitlements earned while they were together. CPP credits can even be split if only one spouse paid into the CPP. If you were legally married and are now divorced the CPP pension credits of you and ex-spouse can be split if:

- You and your ex-spouse had continually lived together for at least a year and
- You or your ex-spouse apply to HRDC (there is no time limitation) and requested information is provided.

If you are separated but not divorced, the credits can be split if:

- You and your spouse had continually lived together for at least a year,
- You and your spouse have been separated for at least a year and

An application is made to the HRDC and requested information is provided. Again, there is no time limit to apply unless your former spouse dies. Then you must apply within three years of the date of death.

If you were in a common-law relationship that has ended, credits can be split if:

- You and your common-law spouse had continually lived together for at least a year,
- You and your common-law spouse have been separated for at least a year and

An application is made to the HRDC and requested information is provided. There is a four-year time limit (from the date you began living apart) to apply.

CPP or QPP overpayments

If you were required to repay a CPP or QPP amount that was paid to you in error and included in your income, you can deduct the amount repaid. Deduct the amount repaid on line 232 of your tax return.

Other Pensions and Superannuation (Line 115)

The first question is what is *superannuation*? The CCRA considers a *superannuation* or *pension benefit* to be any amount received out of a superannuation or pension fund. Hmm . . . we're not sure this definition helps. It gets worse if we look at a dictionary. The definitions for superannuate use words and terms like obsolete, become antiquated, disqualified from active duty because of age, out-of-date, and so on. In the end, it does not matter how superannuation is defined. Pretty well all funds considered superannuation are taxable to the recipient. The dollar amounts of your various pension incomes are to be aggregated and reported on line 115 of your return. This is fairly straightforward — most pension income will be reported on T4A slips or other information slips.

Types of pension income

Here are descriptions of the various types of pension income:

- Payments from a former employer's or union's registered pension plan (box 16 of T4A slip).

  If you transferred a lump sum from a pension plan to your RRSP, see comments below on "direct transfers."

- Payments from a RRIF — a registered retirement income fund (T4RIF slip) and payments from an annuity (T4A slip)

  (If you were under age 65, these amounts are to be reported on line 130 of your return — not on line 115. This is so the income will *not* qualify for the pension credit. The pension credit is discussed briefly below and then in detail in Chapter 18.)

- Certain annuity income. Where you have purchased an annuity with non-RRSP funds, the annuity payments you receive are considered to be part interest and part capital. The capital portion is not subject to tax because it represents a partial return of the purchase price that you funded with tax-paid dollars. The interest portion is usually taxed as "interest" (hey, this makes sense!). However, if you are age 65 or older, receipts from a "mixed annuity" (an annuity payment in which the interest and capital portion are determined by the tax rules), the interest portion is considered pension income and is reported on line 115.

A "mixed annuity" is the street name for the technical term "prescribed annuity." The term "prescribed" implies something has been specifically determined by tax rules.

Foreign pension income

Foreign pension income refers to any pension income that is received from a source outside Canada. A common type is U.S. social security paid to a resident of Canada. To receive this you would have worked in the U.S. for some time in your life. If you had worked in the U.S. or any foreign country you may have been part of a foreign employer's pension plan. When you retire you are entitled to receive your pension even though you are no longer resident in the country that is making the pension payments. You also may have served in a foreign country's armed forces. If so, you may be entitled to a pension from the respective country. Most foreign pension income is subject to tax — but not all! Immediately below, we discuss various sources of foreign pension income. We also comment on the respective tax issues of each source of foreign pension income.

U.S. social security income

The full amount of U.S. social security income you receive is to be included on line 115. Of course, you will need to translate the U.S. dollar amount received into a Canadian dollar amount!

You can translate receipts using the exchange rate as of the day you received the social security payment. Alternatively, you can use the annual average U.S./Canada exchange rate that the CCRA provides. Choose the method that is most beneficial to you — that is, the method that translates into the lowest Canadian dollar equivalent.

On line 256 of your return, you can take a 15-percent deduction of the amount you received in U.S. social security. This results in only 85 percent of your U.S. social security being subject to tax!

Other foreign pension income

The CCRA suggests that you include the foreign pension income on line 115 of your tax return after applying the appropriate exchange rate, and then attach a note to your return indicating the type of pension and its country of origin. If the foreign country withheld tax from your pension payment, do not deduct the tax, but report the gross pension receipt. The foreign tax paid may qualify as a tax credit (referred to as a foreign tax credit) in calculating your tax liability. (See Chapter 19.)

Canada has a number of tax treaties with other countries. A treaty may adjust the amount of a foreign pension that is taxed in Canada. If you determine an amount is not taxable in Canada, it can be deducted on line 256 of your return. The CCRA can assist you in determining whether any part of your foreign pension is exempt from tax in Canada.

Non-Taxable Pension Income

The following should not be included in your tax return:

- Capital element of an annuity. If you are receiving annuity payments, a portion is interest and a portion is capital (in other words, a portion is part of your original purchase price or investment). Since you invested after-tax funds, you are not taxed again.
- Military and civil pensions paid under the
  - *Pension Act* (pension on death of a Canadian armed forces member)
  - *Civilian War Pensions and Allowances Act* (pensions for civilians injured in the Second World War)
  - *War Veterans Act* (pension for veterans, spouse, and dependent children)
- War service pension from other countries allied with Canada
- German compensation in respect of Nazi persecution
- Halifax disaster pension.

Tax treatment of common foreign pensions

- **France.** French pensions are exempt from Canadian tax if they are also exempt from French tax. If the pension is exempt, it should still be reported on line 115 of your Canadian tax return, then deducted on line 256. If the pension is not exempt from French tax, it is fully taxable in Canada.
- **Germany.** There are approximately 50 named pensions from Germany that are exempt from Canadian tax, including German social security and pensions received as compensation for injury or damage as a result of hostilities or past political persecution. Exempt pensions are included on line 115 of the Canadian tax return but then deducted on line 256. The CCRA will help you determine whether your pension is exempt; if it is not, it is fully taxable in Canada.
- **Italy.** Military pensions and pensions received because you rendered services to the Italian authorities are exempt from tax in Canada. Italian pensions usually come with reported instructions in both Italian and French, so if you're unsure if your pension is taxable, read this information for guidance. If it is exempt from tax, it is reported on line 115 and deducted on line 256 of your Canadian tax return; otherwise, it is fully taxable.
- **Spain.** Government pensions from Spain are exempt; otherwise they are taxable in Canada. Report exempt pensions on line 115 and deduct them on line 256 of your Canadian tax return.
- **United Kingdom.** Pensions from the U.K. are reported in the country of receipt; therefore, if you live in Canada and receive a pension from the U.K., it is reported only on your Canadian tax return.

Pension credit

You can claim a pension credit amount if you receive certain types of pension income. The maximum you are allowed is a tax credit amount up to $1,000 of eligible pension income. If your eligible pension income is less than $1,000, your credit amount will be equal to the amount of eligible pension income. For complete details, see Chapter 18.

You should remember that if you incur legal fees to establish your right to a pension benefit, the fees may be fully or partially deducted on your tax return. If so, deduct it on line 232 of your return.

Transferring Pension Income

The tax rules let you, within limits, transfer lump sum pension amounts from one registered pension plan (RPP) to another RPP or to your RRSP. The transfer is tax-free if the funds are transferred directly from one plan to the other. In other words, you don't actually see the money — only the financial institutions do!

If the funds are directly transferred, there will be no income inclusion in your tax return and no need for you to take an offsetting deduction. The institutions involved should not issue you a T4A slip or any kind of tax information slip. You may want to transfer funds when you change jobs or take early retirement. You will often have the choice of leaving the funds or moving them elsewhere — perhaps to a new employer's pension plan. (In practice, we find this form of transfer rare. Most individuals request a transfer to an RRSP.) Your decision to move the funds will rest on the confidence you have in the RPP's investment advisor versus the confidence you have in your ability to take control of the funds (with your own investment advisor's help) through a self-directed RRSP. But be forewarned, if you transfer the funds from an RPP to an RRSP, don't expect to be able to take the funds out of the RRSP (even if you want to pay tax on the RRSP withdrawal). Most provincial pension rules require the funds to be put in a "locked-in" RRSP. This often means you can't get at the funds until you are at least age 60.

The value of your portion of your employer's RPP that you plan to transfer to an RRSP is often referred to as the "commuted value."

Chapter 11

Dealing with Other Types of Income

In This Chapter

- Line 119 — Employment Insurance benefits
- Line 122 — Limited and Non-active partnership income
- Line 126 — Rental income
- Line 128 — Alimony or separation allowances
- Line 129 — RRSP and RRIF income
- Line 144 — Worker's Compensation benefits
- Line 145 — Social assistance

In this chapter we will examine sources of income that are generally classified under that ominous title of "Other income." Far from being unusual, some of these sources are encountered by taxpayers on a regular basis. So hold on tight as we dive headfirst into the not so weird world of other income.

Line 119: Employment Insurance Benefits (EI)

Amounts received as employment insurance (EI) benefits are included at line 119 of your tax return. These benefits are usually the result of unemployment or maternity leave. The government sends a T4E slip to each individual who received these benefits during the year. This slip details the benefits you received, plus the amount of tax withheld on these benefits.

Much to the surprise and chagrin of EI recipients, the government holds back part of your cheques as "tax withheld." The calculation used to estimate your tax generally assumes you will be in the lowest tax bracket and withholds accordingly. The amount in box 14 "Total benefits" of the T4E is the amount to be entered at line 119. The tax withheld in box 22 is deducted at line 437.

Some EI benefits are not included in income. These benefits are payments for a course or retraining program to facilitate reentry into the labour force, and will not appear on the T4E slip.

EI clawback

If you have collected EI benefits in the year, and your net income as determined from line 234 of your income tax return is greater than $48,750, you will be required to pay back a portion of the benefits you've received. In addition, if your income for the year is greater than $39,000 and you have received EI benefits in excess of 20 weeks over the past five years, a portion of these benefits will also be clawed back. The back of your T4E slip contains the details of how to calculate this clawback. If an EI repayment is required, make the deduction for the repayment at line 235 "Social benefits repayment," and record the repayment itself at line 422. Other repayments of EI occur if you become ineligible to receive benefits. This type of repayment typically occurs when you've been receiving EI while injured and off work, and then you get a CPP disability pension that pays you retroactively from the time of injury. These repayments are deducted at line 232 "Other deductions."

If you think that you are going to be faced with one of the above situations, remember your net income will be reduced by contributions to an RRSP, child care expenses, registered pension plan contributions, moving expenses, carrying charges for loans, or any of the other deductions between lines 206 and 233.

EI premiums

For the year 2000, the maximum annual insurable earnings are $39,000 with a premium rate of 2.4 percent. If you earn $39,000 or more, your employer will withhold the maximum premium of $936 ($39,000 × 2.4 percent). All EI premiums paid entitle you to a 17-percent nonrefundable tax credit. If your EI insurable earnings fall below $2,000 for the year, you will receive a full refund of premiums paid for the year. If, on the other hand, you over-contribute to EI because your employer withheld too much or because you had more than one job in the year and both employers withheld the maximum, the over-contribution can be deducted at line 450 of your return.

If you are self-employed, you are not required or permitted to pay EI premiums. Unfortunately, you are also not eligible to collect EI if you find yourself out of work.

Line 122: Limited and Non-Active Partnership Income

The term "limited or non-active partnership" describes a business relationship in which a minority or limited partner is able to invest in a partnership while at the same time being protected from the potential personal liabilities usually associated with partnerships. These partners are not involved in the day-to-day running of the business, but instead are non-active investors. This structure has been used for many years as a form of tax shelter that promoted real estate, oil and gas, films, and so on. More recently, the CCRA has reduced the effectiveness of these investment vehicles by restricting the losses that could be flowed out to the limited partners.

At-risk amount

The losses that a limited partner can claim are now restricted to the partners' at-risk amount, instead of a percentage of the total business loss, as was previously the case.

Your at-risk amount equals the total of your original investment, any subsequent investments to the same partnership, and your share of any profits earned by the partnership.

The T5013

When a limited partnership earns a profit, the information is reported to you on a T5013 or a separate statement of income. You use these documents to complete schedule 4 of the tax return "Statement of Investment Income." After you've completed schedule 4, you transfer the information to line 122 "Net partnership income; limited or non-active partners only."

These profits should then be added to your at-risk amount, for deduction in years of loss. If a limited partnership suffers a loss, that loss will also be reported on the T5013 or on a separate statement of loss. If you have sufficient at-risk room, the loss will be deducted at line 251.

The primary advantage of the limited partnership structure is the flow-through of income and losses to the non-active partners. The limited partnership structure also offers the non-active investors safety, in that they risk only their original investment and are not responsible for all the liabilities of the business. In this way the limited partnership offers both the advantages of a corporation (limited liability) and the advantages of a partnership (direct sharing in the income and losses).

Line 126: Rental Income

Rental income is earned from renting out real property. This real property could be a building, a house, a room in a house, an apartment, office space, machinery, equipment, vehicles, and so on. Rental income can be further classified as income from property or income from a business. Line 126 deals exclusively with income from property.

To determine whether your rental income is from property or a business, you have to look at several factors, including the level of services provided. If you are providing only the basic services associated with rentals (that is, heat, hydro, or maintenance), your income will be classified as property income. If, on the other hand, you are providing a higher level of service (that is, heat, hydro, maintenance, cleaning, maid service, meals), your income may be classified as business income. Business income can also be generated from rentals if the income earned is incidental to your main line of business. This situation often occurs when a company rents extra office space in its building to other businesses.

When trying to determine if your rental income is from property or business, the basic rule of thumb is that the more services you provide, the more likely it is that you are running a business. Check out the CCRA's bulletin IT-434 "Rental of Real Property by Individuals"; it will help you make that determination. To assist you in determining your property rental income, the CCRA provides form T776 "Statement of Real Estate Rentals." This form supports the amount at line 126 of your T1 and should be included in your tax filing.

Rental income is always reported on a calendar-year basis — that is, January to December. If you co-own a rental property, your share of the rental gain or loss will be based on your percentage of ownership. Arbitrary allocations are not acceptable.

Rental income can be reported on the cash basis if the result would be substantially the same as reporting it on the accrual basis. The accrual basis is the usual form of reporting rental income and is the one recommended by the CCRA. When calculating rental income or loss, you cannot use the capital cost allowance deduction to create or increase a rental loss. You *can* use the capital cost allowance deduction to bring your income down to zero, but only after deducting all other expenses. If you are in a loss position after deducting these expenses, no capital cost deduction will be allowed.

Reasonable expectation of profit

The primary motivation of any business is to earn profit. If you don't earn profit, than why are you in business? The reasonable expectation of profit principle is the standard the taxman uses when examining rental businesses (or any business, for that matter) to determine if it's a legitimate business or simply a tax shelter. Any real business has a reasonable expectation that it will soon be earning profit. Even if the business does not earn profit initially, the owner must believe, and be able to prove, that within a short time the business will be profitable. If after examining your rental business the CCRA determines that it has no reasonable expectation of profit, it will conclude that yours is not a legitimate business and deny the rental losses.

Your rental business must have a reasonable expectation of profit to be a business. Generally, the CCRA will allow a start-up business three or four years of losses before questioning its legitimacy. If your rental business loses money year after year, it is very likely that the CCRA will reassess and deny all the losses. We'd love to give you an idea of exactly how long the CCRA will allow you to operate in the red, but they don't adhere to any hard and fast rules about this. So, as we are sure you would anyway, keep a close eye on your books as well as the tax implications of your business's profitability.

If you are denied rental losses in the current year, the CCRA will go back and reassess prior years for the same losses.

Types of rental income

Rental income can be received in the form of cash, services, or payments in kind (that is, goods). If you receive services in payment of rent, you must estimate the fair market value of these services and include it as rental income. Suppose, for example, that you have a tenant who works as a maintenance man in exchange for free rent. In this case, the cost of hiring someone to do this job must be included as "other related income" on the T776. Other forms of rental income include sharecropping or exchange of goods. In all these cases, the fair market value of the goods received should be reported as "other related income" on the T776.

Undeveloped land

The tax treatment of undeveloped land is a tricky issue, and you need to pay special attention to ensure that you do not run afoul of the rules.

Carrying charges

Carrying charges are mortgage interest and property tax. If the land is vacant and is not being used to produce income, you will only be allowed to deduct the interest and property tax to the extent of the net rental income earned on the land (that is, income after other expenses are deducted). In other words, you cannot use the interest and property tax to create a loss on vacant land not used to produce income. If, on the other hand, the land is used or held in carrying on a business, or if the land is held primarily for the purpose of gaining or producing income, the interest and property tax can be deducted in excess of earned income. This distinction allows land under buildings and land used in a business (for example, a parking lot) to avoid the interest and property tax restrictions.

The land must be "used" by the business, not "held" in the course of business. Vacant land held by an active business will still be subject to the property tax and interest restrictions.

Land speculators with insufficient transactions to be considered in the business of selling land will not be allowed to claim interest and property tax in excess of the income earned on the property.

Capital assets

If the vacant land is considered a capital asset, the nondeductible interest and property tax will be added to the cost of the land. This will reduce the capital gain on sale when the land is eventually disposed of.

Inventory

If the vacant land is held as inventory, the nondeductible expenses will be added to the cost of the inventory, thus reducing your income on sale. Here's an example. Mr. Big owns vacant land, which he considers a capital asset. The land was originally purchased for $10,000, one year ago. This year the property tax on the land was $1,000 and the interest on the mortgage was $500. This land was rented to a circus during the year for $700. The *Income Tax Act* will not consider this land to be used in a business or used to produce income. Therefore, the interest and property tax cannot be used to create a loss. The maximum deduction for property tax and interest will be $700 — the income earned on the rental to the circus.

Interest and property tax expenses	$1,500
Maximum deduction (income on rental)	$700
Nondeductible expenses added to cost of land	$800
New cost of land	$10,800

If Mr. B decides to sell the land at year-end for $12,000, his gain on disposal will be $1,200 ($12,000 – 10,800).

Land held but not used in a business, or land held for resale or future development, must not deduct carrying charges in excess of income.

Soft costs

Soft costs are costs incurred during the construction, renovation, or alteration of a building. These include interest, legal fees, property tax, and accounting fees. They must be added to the cost base of the building and amortized. This accumulation of costs must continue until the building is finished or 90-percent rented out.

Real estate rentals — deductible expenses

Unlike vacant land, real estate rentals can create losses. Here is a list of the most common expenses incurred that may be deducted against rental income.

- Mortgage interest
- Property tax
- Insurance
- Maintenance and repairs
- Heat, hydro, water
- Accounting fees
- Condo fees
- Landscaping
- Office supplies
- Fees paid to find tenants

- Advertising
- Management and administration fees
- Salaries or wages paid to take care of property
- Legal fees to collect rent or prepare rental documents
- Lease cancellation fees (amortized over the remaining term of lease to a maximum of 40 years)
- Mortgage application, appraisal, processing, and insurance fees (deducted over five years)
- Mortgage guarantee fees (deducted over five years)
- Mortgage broker and finder fees (deducted over five years)
- Legal fees related to mortgage financing (deducted over five years)

If you own one rental property in addition to your principal residence, you can deduct motor vehicle or travel expenses to conduct repairs and maintenance or to transport tools and material to the rental property, provided the property is located in your general area of residence. If you own only one rental property, you cannot deduct travel expenses to collect rent; this is considered a personal expense. Also, you cannot deduct travel expenses for a property outside your area of residence.

If you own two or more rental properties, you can deduct all the above expenses plus travel to collect rents, supervise repairs, and generally manage the properties. The properties can be located anywhere, not just your area of residence.

Real estate commissions or legal fees paid in connection with the purchase or sale of the property are not deductible as incurred. Instead, they must be added to the cost base of the property.

Nondeductible expenses include the following:

- Mortgage principle
- Land transfer tax (added to the cost of the property)
- Penalties on your Notice of Assessment
- Value of your own labour
- Legal fees incurred to purchase the property (include in cost of property)
- Real estate commissions (part of cost of property)
- Prepaid expenses relating to a future year
- Capital expenditures (additions or major repairs that improve the property, not just everyday repairs and maintenance)
- Personal portion of expenses
- Cost of land.

A common situation that the taxman encounters is that of individuals attempting to represent their cottage or second home as a rental property. In these cases the taxpayers try to deduct all expenses related to this property, plus the travel to get there. Remember, you cannot deduct any personal use portion of expenses or travel to a rental property outside your general area of residence.

To avoid problems with the taxman, it is important to keep detailed records of your rental properties. These records should include a full description of the property, including the purchase and sale documents, plus names and addresses of tenants and former tenants. These records should also include all receipts relating to the property and rental contracts outlining how costs are to be allocated between the owner and the tenants.

Rental of your own residence

When renting all or a portion of your principal residence, you must be careful not to mix personal and business expenses. Remember the following when renting out your principal residence:

- You have to determine which expenses relate solely to the rental activity and which ones are shared with the whole house. The ones that are shared need to be allocated to the rental portion.
- **Expenses of the rental activity.** Expenses such as advertising, cleaning, and cutting keys are incremental costs of owning and renting the property. These expenses are 100 percent deductible against rental income.
- **Expenses shared with rest of house.** Expenses such as taxes, insurance, water, hydro, heat, maintenance, and mortgage interest would have been incurred even if a portion of the house was not rented out. These expenses are allocated between the rental and the rest of the house.

The CCRA accepts two ways of allocating expenses:

- Allocate them based on the number of rooms in the house. If the house has 10 rooms and 2 are rented, allocate 2/10th of the household expenses to the rental units.
- Allocate the expenses based on the square footage. If the house is 2,000 square feet and the rental is 400 square feet, allocate 400/2000th of the house expenses to the rental portion.

Do not claim capital cost allowance (CCA) when renting out part of your home. The reason? Once you claim CCA against your rental income, the part of your home that is rented stops being your principal residence. This means that when you sell your home, part of your proceeds will be taxable because they are no longer exempt under the principal residence exemption.

Capital versus current expenditures

You can divide expenses of a property into two main categories: current expenditures and capital expenditures. Current expenditures are the operating or recurring expenses that provide short-term benefits. These expenditures tend to maintain or keep the property in the same shape. Examples are repairs and maintenance, landscaping, window cleaning, heat, hydro, property tax, and interest expense on the mortgage. Capital expenditures, on the other hand, are the expenses of purchasing the property or substantially improving it. Capital expenditures are expenses that give lasting benefits that improve the property beyond its original condition. Capital expenditures are not expensed in the year of occurrence; rather, they are amortized or deducted over time using the capital cost allowance system. This system is a predetermined amortization plan that tells you how fast you can write off these capital assets. Examples of capital expenditures include major repairs to the property such as a new roof, additions to the property, new windows, new plumbing or electrical wiring, new furnace or coal scuttle.

The key concept in determining if a repair is a capital or current expenditure is the concept of betterment. If a repair improves what was initially there, it will be classified as a capital expenditure. If the repair only restores what was there initially, it is a current expense. Table 11-1 lists common expenses and their classifications

Table 11-1 Classification of Common Rental Expenses

Expenditure	*Current or Capital Expense?*
Re-shingle roof	Current expense
Installing a new roof	Capital expense
Replace a sink	Current expense
Replace the bathroom	Capital expense
Purchase price of the property	Capital expense
Land transfer tax	Capital expense
Equipment purchased for the property	Capital expense
Repairs to equipment	Current expense
Soft costs during construction	Capital expense

The land component of the purchase price plus the land transfer tax, legal expense, and real estate commissions that are allocated to the land part of the rental property (as opposed to the building part), are not treated the same way as other capital expenditures. These costs are not eligible for amortization using the capital cost allowance system because land does not depreciate the way a building or a driveway does.

Capital expenditures to assist the disabled are deductible in the year of occurrence. These expenses are given current expense treatment in an attempt to encourage landlords to install them, and may include the following: installing hand-activated power door openers, installing ramps, modifying bathrooms, elevators, or doorways to accommodate wheelchairs, modifying elevators to assist the blind, and installing telephone devices for the hearing impaired and computer equipment or software to assist the disabled.

Here are some questions to ask yourself in determining if an expense is capital or current:

- Does the expense provide lasting long-term benefits? (capital — yes) (current — no)
- Does the expense maintain or improve the property? (improve — capital) (maintain — current)
- Does the expense purchase a new asset or add to a current asset? (new — capital) (add — current)
- What is the value of the expense? (high — capital) (low — current).

Capital cost allowance

Capital cost allowance is a method of amortizing or deducting the cost of a capital item over time. The cost of capital assets cannot be deducted all at once in the year of acquisition. The length of time that the CCRA requires you to "write off" the asset is supposed to mirror the time it takes for the asset to wear out or become obsolete. The amount that you are allowed to deduct each year is called the capital cost allowance (or CCA).

How do I determine how much CCA I can claim?

The amount of CCA you claim on a yearly basis depends on the type of asset and when the asset was purchased. The *Income Tax Act* puts each asset into specific asset groups or classes. Each class has a predetermined amortization rate. Some assets such as computers are amortized quickly (30 percent per year) because they become obsolete very quickly. Other assets such as business furniture are amortized more slowly (20 percent per year) because they tend to last longer. The amortization allowed in CCA can be on a straight-line basis, a declining balance basis, or a fast write-off basis.

- **Declining balance.** This method allows you to deduct a percentage of the capital cost of the property each year, minus the CCA you claimed in the previous year. The remaining balance declines over the years as you claim CCA.
- **Straight line.** This method requires you to take the cost of the asset and divide it equally over a period of time (for example, 20 years). Each year, you deduct 1/20th of the cost of the asset.
- **Accelerated write-off.** This method may only be used with the CCRA's consent. It is usually designed to encourage the purchase of specific assets or deal with specific problems. For example, the CCRA permitted all Y2K equipment purchases to be written off in one year.

Various CCA classes also have different rules with regard to the treatment of assets in the first year that they are added to the class. Most classes require you to use the half-year rule for new additions. This rule allows you to claim only half the normal CCA in the first year an asset is added to a class. This rule was designed to prevent individuals from buying assets the last day of the year and claiming a full year of amortization.

A further restriction on CCA is that you cannot start claiming CCA until the asset is available for use. This means that assets under construction or assets ordered but not delivered cannot be amortized.

Suppose Andrea buys a building that costs $500,000 and a fashionable chaise lounge that costs $1,000. The building is added to class 1. This class has an amortization rate of 4 percent per year, and the half-year rule applies. The fashionable chaise lounge is added to class 8. This class is amortized at 20 percent per year, and the half-year rule applies.

Year 1	***Building***	***Chaise lounge***
CCA rate	4%	20%
Cost of assets in class	$500,000	$1,000
CCA	($500,000 × 4%) × ½	($1,000 × 20%) × ½
	= $10,000	= $100
Year 2		
Cost	$500,000	$1,000
Less: Prior year's CCA	$10,000	$100
(Undepreciated capital cost)	$490,000	$900
CCA	($490,000 × 4%)	($900 × 4%)
	= $19,600	= $36
Undepreciated capital cost at end of second year	($490,000 – $19,600)	($900 – $36)
	= $470,400	= $864

You do not have to claim the maximum CCA every year. This is a discretionary deduction, and you can claim from zero to the maximum allowed. If you do not owe tax in a particular year, for example, you may not wish to claim CCA that year.

Separate classes

Rental buildings costing $50,000 or more acquired after 1971 need to be placed in separate CCA classes. This means that if you buy two class 1 buildings and they cost more than $50,000 each, they must not be combined into one class 1 group of buildings; instead, they must each be in a separate class 1 group. The reason for this rule is that when buildings are disposed of (usually for a gain), the CCRA wants to recapture, or reverse, the CCA claimed on the building. (If the building was sold for a gain, it obviously did not depreciate, so why allow CCA?) The rules of recapture do not permit the CCRA to reverse CCA on an asset if there is still another asset in the same class. By forcing each building into its own class, the CCRA usually guarantees recapture when the building is sold.

Combining classes to calculate CCA

You cannot use CCA to create a loss on rental income that is property income. The CCRA requires you to combine all rental income and losses from all properties before calculating CCA. In this way, the CCRA prevents you from using CCA to create or increase net rental losses. Let's say Jack owns two buildings. Both buildings are in class 1. The income and loss on the rental buildings are as follows:

	Building 1	*Building 2*
Net income before CCA	$10,000	($15,000)

Since Jack has to combine the income of both buildings, he has a net rental loss of $5,000. As you will recall, you cannot create or increase a rental loss by using CCA. Since Jack is in a net rental loss position, no CCA can be claimed on either building without increasing the rental loss. If this CCRA rule did not exist, he could claim CCA on Building 1 to bring income to zero and claim no CCA on Building 2. The result would be a net rental loss of $15,000.

Recapture and terminal loss

Recapture and terminal loss are adjustments that you must make when assets are either not depreciated enough over time, or depreciated too much. To recapture means to reclaim CCA taken in excess of actual depreciation. To claim a terminal loss means to claim additional CCA when actual depreciation exceeds the allowed capital cost deductions. Neither recapture nor terminal loss can be claimed while assets are still in a CCA class. When all assets in a class have been disposed of, you will be able to determine if you over- or underdepreciated assets. Let's say that Lisa sells her class 1 building for $1,000,000. She originally bought the building for $500,000. Over the years, she has claimed $300,000 of CCA. Since this building is the last asset in the class, we can calculate recapture or terminal loss. At the time of sale, Lisa's undepreciated capital cost balance was $200,000 ($500,000 – $ 300,000) = $200,000.

Since the building increased in value and did not depreciate, the CCRA wants to recapture the CCA she claimed in prior years. As a result, Lisa will be required to include $300,000 in her income for the year of disposition.

Foreign rental income

For tax purposes, you must include in your Canadian income any rental income that you receive on foreign-owned property. The same restrictions apply to foreign source rental income as apply to Canadian source rental income — that is, CCA rules.

All foreign transactions must be converted to Canadian dollars at the exchange rate as of the transaction date. Use the average exchange rate for income transactions that take place throughout the year.

Any withholding tax or income tax paid to a foreign country is eligible for a foreign tax credit when you calculate your rental income for Canadian tax purposes.

Foreign exchange gains or losses

Gains or losses associated with the use of a foreign currency are accounted for as a capital or income item, depending on the nature of the underlying transaction. Gains or losses on rents and expenses are accounted for as an income item to be included on your current tax return. Gains or losses on the sale of the property or the payment of the principal portion of the mortgage are treated as capital items.

Every year, you are allowed to exclude the first $200 of capital gains resulting from currency fluctuations from your income for tax purposes. However, the same holds true for foreign exchange losses: the first $200 in capital losses cannot be deducted.

Restrictions on rental losses

There are several restrictions on the use and creation of rental losses:

- You cannot use capital cost allowance to create or increase a rental loss.
- You cannot charge rent at below the market value in order to create a loss.
- You must show a profit from your rental business within a reasonable amount of time — that is, you must have a reasonable expectation of profit.
- If you own vacant land, you can only deduct expenses to the extent of the income earned on the land, unless it is used in a business or used to produce income.

The CCRA's primary tool in challenging artificial rental losses is the "reasonable expectation of profit rule." This rule requires rental businesses that have losses to prove that the business has a reasonable chance of making profit and that the only reasons it has not made profit is that it is a start-up business or that economic factors or events are preventing it from realizing its potential. If the rental has little chance of showing profit, the CCRA will conclude that it is not a real business and deem all past and future losses to be personal expenses. Increasingly, the CCRA has begun to use another tool to challenge the capital gains on disposition of the rental properties. The CCRA has been reclassifying these capital gains as business income. They claim that the owners of these properties never had any intention to operate a rental business, but instead bought the property as an investment to sell at a profit (hence the property is not a capital asset and is not eligible for capital gains treatment). The CCRA contends that these purchases are merely an "adventure in the nature of trade" and should be treated as business income. As business income, the gains are 100-percent taxable instead of the two-thirds (one-half after October 18, 2000) taxable capital gains. The good news is that those earlier rental losses that were denied can now be used to offset the business income.

Line 128: Support Payments

This particular area of the *Income Tax Act* has undergone significant recent changes because of the Thibaudeau case. This case argued that the rules of support payments severely disadvantaged the receiving spouse and children. The court agreed and changed the rules.

Old rules (pre-May 1, 1997)

Under the old rules of alimony and separation allowance, the payments received pursuant to a court order were deducted from the payer's income and included in the recipient's income. Once included, this payment made up part of the recipient's taxable income and was taxed at the marginal rate, thus reducing the amount of the support payment received.

New rules (post-April 30, 1997)

For court orders or written agreements made after April 30, 1997, child support payments are *not* deductible from the income of the payer or included in the income of the receiver. The net result is that tax does not reduce the amount intended for child support. On the other hand, spousal support payments *are* deductible from income by the payer, and must be included in the income of the recipient. The new rules go on to say that if a court order or written agreement specifies that an individual must make both child support and spousal payments, the CCRA considers payments are allocated first to child support and second to spousal support. This additional provision ensures that all child support must be paid before the payer can claim a deduction for spousal support, and the recipient has to include spousal support in income.

If child support is in arrears, the government will not consider any of the future payments from the payer to be spousal support — at least, not until all back child support is paid. This ensures that the recipient will not be taxed on back child support even if the payer calls it spousal support.

If the court order or agreement does not specify separate amounts for child support and spousal support, all payments will be considered child support and will not be taxable to the recipient or deductible to the payer.

Line 156 of the T1 tax return will include all payments from the payer, both child and spousal support. Line 128 will include only the taxable portion — that is, spousal support.

Specific purpose payments

Specific purpose payments are payments made to third parties on behalf of the spouse or children for things such as rent, tuition fees, medical expenses, or maintenance payments on the recipient's residence. Payments made for specific purposes to a third party are taxable to the recipient and deductible to the payer under certain conditions.

Pre-May 1, 1997 agreements

Payments that are deductible to the payer and taxable to the recipient include the following:

- Payments that are not periodic (one-time payments to dentists or for tuition)
- Payments for certain tangible property (maintenance for the recipient's home)
- Payments to a third party where the recipient has no ability to influence how the money is spent (rent).

The following are some of the conditions that must be met for the payments to be deductible to the payer and included in the income of the recipient:

- The payments were for the recipient's maintenance, or for the maintenance of a child in the recipient's custody, or both (as long as the child was not living with or in the charge of the payer at the time of the payment).
- The payments meet the basic requirements for amounts to be considered support payments — those being that the payer and recipient live apart, the payments were made on a periodic basis, the payments were made for spousal or child support, and the recipient can use the payments as he or she sees fit.
- The court order or agreement indicates that payments will be deductible to the payer and included in the recipient's income.
- The new rules are not being used under a court order or written agreement.

If you are using the new rules, two additional conditions must be met for the payments to be deductible by the payer and included in the income of the recipient:

- The child support must already be fully paid, with nothing in arrears.
- The court order must clearly indicate that the third-party payment is for the benefit of the spouse.

What if I'm under the old rules and would like to use the new rules?

Luckily, you and your former spouse can elect to use the new rules even if your court order or agreement predates May 1, 1997. By using form T1157 "Election for Child Support Payments" the recipient and the payer can agree to treat the child support portion of the payments as nondeductible to the payer and not included in the recipient's income. After this election is filed, however, you cannot return to the old rules.

Under what circumstances do the new rules apply?

The new rules apply automatically in any of the following situations:

- The court order or agreement is made after April 30, 1997, and before January 1, 1999, but does not recognize any payments made before May 1, 1997, as payments made under that court order or agreement.
- The order or agreement is made after December 31, 1998, even if it recognizes earlier payments.
- The order or agreement is changed after April 30, 1997, to increase or decrease the amount of support payable.

Taxable support payments qualify as earned income for RRSP purposes.

Line 129: RRSP and RRIF Income

All amounts you withdraw from an RRSP or RRIF are subject to tax in one form or another. The tax treatment can vary dramatically, depending on when the amounts are withdrawn and how much is withdrawn.

Withdrawals from an RRSP

Amounts can be withdrawn from an RRSP at maturity (when paying retirement income) or before. Funds can also be withdrawn using the Home Buyer's Plan or the Lifelong Learning Plan.

Mature RRSP

An RRSP matures when you retire and decide to start collecting retirement income, or the year you reach 69 years of age — whichever comes first.

In either of these two cases, the RRSP must be converted to an annuity or a Registered Retirement Income Fund (RRIF), with the retirement payments commencing the following calendar year.

It is usually best to delay receiving retirement income from an RRSP until you absolutely need to. The longer it stays in an RRSP earning tax-free income, the better.

You can convert an RRSP to an annuity or RRIF on a tax-free basis using a fund transfer or rollover. If funds are withdrawn from the RRSP as part of the tax-free transfer, they will be included in your income and taxed at your marginal rate. If the funds do not roll directly into the RRIF or retirement annuity, they cannot be put in later on a tax-free basis. Once inside the annuity or the RRIF, withdrawals will be included in your income and taxed at your marginal rate.

Withdrawals prior to RRSP maturity

If you withdraw amounts from your RRSP prior to retirement, or prior to reaching age 69, the amount of the withdrawals is included in income and reported on line 129 of your tax return. In addition, these withdrawals will be subject to withholding tax at source. For federal and Quebec purposes, Table11-2 illustrates amounts withheld on withdrawals of funds prior to RRSP maturity:

Table 11-2 Withholding Rates on Amounts Withdrawn from Unmatured RRSPs

Amount Withdrawn	*Quebec*	*Other*
0 – $5,000	25%	10%
$5,001 – $15,000	33%	20%
$15,001 and greater	38%	30%

At the end of the year in which you withdraw the funds from the RRSP, you will receive a T4RSP. This form will indicate how much you withdrew and how much tax was withheld. You must include the amount withdrawn at line 129, and the corresponding tax withheld at line 437.

Normally, it is suggested that you only withdraw money from an RRSP in situations where you really need the income. If this is the case, you can employ a few simple strategies to save tax in the process:

- **Low-income withdrawals:** Try to withdraw amounts during a year in which you anticipate having a lower income. This will reduce the tax bite when the amounts eventually are included in income.

- **Take out small quantities:** Don't take all the money out at once. Take the funds out in increments of $5,000 or less. This will reduce the withholding tax to 10 percent and give you more money to use when you need it. When filing your return, you will, of course, need to pay tax at your marginal rate for the income inclusion. If you urgently need the money, however, better to have it in your hands than in the taxman's (as withheld tax).
- **Withdraw over two tax years:** Try to take the money out in two different tax years. By taking funds out at the end of December one year and in January of the next year, you will be splitting the withdrawal over two tax years, thus reducing the tax hit in any one year. In addition, tax will not be payable on the January withdrawal until April 30 of the following year — that is, if you withdraw money from an RRSP in January 2001, tax will not be payable on this amount until April 30, 2002.
- **Withdraw RRSP cash from low-income earners:** Remove money from the registered retirement savings plan of the lower income earner first. This will reduce the tax paid by the family, since the lower-income earner probably has a lower marginal tax rate and will pay less tax on the withdrawal.

Withdrawals of unused or over-contributions to an RRSP

Generally, any withdrawals of contributions to your RRSP that exceed the contribution limit are reported on line 129 and taxed as income. This is also the case when you withdraw any undeducted contributions to the RRSP. Luckily, there are relieving provisions that allow you an offsetting deduction against these income inclusions. You will be allowed a deduction equal to your income inclusion for withdrawals of unused RRSP contributions under the following circumstances:

- You withdraw the amount in the year you contributed it.
- You withdraw the amount in the year following your year of contribution.
- You withdraw the over-contribution during the year — or during the year *following* the year — in which you receive a Notice of Assessment or Reassessment for the year of contribution.
- You have not deducted or transferred the unused contribution to your RRSP.

And it is reasonable for the CCRA to consider that:

- You expected to be able to fully deduct the RRSP contribution for the year paid or the following year.
- You did not make the RRSP contribution fully intending to later withdraw the amount and claim the offsetting deduction.

If you meet the above conditions and are going to withdraw your over-contribution, use form T3012A "Tax Reduction Waiver on the Refund of Your Undeducted RRSP Contribution." By submitting this to the CCRA, it will direct your financial institution not to withhold tax on the withdrawal of funds. If you withdraw funds without form T3012A, the issuer of the plan will withhold tax. In this case, use form T746 "Calculating Your Deduction for Refund of Undeducted RRSP Contributions," to calculate the amount of your tax deduction given that you have already paid withholding tax.

Home purchase loans

If you withdraw money from your RRSP to purchase a home under the Home Buyer's Plan, the withdrawal is not included in income, and no withholding tax will apply. If you fail to make the required repayments on this loan, the shortfall will be added to your income at line 129. To learn more about the Home Buyer's Plan, make sure you read Chapter 16.

Lifelong Learning Plan

As was the case with the Home Buyer's Plan, any funds withdrawn under the Lifelong Learning Plan that are not paid back according to the required schedule are included in income at line 129 every year that the payment is missed. Also, if you withdraw the money and do not use it for education, and if you do not return the funds to the RRSP by the end of the calendar year following your withdrawal from the educational institution, the entire amount will be included in income

Spousal RRSPs

A spousal RRSP is an RRSP that you have contributed to but which names your spouse as the "annuitant." This means that all retirement funds out of this RRSP will belong to the spouse and not to you, the contributor. A spousal RRSP is usually used by individuals who have much higher incomes than their spouses and wish to "split" the retirement income rather than have the entire amount included in their income.

Withdrawal from spousal RRSP has very special rules that seek to dissuade individuals from transferring money to the spouse and then withdrawing it using the spouse's lower marginal tax rate. If these rules are violated, the income will be attributed back to the contributing spouse and added to his or her income.

The rules

If your spouse withdraws money from a spousal RRSP that you have contributed to in the year or in the previous two years, the withdrawal will be taxed in your hands and must be included at line 129 of your return. For example, if your spouse withdraws money from a spousal RRSP in 2001 that you contributed to in 2001, 2000, or 1999, the withdrawal will be included in your income, not your spouse's.

To determine how much of the spousal withdrawal to include in your income, complete form T2205 "Calculating Amounts from a Spousal RRSP or RRIF to Include in Income" and file it with both your return and that of your spouse.

If you were separated from your spouse, or were dead, at the time funds were withdrawn, the government will not attribute the income back to the contributor.

RRIF income

A *registered retirement income fund (RRIF)* is the continuation of a matured RRSP. When you reach the age of 69 or wish to receive retirement income, your RRSP can be converted to an RRIF by a tax-free rollover. Like the RRSP, the RRIF earns income tax-free inside the plan. An RRIF is different from an RRSP, however, in that you can no longer contribute to the plan, and a minimum income withdrawal must be made from the plan each year following the year in which the RRIF was established. These withdrawals are considered taxable income. If you are 65 years of age or older, your minimum required RRIF withdrawal should be reported at line 115. Income reported at line 115 is eligible for the $1,000 pension amount at line 314. In all other cases, report income from an RRIF at line 130.

Minimum required withdrawals from an RRIF are not subject to withholding tax. If you withdraw amounts exceeding the minimum, these amounts will be subject to withholding tax and must be reported at line 130. The excess withdrawal from a RRIF will appear in box 24 of the T4RIF and is not eligible for the $1,000 pension amount. RRIFs can be divided into two broad categories: Qualifying RRIFs and Non-qualifying RRIFs:

- Qualifying RRIFs existed before 1993 or after 1992, if the funds used to create them were transferred from another Qualifying RRIF.
- Non-qualifying RRIFs were set up after 1992, or are Qualifying RRIFs that had new funds transferred into them after 1992 from non-qualified sources.

Qualifying RRIF recipients are required to use an old minimum withdrawal schedule until they reach the age of 77, after which they can choose to use the modified schedule. Non-qualifying RRIFs must use the new withdrawal schedule. Table 11-3 is a list of the prescribed minimum RRIF withdrawals. The withdrawal amount is presented as the percentage of total RRIF that must be withdrawn each year.

Table 11-3 Minimum RRIF Withdrawals under the Old, Modified and New Schedules

Age at January 1	*Old*	*Modified*	*New*
65	.0400	.0400	.0400
66	.0417	.0417	.0417
67	.0435	.0435	.0435
68	.0455	.0455	.0455
69	.0476	.0476	.0476
70	.0500	.0500	.0500
71	.0526	.0526	.0738
72	.0556	.0556	.0748
73	.0588	.0588	.0759
74	.0625	.0625	.0771
75	.0667	.0667	.0785
76	.0714	.0714	.0799
77	.0769	.0769	.0815
78	.0833	.0833	.0833
79	.0909	.0853	.0853
80	.1000	.0875	.0875
81	.1111	.0899	.0899
82	.1250	.0927	.0927
83	.1429	.0958	.0958
84	.1667	.0993	.0993
85	.2000	.1033	.1033
86	.2500	.1079	.1079

(continued)

Table 11-3 (continued)

Age at January 1	*Old*	*Modified*	*New*
87	.3333	.1133	.1133
88	.5000	.1196	.1196
89	1.000	.1271	.1271
90	0.000	.1362	.1362
91	0.000	.1473	.1473
92	0.000	.1612	.1612
93	0.000	.1792	.1792
94 or older	0.000	.2000	.2000

In order to defer the tax hit from your RRIF for as long as possible, and if your spouse is younger than you, consider basing your minimum withdrawals on the age of your spouse. This will reduce the amount you are required to withdraw each year, allowing you to defer tax and leave more assets in your RRIF for future growth.

If you are under age 65 or your spouse is under age 65 and you are making your withdrawals based on your spouse's age, the formula to calculate your minimum withdrawal percentage is 1 divided by (90 minus your age).

Line 144: Workers' Compensation Benefits (WCB)

WCB received as a result of injury, disability, or death must be included in income. This amount is found in box 10 on the T5007 sent to you by the Workers' Compensation Board. This income inclusion is then deducted at line 250. The net result is that no tax is payable on this income. By including the benefit at line 144, you increase your net income, thus reducing your entitlement to certain credits and deductions, such as the Child Tax Benefit and the GST credit. This higher income will also reduce the spousal amount that your spouse can claim on you.

If you receive money from your employer as an advance of WCB, the employer will usually put the amount in box 14 of your T4. You should subtract this from your T4 and include it at line 144. Be sure to get a letter from your employer explaining the amount. This letter should be submitted with your return.

Line 145: Social Assistance

Social assistance payments (box 11 on the T5007) are included in your income at line 145 and deducted at line 250, in calculating taxable income. If your spouse has a higher income than you do, the social assistance payments should be included and deducted on your spouse's return instead of yours.

Chapter 12

Interest and Other Investment Income

In This Chapter

- Line 120: Dividends
- Line 121: Interest and other investment income

So you might glance at the notes above and think that this chapter will be really light reading, well, as light as it gets for a tax book of course. Only two lines on your tax return — how much can there be to know? Don't kid yourself, tons of important information is tied to Lines 120 and 121. In this chapter we will look at the taxation of dividends, interest, and other investment incomes, along with the tax treatment of loans from corporations to their shareholders and employees. We will also examine the taxation of income from trust and briefly discuss the implications of distributions from Registered Education Savings Plans. Let's dive right in . . .

Line 120 Dividends

Before we can discuss dividends, it is important to understand what a dividend is and how it differs from other investment income. A *dividend* is a distribution of a company's profits to its shareholders. A dividend comes from the retained earnings of a company after all expenses and taxes have been paid. You need to remember the after-tax part, especially when you distribute the profits to shareholders. When calculating the total tax paid, it is important to recall that both the corporation and the taxpayer have paid tax on this money. Too often we meet with owner–managers who are convinced they are saving tax because the tax rate on dividends is less than that on salary. Needless to say, when the total tax paid is calculated they are quite disappointed to learn that they haven't discovered a new loophole in the tax system!

Dividends can be paid on any class of shares, such as common shares or preferred shares. The important aspect of dividends is that they represent a way owners can remove profits from a company. Since tax advisors and taxpayers are busy beavers when it comes to ways of removing money from a company in the most efficient and tax-effective ways possible, a myriad of sometimes complicated rules follow the taxing and classification of dividends. This next section will help you understand these rules and the rationale behind them.

If you own a company and want to pay dividends, consult a tax professional. You would not believe the problems you could get yourself into if you do it the wrong way.

Canadian source dividends

Canadian source dividends — that is, dividends from a Canadian resident corporation — receive special treatment when it comes to paying the dividends to residents of Canada.

The concept that drives most of the complicated rules in taxation both in Canada and abroad is called the "concept of integration." At its core is the idea that the total tax paid by a corporation and its shareholders should be the same tax paid by an individual who carries on the same business directly without a corporation. By using a separate tax entity — a corporation — and passing the profits to the shareholder, the shareholders pay tax once at the corporate level and again at the individual level. The theory of integration proves that although there are two levels of tax, the total tax bill is no higher than if the profits had been earned personally. Let's work through an example. Corporation A and sole proprietor B run a successful typewriter and Telex repair business. Both entities make $1,000 in the year 2000. As shown in Table 12-1, if there were no integration, the following would happen:

Table 12-1 Non-Integrated Tax System

	Corporation A	*Sole Proprietor B*
Income	$1,000	$1,000
Corporate tax at 20 percent	$200	$0
Income of owner	$800	$1,000
Dividend	$800	$0
Personal tax at 40 percent	$320	$400
Cash remaining after tax	$480	$600

Clearly, if this were the case, no one would want to earn income through a corporation. After all, one could retain more cash after tax by running a sole proprietorship. Since it is not the government's intention to put corporate shareholders at a disadvantage when it comes to earning income, it created an elaborate system to level the playing field.

The system of calculation

The playing field was leveled by using the dividend gross up and dividend tax credit system.

- Dividends from taxable corporations resident in Canada must be included in the income of an individual and grossed up by 25 percent (that is, multiplied by 1.25).
- A federal dividend tax credit is then calculated to offset the grossed-up dividend. The tax credit is two-thirds of the 25-percent gross-up. Calculated another way, the tax credit is 13.33 percent of the grossed-up dividend or 16⅔ percent of the dividend paid.

Let's say T receives a $10,000 dividend from IM Canadian corporation, a Canadian resident corporation. For tax purposes, we will assume T has a high income and pays federal tax at a marginal 29 percent, as shown in Table 12-2. We will also assume T pays provincial tax of 50 percent of the federal tax.

Table 12-2 Integrated Tax System

Dividend received	$10,000
Gross-up (1.25 × $10,000)	$12,500
Federal tax (29 percent × $12,500)	$3,625
Less dividend tax credit (⅔ × $2,500)	($1,667)
Net federal tax payable ($3,625 – $1,667)	$1,958
Provincial tax (50 percent × $1,958)	$979
Total tax	$2,937

As you can see, the net result of this calculation is that T pays about 29-percent tax on the dividend income. When this 29 percent is added to the tax the corporation has already paid, the total tax equals the tax an individual would have paid if he or she had earned the money directly instead of through the corporation. The basic idea behind the gross-up and dividend tax credit is that the gross-up restores the income earned by the corporation before it paid tax, and includes this in your income. The dividend tax credit then represents the tax the corporation paid on this income, for which you are given credit. As a result the tax you pay on the dividend is adjusted to remove the tax already paid by the corporation.

The Quebec tax return has a separate dividend tax credit of 10.83 percent of the grossed-up dividend.

When you receive a T3 or T5 slip reporting your dividend income for the year, you will notice that the slip has boxes that contain both the actual amount of dividends and the taxable amount of dividends paid. Be sure to include only the taxable amount of dividends on your tax return.

As you have probably noticed, individuals are far better off to receive dividend income over interest or wage income, since interest and wages are taxed at the top marginal rate while Canadian source dividends receive the benefit of the dividend tax credit. The only major drawback of dividends when compared to wages is that for purposes of the earned income calculation to determine RRSP contribution room, dividends are not considered earned income; thus, they do not generate RRSP contribution room.

Stock dividends

A stock dividend is a dividend that a corporation pays by issuing new shares instead of cash.

On the balance sheet of the corporation, the dividend will cause a reduction in the retained earnings and a corresponding increase in paid-up capital. A normal cash dividend would see a reduction in the retained earnings and an equal reduction in the cash balance. As was the case previously, if the paying corporation is a Canadian resident, the gross-up and dividend tax credit rules must be used. The only difference is that this time you have no cash to pay the tax. The amount of the dividend on which the gross-up is calculated is your share of the increased paid-up capital. A stock dividend and a stock split are not the same thing. A stock split is simply dividing your shares into more shares with no change to the companies share capital. A stock dividend is the result of and increase in the share capital of the paying corporation. No tax is owed on stock splits, while substantial tax can be owed on stock dividends.

Suppose Helen owns one share of ABC Corporation. The paid-up capital of her one share is $100. If the company has a 2 for 1 stock split, she would have two shares with a paid-up capital of $50 each, and no tax to pay. If instead the corporation issued a stock dividend of 100 percent, she would end up with two shares with a paid-up capital of $100 each, and tax to pay on a $100 dividend.

Foreign dividends

Foreign dividends are dividends received from non-resident corporations. These dividends are treated in a different manner than Canadian source dividends.

- These dividends are not subject to the gross-up and dividend tax credit procedure.
- These dividends are included in income at their full amount. Even if the originating country withheld tax on the dividend, the full amount — not the dividend minus the tax withheld — is included in income as a foreign source of income.

- The dividends must be converted to Canadian dollars when received.
- Tax withheld on a foreign source dividend can be recovered by claiming a foreign tax credit. The maximum credit that can be claimed is 15 percent of the dividend. After entering the full dividend amount including the amount withheld on schedule 4 Part II, you will need to work through schedule 1, method B, to determine your foreign tax credit.

  If the withholding tax exceeds the 15 percent allowable, you can deduct the excess from your income.
- All dividends are included in income in Canada. Even if the dividend you received is not taxable in the country of origin, Canada does not recognize the non-taxability of dividends of other countries.
- If you have interests in foreign property with an original cost of more than $100,000 you will need to file form T1135 "Foreign Income Verification Statement." On this form you must describe the property, the original cost, and the nature of the income earned. You must file this form with your personal tax return. (See Chapter 21 for more information on how to complete this form.)
- If you or a group of Canadians own 10 percent or more of a foreign company, you will be required to file an information return T1134.
- Similar information returns must be filed if you have a 10-percent or more beneficial interest in a foreign trust.

The reporting rules for foreign-owned investment properties are complex, with numerous penalties for deficient or incomplete information. If you are in this situation, you'll require good professional advice.

Let's say you receive a $1,000 dividend from a foreign corporation. The country of origin withholds $250 in tax and pays you the $750 in cash. You have a total income of $10,000 including the foreign income and your basic federal tax is $2,000. The first thing you will notice is that the $250 withheld at source exceeds the 15-percent ($150) foreign tax credit that will be allowed by the CCRA. In response you do the following; you reduce the dividend by the excess tax withheld and include the net amount in income on schedule 4.

Dividends received	$1,000
Less tax paid in excess of 15 percent ($250 – $150 = $100)	– $100
Dividend to include in income	$900

Now that we have adjusted the dividend income, it is time to determine our foreign tax credit (FTC). Here's where it gets ugly.

As per schedule 1, method B, the FTC is the lesser of the following:

A) Actual tax paid less the tax in excess of 15 percent:

($250 less $100)	$150

OR

B) (Net foreign non-business income/net income including foreign non-business income less tax in excess of 15 percent) × Basic federal tax

($900/[10,000 – 100]) × $2,000	$181

This means that the lesser is $150, and you will be able to claim the entire tax withheld as a tax credit against Canadian tax. If it works out that you are not allowed to claim the full foreign tax withheld, you can offset the excess against provincial tax payable or you can claim the excess as a deduction against net income.

Claiming dividends received by your spouse

If your spouse receives dividends from a Canadian resident corporation but has income that is too low to use the dividend tax credit, there is an election available to help. This election allows the higher income spouse to transfer the dividends to his or her return. Once transferred, the dividends will be grossed-up and the dividend tax credit can be claimed.

Why would you want to do this? At first glance, you think this would result in more tax, since the higher-income spouse is paying tax at a higher rate. But by transferring income out of the lower-income spouse's hands, you may be increasing the marital credit that the higher-income spouse can claim. The increase in the credit, together with the fact that the higher-income spouse can use the full dividend tax credit, will offset the higher tax rate paid.

There are several restrictions on this election that you should consider:

- Only dividends received by your spouse can be transferred. Dividends received by other dependants are not eligible.
- Only dividends received from taxable Canadian corporations (that is, dividends eligible for the 25-percent gross-up) may be transferred.
- All the spouse's eligible dividends must be transferred. Partial transfers are not allowed.
- You can only make the election if you increase your married exemption by transferring the dividends to your income. Alternatively, if you create the married credit by making the transfer, you will also be allowed to make the election.

If your spouse has low income, and you are claiming him or her as a dependant, and he or she earns dividends that are eligible for the gross-up and dividend tax credit, you should consider transferring those dividends to you and including them in your income.

Non-taxable dividends

Believe it or not, there are such things as non-taxable dividends. Really, there are. Read on.

Capital dividends

Dividends paid from a private corporation's capital dividend account will be non-taxable in the hands of the shareholders. What is the capital dividend account? Well, it's a special surplus account where companies accumulate income that is non-taxable. These non-taxable incomes include the following:

- Non-taxable portion of net capital gains
- Capital dividends received from other corporations
- The untaxed portion of gains on the disposition of eligible capital property
- The proceeds of life insurance received by the corporation.

Capital dividends received from private corporations are non-taxable and should not be included in the income of the receiving shareholder. In order to pay out a capital dividend to a shareholder, you must file a special election with the CCRA.

Pre-1972 capital surplus on hand

Any dividend received from the "Pre-1972 Capital Surplus on Hand" account on corporate wind up, are non-taxable and should not be included in income. These dividends will be classified as proceeds of disposition and may result in a capital gain.

In some cases it is possible to pay no tax on dividends received, because of the basic personal exemption and the dividend tax credit. In some provinces you may be entitled to receive up to $24,000 in dividends and not pay any tax. Of course, this assumes that you have no other sources of income. The amount of tax-free dividends you are entitled to will depend on your province of residence, since the tax rates will differ. Be sure to visit your tax professional to find out the maximum amount you can receive in dividends and still manage to avoid the taxman.

Line 121: Interest and Other Investment Income

Interest is the compensation paid for the use of money belonging to someone else. Even though this definition appears to be relatively clear, great sections of the *Income Tax Act* are dedicated to identifying and classifying transactions that give rise to interest. The problem with interest is that it is taxed at the same high rate as employment and business income. This rate, as you know, is much higher than the dividend or capital gains rate. With this as a motivation, many individuals and businesses have spent a large amount of time and effort to structure transactions to make it appear that the income reported is of a capital or dividend nature rather than interest. To combat these efforts the *Income Tax Act* has deemed many transactions to be on account of interest, and has brought in requirements on when and how these transactions are to be included in income.

How to report interest income

Paragraph 12(1)(c) of the *Income Tax Act* requires taxpayers to include in income "any amount received or receivable by him in the year as, on account or in lieu of payment of, or in satisfaction of, interest." Simple, eh? Actually, what this means is that taxpayers can't get away with not reporting interest income just because they haven't received any payment. The taxman wants you to report it even if the amount is still owing to you. Reporting interest before you receive it is known as the accrual method. Reporting interest as it is received is called the cash method.

Section 12(4) of the *Income Tax Act* specifies that individuals must report interest on debt obligations using the accrual method. *Accrual* simply means that interest is included in income as earned, not as received. Take Sarah, for example. She owns a $1,000 bond that earns interest of 10 percent, or $100 every year. However, Sarah only receives the interest every three years. Unfortunately, the CCRA doesn't care when Sarah receives the money; every year in her tax return she must report the $100 earned.

The CCRA defines the term *debt obligation* in IT-396R to mean bank accounts, term deposits, GICs, Canada Savings Bonds, mortgages, corporate bonds and loans — that is, the most common sources of interest.

As a result of these definitions, all the interest earned on these sources must be included in income on the yearly anniversary date of the inception of these debt obligation contracts, to the extent that it has not already been included.

Types of interest income

Interest income falls into one of two broad categories: regular interest or compounded interest. *Regular interest* is interest paid on a regular basis during the term of the investment. This interest is usually reported annually to the investor on a T5 slip. *Compounded interest* is interest that is reinvested throughout the term of the investment. Once earned, the interest is added to the principle so that you can earn interest on your interest. The reporting of this type of interest is not as easy or straightforward as the regular interest.

Methods of reporting interest income

Depending on when you purchased your investments, the recording and reporting of interest can vary dramatically. The following section outlines the different reporting methods of interest income.

Interest on investments made after 1989

This is the easy one. All interest earned on debt must be accrued and included in income on an annual basis. All issuers of debt instruments are required to issue information slips to investors detailing their annual income.

Interest on investments acquired before 1990 and after 1981

Interest earned on debt during this period can be reported in several different ways at the option of the investor:

- Interest can be accrued and reported on an annual basis, as above.
- Interest can be accrued and reported on a triennial annual basis from the date of acquisition — that is, interest earned on compounding investments need only be reported once every three years, starting from the year of acquisition. For example, if you bought a compounding investment in 1982, the first time you would have to report interest would be 1985. The next time would be 1988.
- Interest can be recognized as received.
- Interest can be reported as it becomes receivable. Receivable interest is interest that has been fully earned, and you have a full legal right to claim it.

If you receive interest from different types of debt obligations, you may report income from each using any of the above four methods, as long as they are consistently used from year to year. Once you choose to stop reporting interest on a cash basis, you are not permitted to change back to the cash method.

Administratively, the CCRA takes the position that similar investments must report their income in a similar way. For example if you report interest on a government bond using the annual accrual basis, all government bonds must be reported the same way.

To elect to use the accrual basis of income reporting, you must include a statement with your tax return that details the investment and the previous method used, plus you must report all previously unreported income to December 31 of the year of election.

Interest on investments acquired before 1982

Contracts acquired before 1982 are deemed to be issued on December 31, 1988, provided they have been held continuously since 1982. The first three-year anniversary for income recognition will be December 31, 1991, or the day the investment was disposed of, whichever comes first.

If you made an investment prior to November 13, 1981, and you are unable to cancel the contract or require repayment until maturity, you will not be forced to use the three-year reporting method with the deemed December 31, 1988 issue date.

Special reporting methods for certain investments

Certain investments have their own special reporting methods. There are almost as many ways of treating income as there are different types of investing. These are important to consider whenever you're making a investment decision as these special reporting methods do have an impact on your final tax calculation.

Annuity contracts

Annuity contracts acquired after 1989 are subject to annual accrual reporting. If the annuity was acquired before 1990, it will be reported under the triennial method if the premiums paid were fixed before 1990. If the payments were not fixed, the annual reporting method is required.

Life insurance policies

Life insurance policies issued after 1989 are required to use the annual accrual method if they are not exempt from the one- and three-year accrual methods. Since most current life insurance policies are exempt, you do not have to report the income annually or at three-year intervals. Holders of insurance policies issued after 1981 and before 1990 are required to report income on the triennial basis, or may elect to report annually.

Investments acquired at a discount

The difference between the face value of the investment (value at maturity) and the purchase price is considered interest, and will be included in income at maturity. Investments that sell at a discount include bonds and T-bills.

Strip bonds

For investments in strip bonds, you must report a notional interest inclusion each year. The company issuing the bond will calculate this interest and report it to the investor.

Indexed debt obligations

Indexed debt obligations contain a provision that adjusts your return up or down depending on the effect of inflation — that is, if you are to receive 10 percent interest and inflation is running at 3 percent, the obligation will pay 13 percent to compensate for the effects of inflation. For indexed debt obligations, you must report the interest and the adjustment factor annually and include it in income.

Canada Savings Bonds

Canada Savings Bonds have their own unique reporting rules. Here we review several types of bonds and the tax implications of holding them.

- **R bonds:** Interest on the R bond is paid and reported annually until the bond matures or is disposed of.
- **C bonds:** Interest on C bonds (Compounding bonds) is not received until the bond is cashed. C bond interest is reported differently depending on its series.
- **Series 45 and later (1990 to 2000):** Interest is accrued annually and reported to the investor on a T5 slip. This interest must be included in the investor's income for the year.
- **Series 44 (1989):** Interest can be reported either every three years, or annually if the investor chooses. The inclusion years are 1992, 1995, 1998, and 2001 on maturity. No inclusion is required for 2000.

Banks and investment companies will not issue a T5 slip if interest earned is less than $50. You must determine how much interest was earned and report it yourself. Interest earned on tax refunds must be included in income in the year it was received. You must report interest income on joint accounts in the same proportion as your contributions to the account, regardless of whose name appears on the T5. For example, if you and your spouse have a joint account, and you contribute 60 percent of the funds, you must report 60 percent of the interest income.

If you purchase Canada Savings Bonds using the payroll purchase plan, the interest charged by your employer is deductible at line 221 as a carrying charge.

Interest on foreign source income

Interest from foreign sources is subject to many of the same rules as dividends from foreign sources (see above):

- The interest income must be converted to Canadian dollars when received.
- The full amount of the interest must be included in your income regardless of whether you received all the funds, because tax was withheld at the source country.
- A foreign tax credit must be claimed for taxes withheld by the source country.
- If the withholding tax paid to the source country is in excess of 15 percent of the income, you may deduct the excess from the foreign interest income. This deduction is done on Schedule 4 under "carrying charges (specify)." The same rules as were explained in the foreign dividend section determine how much foreign tax credit can be claimed.
- For investments made after 1989, interest earned but not paid on a regular basis must be accrued and included in income on an annual basis.
- For investments made before 1990, you may use the three-year accrual method.

Sign waivers with the CCRA for the years that you had to accrue foreign interest into your income but received no money. By signing the waivers, you keep these years open and will be able to claim the foreign tax credit against this income when the interest payments are eventually received.

Shareholder and employee loans

Shareholder and employee loans have been the focus of numerous court challenges and legislative changes over the years. The primary concern the government has with these arrangements is that, if structured correctly, they can become vehicles for corporations to distribute all their profit and retained earnings to shareholders and employees on a totally tax-free basis. By extending no-interest indefinite loans, the corporations could give you all the money you wanted with no tax implications to you or the company. Banning these loans altogether is not the answer. The government recognizes that in certain situations loans from a company to an employee or shareholder are necessary for the successful operation of the business. With the above parameters in mind, the government has formulated tax legislation that allows corporations to extend loans when necessary, but which places very restrictive rules on these loans in an attempt to prevent a tax-free extraction of earnings. The rules that we will discuss extend not only to shareholders and employees, but also to related individuals, companies, trusts, partnerships, and so on. Through years of experience, the CCRA has seen many variations of the general theme of getting money out of a company with no tax paid, and is therefore prepared to challenge anything that falls outside the strict interpretations of the rules. In general, you must include all loans to shareholders or persons who are not dealing at arm's length with shareholders in the income of the shareholder or the non–arm's length person in the year the loan was made. The same rules apply if you become indebted to a corporation in some manner — for example, you buy a vehicle from the company and pay for it with a promissory note. This being tax, there are exceptions to this general rule. Where would we be without exceptions?

General exceptions to the rule

Shareholder loans will not be included in income in the following situations:

- The indebtedness is between nonresident persons.
- The loan is made in the ordinary course of business of loaning money, provided that bona fide repayment arrangements are made at the time of the loan. This exception prevents loans to shareholders of banks or other financial institutions from being included in their income.
- The loan is repaid within one year from the end of the corporation's taxation year. For example, if the loan is made in 2000 and the corporation's year-end is December 31, 2000, the loan must be repaid by December 31, 2001, to avoid the entire amount being included in the shareholder's 2000 income.

The loan cannot be part of a series of loans and repayments. This means you can't repay the loan, then take out another loan — in theory, you really haven't paid back the original amount. The CCRA will ensure that if you use this strategy, you will be required to report the amount of the loan in income.

Specific exceptions to the rule

The *Income Tax Act*, under the following very specific conditions, allows loans to be made to shareholders who are employees

- The loan is made to an employee who is not a specified employee — that is, who owns less than 10 percent of the shares of the corporation.
- The loan was made to an employee to assist him or her in acquiring a home for his or her own occupation.
- The loan was made to an employee to assist him or her in purchasing previously unissued shares of the corporation.
- The loan was made to an employee to assist him or her in acquiring a motor vehicle required to perform duties of employment.

For these exemptions to be valid, two conditions must also be met:

- The loan arose because of the employee's employment and not because of his or her share holdings. In simpler terms, the loan must be available to all employees, not just share-holding employees.
- There must be a bona fide repayment arrangement in place. Which means that there must be an agreement in place for the loan to be repaid within a reasonable period of time.

Forgiven loans

If a loan or debt is forgiven, the forgiven amount is a taxable benefit and is added to the income of the shareholder or employee in accordance with the debt forgiveness rules.

If you are the beneficiary of a forgiven loan, you should consult a tax professional. In certain situations, the debt forgiveness rules can be complicated.

Imputed interest on shareholder and employee loans

If you receive a low-interest or no-interest loan because of your shareholding or past, present, or future employment, you will be deemed to have received a benefit from employment. The benefit is equal to the difference between the interest paid in the year (or within 30 days after the year-end) and the prescribed interest determined by the CCRA.

A loan received solely because of your shareholding will be included in income if it is not paid back before the second year-end of the corporation making the loan. For the period that the loan is outstanding before the second year-end, an interest benefit will be included in the income of the shareholder if the interest rate charged is below the prescribed rate. If the loan is then taken into income, the interest benefit will be reversed for the years of inclusion. Loans made to a shareholder in your capacity as an employee can escape the income inclusion if the loan falls into one of the above exceptions. This loan will still be subject to the imputed interest benefit if the interest rate charged is below the prescribed rate.

Let's say that Dale receives a loan from his employer for $100,000 at 0-percent interest on January 1, 2000. Dale is not a shareholder and therefore does not have to meet one of the exemptions to avoid income inclusion. The loan is outstanding until December 31, 2000. Assuming a prescribed rate of 5 percent, what is Dale's interest benefit? Dale will be deemed to have an interest benefit of $5,000 ($100,000 × 5 percent). This amount will be added to Dale's 2000 income. Any interest Dale paid on this loan would have reduced the benefit.

If Dale had used the funds to earn income from business or property, or to purchase an automobile or aircraft for use in employment, he would be allowed an offsetting deduction equal to the interest benefit. The prescribed rate on interest benefits is determined by subtracting 4 percent (3 percent in Quebec) from the rate the CCRA charges on late payment of tax. This rate changes quarterly and is linked to the Bank of Canada rate. Contact your local Tax Services Office to obtain this rate. Remember that if you receive a loan from your employer, try to arrange to pay the interest portion on January 30 of the following year. This will save you some cash in the current year and still keep you onside in terms of interest payments.

Special situations

Loans for the purchase or relocation of a home are given special treatment when it comes to calculating the interest benefits.

- **Home loans:** If the loan is made as a home purchase loan, the rate used to calculate the imputed interest benefit for the first five years will never be greater than the prescribed rate at the time the loan was made. When the five years are over, the continuation of the loan is considered a new loan, and the prescribed rate in effect on that day will be the maximum rate charged for the next five years. For example, Maureen receives a home purchase loan on January 1, 2000, at an interest rate of 0 percent. On January 1, 2000, the prescribed interest rate is 5 percent. Over the next five years, Maureen's taxable benefit will be calculated using a prescribed rate that could be less than 5 percent but will never be more.
- **Home relocation loans:** If the loan is a home relocation loan — that is, a loan to purchase a home that is at least 40 kilometres closer to your new work location — you will receive a special deduction in the calculation of the interest benefit. The benefit for the first five years will be reduced by an amount equal to the interest imputed on $25,000. In effect, the benefit on the first $25,000 of the loan will be deducted from the income inclusion.

What is a trust or estate?

The rules relating to trusts and estates are complicated, and your forays into this area should be done with professional advice. Since the area is quite complex, the focus of this section will be to give you an understanding of what trusts are and how they are taxed, without going into too much detail.

A trust is a legal arrangement where an individual (settler) transfers the legal title of property (trust property) to a person (trustee) who controls and administers the property on behalf of another person (beneficiary). A trust is a tax entity that is separate and distinct from the settler, beneficiaries, or the trustee. The key feature of a trust is the separation of the title and *management* of the trust property from the *benefits* of the property.

Why use a trust?

You use a trust when you want someone to benefit from assets but do not want the person to control or own the assets. This is why many trusts are set up for children by their parents. They want the children to have money for things such as education or personal living expenses, but they do not want the children to have access to the capital assets generating the income. Keep in mind that there are two basic types of trusts.

- **Inter vivos:** This is a trust created while the settler is alive.
- **Testamentary trusts:** This is a trust created by a will and comes into effect on the death of the individual. These trusts can be discretionary or non-discretionary, depending on whether the trustee has discretion to decide which beneficiary gets distributions of income, how much to distribute, and when to distribute the income of the trust. In non-discretionary trusts, the trust document specifies the payments of the income.

Income of a trust

In the simplest trust, the income is simply the income generated by the assets held by the trust, less any deductions for amounts paid to the beneficiaries of the trust. Income is paid to a beneficiary when the recipient receives the payment or a payment has been allocated to the beneficiary and when they have a legally enforceable right to receive the payment.

Taxation of a trust

Any income left inside a trust that has not been distributed to the beneficiaries will be taxed. For inter vivos trusts, the income will be taxed at the highest marginal personal tax rate of 29 percent. No deductions for personal tax credits will be allowed in the computation of tax payable for a trust. Testamentary trusts are taxed using the marginal tax rates. But, like inter vivos trusts are denied the deductions for the personal tax credits.

Income of the beneficiaries

Amounts deducted from the trust's net income that are paid or payable to the beneficiaries are taxed in the hands of the beneficiaries as property income. This income retains its original identity even after being paid to the beneficiaries. The term *retaining its identity* means that income that was earned as dividends by the trust remains dividends in the hands of the beneficiaries. This flow-through of income allows beneficiaries to take advantage of the dividend tax credit on dividends from Canadian corporations or the foreign tax credits on foreign source income. Beneficiaries are also allowed the capital gains deductions on qualified farm property and qualified shares of a small business corporation, provided the trust is resident in Canada. Trusts are also permitted to pass on non-taxable dividends that, when received by the beneficiary, are excluded from income. The only exception is net capital losses, which do not flow through to the beneficiaries.

Income allocation

Income is considered allocated to beneficiaries when it is paid or payable to the beneficiary. An amount is considered payable by a trust when the beneficiary has the legal right to enforce payment.

Preferred beneficiary election

In special situations, the CCRA will allow a trust to allocate income to the beneficiaries but not actually pay the money or even give the beneficiaries access to it. The preferred beneficiary election is one of these situations. This election is made when the beneficiary is suffering from severe and prolonged mental or physical impairment. In these cases, the income is allocated to the beneficiary who pays tax at their marginal rate. The only difference is that the income is not paid or payable to the beneficiary; instead, it is retained within the trust as accumulating income. This accumulating income can be paid out at any time, tax-free for the benefit of the disabled beneficiary.

Infants and minors

Another situation in which income is retained in the trust is when the beneficiaries are infants or minors. The income is allocated to the minors and taxed at their marginal rate but are not paid to them until they are 21. To be eligible for this treatment, the income must vest to the children and must be paid to them at age 21 with no additional conditions attached — and it must be the case that the *only* reason for the income to have been withheld in the first place was that the beneficiaries were children.

Generally, the rule is that when a person dies, he or she is taxable on all income earned up until the time of death. If you are the beneficiary of an estate, you become taxable for any income earned after death.

Registered Education Savings Plan Income (RESP)

The investment income earned by an RESP is not taxable in the hands of the contributor. Instead, the income becomes taxable income of the student when he or she removes the money for educational purposes. The advantage of having the tax paid by the student is that the student probably has little or no other income, and the tax will be payable at the lowest marginal tax rate.

Distribution from an RESP

If the beneficiaries of the RESP do not attend an institution of higher education, the contributions and the income earned from these contributions (accumulated income payments) can be returned to the contributor. While the contributions can be withdrawn tax-free, the accumulated income can only be withdrawnal under certain circumstances:

- The plan must have existed for at least 10 years.
- The beneficiaries are at least 21 years of age and will not be attending an institution of higher learning.
- The contributor must be a resident of Canada.

If these requirements are met, the contributions and the accumulated income can be withdrawn. This withdrawal will be taxable in the hands of the contributor.

If the RESP is not used within 25 years of its initiation, it will automatically be returned to the contributor. The income returned to the contributor will be hit with a special penalty surtax of 20 percent on top of the regular tax payable on this income. The surtax can be partially avoided if you transfer the accumulated income directly to an RRSP. The maximum amount that can be transferred is $50,000. In order to transfer funds to your RRSP, you will have to have sufficient RRSP contribution room. If the contributor passes away, the contributor's spouse can use the RRSP transfer option.

File form T1171 "Tax Withholding Waiver on Accumulated Income Payments from RESPs" to avoid tax being withheld on amounts that will be transferred directly to your RRSP.

The withholding rates on amounts withdrawn from an RESP are as follows:

Receipts under $5,000	30 percent
Receipts between $5,001 and $15,000	40 percent
Receipts over $15,000	50 percent

Example: Simon contributed the maximum amount of $42,000 to his son Jacuzzi's RESP. By the time Jacuzzi realized that he did not want to go to university, the plan had been in existence for 20 years and he was 25 years old. The value of the plan had grown to $142,000. Simon decided to end the RESP and take back the contributions plus the accumulated income. At the time Simon decided to take back the money, he had $55,000 in unused RRSP deduction room. How much income will Simon have to pay the 20-percent surtax on?

Amount withdrawn		$142,000
Return of Contribution		$ 42,000
Amount to include in income		$100,000
Less the lessor of		
a) Amount Simon contributed to his RRSP	$55,000	
b) Lifetime RRSP transfer limit	$50,000	$ 50,000
Net income subject to tax and 20-percent surtax		$ 50,000

For RRSP purposes, the return of the RESP income is not earned income, so no additional RRSP room is created.

Other Investment Income

Line 121 of your income tax return is designed to capture all interest and other investment income. Believe it or not, there are still other forms of investment income on which we have not yet touched. In this section we highlight some of the more recognizable forms of other investment income.

Mutual funds

Mutual funds are groups of assets managed by professional managers. The assets managed can range from real estate to mortgages to stocks and bonds. The income that is distributed to the fund investors retains its identity, what I mean is, income earned as dividends by the fund is still regarded as dividends when it is distributed to the investors. As a result, investors can receive interest, dividends, capital gains, foreign income, or capital dividends. Investors in mutual funds receive T5s if they invested in a mutual fund corporation, or T3s if they invested in a mutual fund trust. The shares of mutual funds are capital property that will generate capital gains or losses on disposition. Very often, funds automatically reinvest distributions to the fund holders in new shares of the fund. In these situations, although you never see any of the cash, you will be taxed on the income distributed, and your cost base will be adjusted for the increased investments. If you invest in foreign mutual funds and receive payments from these funds, the payments will be classified as dividend income. Foreign fund payments do not retain the characteristics of the underlying assets when paid to Canadian investors. Amounts withheld are eligible for a foreign tax credit.

Stripped bonds and clipped coupons

These bonds and coupons begin life as long-term government bonds or government-backed bonds that pay interest when the coupons are removed and redeemed for their face value. If the bond is separated from the coupon and sold separately, the bonds and the coupons sell at a discount to the face value. The income earned on the difference between the discounted price of the coupons and the amount you receive on redemption is considered interest. The interest earned on the bond is a notional interest based on the effective interest rate calculated as if the bond was held to maturity. If the bond is sold before maturity and the sale price is more than the purchase price plus all the notional interest included in income, the excess is treated as a capital gain. If the sale price is less, a capital loss will result.

Royalties

Royalties are payments you receive for the use of your property. This income can be classified as business or investment income, depending on its nature. Royalties received for writing a book are business income, while royalties received for the use of property you purchased are investment income.

Annuities

Annuities are amounts payable on a periodic basis according to a contract, will, or trust. Report the interest income earned from an annuity at line 121, unless the recipient is 65 years of age or older and receiving retirement income, in which case you report the interest at line 115.

Labour-sponsored venture capital corporations

Labour-sponsored venture capital funds are sponsored by organized labour to provide venture capital to start-up businesses. Investments in the funds offer special tax credits both federally and provincially. Investments can be withdrawn at any time, but penalties usually apply if money is withdrawn before eight years. If successful, the fund could generate the same income streams mutual funds provide to their investors.

Exempt life insurance contracts

Offered by insurance companies, exempt life insurance contracts allow you to pay life insurance premiums and make deposits to a tax-sheltered investment account. The investments are allowed to grow tax-free inside the plan and can be withdrawn tax-free if they form part of the death benefit paid to the beneficiary. Alternatively, funds can be withdrawn tax-free as a loan against the policy, which is then repaid from the death benefit.

Chapter 13

Capital Gains and Losses

In This Chapter

- Sorting out capital gains versus ordinary income
- Understanding types of capital property
- Calculating a taxable capital gain or loss
- Understanding the lifetime capital gains exemption
- Dealing with cumulative net investment losses
- Getting a handle on the capital gains reserve

So this is an interesting chapter. There is a great deal of important information here. In this chapter we will provide you with the general information you need to report a capital gain or loss. Also right here, right now, you'll be treated to tons of definitions and savvy tips to maximize your tax position. So stick with us — we know you're eager to get a grip on what all this means to you. What is a capital gain or loss, you ask? Well, read on.

Capital Gains Versus Ordinary Income

Usually, you have a capital gain or capital loss when you sell or are considered to have disposed of a *capital property*. The question as to whether or not a property is a capital property can be a difficult one to answer. The judgment depends on both the nature of the property and the manner in which the owner manages the property. If the owner intends to realize a profit from the property versus hold the property for the income it produces, the gain or loss realized on sale is treated as an ordinary income gain or loss as opposed to a capital gain or loss.

Often it helps to understand the difference between capital and income in relation to the taxpayer's intention by thinking about the scenario of a tree and its fruit. If the taxpayer bought the tree with the intention of selling the fruit, then any subsequent sale of the tree would be on account of capital. If, however, the taxpayer purchased the tree intending to sell the tree and make a quick buck, then the transaction would be treated as income — and 100 percent of any gain would be taxable.

In deciding whether the gain or loss is on account of income or capital, the tax courts have used the following tests:

- **The period of ownership:** If property has been held for only a short period, it may be considered to have been purchased to be resold and the profits may therefore be treated as income. A property held for a longer period is more likely to be treated as capital.
- **Improvement and development:** Where a systematic effort has been made to make a property more marketable, it may indicate a business of selling properties.

- **Relationship of the transaction to the taxpayer's ordinary business:** (for example, the sale of a renovated home by a general contractor). The more similar the transaction is to the taxpayer's ordinary business, the more likely it is that the transaction will be treated as income.
- **Reasons for and nature of sale:** If the sale of a property is the result of an active campaign to sell it as opposed to the result of something unanticipated at the time of purchase, the profits will be considered on account of income.
- **The frequency of similar transactions:** A history of buying and selling similar properties, or of quick turnovers, may indicate the taxpayer is carrying on a business.

Falling offside on one of these tests does not mean the transaction will automatically be considered capital or income. The courts look at the larger picture, and you may have the opportunity to argue either way.

Where possible, have your gains treated as capital and your losses treated as income. The reason for this are twofold: one, capital gains are now only 66.66-percent taxable in Canada, while business income is fully taxable; and two, capital losses can only be applied against capital gains, while a business loss can be applied against any source of income to reduce tax.

Types of Capital Property

Capital gains and losses are reported on your tax return on schedule 3. Schedule 3 is divided into the following sections.

Real estate

The real estate section is used to report a capital gain or loss if you sell any real estate property during the year.

Real estate includes the following:

- Vacant land
- Rental property (both land and buildings)
- Farm property, including both land and buildings (other than qualified farm property)
- Commercial and industrial land and buildings.

This section should *not* be used to report the sale of personal use property — that is, your residence, or the sale of mortgages and other similar debt obligations on real property. Report these types of transactions under the appropriately named sections (see below).

Selling land and a building

For each real property you sold in 2000 that includes land and a building, you must do the following:

- Determine how much of the selling price relates to the land and how much is for the building (municipal assessments can be helpful in making this determination).
- Report the sale of your land and building separately on schedule 3.

Mutual fund units and shares

This section is used to report a capital gain or loss when you sell shares or securities that are not described in any other section of schedule 3. These shares or securities include the following:

- Publicly traded shares
- Units in a mutual fund trust
- Shares that qualify as Canadian securities or prescribed securities, provided they are not qualified small business corporation shares or qualified family farm corporation shares
- Shares issued by foreign corporations.

This section should also be used if you make a donation of the following properties:

- Shares listed on a prescribed stock exchange
- Shares of the capital stock of a mutual fund corporation
- Units in a mutual fund trust
- Interest in a related segregated fund trust.

If you donate shares, you'll be deemed to have disposed of them at their current fair market value. The capital that gain results is just one-third taxable — half of the normal inclusion rate of two-thirds. You'll still receive a donation slip equal to the fair market value of your shares. If you donate any of these properties between February 19, 1997 and December 31, 2001, to a qualified donee (other than a private foundation), use form T1170 "Capital Gains on Gifts of Certain Capital Property," to calculate the capital gain to report on schedule 3. If you sold any of the items listed above in 2000, you will receive either a T5008 slip "Statement of Securities Transactions," or an account statement from your investment dealer.

You may buy and sell the same type of property (for example, units of a mutual fund trust or publicly traded shares) over a period of time. If so, there is a special rule that, if applicable, may affect your capital gain (or loss) calculation. See the sections in this chapter on "Calculation of adjusted cost base" and the "Identical properties" rule.

If you own shares or units of a mutual fund, you may have to report the following capital gains (or losses):

- Capital gains (or losses) you realize when you sell your shares or units of the mutual fund (report these amounts in the "Mutual fund units and other shares including publicly traded shares" area of schedule 3); and
- Capital gains realized by the mutual fund from its investment portfolio, which are then flowed out to you. You should receive information slips from your investment dealer detailing the amounts to be reported in this situation.

Bonds, debentures, promissory notes, and other properties

This section is used to report capital gains or capital losses from the disposition of bonds, debentures, treasury bills, promissory notes, bad debts, foreign exchange gains and losses, and options, as well as discounts, premiums, and bonuses on debt obligations.

Donations made to a qualified donee of a debt obligation or right listed on a prescribed stock exchange are treated differently from a prescribed debt obligation. If you make such a donation between February 19, 1997 and December 31, 2001, use form T1170 "Capital Gains on Gifts of Certain Capital Property." If you have a capital gain, report the amount calculated on form T1170 on schedule 3. If you sold any of the types of properties listed above in 2000, you will receive either a T5008 slip "Statement of Securities Transactions," or an account statement from your investment dealer. You may have bought and sold the same type of property over a period of time. If so, a special rule may affect your capital gain (or loss) calculation. For additional information, see the section called "Identical properties."

Treasury bills (T-bills) and stripped bonds

When a T-bill or a stripped bond is issued at a discount and you keep it until it matures, the difference between the issue price and the amount you cash it in for is considered to be interest that accrued to you. However, if you sell the T-bill or stripped bond before it matures, in addition to the interest accrued at that time, you may have a capital gain or capital loss. Before you calculate your capital gain or loss, you have to determine the amount of interest accumulated to the date of disposition. Subtract the interest from the proceeds of disposition, and calculate the capital gain or loss in the usual manner.

Let's look at an example — Lauren bought a T-bill on May 1, 2000, for $98,000. The T-bill's term is 91 days and its maturity value on August 1, 2000, is $100,000. However, she sold it on June 13, 2000, for $99,000. The effective yield rate was 8.19 percent.

Lauren calculates interest on the T-bill as follows:

Interest to be included in income =

$$\text{Purchase price} \times \text{Effective yield} \times \frac{\text{Number of days T-bill held}}{\text{Number of days in the year sold}}$$

$$\$98{,}000 \times 8.19\% \times \frac{44}{365} = \$967.54$$

Lauren calculates her capital gain as follows:

Proceeds of disposition	$99,000.00
Minus: Interest	– $ 976.54
Net proceeds of disposition	$98,023.46
Minus: Adjusted cost base	– $98,000.00
Capital gain	$ 23.46

Mortgage foreclosures and conditional sale repossessions

You may have held a mortgage on a property but had to repossess the property later because the debtor failed to pay all or a part of the amount owed under the terms of the mortgage. In this case, you may have to report a capital gain or a capital loss on this section of schedule 3. The following rules also apply when property is repossessed under a conditional sales agreement.

A *mortgagee* is a person who lends money under a mortgage on a property. A *mortgagor* is a person who borrows money under a mortgage.

If, as a mortgagee, you repossess a property because the mortgagor failed to pay you the money owed under the terms of the mortgage, you are considered to have purchased the property. At the time of repossession, you do not have a capital gain or a capital loss. Any gain or loss will be postponed until you sell the property. If you are the mortgagor and your property is repossessed because you do not pay the money owed under the terms of the mortgage, you are considered to have sold the property. Depending on the amount you owed at the time of repossession, you may have a capital gain, a capital loss, or, in the case of depreciable property, a terminal loss. However, if the property is personal-use property, you cannot deduct the loss.

Capital gains from a mortgage foreclosure or a conditional sales repossession will be excluded from net income when you calculate your claim for the Goods and Services Tax/Harmonized Sales Tax credit, the Canada Child Tax Benefit, and the age amount. You should also exclude this income when calculating your social benefits repayment.

Personal-use property

The personal-use property section is used to report capital gains from the disposition of personal-use property.

Most people are not affected by the capital gains rules because the property they own is for their personal use. When you sell such property — for example, cars, boats, and jewelry — usually you do not end up with a capital gain. This is because this type of property generally does not increase in value over the years. As a result, you may end up with a loss. Although you have to report a gain on the sale of personal-use property on your tax return, you are not ordinarily allowed to claim a loss.

To calculate any capital gain or loss realized when you dispose of personal-use property, follow these rules:

- If the adjusted cost base (ACB) of the property is less than $1,000, its ACB is considered to be $1,000.
- If the proceeds of disposition are less than $1,000, the proceeds of disposition are considered to be $1,000.
- If both the ACB and the proceeds of disposition are $1,000 or less, you do not have a capital gain or a capital loss. Do not report the sale on schedule 3 when you file your return.

The result? When you dispose of personal-use property that has an ACB or proceeds of disposition of more than $1,000, you may have a capital gain or loss. You have to report any capital gain from disposing of personal-use property. However, if you have a capital loss, you usually cannot deduct that loss when you calculate your income for the year. In addition, you cannot use the loss to decrease capital gains on other personal-use property. This is because if a property depreciates through personal use, the resulting loss on its disposition is a personal expense.

These loss restrictions do not apply under the following circumstances:

- If you disposed of personal-use property that is listed as personal property (see the next section); or
- If a bad debt is owed to you from the sale of a personal-use property to a person with whom you deal at arm's length. In this case you can claim the bad debt owed to you as a capital loss; however, your claim cannot be more than the capital gain previously reported on the sale of the property.

Let's say that Barb sold the following personal-use properties in 2000.

Property Sold	***Proceeds of Disposition***	***Adjusted Cost Base***	***Outlays and Expenses***
Canoe	$800	$600	$0
Golf clubs	$1,300	$850	$30
Stereo	$600	$2,100	$50

Based on the information above, Barb would calculate the capital gain or loss for each transaction as follows:

Calculation of Capital Gain or Loss	***Canoe***	***Golf Clubs***	***Stereo***
Proceeds of disposition (greater of sell price and $1,000)	$1,000	$1,300	$1,000
Minus: Adjusted cost base (greater of cost price and $1,000) plus outlays	$1,000	$1,030	$2,150
Capital gain (loss)	$0	$270	($1,150)

Canoe: Both the adjusted cost base and the proceeds of disposition are considered to be $1,000 because they are less than $1,000. As a result, there is no capital gain or loss for this transaction, and Barb does not have to report it on schedule 3.

Golf Clubs: Because the golf clubs' adjusted cost base is less than $1,000, the adjusted cost base is considered to be $1,000. Barb reports $270 as a capital gain.

Stereo: The capital loss from this transaction is not deductible, and Barb cannot use the loss to offset any other capital gains realized during the year.

If you sell your home — your principal residence — for more than what it cost you, you usually do not have to report the sale on your return or pay tax on any gain (see the "Sale of a principal residence" section of this chapter for more details).

Listed personal property

The listed personal property section is used to report capital gains or capital losses from the disposition of such property.

Listed personal property (LPP) is a type of personal-use property. The principal difference between LPP and other personal-use properties is that LPP usually increases in value over time. LPP includes all or any part of, any interest in, or any right to, the following properties:

- Rare manuscripts, or rare books
- Prints, etchings, drawings, paintings, sculptures, or other similar works of art
- Jewelry
- Stamps and coins.

To determine the value of many of these items, you can have them appraised by art, coin, jewelry, book, and stamp dealers. You can also refer to published catalogues. Because LPP is personal-use property, the $1,000 minimum proceeds of disposition and adjusted cost base rules apply. See the previous section, "Personal-use property," for more information about these rules.

If your 2000 gains from dispositions of LPP are more than your 2000 losses from such dispositions, you can use unapplied LPP losses from 1993 and later years to reduce your 2000 gains. If you want to do this, do *not* enter these losses on line 253 of your return. Instead, subtract the unapplied LPP losses of previous years from your 2000 LPP gains. You should only complete the "Listed personal property" area of schedule 3 if after doing these calculations you still have a net LPP gain in 2000. If your 2000 losses from dispositions of LPP are more than your 2000 gains from such dispositions, the difference represents your LPP loss for the year.

Keep a record of your LPP losses that have not expired, so you can apply these losses against LPP gains in other years. An unapplied LPP loss expires if you do not use it by the end of the seventh year after it was incurred.

Foreign currencies

The foreign currencies section is used to report capital gains or capital losses realized by virtue of fluctuations in foreign currencies. Provided that the foreign currency transactions are capital in nature, they are treated in the same way as any other capital gain or loss except that an individual's first $200 of gain realized is exempted from reportable capital gains. Similarly, the first $200 of loss is exempted from capital loss. Before deducting the $200 amount from the capital gain or loss determined, all capital gains and losses from foreign currency must be netted and the $200 exemption applied against the net foreign exchange gain or loss for the year.

Suppose that in 1999 Karen bought 100 shares of ABC Co. for $1,000(US). At this time the exchange rate for Canadian dollars was 1.50, so her purchase cost her $1,500(Cdn). In 2000 she sold these shares for $1,200(US), when the exchange rate was 1.55. Her proceeds were then $1,860(Cdn). Her total gain would be the difference between the price she paid and the price she sold the shares for, or $360(Cdn). The problem is that a portion of this gain resulted from the change in the currency exchange rates. To determine how much of the gain results from currency fluctuations, assume that the exchange rate did not change and calculate the gain. In Karen's case, the gain would be $300. This means that $60 of the $360 gain calculated above was due to the difference in exchange rates. Karen would only need to report $300 on schedule 3 of her tax return.

There is no place on schedule 3 to report your reduction for exchange gains or losses. Therefore, a reduction in the gain can simply be reflected as a reduction in the proceeds of disposition. Remember, if you've increased your loss because of an exchange loss, you must increase your proceeds by the amount of the loss, up to $200.

Depreciable property

The depreciable property section is used to report capital gains or capital losses from the disposition of depreciable property. *Depreciable property* is defined as capital property used to earn income from a business or property. You can write off the cost of the property as capital cost allowance over a number of years.

When you dispose of depreciable property, you may have a capital gain or a loss. In addition, certain capital cost allowance (CCA) rules may require that you add a recapture of CCA to your income or may allow you to claim a terminal loss. Usually you will have a capital gain on depreciable property if you sell it for more than its adjusted cost base plus the outlays and expenses that arose from selling. A loss from the sale of depreciable property is not considered to be a capital loss. You may, however, be able to claim a terminal loss.

Recapture of CCA and terminal losses

Here's an overview of the recapture and terminal loss rules. When you sell a depreciable property for less than its original capital cost, but for more than the undepreciated capital cost (UCC) in its class, you do not have a capital gain. Generally, the UCC of a class is the total capital cost of all the properties of the class, minus the CCA you claimed in previous years. If you sell depreciable property in a year, you also have to subtract from the UCC one of the following amounts, whichever is less:

- The proceeds of disposition of the property, *minus* the related outlays and expenses; or
- The capital cost of the property at the time of sale.

If the UCC of a class has a *negative* balance at the end of the year, this amount is considered to be a *recapture* of CCA. Include this recapture in income for the year of sale. If the UCC of a class has a *positive* balance at the end of the year, and you do not have any properties left in that class, this amount is a *terminal loss*. Unlike with a capital loss, the full amount of the terminal loss can be deducted from income in that year. If the balance for the UCC of a class is 0 at the end of the year, you do not have a recapture of CCA or a terminal loss.

Let's say that in 1994, Kirk bought a piece of machinery, at a cost of $15,000, for his business. It is the only property in its class at the beginning of 2000. The class has a UCC of $11,000. He sold the piece of machinery in 2000 and did not buy any other property in that class. The chart below gives you three different selling prices (proceeds of disposition) to show how Kirk would handle a variety of situations.

Calculation of Capital Gain	***A***	***B***	***C***
Proceeds of disposition	$5,000	$15,000	$20,000
Minus: Capital cost	$15,000	$15,000	$15,000
Capital gain	$0	$0	$5,000

Calculation of Terminal Loss or Recapture of CCA	***A***	***B***	***C***
Capital cost	$15,000	$15,000	$15,000
Minus: CCA (1994–1999)	– $ 4,000	– $ 4,000	– $ 4,000
UCC at beginning of 2000	$11,000	$11,000	$11,000
Minus the lesser of:			
The capital cost of $15,000 and the proceeds of disposition	$5,000	$15,000	$15,000
Terminal loss (or recapture)	$6,000	($4,000)	($4,000)

Example A: Kirk does not have a capital gain, but he does have a terminal loss of $6,000 that he can deduct from his business income in 2000.

Example B: Kirk does not have a capital gain, but he does have recapture of CCA of $4,000 that he has to include in his business income in 2000.

Example C: Kirk has a capital gain of $5,000 and he has recapture of CCA of $4,000 that he has to include in his business income in 2000.

Eligible capital property

This section is used to report capital gains or capital losses from the disposition of eligible capital property.

Eligible capital property is property that does not physically exist but that gives you a lasting economic benefit — for example, goodwill, customer lists, trademarks, and milk quotas.

The taxation rules for eligible capital property are similar to those for depreciable property.

When Does a Disposition Occur?

A disposition usually occurs with an event or transaction where you relinquish possession, control, and all other aspects of property ownership.

You can also have a *deemed disposition* where you are considered to have disposed of property even though you did not actually sell it. This can happen when property is stolen or appropriated, or if there has been a change in the property's use.

The following are examples of cases, other than an outright sale, in which you are considered to have disposed of capital property:

- You exchange one property for another.
- You give property (other than cash) as a gift.
- You convert shares or other securities in your name.
- You settle or cancel a debt owed to you.
- You transfer certain property to a trust.
- Your property is expropriated.
- Your property is stolen or destroyed.
- An option that you hold to buy or sell property expires.
- A corporation redeems or cancels shares or other securities that you hold (you will usually be considered to have received a dividend, the amount of which will be shown on a T5 slip).
- You change all or part of the property's use (for example, the change of use of your primary residence to a rental property).
- You leave Canada (see Chapter 4, "Leaving Canada" section).
- The owner of the property dies (see Chapter 4, "The Sure Things: Death and Taxes" section).

In some of the instances noted above, you will be deemed to have disposed of your property even though you did not receive any proceeds. This, as you might be thinking, may make it difficult to pay the resulting tax bill! Be sure to visit a tax professional to understand the consequences before you cause a deemed disposition.

How to Calculate a Taxable Capital Gain or Loss

To calculate any capital gain or loss, you need to know the following three amounts:

- The proceeds of disposition
- The adjusted cost base (ACB)
- The costs related to selling your property.

To calculate your capital gain or loss, subtract the total of your property's ACB and any outlays and expenses involved in selling your property, from the proceeds of disposition.

Calculation of adjusted cost base

The adjusted cost base of a property is usually the cost of your property plus any expenses to acquire it, such as commissions and legal fees. The cost of a capital property is its actual or deemed cost, depending on the type of property and how you acquired it. It also includes capital expenditures such as the cost of additions and improvements to the property. You cannot add current expenses, such as maintenance and repair costs, to the cost base of a property. In some cases, special rules may apply that will allow you to consider the cost of a property to be an amount other than its actual cost. This section explains these rules.

Identical properties

Properties of a group are considered to be identical if each property in the group is the same as all the others. The most common example of this occurs when you have shares of the same class of the capital stock of a corporation or units of a mutual fund trust. You may buy and sell several identical properties at different prices over a period of time. If you do this, to determine your ACB you have to calculate the average cost of each property in the group at the time of each purchase. You determine the average cost by dividing the total cost of identical properties purchased (usually the cost of the property plus any expenses involved in acquiring it) by the total number of identical properties owned.

A bond, debenture, or similar debt obligation that a debtor issues is considered to be identical, for tax purposes, to another if the same debtor issues both; and all the attached rights are the same. The principal amount of individual debt obligations being the same is not enough for such debts to be considered identical properties. They must still meet the two conditions listed above.

Let's say that over the years, Buffy bought and sold shares of Mudgee Ltd. Table 13-1 shows how the ACB of her shares changes after each purchase.

Table 13-1 Calculating the ACB of Identical Properties

Transaction	*A (Cost)*	*B Number of Shares*	*A/B ACB*
Purchase in 1977 @ $15/share	$1,500	100	$15.00
Purchase in 1982 @ $20/share	+ $3,000	+ 150	
New average cost	= $4,500	= 250	= $18.00
Sale in 1995	– $3,600	– 200	
Average cost	= $900	= 50	= $18.00
Purchase in 2000: $21/share	+ $7,350	+ 350	
New average cost	= $8,250	= 400	= $20.63

Partial dispositions of capital property

When you sell only part of a property, you have to divide the adjusted cost base (ACB) of the property between the part you sell and the part you keep.

Graeme owns 100 hectares of vacant land with a cost base of $100,000. He decides to sell 25 hectares of this land. Since 25 is ¼ of 100, Graeme calculates ¼ of the total ACB as follows:

Total ACB	$100,000
Minus: The ACB of the part he sold ($100,000 × ¼)	– 25,000
The ACB of the part he kept	= $75,000

Therefore, Graeme's ACB is $25,000 for the 25 hectares he sold.

Proceeds of disposition

The proceeds of disposition is usually the amount you received or will receive for your property. In most cases, it refers to the sale price of the property. This could also include compensation you received for property that has been destroyed, expropriated, or stolen.

Selling costs

These are costs that you incurred to sell a capital property. You can deduct outlays and expenses from your proceeds of disposition when calculating your capital gain or capital loss. You cannot, however, reduce your other income by claiming a deduction for these outlays and expenses. These types of expenses include fixing-up expenses, finders' fees, commissions, brokers' fees, surveyors' fees, legal fees, transfer taxes, and advertising costs.

Calculation of taxable capital gains

You have a capital gain when you sell, or are considered to have sold, a capital property for more than its ACB plus the outlays and expenses related to the sale of the property. For transactions occuring after February 27, 2000, you have to report two-thirds of your capital gains as income on your return. Capital gains, once reduced to their inclusion amount, are called *taxable capital gains.*

For the years 1990 to February 27, 2000, you were required to include three-quarters of your capital gains in income on your return. For the years 1988 and 1989, the inclusion rate was two-thirds. For the years 1972 to 1987, the inclusion rate was half. Prior to 1972, capital gains were not taxable.

Calculation of allowable capital losses

You have a capital loss when you sell, or are considered to have sold, a capital property for less than its ACB plus the outlays and expenses related to the sale of the property. For transactions occuring after February 27, 2000, you can deduct two-thirds of your capital losses, or your *allowable capital losses*, against the current year's taxable capital gains. (For transactions prior to February 28, the inclusion rate is three-quarters.)

Unused allowable capital losses become net capital losses and can be carried back three years or forward indefinitely. They can be used against taxable capital gains in carryover years, and will reduce taxable income in those years.

Let's say that in March 2000, Lynne sold 1,000 shares of ABC Public Corporation of Canada for $7,500. She received the full proceeds at the time of the sale and paid a commission of $80. The adjusted cost base of the shares is $3,500. Lynne calculates her capital gain as follows:

Calculation of Capital Gain on Sale of ABC Co. Shares	
Proceeds of disposition	$7,500
Less: Adjusted cost base	$3,500
Less: Outlays and expenses on disposition	$80
Equals: Capital gain	$3,200

Because only two-thirds of the capital gain is taxable, Lynne reports $2,133.33 as her taxable capital gain on her return. When you sell, or are considered to have sold, a capital property for less than its ACB plus the outlays and expenses involved in selling the property, you have a capital loss. You can deduct two-thirds of your capital losses from your taxable capital gains. You should use schedule 3 to calculate and report all your capital gains and losses on your tax return. Do not include any capital gains or losses in your business or property income, even if you used the property for your business.

Before 1972, capital gains were not taxed. Therefore, if you sold capital property in 2000 that you owned before 1972, remove any capital gains accrued before 1972 when you calculate your capital gain or loss.

Sale of a Principal Residence

When you sell your home, you may realize a capital gain. If the property was your principal residence for every year you owned it, you don't have to report the sale on your return. However, if at any time during the period you owned the property it was not your principal residence, you may have to report all or a portion of the capital gain. In this section we'll explain the meaning of a principal residence, how you designate a property as such, and what happens when you sell it.

If after reading this section, you need more information, read the CCRA's interpretation bulletin IT-120 "Principal Residence."

What is your principal residence?

Your *principal residence* can be any of the following: a house, a cottage, a condominium, an apartment in an apartment building, an apartment in a duplex, or a trailer, mobile home, or houseboat. A property qualifies as your principal residence for any year if it meets the following four conditions:

- It is one of the above properties.
- You own the property alone or jointly with another person.
- You, your spouse, your former spouse, or any of your children lived in it at some time during the year.
- You designate the property as your principal residence.

The land on which your home is located can be part of your principal residence. Usually, the amount of land that you can consider as part of your principal residence is limited to one-half hectare (about one acre). However, if you can show that you need more land to use and enjoy your home, you can consider more than this amount as part of your principal residence — for example, this may happen if the minimum lot size imposed by a municipality at the time you bought the property was larger than one-half hectare.

Can you have more than one principal residence?

For 1982 and later years, you can only designate one home as your family's principal residence for each year. If you were married or were 18 or older, your family includes the following: you, a person who throughout the year was your spouse (unless you were separated for the entire year under the terms of a court order or a written agreement), and your children (other than a child who was married during the year or who was 18 or older). If you were not married or were not 18 or older, your family also includes the following: your mother and your father, and your brothers and sisters (who were not married or 18 or older during the year). For 1993 and later years, a spouse includes a common-law spouse. Therefore, common-law spouses cannot designate different housing units as a principal residence for any year after 1992. For years before 1982, more than one housing unit per family can be designated as principal residences. Therefore, for these years a husband and wife can designate different principal residences.

Disposition of your principal residence

When you sell your home or when you are considered to have sold it, usually you do not have to report the sale on your return and you do not have to pay tax on any gain from the sale. This is the case if the home was your principal residence for every year you owned it. If your home was not your principal residence for every year you owned it, you have to report the part of the capital gain on the property that relates to the years for which you did not designate the property as your principal residence.

If you have a loss at the time you sell or are considered to have sold your home, because your home is considered personal-use property, you are not allowed to claim the loss.

If only part of your home qualifies as your principal residence and you used the other part to earn or produce income, you have to split the selling price between the part you used for your principal residence and the part you used for other purposes (for example, rental or business purposes). You can do this by using square metres or the number of rooms, as long as the split is reasonable. Report only the gain on the part you used to produce income. Use form T2091 to designate a property as a principal residence. This form will help you calculate the number of years that you can designate your home as your principal residence, as well as the part of the capital gain, if any, that you have to report.

Complete form T2091, if you did either of the following:

- Sold, or were considered to have sold, your principal residence, or any part of it.
- Granted someone an option to buy your principal residence, or any part of it.

You only have to include form T2091 with your return if you have to report a capital gain.

Calculation of the exempt portion of a capital gain on your principal residence

If you sell a property on which all of the capital gain is not tax-exempt, the following formula calculates what portion of the gain is tax-exempt.

$$\text{Exempt gain equals } \frac{1 + \text{number of years the home was designated as principal residence}}{\text{total number of years you owned the home after 1971}} \times \text{gain}$$

Since an individual can only designate one home as a principal residence for any given year, the 1 + in the formula allows you to protect the principal residence exemption when you sell and purchase a home in the same year.

Say Tiffany is in the process of moving from Toronto to Vancouver, and must sell both her city home and her cottage. She primarily uses the cottage on the weekends to get away from the city smog and traffic. She purchased her city home in 1987 for $120,000, and anticipates that she can sell it for $200,000. She purchased her cottage in 1990 for $100,000, and her realtor assures her that she will get $150,000 for it.

She knows about the principal residence exemption, but isn't sure how it will apply to her since she has owned two homes since she purchased the cottage in 1990.

The first thing Tiffany needs to do is calculate the gain per year from the sale of each property.

	City Home	*Cottage*
Proceeds	$200,000	$150,000
ACB	$120,000	$100,000
Gain	$80,000	$50,000
Number of years	14	11
Gain per year	$5,714	$4,545

Since the city home has a larger gain per year, Tiffany should designate as many years as possible to the city home. Now, initially you would think she should designate 14 years to the city home and none to the cottage. However, remember the formula's 1 + rule. Because of that rule she should designate 13 years to the city home and 1 to the cottage. The result is as follows:

	City Home	*Cottage*
Gain	$80,000	$50,000
Exemption	($80,000)[1]	($9,090)[2]
Capital gain	$0	$40,910

1. (1+13)/14 × $80,000 = $80,000
2. (1+1)/11 × $50,000 = $9,090

Sale of Qualified Small Business Shares

You may be eligible to shelter all or a portion of your gain up to $500,000 from the disposition of qualified small business corporation (QSBC) shares. The next obvious question is, What is a qualified small business corporation share? A share of a corporation will be considered to be a *qualified small business corporation share* if all the following conditions are met:

- At the time of sale, it was a share of the capital stock of a small business corporation, and it was owned by you, your spouse, or a partnership of which you were a member; *and*
- At least 90 percent of the company's assets at fair market value were used by the corporation in its active business, or
- At least 90 percent of its assets are shares or debts in related corporations that meet the 90-percent rule, or
- A combination of assets and shares meet the 90-percent rule.

- Throughout the 24 months immediately before the share was disposed of, while it was owned by you, it was a share of a Canadian-controlled private corporation and more than 50 percent of the fair market value of the assets of the corporation were the following:
  - Used mainly in an active business carried on primarily in Canada by the Canadian-controlled private corporation, or by a related corporation;
  - Certain shares or debts of connected corporations; or
  - A combination of these two types of assets; and
- Throughout the 24 months immediately before the share was disposed of, no one other than you, a partnership of which you were a member, or a person related to you owned the share.

You may find it difficult to determine whether your shares qualify for the capital gains exemption. Be sure to visit a tax professional if you think your shares may qualify.

If you own qualified small business shares, you should consider crystallizing your qualified small business corporation capital gains exemption now — you never know when the CCRA might repeal the exemption. Generally, when you dispose of qualified small business shares, you report any capital gain or loss realized in this section of schedule 3. Up to $500,000 of this gain (or $333,333 taxable gain) will be offset by a deduction on line 254, provided you haven't used up your $500,000 exemption in prior years.

Sale of Qualified Farm Property

If you have a capital gain when you sell qualified farm property, you may be eligible for a $500,000 capital gains exemption. The property will qualify if it meets one of two tests:

- The property must be used by you, your spouse, child, or your grandparents in the 24 months immediately before you sell, and your gross revenue from the farming business for a minimum of two years exceeds your income from all other sources.
- The property must be used by a corporation or partnership where the principal business is farming, for a minimum of 24 months prior to the sale.

Qualified farm property includes the following:

- An interest in a family-farm partnership that you or your spouse own.
- A share of the capital stock of a family-farm corporation that you or your spouse own.
- Real property, such as land and buildings; and eligible capital property, such as milk and egg quotas.

The farm property must be owned by you, your spouse, or a family farm partnership. If a corporation or partnership carries on the farming business, the property will qualify if you, your spouse, or your child is an active participant in the business and more than 50 percent of the fair market value of the property is used in the business of farming. Generally, when you dispose of qualified farm property, you report any capital gain or loss realized in this section of schedule 3. If you dispose of farm property, other than qualified farm property, report any capital gain or loss in the section "Real Estate and Depreciable Property" on schedule 3. For more information on what is considered to be qualified farm property, see the CCRA's Farming Income and NISA guides.

The Lifetime Capital Gains Exemption

Prior to February 23, 1994, everyone had a $100,000 personal capital gains exemption. Many elected, on form T664, to use up their exemption to trigger a capital gain. The election increased the adjusted cost base so that when the property was actually sold, the taxable capital gain was that much less. If you filed form T664, you are considered to have sold your capital property at the end of February 22, 1994, and to have immediately reacquired it on February 23, 1994. The ACB of your property on February 23, 1994, depends on the type of property for which you filed an election. If you filed an election for capital property, your ACB is usually the amount you designated as proceeds of disposition on form T664.

If you sold capital property during 2000, be sure to check back to your 1994 tax return to see if you elected to trigger this gain and increase your adjusted cost base. You don't want to report a higher gain than necessary and pay too much tax.

Cumulative Net Investment Loss

The intent of the *Cumulative Net Investment Loss (CNIL)* account is to prevent a person taking advantage of various "shelter-type" deductions, from compounding his advantage with a capital gains exemption claim.

The CNIL account balance is calculated as follows:

Aggregate investment income (for the years ending after 1987)	–	Aggregate investment expense (for the years ending after 1987).

If the result is a negative balance, that amount is your CNIL account balance. If the result is a positive balance, your CNIL account balance is nil.

Why is the CNIL so important? The CNIL account will limit the capital gains exemption allowable on the disposition of QSBC shares to the extent that you have deducted losses on passive investments. The CNIL account tracks lifetime losses on these types of investments to the extent that they exceed lifetime income from those same investments. (Note: Passive investments are general investments in assets you acquire neither as trading inventory nor for use in carrying on a business.)

For more information on CNIL and how it impacts on your capital gains exemption, make sure you read through Chapter 17, especially the section called "Line 254: Capital Gains Deduction."

The Capital Gains Reserve

When you sell a capital property, you usually receive full payment at that time. However, sometimes you receive the amount over a number of years. For example, you may sell a capital property for $50,000, receiving $10,000 when you sell it and the remaining $40,000 over the next four years. When this happens, you can claim a reserve. Usually, a reserve allows you to report only a portion of the capital gain in the year you receive the proceeds of disposition. Most people can claim a reserve only when they dispose of a capital property. Generally, you cannot claim a reserve if the following apply to you:

- You were not a resident of Canada at the end of the taxation year, or at any time in the following year.
- You were exempt from paying tax at the end of the taxation year, or at any time in the following year.
- You sold the capital property to a corporation that you control in any way.

How to calculate and report a reserve

To claim a reserve, you still calculate your capital gain for the year as the proceeds of disposition minus the adjusted cost base and the outlays and expenses involved in selling the property. From this, you deduct the amount of your reserve for the year. What you end up with is the part of the capital gain that you have to report in the year of disposition.

To deduct a reserve in any year, you have to complete form T2017 "Summary of Reserves on Dispositions of Capital Property." The information provided on the back of the form explains the limits on the number of years for which you can claim a reserve, and the amount of the reserve you can deduct.

If you claimed a reserve in the previous year, include that reserve when you calculate your capital gains for the current year. For example, if you claimed a reserve in 1998, you have to include it in your capital gains for 1999. If you still have an amount payable to you after 1999, you may be able to calculate and deduct a new reserve, which you include in your capital gains for 2000. A capital gain from a reserve brought into income qualifies for the capital gains deduction only if the original capital gain was from a property eligible for the deduction.

The amount of reserve you can take in any particular year is the lesser of the following:

(Proceeds not yet due/Total proceeds) × Gain

1/5 of the gain × (4 – # of preceding taxation years ending after disposition)

Did you catch all that? Let's take Tom, for example. In 2000, Tom sold capital property for proceeds of $200,000. However, he only received $20,000 up front. The remaining $180,000 is not due until 2001. The adjusted cost base of the property was $150,000.

The total gain from the sale of the property is $50,000 ($200,000 proceeds less cost base of $150,000). However, since Tom did not receive all the proceeds in 2000, he is eligible to claim a reserve.

In 2000 his reserve is the lesser of the following:

($180,000/$200,000) × $50,000 = $45,000

(1/5 × $50,000) × (4 – 0) = $40,000

Therefore, in 2000 he can shelter a portion of the $50,000 gain with a $40,000 reserve. He will report only $10,000 of the gain in 2000.

In 2001, he will report another reserve. Keep in mind that he must include the $40,000 reserve he claimed in 2000 in his income for 2001. His 2001 reserve is the lesser of the following:

Nil/$200,000 × $50,000 = $Nil

(1/5 × $50,000) × (4 – 1) = $30,000.

Therefore in 2001, Tom cannot claim any reserve and must include in his income the remaining $40,000 of the capital gain.

You do not have to claim the maximum reserve in the year. You can claim any amount up to the maximum. However, the amount you claim in a later year for the disposition of a particular property cannot be more than the amount you claimed for that property in the immediately preceding year.

Chapter 14

Reporting Other Income on Your Return

In This Chapter

- Reporting retiring allowances
- Reporting scholarships, bursaries, and research grants
- Reporting death benefits
- Reporting legal awards
- Reporting foreign income
- Reporting other income

Here we cover line 130 on the tax return. Just one little line — pretty simple, right? Well, yes and no. You see, we like to call line 130 the "catch-all," since it's basically used to report income that does not belong anywhere else on the tax return. So the bad news is, if you've skipped directly to this chapter hoping you can report all your income here, you're out of luck. If you've read through the chapters leading up to this, and you still can't figure out where to report some particular income you've received, you've come to the right place. This chapter covers some of the most common types of income to be reported on line 130. If you have another form of income and are unsure whether it is taxable, contact the CCRA for help.

And don't worry if you tally up a long list of this type of income — if you're preparing your return by hand, identify the type of income you're reporting in the space to the left of line 130. If you have more than one type of income, attach a note to your return giving the details.

Retiring Allowances

Don't be confused by the term *retiring allowance* — it doesn't apply only to payments you receive when you retire. In fact, it also includes what people normally refer to as "severance" or "termination" pay, as well as to a court award or settlement for wrongful dismissal. Legal awards are discussed in more detail below.

Eligible allowance

Retiring allowances are taxable. However, *eligible* retiring allowances may be rolled directly into your RRSP, tax-free. Confused? Let's take a step back.

When you leave your employer and receive a retiring allowance, a portion of your payment can be transferred into your RRSP. If you choose to do this, you include the full amount of the allowance on line 130 — but a deduction is given on line 208 for the amount transferred to your RRSP. So, how much can you transfer? Well, that depends on when you started working with your employer and how long you have worked there.

The Canada Customs and Revenue Agency (CCRA) sets limits on the amount of retiring allowance you can roll into your RRSP. The limit is calculated as follows:

- $2,000 per year, or part year of service prior to 1996, plus
- $1,500 per year, or part year of service prior to 1989 in which you had no vested interest in any employer's contributions to a registered pension plan, or deferred profit-sharing plan.

Let's suppose Susan left her employer in 2000 and received a $50,000 termination payment. She had started working there in 1985 and had joined the pension plan in 1987.

The amount she can transfer to her RRSP is calculated this way:

$2,000 × 11 years (1985 to 1995)	$22,000
$1,500 × 2 years (1985 to 1987)	$3,000
Qualifying allowance	$25,000

The good news is that *you* don't have to calculate the portion you can transfer to your RRSP. Your employer calculates this amount and reports it in box 26 of your T4A slip.

The amount that can be transferred to your RRSP is over and above your regular RRSP contribution limit. You can still make your maximum RRSP contribution in addition to this *special contribution*. It's not critical that the allowance be transferred directly to your RRSP when it is paid out. However, you must contribute the funds to your RRSP within 60 days following the end of the year in which you receive the payment. For allowances received in 2000, this means the contribution must be made by March 1, 2001.

If you don't make the contribution within 60 days following the end of the year, you lose your right to this special contribution. It is a one-time deal that cannot be carried forward.

If you choose not to transfer your qualifying allowance directly to your RRSP, tax will be withheld from your payment. Table 14-1 lists the withholding tax rates:

Table 14-1 Withholding Rates on Lump Sum Payments

Payment	*Withholding Tax Rate*
0 – $5,000	10 percent
$5,000 – $15,000	20 percent
> $15,000	30 percent

Keep in mind that even though withholding taxes were taken off your retiring allowance, the full amount of the allowance still has to be reported on your tax return. And since the withholding tax rates are probably less than your actual marginal tax rate for the year, be prepared to pay some additional taxes when you file your tax return!

If your employer gives you the option of spreading the retiring allowance over a number of periods, avoid taking a payment of more than $15,000 at one time. This way, you can lower the amount of tax withheld. Of course, this will probably mean that you'll owe tax in April. In addition, spreading the retiring allowance over a number of years can help keep your taxable income at a lower level each year, and may prevent you from being bumped up to a higher tax bracket!

You can avoid withholding tax by transferring your eligible retiring allowance directly to your RRSP. This involves filling out some forms (of course) — namely a TD2 — but your employer can provide these.

Ineligible allowance

Any allowance received in excess of the amount you can transfer to your RRSP is considered to be an ineligible allowance. This amount is reported in box 27 of your T4A, and you must add this to your eligible retiring allowance and report it on line 130.

What is not a retiring allowance?

Obviously, retiring allowances can be very beneficial when they can be rolled over on a tax-free basis to an RRSP or RPP. It is for this reason that Canadians want to receive retiring allowances when they leave a job. However, it's important to note that not all amounts will qualify as a retiring allowance. A retiring allowance does not include the following:

- A superannuation or pension benefit
- An amount received as a result of an employee's death
- Payments for accumulated vacation leave
- A payment made in lieu of a termination notice
- Payments made for human rights violations under human rights legislation.

Scholarships, Bursaries, and Research Grants

Did you receive a scholarship, fellowship, bursary, or prize for achievement in your field of endeavour this year? First off, congratulations! Second, these amounts must be included in your income to the extent that the total for the year exceeds $3,000. (The $3,000 exemption is obviously a little congratulations from the CCRA as well.)

If you receive a scholarship, fellowship, or bursary, you should receive a T4A slip for the full amount received. This total is reported in box 28 of your slip, and there should be a footnote stating that the amount actually relates to a scholarship, bursary, or fellowship, so you'll be entitled to the $3,000 exemption.

The first $3,000 received is not taxable. You should calculate the total amount received in the year, deduct $3,000, and report any balance on line 130.

The $3,000 exemption does not apply to the following:

- Amounts withdrawn from a registered education savings plan (RESP)
- Research grants
- Training allowances under the *National Training Act*
- Amounts received in the course of a business or employment.

What are scholarships and bursaries?

Scholarships and *bursaries* are amounts given to students to help them pay for school — generally a university, college, or similar educational institution. They may apply to any field of study, including an academic discipline (such as the arts or sciences), a professional program (such as law or medicine), or a trade or skill (such as plumbing or carpentry). Normally, a student is not expected to do specific work for the payer in exchange for a scholarship or bursary.

A scholarship from your employer given with the condition that you return to work after completing your studies is not a scholarship at all! In fact, you must report the amount received as employment income on line 104. Say goodbye to the $3,000 exemption — 100 percent of this amount is taxable

What is a fellowship?

Fellowships are like scholarships or bursaries, in that they're given to students to help them pursue their education. The difference is that in most cases they are given to graduate students by a university, charitable organization, or similar body. Fellowships are generally awarded for doctoral studies and postdoctoral work. Normally, fellowships are included in income to the extent that they exceed $3,000, and are reported on line 130. However, when the primary purpose of the fellowship is not education and training but rather carrying out research, the award is considered to be a research grant. Research grants are discussed in more detail below.

If a student receives a genuine loan to assist in financing education, the loan is not considered to be a scholarship, fellowship, or bursary. In other words, the loan is not taxable. For a genuine loan to exist, provisions must generally be made for repayment within a reasonable time.

What is a prize in my field of endeavour?

A *prize in your field of endeavour* sounds pretty impressive, right? Although we're not talking about the Academy Awards, prizes do come in all shapes and sizes. Prizes that fall under this heading are awarded for success in an area of effort. It is a result of accomplishment, rather than luck. For example, if you achieve the highest mark on your bar exam, the $1,000 you receive will qualify as a prize. In this case, you wouldn't have to report anything on your tax return because up to $3,000 of prizes in your field of endeavour can be received tax-free. Take the $1,000 and enjoy it.

These types of prizes should not be confused with prescribed prizes, which are not taxable. That is, even if the prize exceeds $3,000, no tax will result. A prescribed prize is a prize recognized by the public and awarded for achievement in the arts, sciences, or for public service. These prizes are exempt from tax altogether, as long as the amount cannot be considered compensation for services rendered or to be rendered. Although this exemption is aimed at high-profile awards, such as the Nobel Prize, the definition is general enough for other prizes, such as those in recognition of community service, to be exempt from tax.

What is a research grant?

Did you receive a *research grant,* money given during the year to help pay expenses necessary to carry out a research project? If so, you must report any amount you received in excess of expenses in income. Research grants do not qualify for the $3,000 exemption. Grant money received in excess of expenses is classified as employment income and is reported on line 104 of your tax return. If you've been given a research grant this year, you should receive a T4A. The amount you receive is reported in box 28, and the bottom of the slip should indicate the amount related to a research grant.

Death Benefits

A death benefit is an amount paid on the death of an employee to a spouse or other beneficiary, in recognition of service in an office or employment. The first $10,000 of a death benefit paid in respect of any one employee is exempt from tax.

Death benefits paid under the Canada or Quebec Pension Plans do not qualify for the $10,000 exemption.

The spouse gets first use of the $10,000 exemption. If the spouse receives less than $10,000, and there are other beneficiaries who receive funds, the remaining exemption must be split among the other recipients.

Legal Awards

A retiring allowance includes an amount received as a *result of loss of office or employment*. So what does this mean? If you received payment from a lawsuit or out-of-court settlement, for whatever reason, and the complaint arose in relation to your employment, this amount is taxable. For example, amounts paid on account of or in lieu of damages — that is, damages for loss of self-respect, humiliation, mental anguish, hurt feelings, and so on — may be a retiring allowance if the payment arose from a loss of office or employment. The easiest way to look at it is like this: If you sue your employer and you receive payment, it's taxable. If you continue to work, it's included in employment income; otherwise, it's a retiring allowance.

If you win a lawsuit and receive payment that's classified as a retiring allowance, you can deduct any legal expenses incurred. But you can only deduct up to the amount of the allowance you include in income. That is, if you roll the entire amount into your RRSP, you can't deduct any costs. Any legal costs you can't deduct can be carried forward for the next seven years, to offset any retiring allowance you may receive in the future.

Some specific legal payments are excluded from income altogether. For example, all amounts received by a taxpayer or the taxpayer's dependants that qualify as special or general damages for personal injury or death are excluded from income, regardless of the fact that the amount of such damages may be determined with reference to the loss of the taxpayer's earnings. Examples of amounts received as a result of personal injury or death include the following:

- Out-of-pocket expenses such as medical and hospital bills
- Accrued or future loss of earnings
- Pain and suffering
- Shortened expectation of life
- Loss of financial support caused by the death of the supporting individual.

Foreign Income

Keep in mind that if you're a Canadian resident, you're taxable on your entire worldwide income. So if you received money from another country, and no other line numbers are appropriate for reporting your income, you can include the amount on line 130. Make sure you remember to convert it to Canadian dollars first!

More Other Income

In this chapter we've covered some of the more common types of other income. But there's more! Fortunately, you don't have to remember to include these other types of income on your tax return, since you'll receive T slips for them. Simply follow the instructions on your T slips, and you can't go wrong! Table 14-2 lists more types of other income you will have to report on your tax return, and the type of slip on which they'll be reported.

Table 14-2 More Types of Other Income

Type of Income	*Information Slip*
Annuity benefits from an RRIF	T4RIF, box 16
Deemed receipt upon death from an RRIF	T4RIF, box 18
Deemed receipt upon deregistration from an RRIF	T4RIF, box 20
Other income from an RRIF	T4RIF, box 22
Lump sum payments from a registered pension plan	T4A, box 18
Lump sum payments from a deferred profit-sharing plan	T4A, box 18
General annuity	T4A, box 24
Other income	T4A, box 28 or T3, box 26 less box 31 and box 35
Other payments from a deferred profit-sharing plan	T4A, box 28
Maternity allowance	T4A, box 28
Patronage allocations	T4A, box 30
Accumulated income payments from a Registered Education Savings Plan (RESP)	T4A, box 40
Educational assistance payments from an RESP	T4A, box 42
Lump sum pension benefits	T3, box 22
Pension benefits	T3, box 36
Other amounts from a retirement compensation arrangement	T4A-RCA, boxes 14, 16, 18 and 20

Chapter 15

Dealing with Self-Employment Income and Taxes

In This Chapter:

- Understanding the tax realities of self-employment
- Knowing the accrual method of accounting
- Sorting out GST issues if you're running your own show
- Reporting your self-employment income and expenses on your tax return
- Using capital cost allowance as a tax deduction
- Lines 137 and 164 — Professional income
- Lines 141 and 168 — Farming income
- Lines 143 and 170 — Fishing income

Self-employment means running your own business. You are an entrepreneur — someone who accepts the risks and enjoys the rewards of business. In being self-employed, or in being an entrepreneur, you are responsible, either alone or with partners, for operating a business. You need to ensure sufficient cash is available to pay the bills and the salaries of your employees. You hope, after all the expenses of the business are taken care of, that there is something left over for you to take home. The entrepreneur gets paid last!

There are many advantages to self-employment, including the tax savings component. While the tax saving is attractive, most people become self-employed because "they want to be their own boss."

The Tax Implications of Being Self-Employed

First, let's clear up the three fallacies regarding tax savings available from self-employment:

- Just because you don't receive T4s, T5s, and so on, reporting the income of your business does not mean you can understate your actual income when you prepare your tax return.
- You cannot deduct personal expenses in calculating your business's net income.
- If your activities are more like a hobby than a business, you are not considered self-employed.

We've all heard stories about self-employed individuals taking advantage, albeit unscrupulously, of their status. In fact, you have likely been involved in at least the first fallacy. Ever paid someone "cash" so they will charge you a lower price? Ever bought something when the clerk did not ring up the sale on the cash register? Do you think the person you paid is reporting your payment as income subject to tax?

How does self-employment save taxes?

The tax "win" from self-employment is that any expense you incur to build and run the business is generally deductible in computing your business income subject to tax. This is logical since every dollar you earn from the business will be taxed, so every dollar you spend on the business should be tax deductible. If you are running a business and incur a loss, the loss is deducted from other sources of income on your tax return. (An exception to this may be a loss incurred in operating a farm. Farming is discussed near the end of the chapter.)

Generally, self-employment offers you the opportunity to deduct more expenses than if you were employed. As detailed in Chapter 26, Tax Breaks for Employees, only certain employees can deduct expenses they incur to do their job. Even where an employee has the opportunity to deduct a lot of expenses, the self-employed person can usually deduct more. Refer to Chapter 27, Small Business Tax Planning, for ideas on how running your own business can be used to minimize the taxes you and your family pay!

Choosing a taxation year-end for your business

Your business *fiscal year* or *taxation year* does not have to be January 1 to December 31. It can be any 12-month period you choose. Actually, the first year of your business does not even have to be a full 12-month year. If you choose, it could be as short as a day!

Most businesses operate on a January 1 to December 31 taxation year. This is the simplest solution in terms of the complexities of reporting your business's income and expenses. If your business is cyclical or seasonal, it may make sense for you to elect to have a non-December 31 year-end. For example, if your business is extremely busy in late December, perhaps because of the holidays, you would prefer the taxation year-end to be later — say, the end of January or February. If you carry inventory, it would be easier to do a physical count at the end of January or February, rather than at the end of December. Besides, it is only accountants who spend New Year's Eve counting inventory!

Once you have filed a tax return with your business's taxation year-end noted, the taxation year becomes fixed. Though it is possible to change a taxation year-end, it can be difficult: first, you must have a pretty good reason for doing so, and second, you have to ask the CCRA for permission! Our advice is that you take your time in determining the appropriate taxation year-end for your business.

The Accrual Method of Accounting

Most self-employed individuals must use the *accrual method* of accounting in reporting their income and expenses earned from self-employment. (Some people prefer the spelling "a cruel method of accounting.") As we will see near the end of the chapter, self-employed individuals earning commission income or involved in farming and fishing have the option of using the cash method of accounting.

In using the accrual method of accounting:

- Income is recorded as it is *earned* — not when your customer pays you. In most cases you are considered to have earned your income when an invoice is issued. Where, at the end of your business's taxation year, you have invoiced customers but not yet received payment the sale would be recognized as being earned in the year. The unpaid amount would be considered an "accounts receivable" at the end of the taxation year.

- Expenses are recorded as they are *incurred* — whether or not you actually paid for the expense in the taxation year. Often the invoice date is used to indicate when the business has incurred an expense. If you received an invoice from a supplier that was dated for a purchase made prior to the taxation year-end, the expense would be recorded in your business's taxation year as it was incurred in the year. The unpaid amount at the end of the taxation year is considered an "accounts payable."

  The purchase of an inventory item for resale is not recognized as an expense or cost of your business until the inventory item is sold.

The Cash Method of Accounting

Another method of accounting is the *cash method.* Income is reported when cash is *received.* Business' expenditures are recorded when cash is *paid.* The recording of inventory is usually irrelevant when the cash method of accounting is used. (Again, you will see that a farm business is an exception. A farmer's "inventory" may need to be valued — even when the cash method is used. More on this near the end of the chapter!)

The Goods and Services Tax (7 percent GST)/ Harmonized Sales Tax (15 percent HST)

When you report your gross income from operating a business for tax purposes, you exclude the GST/HST and provincial retail sales taxes you have charged customers. These taxes are excluded because they do not represent income of your business. You are simply collecting these taxes on behalf of the federal and provincial governments.

You bill your customers GST on behalf of the federal government. HST is billed on behalf of the federal government and three provincial governments — New Brunswick, Nova Scotia, and Newfoundland. You will send the GST/HST you billed your customers to CCRA net of any GST/HST you have incurred on the expenses of operating your business. As you would expect, any provincial sales tax collected is remitted to the respective province.

As with the reporting of the income and expenses of your business, the GST/HST is accounted for on the accrual basis of accounting. Your GST/HST remittance to the government will be equal to:

- GST/HST you have billed to customers — which is not necessarily equal to the GST/HST you may have collected from customers
- Net of GST/HST that has been incurred or billed to your business by your suppliers — not necessarily what you have paid to your suppliers. If your business has incurred more GST/HST than it has billed then it is entitled to a GST refund.

If you do a lot of billing near the end of your GST/HST reporting period (say you report GST/HST on a monthly or quarterly basis) you may find that your GST/HST liability is due before you collect from your customers! If this is the case, your business will have to pay the GST/HST out of its own money. This cash flow problem can be avoided by doing more billing early in your GST/HST reporting period. By the end of the reporting period, you would hope, your customers will have paid you.

GST/HST — a consumer tax, not a business tax

The GST/HST is designed to be a consumer tax, not a business tax. Where you are entitled to register for GST/HST, the GST/HST is not a source of income or an expense of your business. GST/HST only becomes a cost of a business when the business cannot recover the GST/HST paid.

While in most cases the GST/HST is not an income or an expense, your business must still comply with the paperwork requirements and make the necessary GST/HST remittances. (Just what your business needs — more paperwork!)

Take a look at Gord. Gord is self-employed. His business, Gord's Fence and Deck, operates out of Sudbury, Ontario. Gord builds fences and decks for both residential and business customers. Gord recently completed two projects.

Project 1. Gord built a $3,000 deck in Lori's backyard. He charged her $3,000 plus taxes. He issued Lori a bill for $3,450. The bill was made up of his $3,000 fee (including materials), $240 in Ontario sales tax at 8 percent ($3,000 × 8% = $240) and $210 in GST ($3,000 × 7% = $210).

Project 2. Gord built a $3,000 fence to enclose the parking lot of Northern Paint Inc., a GST registrant. Gord also gave Northern a bill for $3,450 to take into account his fee plus Ontario sales tax and GST.

For income tax purposes, Gord will include only $6,000 in income — two jobs at $3,000 each. The additional funds he collected from Lori and Northern represent taxes he collected on behalf of the Ontario and federal governments. They are not his revenues, they are government revenues. Gord simply served as "an agent" for the governments and collected the tax on their behalf.

Lori's out-of-pocket cost for her deck is $3,450. She cannot recover the GST paid because she is not a GST registrant. Northern's true cost of its fence is only $3,240 — the $3,000 cost and the $240 in Ontario sales tax. The $210 it paid in GST will be recovered from the federal government because Northern is a GST registrant.

Does this seem fair? Why should Lori pay the GST while Northern effectively does not? As noted, the GST (as well as the HST) is designed to be a consumer tax — not a business tax — so, *yes, it is* fair. (Well it's fair in terms of tax theory. Whether we as consumers like paying the GST/HST is another story.) As Northern is a business, it should not, in the end, be subject to the GST — which it is not. If Northern were to sell Lori a can of paint, it would charge her both Ontario sales tax and GST. The GST Northern collected from Lori would be remitted to the federal government. Lori, again, would not be able to recover the GST. (Northern would, of course, remit the Ontario sales tax to the Ontario government.)

Say Northern sold the can of paint to a distributor, who then sold it to a wholesaler, who then sold it to a retail store, which then sold it to Lori. Once again Lori would pay GST and not be entitled to recover it. However, assuming all the businesses in the chain (Northern, distributor, wholesaler, retail store) are GST registrants, these businesses would effectively not have paid any GST on their purchases — the GST they paid would have all been refunded. This illustrates how the GST filters down through various businesses so that only the consumer ends up paying.

Who can register for the GST/HST?

Most businesses can register for GST/HST. It is usually to your advantage to be registered because this is the only way you can recover the GST/HST you have paid on your business expenses. Once registered, you must charge GST/HST on all your services. GST/HST registration is mandatory once your business's annual revenues are $30,000.

If you are starting a business register for GST/HST immediately, don't wait for your annual revenues to exceed $30,000. This way you can recover all the GST/HST you have paid on your business expenses. This will make the cost of your business 7 percent less if you operate in a non-HST province/territory and 15 percent less if your business operates in an HST province. Remember, in running a business, cash flow is one of the most important things to watch. So if you can save 7 percent (or 15 percent), why not?

Who cannot register for GST/HST?

You may have noticed that your doctor or dentist does not charge you GST/HST. Also, no GST/HST is added to your insurance premiums.

Your doctor and dentist are classed as health care providers. People in the health care field are not permitted to register for GST/HST. This is good news for you. Your doctor or dentist bills are 7 percent less expensive than if health care providers were permitted to register for GST/HST. However, as they are not registered for the GST/HST, they also are not entitled to recover the GST/HST they pay on their business expenses.

Fees for financial services do not have GST/HST added. The provision of insurance is considered a financial service, and that is why the premiums you pay for your life, disability, auto, home, and business insurance do not have GST/HST added. The same goes for commissions you pay on the purchase and sale of investments. Like health care providers, providers of financial services are not permitted to register for the GST/HST. However, some organizations provide both financial services and non-financial services. Take the example of your bank. It does not charge you GST/HST on your monthly bank services charges because these are considered financial services. However, when you request cheques to be printed, GST/HST is added to the printing cost because this is not considered a financial service. Banks register for the GST/HST, but only with respect to the non-financial services they provide.

Reporting Your Self-Employment Income and Expenses on Your Tax Return

This section begins with an overview on how your self-employed income and expense are reported on your tax return. We then delve into the completion of form T2124 "Statement of Business Activities." This is the tax form most self-employed individuals need to prepare in completing their tax return. Some bookkeeping tips are offered, and finally we comment on some of the special rules regarding the deductibility of certain business expenses.

Lines 135 and 162: Business income

Business income is the first line on the portion of your return dealing with self-employment income. (Refer to the self-employment section about one-third of the way down on page 2 of the tax return.) You report the gross income from your business on line 162 and the net income or loss of the business on line 135.

Lines 139 and 166: Commission income

Commission income is the third line of your return dealing with self-employment income. This only relates to *self-employed* individuals earning commission income. Do not get this confused with *employees* paid on a commission basis. If you are an employee earning commissions (as opposed to a salary or wages) you will receive a T4 slip from your employer after the end of each year. Like any employee, you will report this income on line 101 of your tax return. Depending on the conditions of your employment, you may be able to deduct some or all of the expenses you incur to earn your commission income. Refer to Chapter 26, Tax Breaks for Employees. If you earn self-employed commission income, you report this on line 166 on page 2 of your tax return, and your net income or loss from your business on line 139.

Whether you earn self-employed commission income or income from any type of self-employment (with the exception of professional, farming, or fishing income), you need to complete form T2124 "Statement of Business Activities." See below for details on form T2124.

Lines 137 and 164: Professional income

Professional income is the second line of the self-employment section on the tax return. If you are a "professional," you report your gross professional income on line 164, and the net income or loss on line 137. A professional needs to report the details of income and expenses on form T2032 "Statement of Professional Activities." This form is very similar to form T2124.

Later in this chapter we have included a section that looks at who or what a professional is and what is "special" about a professional reporting his or her net income on the tax return.

Farming income and fishing income

Line 141 and 168 is where a farmer reports his gross and net income figures. If operating a farm business, you need to complete form T2042 "Statement of Farming Activities" and include it with your tax return. Lines 143 and 170 are saved for reporting gross fishing income and net income. Form T2121 "Statement of Fishing Activities" is completed and sent with your tax return. All the tax stuff in respect of farming and fishing is discussed in the last two sections of this chapter. Stay tuned if you think they apply to your tax situation, we'll fill you in.

Form T2124 "Statement of Business Activities"

Most self-employed individuals should complete the tax form T2124 "Statement of Business Activities." The form serves as an income statement for the self-employed person. All income and expenses of the business are reported on the form. The "net" amount of income (income less expenses) is what the self-employed person pays tax on.

Form T2124 is broken down as follows:

- **Identification:** This is the easy stuff, such as business name and address, your social insurance number, the taxation year of your business, the product or service your business has to offer, and your Business Number or BN. You will have obtained a BN if you are registered for GST, are making payroll remittances to the CCRA, or needed a BN for Customs purposes in running an import/export business.

- **Sales, commissions, or fees (line c, line 8000 to 8299):** You record your self-employed sales, commissions, or fees earned on line 8299. You are responsible for ensuring the amount recorded is correct. You will not receive any T slips from your customers indicating how much you have billed them in the year; it is up to you to track and report the correct amount on your tax return. If you are earning self-employed commission income, you may find that some of your customers will send you an annual T4A slip reporting the amount of self-employed commissions paid to you in the year. Even if you do not receive a slip from all your customers, or if a slip reports an incorrect amount, it's your responsibility to ensure you report the correct amount of gross income earned.

  As noted earlier, the gross income reported is net of any Goods and Services Tax (GST at 7 percent) or Harmonized Sales Tax (HST at 15 percent) and/or provincial retail sales tax charged to customers. If a customer provides you with a deposit for goods or services to be provided after the taxation year-end, the deposit is not included in your gross income. The deposit is not yet considered income because the goods or services for which the deposit was received have not been provided as of the end of your business's taxation year. In other words, the income has not been *earned.* The deposit is treated as *deferred income,* and will be subject to tax in the year it is considered earned.

  The amount of your gross income is noted on line 8299 and is also reported on page 2 of your tax return. It goes on line 162 unless your income comes from self-employed commissions, in which case you report it on line 166.

- **Cost of goods sold (lines 8300 to 8518 and line d):** If you purchase goods for resale, the calculation of your cost of goods sold is detailed on lines 8300 to 8518 of form T2124. If your business only provides services, your cost of sales is zero.

- **Gross profit (line 8519 and line e):** The gross profit of your business (gross income less the cost of sales) is reported on line 8519.

- **Expenses of your business (lines 8521 to 9270):** You simply detail your expenses on these lines. The amounts noted on these lines are to exclude the GST/HST you have paid on these expenses, assuming your business is registered for GST/HST. If your business is not registered for GST/HST, the GST/HST you have paid in connection with these expenses gets included in the expense totals noted. The CCRA discloses on form T2124 that in reporting your business's expenses, you "enter business part only." This is the CCRA's way of saying, "Do not deduct any personal expenses in computing your self-employment income because it is against the law and you will pay dearly if we catch you — so watch out." Many of your business expenses will be 100-percent business use. If you advertise your business in the Yellow Pages, it would be fairly difficult to argue that a part of your advertising cost was personal in nature. However, you probably use your car for both business and personal use. Perhaps you operate your business from your home or apartment. If so, the costs of maintaining your "home office" need to be tracked. Only the "self-employment" or business use portion of your car and home office expenses can be claimed on form T2124. We take a look at deducting a portion of your car and home expenses later in the chapter.

- **Subtotal of expenses (space after line 9270):** Enter a subtotal of lines 8521 to 9270 here.

- **Other expenses of your business (line 9935 and 9936):** Here you report two items that we discuss later in the chapter:
  - Allowance on eligible capital property (line 9935)
  - Capital cost allowance (CCA) (line 9936).

- **Total business expenses (line f, line 9368)**
  - Simply another subtotal.

- **Net income (loss) before adjustments (line 9369)**

  This is the last line at the bottom of page 1 of form T2124. It is simply the gross profit of your business (line e, line 8519) less the total business expenses (line f, line 9366). The amount of this line is to be carried over to line g at the top of page 2 of the T2124.

- **Your share of line g above (line h)**

  If you are operating as a partnership, you put your share of line g on line h. For example, say you have a 33 1/3-percent interest in a contracting business that is operated by you and a couple of partners. If line g on your tax return reported $90,000, your 33 1/3-percent share would be $30,000. You would enter $30,000 on line h. (Refer to Chapter 27, Small Business Tax Planning, for detailed comments on operating a business through a partnership.)

  If your partnership has five or more partners, the reporting of your share of the partnership's income is very simple. There is no need for you to detail the income and expenses of the whole partnership. On behalf of all the partners, the partnership will have sent the CCRA a copy of the partnership's financial statements detailing the income and expenses of the partnership. The partnership will simply issue you a T5013 slip "Statement of Partnership Income" indicating your share of the partnership's net income. If you receive a T5013, simply report your share of the partnership's net income at line 9369 (net income [loss] before adjustment) on the T2124.

  The financial statements of the partnership will probably be prepared under accounting guidelines referred to as *generally accepted accounting principles* (GAAP). In some cases, GAAP guidelines differ from the tax rules. Therefore, it may be necessary to adjust the partnership's accounting income to arrive at the partnership's income for tax purposes. We expect your partnership will provide you with a reconciliation of income on a GAAP basis to income on a tax basis.

- **Minus other amounts deductible from your share of net partnership income (loss) (line i, line 9943):** If you were operating your business through a partnership and you incurred expenses on behalf of the partnership but were not reimbursed by the partnership, you claim these expenses on line i, line 9943. A worksheet (just below line 9946) is provided for you to note the detail of these expenses.

  Common examples of expenses claimed here by a partner are as follows:

  - The costs of meals and entertainment expenses incurred on behalf of customers or potential customers. (As we discuss below, only 50 percent of meals and entertainment expenses can be deducted for tax purposes.)
  - Business use portion of automobile expenses.

- **Net income (loss) after adjustments (line j):** Another subtotal — line h minus line i. (You would think that after this many calculations and subtotals you would be finished, but you're not!)

- **Business-use-of-home-office expenses (line 9945):** This is usually referred to as "home office expenses." If you operate your business from your home or apartment, a portion of the costs of owning or renting the premises is tax deductible. A work chart is provided about halfway down page 2 of the T2124. This chart will assist you in doing a detailed calculation of your home office expenses.

  We provide an example dealing with home office expenses later in the chapter.

- **Your net income (loss) (line 9946):** Finally, you've completed the form! Line minus line 9945. Once you have calculated your total net self-employed business income, you enter the "net" on line 135 on page 2 of the tax return. If you have earned self-employed commissions, the figure is entered in line 139.

Organizing your business by the book

To simplify the preparation of your tax return come tax time (not to mention the preparation of your GST/HST returns), the books and records of your business need to be organized throughout the year. There are a number of small business bookkeeping and accounting software products on the market, all of which work well. They go under names such as

QuickBooks, MYOB, and Simply Accounting. They are available in software stores and office supplies stores, such as Grand & Toy, Business Depot, Staples, and Office Place. (While you are at these stores, you may want to look at tax return preparation software. In Chapter 7 we discuss the various ways in which you can complete your tax return — one of which is to use tax preparation software.)

For those of you who are afraid of computers, we offer the following suggestions to assist you with your bookkeeping:

- **Sales, Commissions, and Fees:** Keeping track of your business's revenue is the easy part of your bookkeeping responsibilities. This is probably the figure you monitor the most because it determines the success of your business — and where your next meal is coming from! Most businesses document sales using numerically numbered invoices. Each invoice notes your business's name, address, phone and fax number, and e-mail address. If you are a GST/HST registrant, you must note your GST/HST registration number on the invoice. The customer gets a copy of the invoice, and you keep a copy. If you sell on credit, you file your copy of the invoice in a binder marked "unpaid" or "accounts receivable." This provides you with instant information on who hasn't paid you. Once an invoice is paid, simply move the invoice to another binder marked "paid." Bookkeeping is not rocket science.
- **Expenses:** Tracking your expenses requires a little more organization — but it is still not rocket science. Take a look at all the expense categories noted on lines 8521 to 9220 of the T2124. Some of these categories will apply to your business and some will not. We suggest you get yourself a bunch of large envelopes or file folders, and simply label them with the various expense categories that apply to your business. If there is a category you would like to have but it is not listed in lines 8521 to 9220, don't worry — simply make up a folder or envelope with the heading you desire. When doing your tax return, you can include this category under "Other" at line 9270. After your business has paid an invoice for an expense, simply file the invoice (or VISA, MasterCard, or AMEX receipt) in the respective envelope or file folder. When tax time rolls around, you simply add up the invoices in each envelope or file folder, and report the total on the appropriate line on form T2124. Remember to exclude the GST/HST from the total of your expenses if you are registered for the GST/HST. (You will need the total of the GST/HST paid to complete your GST/HST return!)

Some of the expenses you can deduct

As we will see, most business expenses are fully deductible in calculating your self-employed income subject to tax. But tax being tax it is always not that straightforward. In this next section, we comment on some of the more interesting rules dealing with the deductibility of expenses.

Overall deductibility

The general rule is that any expense incurred to operate a business is deductible. To be deductible, the amount of the expense must be "reasonable" in the circumstances. If the business pays your spouse a salary that is in excess of what you may have paid someone not related to you, the excess may be considered "unreasonable," should the CCRA query it. If an expense is determined to be unreasonable it is simply not allowed as a deduction.

Salary and payroll costs

In computing the total expenses of your business, a deduction cannot be taken for salaries, wages, fees paid to yourself, or amounts you have taken as "drawings." If you are in a partnership, again no expenses can be claimed in respect of salaries, wages, or fees paid to the partners or amounts drawn out by them. Sole proprietors pay tax on the amount of business income that remains after all other expenses have been recorded. Recall that at the beginning of this chapter we noted that the entrepreneur gets paid last. If you are in a partnership, the bottom-line income is shared among the partners on a basis as agreed to by the partners.

Prepaid expenses

As noted, under the accrual method of accounting, you recognize an expense when it is incurred, not when it is paid. Sometimes you pay for something where the benefit, or a portion of the benefit, of the payment will be in a future taxation year of your business. Take a look at your business insurance. Before the "insurance year" commences, a bill is sent out for the full premium. Say your business taxation year was January 1 to December 31. In September 2000 you arranged to purchase business insurance for the first time. You receive a bill for $1,200 to cover your business for the period October 1, 2000 to September 30, 2001. You make the full $1,200 payment in October 2000.

In preparing the T2124 for your business's 2000 taxation year, you can only deduct $300 for the insurance. This is because only one-quarter (the three months of October through December) of the insurance coverage falls into 2000. The remaining nine months (January to September 2001) of coverage falls into the business's next taxation year — January 1, 2001 to December 31, 2001. You will deduct the remaining $900 of the premium on your 2001 tax return.

Meals and entertainment expenses

Generally, only 50 percent of the amount of meals (including beverages) and entertainment expenses are deductible. Why 50 percent? 'Cause that's the rule!

Say you purchased tickets to a Calgary Stampeders game to take clients to — only 50 percent of the cost of the the tickets would be tax deductible.

In certain circumstances, 100 percent of meals and entertainment expenses can be deducted:

- meals and entertainment expenses provided in the ordinary course of a company's business. For example, a restaurant can deduct 100% of food costs incurred to provide dining services;
- costs incurred as part of fund-raising events for a charity;
- amounts reimbursed in full by a third party. For example, any meal and entertainment costs specifically billed to a customer are fully deductible if disclosed on your invoice, but the customer is only entitled to deduct 50% of the bill on his return;
- any meals and entertainment expenses included as a taxable benefit to an employee;
- costs incurred on behalf of all a business's employees. Christmas parties, staff member recognition get-togethers, and office summer barbeques are examples. This exemption to the 50 percent rule only applies to six such events held each calendar year.

Premiums for health care coverage

If self-employment income is your main source of income, your business can probably take a deduction for the cost of a health care plan. This would be claimed as part of the "other" category at line 9270 of the T2124.

Automobile expenses

Line 9281 is where you report the automobile expenses of your business. If your business needs a car or van that is used 100 percent of the time in the business — say, to make deliveries — the amount included on line 9281 is simply the total of the expenses to keep the vehicle on the road.

However, reporting automobile expenses gets a little more complicated when you use your own car. Your own car is likely driven for two reasons:

- To carry out your business activities
- Personal reasons.

The portion of your car expenses related to carrying out your business activities is deductible in computing your net income from self-employment. The portion of your expenses related to carrying out your business activities is determined using this formula:

$$\text{Total car expenses} \times \frac{\text{\# kilometres driven for self-employment in year}}{\text{\# kilometres driven in year}}$$

You can only deduct the "self-employment use" or "business use" portion of your automobile expenses in computing your net income from self-employment. It is essential that you track the kilometres you drive for self-employment so that, come tax time, you can complete the above formula.

If the CCRA has questions regarding the portion of your car expenses claimed on your T2124, they will want to see a log of your kilometres driven for purposes of operating your business. Get in the habit of having a log in the car. Every time you get in the car, you should make an entry of where you are going, where you have been, and the kilometres traveled. It will make things much easier if you ever need to respond to a CCRA query.

Car expenses include the following:

- Fuel (gas, propane, and oil)
- Repairs and maintenance
- Insurance
- Licence and registration fees
- Leasing costs
- Interest incurred on a loan to purchase a car.

If you own you car and you use it at least partially to carry out business activities you will be able to claim capital cost allowance or CCA. We discuss CCA in detail in a section later in this chapter titled "Capital Cost Allowance (CCA)."

Restrictions on certain automobile expenses

As noted above, where you are entitled to deduct a portion of your automobile costs, you deduct only the "business use" portion of the expenses. However, certain automobile expenses have a "cap" on how much you can use in calculating the business use portion. There are restrictions on leasing costs and interest on car loans.

Restrictions have been put on the lease and interest costs in respect of automobiles because the government does not want to permit tax deductions that it considers to be "in excess" of an "appropriate amount." In other words, the incentive to lease or finance an "expensive" car and be able to deduct a lot of the expenses for tax leaves a bad taste in the government's mouth. You can still lease or finance an "expensive" vehicle, but you will find the amount you can deduct for your lease and interest costs restricted to maximum amounts. Table 15-1 lists the ceilings for maximum amounts that can be deducted for lease and interest costs.

Table 15-1 Maximum Amounts Deductible for Lease and Interest Costs

Lease/Purchased In	*2000*	*1999/1998*	*1997*
Monthly lease cost	$700	$650	$550
Monthly interest cost	$250	$250	$250

Notes

1. The government reviews these limits annually and announces any changes prior to the end of the year so that taxpayers are aware of the rules in advance of the year in which they apply. The rates are set and released by the Department of Finance Canada by press release.
2. All limits are before sales tax. The limits are actually slightly higher when provincial and territorial retail sales tax and GST/HST are added.

The maximum amounts apply *before* you prorate your passenger vehicle expenses between business use and personal use.

Let's look at Angie. Angie is a self-employed commission agent working out of Regina. She sells hair care products to beauty salons. She sells a number of lines for a variety of hair care product manufacturers.

On January 1, 2000, Angie leased a BMW. Her monthly lease cost is $875. Angie uses the BMW 75 percent for her self-employment. Angie expects that her monthly effective tax deduction will be $656 ($875 × 75 percent) or $7,872 per year. She is not worried about the lease cost restriction because she understands the maximum lease cost for leases commenced in 2000 is $700 (see Table 15-1 above).

Oops, Angie is wrong! The effective tax deduction she will have is the $700 per month maximum multiplied by her 75-percent self-employment use. This results in a tax deduction equal to $525 per month, or $6,300 for all of 2000.

We have simplified things here. So don't get thinking you can get around the lease restriction rules by making a big deposit before the lease commences or guaranteeing the car will have a higher value than normal at the end of the lease. Both these ideas would bring your monthly lease costs down. However, the actual calculation to determine the maximum lease costs takes these ideas into account. In fact, one of the calculations focuses on the manufacturer's list price of the car. If the car is considered expensive in the government's eyes, you simply have to live with the restrictions on the amounts you can deduct!

Home office expenses

If you operate your business from your home or apartment (a home office), you can deduct the portion of the expenses related to maintaining the home office workspace. This deduction is particularly attractive because you will find that you can get a tax deduction for a portion of the expenses you must incur anyway, such as monthly utilities, rent, and mortgage interest. For the costs to be deductible, you must ensure your workspace meets one of two tests — but not both!

Under the first test, the workspace must be the chief place where your business is carried out. The CCRA offers the example of the contractor who runs his own business. A contractor spends a great deal of time fulfilling contracts at customer locations. However, the business functions of receiving work orders, bookkeeping, purchasing, and preparing payrolls may be done at home. In this case, the workspace would qualify as a home office and the contractor could deduct related expenses.

If the first test is not met, all is not lost. You may still qualify to deduct home office expenses if your workspace is used exclusively to carry out your business activities. (Note that the word *exclusively* was not used in the first test.) In addition to using the space exclusively for these activities, you must use the space on a "regular and continuous" basis for meeting customers or others associated with carrying out your business. In the CCRA's opinion, infrequent meetings or frequent meetings at irregular intervals are not regular and continuous.

Restrictions on deducting home office expenses

You cannot claim home office expenses to "create or increase a loss" from your business. Say your 2000 business expenses (excluding home office expenses) are greater than your 2000 income: you have a loss from self-employment. (Perhaps you started a new business and your initial expenses exceeded income in the start-up year.) You cannot claim home office expenses to increase the loss. If your non-home office business expenses do not exceed your income, you can only claim home office expenses to the extent that they bring your "net" self-employment income to $nil — you cannot create a loss. Any 2000 home office expenses that can't be used in 2000 are available for deduction in 2001. You may find that on your 2001 tax return you can deduct both 2000 and 2001 home office expenses.

Deductible home office expenses

Subject to the restrictions on deducting home office expenses just mentioned, you can deduct the following expenses — but only the portion of these expenses directly related to your workspace:

- Electricity, heat, and water (utilities)
- Maintenance costs, condo fees
- Rent
- Property tax
- Insurance on your home or apartment
- Mortgage interest (but not mortgage principal).

How to calculate the tax deductible costs of your home office

On page 2 of T2124, a work chart is provided to assist you in calculating your home office expenses. Let's look at how Tara would calculate the portion of her home office expenses. Tara operates an executive recruitment business out of her condo in Montreal. Tara incurred the following expenses in maintaining her condo. Tara is a GST registrant. The amounts below exclude GST.

Gas (heat)	$900
Electricity	$440
Water	$100
Condo fees	$3,500
Insurance on the condo	$300
Property tax	$2,000
Interest on mortgage	$6,000
Total eligible expenses	$13,240

Tara's condo is 1,000 square feet. She estimates that she uses about 150 square feet or 15 percent of the condo as her workspace. Conversely, 85 percent of the home is for personal use. The amount Tara can deduct for her home office expenses is calculated as follows:

Total eligible expenses to maintain her home (as above)	$13,240
Less portion of expenses for personal use ($13,240 × 85%)	($11,254)
	$1,986

Therefore, total expenses relating to the cost of Tara's home office are $1,986. She would enter this amount on line 9945 of her T2124.

Capital Cost Allowance (CCA)

Before looking at the details of capital cost allowance (or CCA, for short), you need to know the answer to these two questions:

- What is a capital expenditure?
- What is a capital asset?

The money you spend in operating your business can be classified in one of two ways.

- **Day-to-day expenditures of running the business:** When these expenditures have been incurred, there is little or no future value associated with the expenditure. The full value from the expenditure is received at the time the expenditure is incurred. (Remember, under the accrual method of accounting, you record an expenditure when it is *incurred* rather than when it is *paid for.*) These types of expenditures are considered "expenses" of your business. Most of these expenses are noted on lines 8521 to 9270 on form T2124. Examples of day-to-day expenditures include salaries paid to employees, office rent, lease payments, bank charges, travel, and telephone.
- **Capital expenditures:** Capital expenditures are made when you purchase a capital asset — an asset that has an expected useful life that will extend beyond the end of your business's taxation year. In other words, the asset is expected to provide value to your business longer than just the taxation year in which it was acquired. Common examples of capital assets are computers, office equipment (photocopiers, fax machines), office furniture, buildings, and machinery. As the value provided by these assets is expected to extend past the end of your business taxation year, you cannot take a full deduction for these expenditures on form T2124. However, as we detail below, you are allowed to deduct a "portion" of the cost of a capital asset for each taxation year it is used in your business. The calculation of the "portion" that can be deducted on your tax return is called capital cost allowance (CCA). This "portion" (or CCA) is calculated using the declining balance method of depreciation, using percentages legislated by the government. (If you disagree with the appropriateness of the percentages — tough!)

Capital cost allowance, or CCA, is simply tax lingo for "depreciation" and "amortization." These are terms often used by accountants. Remember this next time you are at a party and want to impress someone with your vast knowledge!

CCA is an optional tax deduction

CCA is considered an "optional" or discretionary tax deduction. In preparing your T2124 to report your business income, you are not required to claim maximum CCA. In fact, you are not required to claim any CCA at all. The CCA claimed can be any amount between $nil and the maximum amounts determined under the rules we discuss a little later.

You may decide to claim less than the maximum amount of CCA in the following circumstances:

- You have other tax deductions available to you to reduce your personal taxable income to a level where your tax is $nil already.
- You know that when you complete your tax return for next year you will be subject to a higher marginal rate of tax. A deduction next year will be more valuable to you in terms of tax savings than a deduction this year.

Eligibility to claim CCA

Your business can claim CCA on almost all capital assets purchased. The overriding rule is that the capital asset must have been acquired for use in a business — as opposed to being acquired for personal use.

What capital assets are ineligible for CCA?

Land is not eligible for CCA. Why not? Simply because that is the rule. We expect the theory behind this rule is that land does not depreciate with use. It provides ongoing value to your business. This contrasts with a building or a piece or machinery. These capital assets will eventually "wear out" and cease to provide any value to your business. They will need to be replaced.

When your business purchases an asset considered to be "eligible capital property" (ECP), you cannot claim CCA on that asset. An eligible capital property refers to the purchase of an asset that does not physically exist — or as accountants prefer to say, when it is an *intangible* asset.

While CCA cannot be claimed, an annual deduction, referred to as an allowance on eligible capital property, is available. Your business's annual allowance is claimed as an expense of your business on line 9935 of the T2124. Later in this chapter, we discuss ECPs and the allowance on eligible capital property in detail. (Confused with all the short forms yet?)

Calculating CCA — the declining balance method

For most types of assets, you calculate CCA using the *declining balance method* of depreciation. Similar assets are treated as one asset. For example, say your business purchased a meeting room table and bunch of chairs. The table and chairs, both being "office furniture" would be treated as one asset or "pool." CCA is then calculated on the pool balance multiplied by a legislated percentage rate. The remaining "pool balance" is carried to the next year, where again the same percentage is applied to calculate the CCA. Since the pool balance on which the CCA claim is based declines each year, the method is referred to as the declining balance method. This method results in higher CCA deductions in the early years of a capital asset purchase, and lower and lower amounts as the asset ages.

You'll see later that each pool for CCA purposes is referred to as a CCA "class." Specific types of assets are grouped together in the respective CCA "class."

There are some classes of capital assets where CCA is not calculated using the declining balance method. One of these types of capital assets is leasehold improvements. We discuss the CCA calculation for leasehold improvements later in the chapter.

CCA is calculated as of the *last* day of your business's taxation year. The CCA calculation is based on the balance of the CCA class at the end of the taxation year. There is no need to do separate CCA calculations for capital assets owned for only part of a taxation year. As we will see, the rules work to allow for one-half of the regular CCA claim for capital assets purchased at any time in a year — even if the assets were purchased on the last day of a taxation year.

Capital cost

Let's go back to your business's assumed purchase of a meeting room table and a bunch of office chairs. Let's say the total cost of the office furniture is $1,200. This is considered the "capital cost." Capital cost is the starting point for calculating *capital cost* allowance.

Capital cost is equal to all the costs incurred to acquire a capital asset. This can include the following:

- Purchase price
- Freight costs, if paid by your business
- Duty and customs brokerage fees
- Provincial and territorial retail sales taxes
- GST and HST if your business is not registered for GST/HST. (If your business is a GST/HST registrant, the GST/HST incurred on a capital expenditure will be refunded. Since the GST/HST is not a true cost, it is not included in the capital cost of a capital asset.)

Common CCA classes and rates

CCA can best be explained through an example. Don't worry — we will get to one. Let's first look at some common capital assets and the percentage at which CCA is calculated. For simplicity the government has assigned CCA class numbers to similar group of assets (CCA classes).

- Buildings: Class 1: 4 percent
- Fences: Class 6: 10 percent
- Boats: Class 7: 15 percent
- Office equipment and furniture: Class 8[1]: 20 percent
- Cars, trucks, computer hardware, and computer "systems" software: Class 10: 30 percent[2]
- Computer application software, uniforms, linen, dies, jigs, moulds, rental videos, tools under $200: Class 12: 100 percent
- Manufacturing equipment[3]. Class 43: 30 percent

Notes

1. CCA class 8 is where all capital assets eligible for CCA are included if they do not fall into any of the other CCA classes.
2. There is a maximum amount that can be used for the capital cost of a car in terms of calculating CCA. This is discussed under "Restriction on the maximum capital cost of a class 10.1 automobile."
3. Note that manufacturing equipment has a 30-percent CCA rate whereas the rate for office equipment is only 20 percent. In Chapter 1, Canada's Tax System and Rates, we discuss that one of the reasons for some of the tax rules is to encourage spending in ways the government thinks are good for Canada. Well, the

government wants Canada to have a strong manufacturing industry. One way the tax rules assist manufacturers is through the relatively high CCA rate of 30 percent attached to manufacturing equipment. The higher the CCA rate, the greater the tax deduction! The greater the tax deduction, the lower the after-tax cost of purchasing manufacturing equipment.

A CCA example

As promised, here's an example. Let's continue with your business's purchase of a meeting room table and chairs. Remember that the total cost was $1,200. (The $1,200 included all the freight, provincial retail sales tax, and the rest. Assuming you are a GST/HST registrant, the GST/HST on the office furniture is not included in the capital cost.) In preparing your tax return for 2000, you know that you cannot deduct the full $1,200 on form T2124 in determining your net income from self-employment. The meeting room table and chairs are good quality (for $1,200? hmmm) and probably can be used in your business for several years. In fact, the chairs have a 10-year warranty!

Office furniture is considered a CCA class 8 capital asset with a CCA rate of 20 percent. (You're forced to accept the 20 percent rate whether or not the chairs are expected to last 5 years, 10 years, or 30 years!)

You would *think* you could calculate CCA as simply 20 percent of $1,200, or $240. However there's a catch — it's a special rule called the "half-rate" rule. Let's look at what this rule says.

The "half-rate" rule

When calculating CCA for the year in which the asset is purchased, only one-half of the CCA can be claimed (that is, use half the rate you otherwise would to calculate the appropriate claim).

So, the correct way to calculate the 2000 CCA claim on the office furniture is $1,200 × 10% = $120.

Another way to look at it is to calculate the CCA as you otherwise would, and divide the result in half for the first year you are making the claim.

If the office furniture was the only class of capital assets your business had in 2000, you would report the $120 on line 9936 on your T2124. When you complete your T2124, the $120 will be included in the total business expenses noted on line 9368 of the T2124.

If your business had other capital assets (say, computer hardware — a class 10 capital asset), you would need to aggregate the CCA from each class and enter the total CCA on line 6636 of the T2124. The work chart in "Area A" on page 3 of the T2124 allows you to aggregate up to four classes. Of course, if you have more than four classes, you simply prepare your own schedule to calculate and aggregate the CCA amounts.

Don't forget to review the tax planning tips regarding CCA in Chapter 27.

The impact on the CCA of a short taxation year

The above example assumes you had a full 12-month taxation year. Say you started your business on September 1, 2000 and you chose December 31, 2000 as your first taxation year-end. (Remember, your first taxation year does not need to be a full 365-day year — technically, it could be as short as 1 day!) Since your taxation year is not a full year, your CCA claim needs to be prorated to take into account the short year. In this case the CCA claim on the meeting room table and chairs for 2000 would be only $40 ($120 × 122 days/365 days.)

Undepreciated capital cost (UCC)

Undepreciated capital cost is the term used to describe the amount of the capital cost at the end of a taxation year to which CCA has not yet been applied. (In accounting lingo, as opposed to tax lingo, this is called the "net book value.") The UCC at December 31, 2000 in our CCA class 8 office furniture example here would be $1,080. It is calculated as follows:

Undepreciated capital cost (UCC) at January 1, 2000 (assumed)	$nil
Capital cost of additions in 2000	$1,200
Capital cost allowance (CCA) claimed in 2000 (1,200 + 20% × ½)	($120)
Undepreciated capital cost (UCC) at December 31, 2000	$1,080

Sale of capital assets

In the above example we saw how capital asset purchases are treated for CCA and UCC purposes. We will now look at the implications of *when* an asset is sold.

Let's continue with our CCA class 8 office furniture example. As noted above, the December 31, 2000 UCC of the class 8 capital assets was $1,080. Say you decided to upgrade the meeting room table and chairs in 2001. Your new table and chairs cost $1,700. The old table and chairs were sold to a used office furniture retailer for $750.

When a capital asset is sold, the UCC is reduced by the lower of the following:

- The original capital cost of the assets sold. (Remember, this was $1,200.)
- The sale price — the $750 noted above.

When an asset is sold, the half-rate rule comes into play once again.

UCC at January 1, 2001 (same as at December 31, 2000)		$1,080
Add: Additions		$1,700
Sale of chairs:		
Lesser of:		
Original cost:	$1,200	
Proceeds:	$750	($750)
CCA claim for 2001:		
$1,080 × 20% = $216		
($1,700 – $750) × 20% × ½ = $95		($311)
Closing UCC (UCC at December 31, 2000)		$1,799

As illustrated above, if you purchase and dispose of an asset in the same CCA class during the year, you must net the addition and disposal together before applying the half-year rule.

Recapture and terminal loss

So now you know how to handle the CCA calculation where assets are purchased and sold. You can see that as long as assets are continued to be purchased for a cost in excess of the sale price of previously purchased assets, the UCC will never reduce to $nil. However, what if your business sells *all* the assets in a CCA class and does not replace them? Well two things can happen:

- **You sell all the assets in a class for *less* than the UCC balance.**
  - You end up with a UCC balance, but have no assets remaining in the class. From an economic point of view, this means your business did not take sufficient CCA in light of the actual decline in value of the capital assets in the pool.
  - The positive UCC balance is reset to $nil, and the amount needed to do this is referred to as a *terminal loss*. A terminal loss is simply treated as part of the total CCA claim for all the assets of your business. It is fully tax deductible in the taxation year in which it occurs. Example A provides an example of a terminal loss.

    WARNING! The terminal loss rules do not apply to CCA class 10.1 automobiles. We will discuss CCA class 10.1 automobiles shortly.
- **You sell the assets for more than the UCC balance.**
  - Where this occurs, you will end up with a negative UCC balance. From an economic point of view, this means the CCA you claimed was in excess of the actual decline in value of the capital asset.

    For income tax purposes, the negative UCC balance is reset to $nil and the amount needed to do this is referred to as *recapture*. This can be considered "negative CCA" because it is adjusting for excess CCA claims taken in previous taxation years. Recapture is considered income earned by your business and is subject to tax fully in the taxation year when it occurs. We take a look at recapture in example B below.

WARNING! The recapture rules do not apply to CCA class 10.1 automobiles.

Example A: Let's assume that in 2001 you decide to not upgrade your meeting room table and chairs. You admit to yourself that you don't like meeting clients, so the best way not to meet clients is to get rid of your meeting room furniture. (Not a good career move, but it works with the example.) Remember, the table and chairs originally cost $1,200. Again, assume you sell the whole set for $750. In this case, the following would happen:

Opening UCC at January 1, 2001 (same as UCC at December 31, 2000)		$1,080
Sale of chairs:		
Lesser of:		
Original cost:	$1,200	
Proceeds:	$750	
Lesser:		($750)
UCC balance after sale		$ 330

Since you sold all the assets in this class, you shouldn't have any UCC left — there is nothing left to depreciate. However, you have $330 remaining. What this means is that you didn't depreciate the assets fast enough. Therefore, the taxman lets you make this up, by allowing you to claim the full amount remaining as a deduction. After all, you were only using the rate they set — why *shouldn't* you get the deduction? The $330 is referred to as the terminal loss.

Example B: What happens if you sell the table and chairs for $1,800? Sounds good, but there is a downfall. Let's look at the calculation again.

UCC at January 1, 2001 (same as UCC at December 31, 2000)		$1,080
Sale of chairs:		
Lesser of:		
Original cost:	$1,200	
Proceeds:	$1,800	
Lesser:		($1,200)
UCC balance after sale		($120)

See what has happened? Again, you sold everything in the asset pool, so your UCC balance should clear to zero. However, you have a negative UCC balance. What does this mean? Well, it means you've taken too much CCA — the assets did not depreciate as fast as the taxman thought they would. So what happens? Obviously, the CCRA won't let you have too much of a good thing, so it will ask for the extra CCA that you took back (hence the term *recapture*). This means that the amount of the negative UCC must be added to your income in the year the asset is disposed. Oh, well!

Exceptions to the declining balance method

For most capital assets CCA is calculated using the declining balance method of depreciation. However, there are exceptions. A common exception is expenditures made for leasehold improvements.

Leasehold improvements (CCA class 13)

Your business may rent the premises where it operates. If your business incurs costs to make the rented premises more workable for the business, such costs are referred to as leasehold improvements. Say you rented a large warehouse and needed to put up some drywall to make offices. The cost of the drywall (plus the cost of installing it, if you hire someone to put it up) would be a leasehold improvement. Leasehold improvements are the only type of asset included in CCA class 13.

CCA on leasehold improvements is calculated as the lesser of the following:

(i) $\dfrac{\text{cost of leasehold improvements}}{5}$

(ii) $\dfrac{\text{cost of leasehold improvements}}{\text{\# of years in lease plus 1 renewal period}}$

The half-rate rule applies in a taxation year when a leasehold expenditure is made.

To maximize the speed at which CCA is claimed on the cost of your business's leasehold improvements, negotiate your lease to be 4 years with a renewal period of 1 year.

Restriction on the maximum capital cost of a class 10.1 automobile

In a discussion above on the deductibility of automobile expenses, we noted there are restrictions on the amounts that can be deducted in respect of leasing a car and interest incurred on a car loan. The amount of CCA that can be claimed on an automobile is also restricted in certain circumstances. The starting point for claiming CCA is restricted to a maximum amount. The maximum amounts are summarized in Table 15-2 below. The maximum amount that may apply to you will depend on what year the automobile was purchased. Any amount paid for an automobile in excess of the maximum amounts will never be subject to CCA. The excess simply becomes a cost that will never be able to be written off for tax purposes.

Automobiles subject to the CCA restriction are referred to as CCA class 10.1 automobiles. Earlier we noted that there are CCA class 10 automobiles. For an automobile to be considered class 10 its capital cost must be equal to or less than the maximum amounts. In other words, no CCA restrictions apply to CCA class 10 automobiles.

The government simply does not want you driving an expensive car and being able to write off a significant portion in CCA in determining your self-employment income. The CCRA periodically adjusts the maximum amount to take into account rising car prices.

Table 15-2 Maximum Amounts on Which CCA Can Be Claimed on Automobiles

Automobiles Purchased In	*2000*	*1999/1998*	*1997*
Maximum capital cost amount for purposes of claiming CCA on an automobile	$27,000	$26,000	$25,000

The above limits are before provincial/territorial retail sales tax and 7-percent GST/15-percent HST. If you purchased a car in Ontario, you would pay an 8-percent Ontario sales tax and the 7-percent GST — a total of 15 percent. The deemed maximum capital cost for claiming CCA on your car purchase in 2000 would be $31,050 ($27,000 × 115 percent — $31,050). However, if you are a GST registrant any GST you claim back on your automobile would reduce the maximum amount you could use as the starting point for your CCA calculation.

The above limits come into play *before* you prorate your car expenses between business use and personal use. Take a look at Alice's situation. Alice lives in Ontario. She purchased a Toyota Camry in 2000 for $35,000. In 2000, Alice used her Camry 65 percent of the time in carrying out her self-employment activities. Alice is not a GST registrant.

Alice will calculate the CCA on her Camry in 2000 as follows:

Actual cost	$35,000
Alice's deemed maximum capital cost ($27,000 plus 8% Ontario PST and 7% GST)	$31,050
CCA: $31,050 × 30% × ½	$4,658
Percentage used for self-employment	65
CCA claim in 2000	$ 3,028

Special rules in calculating CCA on class 10.1 automobiles

There are a few special rules to consider when you're tallying up CCA on your class 10.1 automobile. Have a look to see if any of these circumstances apply to you.

- CCA on each class 10.1 automobile is calculated on its own. If two cars were used in your business and they both had an actual capital cost above the limits, your business would have two CCA class 10.1 calculations to make. The purchase or sale of one class 10.1 automobile does not impact the CCA calculation of another CCA class 10.1 automobile.

- There is no concept of recapture or terminal loss in dealing with CCA class 10.1 automobiles.
- The half-year rule is not applied in the year a class 10.1 automobile is sold.

Eligible Capital Property (ECP)

In the discussion above on what assets were *not* eligible to claim CCA, we noted that CCA could not be claimed in respect of assets considered *eligible capital property* (ECP). Examples of ECPs are as follows:

- The purchase of goodwill
- A customer or patient list
- A marketing quota and other government right
- An unlimited life franchise, concession, or licence.

These assets do not physically exist. They are referred to as intangible assets. The cost of an ECP is referred to as an eligible capital expenditure (ECE).

An ECE cannot be deducted fully in the taxation year in which the expenditure is incurred. However, a portion of the cost of ECP can be deducted each year. The amount that can be deducted is referred to as the "allowance on eligible capital property" on line 9935 of form T2124.

For calculating the allowance on ECP, one "pool" is used for all ECP purchases. Unlike CCA, there are no separate classes or different rates of deduction. When an ECP is purchased, 75 percent of the cost (the ECE) is added to the continuity of the cumulative eligible capital (CEC) account or "pool." (With respect to the remaining 25 percent, nothing happens with it. It is simply ignored. It will never be deducted for tax purposes!) At the end of each taxation year, 7 percent of the CEC account is claimed as the allowance on eligible capital property. Should an ECP be sold, 75 percent of the proceeds are deducted from the account. While the terms *recapture* and *terminal loss* are not used in discussing the CEC account, they are similar concepts with respect to the sale of ECP.

Look at Andrew. In 2000 Andrew purchased a Quicky oil change franchise in Prince Rupert, British Columbia for $15,000. As the franchise term is unlimited, the cost of the franchise is considered to be ECP.

Andrew would calculate the 2000 allowance on ECP as follows:

Purchase of Quicky unlimited life franchise	$15,000
Portion added to CEC 75% of $15,000	$11,250
Allowance on eligible capital property for 2000: $11,250 × 7% =	($788)
CEC at December 31, 2000	$10,462

In 2001 Andrew will calculate the allowance on ECP as 7% of $10,462 — or $732.

Lines 137 and 164: Reporting Professional Income

The term *professional income* refers to the net income earned by a professional. So what's a professional? The CCRA does not provide an exact definition. However, it is fairly safe to say a professional is a person who earns fees from an occupation for which he or she had to go to school for a long time before being "certified," "licensed," or somehow approved to do what he or she does. If you are a professional, you make most of your money from providing services rather than selling goods. The CCRA offers these examples of professionals: accountants, dentists, lawyers, medical doctors, chiropractors, and veterinarians.

Essentially, professionals calculate their net income from their profession the same way as most self-employed individuals calculate their business income. The comments we have made in this chapter so far with respect to calculating business income apply equally to those who report professional income on their tax return.

The main differences in reporting professional income as opposed to business income are as follows:

- Form T2032 "Statement of Professional Activities" is used in place of form T2124.
- Professionals need to deal with work-in-progress (WIP).

Form T2032 "Statement of Professional Activities"

Form T2032 is similar in design to the T2124. In fact, the numeric line references on the T2032 are identical to those on the T2124. As it is expected that a professional does not sell goods, the T2032 has no section to compute the cost of goods sold.

The income section of the T2032 includes lines to allow you to correctly account for work-in-progress of WIP.

Work-in-progress (WIP)

A unique characteristic of a professional is his or her being able to claim an amount for *work-in-progress (WIP).* WIP represents a professional's unbilled time. Say what? A professional's fees are usually based on time. The value of WIP is based on a professional's fees that have been earned but not yet billed.

We'll walk you through this one by looking at Caroline, who lives in Windsor, Ontario. She plans to see a lawyer about difficulties she is having with her husband. The lawyer's name is Richard — Rick, for short. Caroline wants to clearly understand her rights under Ontario's *Family Law Act.* Caroline makes an appointment with Rick. Rick promotes himself as a specialist in family law. Caroline and Rick plan to meet on December 31, 2000. Rick explained to Caroline the meeting would be an hour in length and that his rate is $200 per hour. Coincidentally, the year-end for Rick's practice is December 31. Caroline and Rick meet as planned. At the end of the meeting, Caroline offers to pay the $200. Rick suggests she wait for a bill that he will get to her in mid-January 2001. Caroline agrees — she likes the idea of keeping her $200 a little longer. (A lawyer not taking money? Whassup? The reason will become obvious in a tip noted soon!) After Caroline leaves his office, Rick makes a record of his meeting in a file for Caroline and records the one hour of time in his bookkeeping system. In entering the time, he records $200 of work-in-progress and $200 of fee revenue earned.

As Rick has only recorded the time but has not billed it, the amount is not yet receivable from Caroline. It will become receivable from Caroline once the bill is issued to her in mid-January 2001. Note that we have not mentioned anything to do with GST. GST will only need to be dealt with once the billing is issued.

Let's assume that for his year ended December 31, 2000, Rick has billed all his clients with the exception of Caroline. (Yes, this is unrealistic, but bear with us as we try to make a point!) Rick's total fees billed in 2000 are $200,000. On line A of schedule T2032, he reports revenue of $200,200. This is because the lawyer has earned the $200,000 he has billed to his clients *plus* the $200 he has yet to bill Caroline. Remember, under the accrual method of accounting you report revenue on an "as earned basis." For businesses such as a retail store, revenue is earned when a sale is made, whether or not it is a cash sale or a credit sale. A professional earns revenues as services are rendered — not when the services are billed.

Where a professional has significant work-in-progress, he or she may end up paying a great deal of tax on income for which a bill has not been rendered. The tax rules recognize this problem and permit certain professionals (the professionals noted above) to deduct year-end WIP in calculating their gross income subject to tax in the year. Where WIP was deducted in the prior year, it must be added back in calculating gross income for the current year. This makes sense because if this was not done, fees in WIP at the end of a year would *never* be recorded as part of gross income for purposes of calculating tax. (The drafters of the tax legislation are smarter than you think!)

Let's continue with Rick. Assume that back at December 31, 1999, Rick's previous tax year-end, he had $50 in WIP.

Rick would calculate his 2000 gross income subject to tax in the following way:

Professional fees — includes WIP — at December 31, 2000 (line A on form T2032)	$200,200
Minus — WIP at December 31, 2000	($200)
	$200,000
Plus — WIP at beginning of taxation year (WIP at January 1, 2000 would equal WIP at December 31, 1999)	$50
Gross income (line 8299 on form T2032)	$200,050

We have seen that WIP at the end of a taxation year is deducted in determining gross income to use in calculating a professional's net income from self-employment. If the professional delays billing clients for services rendered in one year until the next year he or she will defer the tax payable on those services for one year. This is an especially good tax planning idea when tax rates are dropping from one year to the next. The tax is deferred, plus it is subject to tax at a lower rate! However, the longer you wait to bill, the longer you wait for the cash. Make sure your business's cash flow is okay before considering such a tax deferral strategy.

Lines 141 and 168: Farming Income

In this section we start off by taking a look at what CCRA considers to be farming. We will discuss the option farmers have of using the cash method of accounting over the accrual method. Next we present an overview of "inventory adjustments" farmers need to consider in reporting their net income. We wrap up with comments on the restrictions in claiming farm losses. Enjoy!

So what does CCRA think farming is all about? It considers farming to include the following:

- Soil tilling
- Race horse maintenance
- Livestock raising or showing
- Poultry raising
- Dairy farming
- Fur farming
- Tree farming (including Christmas trees)
- Fruit growing
- Beekeeping
- Hydroponics
- Wild-game reserve
- Chicken hatchery
- Feed lot.

Method of accounting

If you are a farmer, the cash method of accounting, rather than the accrual method, can be used to calculate the net income of your farm business. If you had used the accrual method in a prior taxation year, you can switch to the cash method. However, to switch from the cash method to the accrual method, you need permission from the CCRA.

Form T2032 "Statement of Farming Activities"

Form T2032 serves the same purpose as the T2124 "Statement of Business Activities," the T2032 "Statement of Professional Activities," and the T2121 "Statement of Fishing Activities" (discussed later). The form simply acts as a schedule to summarize the income and expenses of operating a farm.

The Mandatory Inventory Adjustment (MIA) (line 9942)

The MIA only applies to those in farming that record their income and expenses on the cash method of accounting.

Why is there an inventory adjustment? The impact of the inventory adjustment rules is to reduce the amount of net loss a farm business can have. (Warning: Do not mix up the inventory adjustment rules with "restricted farm losses." We discuss restricted farm losses later.) Why do the rules work to minimize a farm loss? Like any self-employment loss, a farm loss can be used to "offset" other sources of income you may have — interest, dividends, capital gains, pension, or perhaps employment income or other sources of self-employment income. A large farm loss could significantly reduce your taxable income, which, of course, reduces the tax you pay. You can see why there would be rules to reduce this! In using the cash method of accounting, inventory is ignored. When preparing a T2042 using the cash method of accounting, you deduct the cost of all items purchased for resale — even if they remain unsold at the end of the year.

Say you purchase a number of calves in the year as part of your beef cattle farm operation. You may keep these for a year or a year-and-a-half before they are sold. If you are operating a dairy farm, you may hold onto your cattle for a number of years before they are sold. Under the cash method, the amounts paid are deducted fully in the year purchased. Where significant purchases are made in a year, the farm loss could be, well, significant! (And that's no bull . . . sorry about this one.)

The MIA rules work to minimize the amount of loss that can be claimed when, at the end of the year, products purchased for resale have not yet been sold.

Our interpretation of the MIA is that the government believes the cash method of accounting already provides the tools to manipulate the timing of your farm business's income and expenses. If the cash method is giving you an alleged advantage over other self-employed individuals, the tax rules are certainly not going to give you a further advantage in permitting a significant farm loss to be recognized by not acknowledging inventory your farm holds at the end of the year.

An MIA must be made on your 2000 T2042 if the following exist:

- There is a net loss reported on line 9899 of the T2042
- At the end of your 2000 taxation year, inventory was on hand.

The MIA is calculated as the lesser of the following:

- The net loss reported on line 9899 of the T2042
- The market value of the inventory at the end of the taxation year.

You can see that where the farm inventory is at least equal to the loss on line 9899, the MIA will wipe out the farm loss.

Optional Inventory Adjustment (OIA) (line 9941)

Like the MIA, the OIA is an *addition* you make to your line 9899 net income or loss for 2000. The amount would be deducted on your 2001 tax return.

The maximum amount of the 2000 OIA addition is equal to the following:

The market value of inventory at the end of the taxation year – the Mandatory Inventory Adjustment (MIA)

Why would someone decrease his or her farm loss by making an OIA? A good question! An OIA serves to decrease the loss. Remember, an OIA added to net income or loss in the year is a deduction in the subsequent year. If the expectations are that the net income of the farm will be higher next year, a deduction may prove more valuable next year because the deduction will be worth more in tax savings when it can shelter farm income subject to tax at a higher marginal rate.

What if you have a loss from your farming business?

A unique rule regarding self-employment income generated from farming is the treatment of losses. If your farm operated at a loss for 2000, the net loss would appear on line 9946 of the T2042. This may *not* be the amount you carry to line 141 on page 2 of your tax return. Your farming loss may fall into one of these three categories:

- Fully deductible
- Partly deductible
- Non-deductible.

As with other self-employment income activities, for your net farm loss to be deductible you must operate your farm as a business. The CCRA considers you to be in the business of farming if you have been able to make a profit from farming or at least had the expectation of making a profit in the year or in coming years.

Where you are operating your farm as a business, and farming is your chief source of income in a year, your loss would be fully deductible.

Part-time farmer — the "restricted farm loss" rules

When you operate your farm as a business but farming is not your chief source of income in the year, the loss you claim will be "restricted." In other words, the maximum loss you can claim on your tax return will be *less* than your actual loss — your actual loss will be partly deductible. Any denied loss is called a "restricted farm loss."

The CCRA considers farming to not be your chief source of income when you do not rely on farming alone for your livelihood. Where you have other sources of income, such as employment income or other sources of self-employment income, farming would not be considered your main source of income.

Whether or not your farm loss is fully or partly deductible is a question to answer each year. In some years farming may be your chief source of income and in some years it may not.

The maximum loss that you can claim if farming is not your chief source of income is calculated as follows:

100 percent of the first $2,500 of the loss plus one-half of the remaining loss

The maximum loss that can be claimed is $8,750. If you are mathematically inclined you can calculate that to be able to deduct $8,750 you would need to have at least a $15,000 actual farm loss. Any excess farm loss above the farm loss you can claim is called a restricted farm loss.

The CCRA suggests that when you have entered a of loss on line 141 of your return that is lower than your actual loss, you should note "restricted farm loss" beside the words "farming income" in the self-employment income section on page 2 of your tax return. (We're not sure how you would do this if you e-file your return.)

A restricted farm loss can be used to reduce any net farm income you may have reported in the three prior years — 1999, 1998, and 1997, or may be carried forward for up to 10 years. To carry a loss back (referred to as a loss carryback) to any or all of these years, you must complete a form T1A "Request for Loss Carryback" and file it with your 2000 tax return.

Once the CCRA receives the form, it will apply the loss against the tax return for the year(s) you requested. As this will reduce your taxable income for the year(s), your taxes will also decrease. The CCRA will issue a Notice of Reassessment for the year(s) in which the loss was applied — along with a tax refund cheque!

Even if you are e-filing your 2000 return, the T1A "Request for Loss Carryback" should be paper filed — a fancy word for mailing it in. This allows for quicker processing of your loss carryback request.

When your farm loss is not deductible at all

Where your farm operations are run in a way not considered to be a business, none of your net loss from farming is deductible. As noted above, for your farm to be considered a business, it must operate at least with the expectation that it will make a profit. The CCRA comments that in many cases a profit may never be made given the size and scope of the farm operation. When this is the case, the expenses are considered personal expenses and are not deductible at all. No carryback or carryforward provisions are available. Generally, "farmers" in this category include those that do not look to farming as their chief source of income, and only consider farming to be a hobby.

To determine whether or not farming is your chief source of income, the CCRA will look to a number of factors, including time spent, capital committed, and profitability, both actual and expected.

Lines 143 and 170: Fishing Income

In this final section of the chapter we look at the tax rules that apply to those earning self-employment income from fishing.

What does the CCRA consider fishing income? Let's take a close look. This category includes the following:

- Amounts received from the sale of fish, lobster, scallops, and so on
- Amounts received from other marine products: Irish moss, herring scales, herring roe, seal meat and flippers, seaweed, kelp, roe on kelp, and so on.

If your self-employment income is earned from fishing activities, you report your income in the same fashion as do other self-employed individuals — with a few differences. This section highlights some of these differences. As with farming, you can use the cash method of accounting to calculate the net income of your fishing business.

T2121 "Statement of Fishing Activities"

This form is used to report the income and expenses of your fishing business. It again is similar to the T2124 "Statement of Business Activities."

Expenses

Expenses are detailed on page 2 of the T2121. The expense categories provided are customized a little to reflect items of a fishy nature (we had to say that). For example, the expense categories include "bait, ice, salt, crew shares, gear, and nets and traps."

Food

The cost of food provided to your crew when you fish off-shore is deductible. Food provided on-shore is deductible provided you considered the food as a taxable benefit to your employees.

If it is considered a taxable benefit, the value must be included in the employee's total employment income reported on his or her T4 slip. A deduction can still be claimed when you do not consider the food a taxable benefit, provided your boat is at sea for 36 hours.

Nets and traps

Nets and traps are considered to include lines, hooks, buoys, and anchors. Line 9137 on the T2121 is where your fishing business can claim a deduction for nets and traps. However, the full cost of the nets and traps acquired in the year cannot be deducted. The amount that can be deducted is determined under one of two methods:

CCA method

Your business treats its nets and traps as a capital asset and claims CCA. Nets and traps are CCA class 8 capital assets. You'll recall the CCA rate for class 8 is 20 percent.

Inventory method

Nets and traps are considered inventory. At the end of each taxation year, the value of all the nets and traps is determined. If the value is less than the inventoried cost, a deduction is claimed on line 9137 for the loss in value.

Part III

Tax Deductions and Credits

"Here's what I think happened—He was wounded by Schedule 4. Then he was hit by Schedule 3; this brings him to his knees. Then, as he's crawling to reach his calculator, he gets it square in the pocketbook by Schedule 1, and that's what did him in."

In this part . . .

Now for our favourite part — deductions and credits to reduce your tax. After reading through the last couple of chapters and calculating your income, you may feel like there's no hope, and next year you may as well just hand over your paycheck to the CCRA. Don't fret — there is a light at the end of the tunnel, and it's shinning the words "deductions and credits."

These next few chapters may be the most important in the entire book. So highlight, bookmark, and tag these pages! Do anything you have to do to remind yourself of the deductions to which you're entitled: You can be sure that in most cases, the CCRA won't remind you to claim them! After all, a dollar deduction not claimed means more money in their pockets. Pay close attention to these chapters — you don't want to miss a thing!

"Taxes should be proportioned to what may be annually spared by the individual."

— Thomas Jefferson

Chapter 16

Calculating Your Net Income

In This Chapter

- Understanding what "net income" is and its importance
- Maximizing deductions in calculating net income
- How to make the most out of RRSPs
- Know what you can write off for child care expenses
- Benefit from your moving costs
- Ensure you are up to date on the deduction for support payments
- Know when your legal expenses are tax deductible

So what, exactly, is net income — aside from line 236 on your tax return? It is the amount you arrive at when you take your total income (line 150) less the deductions permitted on lines 207 to 235. You would think that this is the amount of income on which you should pay tax. Well, no. The amount you pay tax on is your taxable income from line 260. The calculation of taxable income is discussed in Chapter 17. Why is calculating your net income so important? Even though we don't pay tax based on net income, it is an important calculation. Take a look at what this one calculation influences.

- The amount of provincial or territorial tax credits (Chapter 20, line 479 of your return) you are entitled to.
- The amount of GST credit (Chapter 21).
- The amount of medical expenses (Chapter 18, lines 330 and 331) you can claim. You can claim the amount of medical expenses that exceeds 3 percent of your net income. (If your medical expenses exceed $1,637 in a year you can claim all eligible medical expenses in excess of $1,637 no matter what your net income is.)
- The calculation of the amount of refundable medical expenses supplement (see Chapter 19 and schedule 10 of your return) available to you.
- The amount of charitable donations (see Chapter 18 and schedule 9 of your return) you can claim. Generally, the amount of charitable donations that can be claimed in one year is limited to 75 percent of net income.
- The amount of social benefits (Chapter 10, Old Age Security; Chapter 11, Employment Insurance Benefits) you must repay.
- The amount of spousal credit (Chapter 18 and line 303) your spouse can claim in respect of you.
- The amount of equivalent-to-spouse credit amount (Chapter 18 and schedule 5 of the return) another may be able to claim for supporting you.
- The amount available for transfer of your disability amount (Chapter 18, line 318) to another.

Let's walk through the tax deductions available in calculating your net income.

Line 206: Pension Adjustment

Well, this line really doesn't provide a tax deduction. Line 206 is a *disclosure line* only. A disclosure line on a tax return is where there is a requirement to note a figure but that figure will not have an impact on the calculation of your tax liability or refund. The amount of your pension adjustment does not impact the calculation of your 2000 net income and therefore, cannot impact on your 2000 tax liability or refund. Your pension adjustment will reduce your 2001 RRSP contribution limit — the amount that you can contribute to an RRSP in 2001 and get a full tax deduction. (We discuss the RRSP deduction below and RRSPs in detail in Chapter 28.) Generally, the *pension adjustment* (PA) is the increase in value of your retirement benefits under an *Registered Pension Plan* (RPP) or *deferred profit sharing plan* (DPSP).

(RPPs, discussed briefly below, and DPSPs are plans set up by employers to assist employees in saving for retirement. The plans are set up in a manner that minimizes taxes to provide for maximum amounts available when the funds are needed. In technical terms, RPPs/DPSPs are tax-assisted retirement plans. Cash placed in these plans can be invested and no tax is payable on the investment income until there is a withdrawal from the plan.) As the value of your Registered Pension Plan increases, the amount you can contribute to your RRSP decreases. The PA is a component used in the formula to calculate your RRSP deduction limit. The pension adjustment reported on your 1999 T4 will reduce your 2000 RRSP deduction limit on a dollar-for-dollar basis. The idea behind the PA is that an individual who is *not* a member of an RPP or a DPSP only has the ability to use an RRSP to save for retirement. To keep Canadians with retirement benefits "equal," the RPP/DPSP member's RRSP deduction room is reduced by his or her PA. Individuals cannot double up on tax-free retirement savings by using both the RPP/DPSP and full RRSP deduction room.

When you receive your tax assessment from the CCRA after filing your 2000 tax return, you will see your 2000 PA amount is included in the formula to calculate your 2001 RRSP deduction limit. CCRA picks up on your PA from you disclosing it on line 206.

The amount you report on line 206 is the total sum of the amounts noted in box 52 of all your T4 slips and box 34 of your T4A slips.

Pension adjustment reversal (PAR)

The *pension adjustment reversal* (PAR) is a relatively new concept. A PAR is essentially a statement showing that the PAs reported on your T4s over the years were too high — your pension adjustments were overstated so your RRSP deduction limits were understated. The PAR simply corrects for the understatement in your RRSP deduction limit. A PAR will often arise when you leave an employer where you were a member of an RPP. If you are entitled to a PAR your employer will report this to you on a T10 slip. A PAR indicates your RRSP deduction limit is being increased — this is good news!

Your employer must send you a T10 slip within 60 days after the end of the calendar year quarter in which you left your job. If you left your job in the last quarter, you should receive your T10 slip by January 30.

Receiving a severance payment? A PAR can be very beneficial as it opens up RRSP room that you can make use of to shelter all or part of the severance from tax. The higher your RRSP contribution, the lower the amount of your severance on which you will be required to pay tax. Caution — don't confuse this tip with the ability some individuals have to transfer a portion of a severance to an RRSP *on top* of their regular RRSP contribution limit. These special rules apply whether or not there is a PAR. Refer to comments below under "Transferring a severance or retirement allowance into your RRSP" in the section dealing with line 208, the RRSP deduction.

How did the understatement of your RRSP deduction limit occur?

If you are a member of a defined benefit pension plan, your yearly PAs are calculated assuming you will continue to work for the company and continue to participate in the pension plan until the "normal" retirement age for the plan.

If you leave the plan earlier than expected, either due to voluntary early retirement or perhaps forced severance, the assumptions used to calculate past PAs were incorrect. The error is that your estimated share of the pension plan used has been overstated because your share will be less than anticipated. It is a bonus to receive a PAR T10 slip — it opens up more RRSP deduction room. The bad news is that you have not had access to the tax-free compounding of the investment growth in your RRSP during the years in which your PA was overstated. Just deal with it and move on. Take advantage of the opened-up RRSP room as quickly as you can. Again, more on RRSPs below and in Chapter 28.

Line 207: Registered Pension Plan Deduction

Enter on line 207 the amount that *you* paid into your RPP during 2000. (Do not include any amount paid by your *employer*.) The amount you paid into your RPP will usually be noted in box 20 of your T4 slip from your employer. It may also be reported in box 32 of T4A slips you received or on receipts provided by your union or the pension plan itself.

The full amount noted on the tax information slips is usually tax deductible. This may not be the case under the following circumstances:

- The amount is greater than $3,500
- Your information slip indicates a past-service amount for services provided *before* 1990.

As well, you may be able to deduct an amount that you contributed in a prior year but have not yet fully deducted fully.

What is past service? The term *past service* refers to work you did for an employer in a prior year that later became pensionable service. (Now it is clear, eh?) Past service can be contrasted with *current service*, which refers to work done for an employer in a current year.

Contributions to your pension plan for past services are considered "past service contributions." (Finally, something that makes sense!). The contributions may also be made to upgrade benefits. Past service contributions are often made in a lump sum. People often refer to past service contributions as "buying back service," or buying increased pension benefits — some money now for an increased pension down the road.

Ask your pension plan administrator if you are entitled to buy back any service. Based on your age, your years to retirement, length of service, and the dollars involved, it can be beneficial in terms of your future pension entitlement to buy back service!

Contributions for current service and past service for 1990 and later years

Your total contributions for current service and past service for 1990 and later years can usually be found in box 20 of the T4 slips you received from your employer. The full amount is to be included on line 207 of your tax return. The full amount must be claimed for a deduction. Any undeducted amount cannot be claimed in an earlier or later year.

The purchase of past service for 1990 and later years can result in a "past service pension adjustment" — a PSPA. A PSPA increases your pension benefits, but decreases your future RRSP contribution room.

Past service contributions for years before 1990

It gets really complicated here. It is such a complex area, in fact, that the CCRA devotes about 2½ pages to it in its guide "RRSPs and Other Registered Plans for Retirement." Your personal circumstances and the amounts you have contributed in the year for current service and for past services provided in 1990 and later years will determine the amount of the pre-1990 past services you can deduct in completing your 2000 tax return.

If your current and past service contributions for 1990 and later years exceeds $3,500, you will find that none of your past service contribution for years before 1990 is deductible on your 2000 tax return. However, all is not lost! Those contributions will be eligible for deduction in 2001 and subsequent years.

Line 208: Registered Retirement Savings Plan (RRSP) Deduction

Next to the ability to sell your house tax-free due to the principal residence exemption (see Chapter 13), the RRSP is Canada's best tax shelter. Yes, we said tax shelter. Many believe a tax shelter is some very creative (perhaps sleazy) tax planning idea available only to the wealthy! Not true. Almost every taxpayer that has a job or is self-employed can take advantage of RRSPs.

What is a registered retirement savings plan?

You can be young without money but you can't be old without it.

Tennessee Williams, Playwright

To more easily understand what a registered retirement savings plan (RRSP) is, think of it as a retirement savings plan that has been CCRA-approved ("registered") and that is eligible for the tax features discussed below. RRSPs are simply an arrangement that allows you to save for your retirement on a tax-friendly basis. Think of an RRSP as your personal pension plan.

Tax savings provided by RRSPs

In Chapter 1 we noted that the government wants you to save for your retirement. To encourage this, an RRSP offers two main tax advantages:

- A tax deduction for contributions made to an RRSP
- Tax-free growth while the funds remain in the RRSP.

Contributions are tax deductible and the funds grow tax-free. No tax is payable until you withdraw from the RRSP. You hope that the tax payable on RRSP withdrawals will be less than the tax saved when you took the deduction for making an RRSP contribution. This will occur if during your retirement years you are subject in a lower tax bracket than the tax bracket you were in when you made your RRSP contributions.

A better idea is to have the withdrawal taxed in your spouse's hands if he or she will be in a lower tax bracket than you are at the time of the withdrawal. This is especially advantageous if you already have significant retirement income (say, pension income from an RPP) and your spouse has little. We know this sounds too good to be true, but you can do it by making spousal RRSP contributions. Spousal RRSP contributions are discussed below.

Setting up an RRSP

Are you reading this after December 31, 2000? Don't worry — it is not too late to set up an RRSP and get a tax deduction for 2000! Contributions made to an RRSP on or before March 1, 2001, qualify for a tax deduction on your 2000 tax return.

You can set up an RRSP in many places: a bank, a trust company, or through your investment planner. It is as simple as filling out a form and providing the money. After you contribute to the RRSP, you will be provided with an "official RRSP receipt." This is what you will use to support the RRSP deduction that you will claim on your 2000 tax return.

Self-directed RRSPs

Banks and trust companies commonly offer deposit-based RRSPs. The money you contribute is usually invested in a number of investment vehicles, although the choice is limited. If you would prefer more diversity and flexibility in your RRSP investing, you should consider a "self-directed RRSP." Don't worry — "self-directed" does not mean that you are on your own. You will work with your investment advisor to decide which investments are appropriate for your RRSP, given your investment goals and risk-tolerance levels. You will usually pay an annual fee to maintain a self-directed RRSP. The fee is about $125 to $150. The fee is not tax deductible and should be paid by you — that is, do not have the fee taken from your RRSP funds.

There is an annual cost to maintain a self-directed RRSP, so in order to justify this cost, you should wait until your RRSP assets reach $20,000 before setting up this type of plan.

RRSP contributions — in kind

Wanna set up an RRSP or contribute to an existing RRSP, but you're short on funds? Well, provided you already hold an investment that is eligible for an RRSP (see list on next page), why not contribute the investment? This is called a contribution in kind. But be careful. If you contribute an investment that has gone up in value from the time you acquired it, a capital gain (see Chapter 13) will be triggered that will be taxed on your 2000 return. If the investment has gone down in value, you would think you would be entitled to a capital loss. No such luck. Why not? Because the CCRA says so.

If you are thinking about contributing investments that have declined in value, you should sell the investment, claim the loss, and then donate the cash. This way you won't lose out on claiming the capital loss.

What investments are "RRSP eligible"?

Once you put money into an RRSP, the RRSP needs to purchase eligible investments. An RRSP is not an investment in itself. The following is a list of investments that you may hold inside your RRSP:

- Cash, guaranteed investment certificates, term deposits, treasury bills
- Canada Savings Bonds
- Canada RRSP Bonds (*no surprise here*)
- Publicly traded shares and bonds, warrants, and options
- Certain private corporation shares where you and your family own less than 10 percent
- Government bonds
- Shares or bonds of a credit union or co-operative
- Mutual funds, segregated funds, and labour-sponsored funds
- Certain mortgages, including a mortgage on your own home
- Units of certain Canadian limited partnerships that are traded on a stock exchange.

Gold, silver, other precious metals, and real estate are not eligible investments. If your RRSP holds an ineligible investment, it will be subject to a 1-percent per month tax on the value of the ineligible investment.

How much can you contribute to your RRSP?

Generally, any person who has "earned income" in Canada can contribute to an RRSP. The amount that a person is allowed to contribute to an RRSP is based on a formula involving three amounts:

- 18 percent of the person's prior years' "earned income," (discussed below) to a dollar limit maximum set by the Department of Finance (currently, the maximum is $13,500),
- the pension adjustment, PA (discussed above at line 206), and
- the pension adjustment reversal, PAR (also discussed at line 206).

Basically, the formula to calculate your current year RRSP contribution limit is:

Lesser of:	
— (a) 18% of prior year's earned income	$XXXX
— (b) Set maximum limit	$XXXX
The lesser of (a) and (b):	$XXXX
Less: Pension adjustment (PA)	($XXXX)
Plus: Pension adjustment reversal (PAR)	$XXXX
Current year RRSP Contribution Limit	$XXXX

What is earned income and how is it calculated?

The main consideration in determining your RRSP deduction limit is 18 percent of your prior year's "earned income." For purposes of determining your RRSP deduction limit, earned income consists of the following:

- Your salary, including taxable benefits (box 14 of your T4)
- Self-employed business income
- Rental income and royalty income
- Taxable spouse and child support payments received

- Amounts from supplementary unemployment benefit plans
- Research grants
- CPP and QPP disability pension (Chapter 10).

In computing earned income, you need to deduct the following:

- union or professional dues deducted on your tax return (line 212),
- employment expenses deducted on your tax return (line 229; see Chapter 26),
- losses from self-employment (see Chapter 15),
- losses from rental operations (see Chapter 11, line 126), and
- support payments deducted (line 220, discussed below) on your tax return.

Limit set by the Department of Finance

As mentioned above, the maximum amount that can be contributed to an RRSP in a given year is limited by earned income and amounts set by the government. The limit has been frozen at $13,500 until 2003, after which it is scheduled to rise to $14,500 in 2004, and $15,500 in 2005. For years following 2005, the limit will be indexed to inflation.

Since the formula is the lesser of 18 percent of earned income and the limit set by the government, an individual would need to have earned income of $75,000 in 2000 to be able to make the maximum contribution in 2001. In fact, even if the individual's earned income exceeded this amount, his contribution would still be limited to $13,500.

Don't forget that even if the "18 percent" calculation works out to $13,500 your RRSP contribution limit is still reduced by your prior year pension adjustment (PA). If you made $75,000 or more in 1999 and had a 1999 PA of $13,500, your 2000 RRSP contribution limit would be zero!

Finding out your 2000 RRSP contribution limit?

There are three ways to find out what your 2000 RRSP contribution limit is:

- **Look at your 1999 Notice of Assessment.** You would have received your assessment from the CCRA after filing your 1999 return. Your 2000 RRSP contribution limit is highlighted on the assessment. Your 2000 RRSP contribution limit is based on information from your 1999 personal tax return. Any unused RRSP deduction room from prior years is added in to compute your contribution limit. If you have not maximized your RRSP contributions in past years, the unused portion is not lost — it carries on indefinitely.

Although you can carryforward all your unused RRSP contribution room, don't wait to make your RRSP contribution. By contributing today, you'll reap the benefits of an immediate tax saving from your RRSP deduction and tax-free growth while your money is inside your RRSP.

- **Call the TIPS toll-free number (1-800-267-6999) and ask what your limit is.** The CCRA operates an automated Tax Information Phone Service — TIPS, for short. All you need is a touch-tone phone and your 1999 personal tax return in front of you. To protect your privacy, you will need to enter your social insurance number as well as requested figures from your 1999 return. Once entered, the CCRA will process your request for your 2000 RRSP contribution limit.
- **Calculate it yourself:**

Shania (no . . . not that one!) had a 1999 RRSP contribution limit of $9,000. In January 2000, she contributed $6,000 to her RRSP. Since the $6,000 was contributed in the first 60 days of 2000, it qualified for a deduction on Shania's 1999 return. Shania's earned income for 1999 was $60,000. Her 1999 T4 from her employer indicated a pension adjustment (PA) of $1,000.

What is Shania's 2000 RRSP contribution limit?

RRSP contribution limit at the end for 1999	$9,000
Less:	
RRSP contributions made in the first 60 days of 2000 and deducted on her 1999 tax return	($6,000)
Unused RRSP contribution limit carried forward to 2000	$3,000
Plus:	
18% of 1999 earned income ($60,000 × 18%) to a maximum of $13,500	$10,800
Less:	
1999 pension adjustment (PA) on 1999 T4	($1,000)
2000 RRSP contribution limit	$12,800

Shania can contribute $12,800 to her RRSP and take a deduction for the full amount on her 2000 return. She must contribute the amount before March 1, 2001, obtain an official receipt, and complete Schedule 7 of her tax return. The amount she will note at line 11 of Schedule 7 is $12,800. She will also note this on line 208 of her return.

Overcontributions to your RRSP

Generally, the amount you contribute to your RRSP will be equal to the RRSP deduction you will take on line 208 of your return. However, the total amount you have contributed to your RRSP may exceed the amount you claim as a deduction if you do one of the following:

- **You accidentally or deliberately over-contribute to your RRSP:** You are permitted to overcontribute to your RRSP. However, the overcontribution is not tax deductible in the year it is made. If your overcontribution exceeds $2,000, you will find yourself in a penalty situation as well as having to withdraw the excess contribution. The penalty is 1 percent per month of the overcontribution in excess of $2,000 — that amounts to 12 percent per year. (By the way, if you were wondering, tax penalties and interest on late tax payments are not tax deductible.)

  Many people will overcontribute by exactly $2,000, since there will be no penalty and the funds can earn income inside the RRSP tax-free. Moreover, the $2,000 can be deducted on a subsequent year's tax return where you may not have contributed up to your maximum.

- **You don't deduct some or all of the RRSP contribution you have made:** Why would you not take a tax deduction when it is available? Well, you may plan on being in a higher tax bracket in the future. Even though you make an RRSP contribution during the year, you don't need to take the deduction that same year. You can save the deduction for a tax year when the deduction is more valuable.

Let's revisit the Shania example. We noted her income was $60,000. After she deducted the $12,800 she contributed to her RRSP, her net income was $47,200. Assuming she had no deductions in calculating her taxable income, she paid tax on $47,200.

At this income, her marginal tax rate is approximately 34 percent. If she earned one more dollar, she would pay an additional 34 cents in tax. However, if she deducted one more dollar, she could save 34 cents in tax. In other words, the tax saving Shania received from the $12,800 RRSP deduction was about $4,352 ($12,800 × 34 percent). Not bad! Let's expand the example and assume Shania knows that in 2001 she will have a salary of $90,000. Her marginal tax rate at this level of income will be about 48 percent. The potential tax saving on the $12,800 RRSP deduction would go up to $6,144 ($12,800 × 48 percent) — an increase of $1,792. Is it worth waiting a year for the additional tax saving? We'll leave this up to Shania to decide.

Removing your overcontribution

There are two ways to remove your overcontribution.

- **Complete form T3012A "Tax Deduction Waiver on a Refund of Your Undeducted RRSP Contributions Made in 2000."** This form authorizes the holder of your RRSP assets to refund your money without withholding any taxes.
- **Request that your bank, trust company, or investment advisor return your overcontribution to you.** This method will result in your having to pay withholding tax on your RRSP withdrawal. However, don't be concerned — you will get the tax back when you file your tax return. The amount of tax withheld will depend on the amount of the RRSP withdrawal. For RRSP withdrawals under $5,000, the withholding tax rate is 10 percent. Ensure you "break" your RRSP withdrawal into components of $4,999 or less to minimize the tax withheld. Withdrawals of amounts of $5,000 to $15,000 are subject to a withholding tax of 20 percent, while withdrawals of $15,000 or more are subject to a withholding tax of 30 percent.

Spousal RRSPs

When you make your RRSP contributions, you have the option of putting the contributions in your own RRSP, or a spousal RRSP, or a combination thereof. A spousal RRSP is an RRSP to which you contribute the funds, although your spouse is the one who receives the funds when withdrawn. This means your spouse — not you — makes withdrawals from the plan and pays tax on those withdrawals.

Ideally, both you and your spouse should have equal incomes in retirement. You should make a spousal contribution if your spouse will be in a lower tax bracket than you when the money is eventually withdrawn. You see, this way you get the deduction at a high tax rate, and your spouse pays the tax at a lower one. How's that for retirement income splitting! (More on income splitting in Chapter 24.) But if your spouse makes a withdrawal from a spousal plan in the year or within two years of when you last made a spousal RRSP contribution, you — not your spouse — will be subject to the tax.

You are not entitled to additional RRSP contribution room in order to make a spousal contribution. The total contributions to your own plan, plus your spouse's, cannot be greater than your total RRSP contribution limit. (The RRSP contribution limit of your spouse does *not* impact how much you can contribute to a spousal RRSP.)

The RRSP Home Buyer's Plan (HBP)

If you wish, you can withdraw up to $20,000 from your RRSP tax-free for buying a home, as long as you haven't owned a home in the past four years. Your spouse can make use of the HBP too, leaving a potential for $40,000 to go toward the home purchase, provided your spouse hasn't owned a home in the past four years either, and you are purchasing the home jointly. The withdrawal is treated as a loan from your RRSP, to be repaid over a period of no more than 15 years. The first repayment, a minimum of 1/15 of your HBP withdrawal, must be paid back in the second calendar year following the year in which you made the withdrawal. If you took out a $20,000 HBP loan in November 1998, for example, you must repay at least $1,333 (1/15 of $20,000) before the end of 2000. If you do not make the repayment, the $1,333 is included in your income. Yikes!

It's easy to make a HBP repayment. You simply make a contribution to your RRSP. On schedule 7, you note the total of your RRSP contributions and then allocate a portion of the contributions to the annual HBP repayment. (It does not qualify for an RRSP deduction because it is simply a repayment of an amount borrowed from your RRSP.) Your remaining contributions are then allocated to the RRSP Life Learning Plan repayment (see below), if applicable, or simply noted as a regular RRSP contribution that is tax deductible in the normal fashion.

If you contribute to your RRSP and then withdraw the funds within 90 days for the HBP, you won't be able to claim a deduction for that contribution. Always allow your contributions to sit for 91 days or more before making a withdrawal under the HBP.

There is no restriction on speeding up your HBP repayment. It makes good financial sense to repay as soon as you can, because the sooner the funds go back into your RRSP, the greater the tax-free growth in value!

To make a HBP withdrawal from your RRSP, provide the holder of your RRSP with a completed form T1036 "Home Buyer's Plan (HBP) Request to Withdraw Funds from an RRSP."

The RRSP and Lifelong Learning Plan (LLP)

The LLP works in a similar way to the HBP. Funds can be withdrawn on a tax-free basis to fund full-time education or training for you or your spouse. The maximum withdrawal is $10,000 per year, or up to $20,000 over a four-year period. Funds need to be repaid to your RRSP over a period of no more than ten years. The minimum repayment is 1⁄10 of the LLP withdrawal. The first repayment is due on the earlier of the following:

- The second year after the last year you (or your spouse) was able to claim the "education amount" on line 323 of the tax return (see Chapter 18)
- The fifth year after your first withdrawal under the LLP.

For each withdrawal you make, you need to complete form RC96 "Lifelong Learning Plan (LLP) Request to Withdraw Funds from an RRSP." You make your LLP repayments in the same fashion as you would make the HBP repayments noted above. You simply contribute to your RRSP, and on schedule 7 designate what portion of your RRSP contribution is for your LLP repayment.

Transferring a severance or retirement allowance into your RRSP

If you are going to receive a severance or retirement allowance from an employer you worked for before 1996, you may be able to put a portion of the payment directly into your RRSP. (Sorry, it can't go into a spousal RRSP.) This is referred to as a "transfer," and is attractive for two reasons:

- No income tax needs to be withheld on the portion of the payment being transferred directly into your RRSP. A direct transfer means the cheque goes from your employer to your RRSP — you don't even get to touch the money!
- The portion transferred to your RRSP is in addition to your regular RRSP contribution limit. You can still contribute up to your RRSP contribution limit in addition to the portion of the severance transferred to your RRSP.

If a portion of your severance or retirement allowance is transferred directly to an RRSP, you need to complete form T2097 "Designations of Transfers to an RRSP" when completing your tax return. The amount of the transfer is noted as an "eligible retiring allowance" (this includes an eligible severance). You note this amount on line 9 of schedule 7, and the amount is added to your regular RRSP contributions to arrive at the total RRSP deduction for the year. You will enter this total on line 208 of your return.

Just after the end of the year in which you received a severance or retirement allowance, you will receive a T4A slip noting both the portion that was eligible to be transferred to your RRSP and the portion that was not. The total of these two amounts is included in your income (line 130). However, the portion included in your income that was transferred to your RRSP is offset by the extra RRSP deduction, so you don't pay tax on this portion. The portion not transferred is, of course, taxable.

It's not critical that you roll your retiring allowance directly into your RRSP — this transfer can be made later. But be sure to make the contribution within 60 days following the end of the year in which you received your payment. If you don't contribute before this time, this special contribution is lost forever!

The portion your retirement allowance or severance that cannot be transferred directly to your RRSP is available to assist in maximizing your regular RRSP contribution for the year. As noted above, if you left an employer where you were part of an RPP you may be entitled to a pension adjustment reversal (PAR, T10 slip) which would serve to increase your RRSP contribution limit.

Line 209: Saskatchewan Pension Plan (SPP) Deduction

If you have made contributions to the SPP, you can deduct the least of the following amounts on your 2000 tax return:

- Amounts contributed to the SPP for yourself or your spouse from January 1, 2000 to March 1, 2001, excluding any contributions deducted on your 1999 tax return.
- Your 1999 RRSP deduction limit less the RRSP deduction you claimed on line 208 (see above), excluding any amounts transferred to your RRSP (that is, a portion of a severance or retirement allowance received that was transferred to your RRSP).
- $600.

Line 212: Deduction for Annual Union, Professional, or Like Dues

Since you are taxed on pretty much all your income, it's logical that costs incurred to earn the income are deductible. It is logical — but no one ever said the *Income Tax Act* was logical. One of the deductions permitted is the cost of belonging to a union or to a professional body, or the cost of carrying professional or malpractice insurance. Union dues paid are noted in box 44 of your T4. Fees paid to professional organizations are usually receipted. If your employer pays the fees for your professional memberships or insurance, the employer gets the tax deduction — you don't, even if the receipt is in your name.

If you paid GST or HST on your union or professional dues you may be able to have the GST refunded to you. Refer to the section near the end of Chapter 26 on the "Goods and Services Tax (GST)/Harmonized Sales Tax (HST) Rebate."

Deductions for Children and Special Care

In this section we will take a detailed look at child care expenses — how much is deductible? What is an eligible child care expense? Who is a supporting person, who gets to claim the child care expenses? What if supporting persons live apart? etc. There are a lot of issues to cover! After our comments on the child care expense deduction we will wrap this section up with an overview of the deduction for attendant care expenses.

Line 214: Deduction for child care expenses

It's kinda hard to work and take care of the kids at the same time, right? Kids need to go to day care or a baby-sitter's house or be watched by a nanny — and all these things cost money!

Our governments recognize that many of us incur child care expenses in order to be able to work. Our government also acknowledges that you may incur child care expenses in order to be able to go to school to train for a job. That's why it offers tax relief for child care expenses that arise when you, your spouse, or other "supporting person" do one of the following:

- Go to work
- Carry on a business (earn self-employment income)
- Go to school to improve occupational skills
- Carry out research.

How much is deductible?

Here are the maximum child care expenses that can be claimed per child in 2000:

Disabled child — regardless of age	$10,000
Child under 7 at December 31, 2000	$7,000
Child aged 7 to 16 at December 31, 2000	$4,000

The above figures are the maximum amounts that can be claimed on a per child basis. The actual claim you can make is the lessor of the following:

- The amounts noted above per eligible child
- The amount of eligible child care expenses incurred
- Two-thirds of your "earned income"

An *eligible child* must meet the following criteria. He or she must be your child, your spouse's child or a child dependent on you or your spouse, one having a net income in 2000 of $7,231 or less. Eligible child care expenses include payments to the following:

- Individuals providing child care services. Payments to the child's mother, father, or a related person under 18, are not eligible child care expenses. Individuals providing child care must provide a receipt with their social insurance number noted. Other child care providers simply need to provide you with a receipt. Receipts must highlight that child care services were provided.
- Day care or child care centres
- Day nursery schools

- Schools where part of the fee is for child care (such as before- and after-school class care)
- Day camps
- Sports camps.

Where payments are made for day camps and sports camps. The eligible amount is restricted in the following situations:

- $175 per week per a disabled child of any age
- $175 per week per child under 7 on December 31, 2000
- $100 per week per child aged 7 to 16.

Earned income is another important concept when it comes to understanding the tax implications of child care expenses. First, do not confuse the concept of earned income for the child care expense deduction with the concept of earned income for purposes of calculating your RRSP deduction limit discussed above. Second, the claim you can make for child care expenses is restricted to two-thirds of your "earned income." Again, the government offers tax relief for child care expenses where they are incurred to let you work, train for work, or carry out research. To ensure you are working, training, or carrying out research, the rules restrict your child care expenses claim to two-thirds of the income earned from these sources. Specifically, "earned income" for determining the maximum amount of deductible child care expenses comprises the following:

- Employment income, including tips and gratuities
- Self-employment income
- Scholarship amounts in excess of $3,000
- Research grants
- CPP and QPP disability benefits
- Government payments under a plan to encourage employment.

Claiming a deduction for child care expenses

You will need to complete form T778 "Child Care Expenses Deduction for 2000." This form has two parts.

Part A — Total child care expenses — This part is simply a summary of the names of the children for whom costs were incurred, as well as the amounts paid to the caregiver individuals and organizations. Where you made payments to a day or sports camp, you need to note the number of weeks the child attended. The number of weeks is important because, as noted above the amounts that can be claimed for child care to these organizations is restricted to weekly dollar amounts.

Part B — Basic limit for child care expenses deduction — Part B details the calculation needed to come up with the maximum child care claim that you can make. It includes the $10,000, $7,000, and $4,000 per child limits noted above, as well as the "two-thirds of earned income" calculation. The lesser of these calculations is then compared to the actual eligible child care expenses incurred.

Who gets to claim the deduction for child care expenses?

If a child lives with both parents, the child care expense deduction is claimed by the parent with the lower income. However, as with everything, there are exceptions to this general rule. These exceptions are discussed as follows.

Where one of two supporting persons has no net income, the deduction for child care expenses will be "wasted." Where possible, the supporting person should arrange their affairs so the deduction can be maximized. This involves ensuring the lower supporting person has "earned income." As noted above, the deduction for child care expenses cannot exceed two-thirds of earned income. So for a maximum claim, the earned income of the lower net income supporting person needs to be 3/2 (or 150 percent) of the eligible child care costs incurred.

Are you the only supporting person? If so, you make the claim for the child care expenses deduction. Can the higher net income supporting person ever deduct child care expenses? Yes! There are instances in which the supporting person with the higher net income can make the claim, because the lower net income supporting person was in one of these situations:

- In school. (The school can be a secondary school, college, university, or an "education institution" certified by the Human Resources Development Canada [HRDC] for courses that develop or improve occupational skills.)
- Not able to take care of children because of a mental or physical disability
- In jail for at least two weeks in 2000.

Also, if you are the higher net income supporting person, you may be able to make a claim if you and your spouse were living apart on December 31, 2000, due to a marriage breakdown, but reconciled before March 1, 2001. A claim will be allowed to you if you and your spouse had been separated for at least 90 days beginning sometime in 2000.

Note that the claim is restricted to the amount of time in the year that the above conditions existed. The claim cannot exceed the following:

- $175 per week per a disabled child of any age
- $175 per week per child under 7 on December 31, 2000
- $100 per week per child aged 7 to 16.

To make a claim as the "higher" net income supporting person, you must complete Part C of form T778 "Child Care Expense Deduction for 2000." In completing this part, the name, social insurance number, and net income of the lower net income supporting person are noted, as is the reason the higher net income supporting spouse is making the claim. Part C also includes a work chart to assist you in calculating the amount that can be claimed based on the $175 and $100 amounts noted above. Part D on page 2 of the T778 also needs to be completed when the higher net income supporting person is claiming child care expenses due to the fact that the lower net income spouse was in school in 2000.

Supporting persons living apart

Where supporting persons were living apart for all of 2000 by virtue of a marriage breakdown (whether a legal or common-law marriage), each is entitled to a deduction for child care expenses. The aggregate claimed by the supporting persons cannot exceed the limits detailed above.

If you separated from your spouse in 2000 and you are the higher net income supporting person, you can make a claim if you and your spouse were living apart on December 31, 2000. A claim will be allowed to you if you and your spouse had been separated for at least 90 days beginning sometime in 2000 and the child care expenses claimed by you were actually paid by you. The claim period is restricted to the period of separation.

Line 215: Deduction for attendant care expenses

If you suffer from a severe and prolonged mental or physical impairment, you may deduct certain amounts paid to an attendant over the age of 18, provided that attendant is needed to enable you to go to work or school. You can claim the deduction on line 215 of your income tax return. Form T929 "Attendant Care Expenses" needs to be completed.

To be eligible to claim this deduction, you must have a severe and prolonged impairment that restricts your activities of daily living and is expected to last for 12 months. As with the disability credit amount, (see Chapter 18, line 316) your doctor needs to complete and sign form T2201 "Disability Tax Certificate" and you must file it with your tax return. If you've already submitted this form to claim the disability tax credit, there's no need to file it again.

Is your attendant required for you to go to work?

Of course, there's a limit to the amount you can deduct. If the attendant is required to enable you to go to work, the limit is the lesser of the following:

- Two-thirds of your "earned income" for the year
- The qualifying amounts you paid to the attendant during the year. The expenses cannot include any that you're already claiming as a medical expense (Chapter 18, lines 330 and 331) — no double dipping!

Qualifying amounts include amounts paid to an attendant to enable you to perform the duties of employment, to carry on a business, or to carry out research for which you receive a grant. The attendant must be over the age of 18, and cannot be your spouse.

As it pertains to deductions for an attendant, here's yet another definition of earned income (you'd think the CCRA could come up with a new name), the sum of the following:

- Net income from a business
- Gross employment income
- Net research grants
- Training allowances paid under the *National Training Act*
- The taxable portion of scholarships, fellowships, bursaries, and similar awards (this is net of the $3,000 exemption).

Is the attendant required for you to go to school?

If the attendant is required to enable you to attend a designated educational institution or secondary school, the limit is the least of the following:

- Two-thirds of your income from other sources (up to a maximum of $15,000)
- Two-thirds of $375, times the number of weeks of attendance at the institution or school
- The qualifying amounts you paid to the attendant during the year.

You are able to claim the disability tax credit and up to $10,000 of attendant care as a medical expense. However, you may only claim the medical expense if you have not claimed the deduction discussed here for attendant care.

Unlike the medical expense credit and the disability credit, the deduction for attendant care cannot be transferred to someone else. You may need to think about which deductions are most beneficial for you.

You must have receipts for all payments made, and that includes the attendant's social insurance number. Although these receipts do not have to be filed (if you are claiming the amounts as an attendant care deduction), you should keep them in a safe place in case the taxman comes looking for them.

Lines 217 and 226: Deduction for a Business Investment Loss (BIL)

In Chapter 13, we discussed the concept of capital gains and capital losses. A capital loss occurs when you sell an investment for less than you paid for it. A capital loss can only be used to shelter or offset capital gains from tax — it cannot be used to shelter other types of income (say, employment income, pension income, interest, or dividends) from tax. If you had a capital loss in 2000 but had no capital gains, the loss can be applied against capital gains reported on your prior three tax returns, or it can be carried forward to be applied against any capital gains that may arise in the future.

A business investment loss (BIL) is a special type of capital loss. A business investment loss, or a portion of that loss, can be deducted in the year incurred to shelter any type of income — not just capital gains — from tax.

A BIL occurs when you sell your shares, or debt of a small business corporation (SBC), at a loss. A BIL loss will also arise if you were deemed to dispose of the shares or debt when the corporation became bankrupt or insolvent.

An SBC is a private corporation with the majority of the ownership in Canadian hands. The corporation must carry on a business in Canada. If the corporation is simply holding investments it likely will not be considered to be carrying on a business for purposes of the SBC rules. (Refer to Chapter 17 for a discussion on SBCs.)

You will be deemed to have disposed of your shares or debt if the corporation is insolvent and no longer carries on business, and if the fair market value of the shares is nil.

Rules in calculating the deductible portion of the BIL

Your true loss is reported on line 228 on your return. The disclosure on line 217 is the amount you are entitled to deduct. As in the calculation of capital losses, 100 percent of a BIL is not tax deductible. This is logical since a gain on the sale of an investment is not fully taxable. The deductible portion of a BIL is referred to as an Allowable Business Investment Loss (ABIL).

If you incurred the loss before February 28, 2000, 75 percent of the loss is deductible. If the loss was incurred on February 28, 2000 or later, 66⅔ percent of the loss is deductible. The change in the rate as of February 28, 2000 and subsequent dispositions resulted from the 2000 federal budget. The rate changes parallel the decrease in the percentage of capital gains now subject to tax.

(Federal proposals announced on October 18, 2000 will decrease the ABIL to be reduced to one-half of the actual loss if the loss is suffered after October 17, 2000.)

Further restrictions in calculating the deductible portion of a BIL

If you have used any portion of your capital gains deduction (Chapter 17, line 254), this will reduce the amount of the BIL that you can deduct.

Let's look at an example. In 1998, Abdul lent $100,000 to assist an SBC in starting up a new Internet business. Unfortunately, in July 2000 the corporation went bankrupt, leaving Abdul with nothing. Back on his 1991 return, Abdul had claimed a capital gains deduction to shelter a $10,000 capital gain he incurred on the sale of some public company shares.

Abdul will report a BIL of $100,000 on line 228. However, his actual BIL eligible for a deduction is reduced by the 1991 capital gain that was sheltered from tax by the capital gains deduction. Therefore, his BIL eligible for deduction is $90,000 ($100,000 less $10,000). He can claim two-thirds of this amount, or $60,000, as his ABIL on line 217. The $7,500 ($10,000 × 75%) that could not be claimed as an ABIL is treated as a regular capital loss.

Line 219: Deduction for Moving Expenses

Did you move in 2000?

Did you move for a new job — even if with the same employer?

Did you move to start a business?

Did you move to attend university or college?

Did you move back from college or university to take a job — even if it was just a summer job?

If you answered yes to any of these questions, you may be eligible to claim a deduction for moving expenses on your 2000 tax return!

When can you deduct moving expenses?

If you moved at least 40 kilometres in 2000 to start a job, start a business, or for full-time post-secondary education, you may be eligible to deduct at least a portion of your moving expenses.

The eligible moving expenses may only be deducted from your employment, self-employment, or scholarship income earned at the new location. If your 2000 eligible moving expenses exceeded your 2000 income at the new location, the excess can be carried forward for deduction on your 2001 tax return.

Look at Ginny's case. She moved from Vancouver to Winnipeg in December 2000 to take a new job. Her total moving costs were $5,000. She was not reimbursed by her new employer (cheapskate!). Since she arrived very late in the year, she only received one month's salary in 2000, totaling $3,000. When Ginny completes her 2000 tax return, she can only deduct $3,000 in moving expenses. She will deduct the remaining $2,000 on her 2001 tax return.

What moving expenses are eligible?

Most moving expenses are eligible for a tax deduction. Specifically, moving expenses that are eligible for deduction are as follows:

- Traveling expenses, including automobile expenses for you and your family
- Meals and accommodation on the way to the new residence
- Costs of moving your "stuff" (moving van, storage, insurance, and so on)
- Costs for up to 15 days for you and your family for meals and temporary stay
- Cost of canceling your lease on old residence
- Costs of selling your old residence (advertising, legal fees, real estate commission, and mortgage prepayment penalty if applicable)
- Costs of maintaining your old residence when vacant (including mortgage interest and property taxes) to a maximum of $5,000
- Legal fees and land transfer fees paid in acquiring the new residence, provided you sold the prior residence as a result of the move
- Utility disconnect and hook-up fees
- Incidental costs related to the move (for example, costs of changing your address, costs of acquiring new auto and driver's licences)

With respect to automobile and meal costs incurred while moving, the CCRA permits you to either claim the actual costs or to use a flat rate. The CCRA refers to the flat rate system as the "simplified method" — appropriately named, we would say.

For meals, the flat rate is $11 per meal per person to a maximum of $33 per person per day. Where you use the flat rate, you don't need to retain receipts.

The flat rate for automobile travel varies by province or territory (see the chart below). If you don't use the flat rate, you need to track all the costs of operating the car for a year (gas, maintenance, insurance, interest on car loans, depreciation, and so on). You then need to prorate the total of these costs on a basis of the # kilometres driven for the move over the total # kilometres driven for the complete year. (Ugh — more math to do.)

Flat rates to use in determining automobile costs

The following flat rates are indicated in cents per kilometre:

All territories	42.5
British Columbia	37.5
Alberta	35.0
Saskatchewan	34.5
Manitoba	37.0
Ontario	38.0
Quebec	41.0
New Brunswick	37.0
Nova Scotia	36.5
Prince Edward Island	36.0
Newfoundland	38.5

Employer paid or reimbursed moving expenses

You can only deduct moving expenses to the extent that the expenses were incurred by you. You cannot deduct expenses that were paid for by your employer (say, at the new location), or that you incurred and which were later reimbursed by your employer. On the other hand, if your employer provided you with an allowance, this amount must be included in your income. Make sure you then claim any eligible moving expenses as a deduction.

When possible, always get your new employer to reimburse you for your moving expenses. This is advantageous for a number of reasons:

- You will not be out any money. Even at the top tax bracket, a tax deduction is only worth about 50 cents on the dollar. This means that each dollar you deduct can only save you 50 cents in tax. Isn't it better to have your employer give you back the full dollar? (The employer can claim a deduction for amounts reimbursed to you.)
- Some moving costs are *not* tax deductible. You definitely want to be reimbursed for these.
- You avoid the hassle of detailing all your moving expenses on your tax return, plus you are far less likely to have the CCRA question your return. Our experience is that the CCRA is fairly diligent in asking taxpayers to provide proof of their moving expenses.
- You do not need to wait for a tax refund to get any of your money back.
- You won't have to read the rest of this section because you will no longer care about the tax rules dealing with the deductibility of moving expenses!

CCRA has stated that your employer can provide you with an up-to-$650 non-accountable allowance as a reimbursement of moving expenses. The allowance will not be considered income provided you certify in writing that you incurred moving expenses of at least an amount equal to the allowance you received.

Coming to or leaving Canada?

In most situations, moving expenses are not deductible if you are moving to or from Canada. (In this situation, you definitely want to have your employer reimburse your moving expenses!) However, if you leave Canada to study full time — say, at a college or university in the United States — your moving expenses would be deductible. These would be deductible against income earned in the foreign country — say, any part-time jobs, scholarships, and so on — that is reported on your Canadian tax return. This assumes that even though you are studying outside Canada, you continue to be a Canadian resident for tax purposes. Therefore, your "worldwide income" is subject to tax in Canada. (Refer to Chapter 2, Who Pays Taxes in Canada?, for a discussion on residency and taxation.) If you are a full-time student and you came to Canada, you can deduct your moving expenses against income earned in Canada.

How do you claim moving expenses on your tax return?

To claim moving expenses, you complete form T1-M "Moving Expenses Deduction." On this form you report where you moved from and to, why you moved (start a job? a business? go to college or university?) and the specific details and dollar amounts of your actual moving costs. Oddly, neither the T1-M nor any moving receipts need to be filed with your tax return. However, you are, as you would expect, required to keep these on hand in case of a CCRA query.

Lines 220 and 230: Deduction for Support Payments

Support is the word that replaced "alimony" and "maintenance" payments a few years back. Support refers both to payments made for spousal support and those made for child support. It is important to differentiate between spousal and child support because each has its own criteria regarding permissible tax deductions.

Line 230 is located just to the left of line 220. Line 230 is simply for disclosure. Here you insert the amount of spouse and child support paid. As detailed below, all support payments may not be tax deductible. Enter the deductible portion on line 220.

Whether you receive the support for yourself or for your children, you should refer to Chapter 11, line 128, to determine what is taxable or not taxable in your hands. You will see that the deduction/income inclusion criteria mirror each other. Where one taxpayer has a deduction, one will have an income inclusion. If no deduction is available, there is no income inclusion. If you are paying a lawyer to help you collect support, your fees may be deductible.

Spousal support

Payments to an ex-spouse (including an "estranged" [separated] spouse) are in most cases tax deductible. To support the deduction, you must have a written agreement or court order signed by both you and your ex-spouse that specifically stipulates the amounts to be paid. The payments must be periodic, that is, monthly. Lump sum payments do not qualify for a tax deduction. If there is no agreement or court order, the amounts paid would not be tax deductible. However, as noted below, it is possible to have an agreement that provides for at least some of the pre-agreement spousal support payments to be tax deductible.

Child support

The rules took a dramatic shift on May 1, 1997. There are now three sets of rules, and you need to determine which ones apply to you. Your child support payments may or may not be tax deductible. The three sets of rules are detailed below.

Child support order or agreement made before May 1, 1997

If you are making payments under an order or agreement made before May 1, 1997, your payments are tax deductible. (Your ex-spouse will include the amounts in his or her income.)

Child support order or agreement made on May 1, 1997 or later

Your payments under a May 1, 1997 or later agreement or order are not tax deductible. (They are not taxable in the hands of your ex-spouse.)

Modification of a pre-May 1, 1997 child support order or agreement

If you are making tax-deductible payments under a pre-May 1, 1997 order or agreement, you may find that your payments suddenly cease to be tax deductible under one of the following circumstances:

- The order or agreement is amended to increase or decrease child support payments (and therefore, considered a new agreement and subject to the new rules)
- You and your ex-spouse elect to have the newer rules apply to your old agreement. This is done by filing form T1157 "Election for Child Support Payments" with the CCRA. As you would expect, the form requires the signatures of both ex-spouses.

Support payments to third parties

Payments you are making to third parties, rather than directly to your ex-spouse, will qualify as support payments for tax purposes provided the payments meet the following criteria:

- They are made by virtue of a court order or written agreement
- They are periodic
- Your ex-spouse has discretion as to the use of the funds.

The ex-spouse is considered to have discretion over the use of the funds if he or she has agreed to have the third-party payments deducted from the support actually received. Where the ex-spouse makes payments to third parties due to a court order for specific living expenses (for example, mortgage or rent payments) of the ex-spouse (or children), the payments are not considered support payments for tax purposes — there is no discretion over the use of the funds.

However, third-party payments made under a court order or written agreement for a specific expenditure (say, for ongoing medical costs of a child) can be deemed to be periodic and at the discretion of the ex-spouse. Here, the CCRA would treat the payment as a legitimate support payment for tax purposes. For this to occur, the written agreement or court order must refer to this intent.

Payments made to a court or provincial authority are considered to have been received by the ex-spouse. The tax implications remain the same as if the funds were actually paid directly to the ex-spouse.

Any payments you have made prior to the date of a court order or a written agreement *can* be considered to have been paid under an order or agreement, and therefore be tax deductible. The order or agreement must stipulate that any prior payments made are considered to have been paid (and therefore potentially deductible) pursuant to the agreement. Only payments made in the year that the order or agreement is finalized, and the preceding year, qualify for the retroactive treatment. Get the separation agreement drawn up promptly!

Though it can be emotionally unbearable to go through the process of finalizing the agreement, our experience in dealing with many separated and divorced individuals is that the agreement is vital in maintaining some sanity and to ensuring your financial protection. You should contact a lawyer specializing in family law as soon as possible to protect your rights to support, your assets, and your children. (There are various health care practitioners and clergy you can turn to for help with the emotional side.)

If you are making payments after the death of your ex-spouse, these payments are not tax deductible, no matter who you are making the payments to. If you die, there can be a claim on your estate for continued support. This kinda contradicts the old "till death do us part" idea.

Line 221: Deduction for Carrying Charges and Interest Expense for Investments

Certain expenses you incur to earn investment income are tax deductible. Briefly, these are as follows:

- Investment counsel fees and investment management fees (only the portion of these fees related to services for your non-RRSP investments outside your RRSP are deductible)
- Safekeeping, custodial, and safety deposit box fees
- Tax return preparation fees, if you have income from a business or a property
- Interest on money borrowed to earn investment income, such as interest and dividends — but not capital gains.

Brokerage commissions are not tax deductible because they form part of the tax cost on the purchase of an investment or reduce the proceeds on the sale.

Eligible carrying costs and interest are to be detailed in Part IV of Schedule 4 "Summary, Carrying Charges and Interest Expenses" of your tax return. The total is then put on line 221.

More on interest that can be deducted

Interest costs are deductible if you've borrowed money to invest in a business or earn *income from property*. Income from property includes interest, dividends, rents, and royalties.

Capital gains are not considered to be income from property. Therefore, if you're earning primarily capital gains, the taxman may deny your deduction. Keep in mind that if you're investing in stocks or equity mutual funds, there's usually the potential to earn dividends. This will normally be enough to keep your interest deductible.

To deduct interest, the CCRA states, you do not have to receive investment income but only need to have an *expectation* that you will. If you are paying interest at a higher rate than what you anticipate your return to be, the excess will not be allowed as a tax deduction. For example, say you took out a loan at 6.5 percent. You used the money from the loan to purchase a bond that is paying 5.5 percent interest. The 1 percent in interest you paid in excess of the return would not be allowed as a deduction. Where you have borrowed money to invest in fixed dividend preferred shares, any interest in excess of 125 percent of the dividend yield would not be allowed as a deduction. The "125 percent" figure is based on the fact that it is 125 percent of dividends that are taxed. (Why should you pay tax on 125 percent of a dividend you ask? Refer to Chapter 12, line 120 — it will make more sense after you read this — honest!)

Interest continues to be tax deductible even if the investment has been sold. This is provided the entire sale proceeds are used to pay down the loan or to purchase another investment.

Line 224: Deduction for Exploration and Development Expenses

We know what you are thinking. How could this deduction possibly apply to me? We know most of you are not out there in the back forty prospecting for gold or drilling for oil. However, you still may be entitled to a deduction for exploration and development expenses incurred by someone else (say, an oil exploration company) on your behalf!

Did you invest in an oil and gas or mining venture in 2000 or in a prior year? The type of investment may have been called a "limited partnership," a "flow-through share" investment, or simply a "tax shelter." Whatever the term, if you did invest, you are probably entitled to some special tax deductions. One of the attractive features promoted in the selling of oil, gas, and mining investments is the tax write-offs (slang for "tax deductions") available from these investments.

If you are contemplating an investment in an oil, gas, or mining venture, ensure you completely understand the risks associated with the investment. A general rule of thumb is that the greater the tax savings, the riskier the investment. Be sure that such an investment falls within your risk-tolerance comfort zone. You should invest based on the quality of the investment — not the tax saving provided by the investment.

Why are these tax deductions made available? Remember that back in Chapter 1 we noted our *Income Tax Act* serves two purposes. The first is to provide cash necessary for the government to operate. And two, the *Income Tax Act* is a tool for many government initiatives. For example, in line 208 we saw that the government wants you to save for your retirement, so we were given the tax saving provisions of the RRSP rules. The government also thinks it is a good idea to encourage oil, gas, and metal exploration in Canada. So the Act contains provisions to encourage this. The Act provides oil, gas, and mining companies with significant write-offs for the following:

- Canadian exploration expenses (CEE)
- Canadian development expenses (CDE)
- Canadian oil and gas property expenses (COGPE).

Since many exploration companies do not have sufficient money to go out and explore for oil, gas, and metals, the Act permits these companies to turn to you for the funds. You are the one actually funding the exploration and development, so you get the attractive tax deductions. This is referred to as the expenses being "renounced" to you. An example below highlights how the write-offs or deductions are calculated. Since "exploration" is the government's main initiative and the exploration phase has the greatest chance of failure, the write-offs are greatest when funds are expended on exploration.

How to claim exploration and development expenses

The promoter of the oil, gas, or mining ventures will provide you with all the information you need. Depending on the structure of the investment, you will receive a T101, T102, or T5013 slip. Instructions are provided on the back of these forms to assist in calculating your deduction. However, to ensure clarity and to illustrate that certain deductions are not all deductible in one year, we provide the following example.

Let's take Norm. Norm is a general contractor operating in Regina. His main source of income is from building and renovating houses — he is not a prospector or miner. In June 1999, Norm's investment advisor suggested he look at an investment opportunity promoted by Sparrow Exploration Inc. Sparrow operated out of Calgary. The opportunity involved the purchase of "flow-through shares." (The offering memorandum indicated they were called "flow-through shares" because certain expenses incurred by Sparrow would not be considered tax deductible for Sparrow but would *flow through* as tax deductible expenses of the investor.) After reading the offering memorandum and considering the appropriateness of the investment and his risk tolerance and investment objectives, Norm decided to invest.

In March 2001, Norm sat down to prepare his 2000 tax return. Sparrow had sent him a T101 slip "Statement — Renunciation of Resource Expenses, Reduction of Amounts Previously Renounced and Allocation of Assistance." (Try saying that five times quickly!)

The slip indicated the following has "flowed through" to him based on his investment:

Canadian exploration expense (CEE)	$1,400
Canadian development expense (CDE)	$800

Have a look at how Norm prepared the following work chart to calculate his 2000 deduction:

	CEE	*CDE*	*Total*
Opening balance	0	0	0
2000 expenses per T101 slip	$1,400	$800	$2,200
Subtotal	$1,400	$800	$2,200
Maximum deduction %	100%	30%	
2000 maximum deduction	$1,400	$240	$1,640

Note that of the $800 allocated to Norm for CDE he was only able to deduct $240 — 30 percent. The amount unable to be deducted on Norm's 2000 tax return, $560 ($800 less $240) will carryover to Norm's 2001 tax return. Norm's 2001 maximum claim will be $168 ($560 × 30 percent). The remaining undeducted amount will carry over to 2002 and the process will repeat itself.

You do not have to take the maximum deduction. Any amount not claimed will carryover to the following year for potential deduction using the same percentage figures. Why would you not want to take a deduction? Perhaps you expect to be in a higher tax bracket next year, so the deduction will be worth more in tax savings if you wait a year. A similar comment was made above in dealing with the RRSP deduction (line 208).

Line 229: Deduction for Employment Expenses

As noted earlier, it is logical that if you are taxed on all your employment income, you should be able to deduct all the expenses you incur to carry out your employment duties. Well, this is not always the case. The fact of the matter is that the deduction for employment expenses is very limited. We warn most of you not to even think about the costs you incur in getting to and from work, your tools, your wardrobe, your makeup, and getting your hair just perfect. (Please, no questions on dry cleaning!) Those most likely to be able to deduct employment expenses are those who have "out of the office" sales jobs and those employed in transportation.

Why worry, if you can deduct your employment expenses? It is always preferable to simply have your employer reimburse you for expenses you incur in doing your job. For example, if you attend a seminar or course to help you do your job better, have your employer reimburse you. The reimbursement would not be a taxable benefit to you.

Did you take a customer out to lunch? Have your employer reimburse you. You are not "out-of-pocket" anything, and you have probably improved your relationship with the customer! Overall, everyone is happy — and you don't need to worry about the income tax return stuff.

For our detailed comments on employment expense we suggest you jump to Chapter 26 which deals with tax breaks available to employees.

ric's Residence

ıs as a clergy person) may be able claim a
respect to his or her residence. We have
(and the changes coming to it in 2001!) in
ole to employees. We suggest you look ahead

s

32 if they apply to you. These include certain
hdrawals of RRSP over-contributions and

g an income tax assessment

r a retirement allowance or a pension benefit.
nt of the payment received in the year — minus
f you cannot claim all your legal fees in the year
ver the next seven years.

arital breakdown, spousal and child support.

and spousal and child support are tax deductible
what is deductible continues to evolve — generally

so that fees for tax deductible services are noted
amily law lawyers are not tax lawyers! You may
ver will understand.A summary of what is tax
ble 16-1.

al Fees Incurred in Respect of Marital and Spousal and Child Support

	Tax Deductible?
er provincial legislation	Yes
ler *Divorce Act*	No
	Yes
	No
	No
t would be taxable to you	Yes
	Yes
Defend against support being reduced	Yes

(continued)

Table 16-1 *(continued)*

Legal Fees Incurred To	*Tax Deductible?*
Terminate or reduce support payments	No
Obtain custody	No
Obtain or enforce visitation rights	No
Obtain a separation agreement	No
Obtain a divorce	No

Repayments of OAS, CPP, QPP, and EI benefits

Sometimes the government sends you too much money. If you have been paid benefits in excess of what you are considered to be entitled to, Human Resources Development Canada (HRDC) — or the Quebec equivalent — will request it back.

If in 2000 you were required to repay any OAS, CPP, QPP, or EI that was included in your 1999 or prior year's tax returns, you can deduct the repayment on line 232 on your 2000 tax return. EI repayments made in 2000 in respect of EI received in 1999 or prior years are noted in box 30 of your 2000 T4E slip.

Repayments of prior year OAS and EI differ from repayments of OAS and EI, referred to as social benefit repayments or clawbacks (see discussion regarding line 235, on the next page). These repayments refer to repayments you may be required to make in connection with OAS or EI received in 2000 — not receipts from prior years. The amount to be repaid is calculated based on your 2000 income, as per line 234 of your return.

Other deductions

- **Withdrawals of over-contributed RRSP amounts:** Remember if you remove an RRSP over-contribution (discussed under line 208), you will be need to include this in your income as with any RRSP withdrawal. Your RRSP holder will issue you a T4RSP slip. The slip will *not* highlight that the amount you are taking out is an over-contribution. The income inclusion can result in double-taxation as you never received a tax deduction for the RRSP contribution as it was an over-contribution. To prevent double-taxation you can claim a deduction on line 232 for the amount of RRSP over-contribution withdrawn. You will need to file a form T746 "Calculating Your Deduction for Refund of Undeducted RRSP Contributions" with your tax return to support the deduction claimed.
- **Unclaimed foreign tax credits:** Foreign tax credits are discussed in Chapter 19. As detailed in that chapter, you may not be entitled to claim a full foreign tax credit. When this is the case, the amount of foreign taxes you paid in excess of the foreign tax credit available to you may qualify for a deduction on line 232.

Line 234: Net Income Before Adjustments

Line 234 is simply a subtotal. It is only relevant for calculating the social benefits repayment on line 235. If you are not eligible to receive OAS or EI, the subtotal will be meaningless to you.

Line 235: Social Benefits Repayment (OAS and EI Clawbacks)

Canada's social welfare programs for seniors (OAS) and the unemployed (EI) have limitations. Essentially, if your income is considered too high, you are required to repay all or a portion of the benefits received.

Old age security (OAS) clawback

The social benefit repayment is in respect of OAS received in 2000. As you may have received the OAS and then may be required to repay all or a portion of it back, it is often referred to a "clawback." The government prefers to use "social benefit repayment" — a far less aggressive term. The clawback of OAS is a calculated amount based on your net income per line 234 ("net income before adjustments") — not per line 236 (simply "net income"). (It would be clearer if line 234 were titled "net income before social benefit repayment.")

As noted in Chapter 10, Human Resources Development Canada (HRDC) may not even have sent you any OAS in 2000 (or sent you a reduced amount), because it expected that you would be subject to the clawback in 2000 and need to repay all or part of your OAS. It has made an assumption based on your 1999 tax return. However, you will still get a T4(OAS) slip indicating that you have received the full OAS. While this will guarantee to confuse you, the slip is correct; the amount clawed back from you will be indicated as a tax paid. (Whether HRDC calls it "tax paid" or a "social benefit repayment" on the slip doesn't really matter because it will "all come out in the wash." You will have to trust us and refer to the detailed discussion on the OAS clawback in Chapter 10.)

As you may remember from Chapter 10, you will be subject to an OAS clawback in 2000 if your line 234 net income exceeds $53,960. For every dollar of income above $53,960 you are required to pay back 15 cents of your OAS income.

The maximum OAS income for 2000 was $5,039. The mathematically inclined can calculate that based on the above formula, the maximum OAS would need to be fully repaid where your line 234 net income is $87,553 or more.

The $53,960 base amount will be increased each year to keep up with inflation. The annual increasing of the amount, referred to as indexing, was introduced as part of the February 28, 2000, federal budget.

You will deduct any social benefit repayment in calculating your net income. This makes sense because the full amount of OAS or EI has been included in calculating your total income. Therefore, since you are not allowed to keep all the income, only the portion that you can keep, if any, is taxed.

If you have received a T4(OAS) slip, ensure that you complete line 235. HRDC may owe you OAS! If it does, the amount is paid to you as part of your tax return — it will decrease your tax liability or increase your tax refund!

Since the OAS clawback is based on the line 234 net income, you should plan, where possible, to minimize this net income figure. This can be done by reducing your income subject to tax — perhaps by rearranging your affairs to shift investment income to a spouse. Other ways may be to reduce the taxable amount of Canada Pension Plan (CPP) benefits you receive by splitting your benefits with your spouse (refer to Chapter 10) and, of course, by maximizing your RRSP contributions.

Employment Insurance (EI) clawback

Like the OAS clawback, a repayment of EI because your income is considered too high is referred to as a social benefit repayment. This differs from the situation where you have simply been paid too much in EI benefits in the view of HRDC. If in 2000 you were required to repay some of the EI you received in 1999 or prior years, the amount repaid can be deducted on line 232 of your 2000 return. We discussed this earlier.

You will need to repay all or part of your current year's EI benefits if one of the following situations apply to you:

- Box 16 ("special benefits paid") of your T4E slip has an amount in it and your line 234 net income is more than $48,750
- Box 15 ("regular and other benefits paid") of your T4E slip has an amount in it, box 7 ("repayment rate") states 30 percent, and your line 234 net income is more than $48,750
- Box 15 of your T4E slip has an amount in it, box 7 has an amount greater than 30 percent, and your line 234 net income is more than $39,000.

To calculate the amount of repayment, complete chart 1 or 2 on the back of your T4E slip.

Just as with the OAS clawback, any amount of EI to be clawed back is deducted on line 235 ("social benefits repayment") in calculating net income. Since the amount is being repaid, it does not make sense for it to be subject to income tax. Report the amount repaid on line 422 of your tax return. In essence, you are simply adding to your tax liability the EI amount to be repaid.

Chapter 17

Calculating Your Taxable Income

In This Chapter

- Defining taxable income
- Taking a look at employee home relocation loans
- Dealing with stock option and shares deductions
- Making the most of loss carryovers
- Applying for a capital gains deduction

Net income, which we discuss in Chapter 16, is basically a snapshot of your current year's income. It takes into account all current sources of income and deductions. This current-year snapshot is then used to calculate your entitlement to certain tax credits, such as the GST/HST credit and Child Tax Benefit, among others. Net income also provides a basis for certain non-refundable tax credits such as the spousal credit and medical expenses. Taxable income, the subject of this chapter, has a different focus altogether. It is the figure used to calculate your income tax liability for the year. The types of deductions allowed under the taxable income category are not necessarily related to current-year activities. This includes deductions for prior year losses. In fact, some of the deductions are permissive in nature, essentially allowing for tax deductions based on your personal situation. For example, there are deductions for employee stock options, for residence in remote areas of Canada, and for certain non-taxable payments received in the year.

On many returns, net income and taxable income will be the same amount; therefore, you won't have to worry about these deductions at all. However, if you do have additional deductions, it's important to keep in mind that there is a difference between net income and taxable income — be sure to use the right figures in the right places! Read your tax forms carefully to ensure that you are calculating your taxes and credits properly.

Ordering of Deductions in Computing Taxable Income

Sometimes you will have so many deductions to claim, you won't need them all to reduce your taxable income to the point where no taxes are owing. If this is the case, ordering of your deductions is key. In fact, the *Income Tax Act* dictates which deductions must be taken before others! The order is as follows:

1. Deductions for employee stock options, employee home relocation loans, non-taxable receipts such as social assistance, workers' compensation, net federal supplements, treaty-exempt income, and vow of perpetual poverty claims. There are also deductions for prospectors' and grubstakers' shares and the disposition of deferred profit-sharing plan shares (there is a one-third deduction allowed so that the disposition of these shares matches the treatment of other types of shares).

2. Loss claims, including non-capital losses, net capital losses, restricted farm loss, farm losses, and limited partnership losses.

3. Capital gains exemption claim for the year.

4. Northern residents' deductions.

If you have more deductions than you need in the year, you must claim deductions in the order specified above. That means you can't claim your northern residence allowances before you apply loss carryovers to your net income.

Always reduce your taxable income to equal your total tax credits for the year. If you reduce your taxable income to zero, you won't owe any taxes, but you might be wasting some deductions. For example, most taxpayers are allowed to claim the basic personal amount of $7,231 — this means the first $7,231 of taxable income is fully offset by this tax credit. Take a look at your non-refundable tax credits and other federal tax credits you have on schedule 1 of your tax return (such as the dividend tax credit, overseas employment tax credit, and alternative minimum tax carryover) to minimize your taxes, and maximize the deductions you can use in future years.

Some deductions can be carried forward to use in future years, while some cannot. So, when given the choice, always try to reduce your "discretionary" deductions, to use up all the deductions and credits that can't be carried forward. Discretionary deductions include some items used to calculate your "net income," such as RRSP deductions and moving expenses. Losses from prior years can also be carried forward (although keep in mind the ordering provisions above), so try to use up other deductions before you dip into these!

Line 248: Employee Home Relocation Loans

This is one deduction that you'll know you're entitled to claim. Why? Because it shows up right on the T4 slip you'll receive from your employer. If you have an amount shown in box 37 of your T4 slip, you can claim a deduction for your employee home relocation loan.

Generally, almost any benefit your employer gives you (including those that pertain to you as a shareholder) is taxable in your hands. This includes all employment perks, unless our tax laws specifically exempt the perks from tax. Lucky for you, an employee home relocation loan is one of these exemptions — albeit a partial exemption.

So what qualifies as a home relocation loan? Unfortunately, a loan to allow you to move down the street because you want a view of the lake does not. A home relocation loan is a loan your employer gives you, usually at a low or preferential interest rate, to help you move for business reasons. Generally, this means you are changing jobs and your new employer is helping you out with a loan, or your current employer is transferring you to a new location.

To qualify for the employee home relocation loan deduction, some criteria must be met. All the following must apply:

- The loan must be received by an employee (or the employee's spouse).
- You must be moving at least 40 kilometres. That is, the distance between your old residence and your new work location must be at least 40 kilometres more than the distance between your new residence and your new work location.
- You must commence work in a new location in Canada, and the move must have been after May 23, 1985.
- The loan must be used to acquire a new residence, and not for any other reason.

- You must not have more than one home relocation loan outstanding. In addition, ensure the loan is designated as a home relocation loan in respect of that move (if your T4 reports the loan, this is sufficient).

When you receive a home relocation loan, the amount received is still included in your taxable income. You'll notice that your gross income reported on your T4 slip is more than you thought you made. But don't worry, your slip is correct. Your employer has to report the imputed benefit on all loans given to you, if the interest rate you're being charged is less than the CCRA prescribed rate.

For example, say your employer gives you a $50,000 interest-free loan to help you transfer from Halifax to Toronto. The prescribed interest rate at the time the loan was granted to you was 6 percent. This means that you will have a taxable benefit of $3,000 ($50,000 × 6 percent), assuming the loan was outstanding for all of 2000.

The CCRA's prescribed interest rates are posted each quarter of the year. They can be found on the CCRA's Web site at `www.ccra-adrc.gc.ca`. The rate that should be used to calculate your taxable benefit is the rate in effect when your employee loan was granted. However, if the rate subsequently drops, you can start using this new lower rate. If the rate increases, you can continue using the most recent low rate.

If you are required to pay at least the prescribed interest rate on your employee loan, no taxable benefit needs to be calculated.

In the past, some employers structured home relocation loans so that the loans did not give rise to a taxable benefit. For example, if the employee had to move to a new city with significantly higher housing costs, the loan would effectively bring the employee to the same economic position as he would be in his old location. After a number of court cases, the 1998 federal budget narrowed this loophole. If you received such a loan in the past, and began work at a new location before October 1, 1998, you can still claim relief from the taxable benefits rules until 2001. However, if you've moved after this date, the rules described in this section will apply to you.

Now for the good part: the deduction! When you have a taxable benefit for an employee home relocation loan, and you meet all the criteria above, you can claim a deduction from your income.

Your deduction will be the lesser of the following:

- The taxable benefit included in your income for the loan
- The amount of interest benefit that would have been computed if the home relocation loan had been $25,000.

In friendlier terms, if you've received a $20,000 interest-free loan from your employer, the prescribed interest rate is 6 percent, and this loan meets the definition of a home relocation loan, your deduction will the lesser of $1,200 and $1,500 ($25,000 × 6 percent). In this case, your entire taxable benefit of $1,200 will be offset by the deduction. Just to keep it interesting, there is another rule surrounding employee home relocation loans. You see, the deduction does not last forever. It is only applicable for a maximum of five years from the day the loan was originally granted, or until the loan is actually paid off, whichever is shorter.

Line 249: Stock Option and Shares Deductions

Stock options are fast becoming one of the hottest benefits offered by employers. But make no mistake about it, they are a taxable benefit. The taxable benefit you receive in the year should be reported on your T4 slip. This amount is included in your total employment income reported on box 14 of your T4 slip. Here's a brief synopsis of the rules (see also Chapter 9).

Public company shares

Normally in the year you exercise your stock options, you will be charged a taxable benefit for the difference between the fair market value of the underlying stock on that day, and your cost. Thanks to the 2000 federal budget, this is no longer the case in all instances. In fact, you may now be able to postpone the taxation of qualifying employee stock options to when the shares are sold, instead of when the option is exercised.

Don't think you're off the hook for taxes on your stock options simply because you didn't sell your shares this year. This new incentive is limited to $100,000 per year, calculated at the time the option was granted to you. For example, say you were granted the option to purchase 100,000 shares of your employer corporation, at a price of $2 per share. At the time you exercise your option, the shares are trading at $5. If you exercise all your options this year, you will only receive a partial deferral of tax. At the time the options were granted to you, they were worth $200,000 (100,000 × $2). This means that you will manage to defer taxes on only one-half of your options ($200,000 less $100,000 divided by $2 per share = 50,000 options). Your taxable benefit this year will be $150,000 ($5 less $2 × 50,000 options), and the other $150,000 will be taxed only when you sell the shares.

The new rule deferring tax on the first $100,000 of employee stock options only applies to options exercised after February 27, 2000 — the date of the federal budget.

If you hold a large number of employee stock options, consider exercising the options over a number of years to take full advantage of the $100,000 per year exemption.

Canadian-controlled private corporations

If your employer is a Canadian-Controlled Private Corporation (CCPC), you're in luck. When you exercise your stock options, you can defer all your taxable benefit until you actually sell the share. The taxable benefit for CCPCs is calculated the same way as that for public companies. That is, the fair market value of the shares on the date you exercise your option less your cost. By the way, your cost includes your exercise price (the amount you must pay for the shares under your option agreement) and any cost you paid to acquire the option itself.

The CCPC rules for stock options will apply to you so long as your employer was a CCPC at the time the option was granted to you (not when the option is exercised). So, if your company goes public in the future, you can still benefit from the more favourable CCPC rules.

Stock option deductions

Now to the part you really want to know about — the stock option deduction. This deduction is available because the taxable benefit you'll be charged when you exercise your stock options (either this year or in a future year when you sell the stock) is taxed as employment income. In other words, 100 percent of the benefit is taxable in your hands. To many people this seems unfair, since the benefit is from a stock, which is normally treated as a capital item. If you recall from Chapter 13, capital gains are only two-thirds taxable (three-quarters for sales prior to February 27, 2000), so you are taxed a full one-third (or one-quarter) more by exercising an employee stock option rather than purchasing the share yourself on the open market and then selling it for a profit.

But don't fret. Our tax laws understand this difference and allow a deduction, known as the stock option and shares deduction. The deduction is equal to one-third of the taxable benefit for options exercised after February 27, 2000, and one-quarter of the benefit for options exercised before the budget date. This means that your stock option benefit will effectively be taxed in the same way as a capital gain would be.

An additional stock option deduction of 33⅓ percent is available if you exercise a stock option, then donate the stock to a registered charity. Yup, that's right. You'll get a tax deduction for 66⅔ percent of your taxable benefit. And in addition, you'll get a donation receipt for the full fair market value of your donation. To take advantage of this 2000 federal budget incentive, you must have acquired the stock after February 27, 2000, and donated it before 2002. In addition, the shares must be donated to the charity within the year and within 30 days of the option being exercised. Like most good things, the stock option and share deduction is not available in every case. In order to qualify, some criteria must be met (you didn't think a tax law would exist without qualifications, did you!).

Shares qualifying for the deduction

The stock option deduction is available if the following conditions are met:

- Your employer corporation, or a corporation that does not deal at arm's length to the employer (a related company), is the seller or issuer of the shares.
- The shares must be common shares of the corporation. There is actually a whole list of qualifications that must be met in Regulation 6204 of the *Income Tax Act* (good reading for anyone with insomnia). Some of these qualifications include (and we must stress *some*) the following:
  - The dividends on the shares must not have a fixed minimum or maximum amount
  - The amount to be received on the dissolution, liquidation, or winding-up of the corporation, by the shareholder, cannot have a fixed minimum or maximum amount
  - The shares cannot be convertible into a non-qualifying share
  - The shares cannot generally be redeemable by the corporation
  - The corporation cannot reasonably be expected to redeem, acquire, or cancel the share in whole or in part, or reduce the paid-up capital of the corporation in respect of the share, within two years after the time the share is sold or issued, except in specific circumstances.
- The exercise price of the option (that is, the amount you must pay to receive the share of your employer corporation) must be at least equal to the fair market value of the share at the time the option was granted to you. If you've paid an amount to acquire the option itself, this amount can be added to the exercise price of the option. For example, if you've paid $2 to acquire the option to purchase a share of your employer, and subsequently pay $5 to exercise the option, you will be eligible for the stock option deduction (assuming all other criteria are met) as long as the fair market value of the employer's shares on the date the option was granted to you was at least $7 ($2 plus $5).
- You must be dealing at arm's length with your employer. This means that if you control the corporation, or are related to a person who controls the corporation (that is, a majority shareholder), you will not be eligible for this deduction.

If the option was granted to you while the corporation was a CCPC, you don't necessarily have to worry about the above rules. You see, if you hold the shares you've acquired under your stock option agreement for at least two years, you'll automatically qualify for the stock option deduction. However, if you don't hold the shares for two years, but meet the above criteria, you'll still qualify.

Although these rules might sound fairly complex, it will not be up to you to determine whether or not you are eligible for the deduction. Your employer should make this determination, and your T4 slip for the year will indicate that your taxable employment benefit is in fact eligible for the "110(1)(d) or 110(1)(d.1) deduction." The amount eligible for the deduction is reported in either box 39 or 41 of your T4 slip. If an amount shows up in these boxes, report it on line 249 of your tax return.

Line 250: Other Payments Deductions

Did you report amounts on line 147 of your tax return? If so, you're likely entitled to a deduction for the full amount reported. You see, the types of payments reported on line 147 are not taxable amounts. And although they must be reported as part of your "net income," they are not intended to be part of your "taxable income." Hence the deduction.

The types of payments reported on line 147, then deducted on line 250, are the following:

- Workers' compensation
- Social assistance payments
- Net federal supplements.

If you've received a T5007 "Statement of Benefits" slip in the year reporting workers' compensation or social assistance payments, or a T4AOAS reporting net federal supplements received in the year, be sure to deduct these amounts on line 250 of your tax return.

If your net income as reported on line 234 is more than $53,960, and you've received net federal supplements in the year, you will have to repay some (or all) of the benefits paid to you in the year. This is the infamous "clawback" discussed in Chapter 10. You'll find that your required repayment will show up on line 422 of your tax return, which makes up part of your taxes payable figure.

Lines 251 to 253: Loss Carryovers

Filing a tax return is one time that being a loser is to your advantage. You see, if you've incurred losses (including limited partnership losses, non-capital losses, and net capital losses) in prior years, and were unable to use those losses on your prior years' tax returns, you are allowed to carry those losses forward to offset some of your current income.

If you've had losses in the past, you may be able to use those losses on your 2000 tax return to offset your taxable income, and reduce your tax bill! If you're unsure what your unclaimed loss balance is, give the CCRA a call. Their computer system tracks unused losses, and they will assist you in claiming the correct amount on your current year's tax return. However, it's up to you to claim the correct loss carryover amount on your tax return. If you forget to claim an amount, the CCRA will not apply your unused losses to your current income because these are optional deductions.

Depending on the type of loss you've incurred, there may be limitations on the amount of loss you can carry forward, and the number of years it can be carried forward.

It's generally most beneficial to apply a prior year's loss to income taxed at a high rate. For example, if your income is low this year, but is expected to increase in future years, you may want to forgo claiming the loss carried forward this year. Instead, you can save the loss for a future year when you know you'll be subject to a higher tax rate. Of course, since certain types of losses have a limited carryforward period, you'll want to be absolutely certain you'll be able to use the loss in future years. If there's any doubt, claim the loss this year — use it, don't lose it — even if you're in a low tax bracket.

Never claim losses to bring your taxable income to zero. Although you'll have no tax to pay with taxable income of zero, you'd also have no tax to pay if you report income equal to your non-refundable tax credits.

Limited partnership losses

Limited partnerships are most commonly purchased as tax shelters. A limited partner, as opposed to a general partner, has limited liability with respect to the partnership's liabilities. You basically invest in the partnership but don't take part in the day-to-day running of the company. And if the partnership gets sued, you're immune from liability. But the main reason people invest in limited partnerships is up-front losses. Although some of these partnerships eventually make a profit, there are often huge losses in the first years. These losses are passed on to investors, to be deducted on their personal tax returns. This means that limited partnerships are most popular with taxpayers subject to the highest rates of tax. You see, the huge losses generated by these partnerships can actually push investors into a lower tax bracket! The tax authorities are not fans of limited partnerships in general, and the tax laws limit the amount of losses that you can claim. Specifically, investors can only deduct cumulative losses up to the investor's at-risk amount.

If you've received form T5013 "Statement of Partnership Income" from your limited partnership in the year, your at-risk amount should be reported in box 45. If not, contact the partnership and ask them for details of this amount — this is something the partnership should track.

Your at-risk amount is the amount you paid to purchase the limited partnership, plus any further capital contributions you made to the partnership (your adjusted cost base). In other words, you can only deduct losses on your tax return up to the amount that you paid for your partnership interest. This differs from other types of losses, where you are generally entitled to deduct the full amount of the losses, whether they are more or less than your adjusted cost base.

Let's work through an example. John purchased an interest in a limited partnership in 1993 for $80,000. Therefore, his at-risk amount was $80,000. From 1993 to 1998 he claimed total losses of $75,000 on his tax returns. His at-risk amount at the end of 1998 was $5,000. In 1999, the limited partnership incurred further losses and allocated $10,000 to John, $5,000 of which will show up on box 18 of his T5013 form and can be deducted in 1999, and $5,000 in box 31. Losses reported in box 31 cannot be deducted this year; they become part of the limited partnership loss carryover amount. So $5,000 of the losses are not deductible since they exceed his at-risk amount.

If John did not need to use any of the losses in 1999, the $5,000 of deductible limited partnership losses would become part of his non-capital loss carryover balance. He can deduct these losses against any source of income in future years by reporting the loss on line 252 of his tax return. The remaining $5,000 of nondeductible losses become part of his limited partnership loss carryover balance. These losses can be deducted on line 251 of a future tax return only if he has limited partnership income from that same partnership, or he increases his at-risk amount.

If your cumulative losses exceed your at-risk amount, you can carry the remaining losses forward for possible use in the future. You can deduct the additional losses in the future to offset any income produced by the partnership or to offset any additional capital you contributed to the partnership. Restricted losses can be carried forward indefinitely.

Your limited partnership losses available for carryover will be reported in box 31 of your T5013 slip. This is the amount that can't be deducted on your current year's tax return, but can be carried forward to offset limited partnership income in the future.

You may be interested to know that the restriction on limited partnership losses has only been in existence since February 25, 1986. Before this date, all losses from a limited partnership were deductible. If you've owned a limited partnership interest since before the new rules were enacted, you may be exempt from the at-risk rules. Your particular limited partnership should be able to provide you with details on whether they meet the exemption criteria.

If you have a limited partnership loss in 2000, this loss can be used to offset income from any source in this year. In fact, the loss must be used this year if it can be. If not, it becomes part of your non-capital loss balance and can be carried back for up to three years to offset a prior year's taxable income or carried forward indefinitely. But don't forget, if any portion of the loss couldn't be used because of the at-risk rules, it can only be carried forward to offset against limited partnership income in the future, unless you increase the adjusted cost base of your limited partnership interest.

Non-capital losses

In general, any business, employment, or property transaction is considered non-capital (see Chapter 13 for details on capital versus non-capital losses). So, if you have your own business and it generates a loss, this is considered to be a non-capital loss. In addition, if you've incurred an allowable business investment loss (an ABIL), this is also considered to be a non-capital loss.

The amount of non-capital loss that is generated in a particular tax year is calculated on form T1A "Request for Loss Carryback." This is also the form that allows you to carry back any current-year losses to prior tax years, and reports the amount of the loss that can be carried forward to future years.

Form T1A is important because not all items on your tax return are figured into the calculation of your non-capital loss. Therefore, if you have a negative net income or taxable income amount (which is actually reported as a zero balance on lines 236 and 260 of your tax return), you should fill out form T1A so you know how much of the losses can be carried over to other tax years.

The items included in the calculation of non-capital losses are as follows:

- **Employment income/loss:** This includes lines 101 and 104 of your tax return less any amounts reported on lines 207, 212, 229, and 231.
- **Investment income/loss:** Add together lines 120 and 121 of your tax return and deduct any amount reported on line 221.
- **Partnership income/loss:** This includes any amounts reported on line 122 of your return. Note that only the allowable loss (not the restricted portion of the limited partnership loss) is included on this line.
- **Rental income/loss:** This is reported on line 126 of your tax return.
- **Business, professional, or commission income or losses:** These are reported on lines 135, 137, and 139 of your return.
- **Farming or fishing income or losses:** These are reported on lines 141 and 143 of your return. The amount of farming losses you can claim may be restricted if farming is not your chief source of income for the year (see Chapter 15 for more information on restricted farm losses). Farming and fishing losses are included in the calculation of non-capital losses; however, they are subject to their own carryover rules. These losses can be carried forward for 10 years (rather than the normal 7) and back for 3 years.

So, once the calculation of total non-capital losses is complete, the amount relating to fishing and farming is removed from the non-capital loss carryforward balance, and put in its own "farming loss" pool to help keep track of the carryforward period.

- **Taxable capital gains:** This is reported on line 127 of your tax return.
- **Non-taxable income:** This is reported on line 147 of your tax return.
- **Net capital losses of other years:** This is reported on line 253 of your return.
- **Certain other deductions:** These include the capital gains deduction, deduction for business investment losses, employee home relocation loan deduction, stock option and shares deductions, other payments deduction, and income exempt under a tax treaty. Amounts are reported on lines 254, 217, 248, 249, and 250 of your tax return.

Form T1A requires you to separate the income and loss items on your tax return. For example, any deductions claimed would be placed in the "loss" column. You must then total all the income and loss items separately.

If you've claimed any amounts on lines 208, 209, 214, 215, 219, 220, 232, or 235 of your tax return, these amounts are deducted from your total income. It's possible that these deductions will cause you to have negative income; however, these amounts do not result in a non-capital loss. If the deductions claimed on these lines result in negative income (before taking into account allowable deductions in the loss column), your total income is deemed to be nil. You then take your total income, less the total amount reported in the loss column, to calculate the net loss for the year. You must then deduct any farming or fishing losses incurred in the year to come up with your total non-capital loss available for carryover (as discussed above, these losses have a longer carryforward period, so are put in a separate pool so you can keep track of the carryforward period). It is this amount that can be carried back to offset taxable income in any of the previous three taxation years, or carried forward.

Calculation of non-capital losses

Pam had more tax deductions than income in the 1999 tax year. She would like to know if she can take advantage of her losses on her 2000 tax return.

Here is a summary of items claimed on her tax return:

Line 121	Investment income	$1,200
Line 135	Business income (loss)	($9,000)
Line 208	RRSP deduction	$2,000

Pam's non-capital loss balance is calculated on form T1A as follows:

Investment income	$1,200	
Business loss		$9,000
Subtotal	$1,200	$9,000
Subtract: Line 208	($2,000)	n/a
Subtotal (if negative = 0)	0	
Subtract: Loss column	$9,000	
Total non-capital loss	$9,000	

By the way, in Pam's situation, she would have been better off not claiming her RRSP deduction in 1999, since she's getting no benefit from it. That is, it is not increasing her non-capital loss, and it is not reducing her taxable income (because she already has losses). This means she's getting no tax reductions in 1999 or any other year for this contribution. She should have opted against claiming the RRSP deduction and saved it for another year.

Non-capital losses can only be carried forward for seven years. Due to the limited carryforward period, you should consider carrying your losses back, if possible, to guarantee that you will receive a tax benefit from the loss.

If you are certain you will have taxable income in the future, you may want to forgo a loss carryback and instead carry the losses forward to offset your future income. You see, it is always most beneficial to claim the losses against income taxed at the highest marginal tax rate. So, if you're expecting to generate significant income in the future that will be taxed at a higher marginal tax rate than you're subject to this year, you may want to keep the losses intact until you're in that higher tax bracket.

For example, say you have non-capital losses carried forward of $20,000 from the 1999 tax year. In 2000, you have taxable income of $30,000, but you expect to have taxable income of $80,000 in 2001. You'd be better off saving your non-capital loss carryforward until 2001, since you'll be taxed at the highest marginal rate in that year, while you're in the lowest tax bracket in 2000. Assuming your marginal tax rate in 2000 is 25 percent and your marginal tax rate in 2001 will be 50 percent, you'll get a tax reduction of only $5,000 ($20,000 × 25%) by applying the loss in 2000, but a $10,000 ($20,000 × 50%) tax reduction by applying it in 2001. When you use the loss carryforwards to offset income taxed at the highest marginal tax rate, you'll get more bang for your buck. To apply a prior year's non-capital loss to your current year's income, report the amount of the loss you want to claim on line 252 of your tax return.

Net capital losses

Capital losses for the year are calculated on schedule 3 of your tax return. Capital losses will arise whenever you sell capital property (such as shares, mutual fund units, or real property) for proceeds of disposition that are less than the adjusted cost base of the property.

You may have both capital gains and capital losses this year. Your capital losses must first be used to offset any capital gains this year. However, if your losses exceed your total gains, you will have a net capital loss for the year. It is this net loss that can be carried back to offset capital gains taxed in any of the previous three taxation years, or forward to offset any capital gains in the future.

Net capital losses can only be used to offset taxable capital gains of other years. They cannot be used to offset any other types of income. Net capital losses can be carried forward indefinitely to offset future capital gains.

Net capital losses are also known as *allowable capital losses*. Only three-fourths of capital gains incurred prior to February 28, 2000 are taxable (as discussed in Chapter 13). Likewise, only three-fourths of any capital losses incurred are deductible. After February 27, 2000, two-thirds of capital gains are taxable or deductible. It is this taxable, or deductible, portion of the gains and losses that is known as taxable capital gains, or net (or allowable) capital losses.

If you've incurred capital losses in prior years, you can deduct these losses on your 2000 tax return against any taxable capital gains reported on line 127 this year. Claim these losses on line 253 of your tax return.

Your Notice of Assessment will normally inform you if you have net capital losses carried forward from prior years. If you haven't kept track of your losses, call your local CCRA office; the CCRA will let you know your net capital loss carryforward balance.

The allowable portion of capital losses (and the taxable portion of capital gains) has been changing over the years. Therefore, when you're claiming net capital losses of other years on your current year's tax return, it's important to note in which year the loss arose, and the capital gains inclusion rate in place during that year. The term *inclusion rate* means the portion of the capital gain that was taxable in that year, and the portion of the capital loss that was deductible. Table 17-1 lists the capital gains inclusion rates.

Table 17-1 Capital Gains Inclusion Rates

Year	*Inclusion*
1987 and earlier	50%
1988 or 1989	66.67%
1989 to February 27, 2000	75%
February 28, 2000, and later	66.67%

If you've incurred capital losses in prior years, and want to apply them to the current year, you'll have to adjust your net capital loss for that year (that is, the loss after the above inclusion rates have been applied). Basically, the amount of the loss is adjusted to match the inclusion rate in effect for the year in which the loss is being applied. These are the steps to take:

1. Determine the year when your net capital loss occurred.
2. Divide your net capital loss for that year by the inclusion rate in effect during that year. For example, if you have a net capital loss of $50,000 carried forward from the 1985 tax year, you will divide that loss by 50 percent. This gives you a total capital loss from 1985 of $100,000.
3. Multiply the total capital loss ($100,000) that you want to apply to your current-year capital gains, by the current-year inclusion rate. If you want to apply the loss to gains incurred prior to February 28, 2000, multiply the total loss by 75 percent. If you want to apply it to gains incurred after February 28, 2000, multiply it by 66.67 percent. Assuming you have taxable capital gains after February 28, 2000, you would multiply your $100,000 loss from 1985 by 66.67 percent. This means you can claim up to $66,667 of net capital losses on line 253 of your tax return this year (assuming you have taxable capital gains on line 127 of at least this amount).

Because of changes in the 2000 federal budget, two different inclusion rates will apply for the 2000 taxation year. Your actual inclusion rate will depend on whether you have realized net gains or losses in one or both periods, or a net gain in one period and a net loss in the other (see Chapter 13 for details).

Line 254: Capital Gains Deduction

If you've claimed a taxable capital gain on line 127 of your tax return, it's possible that you are eligible for an additional deduction. In fact, if you've disposed of qualifying property for a gain, up to $500,000 may be exempt from tax. Of course, not all sales of capital property are eligible for the capital gains deduction. It only applies to disposition of qualified small business corporation shares (QSBC shares) or qualified farm property.

The $500,000 capital gains deduction available is a lifetime limit. In other words, you can't double dip — claim the deduction more than once. Once you've claimed $500,000 in total deductions throughout your lifetime, you'll be cut off from future deductions.

Between 1985 and 1994, there were two capital gains exemptions available in Canada. One was the $500,000 capital gains deduction that is still in effect. The other was a $100,000 deduction available on the sale of any capital property. Now that the $100,000 deduction is gone, the only time you can claim a capital gains exemption is if you sell qualifying property — that is, QSBC shares or qualifying farm property.

If you've claimed any part of the $100,000 capital gains exemption in the past, the amounts claimed will reduce your $500,000 capital gains exemption available on qualifying property. For example, if you claimed the maximum $100,000 prior to 1994, you'll only have $400,000 of the "enhanced" deduction to claim in the future.

Qualified small business corporation shares

If you've disposed of QSBC shares in the year, you may qualify for the capital gains deduction, as long as you are a Canadian resident and you haven't used your entire capital gains exemption in the past.

Not just any share of a Canadian corporation will qualify under the QSBC rules. In fact, these rules are quite stringent. If you own shares in a small Canadian corporation, you should visit a tax professional to ensure that you can claim the capital gains exemption in the future. Even if your corporation does not currently qualify for the exemption, there are steps you can take to ensure the exemption can be claimed.

To qualify as a QSBC, the following criteria must be met:

- The company must be a Canadian-controlled small business corporation (that is, not traded on a prescribed stock exchange).
- You, or a person related to you, must have held the shares for at least 24 months before their disposition.
- Throughout the 24 months prior to the disposition, at least 50 percent of the fair market value of the corporation's assets must have been used in an active business.
- At the time of disposition, at least 90 percent of the fair market value of the assets of the corporation must have been used in an active business carried on in Canada.

Be careful of holding cash and other passive investments in a small business corporation, since these assets will not be considered active business assets. This means your corporation may not meet the QSBC criteria, and you will not be eligible to claim the capital gains exemption.

If you hold shares in a Canadian-controlled small business corporation (for example, a family business), visit a tax professional. There are steps that can be taken to ensure you are eligible to claim the capital gains deduction, even if your shares do not currently qualify. And even if you're not currently planning on selling your business, remember that should you meet an untimely death, you will be deemed to have disposed of all your assets, including these shares, at their fair market value on the date of your death (unless you leave them to your spouse). Some current tax planning could save your family from a significant tax bill on your death!

If you own shares in a QSBC that will be going public in the future, ensure you elect to dispose of these shares on your tax return before they become public company shares. You will have to include the taxable portion of any deemed gains on your tax return, but these will be offset by the capital gains deduction. You can then add the deduction claimed to the adjusted cost base of your new shares, effectively sheltering some, or all, of a future tax bill on the sale of the public company shares.

Qualified farm property

To provide an incentive for Canadians to invest in certain types of farm property, the $500,000 capital gains deduction is available to offset gains on the disposition of certain farm properties as well.

To qualify for the exemption, there are a number of criteria that must be met (are you surprised?):

- The property must be real property (that is, land), a share of the capital stock of a family farm corporation, an interest in a family farm partnership, or eligible capital property used to carry on the business of farming in Canada.
- The property must have been owned by you, your spouse, or either a personal trust or family farm partnership in which you or your spouse has an interest. We'll call these taxpayers "qualified owners."
- The property must have been used by one of the following taxpayers (the "qualified users"):
  - You
  - Your spouse, child (including a grandchild or great-grandchild), parent, or a beneficiary of a personal trust
  - A family farm corporation owned by you, your spouse, your child, grandchild, great-grandchild, your parent, or the beneficiary of a personal trust
  - A family farm partnership in which you, your spouse, your child, grandchild, great-grandchild, your parent, or the beneficiary of a personal trust has an interest.

If the property had been used by a personal trust, the capital gains exemption cannot be claimed by the trust itself. Instead, the capital gains on the disposition of the property are flowed out to the trust's beneficiaries. The beneficiaries then claim the disposition on their personal tax returns, and can claim the capital gains deduction on that gain.

- If the property is real property, it must have been used by a qualified user for farming activities in Canada. Just to make this more confusing, there are more rules to consider, depending on when the property was acquired. If it was acquired before June 18, 1987, the property must have been used by a qualified user to carry on a farming business during the year of its disposition. However, if it was not used for farming in the year of disposition, you may still qualify for the capital gains deduction if a qualified user used it for at least five years during the period of ownership.

  If the property was acquired after June 18, 1987, a qualified owner must have owned the property for at least 24 months immediately before the disposition. In addition, gross revenues from the farming business must have exceeded income from all other sources for a qualified owner for at least two years while the property was owned. There is also the condition that a qualified owner must have been actively engaged, on a regular and continuous basis during a 24-month period, in the carrying on of the farming business.

  If the property was used by a family farm corporation or a family farm partnership, it must have been used to carry on a farming business for at least 24 months (although these 24 months do not necessarily have to be the 24 months preceding disposition). The owner must have been actively engaged, on a regular and continuous basis, in the business of farming, but gross revenues do not have to exceed all other income.
- If the property is a share of the capital stock of a family farm corporation, or an interest in a family farm partnership, the capital gains deduction may be claimed if the property was owned by you or your spouse throughout any 24-month period, if more than 50 percent of the fair market value of the property used by the corporation or partnership

was used by a qualified user principally in the course of a Canadian farming business. In addition, at the time of disposition, more than 90 percent of the fair market value of the property must have been used by a qualified user principally in the course of carrying on a farming business in Canada.

Clearly, the definition of qualified farm property is technical and complex. In fact, since there are so many factors to consider, and the potential tax savings are so high, this is one area where a visit to a tax pro is necessary!

The CNIL problem

With a name that sounds like a horrid disease, it's no surprise that a CNIL spells bad news when you're trying to claim a capital gains deduction. The CNIL's full name is a Cumulative Net Investment Loss. It is basically a cumulation of all your investment expenses, less investment income, claimed since 1988. If you've claimed significant investment expenses or losses in the past, you may have a problem. However, if you've claimed minimal expenses and losses, and mostly income, you probably have nothing to worry about. A CNIL is such a problem because your capital gains deduction will be denied to the extent of your CNIL. So, if you have a CNIL of, say, $10,000, and your capital gain on the disposition of QSBC shares of qualified farm property is $200,000, you'll only be allowed to claim a capital gains deduction of $190,000.

If you're planning on claiming a capital gains deduction, you should know your CNIL balance. Call your local Tax Services Office — they keep track of your CNIL balance and will let you know where you stand.

The CNIL balance is calculated on form 936 "Calculation of Cumulative Net Investment Loss" of your tax return. It's a good idea to fill this form out each year to ensure that you keep an up-to-date total of your CNIL.

What's in a CNIL account?

If you've claimed any of the following income or expense items in the past, you should ensure that you don't have a CNIL problem before you attempt to claim the capital gains deduction:

Investment expenses

- Carrying charges and interest expenses claimed on line 221 of your tax return. This includes deductions for expenses incurred to finance an acquisition of a limited partnership interest.
- Net rental losses reported on line 126.
- Limited or non-active partnership losses claimed on line 122 and limited partnership losses of other years (after 1985) claimed on line 251.
- Deductions for foreign taxes paid.
- 50 percent of exploration and development expenses claimed on line 224 of your return.

Income items

- Dividends, interest, and other investment income reported on lines 120 and 121.
- Net rental income, including recaptured capital cost allowance, reported on line 126.
- Net income from limited or non-active partnerships from line 122.
- 50 percent of natural resource income.

If the total expenses claimed since 1988 exceed the total income claimed, you have a CNIL problem.

Line 255: Northern Residents Deductions

Rainy Hollow, B.C.; Belcher, Manitoba; Flin Flon, Saskatchewan; Pickle Crow, Ontario. What do these places have in common (other than intriguing names)? Well, their residents can claim a northern residents deduction. In recognition of additional costs of living incurred by those living in remote areas of Canada, the CCRA allows special tax deductions to help with the extra burden. Living in a remote area does not mean the nearest McDonald's is an hour away. In fact, the CCRA has a very detailed (and very long) list of specific areas of Canada where you have to live to claim the deduction.

The actual deductions you can claim depend on where you live. There are two different "zones" set out by the CCRA. If you live in a "northern zone," you are allowed the full northern residents deduction. If you live in an intermediate zone, you can deduct half the potential amount.

If you think you may live in a northern zone or an intermediate zone, check out the CCRA's publication "Northern Residents Deductions — Places in Prescribed Zones." You can get this off the CCRA Web site at `www.ccra-adrc.gc.ca`, or by calling your local Tax Services Office. All places in Yukon, Northwest Territories, Nunavut, and Labrador are prescribed northern zones, as are some locations in British Columbia, Alberta, Saskatchewan, Manitoba, Ontario, and Quebec. Prescribed intermediate zones include some places in British Columbia, Alberta, Saskatchewan, Manitoba, Ontario, Quebec, and all of Sable Island, Nova Scotia.

There are two northern residents deductions available:

- Residency deduction
- Travel benefits deduction

If you qualify for the northern residents deduction, you must fill out form T2222 "Northern Residents Deduction – 2000" and file it with your personal tax return. Keep any supporting receipts, in case the CCRA asks to see them.

Residency deduction

To claim the residency deduction you need only live in one of the prescribed zones. Stopping by for a visit won't do. In fact, to qualify, you must have lived, on a permanent basis, in one of the zones for at least six consecutive months beginning or ending in the year.

Even if you live in a prescribed zone on December 31 of the year, you won't automatically get the residency deduction. The deduction only kicks in after you've lived in the northern location for six consecutive months. However, once the six months is complete, file an adjustment to your tax return to request the deduction. For example, Walter moved to Gods Lake, Manitoba (a prescribed northern zone), on December 1, 2000. When he filed his tax return on April 30, 2001, he had only lived in the prescribed area for five months, so he couldn't claim the residency deduction. However, once his six months are up (June 1, 2001, to be exact), he can file a T1 adjustment and request that his 2000 tax return be amended to claim the deduction. This is because he moved to a northern region during 2000.

If you're preparing the tax return for someone who died in the year, the deceased can still claim the residency deduction so long as this person lived in a prescribed zone for at least six months before the date of death.

Two types of residency deductions

There are two separate types of residency deductions you may be able to claim:

- **Basic residency amount.** This is a credit for simply living in a prescribed zone. The credit is $7.50 per day for living in a prescribed northern zone, and one-half of this, or $3.75, for living in an intermediate zone.
- **Additional residency amount.** This is an additional credit of $7.50/$3.75 per day that you can claim if the following situations apply:
  - You maintained and lived in a dwelling during your time up north (generally a house or apartment — sorry, a hotel room or bunkhouse won't qualify).
  - You are the only person claiming the basic residency amount for living in that dwelling for that period.

You are considered to have maintained and lived in a dwelling even if your employer or another person paid for your accommodations and other costs relating to the dwelling.

If more than one taxpayer lived in the same dwelling at the same time during the year, either each taxpayer can claim the basic residency deduction ($7.50 or $3.75 per day), or one taxpayer can claim both the basic deduction and the additional deduction. As soon as one person claims the additional deduction, no other person living in the dwelling during the same period can claim a basic credit. Since you're given a choice, you should consider the income and marginal tax rates of all members of a household before deciding how to allocate the credits.

Board and lodging benefits

Beginning in 1998, if you've received a non-taxable benefit for board and lodging at a special work site in a prescribed northern zone or prescribed intermediate zone (that's a mouthful!), you may have some or all of your residency deductions taken back. Normally, when your employer pays your room and lodging, you would receive a taxable benefit. However, when you work in a "special work site," no taxable benefit is charged if your principal place of residence was not at this special site. For example, if you normally live in New Brunswick, but your employer sent you to Labrador for work (and paid for your room and board there), while your family remained at home in New Brunswick, you would not be charged a taxable benefit for the room and board paid on your behalf.

So what is a "special work site"? It is a place where you were required to work temporarily, and which was too far away from your ordinary residence to commute to daily, and you were required to be away from your ordinary residence, or at this special location, for at least 36 hours.

If you receive a non-taxable benefit for board and lodging at a special work site in a prescribed northern zone, or intermediate zone, the non-taxable benefit (as reported on your T4 or T4A slip) may have to be deducted from your residency deduction. Keep in mind that these rules only apply if you normally reside outside the special work site area (you have a home somewhere else).

If you received non-taxable benefits but the special work site is more than 30 kilometres away from an urban area having a population of at least 40,000, you do not have to reduce your residency deduction.

Travel benefit deductions

The second type of northern residents deduction you may be eligible to claim is the travel benefits deduction. Generally, whenever your employer pays for something on your behalf, you are charged a taxable benefit. This includes some travel benefits that your employer offers to you and your family. When you live in a remote northern area, the fact that your employer will pay for some trips for you and your family could be a popular employment perk. Unfortunately, this could also lead to a tax bill. In recognition of the costs involved in traveling in prescribed and intermediate areas, there is some relief from the taxable benefit rules. You can claim an additional tax credit under these conditions:

- You qualify to claim a northern residents deduction (although you don't have to claim it to meet this criteria — *qualify* is the key word)
- You were an employee and are not related to your employer
- You received taxable travel benefits from your employment in a prescribed zone
- You included the travel benefits in employment income.

Box 32 of your T4 slip, or box 28 of your T4A slip, will report the taxable travel benefits you received in the year. If you received non-taxable benefits, such benefits will not show up on your slips, and you are not eligible to claim the travel benefits deduction.

You must claim the travel benefits deduction in the same year that you report the taxable benefit received from your employer. For example, if you leave for a trip in December 2000 and return in January 2001, you should claim the deduction in the 2000 tax year *if* your taxable benefit shows up on your 2000 T4 (or T4A) slip. If the taxable benefit is not charged until 2001, the deduction can likewise only be claimed in the 2001 tax year.

Types of travel qualifying for deduction

There are different rules depending on your reasons for traveling. If you are traveling for medical services that are not available where you live, there is no limit on the number of trips you can make in the year. However, if you are traveling for any other reason, you can only claim a deduction for two trips a year for each member of your household. Trips for medical or other reasons can be taken by the employee paying tax on the benefit or any member of the employee's household.

If you are claiming a travel deduction for trips made for medical reasons, no one can claim the expenditures as medical expenses as well.

If you are traveling for medical reasons, ensure that your employer notes this fact on your T4 or T4A slip. You should report taxable benefits for medical trips in box 33 of the T4 slip or in the footnotes to your T4A. If this isn't reported properly, have your employer reissue your slip to see that your deduction will be accepted by the CCRA.

Amount of deduction available

Can you take a first class, whirlwind trip, and hope to deduct it as a travel deduction? Let's not be greedy. As with many of our tax rules, there are maximum amounts that can be claimed. Here are the rules. The maximum deduction that can be claimed for each trip in the year is the lowest of the following:

- The taxable employment benefit received for the trip
- The actual total travel expenses for the trip. These travel expenses include such items as:
  - Air, train, and bus fares

- Motor vehicle expenses. You can claim motor vehicle expenses based on actual costs incurred, or on a fixed per-kilometre amount. The per-kilometre amounts are based on Treasury Board mileage rates for civil servants in each province.
- Hotel and motel accommodations, or camping fees
- Other incidental expenses, such as taxis, road tolls, ferry costs

- The cost of the lowest full economy return airfare available at the time for the trip between the airport closest to your residence and the nearest designated city. This airfare amount is part of the calculation, whether or not you traveled by air, or to that city.

So, if you are traveling from a prescribed or intermediate zone to Cape Breton, Nova Scotia, you will have to determine the airfare from the closest airport to your northern location, to Halifax, Nova Scotia (the closest designated city to Cape Breton), even if you didn't fly between these two locations, and even though you're not planning on visiting Halifax!

If you don't know the actual cost of the trip taken (for example, when you're given free airline tickets), include the fair market value of a similar trip as the actual cost.

If you're traveling for medical reasons and cannot travel alone, you can claim a deduction for your travel expenses, as well as those of another member of your household who will act as your attendant (assuming the other conditions for the deduction are met). This is fine.

Line 256: Additional Deductions

Additional deductions — who doesn't like the sound of that! But don't get too excited. Not any old deduction you think you should be entitled to can be written off on your tax return. In fact, the rules for additional deductions are pretty specific. We'll discuss some of them here. And trust us, they're actually not all that common.

Income exempt under a tax treaty

Canada has a number of tax treaties with many countries around the globe. These tax treaties outline, among other issues, how each country will treat certain types of income earned within its borders. Sometimes tax treaties state that certain types of income you earn from a foreign country will not be taxable in Canada. It could be that the income is

Designated cities

The designated cities in Canada for purposes of the travel benefits deduction are as follows:

- Vancouver, British Columbia
- Edmonton, Alberta
- Winnipeg, Manitoba
- Toronto, Ontario
- Montreal, Quebec
- Moncton, New Brunswick
- St. John's, Newfoundland
- Calgary, Alberta
- Saskatoon, Saskatchewan
- North Bay, Ontario
- Ottawa, Ontario
- Quebec City, Quebec
- Halifax, Nova Scotia

taxed in the foreign country, or is altogether exempt from tax. Whatever the case, when you've received income that is exempt under a tax treaty, it is included in your "net" income but not your "taxable" income. This is why you receive an additional deduction. Income exempt under a tax treaty includes the following items:

- **United States social security payments.** These payments are only 85-percent taxable in Canada; therefore, you should deduct 15 percent of the total amounts received, on line 256.
- **Other foreign pensions.** Some pensions received from certain treaty countries, including certain French, German, Italian, and Spanish pensions, are exempt from tax in Canada. If you are unsure whether your pension is exempt from Canadian tax, contact your local CCRA office
- **Child support payments received from residents of the United States.**

If you receive income from a foreign source, and you are unsure how it should be taxed in Canada, check with the CCRA. Under the terms of a tax treaty Canada has with the foreign country, you may be able to claim tax relief.

Vow of perpetual poverty

Living in a dingy basement apartment in downtown Toronto may make you feel as if you've taken a vow of perpetual poverty. However, this tax deduction doesn't apply to you. If you are a member of a religious order, have taken a vow of perpetual poverty, and have turned over your entire earned income and superannuation and pension benefits in the year to your religious order, you're in for some tax relief. In fact, you can deduct the entire amount of this income paid in the year to your religious order, on line 256 of your personal tax return.

Earned income includes any salaries, wages, bursaries, scholarships, or research grants. It doesn't include any income from property (for example, dividends or interest). Even if you pay any investment income earned to your order, you are not entitled to a deduction on line 256.

To claim a deduction for a vow of perpetual poverty, you should include with your tax return a letter from your religious order. This letter should state that you are, in fact, a member of the order, have taken a vow of perpetual poverty, and have given your entire superannuation or pension benefits, and your entire earned income for the year, to that order.

If the above criteria apply to you, and you earn employment income in the year, you should provide evidence to your employer to this effect. The employer can then forgo the income tax and Canada Pension Plan contributions that normally have to be deducted from your pay.

Employment with a prescribed international organization

If you earn employment income from certain international organizations, you can claim a deduction for your net employment income in the year. The international organizations to which this deduction apply include the United Nations and its specialized agencies. If this deduction applies to you, you must include your employment income and any related employment expenses in your "net" income, then deduct the income, net of related employment expenses, on line 256.

Chapter 18

Non-Refundable Tax Credits

In This Chapter

- Understanding how non-refundable tax credits work
- Claiming personal amounts
- Knowing when to claim the spousal amount
- Claiming CPP and EI premiums and calculating CPP/QPP and EI overpayments
- Claiming the disability amount
- Making the most of student loan interest, tuition, and education amounts
- Claiming your medical expenses

Non-refundable tax credits directly reduce the amount of income tax you owe. In this way they differ from exemptions or deductions, which are subtracted from income subject to tax. The deduction allowable against taxes is 17 percent (except for charitable donations) of the total non-refundable tax credits for which you are eligible.

If the total of your non-refundable tax credits is more than the amount of tax you owe, you will **not** get a refund for the difference. The unused portion of the credits will be lost permanently, with a few exceptions to be discussed later in the chapter.

Line 300: Your Basic Personal Credit

For the year 2000, you are eligible to claim $7,231 as a personal amount credit for yourself on line 300.

Part-year residents

If you immigrated to or emigrated from Canada in 2000, you have to reduce your claim for personal amounts (lines 300 to 307, and 315). These amounts should be prorated for the number of days you were a resident in Canada over the number of days in the year, 365.

Non-residents

Non-residents are denied personal amount credits unless all or almost all of their employment and business income is from Canada and is not treaty protected.

Line 301: Age Amount

You qualify for an age amount of $3,531 if you were 65 years or older by December 31 of the year for which you want to claim this credit.

The amount you are able to claim is reduced by 15 percent of your net income (from line 236 of your return) in excess of $26,284, so that the age amount is reduced as income exceeds this level. For example, suppose Alice turned 65 in 2000, and she is wondering if she is entitled to claim the age credit. Her income for the year as reported on line 236 is $35,000. Her age credit is reduced by $1,307 ([$35,000 less $26,284] × 15%). This means that she can claim $2,224 on line 301 of her tax return.

You won't be entitled to any age credit if your net income exceeds $49,824.

If your spouse is eligible for the age amount and does not need the full credit to reduce his income tax to nil, the unused portion is available to you as an additional deduction. Calculate the additional deduction available on schedule 2 of your tax return.

Line 303: Spousal Amount

You may claim a spousal amount of $6,140 if you were married or had a common-law spouse at any time in the year, and if you supported that spouse at any time while you were married.

Just being married isn't enough to claim the spousal amount — you must also have supported your spouse. What does this mean? Well, it doesn't mean you have to pay for everything, but it does mean you must pay for a reasonable proportion of the expenses for your spouse. These expenses may include items such as food, utilities, taxes, insurance, repairs, and clothing.

If your spouse had income for the year, the $6,140 amount is reduced by the amount of your spouse's income over $614. Therefore, if your spouse's income was greater than $6,754, the credit available to you is reduced to nil.

For the purposes of this calculation, the following payments would be considered your spouse's income: salary, wages, tips and other remuneration, dividends, interest, taxable portion of any capital gains realized, Old Age Security pension or supplement, rents, income from any business, social security payments, and any Guaranteed Income Supplement received.

Your spouse's net income is the amount reported on line 236 of your spouse's tax return. If you separated in the year and were not back together by December 31, reduce your claim by your spouse's net income before the separation only. If you cannot claim the spousal amount, or you have to reduce your claim because of a spouse's dividend income from taxable Canadian corporations, you may be able to reduce your tax if you report all of your spouse's dividends on your return.

Who is your spouse? Well, currently it includes the person you are legally married to or your common-law spouse. Under proposed amendments to tax laws, this will change in 2001 to include same-sex partners, who will be referred to as "common-law partners." This will be two persons, regardless of sex, who cohabit in a conjugal relationship for at least 12 months. Common-law partners can jointly elect to be treated as spouses for taxation years commencing 1998.

Line 305: Equivalent-to-Spouse Amount

No, contrary to popular belief, the equivalent-to-spouse credit is not for people who are *almost* married. Instead, this credit of $6,140 is available to you if you have a dependant and you were single, divorced, separated, or widowed at any time during the year. Not just any dependant will qualify for this credit, so unfortunately you can't claim a credit for your 28-year-old son who still lives in your basement, even if he does eat all your food. Your dependant must satisfy the following requirements:

- Been under 18, your parent or grandparent, or mentally or physically infirm
- Related to you by blood, marriage, or adoption
- Lived with you in a home that you maintained
- Wholly dependent on you for support.

This claim is usually made by a single parent for a child, although claims by children for a parent and by one sibling for another are fairly common as well.

Like the spousal amount, the equivalent-to-spouse amount of $6,140 is reduced by the dependant's income over $614.

You cannot claim this amount if you are claiming a spousal amount, or if someone else in your household is claiming this amount for the same dependant.

You can claim equivalent-to-spouse for a dependant who lives away from home while attending school, if that dependant ordinarily lives with you when not in school.

Line 306: Amount for Infirm Dependants

You may be able to claim a deduction of up to $2,386 for each relative dependent on you or your spouse who is 18 years or older and was dependent on you during the year by reason of physical or mental infirmity. The credit is reduced by the dependant's income in excess of $4,845. The credit is completely eliminated once the dependant's income reaches $7,231.

A dependent relative may include either your or your spouse's father, stepfather, mother, stepmother, grandfather, grandmother, brother, sister, uncle, aunt, niece, or nephew.

To claim this amount the dependant must meet the following criteria:

- Eighteen years of age or older at the end of the year for which the tax return is filed
- A resident of Canada at some time during the year, if claim is made for a dependant other than a child or grandchild
- Dependent on you by reason of mental or physical infirmity
- Dependent on you for support at some time during the year.

You may be able to claim a personal amount for children or grandchildren even if they live outside Canada, provided they depended on you for support. You must provide proof of support paid. Dependants other than your children or grandchildren must have been resident in Canada at some time during the year. You cannot claim an amount for any other relatives who lived outside Canada for all of 2000.

To claim the credit, the child, grandchild, or other dependant must be dependent on you by reason of physical or mental infirmity. Unfortunately, *infirmity* is not defined in our tax law. The taxman has said that it does not mean the person is unable to work. Rather, the infirmity must be such that it requires the person to be dependent on the individual for a considerable period of time. Temporary illness is not classed as infirmity. Neither is infirmity the same as "severe impairment," which is required to claim other tax credits. Although you do not have to file a medical certificate to prove infirmity, you are required to keep on file a doctor's statement confirming the nature, commencement, and duration of the infirmity.

You cannot claim this credit if you are already claiming the equivalent-to-spouse credit for the same dependant.

Generally an individual is dependent on you for support if the individual does not have income in excess of the basic personal amount and you have contributed to the maintenance of that person — that is, paid for food, clothing, and other bills.

Lines 308 to 310: Canada Pension Plan/ Quebec Pension Plan Premiums

Enter the total of the amounts shown in boxes 16 and 17 of your T4 slips. Do not enter more than $1,329.90. If you contributed more than $1,329.90, enter the excess amount on line 448 of your return. The CCRA will refund this overpayment to you, or use it to reduce your balance owing. If you lived in Quebec on December 31, 2000, and contributed more than $1,329.90, claim the overpayment on your Quebec provincial return. In some cases, you may have an overpayment, even if you contributed less than $1,329.90. For example, your CPP or QPP contribution will be prorated if, in 2000, the following was true:

- You were a CPP participant and you turned 18 or 70, or received a CPP retirement or disability pension
- You were a QPP participant and you turned 18 or received a QPP disability pension.

If you would like to calculate your CPP overpayment yourself, use form T2204 "Employee Overpayment of 2000 Canada Pension Plan Contributions and 2000 Employment Insurance Premiums." Otherwise, the CCRA will calculate the overpayment for you and will adjust your T1 return for the difference.

Canada or Quebec Pension Plan contributions payable on self-employment and other earnings

You can claim an amount for the Canada Pension Plan (CPP) or Quebec Pension Plan (QPP) contributions that you have to make on self-employment earnings and on limited or non-active partnership income. If you have both employment and self-employment earnings, the amount of CPP or QPP contributions that you have to make on your self-employment earnings will depend on how much you have already contributed to the CPP or QPP as an employee.

You cannot use self-employment losses to reduce the CPP or QPP contributions that you paid on your employment earnings.

How to calculate your allowable contributions for CPP or QPP

Complete schedule 8 to calculate your CPP or QPP contributions payable, and attach it to your paper return. If you were a member of a partnership, you should include only your share of the net profit or loss. If you were not a resident of Quebec, use the amounts on lines 135 to 143 and line 122 of your return. Enter on line 310 and line 421 the required contribution. If you were a resident of Quebec, use the amounts on line 164 of your Quebec provincial return. Enter on line 310 the amount of the contribution.

Making additional CPP contributions

You may not have contributed to the CPP for certain income you earned through employment, or you may have contributed less than you were allowed. This can happen if any of the following apply:

- You had more than one employer in 2000
- You had income, such as tips, from which your employer did not have to withhold contributions
- You were in a type of employment that was not covered under CPP rules, such as casual employment.

If the amount you have reported on line 308 is less than $1,329.90, you can contribute 7 percent on any part of the income on which you have not already made contributions.

To make additional CPP contributions for 2000, complete the CCRA's form CPT20 "Election to Pay Canada Pension Plan Contributions." You should attach a completed copy of the form to your tax return or send it to the CCRA separately before May 1, 2001. You must also complete schedule 8 to calculate your additional CPP contributions. Include the amount of these contributions on lines 310 and 421. The 2000 income limit for contributing to the CPP is $37,600.

Making additional contributions will increase the pension you receive later.

Line 312: Employment Insurance Premiums

Enter the total of the amounts shown in box 18 of all your T4 and T4F slips. Do not enter more than $936.

If you contributed more than $936, enter the excess amount on line 450 of your return. The CCRA will refund this overpayment to you, or, if applicable, will use it to reduce your balance owing.

In some cases, you may have an overpayment even if you contributed less than $936. If so, the CCRA will calculate your overpayment and show it on your Notice of Assessment.

If you would like to calculate your overpayment, use form T2204 "Employee Overpayment of 2000 Canada Pension Plan Contributions and 2000 Employment Insurance Premiums."

If the total of the Employment Insurance (EI) insurable earnings shown in box 24 of all your T4 slips (or box 14, if box 24 is blank) and box 16 of your T4F slips is $2,000 or less, the taxman will refund your total EI premiums to you or will use the amount to reduce your balance owing. In this situation, do not enter your total EI premiums on line 312. Instead, enter the amount on line 450.

If your total EI insurable earnings are more than $2,000 and less than $2,059, the CCRA will refund a part of your EI premiums to you or use the amount to reduce your balance owing. In this situation, enter your total EI premiums on line 312. The CCRA will calculate your refund and show it on your Notice of Assessment.

If you would like to calculate your refund yourself, use form T2204.

Line 314: Pension Income Amount

You can claim up to $1,000 if you reported pension or annuity income on line 115 or line 129 of your return. Only pension or annuity income you report on line 115 or 129 qualifies for the pension income amount.

Amounts such as Old Age Security benefits, Canada Pension Plan benefits, Quebec Pension Plan benefits, Saskatchewan Pension Plan payments, death benefits, and retiring allowances do not qualify for the pension income amount.

If you are age 65 and over, but do not have sufficient pension income to qualify for the full credit (that is, your pension income is less than $1,000), you can create pension income by converting all or part of your RRSP to an RRIF or a life annuity. Or you can purchase a life annuity with other available funds. If you are under 65 and can begin receiving a pension from a life annuity or RRIF because of job loss or some other reason, this will also create pension income.

If you do not need your entire pension income amount to reduce your federal income tax to zero, you can transfer the unused credit to your spouse. Alternatively, you may be able to claim all or part of your spouse's pension income amount.

Line 315: Caregiver Amount

If, at any time in 2000, you maintained a dwelling where you and a dependant lived, you may be able to claim this $2,353 credit.

Your dependant must have been one of the following individuals:

- Your child or grandchild
- Your brother, sister, niece, or nephew, parent, or grandparent (including in-laws) who was resident in Canada
- Your aunt or uncle who was resident in Canada.

In addition, the dependant must meet all of the following conditions:

- Been 18 or over at the time he or she lived with you;
- Had a net income of less than $13,853
- Been dependent on you due to mental or physical infirmity, or, if he or she is your parent or grandparent (including in-laws), born in 1935 or earlier.

The credit of $2,386 is reduced dollar for dollar by your dependant's income in excess of $11,661. Once your dependant's income reaches $14,047, the credit is completely eliminated.

This claim is different from the infirm dependant amount claimed on line 306. To claim this amount, the dependant must have lived with you at some time during the year. This was not a requirement to claim the infirm dependant credit. Since this credit will always be greater than or equal to the infirm dependent credit, you should claim this credit if the dependant has lived with you. You cannot claim both credits.

Claims made by more than one person

If you and another person support the same dependant, you can split the claim for that dependant. However, the total of your claim and the other person's claim cannot be more than the maximum amount allowed for that dependant.

You cannot claim this amount for a dependant if anyone claims an amount on line 306 for that dependant or anyone other than you claims an amount on line 305 for that dependant.

Line 316: Disability Amount for Yourself

You may be able to claim a disability amount of $4,293 if a qualified person certifies both of the following:

- You had a severe mental or physical impairment in 2000, which caused you to be markedly restricted all, or almost all, of the time in any of the basic activities of daily living.
- Your impairment was prolonged, which means it has lasted, or is expected to last, for a continuous period of at least 12 months.

The only persons that qualify to certify that your impairment was severe and prolonged are doctors, optometrists, psychologists, occupational therapists, and audiologists.

You may be markedly restricted in a basic activity of daily living if you are blind or are unable to feed and dress yourself, control bowel and bladder functions, walk, speak, hear, or perceive, think, and remember.

You may also be markedly restricted if it takes you an extremely long time to perform any of these activities, even with therapy and the use of appropriate aids and medication.

The 2000 federal budget extended eligibility for the disability tax credit to include individuals who must undergo therapy several times each week, totaling at least 14 hours per week in order to sustain their vital functions. Individuals who would qualify under this extended definition include, for example, individuals with severe kidney disease requiring dialysis, or individuals with cystic fibrosis who require clapping therapy in order to breathe.

If you are making an application for this amount for the first time, you have to submit a completed and certified form T2201 "Disability Tax Credit Certificate." The CCRA will review your claim before it assesses your return to determine if you qualify. Once your claim is approved, you will be able to claim this amount for future years, as long as your circumstances do not change.

If your spouse does not need to use all of his or her disability amount, you may be able to claim the unused portion on line 326. If you have another dependant who does not need to use this entire amount, you may be able to claim the unused portion on line 318.

Line 318: Disability Amount Transferred from a Dependant Other Than Your Spouse

You may be able to claim all or part of any disability amount on line 316 for which your dependant qualifies. You can claim the unused portion if he or she lived in Canada at any time in 2000, and was dependent on you because of mental or physical infirmity.

In addition, one of the following must apply:

- You claimed an equivalent-to-spouse amount on line 305 for that dependant.
- The dependant was your or your spouse's child, grandchild, parent, or grandparent, and you could have claimed an equivalent-to-spouse amount on line 305 for that dependant if you did not have a spouse and if the dependant did not have any income.
- The dependant was your or your spouse's child, grandchild, parent, or grandparent, and you made a claim on line 306 or 315 for that dependant.
- The dependant was your or your spouse's child or grandchild, and you could have made a claim on line 306 or 315 for that dependant if he or she had no income and had been 18 years of age or older in 2000.
- The dependant was your or your spouse's parent or grandparent, and you could have made a claim on line 306 or 315 for that dependant if he or she had no income.

If you are required to make child support payments for your child, you cannot claim a disability amount for that child.

To claim the credit, you must attach to your paper return a properly completed and certified form T2201 "Disability Tax Credit Certificate" for each dependant.

If you were allowed a disability amount in a previous year and the dependant still meets the eligibility requirements in 2000, you can claim the disability amount in 2000 without sending in another form T2201. If you are not attaching the T2201 for a dependant, you should attach a note to your tax return stating the dependant's name, social insurance number, and relationship to you.

If you are splitting this claim for a dependant with another supporting person, attach a note to your tax return including the name and social insurance number of the other person making this claim. The total claimed for one dependant cannot be more than $4,293.

You can claim this credit only if the spouse of the person with a disability is not already claiming the disability tax credit or any other non-refundable tax credit (other than medical expenses) for the person with a disability, and you supported that person.

If you can claim this amount, you also may be able to claim an amount on line 315 for the same dependant.

Line 319: Student Loan Interest

You can claim the amount of the interest you, or a person related to you, paid on loans made to you for post-secondary education under the *Canada Student Loans Act*, the *Canada Student Financial Assistance Act*, or similar provincial or territorial government laws.

Interest on personal or family loans will not qualify for this credit. You can claim an amount only for interest that you have not previously claimed.

If you do not wish to claim these amounts on the return for the year they are paid, you can carry them forward and apply them on any one of the next five years' returns. Receipts should be attached to your paper return for the amounts you claim.

Line 323: Tuition and Education Amounts for Yourself

You can claim eligible tuition and education amounts for 2000, and any unused amounts carried forward from previous years, that are shown on your 1999 Notice of Assessment for credit on your 2000 tax return.

Tuition amount

You can claim only the tuition paid for courses you took in 2000. Qualifying courses include most at the post-secondary level or those that develop or improve skills in an occupation. You won't be eligible for a credit in any of the following circumstances:

- You pay tuition fees to a university, college, or other educational institution in Canada offering post-secondary courses, but the course you took is not at the post-secondary level.
- You paid tuition fees to a certified institution that provides courses for occupational training; however, you did not reach the age of 16 before the end of the year in which the courses were taken. Or it was not reasonable to conclude that the purpose for which you were taking the course was to provide occupational skills.

You must have paid more than $100 during the year to each educational institution whose fees you claim.

You cannot claim other expenses related to pursuing your education, such as books, or board and lodging. Credit for these amounts is allowed for in the education amount (see below). To claim tuition fees paid to an educational institution in Canada, you must obtain from your educational institution an official tax receipt or a completed form T2202A "Tuition and Education Amounts Certificate."

To claim tuition fees paid to an educational institution outside Canada, you must receive from your institution a completed form TL11A "Tuition Fees Certificate — University Outside Canada," which you can obtain from any Tax Services Office. In order to qualify, you must attend a university outside Canada, and must be enrolled in full-time attendance in a course that lasts at least 13 weeks and leads to a degree.

Education amount

You can claim this amount for each whole or part month in 2000 in which you were enrolled in a qualifying educational program. Your educational institution has to complete and give you form T2202 "Education Amount Certificate," or form T2202A "Tuition and Education Amounts Certificate" to confirm the period in which you were enrolled in a qualifying program.

The following amounts apply:

- You can claim $200 for each month in which you were enrolled as a full-time student.
- You can claim $60 for each month in which you were enrolled in a qualifying part-time program.

You cannot claim more than one education amount for a particular month.

A full-time program is a program at the post-secondary level that lasts at least three weeks, and requires at least 10 hours per week on courses or work in the program. A part-time program must also last at least three weeks, but it does not have a 10-hour per week course or workload requirement.

You can claim $200 a month if you attended your educational institution only part-time because of a mental or physical impairment. In this case, you have to complete form T2202 "Education Amount Certificate," to make your claim.

Generally, you cannot claim an education amount for a program for which you received a reimbursement, benefit, grant, or allowance, or for a program related to your job if you received a salary or wages while studying.

Transferring and carrying forward amounts

You have to report your tuition and education amounts first on your own return, even if someone else paid your fees. However, you can transfer to your spouse the part of your tuition and education amounts that you do not need to use to reduce your federal income tax to zero. Your spouse would then claim the unused portion of your tuition and education amounts on line 326 of his or her return.

You must use all the credits necessary to reduce your taxes to nil before you can transfer the credits to another person. If you do not transfer your unused amount to your spouse, you can transfer it to your or your spouse's parent or grandparent, who would claim it on line 324 of his or her return. Complete the back of form T2202 or form T2202A, as well as schedule 11 on your tax return, to calculate and designate this transfer. The maximum amount you may transfer is $5,000.

You can carryforward and claim in a future year the part of your tuition and education amounts that you do not need to use and did not transfer for the year in which they were incurred. However, if you carryforward an amount, you will not be able to transfer it to anyone else. You must claim your carryforward amount in the earliest year possible. The carryforward amount should be calculated on schedule 11 of your tax return.

If you are transferring a tuition or education amount to another person, do not transfer more than the person needs to reduce his or her federal income tax to zero. That way, you maximize the benefit of the credit and can carryforward the unused amount to a future year.

If your spouse does not need to use all of his or her tuition and education amounts, you can claim the unused part on line 326.

Line 324: Tuition and Education Amounts Transferred from a Child

A student who does not need all of his or her 2000 tuition and education amounts to reduce federal income tax to zero may be able to transfer the unused portion to you if you are a parent or grandparent of the student or of the student's spouse. The maximum amount that each student can transfer is $5,000 minus the amount the student needs, even if there is still an unused amount. To make the claim, the student has to complete form T2202 "Education Amount Certificate," or Form T2202A "Tuition and Education Amounts Certificate," to calculate the transfer amount and to designate you as the parent or grandparent who can claim the amount. If the tuition fees being transferred to you are not shown on the student's form T2202 or form T2202A, you should have a copy of the student's official tuition fees receipt.

If a student's spouse claims amounts on line 303 or 326 for the student, a parent or grandparent cannot claim the tuition and education amounts transfer.

If no amounts are claimed for the student by the student's spouse, or if the student does not have a spouse, the student can choose which parent or grandparent will claim the tuition and education amounts transferred. Only one person can claim the transfer from the student. However, it does not have to be the same parent or grandparent as the person who claims the student as a dependant on line 305 or 306.

Line 326: Amounts Transferred from Your Spouse

Your spouse can transfer to you any part of certain amounts, as discussed above, that he or she qualifies for but does not need to reduce federal income tax to zero.

The credits that may be transferred from one spouse to another are the age credit, the disability credit, the pension credit, and tuition and education credits. For additional details and to calculate your allowable claim, see Schedule 2 of your tax return. In the identification area on page 1 of your return, be sure to report your marital status and your spouse's name and social insurance number.

Lines 330 and 331: Medical Expenses

You can claim medical expenses you or your spouse paid for any of the following persons:

- Yourself
- Your spouse
- Your or your spouse's child or grandchild, who depended on you for support
- Your or your spouse's parent, grandparent, brother, sister, uncle, aunt, niece, or nephew, who lived in Canada at any time in the year and depended on you for support.

You can claim medical expenses paid in any 12-month period ending in 2000 and not claimed in 1999. Generally, you can claim all amounts paid, even if they were not paid in Canada. Your total expenses have to be more than either $1,637 or 3 percent of your net income (line 236), whichever is less. If you claim medical expenses for a dependant (other than your spouse) whose net income is more than $7,231, you have to reduce your claim.

There is a refundable tax credit for working individuals with low incomes and high medical expenses (see Chapter 19 for details).

Checklist of allowable medical expenses

- **Fees for professional medical services:** These include the services of doctors, dentists, surgeons, chiropractors, acupuncturists, registered or practical nurses, physiotherapists, speech therapists, naturopathists, professional tutors that a medical practitioner certifies as necessary because of a person's learning disability or mental impairment, and so on.
- **Payments for apparatus and materials, and repairs thereto:** Eligible apparatus and materials might include artificial limbs, wheelchairs, crutches, hearing aids, prescription eyeglasses or contact lenses, dentures, pacemakers, iron lungs, orthopedic shoes, reasonable expenses relating to renovations or alterations to a dwelling of an impaired person, reasonable moving expenses if incurred by an impaired person moving to a more accessible dwelling, and so on.
- **Medicines:** These might include costs of prescriptions, insulin or substitutes, oxygen, and so on.
- **Fees for medical treatments:** These treatments might include blood transfusion, injections, pre- and post-natal treatments, psychotherapy, speech pathology or audiology, and so on.
- **Fees for laboratory examinations and tests:** These include blood tests, cardiographs, X-ray examinations, urine and stool analyses, and so on.
- **Fees for hospital services:** These include hospital bills, use of the operating room, anesthetist, X-ray technician, and so on.
- **Amounts paid for attendant care, or care in an establishment**
- **Ambulance charges**
- **Expenses for guide and hearing-ear animals**
- **Premiums paid to private health services plans** (other than those paid by an employer) and premiums paid under the Quebec Medical Insurance Plan.
- **Group home:** If you paid fees to a group home in Canada for individuals who qualify for the disability amount (line 316), the portion of those fees paid to someone to care for or supervise such an individual, if nobody has claimed it as an attendant- or institutional-care medical expense on line 330, a child care expense on line 214, or an attendant care expense on line 215 for that person.
- **Travel expenses, if medical treatment is not available locally**

Items you cannot claim as medical expenses

Things you cannot claim as medical expenses include such items as the following: toothpaste, maternity clothes, athletic club memberships, funeral, cremation or burial expenses, illegal operations, treatments or illegally procured drugs, and so on. In addition, you cannot claim the part of an expense for which you have been or can be reimbursed. However, you can claim all of the expense if the reimbursement is included in your income — such as a benefit shown on a T4 slip — and you did not deduct the reimbursement anywhere else on your return.

How to calculate your medical expenses claim

Follow the steps below to calculate the amount you can claim for medical expenses:

- Choose the 12-month period ending in 2000 for which you will claim medical expenses. You cannot include any expenses you deducted on your 1999 return.
- Add up your allowable medical expenses for that period, and enter the total on line 330.
- Subtract $1,637, or 3 percent of your net income (line 236), whichever is less.
- Compare the result with the amount your spouse would be allowed. Generally, it is better for the spouse with the lower income to claim the allowable medical expenses. You can make whichever claim you prefer.

Attach your receipts and other documents (other than your health services plan premium receipts) to your paper return. Receipts for attendant care or therapy paid to an individual should show the individual's name and social insurance number.

The medical expense adjustment

If you claimed medical expenses for a dependant, other than your spouse, whose net income was more than $7,231, you have to reduce your medical expenses by making the following adjustment:

- Subtract $7,231 from the dependant's net income (line 236 of his or her return) or the amount that it would be if he or she filed a return.
- Multiply the result by 4.
- Complete this calculation for each such dependant.
- Enter on line 331 of your return the total of the amounts you calculated.

If the medical expenses adjustment you calculate for a dependant is more than the medical expenses you claimed for that dependant, it is not to your benefit to claim the medical expenses for that dependant.

Line 349: Donations and Gifts

You can claim donations made by either you or your spouse. Enter your claim from the calculation on schedule 9 and attach it to your return.

These donations and gifts do not include contributions to political parties. If you contributed to a federal or provincial political party, see Chapter 19 to find out about claiming a credit.

Allowable charitable donations and government gifts

Add up all of the donations made in 2000, plus any donations made in any of the previous five years that have not been claimed before. Generally, you can claim all or part of this amount, up to the limit of 75 percent of your net income reported on line 236.

For the year a person dies and the year before that, this limit is 100 percent of the person's net income.

You do not have to claim on your 2000 return the donations you made in 2000. Your credit is 17 percent of the first $200 of the donations and gifts you claim, and 29 percent of the balance. Therefore, it may be more beneficial for you not to claim them for 2000, but to carry them forward and claim them on your return for one of the next five years. You should attach your official receipts to your paper return, showing either your name or your spouse's name. The CCRA will not accept as proof of payment cancelled cheques, credit card slips, pledge forms, or stubs.You do not have to attach receipts for amounts shown in box 46 of your T4 or T4A slips, in box 36 of your T3 slips, in box 34 of your T5013 slips, or on financial statements showing an amount a partnership allocated to you.

You can claim only amounts you gave to Canadian registered charities and other qualified donees.

Cultural and ecological gifts

Unlike other donations, your claim for these types of gifts is not limited to a percentage of net income. You can choose the portion you want to claim in 2000, and carryforward any unused portion for up to five years.

Donations of cultural property enjoy an exemption from capital gains tax and an eligibility for the charitable donations tax credit for individuals. Institutions must retain the donated cultural property for ten years.

Donations of publicly traded securities

Capital gains on shares of publicly traded companies that are donated to charities between February 19, 1997 and December 31, 2001 will be included in income at 50 percent of the normal two-thirds inclusion rule for capital gains — that is, 33.33 percent. Rather than selling the security and donating the cash, you should consider donating the security instead. This way, you'll pay less tax and still get the same donation credit.

Donations to U.S. charities

Generally, donations to foreign charities are not deductible. However, you can claim donations to U.S. charities, subject to a limitation of 75 percent of your *U.S. source* income, as long as the charitable organization is recognized as such by U.S. law and would have qualified in Canada if it had been a Canadian organization.

The CCRA keeps a list of foreign registered charities. You can find out if your donation qualifies by visiting the following Web site: `www.ccra-adrc.gc.ca/charities`.

If you make a donation to a qualifying foreign university, the donation can be treated as if it were a Canadian donation. A qualified university is one where the student body normally includes students from Canada. A listing of these universities can be found in Schedule VIII of the Income Tax Regulations.

Part IV

Calculation of Federal and Provincial Taxes and Credits

"I put an extension on my tax return like you suggested, but I still don't think it's going to get there on time."

In this part . . .

Now we're through with the additions, deductions, and non-refundable credits, it's time for the moment of truth: How much tax do I owe? If this book were a movie, this would be the climax — not the part you want to miss with a trip to the refrigerator.

With the majority of provinces moving away from the traditional tax-on-tax system to the tax-on-income system, it's safe to say that there will be more work to do this year for those of you who complete your return the old fashion way — by hand. But don't worry, we've made sure that by the time you finish reading, you'll have calculated your tax properly and taken advantage of every federal and provincial or territorial credit possible.

"The avoidance of taxes is the only intellectual pursuit that still carries any reward."

— John Maynard Keynes

Chapter 19

Figuring Out Your Federal Tax

In This Chapter

- How to apply federal tax rates
- Calculating alternative minimum tax
- Calculating refundable federal and provincial tax credits
- Calculating federal surtax
- Calculating social benefits repayment
- Calculating the Goods and Services Tax Rebate

The dreaded moment has arrived! We're about to calculate the total federal tax you get to pay based on your taxable income. In this chapter we guide you through the steps required in that calculation. Here we go . . .

Schedule 1: Federal Tax Calculation

In Canada you are liable for two types of income tax: federal and provincial. Your federal tax amount is an especially important number — not only does it represent your tax liability to the federal government, but also many provinces base *their* tax on the federal tax liability. This is one number you don't want to get wrong!

Federal taxes are calculated on schedule 1 of your tax return. If you have any taxable income this year, you must complete at least page 1 (part 2) of schedule 1. After computing the initial tax calculation, schedule 1 then divides into two calculations, Method A or Method B.

Method A is for straightforward situations. Method A therefore should *not* be used by taxpayers who have claims or liabilities for the following:

- Dividend tax credits
- Foreign tax credits
- Overseas employment tax credits
- Minimum tax liability
- Minimum tax carryforward applied

Method B is required when you have any of the above credits or liabilities.

Method A uses the initial tax calculation result, then applies nonrefundable credits (Chapter 18) and any surtaxes owing.

Method B (schedule 1, page 2) takes into account any of your special credits and liabilities (the situations disqualifying you from using Method A) and has its own calculation of nonrefundable tax credits and surtax.

Federal tax rates

The first step in calculating your federal tax payable is to apply the following rates of federal tax to your taxable income figure, as calculated in Chapter 17. And don't worry — these numbers are provided for you on schedule 1.

Taxable Income	*Tax Rate*
$30,004 or less	17%
In excess of	
$30,004	$5,100 + 26% of taxable income in excess of $30,004
$60,009	$12,902 + 29% of taxable income in excess of $60,009

These tax brackets will be adjusted in future for changes in the consumer price index in excess of 3 percent. Due to the low levels of inflation we have been experiencing recently, there has been no indexing of these rates since 1992.

Your basic federal tax is a subtotal that you use for certain calculations. For example, the federal individual surtax is generally a percentage of your basic federal tax. You will want to double-check this number.

After you calculate your basic federal tax, you will move on to use either Method A or Method B. In either case, your basic federal tax will generally end up being less than the amount calculated in part 1 of schedule 1. Why? Because your nonrefundable tax credits (among others, if you use Method B) actually reduce your basic tax owing.

Method A simply requires you to go line by line and fill in numbers. There's no rocket science here. Method B is where you could run into trouble, so we'll now spend some time explaining some of the items you may need to consider.

Alternative Minimum Taxes

How do you know when you owe AMT? Well, for starters, keep in mind that this isn't something the average Joe taxpayer will ever have to worry about. But if you have some less-than-common tax deductions this year, take a look at form T691 — Alternative Minimum Tax. This is where AMT is calculated. And here is a list of some tax deductions that may subject you to AMT:

- Capital cost allowance and carrying charges claimed on certified film property acquired before March 1996, or rental and leasing properties
- Losses from limited partnerships, including carrying charges relating to your acquisition of a limited partnership
- Resource expenditures, depletion allowances and carrying charges related to resource properties and flow-through shares
- The non-taxable portion of capital gains reported in the year (one-quarter of gains February 27, 2000 or before, and one-third of gains after February 27, 2000). This includes any capital gain on which the capital gains exemption is claimed.
- Employee home relocation loans
- Stock option and share deductions.

AMT may also apply if you've claimed tax credits such as the investment tax credit, overseas employment tax credit, federal political tax credit, or labour-sponsored fund tax credit.

If you've claimed a significant amount of any of the above deductions or credits, complete form T691 to see if you have to pay AMT this year. This form requires you to recalculate your taxable income without the deductions. If taxes on this new income, less a $40,000 exemption, are greater than your regular federal taxes owing, you'll have to pay AMT. Simply follow this form to crunch the numbers.

If you've just learned that you have to pay AMT this year, you probably have steam coming out your ears. Cool down. Your AMT can be carried forward to offset against regular taxes (that is, not AMT) owing in future years. You'll have to bite the bullet this year, but as long as similar tax deductions don't keep cropping up year after year on your tax return, you'll eventually get credit for this awful tax.

If you paid alternative minimum tax on any of your 1993 to 1999 returns, but you do not have to pay minimum tax for 2000, you may be able to claim a credit against your 2000 taxes for all or part of the minimum tax you paid in those years. To calculate your claim, complete parts 1, 2, and 8 of form T691, "Alternative Minimum Tax." Attach a completed copy of the form to your return.

Line 425: Federal dividend tax credit

In Chapter 12 we talked about the fact that dividends you received from taxable Canadian corporations had to be multiplied by 1.25. This is one rule that's hard to forget because the amount of dividends reported on line 120 of your tax return is actually 25 percent higher than the amount you received this year. What's the catch?

Due to some heavy-duty corporate and personal tax rules that we won't bore you with here, the dividend gross-up actually works in your favour. You see, you are now entitled to a dividend tax credit. So, if you reported dividends on line 120, enter on line 425 of schedule 1 the total of the dividend tax credits from taxable Canadian corporations shown on your information slips. These credits normally show up on T5, T3, T5013, and T4PS slips. If you did not receive dividend information slips, don't fret. You can actually calculate this amount yourself. It is 13.33 percent of the taxable amount of dividends you received from taxable Canadian corporations.

Foreign dividends do not qualify for this credit. So, remember that foreign dividends should not be grossed up on your tax return and should not be reported on line 120, and you should not claim a dividend tax credit.

Lines 431 and 433: Federal foreign tax credit

If you've received income from foreign sources this year, you may have paid tax to some foreign tax authorities. But as we've learned throughout this book, Canadians are taxed on their worldwide income, which means that this same income is being taxed in Canada. Does this mean you're being double taxed? Probably no. Lucky for you, Canada lets you claim a credit for the foreign taxes you've paid.

The federal foreign tax credit is for foreign income taxes you paid on income you received from outside Canada and reported on your Canadian return.

Claiming this credit may take a bit of work. If you paid tax to more than one foreign country, and the total non-business income tax you paid to all foreign countries is more than $200, you have to do a separate calculation for each country for which you claim a foreign tax credit. In addition, a separate calculation is required for business income for each country. (You normally can tell if you've received non-business or business income from a foreign source because these are separately reported on your information slips.) Use form T2209 "Federal Foreign Tax Credits" to calculate your credits.

Once you've calculated the amount of foreign tax credits you're entitled to, enter the total on line 36 of schedule 1.

If you can't use all your foreign taxes this year, remember that you can carry unclaimed foreign business income taxes back three years and forward seven years.

Generally, the foreign tax credit you can claim for each foreign country is the *lowest of* the following:

- The foreign income tax you actually paid
- The tax due to Canada on your net income from that country.

If you paid tax on income from foreign property, your foreign tax credit for the income from that property cannot be more than 15 percent of your net income from that property. However, you can deduct the excess amount on your return at line 232.

TIP

If you were a member of a partnership and are entitled to claim a part of the foreign taxes the partnership paid, include in your calculation the amount shown in the financial statements or in box 33 of your T5013 Statement of Partnership Income slip.

How to claim the federal foreign tax credit

There is red tape that comes with claiming a foreign tax credit. Here are some things to remember:

First, ensure you complete the federal foreign tax credit area in Method B on schedule 1 and attach the schedule (and form T2209, if you use it) to your return. Then, attach the following to your tax return:

- A note showing your calculations. Show all amounts in *Canadian* dollars.
- Proof, such as an official receipt, showing the foreign taxes you paid. For example if you paid taxes in the U.S., attach your W-2 information slip, U.S. 1040 return, and any other supporting documents.

If your federal foreign tax credit on non-business income is less than the tax you paid to a foreign country, you may be able to claim a provincial or territorial foreign tax credit. You should complete form T2036 "Provincial Foreign Tax Credit" to determine the amount, if any, of the credit available.

You may also be able to use form T2209 to reduce your federal individual surtax by any unabsorbed foreign tax in excess of the foreign tax credit limit.

Line 429: Overseas employment credit

The overseas employment tax credit is available to you if you were a Canadian resident but were working abroad for six months or longer in connection with a resource, construction, installation, agricultural, or engineering project. To claim your credit, you have to fill out form T626 "Overseas Employment Tax Credit," and have the form certified by your employer.

When you claim an overseas employment tax credit, you use form T626 to actually calculate your taxes owing. Therefore, you should enter the result of your calculation from form T626 on line 429 of schedule 1 — that is, this becomes your basic federal tax.

If you have severed your ties with Canada and have become a non-resident, you will not be eligible for the credit because your income as a non-resident will generally not be taxable in Canada.

Lines 409 and 410: Federal political tax credit

If you contributed to a registered federal political party or a candidate for election to the House of Commons in 2000, enter the total amount of your contribution directly on page 4 of the T1 jacket, on line 409.

You may deduct from your federal tax payable a portion of the political contributions you made. The amount of the credit deductible depends on the amount contributed.

The credit is calculated as the total of the following:

75 percent of the first $200 contributed + 50 percent of the next $350 contributed + 33⅓ percent of the next $525 contributed

Therefore the *maximum* credit you will be able to claim in a year is $825, and that's when $1,075 has been contributed. Credit is not available for contributed amounts over $1,075.

Enter the amount of the credit calculated on line 410.

Attach your official receipts to your return. You do not have to attach receipts for amounts shown in box 36 of your T5013 slips, or on financial statements showing an amount a partnership allocated to you.

Since the amount of the available credit diminishes with the size of the contribution, consider spreading your political contributions over two tax years. For example, two annual contributions of $750 will result in a larger credit amount than a contribution of $1,500 all in one year ($780 versus $500). Before you make your contributions, consider how to maximize the available credit.

The federal political contributions tax credit only applies to federal political contributions. If you've made provincial political contributions, these may be eligible for credit against your provincial taxes owing.

Line 412: Investment tax credit

You may be eligible for this credit if any of the following apply:

- You bought certain new buildings, machinery, or equipment, and they were used in certain areas of Canada in qualifying activities such as farming, fishing, logging, or manufacturing
- There's an amount shown in box 13 of your T101 or T102 slip
- There's an amount shown in box 41 of your T3 slip
- There's an amount shown in box 38 of your T5013 slip
- There's an amount shown on the financial statement given to you by a partnership.

The investment tax credits once available have been cut back to the point where the only qualifying expenditures are the following:

- Scientific research and development expenditures for research anywhere in Canada
- General expenditures for equipment used in a variety of activities if carried on in the four Atlantic provinces or the Gaspé Peninsula of Quebec.

To be able to claim a credit for an eligible expenditure, you have to send a completed T2038 — Investment Tax Credit (IND) to the CCRA no later than 12 months after the due date of your return for the year in which the expenditure arises.

If you have not used your investment tax credits generated in earlier years, under the more liberal rules you may carryforward these amounts to offset future taxes.

You may be able to reduce your federal individual surtax by any unclaimed investment tax credit, or claim a refund of your unused investment tax credit. See lines 419 and 454 of the T1 jacket.

Lines 413 and 414: Labour-sponsored funds tax credit

An LSVCC is a venture capital fund established under specific federal or provincial legislation and managed by labour unions or employee groups. You can claim the labour-sponsored fund tax credit if you purchased an approved share of the capital stock of a prescribed labour-sponsored venture capital corporation (LSVCC) from January 1, 2000 to February 28, 2001. If you bought a share between January 1, 2001 and February 28, 2001, you can claim a credit for that share either on your 2000 return or on your 2001 return, but not both.

If you bought an LSVCC share from January 1, 2000 to February 29, 2000, and claimed the credit for it on your 1999 return, you cannot also claim a credit for that share on your 2000 return.

Enter the net cost of purchasing your share of the LSVCC on line 413 of your T1 jacket. The net cost is the amount you paid for your shares. Enter the amount of the credit on line 414. The allowable credit cannot be more than 15 percent of the net cost, to a maximum of $750.

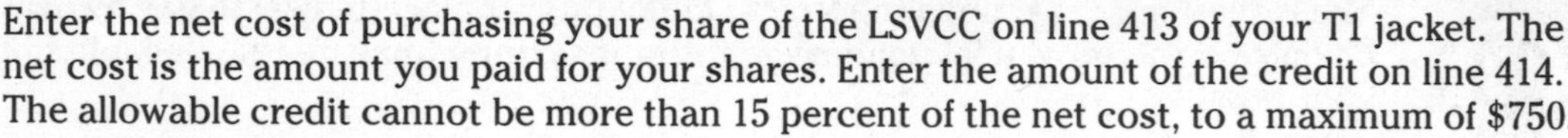

Labour-sponsored funds can be contributed to your RRSP. If you choose to do so, don't forget to claim an RRSP deduction as well as the federal (and perhaps provincial) tax credit for your investment!

For 1998 and later years, if a spousal RRSP became the first registered holder of the share, either the RRSP contributor or the payee may claim the credit for that share.

Attach to your return either a T5006 slip "Statement of Registered Labour-Sponsored Venture Capital Corporation Class A Shares," or an official provincial or territorial slip.

Line 418: Additional tax on RESP accumulated income payments

Many Canadians are purchasing Registered Education Savings Plans (RESPs) to help fund their children's education. But when the moment of truth arrives, and your child decides to forgo post-secondary school, guess who's stuck paying the tax? You guessed it, you are.

Don't get us wrong, ***we*** think RESPs are a great tax deferral and income splitting tool. We're just warning you of one of the repercussions. You see, if you received an accumulated income payment from an RESP in 2000, you may have to pay an additional tax of 20 percent on all or part of the amount in box 40 of your T4A slip.

You are liable for additional tax when you have contributed to an RESP that has been running for at least ten years, and the beneficiary of the plan does not pursue a post-secondary education by 21 years of age. You are then entitled to the accumulated investment income in the plan. There are some ways you can use this accumulated income to avoid the additional tax. For example, you are able to transfer the income to your RRSP or that of your spouse, subject to your contribution limit and an overall total of $50,000. However, any surplus amount will be subject to an additional 20 percent tax.

You can withdraw the capital you contributed to the RESP at any time without paying additional tax because you have already paid tax on these funds.

Line 419: Federal surtax

Nothing like kicking you when you're down. On top of your federal tax calculated on schedule 1, there's more federal tax to worry about. This is the federal individual surtax.

The federal individual surtax is an additional tax of 5 percent that applies to taxpayers with basic federal tax above a threshold amount. This level was $12,500 but was raised to $18,500 in the 2000 federal budget. Since the increased threshold amount comes into effect on July 1, 2000, for the 2000 tax year the 5 percent surtax effectively applies on basic federal tax in excess of $15,500. Use schedule 1 to calculate your federal individual surtax, if any. The surtax applies to the tax payable after you deduct personal amount credits and the dividend tax credit, but before other credits are applied.

The February 2000 federal budget announced that this surtax is in the process of being phased out over the next five years. For 2001, the surtax rate is to be reduced from 5 percent to 4 percent, effective January 1, 2001.

You may be able to reduce the federal individual surtax you have to pay by using the unclaimed part of any foreign tax credits or investment tax credits available.

Line 421: Canada Pension Plan contributions on self-employment earnings

Enter the Canada Pension Plan contributions you have to pay, from line 310 of your return. If you were a resident of Quebec, this line does not apply to you; enter on your Quebec provincial return the Quebec Pension Plan contributions you have to pay.

If you are self-employed, you must fill out schedule 8 to see if you owe any CPP on your self-employment earnings.

Canada Pension Plan and Employment Insurance Overpayment

In this section we discuss what to do when you have paid too much CPP or EI. Here are the steps that you take if you've handed over too much of your hard-earned cash.

Line 448: CPP overpayment

Finally, a breath of fresh air! After pages of pay this, pay that, here is one area where you can recoup some of the money you've paid in the year. As you probably know, your employer has to take CPP premiums off your pay. However, it's possible that you paid too much! This most commonly happens when you held more than one job in the year. You see, since each employer is obligated to withhold CPP without regard to your other employers, you may have maxed out your payments for the year. However, it is also possible that your employer messed up and took too much CPP off your pay. Either way, relief is on its way — you're entitled to a refund of your CPP overpayment.

If you were not a resident of Quebec and you contributed more than you were required to, as explained in Chapter 18, enter the difference on line 448. The CCRA will refund the excess contributions to you, or will apply them to reduce your balance owing. If you were a resident of Quebec, this line does not apply to you; claim the excess amount on your Quebec provincial return.

Line 448: EI overpayment

As with the CPP overpayment, you may have had too much EI deducted from your pay in the year. If you contributed more than you had to, enter the difference on line 450. Refer to Chapter 18 if you need help calculating the correct amount. The CCRA will refund the excess amount to you or use it to reduce your balance owing.

If you repaid some of the Employment Insurance benefits you received, do not claim the repayment on this line. This is considered a social benefits repayment.

Line 422: Social benefits repayment

Did you receive social benefits such as the Old Age Security pension (including net federal supplements) or Employment Insurance benefits this year. Well, you could be in for a surprise. You see, you can't always have your cake and eat it too. Some taxpayers will actually have to repay the benefits they received in the year. If this applies to you, you must enter the amount of social benefits you have to repay, from line 235 of your return on line 422.

Employment Insurance (EI) clawback

Your EI payments are subject to a "clawback" to the extent that your net income is greater than 125 percent of maximum insurable earnings, being $39,000. The government claws back payments at a 30-percent rate to the extent they exceed 125 percent of $39,000, which is $48,750.

Old Age Security (OAS) clawback

Your Old Age Security benefits will be taxed back at a 15-percent rate if your income is greater than $53,960. At $87,293, 100 percent of your Old Age Security benefits will be clawed back.

The $53,960 threshold for OAS is indexed and will be adjusted in future for changes in the consumer price index in excess of 3 percent.

Line 452: Medical expense supplement

You can claim a credit of up to $500 if you have an amount at line 332 (that is, a medical expense credit) and both of the following apply:

- You were resident in Canada throughout 2000
- You were 18 or older at the end of 2000.

In addition, the total of the following two amounts has to be equal to or greater than $2,500:

- Your employment income on lines 101 and 104 minus the amounts on lines 207, 212, 229, and 231 (but if the result is negative, use "0")
- Your net self-employment income (not including losses) from lines 135 to 143.

To claim this credit, complete and attach schedule 10 to your return.

You can claim both the medical expense supplement and a medical expense credit for the same expenses.

You cannot claim this credit if the total of your net income (line 236) and your spouse's net income is $26,745 or more.

Line 457: Goods and Services Tax rebate

If you were able to deduct expenses from your income as an employee or as a partner, you may be eligible for a rebate of the GST/HST you paid on those expenses. You see, if your employer (or partnership) paid for these expenses directly, the employer would have been able to claim an input tax credit for the GST/HST paid. Since you paid for the expense yourself, the GST/HST rebate works as if you are getting the input tax credit instead.

Generally, you can claim this rebate if either of the following applies:

- Your employer has a GST/HST registration number
- You are a member of a GST/HST-registered partnership, and you have reported on your return your share of the income from that partnership.

If your employer is not registered for GST purposes and is a listed financial institution, health care provider or nonprofit organization, you won't be able to take advantage of this rebate.

You can only claim a GST/HST rebate if you paid GST/HST on your expenditures. If you've paid for zero-rated or exempt expenses, such as insurance or interest, you're out of luck. To claim this rebate, complete form GST 370 "Employee and Partner GST/HST Rebate Application." Attach a completed copy of this form to your return, and enter on line 457 the rebate you are claiming.

You have to include in income any rebate you receive, in the year you receive it. For example, if you claim a rebate on your 2000 return and you receive your rebate in 2001, you have to report the rebate on your 2001 return.

There! That wasn't so bad, was it?

Chapter 20

Looking at Provincial and Territorial Taxes and Credits (Line 428)

In This Chapter

- Taking a look at provincial and territorial tax rates
- Doing the tax calculation for multiple jurisdictions
- Understanding provincial foreign tax credits
- Assessing the taxes for all provinces and territories

In Canada, we pay taxes to both the federal government and a provincial or territorial government, although in every province but Quebec it may not seem this way since the Canada Customs and Revenue Agency (CCRA) administers income taxes on their behalf.

Provincial and territorial taxes have been evolving over the past few years. While Quebec has had its own system of taxation for many years, the other provinces and territories have all imposed taxes based on a percentage of the federal tax liability. Beginning in 2000, this has begun to change. Most provinces, including Quebec, will now directly impose taxes on your taxable income, as opposed to basing it on federal taxes payable. The reason for this change is that some of the provinces would prefer to be able to directly influence the provincial taxes with their tax laws, as opposed to being dependent (and maybe at the mercy of) the federal tax system.

In this chapter we will discuss the tax rates that apply in your province or territory of residence, the method of taxation, and any special tax credits that may apply to you. With the number of changes that were introduced in the 2000 provincial and territorial budgets, you're sure to learn something new! And by the way, any time we refer to "provincial tax," we mean the territories too!

Provincial and Territorial Tax Rates

As we cover in Chapter 1, our federal government levies taxes based on the taxable income you earn in a year. It is this federal tax amount that becomes the basis for tax in some provinces and territories in Canada. This is the concept of tax on tax. The federal tax rates that apply in 2000 are as follows:

Taxable Income	*Marginal Tax Rate*
$0–$30,004	17%
$30,005–$60,009	25%
Over $60,009	29%

Your basic federal tax is calculated by using the above rates, then deducting any federal tax credits such as non-refundable tax credits, dividend tax credits, foreign tax credits, and others. This basic federal tax calculation is done on schedule 1 of your personal tax return. To calculate provincial taxes in provinces where there is still tax on tax, you simply have to take the basic federal taxes payable figure as calculated on schedule 1 of your tax return, and multiply it by the provincial or territorial tax rate. Provincial and territorial taxes calculated as a percentage of basic federal tax are shown in Table 20-1 as follows:

Table 20-1 Provincial Tax Rates for 2000

Province/Territory	*Basic Tax Rate as a % of Basic Federal Tax*
Alberta	44
Saskatchewan	48
Newfoundland	62
Prince Edward Island	57.5
Northwest Territories	45
Nunavut	45
Yukon	49

Depending on your province of residence, your provincial tax liability may not be based on federal taxes at all. Beginning in 2000, many provinces will have a tax calculation based on your taxable income in the year. The provinces that now have a tax on income system are Quebec, Ontario, Manitoba, British Columbia, New Brunswick, and Nova Scotia. In these provinces, you must take your taxable income figure and multiply it by the provincial tax rates. You may then deduct tax credits available in that province to come up with your provincial tax payable.

British Columbia, Manitoba, Ontario, New Brunswick, and Nova Scotia will implement the tax on income system beginning in 2000. Alberta, Saskatchewan, Prince Edward Island, and Newfoundland will stick with the tax on tax system until 2001. No word yet on when Yukon, Nunavut, and the Northwest Territories will make the switch.

Those provinces that move to a tax on income system have control over the non-refundable tax credits. Since 2000 is the first year, all provincial non-refundable credits must be the same as the federal credits. Table 20-2 shows the provincial tax rates as a percentage of taxable income.

Table 20-2 Provincial Tax Rates for 2000

Taxable Income	*Tax Rate as a % of Taxable Income*
British Columbia Taxes	
$0–$30,004	8.4
$30,005–$60,009	12.4
Over $60,009	14.4
Ontario Taxes	
$0–$30,004	6.37

Taxable Income	*Tax Rate as a % of Taxable Income*
$30,005–$60,009	9.62
Over $60,009	11.16
Manitoba Taxes	
$0–$29,590	8
$29,591–$59,180	12.22
Over $59,180	13.63
New Brunswick Taxes	
$0–$29,590	9.94
$29,591–$59,180	15.21
Over $59,180	16.96
Nova Scotia Taxes	
$0–$29,590	9.77
$29,591–$59,180	14.95
Over $59,180	16.67
Quebec Taxes	
$0–$26,000	19
$26,001–$52,000	22.5
Over $52,000	25

Prince Edward Island, Alberta, Newfoundland, and Saskatchewan will move to a tax on income system in 2001.

Of the five provinces adopting the tax on income system this year, only Ontario and British Columbia have decided to index their tax brackets to inflation, like the federal government announced they would do in the 2000 federal budget. Manitoba, New Brunswick, and Nova Scotia are continuing with the unindexed brackets.

If you've lived in more than one place in 2000, you may be wondering which province or territory you should pay tax to. It's surprisingly easy. Wherever you live on December 31, 2000, is your province of residence for the entire year. So even if you moved from Nova Scotia to Ontario on December 29, 2000, if Ontario is now your new permanent home, you will file a tax return stating Ontario is your province of residence. All your income from the entire year will be subject to Ontario tax rates.

If you are planning to move this year, time your move carefully to save taxes. Since each province and territory has different tax rates, if you're moving from a high taxed place to a lower taxed place, you're better off moving during this taxation year. This means that all your income from the entire year, even when you lived in the higher taxed jurisdiction, will be subject to the lower tax rates in your new province or territory of residence. On the other hand, if you're moving to a higher taxed jurisdiction, consider postponing your move until next year.

Tax Calculation for Multiple Jurisdictions

Although your provincial and territorial taxes are normally calculated based on where you lived on December 31 of the year, there is a special calculation that must be done if (and only if) you earned self-employment income in more than one province where you had a permanent establishment during the year. This is the tax calculation for multiple jurisdictions found on form T2203 "Provincial and Territorial Taxes for 2000 — Multiple Jurisdictions."

You only have to fill out form T2203 if you earned self-employment income in a province where you had a permanent establishment other than your province of residence (that is, where you lived on December 31), or outside Canada, in the year. You must also fill out form T2203 if you were a non-resident and earned self-employment income in more than one province or territory in Canada. You do not have to fill out form T2203 if you've lived in more than one province in the year or if you earned any types of income other than self-employment income in more than one province or territory.

For example, John lived in Manitoba on December 31, 2000. John is an accountant whose firm has offices, and earned income, in Manitoba, Saskatchewan, and Alberta during 2000. Therefore, when John files his 2000 tax return, he will put Manitoba as his province of residence on page 1 of his tax return, but show his province of self-employment as multiple jurisdictions. All his income, other than his self-employment earnings, will be taxed using Manitoba tax rates. To calculate the tax on his self-employment earnings, he will use form T2203.

What is a permanent establishment?

You'll notice that you only have to file form T2203 if your business has a "permanent establishment" in more than one province or territory in the year, or in a country other than Canada. The term *permanent establishment* is actually quite important. It's not enough that you earned some self-employment income in another province during the year. For example, if you are a consultant in Nova Scotia and took on a job in Prince Edward Island during the year, you don't necessarily have a permanent establishment in Prince Edward Island. And you don't necessarily have to calculate tax for multiple jurisdictions.

A *permanent establishment* is defined in the *Income Tax Act* as a fixed place of business, including an office, a branch, a mine, an oil well, a farm, a timberland, a factory, a workshop, or a warehouse. In addition, if you have an employee or agent carrying on business for you who has general authority to contract on your behalf or who has a stock of merchandise used to fill orders, you will be deemed to have a permanent establishment in that place. If you have substantial machinery or equipment in a particular place, you may also be deemed to have a permanent establishment there. On the other hand, if you do business through a commission agent, broker to an independent agent, or you maintain an office solely for the purchase of merchandise, these factors alone will not deem you to have a permanent establishment in that location.

Completing form T2203

When you earn self-employment income through a permanent establishment in more than one province, territory, or country, you will have to allocate your total business income in the year to a particular jurisdiction. In addition, all your non-business income should be allocated to your province of residence at year-end.

Based on the percentage of your total income allocated to each jurisdiction, you must then calculate your provincial taxes owing. Remember, there will be taxes owing to more than one province, since you earned business income in more than one province.

The actual calculation of provincial taxes will depend on the tax system in the province or territory. If the province or territory still has a tax on tax system, you will simply allocate part of your basic federal tax to that province or territory, then multiply it by the provincial tax rate.

For example, say you earned total business income of $100,000 in 2000. This was your only source of income in the year and you earned $32,000 of this income in Prince Edward Island. This means that 32 percent of your net income is allocated to Prince Edward Island in the year. Therefore, if you paid $23,000 in basic federal tax in the year, 32 percent of that tax, or $7,360, should be allocated to Prince Edward Island. You would then multiply the $7,360 in basic federal tax by the province's 57.5-percent tax rate to come up with total Prince Edward Island taxes payable of $4,232 (assuming there were no provincial tax credits available to offset this amount).

If you have allocated some business income to a jurisdiction with a tax on income system, to calculate provincial taxes payable you will simply take the total income allocated to that jurisdiction and multiply it by the provincial tax rate in effect for that income level.

For example, if you've allocated $15,000 of your business income to the province of Ontario in 2000, you owe $956 (6.37% × $15,000) in taxes to Ontario (less any Ontario nonrefundable tax credits and provincial tax credits available).

If you've earned business income outside Canada, a special federal surtax will apply to that income. This surtax is meant to replace the provincial taxes that would otherwise be owing. To calculate this surtax, simply take the amount of income allocated to the jurisdiction outside Canada over total income earned in the year. You should then multiply the basic federal tax owing by this percentage to come up with basic federal tax allocated to this other jurisdiction. You then multiply by 48 percent to come up with the special surtax owing.

For example, if you earned business income of $50,000 in a country outside Canada, and total income of $100,000, 50 percent of your income in the year is attributable to this other jurisdiction. If you paid $23,000 in basic federal taxes in 2000, 50 percent of this, or $$11,500, is attributable to the other jurisdiction. You would then multiply the $11,500 of federal taxes by 48 percent to come up with federal surtax on income earned outside Canada of $5,520.

Only income earned in a year must be allocated to the jurisdiction in which it was earned. If your business had a loss, you can use that loss to offset income taxed in your province of residence on December 31 of the year.

Provincial Foreign Tax Credits

If you paid foreign taxes on foreign non-business income you earned this year, but could not receive a full federal foreign tax credit for these taxes, relief is available. You can deduct all or a portion of the foreign taxes from your provincial taxes payable. The provincial tax deduction allowed is calculated on form T2036 "Provincial Foreign Tax Credit" (unless you live in the province of Quebec). The actual deduction is the lesser of the following:

- Actual foreign taxes not claimed as a foreign tax credit
- Net foreign non-business income divided by net income, times provincial tax otherwise payable.

When you have a provincial foreign tax credit, enter that credit on the tax calculation form for your province of residence.

British Columbia

British Columbia is one of the many provinces of Canada that in 2000 is moving to the tax on taxable income system of calculating provincial taxes. There are several reasons for this move, including the fact that the provinces expected the federal government to lower federal tax rates in 2000 and beyond (which it did). You see, with a tax on tax system, a decrease in federal tax rates would also mean a decrease in provincial tax revenues. In addition, the provinces want more control over their tax revenues and would like to be able to directly influence tax policy. But enough of the political nonsense — let's get on to the rules.

As well as moving toward the tax on taxable income, B.C. will continue to charge surtax in 2000. The surtax prior to July 1, 2000 was 30 percent of B.C. tax in excess of $5,300 and 19 percent of tax in excess of $8,660. Effective July 1, 2000, the first surtax remained the same while the second surtax was reduced to 15 percent of tax in excess of $8,660. This surtax is reduced if you have dependants.

If you live in British Columbia, you'll also have to calculate provincial nonrefundable tax credits in 2000. The credits are almost identical to the federal credits, except that you must apply the lowest rate of B.C. tax (8.4 percent) to come up with your provincial credits. In addition to the federal credits, there is a supplemental basic personal amount and spousal amount of $300 available provincially. And if you've made charitable donations in the year, the low 8.4 percent rate only applies to the first $200 of donations. Any donations in excess of this will give rise to a 14.4-percent nonrefundable tax credit.

British Columbia tax credits

The 2000 provincial budget did not propose any changes to British Columbia tax credits. Therefore, you won't find filling in form T1C – British Columbia (where the tax credits are found) to be much different this year from last year. Some of B.C.'s tax credits are free money types of credits — that is, you don't have to be taxable in B.C. to receive the credits — while others can only be claimed to the extent that you owe provincial tax in the year. Either way, take a look at the credits to see if they can help you out!

- **Sales tax credit:** If you were a resident of B.C. and were 19 or older on December 31, 2000, or you were under 19 but were married or are a parent, you may be eligible for the sales tax credit. This credit is available whether or not you owe B.C. taxes this year — in fact, even if you didn't work this year, you'll probably qualify! The available credit is $50 for you, plus an additional $50 for your spouse (although only one of you can make this claim). Unfortunately, your claim is reduced by 2 percent of your net family income over $18,000.
- **Political contribution tax credit:** If you've made contributions to political parties or constituency associations registered in B.C. or to candidates seeking election to the B.C. legislature, you may receive a credit for part of these contributions. The credit is calculated as follows:
  - 75 percent of contributions up to $100
  - 50 percent of the next $450 of contributions
  - 33⅓ percent of contributions over $500
  - The maximum credit you may claim is $500, which is reached when you've made $1,150 in contributions.

- **Other tax credits:** Credits are also available if you've invested in a registered British Columbia employee shares ownership plan (ESOP), or employee venture capital corporation at any time during 2000, or in the first 60 days of 2001. You will receive form ESOP 20 "Employee Share Ownership Plan" or form EVCC 30 "Employee Venture Capital Corporation" as evidence of your qualified investment. These forms will detail the amount of credit to which you're entitled. The maximum credit you may claim this year is $2,000, unless your B.C. tax is less than this amount, in which case your credit will be capped.
- **Venture capital tax credit:** Did you receive form VCC 10 "Venture Capital Corporation" this year? If so, you've acquired shares from a registered British Columbia venture capital corporation. And from a tax standpoint, at least, this is a good investment. You see, you are entitled to a credit of up to $60,000 this year. Your form will tell you exactly how much of a credit you're entitled to.
- **Mining exploration tax credit:** This is a credit available to individuals who incurred qualified mining exploration expenses in British Columbia during the year. Qualifying expenses include expenditures to determine the existence, location, extent, or quality of a mineral resource in the province. You must fill out form T88 BC "Mining Exploration Tax Credit" in order to claim this credit.

Alberta

If you don't like paying high income taxes, Alberta is the place to be. Although Alberta is not changing its tax on tax system in 2000 (the basic Alberta tax will remain at 44 percent of the basic federal tax), the 8 percent surtax that was in place in prior years has been eliminated. In addition, the year 2001 promises greater changes for Alberta. Alberta will implement a flat tax: here will be a single rate of provincial tax (11 percent) of taxable income, regardless of the amount of income you earn. And to top it off, there will be no additional flat taxes or surtaxes! But let's stick to the year at hand.

So for the year 2000, at least, there are few changes to the Alberta tax system. Your basic Alberta tax is simply 44 percent of your basic federal tax. You also have to calculate an additional flat tax, which is .5 percent of your taxable income from line 260 of your tax return. The basic tax plus the flat tax becomes your adjusted Alberta income tax. You can reduce this adjusted tax through the following items:

- **Alberta royalty tax rebate:** This rebate is available if you paid royalties or similar payment to the federal or a provincial government for production from a Canadian resource property. This will occur if you have attributed Canadian royalty income for the year. You must fill out form T79 "Alberta Royalty Tax Rebate" to receive this rebate.

  There is also a royalty tax credit available from the Alberta government if you've paid Alberta Crown Royalties in the year. This credit is not part of your regular tax return. In fact, to receive this credit you must fill out a special form AT60 "Alberta Royal Credit Application" and send it to the Alberta Tax and Revenue Administration Office in Edmonton. If you've paid these royalties in the year, you will receive a refund cheque for a percentage of the total amounts paid — the percentage changes each quarter of the year depending on the price of oil.
- **Alberta selective tax reduction:** If your adjusted Alberta income tax, less royalty tax rebate, is less than $860, you may be eligible for an additional tax reduction. The reduction is $430 less one-half of your adjusted income tax, less the royalty tax rebate amount.

Alberta also has a political contribution tax credit. Although this credit does not directly reduce your Alberta taxes owing, the credit claimed cannot exceed your Alberta income taxes payable. Your credit is calculated as follows:

- 75 percent of the first $150 of contributions to a registered Alberta political party or a registered Alberta constituency association or to a registered candidate seeking election to the Alberta Legislature
- 50 percent of the next $675 of contributions
- 33⅓ percent of contributions over $825
- The maximum credit that can be claimed in the year is $750 (unless your Alberta tax is less than this, in which case the credit is capped).

Saskatchewan

Like Alberta, Prince Edward Island, and Newfoundland, Saskatchewan opted to delay the transition into a tax on income system until 2001. There are lots of goodies in store under the new tax system, which Saskatchewan is saying will save the average family about $1,000 per year. But alas, all of you in that neck of the woods will have to wait.

According to the 2000 federal budget, it looks like Saskatchewan was too busy thinking about 2001 to make many changes to your tax system in 2000. (Which is only good for those of you who hate change!)

As in 1999, your provincial tax is calculated as 48 percent of federal tax. Of course, you'll have to add that flat tax of 1.5 percent of your net income for the year. The flat tax was actually reduced in the budget to 1 percent, but it only became effective July 1, making the effective rate for the entire year 1.5 percent. On top of that, you'll pay a 10-percent "deficit surtax." If you think you're done, guess again. If your provincial tax is greater than $4,000, the taxman will ask you to hand over another 15 percent of the tax in excess of $4,000.

Now for the good news. If your net income is less than $40,000, you may be eligible to claim some deductions against this tax. Make sure you complete the bottom of form T1C (Sask) to claim your deductions. Here are the details.

- **Saskatchewan tax reduction:** Saskatchewan introduced the tax reduction to help low- and middle-income taxpayers by reducing their net provincial tax payable. You can only claim this reduction if you were resident of Saskatchewan at the end of the year. You may claim all applicable credits, as follows:
  - A sales tax reduction of $200.
  - A reduction of $300 if you made a claim for a spouse amount (line 303) or equivalent to spouse amount (line 305).
  - A reduction of $250 for each dependent child (to a maximum of $1,000) who was living with you during the year and was 17 or younger at the end of the year.
  - The total of all applicable reductions is reduced by 5 percent of adjusted net income over $10,000.
- **Labour-sponsored venture capital tax credit:** Did you receive form T2C (Sask) this year? If so, you must have invested in a labour-sponsored venture capital corporation. If the corporation is registered in Saskatchewan, you'll receive a credit to a maximum of $1,000. If the corporation is only registered federally, you can only claim a credit to a maximum of $525 — but at least it's something. Either way, report the details from your T2C slip in boxes 31 and 32 of your T1C (Sask).

Saskatchewan tax credits

Something new for 2000 — Saskatchewan has introduced the Saskatchewan Sales Tax credit. This new credit was introduced in April 2000, and will help offset the effect of sales taxes on lower-income earners.

You don't need to have paid Saskatchewan tax in order to be eligible for the credit. All you need to do is file an income tax return and meet the income and family criteria to be eligible for a quarterly cheque. Now there's *really* no excuse for not filing a tax return!

There are two components to this credit: the adult component and the child component. The program will provide a refundable tax credit of $77 per adult and $55 per child, to a maximum of $264 per year. The adult component will max out at $77, once your income reaches $7,700. It will then fall at a rate of 1 percent as family net income reaches above $27,300. If you have a dependent spouse or equivalent to spouse, you'll be eligible for an additional $77. The child component will provide an additional $55 per child, but will be reduced at a rate of 1 percent of the family income in excess of $14,100 ($8,600 if there is more than one qualifying child).

Manitoba

The year 2000 is one of great tax changes in Manitoba. Like many other provinces, the Manitoba government has decided to change from a tax on tax system to a tax on income system. This change is being partially implemented for the year 2000, and will be fully implemented in the 2001 tax year.

Manitoba has a three-tax system. It levies a basic income tax, a net income tax, and a net income surtax. However, now that it is changing to a tax on income system, the three-tax system will be replaced with one tax. This is meant to offer a less complex tax system for Manitoba, although we can't say that the 2000 tax rules will accomplish this.

For 2000, the basic income tax will be calculated directly on taxable income (rather than on basic federal taxes). However, the net income tax and the net income surtax will still exist. The flat tax is calculated as 2 percent of your net income in the year. The surtax is calculated at 2 percent of your net income over $30,000, less credits for yourself and your dependants.

You may be eligible for an additional refund of the net income flat tax and surtax. If you claimed more than $2,500 of medical expenses on line 332 of your tax return, declared capital gains as a result of a forced disposition of farm properties, or were a member of a religious order and took a vow of perpetual property, you may be able to claim this refund. To see if you qualify, you must apply to the Manitoba Tax Assistance Office, Room 309, Norquay Building, 401 York Avenue, Winnipeg, MB, R3C 0P8. Do not send your application to the CCRA. Once you receive your 2000 Notice of Assessment, send to the above address your 2000 personal tax return and the Notice, along with a note stating that you are requesting a refund of your flat tax and surtax.

Although Manitoba will levy taxes based on taxable income in 2000, you still only have to file one tax return this year. You simply have to fill out the Manitoba tax schedules to figure out what your provincial tax liability is, and send your whole return to the CCRA. No other special tax filings are required.

Since basic income taxes are now being calculated on taxable income, as opposed to federal taxes, it stands to reason that you also have to calculate nonrefundable tax credits independent of the federal tax system. See Table 20-3 for the most common nonrefundable tax credits that will apply in Manitoba:

Table 20-3 Manitoba Nonrefundable Tax Credits

Credit	Amount
Basic personal credit	$587
Spousal credit	$491
Equivalent-to-spouse credit	$491
Age credit	$282
Disability tax credit	$343
Caregiver tax credit	$191

These credits represent the same nonrefundable tax credits that apply federally, except that you must multiply the total credits by the lowest Manitoba tax rate of 8 percent, rather than the federal rate of 17 percent. The only exception is charitable donations. To parallel the credits available federally, the first $200 of donations will receive an 8-percent nonrefundable tax credit in Manitoba, while any further donations will receive a 13.63-percent credit.

Once you take your taxable income, multiply it by the appropriate tax rates, calculate any flat tax or surtax payable, and deduct your nonrefundable tax credits, you will have your adjusted Manitoba tax. You may then reduce your taxes further by claiming the following:

- **Manitoba tax reduction:** This reduction is based on your eligibility for certain personal amount credits for yourself and dependants.
- **Manitoba labour-sponsored funds and equity tax credits:** These are credits available to individuals who purchase qualifying shares of a labour-sponsored fund or eligible Manitoba-based company in the year. If you are eligible for the labour-sponsored fund tax credit, you will receive form T2C (MAN) outlining your credit. The maximum credit is $750 in 2000. If you are eligible for the equity tax credit, you'll receive form T2ETC (MAN). The maximum equity tax credit this year is $1,500. In addition, these credits can only be claimed to the extent that you have Manitoba taxes owing in the year — once your taxes are nil, you'll lose the advantage of these credits.

Manitoba tax credits

Manitoba offers a number of tax credits that are not (except for the political contribution tax credit) limited by the amount of Manitoba tax you'll have to pay this year. Some of these credits are limited by the total of your net income and that of your spouse.

If you lived in Manitoba on December 31, 2000, take a look at form T1C (MAN). You may just be entitled to some free money! This form outlines various tax incentives offered by the Manitoba government, and you don't even have to be taxable in the year to claim them. Even if you haven't earned any income in the year, file a tax return so that you can receive the free money these credits can offer you.

Here is a summary of Manitoba tax credits that you may be eligible to receive:

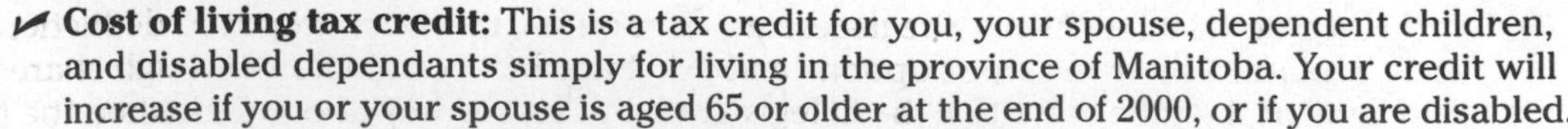

- **Cost of living tax credit:** This is a tax credit for you, your spouse, dependent children, and disabled dependants simply for living in the province of Manitoba. Your credit will increase if you or your spouse is aged 65 or older at the end of 2000, or if you are disabled.

  The cost of living tax credit is not available to everyone. Your total credits will be reduced by 1 percent of the total of your and your spouse's net income.

- **Property tax credit:** If you paid property taxes or rent in Manitoba, you may be entitled to a credit for some of the taxes or rent paid, depending on your income level. The minimum credit is $325 in 2000, and the maximum credit is $600. If you are a senior, the maximum credit is increased to $700. Like the cost of living tax credit, your claim will be reduced by 1 percent of the total of your and your spouse's net income in the year.

  You must fill out the bottom of form T1C (MAN) in order to claim a property tax credit. This means providing details of your addresses, your roommates, and the names of municipalities or landlords you made payments to in the year.
- **Homeowner's school tax assistance:** This is another type of property tax credit available to taxpayers who are age 55 or older at the end of the year and who have a net family income of less than $23,800 in 2000.
- **Learning tax credit:** In order to provide additional incentives for residents of Manitoba to further their education, the government offers a tax credit for tuition and education amounts incurred in the year (capped at $10,000). You can even claim this credit if you are claiming tuition and education amounts transferred from a child, grandchild, or spouse! The total credit is 7 percent of the lesser of $10,000 and the amount reported on line 5 of schedule 11 of your tax return.
- **Political contribution tax credit:** Like many of the other provinces, Manitoba offers a tax credit to those contributing to recognized Manitoba political parties and candidates seeking election to the provincial legislature. The credit is calculated as follows:
  - 75 percent of the first $100 of contributions
  - 50 percent of the next $450 of contributions
  - 33⅓ percent of contributions over $550
  - The maximum credit allowed in the year is $500, or your Manitoba tax otherwise owing, whichever is less.

Ontario

If you live in Ontario, you'll find that preparing your tax return has changed this year. This is because Ontario has changed from a tax on tax system to a tax on income system. In other words, instead of simply taking your federal taxes payable amount and multiplying it by the Ontario tax rate (the way you did in the past), you'll have to do a separate calculation based on your taxable income for the year.

One thing you'll probably be happy about is that Ontario will not require you to file a separate tax return. Your Ontario taxes will still be calculated on your regular tax return and filed with the CCRA. Of course, there are more lines and schedules to fill out now, but you have to admit that this is easier than filling out a whole new return.

Calculating Ontario taxes

For 2000, the taxable income figure you'll use for Ontario tax purposes will be the same one you use for federal purposes. In the future, this may change. You see, Ontario plans to reduce the capital gains inclusion rate to 50 percent over the next five years, so two separate taxable income calculations may be necessary. In addition, there are proposed deductions for Ontario research employee stock options and purchasers of certain flow-through shares that have not, at the time of writing, been legislated. But let's worry about that when the time comes.

Once you've calculated your Ontario taxes owing, you can reduce this number by applying nonrefundable tax credits and certain Ontario tax credits. Nonrefundable tax credits will be calculated by taking the total credits that apply federally (except donations), and multiplying them by the lowest Ontario tax rate (6.37 percent). This is essentially the same system that applied before — it only looks different.

For example, if you only qualify for the basic personal amount in 2000, you will receive a federal nonrefundable tax credit of $1,229 ($7,231 × 17%). This amount is used to offset your federal taxes otherwise owing (see chapters 18 and 19). In addition, you will receive a provincial credit of $461 ($7,231 × 6.37%). This credit will offset your Ontario taxes otherwise owing.

The nonrefundable tax credit for charitable donations will also mirror the federal credit. The first $200 of donations will receive a credit calculated at the lowest Ontario tax rate of 6.37 percent, and any donations above this level will receive a credit at Ontario's highest tax rate of 11.16 percent.

In addition to nonrefundable tax credits, there are some Ontario tax credits available that will reduce your Ontario tax payable. These are the Ontario investment and employee ownership tax credits. If you invest in certain labour-sponsored funds in the year, the Ontario government will give you a 15-percent tax credit, to a maximum of $750, to offset your Ontario taxes. This is in addition to any federal credit that may be available. The employee ownership tax credit is available when employees invest in, or buy out their employer corporations. The corporation in essence becomes a labour-sponsored venture capital corporation, and your investment will entitle you to a tax credit of 20 percent of the first $3,500 of investment and 30 percent on the balance of the investment, up to $15,000. The maximum credit that can be claimed in one taxation year is $4,150.

If you make an investment in an employee ownership labour-sponsored venture capital corporation, but cannot deduct all your tax credits this year, you can carryforward your unused credits for five years. On the other hand, unused labour-sponsored fund credits (in Ontario called labour-sponsored investment fund credits, or LSIFs) cannot be carried forward if they're not used this year.

Ontario surtax

In addition to basic Ontario tax, there is also surtax to calculate. This surtax has a fancy name, the "fair share health care levy." Sounds like a Dr. Seuss book, don't you think? You see, although Ontario has been decreasing its personal tax rates in recent years, the decrease in basic rates is being replaced with an increase in surtaxes for certain taxpayers. So for some taxpayers, the tax cuts are really a facade.

The surtaxes for the 2000 taxation year are calculated as follows:

> 20 percent × Ontario income tax in excess of $3,561, plus
>
> 36 percent of Ontario income tax in excess of $4,468.

For example, if you have taxable income of $60,000 in 2000, your basic Ontario tax before applying nonrefundable tax credits would be $4,797 ($30,004 × 6.37% plus $60,009 less $30,004 × 9.62%). Assuming you will claim the basic personal credit of $461 ($7,231 × 6.37%), your basic Ontario tax will be $4,336. This means that you will have surtax to pay. Your surtax will be as follows:

> $4,336 less $3,561 × 20% = $155, plus
> $4,336 less $4,468 × 36% = $0
>
> For a grand total of $155.

Ontario tax reductions

You may be eligible for an Ontario tax reduction if the government considers you to have a low or moderate income! For the 2000 tax year, you can receive a tax reduction of up to $156 for yourself plus $317 for each dependent child age 18 or under and each dependant with a disability.

You can only claim this reduction if two-times the reduction is greater than your basic Ontario tax plus surtax owing.

For example, say you have two children under the age of 18. You will have a potential reduction of $790 ($156 plus $317 × 2). Two-times $790 is $1,580, so if your Ontario tax figure is greater than $1,580, you cannot claim the reduction. In this example, it will occur at approximately $25,000 of income. Keep in mind, however, that the actual amount will depend on your level of nonrefundable tax credits in the year and your actual tax reduction amounts.

Ontario tax credits

In addition to tax credits that directly reduce your provincial taxes payable, Ontario has a number of special purpose tax credits for which you can receive a direct refund.

If you are a resident of Ontario, take a look at form T1C. This form outlines the various Ontario tax credits available to you. Even if you don't have any taxes owing in the year, if you qualify for any of these credits you will receive a cheque from the government. This is not a refund of taxes you've already paid — it's free money! Here is a summary of Ontario tax credits:

- **Property tax credit:** This is a credit to help reimburse Ontario taxpayers for their occupancy costs in the year. You simply have to enter either your rent paid, your property tax paid, or a whopping $25 for college residence fees, on form TIC; then go through the calculation to see if you qualify. Remember, in order to qualify, the rent, property tax, or college residence fees must be paid toward an Ontario residence — if you've paid amounts in another province, you're out of luck. Also, you'll notice that if you're over the age of 65, you'll be entitled to a higher property tax credit than the younger folk.
- **Sales tax credit:** The sales tax credit is a credit available to help reimburse you for sales taxes you pay throughout the year. You can receive $100 each for you and your cohabiting spouse, plus $50 for each dependent child under the age of 18 who lived with you in Canada during the year and for whom you (or your spouse) received Canada Child Tax Benefits during the year.

If you are age 16 or older in 2000, you should complete form T1C (Ont). Even if you didn't work in the year, you may qualify for a sales tax credit of $100 if one of your parents didn't claim a credit for you already.

Even though you've incurred occupancy and sales tax costs in the year, you will not necessarily receive Ontario tax credits for these amounts. Part, or all, of your credits will be reduced by your and your spouse's net income in the year. If you' re under age 65, your credit is reduced by 2 percent of each dollar of net income over $4,000. For example, if your net income is $12,000 in 2000, your credit will be reduced by $160. If you're age 65 or older, your credits are reduced by 4 percent of each dollar of net income over $22,000. So, if you and your spouse have a combined net income of $40,000, your credits will be reduced by $720.

Since the credits available to those age 65 or older are greater than those available to other taxpayers, claim the credits on the return of the older spouse if one partner is over age 65 and one is under age 65.

You must detail the rent and property tax paid for each address where you lived during 2000 on form T1C (Ont). This includes listing each address you lived at, the number of months you lived in each place, the rent or property tax paid for each location, and the name of the landlord or municipality to which you made your payments. However, if you have more than one residence at one time (for example, if you have a house and a cottage), you can only include the property tax or rent paid on one residence (your principal residence).

- **Ontario political contribution tax credit:** This is a credit available to any taxpayer who made a contribution to a registered Ontario political party or to a registered candidate who is running for election on the Ontario Legislative Assembly in 2000. The credit is calculated as follows:
  - 75 percent of the first $300 of contributions
  - 50 percent of the next $700 of contributions
  - 33⅓ percent of contributions over $700
  - The total credit is maxed out at $1,000, so if you make more than $2,275 of contributions you will not receive any additional tax relief.
- **Ontario Home Ownership Savings Plan tax credit:** This is a credit available to encourage Ontarians to save for a home. You will receive a credit of up to 25 percent of your contribution to the plan, although the maximum annual contribution you can receive a credit for is $2,000 for each of you and your spouse. The 25-percent credit is reduced as your net income increases — form T1C contains a factor table to help you calculate your credit. If your income exceeds $40,000, or you and your spouse's net income exceeds $80,000, you won't qualify.

If you contribute to an OHOSP, you must purchase a home by certain deadlines. If you do not use the funds for the intended purpose, you will have to repay your Ontario Home Ownership Savings Plan tax credits.

OHOSPs are offered through many bank and trust companies. There are some qualifying rules, but if you are at least 18, and you and your spouse are first-time homebuyers, you should qualify.

- **Ontario Tax Credits for Self-Employed Individuals:** There are a number of special credits available if you are self-employed and made qualifying expenditures in the year. These credits include the following:
  - **Co-operative education tax credit:** A credit of 10 to 15 percent of remuneration paid to a co-op student or apprentice in the year. The students must be enrolled in a qualifying institution, and there are minimum and maximum employment period criteria to be met.
  - **Graduate transitions tax credit:** A credit for hiring new post-secondary graduates for a minimum of six months. A credit of 10 to 15 percent of remuneration paid to the graduate, to a maximum of $4,000 for each graduate hired, can be claimed if the criteria are met.
  - **Workplace child care tax credit:** This is a credit for 5 percent of qualifying expenditures you incurred to create additional licensed child care facilities or to improve existing facilitates.
  - **Workplace accessibility tax credit:** A credit of 15 percent of eligible expenditures you incurred to accommodate an employee with a disability.

If you think you may qualify for any of these self-employed Ontario tax credits, contact the Ontario Ministry of Finance. There are information bulletins available on each of these credits that will help you see if you do, in fact, qualify, and help you calculate your credits.

Quebec

As a resident of Quebec, you have your work cut out for you. Not only does Quebec have its own system of taxation, you also have to file a whole separate tax return each year to calculate your provincial taxes. Yes, this is in addition to your federal tax return.

If you are a resident of Quebec, you must file two tax returns this year. Your federal return will be sent to the Canada Customs and Revenue Agency (CCRA), while your Quebec return must be sent to the Ministère du Revenu. Your Quebec return is due on the same day as your federal return.

There are two tax systems in place in Quebec. If you have few deductions and credits, you may use the simplified tax system. Otherwise, you must use the general tax system. If you were not a resident in Quebec on December 31, 2000, were not a resident of Canada throughout the year, went bankrupt in 2000, or are preparing a date of death return, you must use the general tax forms. The basic difference between the two systems is that under the simplified system, many of the deductions and tax credits (QPP contributions, EI premiums, union or professional dues, and medical expenses) are replaced by a flat amount of $2,430. The simplified system also allows you to file a return jointly with your spouse. Depending on your personal circumstances, this may or may not be beneficial to you — obviously, if your deductions and credits would exceed $2,430 and you need these credits to reduce your taxes to nil, you'll want to use the general system.

Preparing your Quebec tax return is, for the most part, the same as preparing your federal tax return. The types of income you must report and many of the deductions are identical, although they may be reported on different slips. For example, for Quebec taxation purposes, a T4 slip is called the RL-1. In addition, many of the forms that apply to your federal return also apply to your provincial return — the only difference is the names. For example, if you've moved in the year, you should fill out form T1M "Moving Expenses" with your federal return, and form TP-347-V "Moving Expenses" with your Quebec return. Therefore, you can safely use the rules in the rest of this book to calculate your Quebec income.

If you are a resident in Quebec, you must report your income from all sources on your Quebec tax return. Even if you worked outside Quebec during the year, you must still report this income on your return.

Differences between your federal tax return and your Quebec tax return

Of course, there are some differences between the Quebec tax return and federal return other than the schedule and form names. Let's look at some of the major differences.

We haven't made note of all the differences here. Since residents of Quebec must file a separate return, it is safe to say that there are enough differences to warrant another book. We'll see about that. In the meantime, for more details, refer to the package sent to you by the Ministry of Quebec.

Schedule A: Dependent children

You may be eligible to claim a non-refundable tax credit for dependent children who lived with you during the year. The dependant must be 18 years or younger, or attended school or university full time in 2000. The credit is composed of three parts. First, an amount equal to $2,600 for the first child and $2,400 for each additional dependant. Second, if the dependant attended full-time post-secondary studies during the year, you can claim an additional credit of $1,650 for each completed term to a maximum of $3,300 per child. Third, an amount for a single-parent family equaling $1,300. This amount may be claimed for only one child. The total of these three components is reduced by each child's income, reported on line 220 of his or her income tax return. Any remaining amount should be reported on line 367 of your return.

A dependent child may be your or your spouse's child, grandchild, brother, sister, nephew, or niece, or your brother-in-law or sister-in-law.

Schedule B: Tax relief measures

There are a number of schedule B tax relief measures that deal with such important tax situations as relief for the aged, for medical needs, and family issues.

Amount with respect to age, for persons living alone or for retirement income

As with the federal rules, if you were age 65 or older at the end of the year, you may be eligible for a nonrefundable credit equal to $2,200. You may also claim the credit for your spouse if he or she was 65 or older at the end of the year. This credit is reduced by 15 percent of family income in excess of $26,000. The credit is eroded to nil once family income reaches $40,666.

Something different from the federal return is a nonrefundable credit for living alone or with a dependant. The dependant must be under 19 years or attending post-secondary school full time during the year. The credit is $1,050 and is reduced by 15 percent of family income in excess of $26,000. The credit disappears once family income reaches $33,000.

There is also a credit on schedule B for a portion of your retirement income. It is similar to the $1,000 pension credit on the federal return, except that it is ground down by 15 percent of net family income in excess of $26,000.

You should report the sum of these three credits (if applicable) on line 361 of your Quebec return.

There is no Quebec equivalent to the federal credit for "equivalent to spouse." This credit is effectively replaced with three credits: the person living alone amount, the first child amount, and the single parent amount.

Medical expenses and refundable medical tax credit

In this area you'll calculate both a refundable tax credit and a nonrefundable tax credit relating to medical expenses. Let's start with the nonrefundable amount for medical expenses.

The nonrefundable medical credit is similar to the federal medical expense tax credit in that it is calculated as the excess of total medical expenses paid for a 12-month period ending in 2000, over 3 percent of your family income. Report any excess on line 381 of your Quebec return.

Did you catch the differences between this and the federal calculation? Two things. One, the credit is calculated with reference to family income, not just the income of the person claiming the credit. So much for reporting medical expenses on the return with the lowest income! Second, notice there is no threshold the way there is for the federal calculation. If your 3 percent of family income is higher than your expenses, you cannot make a claim.

Quebec also has a refundable tax credit for medical expenses. This is similar to the federal version called the refundable medical expense supplement. In Quebec, it is calculated by taking 25 percent of the medical expense amount discussed above (to a maximum of $500), and reducing this by 5 percent of family income in excess of $17,500. Report any remaining amount on line 462 of your Quebec return.

Tax reduction in respect of families

If you have dependent children during 2000, you may be entitled to a tax reduction. If you are married your basic reduction is $1,500, while if you are a single parent your basic reduction is $1,195. You must then reduce your claim by 5 percent of your net family income in excess of $26,000 to come up with your reduction.

Schedule C: tax credit for child care expenses

At the federal level, child care expenses are a deduction from total income (see Chapter 16). This is not the case in Quebec. Instead, child care expenses are a refundable tax credit. The types of expenses that qualify as child care expense in Quebec are quite similar to those claimed federally; however, the actual calculation of the credit is quite different. The refundable tax credit rate will vary depending on your family's net income. For example, if your family's net income is less than $27,000, the applicable rate is 75 percent. This rate decreases by 1 percent for every $1,000 of income. Once family income exceeds $75,000, the applicable rate remains at 26 percent.

Schedule D: deduction for strategic investments

You may be eligible for a deduction from income if you made investments in any of the following:

- Quebec stock savings plan (QSSPs)
- R&D venture capital corporations
- Quebec business investment companies (QBICs)
- Co-operative investment plans (CIPs)
- Certified Quebec films
- Exploration respecting Quebec resources
- Scientific research and experimental development.

Schedule F: contribution to the Health Services Fund

Residents of Quebec whose total income on line 199 exceeds net employment income reported on line 104 by $11,000 or more are required to complete schedule F of the Quebec tax return. Based on the results of this form, you may be required to make a contribution toward Quebec's provincial health insurance; however, you can also claim 22 percent of the contribution as a nonrefundable tax credit.

Schedule K: premium payable under the Quebec Prescription Drug Insurance Plan

If you were not a member of a group insurance plan in 2000, you were required to take part in the Quebec prescription drug insurance plan. As a part of being a member of this plan, you are required to pay a premium. There are certain exceptions to the requirement to pay a premium, and the list is shown in schedule K "Quebec Prescription Drug Insurance Plan."

The premium for each spouse is essentially the lesser of the following:

- 4 percent of net family income reduced by certain basic allowances
- $350 prorated for the number of months each spouse was not covered by a group insurance plan.

Anti-Poverty Fund

The Quebec government makes you contribute to the Anti-Poverty Fund if you are reporting an amount on line 441 of your tax return. This basically means that you owe provincial tax after taking into account nonrefundable tax credits and certain other credits. The actual contribution you must make is .3 percent of the amount you reported on line 441.

Refundable tax credits

Refundable tax credits provide a much-needed respite for taxes for some special circumstances. We discuss some refundable tax credits and how they work in detail below.

Adults housing their parents

Quebec provides for a refundable credit of $550 to you for each live-in parent age 70 or older at the end of the taxation year. The parent does not need to be dependent on you, but must live with you for 365 consecutive days, of which 183 were in this taxation year.

A "parent" means a parent, grandparent, great-grandparent, uncle, aunt, great-uncle, or great-aunt of either yourself or your spouse.

By "live-in," the taxman means that the parent must share with you your house, apartment, or other place of residence where you primarily eat or sleep. There has been some debate as to whether or not an in-law suite would qualify. It probably depends on the actual layout of the suite and how integrated it is with the rest of the home.

Treatment of infertility

Instead of providing a medical credit for the treatment of infertility, beginning in 2000 the Quebec government will offer a refundable tax credit equal to 25 percent of all eligible expenses. The maximum credit that may be claimed in a year is $3,750.

Adoption expenses

There is also a refundable tax credit available to help adoptive parents with the high cost of adoption. In 2000, a credit is available of 25 percent of expenses incurred for final adoption judgments handed down after December 31, 1999. The maximum credit that can be claimed in 2000 is $3,750.

Support for top-level athletes

In order to support Quebec's top-level athletes, the 2000 Quebec budget introduced a refundable credit. The amount of the credit varies depending on the level of performance in the year, the type of sport involved, and the number of days to which the recognition applies.

Non-refundable tax credits

As a recap, here is a list of some of the more common nonrefundable tax credits. Keep in mind that this list is not exhaustive. The majority of these credits were described above because the credit was calculated on one of the schedules. For credits we did not talk about, the rules are similar to the federal rules. You should refer to your 2000 income tax package from your provincial ministry to determine the value of the credit and how it is calculated.

- Amount with respect to age
- Amount for a person living alone
- Amount for retirement income
- Amount respecting a spouse
- Contribution to the health services fund
- Union or professional dues
- Amount respecting a severe and prolonged mental or physical impairment
- Amount for medical expenses
- Amount for tuition or examination fees
- Amount for interest paid on a student loan

If you worked in another province during the year and had withholding taxes taken off your pay, you can request that up to 40 percent of these taxes be transferred to Quebec to help offset your Quebec taxes otherwise payable. You must request this transfer on your federal income tax return.

If you are receiving a tax refund in 2000, but your spouse owes money, you can request that your refund be used to pay your spouse's tax bill! Simply enter the amount you'd like to transfer on line 476 of your Quebec return.

Newfoundland

Newfoundland has decided, as have some of the other provinces, to wait until 2001 to implement the new tax on income system. So for this year, at least, your taxes will be calculated pretty much the same way they were for 1999. One change is that the provincial tax rate as a percentage of federal tax was reduced from 69 percent to 62 percent. That's the good news. The bad news is that the government introduced a second surtax equal to 6 percent of provincial tax in excess of $250. This is on top of the original surtax of 10 percent of the basic personal tax in excess of $7,050.

Once you've calculated your Newfoundland taxes owing, there are a number of credits available that may help you reduce these taxes. These include the following:

- **Venture capital tax credit:** New for 2000, investors will receive a tax credit to invest in local businesses.
- **Newfoundland research and development tax credit:** This credit is available to individual business owners who made eligible expenditures for scientific research and experimental development in Newfoundland in 2000. A special form T1129 "Newfoundland Research and Development Tax Credit" must be completed to claim this credit. Although the figures on this form do not directly affect your personal tax return, the T1129 should be sent in with your return. Your claim will be assessed, and if you qualify you will receive a separate cheque for the allowable credit.
- **Newfoundland political contribution tax credit:** If you've made contributions to a registered Newfoundland political party, a district association, or a registered Newfoundland independent political candidate during an election period in 2000, you will receive a special tax credit. The credit is calculated as follows:
  - 75 percent of the first $100 of contributions
  - 50 percent of the next $450 of contributions
  - 33⅓ percent of the next $600 of contributions
  - The maximum credit in the year is $500, which is reached once you've made contributions of $1,150.

New Brunswick

New Brunswick is another province that has moved to a tax on income system effective in 2000. Therefore, if you lived in the province of New Brunswick at the end of 2000, you will have to calculate your provincial tax owing based on your taxable income in 2000. For 2000, the provincial system must mirror the federal system; therefore, you can offset your New Brunswick taxes owing by the same tax credits that are used to offset your federal taxes, except that you will use provincial tax rates for this calculation.

Once you calculate your New Brunswick taxes owing, there are a number of tax credits that can help lower your tax bill. These include the following:

- **Political contribution tax credit:** If you made contributions in 2000 to registered political parties, district associations or independent candidates in New Brunswick, you can offset your New Brunswick taxes owing by the following amounts:
  - 75 percent of the first $100 of contributions
  - 50 percent of the next $450 of contributions
  - 33⅓ percent of the next $600 of contributions
  - The maximum credit in the year is $500, which is reached once you've made contributions of $1,150.
- **Stock savings plan tax credit:** If you've invested in a new issue of certain shares of a public company operating in New Brunswick, you've made a wise investment (from a tax standpoint, at least!). You may now claim a tax credit of up to 30 percent of this investment. You should have received certificate NB-SSP-1, showing your eligible investment. You can use this credit to offset your New Brunswick taxes otherwise owing; however, if the credit exceeds your New Brunswick taxes, you can carryforward the unused credits for up to seven years.
- **Labour-sponsored venture capital fund tax credit:** Similar to the federal labour-sponsored fund tax credit, this credit is offered to you by the province of New Brunswick if you've invested in a qualified New Brunswick labour-sponsored fund. How do you know you've invested in a qualifying fund? You'll receive certificate NB-LSVC-1, issued by the corporation. The maximum credit you can claim this year is $750 (but don't forget to claim your federal credit too!). You can only claim this credit to the extent that you have New Brunswick taxes owing in the year. If you've reduced your taxes to nil, you'll lose the value of the credit.

Nova Scotia

Canada's Ocean Playground is yet another province moving to the tax on taxable income system in 2000. The province set its tax on income rates equivalent to the effective tax on tax rates that were in place in 1999; therefore, you can be assured that your tax bill won't increase due to the new system. In addition, Nova Scotia adopted the federal non-refundable credit amounts in 2000. This means that you will qualify for the same nonrefundable tax credits provincially that you do federally. You simply have to multiply the credits by the lowest Nova Scotia marginal tax rate to come up with the amount that can be used to reduce your Nova Scotia taxes in the year.

Nova Scotia also offers a number of provincial tax credits that you can use to offset your provincial taxes owing. Here are the details:

- **Political contribution tax credit:** This credit is available if you contribute funds to a recognized Nova Scotia political party or to a candidate seeking election to the Nova Scotia House of Assembly during 2000. The credit is calculated as follows:
  - 75 percent of the first $100 of contributions
  - 50 percent of the next $450 of contributions
  - 33⅓ percent of the next $600 of contributions
  - The maximum credit in the year is $500, which is reached once you've made contributions of $1,150. If your credit is greater than your actual provincial tax in the year, you will not get a full credit.

- **Labour-sponsored venture capital tax credit:** To mirror the federal tax credit for investing in certain labour-sponsored funds, Nova Scotia offers a provincial credit for investments in Nova Scotia labour-sponsored funds. The actual credit is equal to 15 percent of eligible investments made in 2000, or the first 60 days of 2001. The maximum credit available provincially is $525.
- **Equity tax credit:** In order to stimulate investments in certain Nova Scotia businesses, an equity tax credit is available if you invest in eligible shares. You will receive form NSETC-1 from the Nova Scotia Department of Finance if you've made an eligible investment. The maximum credit you may claim this year is $9,000; however, if your credit this year is greater than your Nova Scotia taxes payable, you can carryback your unused credit for three taxation years, or carryforward for seven years.

If you look at your 1999 Nova Scotia tax forms, you'll see that there used to be a stock savings plan tax credit and a homeownership savings plan tax credit. The year 1999 was the last in which you could claim unused credits under the stock savings plan tax credit; therefore, if you still have unused credits you're out of luck. The homeownership plan expired on January 1, 2000, so no new savings plans under this program could have been established this year.

Prince Edward Island

Prince Edward Island (PEI) is one of the few provinces in Canada to opt out of the tax on income system in 2000. However, the home of Anne of Green Gables will move to this system in 2001. So for this year, at least, there are few changes to your tax return if you live in PEI.

One change you'll be happy about (unless you really like to pay tax) is that effective January 1, 2000, the personal income tax rate was reduced to 57.5 percent of basic federal taxes. This is a 1-percent decrease over 1999.

In addition, there is a Low Income Tax Reduction Program effective January 1, 2000. Under this program, there is an additional $250 nonrefundable tax credit available against your PEI tax payable. In fact, you can receive $250 for yourself, another $250 for your spouse or equivalent to spouse, and $250 for each of your children. Of course, this credit is not available to everyone. If your family's taxable income is less than $15,000 this year, you'll receive a full credit; however, as your income creeps over the $15,000 level, the credit will be reduced. This credit only reduces your PEI taxes payable; if the credit is more than the tax you otherwise owe, you will not receive a refund for the difference.

Prince Edward Island also offers a political contribution tax credit. If you made contributions in 2000 to a recognized PEI political party or to a candidate seeking election as a member of the PEI Legislative Assembly, you will receive a credit as follows:

- 75 percent of the first $100 of contributions
- 50 percent of the next $450 of contributions
- 33⅓ percent of the next $600 of contributions
- The maximum credit in the year is $500, which is reached once you've made contributions of $1,150. Of course, if this is greater than your actual PEI taxes in the year, you will not get a full credit. You can only claim the political contribution tax credit to the extent that you have PEI taxes owing in the year.

Yukon

Yukon was first out of the gate with their 2000 budget, which continued the territory's measures to reduce personal tax over the next two years. The only major development was a reduction in the territorial tax rate as a percentage of federal tax from 50 percent to 49 percent. It is expected that by January 1, 2002, the rate will have dropped to 44 percent. (Which, for those of you who like the sound of it better, means you'll be paying 12 percent less tax.)

In addition to the basic Yukon tax, don't forget the additional 5-percent surtax for those of you whose Yukon tax exceeds $6,000.

After calculating total Yukon tax, there is some relief available with the Yukon tax credits.

Yukon tax credits

Yukon tax credits can be found on form T1C (Yukon). Some are new for 2000, while others are around from their introduction in the 1999 budget. Take a look at the ones noted below. You never know — you may be entitled to a credit without even knowing it.

- **Low-income family tax credit:** This credit provides a benefit of up to $300 for those with less than $25,000 in annual net income. Unfortunately, this credit isn't refundable, meaning that you will only get relief to the extent of your Yukon tax payable. If you were married on December 31, only the spouse with the higher income can claim this credit.
- **Small business investment tax credit:** Did you invest in a local business this year? Are you 19 years of age or older, and a resident of Yukon? Well, if so, there's good news for you. You may be eligible for a refundable credit of up to 25 percent of eligible investments made in local businesses. The maximum credit available is $25,000 per investor per year. If your credit is more than this, you can carry any unused amounts forward for seven years, or back three years. If you qualify for this credit, you'll receive certificate YSBITC-1 in the mail.
- **Mineral exploration tax credit:** Yukon's newest goal is to make the tax benefits from investing in mining and forestry as competitive as possible with other jurisdictions. In 1999, the territory introduced this credit that provides for a 22-percent refundable credit on eligible new mineral exploration work in the Yukon. But you'd better act fast if you want to take part in this program — it's only around until March 31, 2001.
- **Research and development tax credit:** This credit is calculated as 15 percent of all eligible expenditures. Combined with the federal tax credit available for research and development, the total tax credit is between 35 percent and 50 percent of eligible expenditures.
- **Investment tax credit:** This new credit is set at 25 percent of investments made under the Fireweed Fund, a labour-sponsored venture capital fund. With the federal credit of 15 percent, this brings the total tax credit for eligible investments to 40 percent.
- **Political contribution tax credit:** You can deduct part of the contribution you made in 2000 to a registered Yukon political party or a candidate seeking election to the Legislative Assembly. The credit is calculated as follows:
    - 75 percent on the first $100 of contributions
    - 50 percent on the next $450 of contributions
    - 33⅓ percent on contributions over $550.
    - For total contributions over $1,150, enter $500 on line 19 of form T1C (Yukon).

You'll only receive a political tax credit to the extent of Yukon tax paid.

- **First Nations tax credit.** This credit is available to those who lived on a First Nations settlement on December 31, 2000. The credit is equal to 95 percent of Yukon tax less any other Yukon tax credits you are entitled to. Although it is called a credit, it is not exactly a reduction in total taxes. You see, the reduction is simply paid to the First Nations Government. Sorry to get your hopes up. Eligible settlements include the following:
  - Champagne and Aishihik
  - Little Salmon/Carmacks
  - Nacho Nyak Dun
  - Selkirk
  - Teslin Tlingit
  - Tr'ondëk Hwëch'in
  - Vuntut Gwitchin

Members of a First Nation are entitled to reduce their federal and Yukon income tax payable and instead remit a corresponding amount of tax to the First Nations Government. The reduction is 75 percent of basic federal tax, and 95 percent of net Yukon tax. You can calculate these reductions by completing form T1C (Yukon) AG "Yukon First Nations Tax," and entering the results on line 432 of your income tax return.

In addition to the abovementioned credits, there is also a child tax credit available for families. Although this credit is not available on your income tax return, you do need to complete a tax return in order to be eligible. This credit provides up to $300 a year per child for families with a net annual income below $16,700.

Northwest Territories

The bad news is there were no significant changes to the tax rates and credits in the Northwest Territories this year. The good news is, you should have no trouble completing your tax return this year, since it will be pretty much the same as last year. For those of you who would like a bit of a refresher, here is a recap of the taxes and credits applicable in the Northwest Territories.

The Northwest Territories works on, and will continue to work on, a tax on tax system. Northwest Territories tax is calculated at 45 percent of federal tax. From this you may be eligible to deduct certain tax credits. To claim any of the credits that apply to you, you must complete the bottom of form T1C (NWT).

Northwest Territories tax credits

- **Cost of living tax credit:** If you were a resident of the Northwest Territories at the end of 2000, you may be eligible to claim the cost of living tax credit, which is a refundable credit. The amount of credit you are entitled to depends on your adjusted net income, which is the amount you reported on line 236 of your return less any social assistance payments and exempt foreign income reported on lines 250 and 256. Your credit is calculated as 1.25 percent of the first $12,000 of income, 1 percent of the next $36,000, and 0.75 percent on the remaining income up to $66,000. If your adjusted net income exceeds $66,000, report a credit of $645 on line 11 of form T1C (NWT).

- **Political contribution tax credit:** This credit is available if you contributed funds to a candidate seeking election to the Northwest Territories Legislative Assembly. The actual amount of the credit is as follows:
  - 100 percent of the first $100 contributed
  - 50 percent of the next $800.
  - For contributions over $900, the maximum credit you can receive is $500.

Your political tax credit can only be used to offset Northwest Territories tax. If you have no taxes owing, you won't get credit for your contribution.

- **Risk capital investment tax credits:** The Northwest Territories offers tax credits for those residents who invest in one or more of a variety of investments offered. The eligible investments include labour-sponsored venture capital corporations, employee venture capital corporations, community-endorsed venture capital corporations, and direct investment in territorial business corporations.

  Don't have a clue whether any of your investments will qualify? No need to worry. If you are eligible for the credit, the taxman will send you form T2C (NWT). Simply fill in the bottom of form T1C (NWT) according to the boxes marked on your slip, and you're off to the races. The credit is equal to 15 percent of the first $5,000 invested and 30 percent of the next $95,000. The maximum credit you can claim is $30,000, or 30 percent of your investment.

As with the political contribution tax credit, you'll only be eligible for this credit to the extent of Northwest Territories tax paid. However, don't panic if your credit exceeds your taxes owing. Any unused credits can be carried forward seven years or back three years (but not to a year before 1998).

Nunavut

We'll end off this chapter with the newest addition to our country and the area with the least number of changes in 2000. For 2000, Nunavut has decided to keep the tax on tax system that was in place in 1999. In addition, no new tax credits were introduced this year. So all that's left is to review the existing tax credits in the territory.

Nunavut tax credits

Once you've calculated your Nunavut tax, you may also have some credits to claim. These credits are calculated on form T1C (NUN). Some of these credits are available to you whether or not you've paid Nunavut tax in the year. Therefore, take a look at what's available — you may find that you can receive some free money! Here are some credits that may apply to you in 2000:

- **Cost of living tax credit:** A credit is available to each taxpayer in Nunavut to help out with the cost of living there. This credit is based on net income from line 236 of your return, less any social assistance payments and foreign treaty–exempt income reported on lines 250 and 256. The actual credit is calculated at 1.25 percent of your first $12,000 of income, 1 percent on the next $36,000, and .75 percent on the next $18,000. The maximum credit in 2000 is $645. This limit is reached at $66,000 of adjusted net income.
- **Political contribution tax credit:** Nunavut offers a tax credit to those contributing funds to candidates running for election to the Nunavut Legislative Assembly. However, contributions to local political parties will not qualify. You can only use this credit to reduce Nunavut tax owing in the year. If you don't have any taxes owing, you will not get any credit for your contributions.

The actual credit is calculated as follows:

  - 100 percent of the first $100 contributed
  - 50 percent of the next $800 contributed.
  - The maximum credit in the year is $500, which occurs at a $900 contribution level.

- **Risk capital investment tax credits:** Nunavut offers some tax credits to encourage investment in that territory. These include the labour-sponsored venture capital corporation tax credit; and the employee venture capital corporation, community-endorsed venture capital corporation, and territorial business corporation direct investment tax credits. We know, the names sound scary, but it's not actually that complicated. If you qualify for these credits, you will receive a form called T2C "Risk Capital Investment Tax Credit."

  If you invest in any of these corporations, you will receive a credit of 15 percent of the first $5,000 invested and 30 percent on the next $95,000 of investment. The maximum credit is $30,000, or 30 percent of the investment made. Similar to the political contribution tax credit, these credits are only available if you owe Nunavut tax in the year.

Once your Nunavut taxes are reduced to nil, the unused credits may be carried forward for seven years, or back three years (but not to a year before 1998). Since Nunavut only came into existence in 1999, if you want to carry a credit back to 1998, it should be used to offset your Northwest Territories tax payable in that year.

Chapter 21

Other Items: Questions and Opportunities for Taxpayers

In This Chapter

- Dealing with Elections Canada
- Reporting foreign income
- Applying for a Goods and Services Tax credit
- Understanding the Child Tax Benefit

This chapter takes you through some additional, yet sometimes forgotten, items on your tax return. Two of them represent questions that the CCRA wants you to answer, while the other two relate to free cash from the government for which you may be eligible. Yes, free cash! So now that we've got your attention, let's go through them. We'll talk about the questions first, and keep you in suspense about the free cash.

Elections Canada

In 1997, the CCRA introduced a new question to the front of the tax return. It asks, "Do you authorize CCRA to provide your name, address, and date of birth to Elections Canada to update information on the National Register of Electors?" You'd think that once you answered the question back in 1997, they wouldn't ask again. However, as you know, things aren't always as they should be. You need to answer this question every year, whether or not any of your information has changed. Prior to including this question, the CCRA used to spend approximately $30 million per year conducting door-to-door enumerations, finding out information about taxpayers. Now, if only they would include questions asking if you already owned a vacuum cleaner, needed your ducts cleaned, or wanted your driveway repaved. If you answer "yes" to this question, the CCRA will provide *only* your name, address, and date of birth to Elections Canada, to ensure that the National Register of Electors is up to date.

If you answer "no," the CCRA will not provide any information to Elections Canada. Answering "no" does not mean you are giving up your right to vote. It does mean that your information may not stay up to date, and if this is the case, come election time, you will need to take the necessary steps to correct your information. If you want to e-file your return, you must answer the Elections Canada question first. If you don't, your return can't be filed electronically.

Under the *Canada Elections Act,* information on the National Register of Electors can be used for electoral purposes only. No need to worry that your name will suddenly appear on mailing lists offering you free magazines.

Foreign Income Reporting

On page 1 of your return, you'll also find a question asking if the total cost of all foreign property owned in 2000 was greater than $100,000(Cdn). If so, you'll need to answer "yes" to this question, then complete form T1135 and file it along with your tax return.

There are substantial penalties for failing to file form T1135 by April 30. And these penalties increase if the CCRA asks you to file a return and you don't comply, or if you're found to have given false information amounting to gross negligence.

If you e-file your tax return, form T1135 must be sent separately to the CCRA. Send your completed form to the following address:

Ottawa Tax Centre
Employer Services Division
Other Programs Unit
875 Heron Road
Ottawa, Ontario
K1A 1A2

Also, you should note that if you are a new resident of Canada, you do not have to file form T1135 in the first year you become a resident of Canada. You will, however, have to file this form in subsequent years.

What constitutes foreign property? you ask. Well, the CCRA has provided a detailed list in the instructions accompanying form T1135, but just for fun we'll go over some of the more common types of foreign property:

- Funds in foreign bank accounts
- Shares of a non-resident corporation
- Land and buildings located outside Canada, such as foreign rental property
- Interests in mutual funds organized in a foreign jurisdiction
- Debts owned by non-resident persons, such as government or corporate bonds
- Property that is convertible or that can be exchanged for a right to acquire specified foreign property.

Specified foreign property does not include the following:

- Property used or held exclusively in the course of carrying on an active business
- Personal-use property, such as vacation property used primarily as a personal residence
- An interest in a U.S. Individual Retirement Account (IRA)
- Shares of the capital stock, or indebtedness, or a non-resident corporation that is a foreign affiliate
- An interest in, or indebtedness of a non-resident trust that is a foreign affiliate.

As mentioned, form T1135 only needs to be filed if the total cost of all foreign property holdings exceeds $100,000. Normally, this cost is what you originally paid for the asset. However, there are some cases in which your cost base will change. If you're not sure what your cost base should be, you might want to read over Chapter 13, where we go over how to calculate the adjusted cost base of assets.

Since you likely purchased your foreign property using foreign funds, you will have to convert the cost into Canadian dollars to see if the property cost more than $100,000 Canadian. To do this, you will have to find out the foreign exchange rate that was in effect at the time you purchased the asset.

If you've immigrated to Canada, the cost base of any foreign property you own is the fair market value of the property on the day you became a resident of Canada.

Let's take a look at some examples. Suppose Karen owns shares in a non-resident corporation with a cost base of $85,000. She also holds $20,000 in a U.S. bank account. Does she have to file form T1135? Yes! Although the cost of each property is less than $100,000, the total of all foreign property held exceeds $100,000.

What about Dave? He holds approximately $120,000 of foreign securities in his RRSP. Does he have to file a T1135? No. You do not have to file form T1135 for a trust governed by an RRSP.

Form T1135 must be filed if the cost base of specified foreign property exceeded $100,000 at any time during the year. The $100,000 test doesn't apply only at the end of the year! Even if you own shares of non-resident corporations that are held by a Canadian stockbroker, you have to report these shares on form T1135 (if they exceed the $100,000 cost threshold). In fact, you must report all shares of non-resident corporations, whether they are physically held inside or outside Canada.

Checking Out the Goods and Services Tax Credit

As discussed in Chapter 2, the Goods and Services Tax (GST) credit may be available to you. But only if you apply for it. Even if you received this credit before, you must reapply every year, since eligibility is based on information provided in your return — such as your income and your spouse's income. To apply for the credit, simply answer "yes" when asked on page 1 of your tax return whether or not you are applying. The CCRA will do the rest.

Who can apply?

You can apply for the GST credit if at the end of the year you were resident in Canada and any of the following apply:

- You were 19 years of age or older
- You had a spouse
- You were a parent.

You cannot apply if at the end of the year you were in either of the following situations:

- Confined to a prison or similar institution, and had been there for more than six months during the year
- Did not have to pay tax in Canada because you were an officer or servant of another country, such as a diplomat, or a family member or employee of such a person.

You cannot claim the credit for a spouse or child who met either of these conditions at the end of the year.

The amount of credit for which you are eligible depends on whether you are married, the number of children you have, and your total family income. If you have a spouse, only one of you can receive the credit. It does not matter which one of you applies; the credit is the same. You can claim a GST credit for each of your children to whom, at the end of the year, all of the following apply:

- He or she was under 19 years of age.
- He or she did not have a spouse.
- He or she was not a parent.
- He or she either lived with you or was claimed as a dependant by either you or your spouse.

If your child does not meet the above criteria and you cannot claim the GST credit on his or her behalf, make sure your child files a tax return for the year, since he or she will be eligible for a GST credit.

How much can I get?

As mentioned, your eligibility to receive the GST credit depends on the number of children and your total family income. Once your income reaches a certain point, you will no longer receive the credit. Table 21-2 shows whether you should apply in 2000, and the maximum credit you could receive. For 2000, if your total family income is higher than $11,796, you may be eligible to receive the highest credit. The credit begins to decline once your income reaches $26,284. Look up the number of children you have. You can see the approximate amount of your credit if your income is between $11,796 and $26,284. If your total family income exceeds the amount indicated, however, you won't be eligible for the credit.

Table 21-2 Maximum GST Credit Available in 2000

Number of Children	*If Total Family Income $11,796–$26,284, Max Credit*	*Family Income*
0	$404	$34,364
1	$510	$36,484
2	$616	$38,604
3	$722	$40,724
4	$828	$42,844
5 or more	$934 +	Apply

If you apply, you will find out two things by July of the same year: whether you are eligible, and what quarterly amount you will receive. Payments are made in July, October, January, and April.

Jon and Cathy work out their GST credit

Jon and Cathy are married. His total income for 2000 is $30,000. Cathy stayed at home with their three-year-old daughter during the year, so she had no income. They are entitled to a quarterly GST credit of $107, as follows:

Jon's income on line 236 of his return	$30,000
Cathy's income on line 236 of her return	$0
Total	$30,000
Basic goods and service tax credit	$202
Credit for spouse	$202
Credit for one qualified child	$106
Total	$510

Total family income	$30,000	
Subtract: base amount	$26,284	
Excess	$3,716	
5 percent of excess		$186
Goods and Services tax credit		$324
Quarterly credit	$81	

The Child Tax Benefit

The *Canada Child Tax Benefit* (CCTB) is a tax-free monthly payment made to eligible families to help them with the cost of raising children under the age of 18. Along with the CCTB goes the National Child Benefit Supplement (NCBS), which is paid monthly to benefit low-income families with children.

Who can receive the CCTB?

To be eligible to receive the CCTB, you have to live with the child and be a resident of Canada for income tax purposes. (If you are unsure whether you are a resident, you should refer back to Chapter 2.) In addition, you or your spouse has to be one of the following:

- A Canadian citizen
- A permanent resident or landed immigrant, under the *Immigration Act*
- A Convention refugee under the *Immigration Act*
- A visitor to Canada or a holder of a minister's permit under the *Immigration Act* who has lived in Canada throughout the previous 18 months and has a valid permit in the 19th month.

To be eligible, you must be the person who is primarily responsible for the care and upbringing of the child. This means that you are the one who supervises the child's activities and ensures that his or her needs, including medical and child care needs, are met. The primary caregiver is generally the mother, if she lives with the child, but can also be the father, grandparent, or legal guardian.

If I'm eligible, how do I receive the credit?

If you are eligible for the CCTB, you can apply as soon as any of the following conditions are met:

- The child is born
- The child starts to live with you
- You or your spouse meet the eligibility requirements.

Don't delay in applying for the credit, since you will only be eligible for retroactive payments for up to 11 months.

To apply for the CCTB, you must complete and mail form RC66 "Canada Child Tax Benefit Application." You can pick up this application at your Tax Services Office, or download it from the CCRA Web site. You and your spouse must also file a tax return, so that the CCRA can calculate the amount of your benefit. If you have not filed a return, you must do so before any payments can be made.

To continue receiving the CCTB, both you and your spouse have to file a tax return every year, even if you have no income to report.

If your child was born outside Canada, or was born in Canada but is over the age of one, you need to attach proof of birth to your application. Proof of birth includes one of the following:

- Birth certificate or birth registration
- Hospital record of birth; or the record of the physician, nurse, or midwife who attended the birth
- Baptismal or cradle roll certificate, or other church record.

For a child born outside Canada, include one of the following:

- *Record of Landing* issued by Citizenship and Immigration Canada
- *Notice of Decision* issued under the *Immigration Act*
- Passport of citizenship certificate. After you have completed the application, you need to wait patiently for about two months for the CCRA to process it. (Don't ask why.) Once the CCRA has processed the application, it will send you a Canada Child Tax Benefit Notice telling you the amount you are entitled to (if any), along with your first payment.

How much will I receive?

The amount of your benefit depends on the number of children you have and their ages, your province or territory of residence, your total family income, and whether you or your spouse have claimed any child care expenses. The system operates on a time lag basis. For example, the benefits payable in January to June 2001 will be based on a calculation using your family income from 1999. The benefits payable from July to December are calculated using your income from 2000. The reason for the time lag is due to the fact that the CCRA doesn't know what your income is until you file your return. Since you don't file your return for 2000 until April 2001, your benefits for the beginning of that year are based on income from the second preceding year.

The 1999 federal budget introduced some changes to the CCTB. The budget proposed to increase the CCTB benefits by $2.5 billion annually by 2004. This is being done in three ways. First, the CCTB is now fully indexed to inflation, meaning that as the cost of living increases, the amount of the CCTB also increases. Second, both the base benefit and the NCB supplement are increased beyond indexation. Third, the income thresholds at which the base benefit begins to be reduced, and the income level where the NCB supplement is eliminated, are higher. Finally, the reduction rate for the base benefit is lower than in previous years. As a result of these changes being phased-in, the CCTB benefit will fluctuate over the next couple of years. Table 21-2 shows the maximum monthly benefits available in 2000.

Table 21-2	Maximum CCTB Benefits for 2000	
Base Benefit	***Starting January 1, 2000***	***Starting July 1, 2000***
Basic amount	$86.17	$90.83
Additional benefit for third child	$6.33	$6.33
Additional benefit for children under 7 years	$18	$18

Starting July 1, 2000, the benefit is reduced if your family net income is more than $30,004. The reduction equals 2.5 percent for a one-child family, and 5 percent for families with two or more children. Table 21-3 shows these amounts.

Table 21-3	National Child Benefit Supplement (NCBS)	
NCBS	***Starting January 1, 2000***	***Starting July 1, 2000***
First child	$66.33	$80.50
Second child	$49.67	$63.58
Third child	$43.08	$57.25

There is a reduction of the NCBS if family income exceeds $21,214. The reduction is 11.1 percent for a one-child family, 19.9 percent for two-child families, and 27.8 percent for families with three or more children. The benefit will be completely eliminated once your family income reaches $30,004.

Suppose Karen and Jason have one son, age 2 (named Nicolas, if you care). Their total family income for 2000 was $38,000. From July 2000 to June 2001, they can expect a Child Tax Benefit of $92.17. Here's how it works.

Base benefit: $90.83 × 12		$1,090
Supplement for children under 7: $18 × 12		$ 216
Total		$1,306
Benefit reduction:		
1999 family adjusted income	$38,000	
Less:	$30,004	
Subtotal	$ 7,996	
Reduction of 2.5 percent of difference for 1 child	$ 200	$1,106
National Child Tax Benefit supplement: $80.50 × 12	$ 966	
Benefit reduction:		
1999 family adjusted income	$38,000	
Less:	$21,214	
Subtotal	$16,786	
Reduction of 11.5 percent of difference for 1 child	$ 1,930	$ 0
Estimated Child Tax Benefit for July 2000 to June 2001	$ 1,106	
Estimated monthly benefit	$ 92.17	

You should apply for the benefit even if you think you're not entitled to it based on your current family income. The CCRA will automatically recalculate your entitlement every July after your tax return is filed. If your income changes and you have already applied, you don't have to worry about applying at that time. A toll-free telephone number (1-800-387-1193; 1-800-387-1194 for French) has been set up to provide you with information on the Child Tax Benefit. In addition, you can find out information on your personal situation by contacting your local Tax Services Office.

Part V
After You've Filed

In this part . . .

So you've filed your return, now what? Well, you sit and wait for a thank-you card in the mail from the CCRA called a Notice of Assessment. Does getting this hot little item in your hands mean you're free and clear? Unfortunately, not always. You see, the CCRA likes to perform random checks on people — think of it as a lottery you don't want to win. Sometimes they are requests for little pieces of information, while sometimes they are larger requests for all your information. These larger requests are simply a nice term for "audit."

So, even the nice, law-abiding folks out there will sometimes find themselves hassled by the tax police. For those of you in that boat, all we can say is, we're sorry, and you'll live. But don't panic. This part will tell you everything you need to know when dealing with the CCRA.

'The best measure of a man's honesty isn't his income tax return. It's the zero adjust on his bathroom scale."

— Arthur C. Clarke

Chapter 22

CCRA Administration

In This Chapter

- Understanding your Notice of Assessment
- Deciphering reassessments
- Entering a notice of objections
- Requests for Information
- Fixing your mistakes
- Avoiding penalties and interest

Congratulations! You have completed your tax return and sent it in. One day (two to three weeks if you e-filed your return, or four to six weeks if you mailed it), you will receive a Notice of Assessment. What does this mean? Has the Canada Customs and Revenue Agency (CCRA) audited your return and given it final approval? Unfortunately, the answer is no.

What you have is an acknowledgment that your return has been received and a confirmation that a basic review of your calculations has produced no obvious errors or omissions. "Obvious" means things like: arithmetically the return adds up, you have not claimed a northern residents deduction from your home in Windsor, and you have filed your return in the correct province of residence. You can interpret your receipt of the notice to mean that the CCRA accepts your return as filed and does not require any more information at this time. In the majority of cases, you will never need to concern yourself with this return again.

Not surprisingly, most of this early assessing is done by computer. The information is entered into the CCRA computer using the line numbers or keypunch summaries that accompany most returns. The computer then checks the math and runs cross-checks between information that is entered and information it expects to find. The computer also matches up all your T4s, T4As, T5s, T3s, and so on with the matching slips sent in by your employer, bank, or investment company, to ensure you have included all this income on your return.

Don't forget to include **all** the income on **all** your information slips when filing your tax return. If you omit them, the CCRA's computer will find them and assess you for any additional taxes owing.

Beyond the basic review, the Notice of Assessment gives you no assurance that the CCRA will not review your return at some later date. It does mean that your return is safely tucked away and that for now the taxing authority has no further questions.

Understanding Your Notice of Assessment

The typical Notice of Assessment (form T451 E) contains a date, your social insurance number, the tax year being assessed, the address of the Taxation Centre where the return was assessed, a summary of your return by line number, the amount you owe or are owed, plus an explanation of any changes.

The explanation of changes typically includes the information that the return was assessed as filed, or that some changes were made due to calculation errors or omissions. The notice will go on to say that no additional interest will be charged on amounts owed if the debt is paid within 20 days, and it gives you a number to call if you have any questions. At the bottom of the notice is an RRSP deduction limit statement that tells you how your limit was calculated and how much deduction room you have for next year.

Your Notice of Assessment contains some useful information for future years, including your RRSP contribution limit, loss carryforward figures, and alternative minimum tax carryforwards, among others. Keep this notice to help you in preparing your tax return for next year.

The date on your Notice of Assessment is of particular importance — it represents the day the assessment was mailed to you and is referred to as the "assessment date." This date is important because if you don't agree with any changes made by the CCRA, you have the later of 90 days from the assessment date and one year from the original due date of your tax return to object to the changes.

If you don't agree with any change made by the CCRA on your Notice of Assessment, don't wait too long to follow up! There is a time limit to file an objection, and if you miss this deadline you'll be out of luck.

Help! I've Been Reassessed

Unfortunately, one of the realities of our tax system is that occasionally the CCRA will disagree with the preparation of your tax return. If the CCRA disagrees with you the first time it assesses your return, you will receive a Notice of Assessment detailing the changes. Any adjustments after the original Notice of Assessment will be communicated to you by means of a *Notice of Reassessment.* The reassessment could be for a higher or lower amount than you actually paid. A reassessment can be the result of audit, compliance review, or a taxpayer-requested change.

Before a reassessment is processed, you will receive a letter outlining the proposed changes and indicating that if you wish to make representation with respect to these changes you must do so within 30 days. If you want to dispute the proposed changes, you will need to provide additional information or make arguments to the auditor within this period. If no representations are made, the CCRA will process the changes as proposed.

If you need more time to get information, request an extension to the original 30-day limit. One extension of 30 days will almost always be granted.

All discussions with the CCRA should be documented. All requests and explanations should be put into letters and sent to the auditor. This way there are no misunderstandings and a trail exists that can be used if you decide to appeal.

Unfortunately, almost every reassessment carries interest charges that will date back to the day after the original filing deadline of the return. The rationale is that the money was owed at the original deadline and the reassessment corrects your original filing error. Penalties may also be applied in certain circumstances. Later in this chapter we will discuss how penalties and interest arise.

Dealing with Objections

A *Notice of Objection* is a formal document through which you notify the CCRA that you disagree with its assessment or reassessment and that you would like the return transferred to the independent Appeals Division for a review and judgment.

A Notice of Objection is filed by completing form T400A or by writing a detailed letter outlining the reasons for your objection. You then send the form or letter to the Chief of Appeals in your local Tax Services Office or the Taxation Centre where you filed your return.

If you feel that the local CCRA office is biased against you, you can send the objection to any office for appeal. In your letter, specifically indicate that you wish to have the issue dealt with in the alternative office.

Appeals divisions are usually separated physically from the rest of the Tax Services Office. Its officers are required to have limited interaction with the rest of the audit division. This process ensures that an unbiased person will be reviewing and deciding on your objection.

Appeals officers are also required to make available to you all documents in the CCRA file that are relevant to your appeal. In addition, officers must fully report to you any meeting or discussions with the original auditors. You may also request to be present at these meetings.

Use form T400A if you file an objection. Though not mandatory, it will act as a precise guide as to the information that the Appeals Division will need in order to deal quickly with your situation.

When can I file a Notice of Objection?

A Notice of Objection must be filed before the later of the following:

- 90 days from the mailing date of the Notice of Assessment or Notice of Reassessment (assessment or reassessment date)
- One year from the due date of the return.

Let's say that the due date of your 2000 tax return is April 30, 2001. Assume your return's assessment date is July 1, 2000.

You will have until the later of 90 days after the date of mailing of the Notice of Assessment (assessment date), September 29, 2001 or one year after the return was due, April 30, 2002, to object to the assessment. In this case, you will have until April 30, 2002 to object to the assessment. In the case of a Notice of Reassessment, the rules are slightly different. Since a reassessment is usually well after the original Notice of Assessment, the date of one year after the return was due has usually passed. As a result, you must file your Notice of Objection within 90 days of the mailing date of the Notice of Reassessment.

In certain special circumstances the right to object to a reassessment is limited. If a reassessment is the result of any of the following situations;

- A court decision on a previous appeal
- A late-filed election
- Losses carried back
- Denial of expenses related to a criminal activity
- Change due to a tax avoidance issue.

The objection must be limited to the specific issues raised in the reassessment only. No new issues will be considered.

TIP

When your return is opened on a reassessment that does not involve any of the above circumstances, you can request adjustments of any issues in the return(s) in question.

When the CCRA goes back beyond the normal three-year limit to give you a refund, they will refuse to allow you to object to their assessment, unless a waiver was filed for that year.

If I file an objection, should I pay the disputed amount?

The answer is yes. This may seem strange, since the core of your argument is that you do *not* owe this money. The truth is that the CCRA will begin charging interest on the disputed amount if it is not paid within 20 days of your assessment or reassessment date. If you win the appeal, you will get your money back plus interest. If there's a chance you'll lose, why pay the extra interest?

Will collection actions start against me while my case is under appeal?

No. The CCRA will stop collection actions against you while your case is under appeal. Unfortunately, you will still continue to receive notices of outstanding amounts from the CCRA collections division throughout the period, but no action will be taken against you — yet. If you lose your appeal, however, watch out. The collections people at the CCRA mean business, and you should make every effort to cooperate with them.

Remember when dealing with the CCRA that it is always better to resolve issues before an assessment or reassessment is issued. Not only because of the time and trouble it takes to file a Notice of Objection, but because once you receive an assessment or reassessment, the onus is on you to prove the assessment or reassessment is wrong. The courts have accepted that the CCRA only needs to prove its case on a balance of probabilities and not beyond a reasonable doubt. This puts you at a distinct disadvantage once the assessments arrive.

How long does it take for my appeal to be heard?

Generally speaking, appeals take many months to be resolved. It can take from six months to a year for a decision to be rendered.

What if I lose the appeal but still think I'm right?

Once your appeal has been rejected by the CCRA, Tax Court is your next stop.

We will look more closely at the court system in the next chapter, but for now you need to know that to be able to advance to Tax Court you must have filed a Notice of Objection within the time limit set out above. If you didn't follow the rules, the Tax Court will not hear your case.

As you can see, the Notice of Objection, filed correctly and within the required time limit, is a powerful tool for protecting your right to appeal.

If in doubt, file a Notice of Objection to protect your rights to appeal.

How long after I originally file my return can I be reassessed?

The general rule is that a return can be reassessed any time within three years from the mailing date of the original Notice of Assessment (the assessment date). After the three years has passed, the return becomes *statute barred*. When a return is statute barred, neither you nor the CCRA can go back and reopen the year for reassessment.

Let's say you mailed your 1994 return on April 30, 1995. A month later you receive your Notice of Assessment. On this notice is a date of May 30, 1995. If the CCRA wants to reassess the 1994 tax return, it must do so before May 30, 1998. Even if your return is reassessed, the original Notice of Assessment date is the key date used to determine when the return goes statute barred. Subsequent Notices of Reassessment do not affect this original date.

Reassessment outside the three-year limit

The *Income Tax Act* does allow the CCRA the discretion under specific circumstances to reassess beyond the normal reassessment period of three years. Reasons for reassessment outside the three-year limit include the following:

- The taxpayer has made misrepresentations in his tax return due to fraud, neglect, carelessness, or willful default.

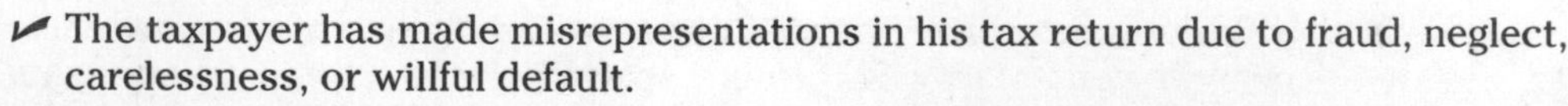

  If the CCRA can prove that you intentionally or unintentionally misrepresented information on your return because of fraud or carelessness, you can be reassessed at any time with no limitations.

- The taxpayer signs a waiver of the three-year limit. (We will discuss this later.)
- The special six-year rules apply, which include carrybacks.

Since the law allows you to carry losses back three years, any prior return within that carryback period stays open for six years from the original assessment date rather than the usual three.

For example, say you have a non-capital loss in 1994 that you request to be carried back to 1991. The CCRA then reassesses your 1994 tax year, adjusting the loss previously claimed. This reassessment takes place in 1997 (which the CCRA can do because this is before the statute-barred date for the 1994 tax year). However, the CCRA has to be able to return to the 1991 tax year as well, so that the loss you carried back can also be adjusted.

If not for this rule, the 1991 year would be statute barred by the time the 1997 reassessment took place and the loss could not be adjusted.

- Transactions with related non-residents.
- Transactions involving the payment of tax to a foreign government.
- Consequential changes.

Consequential changes are changes that occur in a year as a result of a court decision or a settlement with the CCRA, that affect other taxation years. In these cases the CCRA can reassess returns for otherwise statute-barred years.

In addition to the above rules, the CCRA was given special discretionary powers to reassess beyond the normal statue-barred period in the following circumstances:

- The CCRA receives a written reassessment request from the taxpayer, and
- The year of reassessment is after 1985, and
- The effect of the reassessment will be to reduce the tax originally assessed or give rise to a refund, and
- The CCRA is satisfied that the request for the adjustment would have been accepted if it had been made within the normal reassessment period.

For further information on these special rules, you can consult the CCRA bulletin IT-241 "Assessments Beyond the 3-Year Limit."

Waivers

Sometimes you won't want the regular three-year assessing period to apply to you because it is to your benefit to have the tax year remain open. In these cases, you should file a waiver with the CCRA. A waiver is a document that specifies the items reported on your T1 that you don't want the regular three-year assessing period to apply to. You must file a waiver on form T2029, and it must be received by the CCRA within three years of the assessment date in question.

When signing a waiver, be very specific about which items you want to remain open. If you are too general, you are leaving the door open for the CCRA to reassess items you had not intended them to consider. The CCRA is limited to looking at only the items mentioned in the waiver. Since the CCRA is allowed to assess more tax, only include items that you expect will *reduce* your tax liability.

Why and when to sign a waiver

There are basically two situations in which waivers come into play:

- The CCRA asks you to sign a waiver on a particular issue because the three-year limit is approaching and the issue may not be resolved before the return goes statute barred. If you do not sign the waiver, the CCRA will assess the issue and force you to file a Notice of Objection and appeal its decision. This can be a long process, so you'll save a lot of time, effort, and money if you simply sign the waiver and hope the issue is resolved without additional tax being levied. The CCRA usually takes this approach if an issue is in dispute and it believes that additional tax is owed. By getting a waiver, the CCRA protects its right to enforce an assessment, while giving you more time to consider the issue and to help rectify the situation.
- You are asking the CCRA to reduce the tax you owe, and the three-year limit is approaching. By signing the waiver you can ensure that the issue will still be open for discussion, and you can avoid taking the entire return to appeal.

As mentioned earlier, the CCRA is given the discretion to reassess returns beyond the three-year limit if the effect is to reduce the tax originally assessed and the CCRA is satisfied that the adjustment would have been accepted if filed on time. By filing a waiver, you can avoid being victim to the CCRA's discretion and protect your right to appeal.

Can I revoke a signed waiver?

Yes, a waiver can be revoked on six months' notice by filing form T652 "Revocation of Waiver." After revocation, the waiver is permanently revoked and no reassessment can be made after this date.

In some cases, it's a good idea to sign a waiver and file the revocation at the same time. For example, if the CCRA requests the waiver, your filing both forms at once gives them only six months to resolve the issue and does not leave your return open for years to come.

Requests for Additional Information

During the initial tax assessment, or as a result of a re-review of your return, the CCRA may have additional questions. To obtain information to answer these questions, the CCRA will send you a letter called a Request for Additional Information." This letter will usually ask for specific information and will include an address where this information is to be sent, the name and phone number of the person requesting the information, and a date the information must be received by (usually 30 days from the date of the request).

Is this letter the beginning of a full audit of your return? Should you seek professional advice? The answer is no.

The first thing to remember is that a request for information is not an unusual thing. It is a normal part of the CCRA's verification process. Second, a request for information does not automatically mean you will owe more tax.

In fact, there are many reasons why a request might be sent to you. One of the most common is that a particular receipt or slip of paper was not included in your paper-filed return. Examples of this are charitable donation receipts or RRSP receipts. Perhaps the information you supplied was unclear or incomplete, or the CCRA is doing random compliance checks to test the accuracy of returns. For example, if you are claiming carrying charges or child care expenses, the CCRA may ask to see proof of these deductions.

This later request is usually the result of a desk audit. Such audits are done at the Tax Services Office and are primarily directed at testing a large number of returns and identifying potential problems that will be forwarded for a full audit. As long as the information you've reported on your tax return is truthful, supportable, and within the tax laws, you should have nothing to worry about.

If you did not send receipts to the CCRA because you electronically filed your return (e-filed), a request for information is very common. You see, when you e-file, no receipts are sent to the CCRA. By asking you to send in receipts, the CCRA is trying to maintain the integrity of the system by testing the accuracy of your return. With this in mind, it's best to read the letter carefully and respond with the correct information within the time limit set out.

If you cannot get the information within the time limit, call the number on the request and ask for an extension. In most cases, a further 30-day extension will be granted. This extension is usually a one-shot deal, however, and will not be granted a second time.

Record the name and phone number of the person on the letter. Most Tax Services Offices have hundreds of people with hundreds of phone numbers, and it's unlikely that you'll be able to locate this person if you lose the name and contact number.

If you ever have contact with someone at the CCRA and find them to be helpful, keep a record of their name and number and call them if you have a question in the future. A knowledgeable person inside a huge bureaucracy can be worth his or her weight in gold.

The worst thing to do if you receive a request for additional information is to ignore it. Ignoring the CCRA will not make your problems magically disappear. You see, if you don't provide the information in the time allowed, or if you do not make suitable arrangements for an extension, the auditor will simply conclude that the information does not exist and reassess you accordingly. This type of reassessment usually includes penalties and interest. As well, once this reassessment is complete, the CCRA is under no compulsion to accept supporting information at a later date and can legally refuse to accept it.

For more serious situations where substantial amounts of money are involved or potential criminal activities are suspected, the CCRA can invoke a requirement or a judicial authorization forcing you to provide information. The *Income Tax Act* gives them authority to do so.

Fixing Your Mistakes on a Return You've Sent

If you think you have forgotten or omitted information on your already filed return, or if you discover new information that pertains to a previously filed and assessed return, will the CCRA allow you to submit this information late? The answer is yes!

As you can imagine, this is a common problem. But don't worry, there is a process to allow you to change or add information to both assessed and un-assessed returns. The process is as follows:

- The CCRA asks that if you need to make a change to a return already sent in, you *do not file another return for the year.*
- Complete either form T1-ADJ "Adjustment Request," available at all CCRA Tax Services Offices, or a letter detailing the changes (including the years involved, the specific details, your address and social insurance number, your home and daytime phone numbers). This letter must be signed and dated by you.
- Provide *all* supporting documents for the requested changes.
- Send this adjustment request to the Taxation Services Offices where you filed your return.

If you follow this process, you will greatly assist the CCRA in making the correct changes in a timely manner. Upon review of the information, the CCRA will take one of three steps:

- Accept your changes and send you a Notice of Reassessment (or Notice of Assessment, if the return had not yet been assessed).
- Deny your request. A letter will explain the reasons.
- Request additional information.

What if you discover an error several years back that would have resulted in a refund had you filed correctly the first time?

The CCRA will allow you to ask for a refund for years as far back as 1985 if it is satisfied that the request would have been accepted had it been made in the normal reassessment period and if all the relevant information is provided. The policy of allowing late refund requests is covered in the CCRA's information circular 92-3 "Guidelines for Refunds beyond the Normal Three-Year Period," available at Tax Services Offices or on the CCRA's Web site.

If the filing deadline is approaching (that is, April 30) and you are missing slips or information, it is best to file your return on time to avoid the late filing penalties. Do your best to calculate your income and deductions, then follow the above adjustment process when the information is available. The CCRA suggests that you include any partial information you have, a description of the missing information, and an explanation as to what you are doing to obtain it.

Late-filed elections

The *Income Tax Act* contains various elections that allow you to adopt special treatment for particular tax issues. However, to take advantage of them, the elections must be filed within certain time frames, and the CCRA must be aware that the election is being made. Sometimes the election requires special tax forms to be filled out, while other times a note attached to your tax return is enough. If you don't take advantage of a favourable election on your tax return, you may not be totally out of luck. In certain circumstances, the CCRA will allow you to file an election late.

The CCRA has issued information circular 92-1, in which it outlines the circumstances under which it will allow you to late-file, revoke, or change elections. These situations generally involve honest mistakes or circumstances out of your control where you made a reasonable effort to do the right thing. If, on the other hand, it appears that you were simply negligent, careless, or trying to engage in retroactive tax planning, the CCRA will not permit a change to the election.

Refunds: Show Me the Money!

The rule is simple — to get a refund, you need to file a tax return. However, if you failed to file a return in the past, and you would have received a refund had you filed, you should still file a tax return for the missing years. The CCRA is prepared to accept returns requesting refunds back to 1985 if you provide *all* the pertinent information and the CCRA is satisfied that the refund would have been issued if the information had been supplied on time. Remember, a return must normally be filed within three years of the end of the year to which it pertains, in order to be eligible for a refund.

The CCRA doesn't have to accept your return if you file late. By filing outside the three-year limit, you are putting yourself at the mercy of the CCRA's discretion as to whether it will accept or reject your request. Information circular 92-3 "Guidelines for Refunds beyond the Normal Three-Year Period," available at CCRA offices or on CCRA's Web site, provides details of this policy.

The real scoop on refunds

An important point to mention at this juncture is that refunds come from taxes you've already paid. Creating a big loss on a tax return will not get you a refund unless you have already paid tax. The *Income Tax Act* requires the Minister (through the CCRA) to determine if an overpayment of tax has occurred and to pay a refund. Usually the refund arrives with your Notice of Assessment. If a refund is owed and you have not received it with your assessment, the CCRA is required to issue a refund upon receipt of your application in writing.

If you have any other tax liabilities outstanding, the CCRA will use your refund to pay these taxes instead of giving you the money directly.

Interest on refunds

The CCRA pays interest on refunds based on a prescribed interest rate that is set quarterly. The amount it pays on refunds is set at 2 percent below the interest it charges on balances owing. In 1999, the prescribed interest rate was the same for all four quarters: 7 percent for refund interest and 9 percent for balances owing.

Interest on refunds is compounded daily starting on the latest of the following three dates:

- The day after you overpaid your taxes
- 45 days after you file your return
- 45 days after the balance due date for the year (June 15).

If a refund arose as a result of a loss carryback, no interest is payable for the period before you filed your tax return.

Direct deposit

Your refund can be automatically deposited into your bank account. If you paper file, complete form T1-DD "Request for Direct Deposit of Refund" and send it with your tax return. For e-filing, prepare and send in form T183 "Request for Direct Deposit of Refund."

Refunded interest as income

Refund interest is income and must be included in your return in the year you received it. If you also paid interest on an underpayment of income tax, the income inclusion can be reduced by the amount of arrears interest accruing over the same period.

Balances Owing

The *Income Tax Act* requires that all tax for a year be paid by the balance due date. This date is April 30 of the year following the taxation year in question. For 2000, the balance due date is April 30, 2001.

Even if your tax return is not due until a later date (for example, if you are self-employed, your tax return is not due until June 15), you must estimate your taxes payable and remit the amount to the CCRA by April 30.

If you are filing a tax return for a person who has died in the year, any balance owing is due on April 30, unless the person died after October 31 of the taxation year or before May 1 of the following year. In these cases, any outstanding tax bill is due six months after the date of death. For example, if George died on February 1, 2001, his 2000 tax bill is not due until August 1, 2001.

Your tax bill is considered to be paid on the day that it was mailed to the CCRA, if it is sent by first-class mail or courier. If you're filing your tax return at the last minute, don't just drop it in any old post box. Ensure that your return is postmarked April 30 so it will not be considered late-filed. If the mail doesn't get picked up until the next day, you'll be stuck with a late-filed tax return!

Interest on balance due

If you have a balance owing for the current year, the CCRA charges compound daily interest starting May 1 on any unpaid taxes. As we discussed earlier, this also applies to reassessments. If you are reassessed for 2000, the interest calculation starts May 1, 2001 — one day after the tax should have been paid. If you incur any penalties, interest is also charged on the penalty starting the day after your return is due. The interest rate charged is a prescribed rate that is adjusted quarterly. To obtain a rough estimate of the interest rate on balances owing, take the Bank of Canada rate and add 4 percent. This high rate is then further inflated by daily compounding.

Pay your tax by April 30 to avoid significant interest charges. This also applies if you are filing your return late. Estimate your tax payable and send it in.

Instalments

If you are required to pay instalments in the year, be aware that late or deficient instalment payments also attract interest at the high prescribed rate.

If you are deficient or do not make an instalment payment, you can avoid interest by paying your next instalment early. The CCRA will give you credit for the overpayment interest (at the same rate as the late payment) and net the interest owed against the interest earned.

Nondeductible interest

Interest paid to the CCRA is nondeductible for tax purposes, although it can be used to offset refund interest, which is considered taxable income.

Penalties and Interest

Penalties are in addition to the interest payments made on late or deficient taxes. Penalties also attract the same interest as do unpaid balances.

Late-filing penalty

If you file your return late (after April 30) a penalty of 5 percent of the tax owing will immediately be applied. A further penalty of 1 percent of the unpaid tax will also be added for each full month the return is late, up to a maximum of 12 months (additional 12 percent maximum).

If you are late a second time within three years of the first late filing and you have received a demand-to-file request from the CCRA, the penalty is bumped up to 10 percent of the unpaid tax plus 2 percent per month, to a maximum of 20 months (40 percent maximum).

Even if you cannot pay your tax, make sure you file your return on time to avoid the late-filing penalties.

Repeated failure to report income

If you have failed to report income, and this has been reassessed by the CCRA, any subsequent failure to report income within the next three years will earn you a penalty of 10 percent of the unreported income.

Failure to provide complete information

If you fail to provide complete information, you'll face a fine of $100 per occurrence. Some examples include not providing a SIN number on your return or omitting information that the CCRA requires to correctly assess your return. Don't be sloppy — complete all information asked for on your tax return.

If the information you need had to be obtained from a third party, and this person (or company) would not cooperate, the CCRA will waive your penalty. Attach a note to your tax return outlining the steps you took to try to obtain the information.

Failure to file information returns

You may be required to file information returns along with your income tax return. Failure to file such an information return comes with its own set of penalties. The fine is the greater of the following:

- $100
- $25 per day to a maximum of 100 days ($2,500).

These returns include tax shelter information returns and foreign property information returns.

Tax evasion, gross negligence, false statements, or false credit returns

For serious situations where the taxpayer has intentionally tried to misstate or misrepresent their return, a penalty of 50 percent of the tax avoided will be added to their tax liability. Cheating definitely does not pay off!

Criminal prosecutions

Tax evasion usually involves a criminal prosecution in addition to the above penalties. The courts can impose fines of up to 200 percent of the tax evaded and sentence you to five years in prison.

Waiving of interest and penalties

As we will discuss in the next chapter, the CCRA, through its Fairness Committees, can waive penalties and interest in certain circumstances, such as illness or natural disaster.

Chapter 23

Dealing with Canada Customs and Revenue Agency

In This Chapter

- Getting to know the "new" tax collector — the CCRA
- Avoiding the dreaded audit
- Making an application for fairness
- Understanding Voluntary Disclosures
- Sorting out tax evasion, tax planning, and tax avoidance

Let's start with just a little history — on November 1, 1999, Revenue Canada ceased to exist. Now before you get all choked up: To replace Revenue Canada, the government created the Canada Customs and Revenue Agency (CCRA). The new agency has all the same people, offices, policies, and rules of the old Revenue Canada. And yes, they still collect tax. Too bad for us. Under the old regime, the Department of Finance formulated tax law and policy. The Department of National Revenue (a.k.a. Revenue Canada) would then administer and supervise the tax system, and the Receiver General would accept payments of taxes owing. Revenue Canada was run by the Minister of National Revenue (a member of Parliament) who reported to Parliament. The new agency works exactly the same way, albeit with a few subtle but important changes.

The agency format was designed to solve some of the perceived problems with the taxation system. Unlike the old Revenue Canada, the CCRA is not a government department. Instead, it's a separate entity with its own autonomous management board that essentially reports directly to Parliament. The government intends this structure to separate the CCRA from the influences of Treasury Board, the federal public service, and politics in general.

The new management board is made up of representatives from both the federal and provincial government, plus individuals representing business and industry. The agency's long-term goal is to bring all taxation under one roof. The CCRA hopes to eliminate the overlap of administration of the tax system by convincing the provinces, and eventually municipalities, to allow the agency to control and administer all aspects of taxation within Canada. Also, by having business and industry involvement, the CCRA hopes to better serve these segments.

The federal government also hopes that this agency structure will allow it to better manage the tax system by giving it more flexibility in the areas of employee relations and management structure. It is hoped that the CCRA, now less fettered by the influences of politics, Treasury Board, the public service, and its unions, will be in a position to introduce a more goal-oriented business approach to taxation in Canada. All this sounds wonderful until you realize that with all other tasks out of the way, the CCRA's only remaining mandate is to generate revenue. And guess what brings revenue to the CCRA? You guessed it — our taxes! The CCRA will, in all likelihood, have a much greater focus on pursuing and collecting tax than the "old" Revenue Canada. Only time will tell! In this chapter we'll take a close look at the role of the CCRA and give you the inside track on dealing with the various processes they can put taxpayers through if things go awry — audits, hearings. We'll wrap up with some stern words about tax evasion and the benefits of tax planning. Let's get started.

Avoiding the Dreaded Audit

Most people find the very idea of an income tax audit stressful for the following reasons:

- You feel that the situation is not in your control.
- You feel like a criminal who must prove your innocence.
- You feel guilty because you may have taken some liberties with your return.
- You feel helpless because you don't know the rules.
- You feel vulnerable in the face of the awesome power of the CCRA.
- You are afraid that you will owe substantial amounts of money.

The key to avoiding this stress is to avoid an audit — and if it's too late for that, you should at least know what to expect.

Types of audits

The CCRA conducts investigations at several points along the assessment path. In fact, your return could be the subject of an intense review — and you might never even know it. As we will discuss in the next section, the CCRA compares your return to norms and averages for your region of the country, income levels, and types of income. If a variation outside the acceptable level occurs, your return starts winding its way through the audit system.

What you should know about audits

- The actual percentage of returns selected for audit is a guarded secret but it would be safe to say that between 5 percent to 7 percent of personal tax returns are selected for review on a yearly basis. In fact, in 1999 the CCRA assessed about $5 billion in additional tax due to audit.
- If you do get selected for audit, remember the burden of proof is on you to disprove the auditor's conclusions. The CCRA need only prove its case on a balance of probabilities. Once this is done, it becomes your problem to prove them incorrect.
- Keep in mind that the CCRA may enter any place where records are kept in connection with your business or employment to conduct investigations. If the records are kept in your place of dwelling, the auditors need permission from you or must obtain a court-issued warrant.
- You are required to assist the auditor by providing all requested information and answering all questions pertaining to the audit.
- There is no client–solicitor confidentiality protection between an individual and his or her accountants. The CCRA can demand information from third parties.
- If an audit becomes a criminal investigation, you must be read your rights — and it's recommended that you seek legal representation.
- To satisfy debts, the CCRA can force the seizure and sale of personal property or garnish payments owed to you.

This brief list of things to know about a CCRA audit is only the tip of the iceberg when it comes to the powers that can be wielded. Believe it or not, in comparison to the IRS in the United States, the CCRA has far greater power and reach to enforce the tax law and collect outstanding amounts!

Verification audits

These audits take place within the CCRA. The primary focus of these reviews is to compare your tax return against information already on hand at the CCRA. This is where your T4 is matched against the T4 filed by your employer.

Non-filer audits

This audit attempts to identify non-filers by matching past returns to the current year. This group also compares information produced by employers and institutions against filed returns to make sure everyone getting T4s, T5s, or UIC is filing tax returns.

Benefit audits

A benefits audit involves checking to see that the benefits recorded on your T4s or other documents are calculated correctly.

Office examinations

These audits examine the deductions and expenses claimed by comparing the amount on the tax return with the receipts or supporting documentation provided by the taxpayer. Of particular interest to these auditors are individuals with rental income, farmers and fishermen, individuals with commission income, or individuals involved in other commercial activities that have a history of noncompliance. These initial reviews attempt to identify areas of noncompliance or systemic problems so that they can be addressed before too much damage is done. Another benefit of this early work is the detection of noncompliance related to variables such as income type or deduction categories. The CCRA uses this knowledge to prepare a profile of high-risk returns that are likely to have noncompliance problems. Finally, this early analysis creates leads that will be passed on to the next level of audit.

Desk audits

Desk audits are the traditional audits with which people are most familiar. These audits are done from the local Tax Services Office and usually result from a lead from previous reviews. This audit is conducted after your return has been assessed and usually focuses on a few specific areas, such as rental income or deductions for travel expenses.

If you make a request to change a return that has already been filed, the return can be sent to audit for review. Before making such a request, be sure that the return does not contain other errors that will be negatively reassessed if caught by the auditor. Also, make sure that your request is well researched and in accordance with the law. If the initial processor does not understand the request, or it is unclear, the return will be sent to audit for follow-up. During a desk audit, you will receive letters asking for support for deductions or verification of income. If you e-filed your return, typical requests are for RRSP deduction slips or proof of travels expenses. If the auditor is satisfied that his or her questions have been fully answered and adequate support has been provided where needed, the audit will usually end. If, on the other hand, problems arise, the auditor is likely to expand the scope of the audit and look into other areas of the return.

In general, most desk audits are concerned with employee business expenses, rental income, business income and deductions, child care, and interest expenses.

If you send information to an auditor either through the mail or in person, be sure you make copies. Sometimes important documents go missing, and if you can't support your claims you will probably be reassessed.

Field audits

These are the most comprehensive audits and are usually reserved for business or complex individual returns. A field audit involves an auditor coming to your home or business to do the examination in person. Field audits are not simply big desk audits. They involve numerous audit techniques and have a focus distinct from other audits. Usually, several years are audited at once. The standard audit starts by looking at two consecutive years. If the results indicate problems, the audit can be expanded to encompass all years that are not already statute barred. If fraud or willful negligence is discovered, all years can be opened for examination.

A field auditor is looking not only at your books, but also examining more intrinsic things such as your lifestyle or evidence that all income might not be reported. You'll also find that a field auditor will be your best audience when it comes to conversations. You see, field auditors are very interested in what the taxpayers say. Very often nervous taxpayers unintentionally betray elaborate tax avoidance schemes during a seemingly innocent conversation. Field audits are not limited to a narrow focus. A field audit could ask you to verify any amount or any numbers in your tax return. This audit is an intense in-depth review of any and all transactions that make up your financial statements and tax return.

If you find yourself fallen victim to a field audit, try to control the flow of information to the auditor. Rather than give the auditors access to all the records, it's best to position the auditors away from the records and make them ask you for the information they require. This will prevent them from going through everything without your knowledge. By supplying the records as required, you are aware of the potential issues that might arise.

Make sure your records are well organized and easy to understand. The easier it is for the auditor, the sooner the audit will end.

Once the audit is complete, you will receive one of two letters. If you're very lucky, you'll receive a letter indicating that no changes were made and that the audit is complete. However, it's more realistic that you'll receive a letter outlining the auditor's proposed adjustments. After you receive the letter, you'll have 30 days to respond if you want to make representations regarding the proposal. If you make no representations, the next letter you receive will be your Notice of Reassessment. If you disagree with the proposals, now is the best time to object — before the reassessment is done.

If you feel you are not getting anywhere with the auditor, ask to meet with the auditor's supervisor. The supervisor has more experience and can usually deal with your concerns. It is always best to deal with your objections or concerns at this proposal stage rather than after the reassessment, when the burden of proof moves from the CCRA to you (see Chapter 22).

Avoiding an Audit

By far the best way to deal with an audit is to avoid it. However, to avoid an audit, you have to know how returns are selected for audit in the first place. The CCRA uses three methods to select returns for audit. The first method is the scoring method. The CCRA scores each return using criteria such as types of income and deductions and the dollar amount involved. When the scores reach a certain amount, the file is pulled for review. If the review indicates the likelihood that an error has occurred, and the dollar amounts are high enough, the return will be sent to audit. Returns are also selected for audit as a result of errors detected on initial processing or the inclusion of the return in a special project (see below for details).

Scoring your return

Years of experience have allowed the CCRA to identify streams of income or deductions that are more likely to contain errors or misrepresentations. By knowing these areas, you will be better able to avoid initiating an audit. Basically, the CCRA divides potential problem areas into the following three main categories:

- Underreported income
- Overstated deductions
- Non-filers.

Underreporting income

Underreported income is one of the most common errors encountered by the CCRA. This section breaks the problem down into the areas of most frequent occurrence to examine them in more detail.

Income from self-employment

Income from self-employment has been identified as one of the primary areas where underreported income occurs. In the past five years, the CCRA estimates that only about 85 percent of income earned through self-employment is reported. The primary areas that traditionally underreport income are building contractors, automobile repair businesses, restaurants, and wholesale businesses. The reason for the low reporting is that these are primarily cash businesses, so it is relatively easy for them to offer customers special prices for cash sales.

Remember that the CCRA and the various provincial tax ministries have over 100,000 employees Canadawide. And it is very common for these people to report individuals who unknowingly offer them the no tax, cash payment option. If you are in this business you may have already been reported and it is only a matter of time until the audits begin. Knowing as it does that these areas have problems in income reporting, the CCRA carefully examines these returns for signs of trouble. Individual returns are compared to industry averages, and suppliers are contacted and asked to provide listing of sales that are then compared to reported incomes of their customers. The CCRA has also initiated special groups within each district office to combat this underground economy. These groups tend to focus on specific industries and become familiar with some of the more common tricks of the trade.

The most powerful tool that the CCRA currently employs to combat income underreporting is the net worth assessment. Basically, the CCRA values all your assets and asks you to show how they were purchased. If you are unable to show that the money was earned, inherited, or gifted to you, the CCRA assumes that you purchased the items with unreported income. And you know what unreported income means — you're right: interest and penalties. In this case, the penalties are usually double or triple the amount owed. Once the CCRA has made this assessment, the onus is on you to go to appeals and prove, if you can, that these assets were *not* purchased with unreported income.

Telling the auditor that this additional money was given to you by relatives overseas is the defence most often heard during net worth assessments. Unfortunately, the CCRA has adopted a policy that requires you to show them indisputable proof of this payment. So, unless you have a bank statement showing the money coming into your account and your overseas relative can provide proof that they sent the money, this defence will not be accepted. The best way to avoid an audit is to report all your income and keep accurate records.

Contrary to popular belief, inaccurate records work against you because they allow the auditor to pick an amount they believe represents your income. After the auditor has finished the assessment, you're left with the burden of disproving the income inclusion — with few records to support you.

Rental income

Another area that attracts the CCRA's eye is rental losses. The primary concern for the government is that rental losses are used to offset other forms of income, particularly employment income. The CCRA monitors the losses reported by taxpayers each year. The first time a return shows a rental loss, the computer marks the return for future review. A second loss moves the return up the priority list. A third loss will cause the return to be removed for review. If the file is selected for audit, the auditor will initially try to verify the income and expenses associated with the property. If the income and expenses appear legitimate and can be supported, the auditor may then assert that this rental business has no reasonable expectation of profit, which is a critical assumption of all business. You see, if the CCRA doesn't believe that you have a reasonable expectation of profit, it views you as not having a business at all. Since no business exists, your losses will be denied and you must pay the back tax, plus interest and penalties.

If you own rental property, it's not wise to have continuous losses year after year. The CCRA will allow you start-up losses as with any business, but within two years of start-up, the rental business should start establishing a record of profitability, even if it is very small.

Investment income

If you own shares, bonds, bank deposits, annuities, mutual funds, mortgages, and other debt or ownership instruments, chances are that you have investment income. Investment income includes interest, dividends, capital gains, and royalties. This type of income is generally reported on a T5 or T3 slip. The reason the CCRA is interested in investment income is that it knows taxpayers avoid reporting certain types of investment income. Areas scrutinized by the CCRA include the following:

- Foreign income
- Income from tax shelters or limited partnerships
- Gain or losses on disposal of investments.

The federal government has introduced new legislation in recent years to try to combat potential underreporting of income.

Foreign Income: In 1998, taxpayers with foreign holdings were required to report all these holdings on forms T1135 "Foreign Property Holdings" and/or T1141 "Transfers and Loans to Foreign Trusts." These forms are intended to capture all offshore investments, transfers, and income.

Make sure you fill out forms T1135 and T1141 as completely as possible — since the fines for not reporting or incorrectly reporting are substantial. The fines for failure to file the T1135 or T1141 are $25 a day, up to a maximum of $2,500. If the CCRA issues a filing demand, and you choose not to comply, the fine is $500 per month up to a maximum of $12,000. The CCRA will double the fine if it has to issue a second demand. False statements or omissions get an additional fine of the greater of $24,000 or 5 percent of all the amounts that should have been reported.

If you receive distributions from off-shore trusts, or if you have beneficial interest in an off-shore trust or estate, disclose this on forms T1135 and T1141.

Tax Shelters: Tax shelters are becoming a thing of the past. The CCRA is actively shutting down most of the loopholes that have allowed tax shelters to exist. Likewise, the at-risk rules have limited the effectiveness of limited partnerships.

Capital Gains and Losses: Gains or losses on share dispositions are not directly reported to the CCRA. To combat this potential loss of income, the CCRA runs special projects to identify all holders of particular investments and then examine their returns to see how transactions are being recorded.

Investment gains and losses are tracked by the CCRA and accumulated in the cumulative net investment loss account (CNIL). If you claim the capital gains exemption on qualified small business shares or qualified farm property, a negative CNIL account will reduce the exemption you can claim (see Chapter 17 for more details).

Non-residents earning income in Canada

The risk is that non-residents earning income in Canada will gladly accept their money and then leave the country without paying tax. To combat this situation, the CCRA places the onus of paying this tax on the payer and not the receiver. Companies employing people like this are required to withhold tax on the pay to these people at the high rate. If the receiver wants to reduce this rate, he or she must file a T1 in Canada and request a refund.

Overstated deductions

As with understated income, the CCRA has traced errors in deductions over many years and compiled a list of some of the most common errors:

- Moving expenses — 50-percent error rate.
- Amounts for infirm dependants — 40-percent error rate.
- Child care expenses and northern residents deduction — 30-percent error rate.
- Education amounts, medical expenses, and tuition fees — 20-percent error rate.
- Equivalent to spouse, and charitable donations — 15-percent error rate.
- Political donations, and amounts transferred from spouse — 8-percent error rate.

Knowing the error rates, the CCRA factors in the amount of the deduction and determines if a particular return meets the criteria for examination. It is safe to say that high dollar amounts or deductions that reduce a significant amount of the taxpayer's income will often be removed from processing for a closer look.

If you are claiming any of the above deductions, check the calculations, make sure that they are done correctly, and see that all the supporting documentation is attached and easy to review. This will reduce the risk of your return being held for audit.

Non-filers

Many taxpayers are under the mistaken belief that by not filing a return they will never be selected for audit. The fact is, the CCRA has entire groups within each Tax Services Office that do nothing but look for non-filers. The search begins by cross-checking social insurance numbers with filed returns. This group also cross-checks T slips against returns filed. On occasion, even driver's licences can be cross-checked against returns filed.

Eventually, all non-filers get caught, and penalties and interest charges are applied to outstanding amounts.

If you have not filed, and the CCRA is not actively pursuing you to file, consider making a voluntary disclosure. By voluntarily coming forward and providing tax returns, you can avoid late filing penalties, and occasionally interest. See the upcoming sections "Making an Application for Fairness" and "Voluntary Disclosures" for more details.

Initial processing errors

Often an audit is triggered by processing errors found when the computer initially tries to assess your return. Examples of these errors include the following:

- Your return has no social insurance number
- The social insurance number provided is incorrect or belongs to someone else
- The T slips are missing or do not match the slips sent in by your employer or other source.

Basically, these errors are fundamental errors that stop the computer from processing your return and cause it to be removed and examined. These errors are usually very avoidable, and can be eliminated by your carefully preparing your return or reviewing the return prepared for you by someone else.

Special projects

An example of a special project is the underground economy project, in which the CCRA auditors go out looking for individuals who claim little or no income in specific areas of the economy (construction, home renovation, jewelry). Other special projects are the examination of all returns claiming deductions from tax shelter schemes. Usually these projects are aimed at perceived abuses or loopholes in the tax system.

Avoid situations that promote tax avoidance or evasion as a primary motivation. These areas are usually under close scrutiny by government agencies and often result in audits of the participants. Cash or under the table transactions in the auto repair or home renovation industries are currently of particular interest to the CCRA.

Here Comes the Judge

As was mentioned in the previous chapter, the Appeals Division is the last level of recourse within the CCRA. If you continue to disagree with the decision, your next step is Tax Court. To proceed to tax court, you must have filled a timely Notice of Objection to your original assessment (see Chapter 22). If this was the case, then your appeal to the court must be filed either:

- within 90 days of the date of mailing of the confirmation of assessment or the reassessment to the Notice of Objection; or
- after 90 days have passed since you filed the Notice of Objection if you have not received a confirmation of assessment or reassessment from the CCRA appeals division.

If you fail to file an objection as required, you lose your right of appeal. The Tax Court has two divisions, Informal and General. If the amount of tax in dispute is less than $12,000 or $24,000 of losses in dispute, you can choose to have your case heard in the Informal division. If the amount of tax owed is more than $12,000 or $24,000 of losses in dispute, you must proceed to the General division.

Informal division hearings

Under the Informal procedures, the taxpayer need not be represented by a lawyer. You may appear on your own or be assisted by a lawyer, accountant, or advisor. This court does not necessarily follow the "normal" rules of evidence and procedure, nor are decisions precedent-setting. The decisions of this court are required to be quick and are usually delivered within a year of your appeal. If you want to appeal a decision of this court, you are limited to issues of law or gross error, and must apply for a "judicial review" before the Federal Court of Appeal.

If you go to Tax Court using the informal division, it is advisable that you seek the advice of an experienced tax professional (although you are not required to do so). The expert's advice can better prepare you for the proceedings and help you to avoid costly errors that could jeopardize your case.

General division hearings

General division is a formal court proceeding, and lawyers are required. These cases will involve all the usual aspects of a trial in provincial court. You can only appeal the decisions of these cases to the Federal Court of Appeal on issues of fact and law. As is the case in most formal court proceedings, the time involved can be several years from the initiation of the process until a decision is made. The amount of money involved is also substantial, with the added downside that you could end up paying the court costs if the decision goes against you. Beyond Tax Court, cases heard in the General division can be appealed to the Federal Court of Appeal and eventually to the Supreme Court of Canada — but only if leave to appeal is granted by the justices of the Supreme Court.

Obtain form TLA7 "Appealing to the Tax Court" from your local Tax Services Office if you intend to appeal to the Tax Court. It will clearly explain your options and time constraints.

Making an Application for Fairness

Within each Tax Services Office there exists a committee responsible for reviewing taxpayers requests to do the following:

- Waive penalties and interest on assessment
- Accept late, amended, or revoked elections
- Allow refunds beyond the normal three-year period.

Adjustments to returns are made for compelling reasons on compassionate or equitable grounds, or for circumstances beyond the control of the taxpayer. Examples would include serious illness or accident, incorrect information supplied to you by the CCRA in a written form, a natural disaster, strike, or civil disobedience. In the case of late-filed elections, the CCRA is also willing to accept honest mistakes as a legitimate reason for filing incorrectly.

Visit the CCRA's Web site at `www.ccra-adrc.gc.ca` to get a copy of information circulars IC 92-1 "Guidelines for Accepting Late, Amended or Revoked Elections," IC 92-2 "Guidelines for Cancellation and Waiver of Interest and Penalties," and IC 92-3 "Guidelines for Refunds Beyond the Normal Three-Year Period." These guidelines will help you to better understand the situations where fairness may be applied. In addition to the above factors, the Fairness committee wants to see that the taxpayer has made every effort to minimize or correct the errors where possible. It will also check the individual's history with the department to ensure that there are no problems related to evasive or criminal behaviour. To submit an application for fairness, you must make the request in writing and give all the reasons and details supporting the request. Send this request to the attention of the director of the local Tax Services Office.

Voluntary Disclosures

If you have never filed a return, or you sent a return that was incomplete or incorrect, or you stopped filing returns for two or more years, a voluntary disclosure could help you out of this situation. As you recall from the previous chapter, late returns and false or incomplete information can attract heavy penalties. To avoid these penalties, you can voluntarily come forward and provide the missing information. Under these circumstances, the CCRA will always waive penalties if you tell them before they catch you, and you will only be responsible for paying the tax you owe and any associated interest. Here are the CCRA's only stipulations:

- You must provide full and complete information. If you intentionally provide incomplete information, the CCRA will not consider this a voluntary disclosure and will assess penalties.
- The CCRA must not have requested the information or started an action against you prior to the voluntary disclosure. If the CCRA has already requested the information, or if an audit has been initiated, it is not considered a voluntary disclosure.

Tax Evasion

The term *tax evasion* is usually associated with knowingly falsifying or omitting information in an attempt to artificially understate tax owing. Evasion also includes gross negligence or intentionally allowing a misstatement of information to be presented in your tax return (see Chapter 22 for more details). The key to evasion is a willful attempt to misrepresent or deceive. Information circular IC 73-10R3 "Tax Evasion" outlines the penalties for tax evasion — and these should not be taken lightly! Generally, the fine for tax evasion is 50 percent of the tax avoided, plus interest calculated from the day the return was due. In addition to the above penalties, tax evasion also carries criminal consequences: jail time of up to five years and additional fines of up to 200 percent of the evaded tax. It is important not to confuse tax evasion with tax planning or tax avoidance. According to the Declaration of Taxpayer's Rights, it is not illegal for you to reduce your tax payable to the minimum under the law. So where is the line that divides evasion from avoidance or tax planning?

Tax Avoidance

Tax avoidance is a situation in which a taxpayer has legally circumvented the law by using an elaborate web of multiple transactions or schemes that distort the truth and result in reduced or eliminated tax payable. Since the net result is a violation of the spirit or intent of the law, the CCRA routinely challenges these transactions. This can be done by attacking aspects of the plan that the CCRA considers legally vulnerable or by lobbying the government to change or alter legislation. Even though these transactions are not illegal, you risk having your returns reassessed when the CCRA finds a way to attack the plan. These reassessments usually carry interest charges dating back to your original involvement in the plan.

Tax Planning

This is simply the process of reducing tax by using legal means that do not violate the spirit or intent of the law. In an attempt to better prevent tax avoidance schemes, the Department of Finance introduced section 245 to the *Income Tax Act.* Section 245 is the General Anti-Avoidance Rule (GAAR). The legislation's intention is to give the CCRA a tool that it can use against any and all tax avoidance schemes. The CCRA only has to prove that tax avoidance was the primary thrust of any transaction, and GAAR is the legislative support to reassess the scheme. Unfortunately, the fine line between tax avoidance and tax planning, plus the generalized wording of this section, have made it difficult to apply. Only recently has the CCRA had any success in using GAAR. The success rate will increase as more cases are brought to court, and precedents are established.

Tax avoidance and evasion techniques never pay in the end. It is always easier to play by the rules and avoid costly audits and reassessments.

Part VI
Tax Planning Tips

"I set up everything for you to do your taxes. I put out your calculator, plenty of pencils, and a large morphine drip."

In this part . . .

So you've filed your tax return, and managed not to win the CCRA's random lottery (or so far, at least). Does this mean that you're through with your taxes for another year? Well, that's really up to you, but we recommend that tax planning be a year-round activity. After all, a day without tax planning is like a day without sunshine. Well, maybe not quite, but how many of you find yourselves in shock come April each year, horrified that your tax bill is enough for a down payment on a house?

To avoid the April shock, it's best to think about your taxes every time something big happens in your life. This part will give you some handy pointers to save tax (and a headache) when it comes to income-splitting with your family, planning for your estate, retirement, owning your own business, or delving into the world of investments. So read on to learn how you can keep more money in your pockets come April.

"I believe we should all pay our tax bill with a smile. I tried but they wanted cash."

— Anonymous

Chapter 24

Income Splitting with Your Family

In This Chapter

- Understanding income splitting — why bother?
- Reviewing the attribution rules
- Identifying the best ways to split income

So first things first — what is income splitting? Income splitting involves shifting income from the hands of one individual who pays tax at a high rate to another who will pay tax at a lower rate. For example, if a husband gives money to his wife for investment purposes, and the wife is taxed at a lower tax rate than the husband, income splitting is achieved if the investment income can be taxed in the hands of the wife as opposed to the husband. The tax savings from income splitting can be substantial. In this chapter you will learn how you can save your family real tax dollars by splitting your income with your spouse or children. We'll also give you ideas of how you can income split with your family, and manage to avoid the dreaded attribution rules.

Income Splitting in Action

Let's look at an example. Rick lives in Ontario and currently earns $60,000 per year. Of this $60,000, the taxman comes along and takes about $15,500. *Ouch!* But suppose both Rick and his wife Faye work and each bring home $30,000. The total family income stays the same, but the taxman's cut is greatly reduced. In this case, the total family tax bill is just $11,000 — a tax saving of $4,500. Why the tax saving? Well, when Rick and Faye each earned $30,000, every dollar earned was taxed at the low rate of about 22 percent. However, when Rick was the sole income-earner, every dollar earned in excess of $30,004 was taxed at a higher marginal rate — almost 36 percent, in fact. This higher tax rate naturally results in a higher tax bill.

Every Game Has Its Rules

Splitting income sounds really easy and straightforward, right? Wrong! If a tax strategy makes big promises, and is easy to do, you're in for a disappointment because it probably won't work. And just to prove this theory holds true the CCRA came in and rained on everyone's parade by introducing the attribution rules. If you're looking for some light reading (huh!) the attribution rules can be found in section 74.1 of the *Income Tax Act.* Fortunately for those who don't require any leisure reading, we'll present a summary of how the attribution rules work. These rules state that if you try to pass income-producing property (for example, property that earns dividends, interest, rents, and royalties) to your spouse, or to a child, grandchild, in-law, niece, or nephew under the age of 18, *you* — not they — will be taxed on the income earned on this property.

Notice that capital gains are not included in the list of income that gets caught under these rules. Although capital gains from property transferred to a spouse will be subject to attribution rules, capital gains earned in the hands of a minor child are not subject to the attribution. This means that it is possible to split income with a minor child by having the child place the funds in investments that will primarily earn capital gains. Does this mean that the days of income splitting are over? Of course not. Remember, we said that the attribution rules made this more difficult, but not impossible. Here are some ways to sidestep the rules, and still reap the benefits of tax savings!

Transfers to a spouse

If you gift, or loan money to your spouse, here's how the attribution rules will impact you:

- **Gift money.** Attribute all investment income (interest, dividends, rents, and royalties) and capital gains back to transferor.
- **Loan money with no interest.** Attribute all investment income (interest, dividends, rents, and royalties) and capital gains back to transferor.
- **Loan money with interest.** No attribution if interest is charged at the lower of lending rate or the CCRA prescribed rate, and paid by January 30.

Transfers to minor children

If you're thinking of gifting or loaning money to a minor child, be sure to check this list, to make sure you don't get caught by the attribution rules:

- **Gift money.** Attribute all investment income, but not capital gains, back to transferor.
- **Loan money with no interest.** Attribute all investment income, but not capital gains, back to transferor.
- **Loan money with interest.** No attribution if interest is charged at lower of the lending rate or the CCRA prescribed rate, and paid by January 30.

Transfer to an adult child

The attribution rules provide you with a little slack when you give or loan money to an adult child. However, some income is still caught under the rules, so check out the list below:

- **Gift money.** No attribution.
- **Loan with no interest.** Attribute all investment income and capital gains if loan is made specifically to avoid tax.
- **Loan money with interest.** No attribution if interest is charged at the lower of the lending rate and the CCRA prescribed rate, and paid by January 30.

Ideas for Splitting Income

Now that you understand what income splitting is, and why it is important, here are a few ideas of how you can minimize your family's total tax bill and manage to side-step the attribution rules.

Lend money or investments to a family member

You may loan money to a minor child or a spouse to be used for investment purposes — but as with everything, there's a catch. You see, interest-free loans or even low-interest loans won't cut it. To avoid the attribution rules, you must charge interest on the loan at the CCRA's prescribed rate, or the current commercial rate (you should choose whichever rate is lower). The interest must be paid to you by January 30 every year, and must be included in your income. Your family member can deduct this interest from the income he or she earns on the investment.

The CCRA announces the prescribed rates every quarter. The rates can be found on their Web site at `www.ccra-adrc.gc.ca`. At the time of writing, the prescribed rate on non–arm's length loans was 6 percent.

Consider Julie, who wants to transfer some income to her husband, Jim, because he is in a lower tax bracket. She knows that she can't give him money, so she decides to loan him $100,000 at 6-percent interest. Jim takes this money, invests it, and in the first year earns $8,000. If Jim pays Julie $6,000 in interest in January, he can report the $8,000 on his tax return — saving her from reporting it on hers. As well, he can deduct the $6,000 paid to Julie, so his total income is just $2,000. Julie must report the $6,000 interest in her income. If your head is spinning, here's the end result. Julie managed to transfer $2,000 of her income to Jim, who will pay tax at a lower rate.

You'll only manage to split income if your investments earn a rate of return higher than the prescribed rate set by the CCRA.

When a family member borrows money to invest, make sure that a higher-income family member doesn't guarantee the loan or give the borrower funds to make the repayment. The attribution rules will apply, causing any income earned on these borrowed funds to be taxed in the hands of the person guaranteeing the loan or providing the funds to make repayments.

You may loan money without charging interest to related adults (that is, individuals over the age of 18), as long as you're not lending the funds only to split income and reduce taxes. This means, for example, that you may lend money to an adult child to be used for school or a trip.

Split tax on CPP payments

You know how it works when you're married: "What's mine is yours, and what's yours is mine." Well the same holds true for CPP payments. You see, if both you and your spouse are over age 60, you're allowed to share up to 50 percent of your CPP payments. Since a portion of your payments will now be directed to your spouse, this means less income for you to report. If your spouse is in a lower tax bracket, it means tax savings!

The assignment of a retirement pension plan redistributes a couple's CPP retirement pension or pensions. It does not increase or decrease the overall pension paid. You can't just arbitrarily decide how much of your pension you'd like your spouse to pay. We're dealing with the CCRA, remember? That means there's a formula to determine how much you can split. The amount that can be split is based on the length of time you and your spouse have been together as a percentage of your total contributory period, to a maximum of 50 percent. The following examples explain how it works.

Mark and Jane have been living together since 1967. Jane has never worked outside the home. Mark's CPP payment is $800 per month. After Jane completes the application for assignment, they will each began to receive $400 per month.

Sandra and Keith have been married since 1980. Keith's monthly CPP payment is $400. He earned $100 of pension before he and Sandra were married and the other $300 after they were married. Sandra's monthly pension is $550. Sandra did not work prior to her relationship with Keith.

Keith submitted an application to split CCP payments with his wife. Sandra and Keith have earned $850 in CPP payments since they've been married. One half of this amount is $425. Therefore, Keith will receive the $100 he earned prior to his marriage, plus one-half of the money he and Sandra earned while together, for a total of $525. Since Sandra did not earn any CPP benefits prior to her marriage, she will receive $425 per month after the application is approved.

Both these examples show how the spouse earning higher CPP payments can transfer a portion of these payments to the lower-income spouse in order to have the payments taxed in his or her hands.

You should apply to split CPP payments with your spouse if you're both over age 60, your CPP payments are higher than your spouse's, and you are in a higher tax bracket.

Your pension-sharing arrangement will end 12 months after you separate from your spouse, the month you divorce, the month of death of you or your spouse, or when you ask for the assignment to stop.

For further information about assigning pension benefits to your spouse, contact Human Resources Development Canada at 1-800-277-9914 or visit its Web site at `www.hrdc-drhc.gc.ca`.

Pay salary or wages to family

If you have your own business, consider paying a salary or wage to members of your family. Of course, they must actually work in the business (and no, you won't get away with paying your four-year-old son to colour pictures you use for advertising). And the salary you pay them must be reasonable for the work they do.

The advantage to this is that you can claim the amount paid as a deduction on your business statement, so your taxable income is reduced. On the flip side, the family member includes this amount in his or her income. You can pay a child that has no other source of income up to $7,123 in 2000 without generating a tax bill for that child. Assuming your marginal tax rate is 50 percent, that's a savings of $3,500 in tax!

By paying your child or spouse a salary, you'll generate earned income in their hands. This gives rise to valuable RRSP contribution room. Make sure you read Chapter 28 on the benefits of contributing to an RRSP early.

Transfer money for business purposes

You can either give or lend money to family members to be used in a business, and thereby avoid the dreaded attribution rules. Even if it's a loan, there's no need to charge interest. Since the funds will earn business income and not income from property, you'll avoid having the income come back to be taxed in your hands.

Your investment may be protected if the business goes sour. The company you invest in must be a Canadian-controlled private corporation, and at least 90 percent of the assets must be used in active business that operates primarily in Canada. If the business takes a downturn and you won't recover your loan, you may be eligible to claim an allowable business investment loss on your tax return. See Chapter 16 for more details on allowable business investment losses.

Pay an allowance to a working child

If you're paying your child an allowance for work around the house, don't stop paying once your child starts working. We know, you're probably thinking, "Why should I pay them, if they have their own spending money?" Here's why: Paying your child an allowance will free up their earnings for investment. When they invest their own income, the attribution rules won't apply and you effectively will have split income.

Another option is to lend money to your adult child, interest free, to help pay for school. Suppose you have a daughter who attends university and earns $8,000 over the summer. In prior years she has used her income from the summer to help pay for school and books. Instead, consider lending her the $8,000 to help pay for school. She can then invest the money she made over the summer. Since the investment represents her own money, any income earned will not be attributed back to you, and will be taxed at her marginal rate (or not taxed at all, if her income is low enough). When she graduates, she can pay the loan off using the funds she's invested.

Higher-income spouse should pay the household expenses

Another way to get more funds into the hands of the lower-income spouse is to have the higher-income spouse pay all the daily living expenses. This includes groceries, mortgage or rent payments, credit card bills, and so on. This frees up more cash in the hands of the lower-income spouse to earn income that is taxed at the low rate.

Similarly, another way to transfer funds is for you to pay the income tax liability and instalments of your spouse. Since the amount you pay is paid directly to the CCRA and is not invested by your spouse, the attribution rules won't apply. This means any funds your spouse would have used to pay the liability are now free to be used for investment purposes.

Invest Child Tax Benefits in the child's name

The government pays Child Tax Benefits monthly to qualifying families until their children reach 18 years of age. These benefit payments can be invested in your child's name and earn any type of income without the attribution rules kicking in.

Make sure these funds are deposited directly into an investment account for your child. Keep them separate from other funds that you may have given your child previously, because the attribution rules still apply to these gifted funds.

Before opening an investment account, obtain a social insurance number for your child. Having your child's name directly on the account will help avoid any confusion with the taxman when it comes time to report the income on your child's tax return.

Contribute to a spousal RRSP

The optimum goal is for spouses to have equal incomes during retirement. This will accomplish perfect income splitting and keep the total family tax bill to a minimum. To make this happen, the higher-income spouse may have to make contributions, in advance, to his or her spouse's RRSP. Spousal RRSP contributions work like this: You contribute to an RRSP under which your spouse is the annuitant. This simply means that your spouse will withdraw funds from the RRSP in the future and pay tax on the withdrawals. Although your spouse withdraws the funds, you are entitled to the deduction when the money is put into the fund. Talk about shifting income from one spouse to the other!

Your spouse must keep the funds inside the RRSP for a minimum number of years, or else the withdrawal is taxed in your hands. Don't take funds out if the contribution was made in that same year, or in either of the two previous years. Wait until the third calendar year after your last contribution to withdraw the funds.

Suppose you contributed $4,000 to a spousal RRSP in 1999, and your spouse withdrew $5,000 from the plan in 2001. The first $4,000 would be taxed in your hands since that amount can be attributed to contributions you made in the year of withdrawal or the previous two years. Only the remaining $1,000 would be taxed in your spouse's hands.

Make a spousal contribution on December 31. You'll then only have to wait two years plus one day to begin making withdrawals.

Say you make your contribution on December 31, 2000. Your first withdrawal can be as early as January 1, 2003, and you can still avoid the attribution rules! You see, you will not have made a contribution in the year of withdrawal (2003) or in either of the two preceding years (2001, 2002). If you had made your contribution even one day later, your spouse would have to wait an extra year to make a withdrawal.

Contribute to an RESP

Registered education savings plans (RESPs) are used to help build an education fund for your child or grandchild. But did you realize that RESPs are a great way to income split with your family?

Although contributions made to an RESP are not tax deductible like contributions to an RRSP, they do grow tax-free. This doesn't mean they are never taxed, but as with an RRSP, you won't be taxed on any of the income earned in the plan. And what's more, when the funds are taken out for educational purposes, you won't be the one to foot the tax bill. You see, the income earned in the plan is taxed in the child's hands, not yours. As a student, that child will probably have minimal income and will be eligible for the education and tuition credit, and therefore won't likely pay tax.

Did you catch the income splitting implications? By setting up an RESP, you can essentially give funds to your child to be used for education, and all the income earned on those funds is taxed later in your child's hands.

Not all RESPs are created equal. You can choose either a family plan or an individual plan. Depending on your circumstances one may be better suited to you than the other. Be sure to talk to your advisor to determine what type of plan is best for you.

The scoop on RESPS

Here, in a handy sidebar no less, is a summary of all the fast facts you need to know about Registered Education Savings Plans.

- The maximum amount of contributions that can be made to an RESP for any one beneficiary is $4,000 per year.
- There is an overall lifetime contribution of $42,000 per beneficiary.
- If you contribute less than $4,000 in one year, you can't carry forward the unused room and then contribute more than $4,000 the next year.
- The government provides a direct grant to the RESP worth 20 percent of the first $2,000 of contributions made to the plan each year. The grant is worth $400 per beneficiary under the age of 18.
- Entitlement to the grant may be carried forward to a later year if the $2,000 contribution is not made. The maximum grant per beneficiary is capped at $800 (20 percent of the maximum annual contribution of $4,000).
- Contributions can be withdrawn from the plan tax-free. However, income cannot be withdrawn tax-free.
- Students attending post-secondary education can withdraw funds from the plan to pay for living and educational expenses. These withdrawals are taxed in the student's hands.
- There may be penalties to pay if the student does not attend post-secondary education.

Chapter 25

Taxes and Estate Planning

In This Chapter

- Grasping the basics of planning your estate
- Working to minimize the effect of death on your tax bill
- Deciding how to leave assets to your spouse
- Making use of your RRSP — and those of family members
- Leaving your assets to charity

Probably the last thing anyone wants to think about is their own death. It really is a morbid subject. However, avoiding the unavoidable can cost you — or the friends and family you leave behind — money. You see, death can have some pretty severe tax consequences. And depending on what province you live in, you may also have probate fees to contend with. In this chapter we will work through the issues that influence your estate plan, let you know what types of taxes may apply when you die, and offer some valuable tips on how to minimize taxes and probate fees when you pass away.

The Big Wide World of Estate Planning

Estate planning involves a wide variety of issues including the following:

- Minimizing taxes and probate fees on death
- Minimizing the tax hit to the beneficiaries of your estate
- Planning ways to cover a tax liability on death
- Ensuring an efficient transfer of your assets to your intended heirs
- Business succession planning
- Ensuring your family's needs will be met after you're gone.

Even if your affairs are not overly complicated, estate planning is important. You should visit a lawyer to ensure that you have an up-to-date will, and a tax professional to ensure that you take full advantage of tax planning opportunities. The money your heirs will save, and the headaches that will be avoided, will be well worth the cost.

Do I need to plan my estate?

How do you know when your affairs are complicated enough to require estate planning? Here are the top 10 reasons Canadians need estate planning help:

- You own assets that have appreciated in value since they've been acquired.
- You do not intend to leave all your assets to your spouse on death.

- You live in a province or territory where probate fees apply.
- You own your own business.
- Your family depends on your income for support.
- You have a young family or other dependants (such as a disabled child) and are concerned about their well-being after your death.
- You own assets in a country other than Canada.
- You are concerned about leaving as much of your estate as possible to your heirs, and not the government.
- You are concerned about the tax burden on your heirs after your death.
- You want to minimize family squabbles after you're gone.

Some of these concerns are easy to address. In fact, you can deal with some of these items on your own with the help of this chapter. Others, however, require a little more thought. And this probably means getting help from a tax professional, lawyer, financial advisor, or insurance expert.

The importance of having a will

A properly drafted will is one of the most important estate planning tools you can have, for both tax and non-tax reasons. Carefully worded, the will can accomplish the following:

- Prevent family disagreements about who will inherit your assets.
- Ensure your assets are distributed to your intended heirs. If a will doesn't exist, your assets will be distributed according to provincial law.
- Ensure that the executor of your choice will handle your estate. If you don't leave a will, the courts will appoint an administrator — and this person may not have been your first choice!
- Reduce administration costs on death. If you die intestate (without a will), the court will make decisions on your behalf, and charge your estate accordingly.
- Ensure that your dependants are cared and provided for, if you've clearly stated in your will who will be their guardians. A will can also help to ensure funds to be used to support the children are not held up in court.
- See that the executor of your estate is given full powers to take advantage of beneficial tax elections. Many tax elections will be unavailable unless your will specifically states that your executor has the right to use them on your behalf.
- Outline which of your assets will be passed to particular beneficiaries, and therefore help reduce taxes on the transfer of assets (since different types of assets will give rise to tax implications depending on whom they are passed to).
- Allow trusts to be set up on your death. Unless your will specifically allows for this, you'll lose this tax planning opportunity.

Death and Your Tax Bill

As the saying goes, two things are guaranteed in life, death and taxes. And you can be sure the taxman will get his share of taxes when you die. The thought of leaving up to half your estate to the government may not exactly thrill you, but don't worry. There are ways to minimize your taxes on death, and to be sure you leave as much as possible to your heirs.

Before we go into the details on how to minimize your tax exposure on death, we should explain the tax implications of death. Canada does not have estate taxes like that of some other countries (such as the United States). Instead, in Canada you are deemed to have sold all your capital assets at their fair market value immediately before your death. So, even though you haven't actually sold anything and have no proceeds of disposition, you are still considered to have disposed of your assets. This may result in a hefty tax bill if any of your assets have appreciated in value since you purchased them.

For example, Bernadette passed away this year. At the time of her death, she owned stocks with a fair market value of $250,000. The adjusted cost base of these shares was $100,000. Therefore, due to the deemed disposition rules on death, a capital gain of $150,000 ($250,000 less $100,000) will have to be reported on her final tax return.

The implications of this are obvious. You'll be triggering a tax bill, but your heirs may have no funds to pay the bill since no actual proceeds have been received. This means that unless your family has excess cash on hand (perhaps from a life insurance policy), they will have to liquidate some of your estate to pay your final tax bill.

Before you freak out, it's important to note that there are some assets that will not generally give rise to taxes on death, despite the deemed disposition rules. We'll call these tax-friendly assets. If you own these types of assets, you probably won't have to worry about burdening your family with a huge tax bill on death. Here are some tax-friendly assets:

- **Cash and near-cash investments:** Cash and near-cash investments will not generally give rise to a tax liability on death since these assets do not generally appreciate in value. For example, a $10,000 GIC will be deemed to be disposed of at its fair market value, which is, of course, $10,000. As a result, no taxable capital gain arises.
- **Life insurance proceeds:** Death benefits paid on a life insurance policy after the death of the insured are paid on a tax-free basis to the beneficiaries of the policy.

  Make sure you're adequately insured. Since life insurance proceeds are not taxable on your death, these could be an important source of funds to pay your final tax bill. In addition, life insurance can be used to replace your income after your death.
- **Death benefits:** Up to $10,000 of death benefits paid by your employer to your heirs can be paid on a tax-free basis.
- **Principal residence:** The disposition of a principal residence in Canada is typically sheltered from tax through what is known as the principal residence exemption. This exemption is available on death to shelter the gains that might arise from the deemed disposition rules. As a result, the death of a taxpayer does not usually create a tax liability in respect of a principal residence.

  If you own more than one property on the date of death, there could be additional tax to pay because only one property can qualify as your principal residence.
- **QSBC shares and qualified farm property:** Up to $500,000 of capital gains triggered on the disposition of QSBC shares and qualified farm property may be eligible for the capital gains deduction (see Chapter 17). This deduction is also available on death, although due to the stringent criteria that must be met, it is imperative that you contact a tax pro before your death to ensure that the deduction will be available to you.
- **Assets with low or no gains:** This may seem obvious, but if you own assets that have low or no accrued capital gains, the deemed disposition on death may have no tax consequences to speak of. In addition, if you have a number of assets with gains, but others with accrued losses, the two may offset each other, resulting in no tax.
- **Capital losses available for use:** Do you have unused capital losses from other years? Normally, capital losses can be carried forward indefinitely to be applied against any capital gains realized. However, on death the capital losses can be used against other sources of income in the year of death and the immediately preceding year. Where capital losses are available, any capital gains (and therefore taxes!) triggered by the deemed disposition on death may be fully or partially offset.

There are a variety of assets that are subject to the deemed disposition rules on death. If you own any of these items, your estate may have substantial tax liabilities on death: RRSPs and RRIFs, capital assets including shares of public and private companies, mutual fund units, real estate, depreciable assets, bonds, a residence (other than a principal residence), partnership interests, eligible capital property, and so on.

Probate fees

Probate fees are fees that the provincial and territorial probate courts charge to validate your will and authorize the executor to administer your estate. The probate process is not mandatory. That said, there are sometimes statutory reasons for requiring probate, or an interested party (such as a bank that holds the assets) may request it. Each province in Canada, with the exception of Quebec, imposes probate fees on death (in Quebec, there are no probate fees for notarial wills and a nominal fee for English form wills).

The actual probate fees charged vary by province. See Table 25-1 for a summary of these fees, which are based on the fair market value of your estate at the time of death. In some provinces (most notably Ontario and British Columbia) the liability for probate fees could be substantial, while in other provinces, such as Alberta, probate fees are minimal.

Table 25-1 Probate Fees Levied by Province or Territory

Province/Territory	*Fees Charged*
Alberta	Flat charges ranging from $25 for first $10,000 of estate to $6,000 for estates over $1 million
British Columbia	Fees ranging from $0 for estates under $10,000 to 1.4% of the gross value of estates over $50,000
Manitoba	Flat charge of $25 for the first $5,000 of estate and .6% of the gross value of estates over $5,000
New Brunswick	Flat fees of $25 to $100 for the first $20,000 of estate and .5% of the gross value of estates over $20,000
Newfoundland	Flat fee of $80 for the first $1,000 of estate and .5% of gross value of estate plus flat fee of $75 for estates over $1,000
Northwest Territories/ Nunavut	Flat fees of up to $15 for first $1,000 and .3% of gross value of estates over $1,000
Nova Scotia	Flat fees of $75 to $800 for first $200,000 of estate to .5% of gross estates over $200,000
Ontario	.5% of gross estates below $50,000 and 1.5% of gross value of estates over $50,000
Prince Edward Island	Flat fees ranging from $50 to $400 for first $100,000 of estate and .4% of gross estates over $100,000
Quebec	$65 flat fee for English form will
Saskatchewan	.7% of gross value of estate
Yukon	No fees for estates under $10,000, flat fee of $140 for estates of $10,000 to $25,000 and .6% of estates with gross value over $25,000

Minimizing the Taxes You Pay on Death

For those concerned about the potential tax bite on death, there are steps you can take now to minimize the hit. Remember, once you're gone, it's too late for tax planning. So, act now to ensure that your heirs, not the tax authorities, get your assets.

Giving your assets away today

It makes sense that if you don't own assets on death, there is no way to tax you on death. So if you're concerned about the deemed disposition, give your assets away today!

Giving assets away today does not necessarily avoid tax altogether. You see, if you give your assets away now, you are deemed to have disposed of these assets now (instead of on death). So, if you give away assets that have appreciated in value, you'll trigger a tax liability when the gift is made.

The assets most suited to this strategy are those that have not greatly appreciated in value, but which you expect will rise in value in the future. This means that you won't trigger a significant tax liability on their transfer, and when you die you won't own the asset, so there will be no tax to pay on your final tax return.

If you own assets that have appreciated in value, consider giving these assets away to your heirs slowly over time. You'll still trigger a tax liability at the time of the gift, but you'll spread your tax bill over a number of years. In addition, this may prevent you from bumping yourself up to a higher tax bracket in one particular taxation year.

By giving assets away today, you can also avoid probate fees. Since you no longer own the assets, these assets will not form part of your estate. For this reason, you may want to consider giving away "tax-friendly" assets — that is, assets that will not trigger a tax liability when you give them away as a strategy to minimize your probate fees.

To avoid probate fees, many Canadians are changing their investment accounts to joint ownership with right of survivorship. Though this is a valid strategy, it's not without tax consequences. You see, when you place your assets into joint ownership, you're effectively giving up beneficial ownership of half those assets. So guess what? You've managed to trigger a deemed disposition for tax purposes. This isn't a problem if your spouse is the joint owner; however, if any other person is named joint owner, including your children, you will have to claim a capital gain for the disposition of your one-half ownership on your tax return (assuming the assets have appreciated in value).

Leaving them to your spouse

There is one very important exception to the deemed disposition rules on death. If you leave assets to your spouse, or a qualifying spousal trust, you will not be deemed to have disposed of your assets at their fair market value. Instead, the assets can be rolled over to your spouse at their adjusted cost base. This can spell major tax relief when you die owning assets that have appreciated in value!

If you leave assets to your spouse on death, your spouse will inherit the assets at their adjusted cost bases. This means no tax will be triggered on your death. In fact, any potential tax bill will be deferred until the death of your spouse or until your spouse disposes of the assets, whichever comes first.

Spousal trusts

A transfer on death can be made on a tax-deferred basis to a spousal trust, no differently than a direct transfer made to a spouse. To qualify as a spousal trust, the trust must provide that the surviving spouse is entitled to receive all the income of the trust that arises before the surviving spouse's death, and no person except that spouse may, before his or her death, receive any of the capital of the trust. It's not necessary that capital be paid during the spouse's beneficiary's lifetime, but it is required that no other beneficiary shall have access to the capital of the trust during the spouse's lifetime.

The spousal trust is, in many situations, a preferred option to leaving assets directly to a spouse because it allows the deceased to maintain some control over ultimate distribution to his or her children and any other residual beneficiaries. Keep in mind, however, that a properly drafted will is imperative if you want to achieve your desired results!

If you're planning on leaving some of your assets to a person other than your spouse, tax planning is imperative! Because of the spousal rollover, it is best to leave assets that have significantly increased in value to your spouse, because the transfer will not trigger tax. You should leave assets that have not appreciated in value, or which will not trigger a tax liability (back to those "tax-friendly assets"), to your other heirs.

In order for the spousal rollover to apply, certain tests must be met. In most cases, these tests are quite easy to meet:

- The deceased is a resident of Canada at the time of his or her death.
- The property is transferred as a consequence of his or her death.
- The transferee spouse or spousal trust is a resident of Canada at the time of death, or, alternatively, the spousal trust must be a resident of Canada immediately after the property vested in the trust.
- The property has become vested indefeasibly in the spouse or the spousal trust within 36 months of the date of death (this period can be extended in certain circumstances). Yes, this sounds scary. But don't worry. This just means that the spouse or spousal trust has a right to absolute ownership of the property, no matter what, within 36 months.

Electing out of the spousal rollover rules

In some cases, a rollover of your assets to your spouse at cost is not the most tax-efficient choice. For example, if you own some assets at the time of your death that have decreased in value, it would be helpful to trigger at least some tax to fully use the losses. In addition, you may have losses carried forward from other tax years that should be used up. In these cases your legal representative should elect, in your terminal return, to have the property disposed of at fair market value, instead of at its adjusted cost base. Since the spousal rollover at cost occurs automatically, it's important that your representative file this special election to ensure the transfer occurs at fair market value in these circumstances.

For example, a capital property with an adjusted cost base of $50,000 acquired in 1990 has a fair market value of $20,000 at the date of death. If the deceased spouse leaves the property to a surviving spouse or a spousal trust and no election is made, the surviving spouse or spousal trust receives the capital property at its adjusted cost base of $50,000. On a subsequent disposition, assuming no change in value, the surviving spouse or spousal trust will realize a capital loss of $30,000 ($50,000 less $20,000). However, unless the spouse or spousal trust has capital gains to offset the loss, it may be unusable. On the other hand, if the property was transferred at its fair market value, the capital loss would be triggered on the deceased's final tax return and could be used to offset any source of income in that year or on the prior year's return.

The election to transfer assets to your spouse at fair market value is inflexible in that you don't have the option to elect other than the fair market value of the asset at the time of your death. So, if you want to use this election to increase the adjusted cost base of a significant capital asset going to your surviving spouse, you will need to recognize the whole of the gain on the appreciated asset. You can't pick and choose the elected amount. However, you can make the election on a property-by-property basis. That is, you can elect out of the rollover rules for one property, and this election does not force you to make the election for all other property owned at the time of death. So, what you *can* pick and choose are which assets you wish to transfer on a rollover basis and which properties you wish to transfer at fair market value.

To transfer assets to your spouse at fair market value, you must file a special election with your tax return. This election is easy to complete. In fact, there is no form or specific format required for the election. Simply include a separate statement on the terminal return indicating that a subsection 70(6.2) election is being filed, and state which properties you are transferring at fair market value.

Leaving your RRSP or RRIF to a dependent child

Registered retirement savings plans (RRSPs) and Registered Retirement Income Funds (RRIFs) are often the most valuable assets owned on death. And since RRSPs and RRIFs are subject to the deemed disposition rules, it's no surprise that they can lead to huge tax liabilities. Because of the spousal rollover rules, it's usually good estate planning to ensure your spouse is named the beneficiary of your RRSP or RRIF. This means that no tax will be triggered on your death, but rather it will be deferred until withdrawals are made from the RRSP or RRIF, or until the death of your spouse. In addition to passing your RRSP or RRIF on a tax-deferred basis to your spouse on death, another exception to the deemed disposition rules exists specifically for RRSPs and RRIFs. This exception is when you leave your RRSP or RRIF to a dependent child.

Be careful when leaving RRSPs and RRIFs to your children or grandchildren. There are criteria that must be met in order to receive a tax-free rollover of these assets. The child or grandchild must have been financially dependent on you at the time of your death due to a physical or mental infirmity or must have been a minor. An infirm dependant can be any age at the time of your death, while a minor child must be under the age of 18.

A child or grandchild who was financially dependent on you due to physical or mental infirmity may transfer your RRSP or RRIF assets tax-free to his or her own RRSP, RRIF, or annuity. A minor child or grandchild, financially dependent on you at the time of your death, must purchase an annuity to age 18 with your plan's assets.

"Financially dependent" does not mean what you might think it should mean. If fact, even if your child or grandchild lives with you, and you provide this person with food, shelter, and some pocket money, the tax authorities may not consider him or her to be dependent on you. The child or grandchild must have had income for the year preceding death that was less than the basic personal amount plus the supplementary personal amount. So, for a death that occurs in 2000, you'll have to consider the child or grandchild's income in 1999. If that income exceeded $7,044 (the 1999 basic personal amount plus supplementary personal amount), you cannot make a tax-free transfer.

Making a final RRSP contribution

February is usually a frantic month in most financial institutions. Why? Because of the RRSP contribution deadline, of course. As you probably know, you normally have 60 days after a taxation year in which to make an RRSP contribution. Since death is usually an unplanned event, it's highly probable that you could never have the chance to make an RRSP contribution for the year to help reduce your taxes. This would simply be unfair. Therefore, to help minimize your taxes on death, your executor is allowed to make a contribution to a spousal RRSP on your behalf. This contribution can be made either in the year of death, or in the first 60 days of the following year. In order to be eligible for this final RRSP contribution, the following criteria must be met:

- The surviving spouse must be eligible to have an RRSP (be age 69 or younger in the year)
- The deceased must have RRSP contribution room.

If you'd like your executor to make a final RRSP contribution on your behalf in the year of death, say so in your will. Without direction in your will, it's likely that this tax saving will be forgotten altogether.

Donating to charity after death

For those who are charitably inclined, there are some steps you can take prior to death to help minimize the tax hit. You see, in recent years our government has been making enhancements to the tax laws to help promote charitable giving. Therefore, if you do intend to give to charity on your death, read on. You may find that there are some ways to give to charity that you never knew existed. Normally, individuals are eligible to claim donations of up to 75 percent of their net income annually. This is actually increased to100 percent of net income in the year of death. This means that a significant donation made on death may actually eliminate the tax that would otherwise be owing. And if the total donations made during the year of death exceed the limit noted, any excess may be carried back and claimed in the year before death — up to 100 percent of income in that year as well.

If you're planning on giving a substantial sum to charity, you will want to ensure you're getting a full tax advantage for the donation. Due to the net income limitations noted above, however, this may not be possible. If this is the case, you may be better off making some of your donations during your lifetime. Not only will this give you the opportunity to see your gift put to good use, but also, with some planning, you can help ensure the full donation is deductible on your tax return and reduce the probate fees (since the assets are no longer owned by you at the time of death).

Donating to charity on your death can also help to wipe out a tax bill. Here are some ways to donate after your death *and* receive a tax credit on your final return:

- **Donate through your will:** When you make bequests to charity in your will, the subsequent donation made to the charity is eligible for the donations tax credit on your final tax return. Bequests made in your will are deemed to have been made in the year of death. However, if the bequest is not made in your will, be warned: The subsequent donation cannot be claimed on your final tax return.
- **Make a gift in kind:** Instead of donating cash, you may wish to make a gift of tangible property. Donations other than cash are referred to as gifts in kind, and may include items such as mutual funds, real estate property, pieces of artwork, vehicles, clothing, or securities, just to name a few. When you make a gift in kind, you'll receive a donation receipt based on the fair market value of the item at the time it's donated. Whenever a

gift in kind is made, you are deemed to have disposed of the property at its fair market value on that date. This could give rise to taxable capital gains if the property has appreciated in value since you acquired it. Keep in mind, though, that the donation credit will help to offset the tax on the gain.

- **Donate publicly traded securities:** Donating securities is really a gift in kind; however, there are special tax treatments for the gift of publicly traded securities. By donating shares traded on a prescribed stock exchange, you will need to report only one-half of the taxable capital gain that would otherwise result from the disposition of the security. This means paying half the tax you otherwise would have if you'd sold the shares and donated the proceeds.

Instead of liquidating investments and then donating the net proceeds to charity, save tax by directly donating your publicly traded securities. Although you must still report the disposition of the shares on your personal tax return, only one-half of the normal capital gains rate will apply to the disposition. And don't forget, you'll get a donation receipt for the full fair market value of the securities at the time of the donation.

- **Donate life insurance:** There are three ways to donate life insurance to charity.
    - First, you could take out a life insurance policy and irrevocably designate a charity as the beneficiary of the policy. Since the 2000 federal budget, naming a charity as a direct beneficiary of your policy will get you a donation credit on your final income tax return. If you designate a charity as the beneficiary of your life insurance policy, you cannot name a new beneficiary *under any circumstances.*
    - Second, you could transfer the ownership of the policy to the charity and make the charity the beneficiary. Under this scenario, a donation credit is available for any cash surrender value that exists at the time the policy is transferred. You will also receive a donation credit for any insurance premiums paid on the policy after this date.

When you transfer the ownership of a life insurance policy, a deemed disposition occurs. This means that there may be a tax liability if the cash surrender value exceeds the adjusted cost base of the policy — although the donation credit will probably outweigh this.

    - Third, you may choose to name your estate as beneficiary of the life insurance policy and then direct in your will that the death benefit be given to a charity. The insurance premiums paid would not be eligible for a donation credit; however, the death benefit would qualify as a testamentary donation and would be eligible for a donation credit on your final tax return.

- **Use a charitable remainder trust:** A *charitable remainder trust* (CRT) is an irrevocable (that is, you can never get your donated capital back) trust, with a charity named the capital beneficiary, and you as the income beneficiary. This means that although you are donating some of your assets to charity, you still have a right to the earnings of those assets during your lifetime — but not the assets themselves. A CRT works as follows. First, you will transfer assets into a trust. These assets may include property, stocks, bonds, mutual funds, securities, and anything else of value. You will receive a donation credit at the time that the assets are transferred to the trust. Keep in mind, however, that the amount that is eligible for the donation credit is not the fair value of the assets at the time they are transferred. Instead, the value of the credit must be determined by an actuarial calculation based on your age and the projected value of the assets when the charity is due to receive them. Since you still retain some interest in the property transferred, the calculation works in such a way that the older you are, the greater the tax credit.

A CRT makes sense for people who still want to enjoy the right to use a property or the right to receive any income earned on the property. This is especially important to those who depend on the earnings from the assets for day-to-day living.

Remember that there can be costs associated with CRTs. As with all donations of capital property, when you transfer them to a CRT, the action may give rise to a taxable capital gain if that property has appreciated in value since it was purchased. The good news is that the donation credit will probably reduce, if not offset, the tax liability resulting from the gain. As well, there will be initial costs to set up the trust, as well as fees for the annual tax returns required. Be sure to weigh these costs against the tax saving before setting up a CRT.

- **Use a charitable annuity:** Sometimes you know how much money you want to donate to charity when you die, but currently that amount is tied up in investments. And if you are using the income from the investments to support your daily expenses, you may not want to part with the money now. A charitable annuity may be a solution. With such an annuity, the charity will receive a donation now, and you will continue to receive funds from the donated investments to meet your living expenses.This is how it works. You will give a set amount of assets to your favourite charity and take back a life annuity. The amount of the annuity is fixed based on the amount you determine that you need annually. The donation credit is calculated based on your life expectancy. Therefore, based on the amount you want to take back annually and some number-crunching based on your life expectancy, you may or may not get a donation credit today.

If your gift is likely to exceed the total payments made during your lifetime, the excess is treated as a donation at the time the gift is made. Obviously, a charity will not agree to pay an annuity so large, or for such a long period of time, if the present value of estimated payments exceeds the cash value of the initial gift. However, should the current value of the payments exceed the cash value of your gift, no donation slip will be issued.

Set up a testamentary trust in your will

A testamentary trust is a great way to income split and save tax in the hands of your heirs after you're gone. You see, if your heirs are financially independent, any investment income generated annually on the inheritance you leave to them is likely to be taxed at the top marginal tax rate in their hands. By comparison, if it were possible to have a testamentary trust pay the tax on those earnings annually, tax savings would generally result because the trust is taxed at low marginal tax rates on its first $30,004 of income. What is a testamentary trust, and why haven't you heard of one before? A testamentary trust (like any trust) is a relationship between three parties:

- The settlor who transfers assets into the trust (that would be you)
- The beneficiaries who will receive income and/or capital from the trust (your heirs)
- The trustee who maintains and controls the trust's assets for the beneficiaries (any trusted person).

A testamentary trust is taxed in the same way as an individual. This means that it is subject to the same graduated tax rates that we all must pay. So, when taxable income is generated within the trust, the trust can take advantage of these low tax rates. If your heirs received the inheritance directly, any earnings from the inheritance would be tacked on to that heir's taxable income from other sources, and probably be taxed at higher marginal tax rates than the trust.

A testamentary trust must be set up through your will. Rather than leaving all your assets directly to your heirs, consider leaving all or a portion of them to a testamentary trust for each heir. Annually, the trustee of each trust can determine whether the income earned in the trust should be taxed in the hands of your heirs, or in the trust itself. This flexibility will ensure that there will be tax savings enjoyed annually. In fact, the tax savings will be up to approximately $11,000 annually, for each trust set up, if your heirs are in the highest marginal tax bracket. The actual tax savings will depend on the level of income earned in the trust each year, and the tax rates in effect at that time.

If you plan on leaving all your assets to your spouse on death, you can set up a spousal testamentary trust in your will. This means that all your assets will transfer to the trust at cost, deferring tax until the death of your spouse.

You can only establish a testamentary trust by providing for one in your will. Therefore, if you'd like your executor to have the option of setting up testamentary trusts on your death, say so now! A complete and properly drafted will prepared today can help your heirs save big money down the road.

Chapter 26

Tax Breaks for Employees

In This Chapter

- Boosting your salary with non-taxable benefits
- Understanding tax deductions available to employees
- Sorting out what employee expenses are deductible and which are not
- Figuring out automobile expenses
- Getting the most out of your home office expenses
- Applying for the Goods and Services Tax (GST)/Harmonized Sales Tax (HST) rebate

Did you know that there are ways to increase your take-home pay without getting a raise? We expect that when you are thinking about your annual compensation review or considering a job offer, you focus on salary. (We would do the same thing!) But there are some tax-saving non-salary perks you may want to consider. (Especially if your compensation review starts off with ". . . well the company hasn't done too well this year and the raises are going to reflect this . . ." We know — you've heard it before.) This chapter will get you thinking about other forms of compensation, such as non-cash perks like club and gym memberships, stock options, cars, loans, employee discounts, day care, education, pension plans, profit sharing, health/dental insurance, and so on! Stay tuned for all the latest information on tax breaks for employees.

Taking a Look at Non-Taxable Benefits

Salary is fully taxable as it is received. (And yes — before you ask, signing bonuses are fully taxable too!) However, your employer can also provide non-salary benefits — some of them completely tax-free. Consider these items at your next compensation review or when looking at a new job opportunity. These are discussed in detail in Chapter 9. Here, we'll list them for you, since they're important to remember:

- Recreational club fees when membership can be said to be for your employer's benefit. Are you good at "networking"?
- Employer-provided fitness facilities. Hey, ya gotta be fit to do a good job!
- Stock options. Do you work for the next dot-com to be taken over and make its shareholders millionaires — or at least thousandaires?
- Interest-free or low interest loans from your employer. Use your employer as a cheaper alternative to a bank! Ask for a loan for the following:
    - An investment (it doesn't need to be an investment in shares of your employer).
    - An automobile to use in carrying out your job responsibilities. If you have to travel to do your job you're probably going to need a car!

  - A home to live in. There would be deemed interest benefit included in your T4 equal to the market rate of interest you didn't pay. At worst, for those taxed at the higher rates, the tax on the interest benefit is equal to about 50 percent of the interest you would have had to pay with conventional financing. This can turn a 7-percent mortgage into an effective 3.5-percent mortgage. Not a bad rate, we would say! Moreover, if the loan is a "home relocation loan" (at least a 40-kilometre move for work), there is no interest benefit on the first $25,000 of the loan. You can truly get a $25,000 loan, interest- and *tax-free* if your employer is willing!

- Expense reimbursements. Get your money back for expenses you incurred for your employer. Consider the following:
  - Reimbursement of moving expenses incurred to take on a job (see Chapter 16, line 219).
  - Reimbursement for the loss you incurred on the sale of your old home so you could move to take the new job. The first $15,000 is completely tax-free and only half of the amount above $15,000 is taxed. (This is important because the loss on your previous home is not eligible for the moving expense deduction. Refer to Chapter 16, line 219.)
  - Reimbursement of expenses you incur to carry out your work. The majority of this chapter deals with employees being able to deduct expenses they incur in carrying out their job. It is still better for the employee to receive a dollar-for-dollar reimbursement of expenses!
- Employee merchandise discounts. Discounts are normally available to retail employees.
- Employer-operated day care. Do your employer facilities include a day care? If so, this could save you a ton in child care costs — plus, your kids would be close by!
- Travel when there is a business purpose. Often, your spouse can go along too! Perhaps you can combine a business trip with a vacation.
- Subsidized cafeterias when there is a reasonable charge to cover cost of food, preparation, and service.
- Employer-paid counseling for retirement, reemployment, substance abuse, and stress management. (Stress management counseling is pretty popular these days — especially when editors set unrealistic deadlines!)
- Education costs — again, where there is a perceived benefit to the employer. Are there courses or seminars you would like to take to help you in carrying out your job's responsibilities?
- Parking, provided your employer does not pay for the space.
- Transportation passes provided to bus, rail, and airline employees.
- Employer contributions to the following deferred compensation/pension plans:
  - Registered pension plans (RPP)
  - Deferred profit sharing plans (DPSP)
  - Retirement compensation arrangements (RCA).
- Employer-paid premiums for private health/dental insurance (except for Quebec tax purposes) for yourself and family.
- Employer-paid death benefits. The first $10,000 is tax-free! (Of course, you don't get the $10,000 — your estate does!)
- Retirement and severance payments to the extent transferred to your RRSP (see Chapter 16, line 208).
- Uniforms, necessary special clothing (including safety footwear), and cleaning of these items.

Tax Deductions Available to Employees

In Chapter 16, The Calculation of Net Income, a number of tax deductions are detailed. Of all the deductions noted, many were available to employees (and perhaps to non-employees as well!). Here are some tax deductions available to employees:

- Deduction for contributions to a Registered Pension Plan (RPP) [line 207 on tax return]
- Deduction for contributions to a registered retirement savings plan (RRSP) [line 208]
- Deduction for annual union, professional, or like dues [line 212]
- Deduction of child care expenses [line 214]
- Deduction for attendant care expenses [line 218]
- Deduction for moving expenses [line 219]
- Deduction for legal fees to collect a severance or retirement allowance [line 232].

In addition to these deductions, certain types of employees can deduct expenses they incur in doing their job. The rest of this chapter deals with the type of employee expenses that can be deducted and how these deductions are calculated and reported on the tax return. The chapter concludes with a discussion on the GST/HST rebate for GST/HST incurred on employment expenses.

Employment Expenses

You may be one of many employees that are required to fund the costs of carrying out your employment duties. These costs can vary from taking prospective customers out to lunch to using your own car for sales calls to perhaps using space in your home or apartment for work purposes. These next few sections of this chapter apply to you if you're in the following situation:

- Your employer pays you an allowance to cover your expenses but the allowance is included in your T4 employment income. In other words, you pay tax on the allowance.
- Your employer does not pay you an allowance. You are simply required to pay your own expenses.

If you fall into one of these criteria, you should be able to claim a deduction for at least some, if not all, the expenses you incurred to do your job.

If you do not fall into one of these categories, don't be overly jealous of those who do. Though it is nice to be able to deduct employment expenses, it would be better if your employer simply reimbursed them. With a reimbursement, you would not be out any money. Your employer would return to you every dollar you spent in doing your job. In deducting employment expenses, the best you can do is receive about a 50-cent refund for every dollar deducted — and this assumes you are in the top tax bracket, which means your taxable income after all deductions (including the deduction for employment expenses) exceeds $60,009.

Who is eligible to deduct employment expenses?

To deduct the expenses you incur to carry out your employment duties, the following must apply to you:

- You must be required to pay expenses to earn your employment income (in the CCRA's words, you must be required to incur the expenses under the terms of your employment contract, whether or not you have a written contract).
- Your employer must provide you with a form detailing the expenses you are required to incur. The form is T2200 "Declarations of Conditions of Employment." It is completed and signed by your employer — not you. The form is to be included with your mailed-in tax return. If your return is being net-filed or e-filed, you must keep the form in case the CCRA asks to see it — and in many cases they do so!

Form T777 "Statement of Employment Expenses"

The CCRA publishes this form to assist you in gathering and summarizing your employment expenses. This is the form used by the majority of employees. The total of your eligible employment expenses from the T777 is carried over to line 229 on your tax return. A second employee expense form, TL2 "Claim for Meals and Lodging Expenses," is used by employees involved in air, rail, bus, and trucking industries. This form is discussed later in the chapter. Another form that can come into play is form GST370 "Employee and Partner GST/HST Rebate Application." Most employees like this form because it works only one way: it assists you in calculating the amount of GST/HST you can recover from the government!

The employment expenses you deduct are to include the GST, HST, and provincial and territorial sales taxes you paid. Do not separate the GST/HST or provincial/territorial sales taxes from the non-tax portion of your expenses. If you lived in Alberta (no provincial sales tax) and purchased $100 of deductible supplies to do your job, you would actually pay $107 when the GST is added. It is the $107 that is included in your employment expenses on the T777.

Do not get confused with self-employed individuals who are registered to collect and remit GST/HST. Many self-employed individuals need to separate the GST/HST components from their self-employment expenses. This does not apply to employees. An employee is not permitted to register for GST/HST. However, the employer is probably registered for GST, unless the employer carries on a GST/HST-exempt activity (for example, health care or financial services). The GST/HST included in your employment expenses can be rebated (another word for refunded!) to you! This is discussed in the last section of this chapter.

Where you are eligible to claim a deduction for employment expenses, record keeping is vital for a number of reasons. One, you don't want to miss out on claiming a legitimate expense. If you do, you overstate your tax liability! Two, the CCRA can request employees to provide support for the expenses claimed on their tax return. You do not send in support for your employment expenses with your tax return. The CCRA is usually happy to accept the deduction for employment expenses, provided the support (receipts, invoices, ticket stubs, kilometre log, and so on) is organized and available for inspection should it be requested. Third, you simplify your tax return preparation. Don't even think of bringing a shopping bag (or the infamous shoe box) full of receipts and stuff to an accountant in late April and expect to be pleasantly welcomed!

What's Deductible and What's Not?

Let's look at an example. Fiona took an industrial sales job with Warton Products Inc. of Stratford, Ontario, on February 1, 2000. Her conditions of employment were that she was to be paid on a commission basis and that she was required to do the following:

- Pay for her own office supplies (paper, toner, postage, and so on)
- Pay the salary of her part-time assistant, Katy
- Provide a home office for her and Katy. Fiona was not provided with a workspace at Warton
- Provide her own car because the job involved significant travel in southern Ontario.

During 2000, Fiona made commissions of $90,000. She paid GST on her expenses when applicable. All her expenses were incurred in Ontario, so she did not pay any HST in 2000.

HST, or the 15-percent Harmonized Sales Tax, is paid on the purchase of goods and services made in New Brunswick, Nova Scotia, and Newfoundland. These provinces are referred to as the "participating provinces" because they are participating with the federal government in integrating the federal Goods and Services Tax (GST) with provincial sales taxes. The other provinces (and the territories) charge the 7-percent GST and their own version of a provincial or territorial sales tax. (Fortunate Albertans pay no provincial sales tax!) The provincial and territorial sales taxes are not integrated with the federal GST. Provincial and territorial sales taxes operate completely separately from the GST and are based on different taxing concepts.

Table 26-1 compares the expenses that can be deducted by an employee earning a salary and those that can be deducted by an employee being paid on a commission basis.

Table 26-1 Can It Be Deducted?

Expense	*Earning Salary*	*Earning Commissions*
Legal fees to collect wages, salary, or commissions owed	Yes	Yes
Accounting fees for tax return preparation	No[1]	Yes
Advertising and promotion	No	Yes
Entertainment for customers	No	Yes[2]
Food and beverage[3]	Yes[2]	Yes[2]
Lodging and travel	Yes[4]	Yes
Parking[5]	Yes	Yes
Automobile expense	Yes	Yes
Office supplies[6]	Yes	Yes
Uniforms	Yes	Yes
Clothing, dry cleaning, makeup and hairstyling	No	No
Computer or fax purchase	No	No
Computer or fax lease	No	Yes
Cell phone purchase	No	No
Cell phone lease	No	Yes
Cell phone airtime[7]	Yes	Yes
Long distance calls[7]	Yes	Yes
Internet[8]	Yes	Yes
Licences[9]	No	Yes

(continued)

Table 26-1 *(continued)*

Expense	*Earning Salary*	*Earning Commissions*
Salaries to assistants[10]	Yes	Yes
Office rent[10]	Yes	Yes
Home office[10]	Yes	Yes

Notes

1. An alternative filing opportunity is to claim the accounting fee as a carrying charge on schedule 4. Refer to Chapter 16, line 221. It deals with the deduction available for carrying charges and interest expense.
2. Only 50 percent of entertainment, food, and beverage expenses can be deducted.
3. Food, beverage, and lodging are only deductible if your employer requires you to be away from the municipality or metropolitan area where your employer is located for at least 12 hours.
4. You can deduct travel expenses if you were normally required to work away from your employer's business or in different places, and you did not receive a non-taxable allowance to cover traveling expenses.
5. The CCRA's position is that parking costs at your employer's office are not deductible because they are considered a personal expense. However, if you need to go to the office before or after seeing a customer, or to work at a different location, we would argue that the parking in these circumstances should be deductible.
6. Supplies must be used directly in your work and for nothing else. The CCRA takes the position that this includes "pens, pencils, paper clips, stationery, stamps, street maps, and directories." Supplies do not include items such as briefcases or calculators. Tools are not deductible.
7. Restricted to work-related cost of calls and airtime.
8. The CCRA's guide "Employment Expenses" is silent on Internet charges. We would expect the CCRA to permit at least a portion of Internet fees if the Internet is needed to do your job. (Hey, you need an e-mail address, don't ya?)
9. Annual licence fees are deductible if needed to carry out work (for example, real estate and insurance licences).
10. Your employer must specifically indicate on form T2200 that you are required to incur these costs.

Assuming Fiona spent $5,350 on office supplies and $4,000 for Katy's salary, she would be entitled to a full deduction of $9,350. This is a hint to what comes later. The amount spent on supplies includes 7-percent GST. Again, GST, HST, and provincial and territorial sales taxes are not subtracted when you are determining your deductible employment expenses.

Automobile Expenses

If you pay your own automobile expenses and are required to use your car to carry out your employment duties, you can deduct a portion of your costs in completing your income tax return. As noted above, your employer would indicate on form T2200 that you need to supply your own car and incur expenses to keep it on the road. Here are some types of automobile expenses that can be deducted:

- Fuel (gas, propane, and oil)
- Repairs and maintenance
- Insurance
- Licence and registration fees
- Leasing costs
- Interest incurred on a loan to purchase a car
- Capital cost allowance (CCA or tax depreciation).

It is only the "employment use" portion of automobile expenses that is included in your deductible employment expenses. The CCRA states that driving only to and from work is personal use — not employment use. However, if you need to go out in your car in the middle of the day (say, to see a potential customer) or perhaps on your way to or from work, the trip can be considered employment use.

Remember that Fiona started working at Warton on February 1, 2000. She was required to provide her own car. Fiona used her Honda Civic, which she had leased a few years back. Her lease costs for the period were $3,300 ($300 per month for 11 months). From February to December 2000, Fiona drove the Civic a total of 20,000 kilometres — 15,000 were work-related. Fiona, being ever fearful of a CCRA query, kept a log in her glove compartment that detailed the work trips and kilometres driven. She updated the log daily. Based on the kilometres, you can see that Fiona used her car 75 percent of the time for work and 25 percent for personal use. Fiona can deduct 75 percent of her automobile expenses in calculating her deductible employment expenses.

Do you really need to keep a log of your kilometres driven for employment use? If you are asked by the CCRA to support your automobile expenses, they will ask to see your log of kilometres. So get in the habit of keeping the log in the car. Every time you get in the car, you should make an entry of where you are going, and later where you have been and the kilometres traveled. You will thank us if the CCRA comes knocking!

Let's calculate Fiona's automobile expenses using the chart in the middle of form T777.

Expenses	*Dollar Value*
Fuel (gas, propane, oil)	$2,000
Maintenance and repairs	$1,500
Insurance	$1,100
Licence and registration	$125
Lease	$3,300
Other — car washes	$100
Total expenses	$8,125
Employment use portion	75 percent
Allowable amount of automobile expenses that Fiona can deduct on her tax return	$6,094

Capital cost allowance (CCA) when an automobile is owned rather than leased

In the above example Fiona leased the car she used to carry out her employment duties. What would the impact be if Fiona owned the car? Before heading back to our example let's look at something called *capital cost allowance* — CCA for short. It is the tax term for depreciation.

As your car is expected to last more than a year the cost of your car cannot be completely deducted in computing your employment expenses. However, a percentage of the car's cost can be deducted each year. This deduction each year is referred to as capital cost allowance (CCA). The first step in determining the CCA you can deduct is to decide whether your automobile is "class 10" or a "class 10.1" for CCA purposes. Both CCA classes 10 and 10.1 calculate the maximum CCA that can be claimed at a rate of 30 percent calculated on the declining balance method of depreciation. Where an automobile is purchased in a year the "half-rate" rule applies. This results in a CCA calculation at 15 percent (30 percent × ½ = 15 percent). The determination of whether your car is considered a "class 10" or "class 10.1" automobile is important as the CCA on class 10.1 automobiles is restricted to a maximum amount. The restrictions on CCA and other automobile expenses are discussed shortly.

There are many, many CCA classes. For example, a building is usually class 1 that has a 4 percent CCA rate. Furniture and fixtures are part of class 8 with a 20 percent CCA rate. The determination of the CCA class is important because each class has it own particular rules. Most CCA classes have different percentage figures that are used to determine the maximum amount of CCA that can be claimed in a year.

Rather than leasing her Honda Civic, assume that Fiona purchased the Civic in 2000 for $23,000 taxes included. (By the way, this car qualifies as class 10 — therefore, no restrictions apply in calculating CCA). Let's take a look at how Fiona would calculate CCA for 2000 and 2001.

Before calculating CCA, Fiona would calculate her employee expense deduction for the operating expenses of her car in the same way as above. She would total up the amounts she spent for fuel, repairs, licensing, insurance, etc. (Of course there would be no leasing costs as we assume here she owns the car!) The total amount of expenses would then be multiplied by the employment use portion. In the preceding example 75 percent was used for the 2000 year. We'll assume the appropriate employment usage figure was also 75 percent for 2001.

The claiming of maximum CCA available, whether for an automobile or any asset on which CCA can be claimed, is optional. A taxpayer (whether employed or self-employed, or perhaps a corporation) may decide to claim less than the maximum CCA or no CCA at all! While, at first, it may seem odd that a taxpayer would not take maximum advantage of a tax deduction available, there are some logical reasons for this. For example, an employee may benefit by *not* taking CCA in one year as a higher CCA claim will be available next year. Perhaps the taxpayer will be in a higher tax bracket next year. This will result in a greater tax reduction than if the CCA is taken this year.

Table 26-2 summarizes how Fiona would calculate CCA for 2000 and 2001.

Table 26-2 Fiona's Capital Cost Allowance (CCA) schedule for 2000 and 2001

Year: 2000		
Undepreciated capital cost (UCC) at January 1, 2000		$0
Acquisitions in year	$23,000	
Subtract – one-half (note 1)	($11,500)	
	$11,500	$11,500
Base for 2000 CCA calculation		$11,500
CCA at 30 percent (note 2)		($3,450)
Add-back one-half subtracted above		$11,500
UCC at December 31, 2000		$19,550
Year: 2001		
UCC at January 1, 2001 (as above)		$19,550
CCA at 30 percent (note 2)		($5,865)
UCC at December 31, 2001		$13,685

Notes

1. This part of the calculation results in only half of the capital cost of the acquisitions in 2000 being depreciated. While the CCA rate is 30 percent, the subtracted amount results in the CCA being only 15 percent — half of 30 percent. This calculation is referred to as the "half-rate" rule.
2. Remember that Fiona only used her car 75 percent of the time to carry out her employment duties. Therefore, her tax deduction is 75 percent of the CCA calculated. In 2000 — $3,450 × 75% = $2,587.50. In 2001 — $5,965 × 75% = $4,398.75.

Restrictions on certain automobile expenses

Where you are entitled to deduct a portion of your automobile as employment expenses, you deduct only the "business use" portion of the expenses you actually paid. For most of your expenses, this is true. The amount you pay is the starting point in determining what you can deduct. However, there are three exceptions to this:

- Automobile leasing costs
- Interest on car loans
- Capital cost on which CCA will begin to be calculated. (CCA class 10.1 automobiles are subject to this restriction.)

When these exceptions apply, you will find that the amounts you use to begin calculating your deductible automobile expenses are less than you actually paid.

Restrictions have been put on the lease, interest, and capital costs in respect of automobiles, because the government does not want to permit tax deductions it considers to be in "excess" of an "appropriate amount." In other words, the incentive to lease or purchase an "expensive" car and be able to deduct a lot of the expenses for tax leaves a bad taste in the government's mouth. You can still lease, buy, and finance an "expensive" automobile, but you will find your lease, interest, and CCA deductions are restricted to maximum amounts.

Maximum amounts for automobile lease, interest, and capital costs

Remember, these maximums apply *before* you prorate your automobile expenses between employment use and business use.

Let's look at Rashid's situation. Rashid is a salesman. On January 1, 2000, he leased a Mercedes. His monthly lease cost is $850. Rashid uses his car 60 percent for work. Rashid expects that his monthly effective tax deduction will be $510 ($850 × 60 percent), or $6,120 per year. He is not worried about the lease cost restriction because he understands the maximum costs for leases commenced in 2000 is $700 (see Table 26-3 below). Rashid is wrong! The effective tax deduction he will have is the $700 per month maximum multiplied by his 60-percent employment use, which results in a tax deduction equal to $420 per month, or $5,040 for all of 2000.

Oh, by the way, we have simplified things here. So don't get thinking you can get around the lease restriction rules by making a big deposit before the lease commences or guaranteeing the car will have a higher value than normal at the end of the lease. Both these ideas would bring your monthly lease costs down. However, the actual calculation to determine the maximum lease costs takes these ideas into account. In fact, one of the calculations focuses on the manufacturer's list price of the car. If the car is expensive, you will simply have to live with the restrictions on the amounts you can deduct! (Also, don't think you can avoid the restrictions because you drive a van or a SUV rather than a car. You'll still be caught by the rules.)

Table 26-3 lists the ceilings for maximum amounts that can be deducted for lease and interest costs, as well as the maximum amount that can be used for capital cost allowance (CCA):

Table 26-3 Restrictions on Automobile Expenses[1]

	2000	*1998 & 1999*	*1997*
Maximum cost for CCA purposes[2, 3]	$27,000	$26,000	$24,000
Maximum deductible monthly lease payment[2]	$700	$650	$550
Maximum monthly interest cost[2]	$250	$250	$250

(continued)

Notes

1. The government reviews these limits annually and announces any changes prior to the end of the year so taxpayers are aware of the rules in advance of the year in which they apply. The rates are set and released by the Department of Finance Canada by press release.
2. All limits are before sales tax. The limits are actually slightly higher when GST/HST and provincial and territorial sales tax are added in.
3. Automobiles that have a capital cost above these limits are considered "class 10.1" automobiles.

Home Office Expenses

If your employer requires you to provide space in your home or apartment to carry out your employment duties, your employer must indicate this on form T2200, provided to you. If you do maintain a home office, you can deduct a portion of the expenses related to maintaining the workspace. This deduction is particularly attractive, since you'll be getting a tax deduction for a portion of the expenses that you incur anyway, such as monthly utilities and rent.

A tale of two tests

For the costs to be deductible, you must ensure your workspace meets one of two tests — you don't have to meet both! Under the first test, the workspace must be the primary place where your employment duties are carried out. A sales representative employed by a company may work from home and rarely "go to the office." A part-time night school teacher may not have an office at a school and must plan lessons and mark exams at home.

If the first test is not met, all is not lost. You may still qualify to deduct home office expenses if your workspace is used exclusively to carry out your employment duties. (Note that the word *exclusively* was not used in the first test.) In addition to using the space exclusively for these activities, you must use the space on a "regular and continuous" basis for meeting customers or clients or others associated with carrying out your employment duties. In the CCRA's opinion, infrequent meetings or frequent meetings at irregular intervals are not regular and continuous.

Restrictions on deducting home office expenses

You cannot claim home office expenses to "create or increase a loss" from employment. Say your 2000 employment expenses (excluding home office expenses) are greater than your 2000 employment income — you have a loss from employment. (Perhaps you started a new job and your initial expenses exceeded income in the start-up period.) You cannot claim home office expenses to increase the loss. If your non-home office employment expenses do not exceed your employment income, you can only claim home office expenses to the extent that they bring your "net" employment income to nil — you cannot create a loss. Any 2000 home office expenses that can't be used in 2000 are available for deduction in 2001. You may find that on your 2001 tax return you can deduct both 2000 and 2001 home office expenses.

Deductible home office expenses

As Table 26-4 details, an employee paid on a commission basis is able to deduct more home office expenses than an employee paid by salary.

Table 26-4	Home Office Expenses Deductions	
	Earning Salary	*Earning Commissions*
Electricity, heat, and water	Yes	Yes
Maintenance	Yes	Yes
Rent	Yes	Yes
Property tax	No	Yes
Home insurance	No	Yes
Mortgage interest	No	No
Mortgage principal	No	No

Expenses such as telephone and Internet charges are not mentioned here. Though you may think of these as a home office expense, they can be deducted as "supplies" in completing form T777. The CCRA's position is that long distance charges for calls made to carry out your employment duties can be deducted, but that the monthly charges for your residential phone line cannot — not even a portion of them. However, if you have a separate phone line for your employment, the full costs associated with this phone can be deducted.

How to calculate the deductible costs of your home office

To calculate and report the tax deductible costs of your home office expenses, go through these four steps:

(1) Summarize the total expenses of your apartment or home at the bottom of form T777; refer to lines 17 to 22.

(2) Determine the total of the expenses that represent the personal use of your home rather than employment use. The CCRA suggests that this can be done on a square-foot or square-metre basis. Say you have a 1500-square-foot house. Your office is about 150 square feet, or 10 percent of the house. Therefore, 90 percent of your house expenses are incurred for personal use. Note the personal use portion on line 23 of the T777.

Maximize the business portion of your home by including a portion of the hallways and washroom as business space if they are used in the business. Also, exclude certain non-usable space (for example, an unfinished basement) from your calculation of the total square footage of your home.

(3) Subtract the personal use expenses from the total expenses to arrive at the total expenses that represent the cost of maintaining your home office. This amount is noted on line 24 of the T777.

(4) Provided your home office expenses do not create or increase an "employment loss," the amount noted on line 24 of the T777 will be entered at line 2 of the "Expenses" section at the top of the T777.

Let's revisit Fiona's situation. Remember that Fiona was required to have a home office to carry out her employment duties in 2000. Fiona incurred the following expenses in maintaining her home for the eleven months she was working for Warton Products Inc. (the amounts include GST where it was paid).

Gas (heat)	$856
Electricity	$428
Water[1]	$100
Maintenance	$963
House insurance[1, 2]	$300
Property tax[1, 2]	$2,000
Interest on mortgage[1, 3]	N/A
Total eligible expenses	$4,647

Notes

1. GST exempt. No GST paid on these costs.
2. Fiona is able to claim for house insurance and property tax because she is paid by commission. If she earned salary, no claim for these items would be permitted.
3. An employee, whether paid by salary or commission, cannot claim mortgage interest in computing the costs of maintaining a home office. However, a self-employed person can (refer to Chapter 15, Dealing with Self-Employment Income and Expenses).

Fiona's house is 1500 square feet. She estimates that she uses about 150 square feet, or 10 percent, of the house for her workspace. Conversely, 90 percent of the home is used for personal use. The amount Fiona can deduct as her employment expense in maintaining her home office is calculated as follows:

Total eligible expenses to maintain her home (as above)	$4,647
Less portion of expenses for personal use ($4,647 × 90 percent)	($4,182)
Expenses representing cost of maintaining her home office	$465

Additional Deductions

Certain types of employees can find themselves in "special circumstances" when it comes to the deduction of employment expenses. These types of employees include the transport employees, employed musicians, employed artists, and clerics, perhaps better known as clergy persons. This next section provides the details of the "special" rules that impact these employees and their deduction for employment expenses they incur in doing their jobs.

Transport employees

If you are employed in the transport industry (air, rail and bus travel, and trucking), you and your employer are required to complete form TL2 "Claim for Meals and Lodging Expenses." You complete part 1 of the form (name, period of employment, and so on) and part 2 (details of your trips and costs incurred for meals and lodging). If any of your costs were reimbursed, deduct the amount of reimbursement. Only 50 percent of your meals are deductible, but 100 percent of your lodging costs can be deducted. The total of the amount deductible is to be included on line 229 of your tax return. Like non–transport industry employees, you may be eligible for a GST/HST rebate. This is discussed in the next section. Your employer needs to complete and sign part 3 of the TL2. In signing, your employer is agreeing to the claim for meals and lodging that you have calculated.

Musician's instruments

There's good news if you're an employed musician. In addition to the costs noted above for employees, you're entitled to deduct capital cost allowance on your instrument (Class 8 — 20-percent declining basis), as well as any amounts paid for the maintenance, rental, and insurance of the instrument. To claim these amounts, you must be required, as a term of your employment, to provide your own musical instrument.

If you are an employed musician, you can only deduct expenses for maintenance, rent, insurance, and capital cost allowance to the extent of your employment income. This means you cannot create or increase an "employment" loss from your musical career. However, should you be a self-employed musician the treatment is different. Again, we refer you to Chapter 15 that deals with self-employed income and expenses.

Artist's expenses

If you're an employed artist, there are some additional deductions you'll enjoy in addition to the "regular" employee expenses discussed in this chapter. CCRA considers you an artist if you do any of the following:

- Create (but don't reproduce) paintings, prints, etchings, drawings, sculptures, or similar works of art
- Compose dramatic, musical, or literary works
- Perform dramatic or musical work, as an actor, singer, or musician
- Belong to a professional artists' association that is certified by the Minister of Canadian Heritage.

An artist who earns income from any of the above activities may deduct related expenses incurred to earn this income. Again, these "related" expenses are in addition to the regular employment expenses deductible by all types of employees that are required to incur these expenses as part of their job. But of course, just as with many things in our tax system, there's a limit. The deduction for employed artists' expenses is limited to the lesser of the following:

(i) expenses incurred and

(ii) the amount determined by the formula

- the least of 20 percent of the employment income from artistic activities and $1,000
- less expenses already claimed for capital cost allowance (CCA) on an automobile and any expenses claimed in connection with musical instruments (see above discussion on "musician's instruments")

To the extent an artist's expenses cannot be deducted in the year they are incurred the amount can be carried forward to the next year for possible deduction in that year.

How about an example? Heather was employed by Painters R Us, and earned $25,000 during 2000. During 2000 she incurred $750 in expenses for advertising and promoting paintings done by her plus $1,000 in travel costs. She also calculated that the capital cost allowance (CCA) on her car was $350. Heather is unsure about how much she can deduct for employee expenses on her 2000 income tax return. Heather incurred a total of $750 in artist's expenses. The $350 of CCA, and the $1,000 in travel costs are deductible under other categories discussed earlier in this chapter. Remember artist's expenses are only those that are not already deductible under regular employment expenses. Heather's deduction for artist's expenses is limited to the lesser of the following:

20 percent of $25,000 (which is $5,000) and $1000 — the lesser is $1,000

less the $350 claimed for CCA on her car

The answer is $650 ($1,000 less 350)

Heather is eligible to deduct a total of $650 of the $750 artist's expenses she incurred. The remaining $100 that she is not able to deduct can be carried forward to 2001 and added to any artist's expenses she incurs in 2001.

Cleric's residence deduction

A cleric may be able to claim a deduction in computing net income. The deduction is permitted where the individual is

- in charge of or ministering to a parish, congregation, or diocese, or
- engaged exclusively in full-time administrative service by appointment of a religious order or religious denomination.

Where a member of the clergy has free accommodation the value of this benefit is included in his or her income. It is usually reported on a T4. The amount is included in the total employment income noted in box 14 and highlighted separately in box 30. The deduction available is equal to this benefit. Hence the cleric is subject to tax only on the salary component of his or her employment income.

Where free accommodation is not provided a claim can be made for the amount paid as rent or the fair rental value of the accommodation owned by the cleric. The deduction cannot exceed the employment income earned as a cleric. If the cleric receives a housing allowance from an employer the allowance is included in income. However, the income inclusion can be offset with the cleric's residence deduction. In fact, many clerics claim a cleric's residence deduction *in excess* of the housing allowance that was included in their income. For 2000 this is permissible, as the cleric's residence deduction is not limited to the amount of the housing allowance but to the total of the cleric employment income.

Changes are proposed to prevent this "excess" deduction. ("Excess" in CCRA's mind, perhaps not "excess" in a cleric's mind.) Beginning in 2001 where a cleric provides their own residence (whether rented or owned) the cleric's residence deduction will be limited to the lesser of the amount of the housing allowance included in the cleric's income and the greater of $10,000 and 50 percent of the cleric's remuneration (excluding the housing allowance). (Employers who do not pay a housing allowance can earmark a reasonable portion of the cleric's income as being an allowance.)

These rules may dramatically decrease the amount of deduction available to some clerics. Suppose that Peter, a cleric, rents his home for $800 per month. His current salary is $35,000 per year. In 2000 he may deduct $9,600 ($800 × 12 months) for the cleric's residence deduction. However, commencing in 2001, he must calculate his deduction under the new rules. Although his employer does not pay him an allowance, say his employer indicated that Peter's salary includes $250 per month as a housing allowance. His 2001 deduction is limited to the lesser of the following:

His housing allowance of $3,000 ($250 × 12)

The greater of

$10,000 and 50 percent of $32,000 ($35,000 – $3,000) which is $16,000

Therefore, for 2001 his deduction is reduced to only $3,000 — far less than the $9,600 deduction for 2000.

Since these new rules don't come into effect until 2001, now is the time to renegotiate salary and housing alternatives with your employer.

No changes are proposed that will impact a cleric who lives in employer-provided accommodation. The employment benefit included in income from this will be able to be completely offset with the cleric's residence deduction.

The amount of a cleric's residence deduction is entered on line 231 of the cleric's tax return. It is not reported on the T777 form.

Goods and Services Tax (GST)/ Harmonized Sales Tax (HST) Rebate

The *Goods and Services Tax* (GST) and *Harmonized Sales Tax* (HST) are consumer taxes. This means that if you incur GST or HST in carrying out your employment duties, you are really incurring it on behalf of your employer's business — not as a consumer. Therefore, the GST or HST should be refunded or rebated to you because it was not incurred for a consumer purchase.

Say you purchase a gift to give to one of your best customers. The actual price of the gift was $100, but you paid $107 when GST was added. (For simplicity, we've assumed you bought this gift in a non-HST province and we've ignored retail sales tax.)

The $7 paid was not in respect of a consumer purchase. Therefore, the $7 should be refunded or rebated to you. This is referred to as a GST rebate. It is calculated using form GST 370 "Employee and Partner GST/HST Rebate Application." You will note the $7 on line 457 of your tax return and it will either decrease the income tax you owe or increase your tax refund!

What if the gift was for your mother? Well, there is no employment aspect to this purchase, so the $7 is not refundable — it becomes a true cost to you because you are acting as a consumer in making this gift purchase. The $7 is not going to be returned to you . . . but your mom will appreciate the gift.

Assessing your eligibility for GST/HST rebate

If you have to pay your own expenses to carry out your employment duties, you are probably able to claim a rebate for the GST and HST included in your expenses. You are not eligible to claim the GST/HST if either of the following applies to your situation:

- Your employer is not a GST/HST registrant
- Your employer carries on a GST/HST–exempt activity, which includes both the following:
  - Health care (for example, a medical or dental practice)
  - Financial services (for example, banking, insurance, and investing)

Expenses that qualify for the GST/HST rebate

Deduct expenses you paid GST/HST on and deducted on form T777, plus the GST/HST component of the union or professional dues deducted on line 212 of your tax return.

Expenses that do not qualify for the GST/HST rebate

You probably did not pay GST/HST on *all* your expenses because some did not attract GST/HST.

- Expenses where no GST/HST was incurred.
  - You may have paid for goods or services that are GST-exempt, such as some membership fees and dues, insurance, licences, and salaries to assistants.
  - You may have incurred employment expenses where no GST/HST was paid because the vendor of the goods or provider of the service was not registered for GST and therefore, did not charge GST.
- Personal use portion of employment expenses.
  - You cannot claim a GST/HST rebate in connection with GST/HST paid on the personal portion of your automobile and home office expenses.

How to calculate and claim your GST/HST rebate

The rebate you are entitled to is calculated on form GST370 "Employee and Partner GST/HST Rebate Application."

The title of form GST370 includes "partner" because the form is used by a partner to calculate the GST rebate on expenses he or she incurs to earn income that is not reimbursed by the partnership. The partnership is the GST registrant — not the individual partners. Common partnerships in Canada are law and accounting firms. Many health care practitioners (doctors, dentists) operate in partnerships as well, but their activities are GST-exempt, so they are not eligible for the GST/HST rebate. Partners do not complete form T777 because this form is specifically for employees. Refer to Chapter 15 for a discussion on reporting partnership income and expenses.

Form GST370 (page 2) provides a work chart to separate your expenses among the following:

- Expenses on which you paid 7-percent GST
- Expenses on which you paid 15-percent HST
- Expenses eligible for the GST/HST rebate
- Expenses not eligible for the GST/HST rebate.

In this chapter we saw that Fiona was able to deduct the following employment expenses:

Office supplies	$5,350
Salary to Katy, Fiona's assistant	$4,000
Automobile expenses (under the scenario where her car was leased)	$6,094
Home office expenses	$465
Total employment expenses	$15,909

Fiona would use form GST370 to calculate her 2000 GST/HST rebate. As Fiona incurred GST only (no HST), she will only use the GST portion of form GST370.

GST rebate on eligible expenses		
Total employment expenses per T777		$15,909
Less non-eligible expenses (expenses on which no GST was paid)		
Salary to Katy		$4,000
Employment-use portion claimed of:		
Car insurance	$1,000 × 75 percent business usage	$750
Car licence and registration	$125 × 75 percent business usage	$94
Water	$100 × 10 percent business usage	$10
House insurance	$300 × 10 percent business usage	$30
Property tax	$2,000 × 10 percent business usage	$200
Total expenses eligible for the GST rebate		$10,825
Multiply by factor to "back out" 7% from total		7/107
GST employee rebate (to line 457 on tax return)		$708

Fiona will put the $708 on line 457 of her tax return. It will serve to reduce the total tax owing on her tax return or increase the refund owing to her.

Now you say, *HOLD IT!* You've just realized that Fiona received two benefits:

- She got a tax saving from being able to deduct the GST component of her employment expenses.
- She received back the GST she paid.

Isn't this double-dipping on a tax/GST break? Congratulations on being so observant. Fiona has indeed received a double benefit. In fact the government purposely designed the system this way! (Who else could?) However, when Fiona does her 2001 tax return, the double benefit will be taken away.

In Chapter 9, we discussed the employment income inclusions under line 104 of your return. One of the inclusions was the prior year GST/HST rebate. The prior year GST/HST rebate relates to the GST/HST included in employment expenses deducted on the previous year's tax return. So effectively, the GST/HST portion of employment expenses deducted on a tax return in one year are added back to income in the immediately subsequent year's tax return. In year one you have the benefit of deducting the GST/HST portion of the employment expenses. In year two the amount is added back to income. Therefore, the benefit of the deduction in year one is nullified by the income inclusion in year two. That's okay because don't forget you actually received a refund of the GST/HST you paid on your employment expenses through the GST/HST rebate mechanism.

So, if we get back to Fiona's situation we will see that she'll include the $708 on line 104 of her 2001 tax return. It will be fully subject to tax in 2001.After two years and two tax returns, the only double-dipping Fiona will do is at Dairy Queen.

We expect that the government designed the employee expense and GST/HST rebate system the way it did so that employees would not need to keep track of the GST/HST component separate from the non–GST/HST cost of every expense they incur. This would be necessary if the amounts on form T777 needed to be reported without the GST/HST component. So, although it may be difficult to understand the logic behind the employee expense and the GST/HST rebate system, it is easier to comply with the system than it is to understand it.

Provincial and territorial sales taxes

There is no rebate for provincial and territorial sales taxes. They simply remain part of the costs you incurred in carrying out your employment responsibilities.

Chapter 27

Tax Planning for Your Small Business

In This Chapter

- Deciding what business ownership structure is right for you
- Making the most of your small-business tax planning
- Understanding what expenses are tax deductible, partially deductible or not deductible at all

As most owners will attest, running a small business is no "small" feat. Issues arise continually that need an owner's attention — customers, manufacturing, marketing, sales. labour relations, etc. Another area owners must look to is the tax side of owning and operating a small business. As we delve into this chapter we will tackle many tax issues that a small business owner must face. Tons of these issues can lead to positive tax planning opportunities in terms of maximizing after-tax income for the business owner and his or her family. If you're a small business owner, like any taxpayer, remember that tax planning is a year round activity. By planning ahead you can take advantage of many of the excellent tax tips and breaks we look at in this chapter. Once the tax year of your business is over, it is difficult to do any "retroactive" tax planning. So take action today and get planning — prompt implementation of these strategies will get you on the road to maximizing your tax savings.

Choosing the Right Business Ownership Structure

Businesses can be operated through one of three main types of ownership structures:

- Sole proprietorship
- Partnership
- Corporation.

The structure you choose at the start of your business, and as the business grows, will be a key factor in the business's future growth, profitability, tax minimization, and cash flow.

Many people starting a business have the idea that they should use a corporation immediately. In other words, that they should begin an incorporated business on day one. The reason they most often give is that they understand a corporation pays less tax than other forms of business ownership structures and that it is therefore the superior structure. As we will see, it's true that a corporation's tax rate may be lower than the owner's personal tax rate. (The lower tax rate is mainly due to the "small business deduction." We discuss this tax credit in detail later in the chapter.) However, what some small business owners fail to see is that they will need to have the corporation "pay" them in order for them to have personal funds to buy groceries, pay the home mortgage, and fund kids' birthday parties. When a small business owner pays himself or herself, he or she will of course have to pay personal income tax on their pay. Therefore, both corporate and personal income taxes are paid. The tax rules are designed so that when you add the corporate and personal tax together the aggregate is approximately equal to the total personal tax an unincorporated business owner would have paid. Tax geeks refer to this as the integration of the corporate and personal tax systems.

Sole proprietorships

A sole proprietorship is a common business ownership structure when there is one owner. Unlike a partnership or a corporation, a sole proprietorship is not a separate legal entity — it is simply treated as an extension of the owner, or "the proprietor." The owner reports revenues and expenses of a business operated through a sole proprietorship on his or her personal tax return. No separate tax return is needed for the business. The owner reports the net income (refer to Chapter 15, Self-Employment Income) from the business on one of the following lines of the personal tax return:

- Line 135 — Business income (form T2124 "Statement of Business Activities" needs to be completed)
- Line 137 — Professional income (form T2032 "Statement of Professional Activities" needs to be completed)
- Line 139 — Commission income (form T2124 is used here again)
- Line 141 — Farming income (form T2042 "Statement of Farming Activities" needs to be completed)
- Line 143 — Fishing income (form T2121 "Statement of Fishing Activities" needs to be completed).

A sole proprietorship is generally the way to start any business. An exception may be where the business may incur significant liabilities — both actual liabilities for money owed (say from financing start-up activities) and potential litigation liabilities. The reason? If you own a sole proprietorship, you own all the *assets* of the business but you are also responsible for all the *liabilities* of the business. In other words, the amount of liabilities you are responsible for is "unlimited." (We discuss later that operating a business through a corporation may be a way to limit your liability.) Also, don't forget, no matter what the form of your business ownership, you will want to purchase some type of liability insurance — in many industries it is mandatory. The advantage of starting as a sole proprietorship is that any start-up losses are claimed on your personal tax return. These losses are deducted from your other sources of income in the year. Therefore, your net income and taxable income will be lower — meaning the taxes you pay will also be lower! Losses are generally bad from a cash flow point of view, but good from a tax savings point of view.

Rebecca opened up her very own florist shop in Edmonton, Alberta, on January 2, 2000. Prior to opening, she went to see an accountant for advice on the business ownership structure she should use. She decided that a sole proprietorship made the most sense. Previously, Rebecca was employed by a florist shop in Red Deer, Alberta. Over the past five years, she has reported about $30,000 of taxable income each year on her personal tax returns. Rebecca expects to lose money in the first two years. She expects to lose $15,000 in 2000 and $8,000 in 2001, due to start-up costs and low revenues while she builds her customer base. If Rebecca had incorporated her florist shop when she started her business, the losses would be "trapped" in the corporation until she made a profit — three years from now, in 2003! At that time, the $23,000 in losses incurred in 2000 and 2001 could be used to offset the profits in 2003.

A loss from a business, whether incorporated or not, can be used to offset business profits of the subsequent seven years or prior three years. Note that a business loss, referred to as a *non-capital* loss, can be used to offset any other type of income, including capital gains. This is in contrast to a *capital* loss, which can only be applied against capital gains. A capital loss can also be carried back to the three previous years. However, a capital loss carryforward period is indefinite. Refer to Chapter 17, lines 251 to 253 for comments on claiming losses of prior years on your 2000 tax return.

By operating her business as a sole proprietorship from its commencement, Rebecca's losses in 2000 and 2001 can be carried back and applied against the taxable income she reported in the past three years (1997, 1998, and 1999) on her personal tax returns. The result: She can immediately recover some of the taxes she paid in those years. Obviously, Rebecca prefers to recover some of the taxes now than to wait for the tax savings three years from now. Also, let's say Rebecca had, in addition to her business loss of $15,000 in 2000, investment income of $10,000 in 2000. Before carrying the loss back to 1997, Rebecca would first claim a portion of the loss against the $10,000 in investment income so no tax would be payable in 2000. The excess loss remaining would then be carried back to 1997.

To request a loss be carried back to a prior year, you complete form T1A "Request for Loss Carryback" at the time you are preparing your personal income tax return. To ensure speedy processing of your loss carryback request, you should mail your T1A to the CCRA separately from your tax return. If you e-file your return, you must still mail a paper copy of the T1A to the CCRA. Once a T1A is processed by CCRA you will receive a Notice of Reassessment for the year in which the loss was carried back to. You will also receive a cheque!

Sole proprietorship: The good news

A sole proprietorship has a number of advantages. These advantages stem from the simplicity and low cost of setting up a sole proprietorship to the uncomplicated requirements of reporting the results for tax purposes. Let's take a detailed look at the advantages of a sole proprietorship:

- Ease of operation — it's the easiest of the three business ownership structures.
- Simplicity of record keeping. However, the CCRA still requires you maintain a set of books separate from your personal affairs.
- Simplicity of income tax filing — no separate tax return required. Minimal accounting fees if you need an accountant to assist you with your personal tax return.
- Low cost to begin business — no incorporation fee. Depending on where you live and the name of the business you choose, you may need to register the business's name. In Ontario the registration fee is about $80.
- Opportunity to apply losses against other sources of personal income in the year the loss was incurred and the previous three years. Where a loss is carried back, you can recover some of the taxes paid in those years.
- Ease of change to an incorporated business. The income tax rules permit a sole proprietor to convert the business to an incorporated business without tax being triggered, provided the correct tax election is made, documented as required, and filed with the CCRA within statutory time limits. It often makes sense to defer the conversion of a sole proprietorship to an incorporated business until the business is profitable.

Sole proprietorship: The not-so-good news

With every bit of sunshine comes a little rain. With the many advantages of a sole proprietorship come a few disadvantages:

- Your liability is unlimited. All your personal assets (your home, car, jewelry, and so on) are exposed to creditors, even though these assets are not used in the business.
- You can't take advantage of the low corporate tax rate available on the first $200,000 of a corporation's business (non-investment) income provided by the tax credit referred to as the "small business deduction." When compared to a corporate business ownership structure, fewer after-tax funds are available to the business owner to reinvest in the business. We discuss the small deduction in detail.

- You can't take advantage of the $500,000 capital gains exemption. To make use of the exemption the business must operate through a corporation. We explain the exemption below in our comments dealing with corporations. The exemption is also discussed in Chapter 17, line 254.

While we have noted these disadvantages it is fairly easy to avoid them. As noted above, one of the advantages of a sole proprietorship is the ease of changing to a corporate ownership structure. So, to avoid the disadvantages of a sole proprietorship, simply convert your proprietorship to a corporation!

Partnerships

A partnership ownership is similar to a sole proprietorship, except that there is more than one owner. There are at least two owners, and they are referred to as "partners." Partnerships and partners comply with the same tax rules we all do. A partnership is a separate legal entity. This contrasts with a sole proprietorship, which is considered merely as an extension of the business owner. The partners determine how they will split the profit (or loss) of the partnership. The partnership does not pay any income tax. Its profit (or loss) is allocated out to the partners, who then become responsible for paying income tax on their share, or, where a loss has been allocated to them, making the best use of the loss in minimizing taxes.

Which type of partnership is for you?

There are three forms of partnerships: a *general partnership*, a *limited liability partnership* (LLP), and a *limited partnership* (LP). Each form has slightly different characteristics. The type of partnership you use will depend on the business or investment undertaking, your faith in the business or investment, as well as your faith in your partner's capabilities.

General partnerships

This is the most common partnership where the partners are actively involved in running a business. The partners share the ownership of the assets and the liabilities. Just as with a sole proprietorship, general partners have unlimited liability with respect to debts of the partnership. Even worse, they have "joint and several liability." This means that if one of the partners can't fund his share of the liability, creditors can still come after the other partners for the full debt. So, if a partner in a law practice "screws up" really badly and litigation is commenced against the law firm, all the other partners are on the hook for the potential debt even though they had nothing to do with the "screw up"! This quite obvious negative characteristic of a general partnership has been somewhat softened by the introduction of limited liability partnerships (LLPs).

Limited liability partnerships (LLPs)

Don't confuse this with a limited partnership (discussed below). An LLP works to limit the liability of the partners in a partnership who were not responsible for the liability. In other words, it is the partner(s) responsible for the liability that is (are) exposed to creditors. The "joint and several" liability characteristic of a general partnership does not exist in an LLP. Due to fairly recent changes in many provincial partnership laws over the past few years, many accounting and law firms have converted from a general partnership to an LLP.

Limited partnerships (LPs)

This is a partnership where each partner's liability is limited to the investment each has made in the LP and any financial commitments to which they have agreed. LPs are generally used for investments. By definition, a limited partner cannot be active in the day-to-day running of the partnership. Each LP has one general partner. It is the general partner, usually the operator of the LP, that assumes all the responsibilities for the LP's debts in excess of the limited partners' investments and financial commitments.

Tax implications of a partnership

As noted above, the partnership itself does not file an income tax return. The income or loss of the partnership is allocated to the partners based on their agreement for sharing income and losses. When there are more than five partners, the partnership is required to file financial statements and a form T5013 "Partnership Information Return" with the CCRA. Also, each partner's share of the partnership's income or loss needs to be documented on a T5013 slip prepared for each partner. The T5013 slip is included with the partner's personal tax return. The amount of partnership income is usually reported on one of the self-employment forms discussed above under "Sole proprietorships." Then the partner will deduct any expenses incurred by the partner personally in carrying out partnership duties. These expenses would be for any expense that a partner incurred to earn his or her partnership income. A partner's expense that has been paid for or reimbursed by the partnership cannot be claimed as it has already been taken into account in determining the partnership income. Common items claimed by partners on their tax returns include promotional costs such as meals and entertainment expenses, and automobile expenses. The partner's "net" income or loss (partnership share of income or loss, less expenses incurred personally by the partner) is then reported on one of lines 135,137,139,141, or 143 of their tax return.

Partnerships: The good news

Using a partnership as your form of business organization offers many of the same advantages provided by a sole proprietorship.

- They are relatively easy to set up.
- Minimal government regulations are imposed on partnerships. (A limited liability partnership and a limited partnership have a few more regulations than does a general partnership.)
- Simplicity of income tax filing — no separate tax return required. (However, form T5013 "Partnership Information Return" and T5013 slips for each partner may be needed.)
- Skills of others are available to help run the business.
- Risks of the business can be shared with other partners.
- You can use your share of the partnership loss to shelter other sources of personal income from tax.
- Like a sole proprietorship, it is fairly easy to convert a partnership into a corporation.

Partnerships: The not-so-good news

Disadvantages of owing a business through a partnership are similar to the disadvantages faced by sole proprietors. These disadvantages are noted below:

- With a general partnership, your liability is unlimited. As in a sole proprietorship, your personal assets are exposed to creditors, even if you had nothing to do with the liability. (An LLP works to minimize this disadvantage.)
- If relationships between partners deteriorate, it may be necessary for a partner to leave the partnership. This can be a very unpleasant task to deal with. To minimize the unpleasantness, your partnership agreement should deal with how partner departures will be handled.
- If you are operating your business through a partnership you can't take advantage of the low corporate tax rate available on the first $200,000 of a corporation's business (non-investment) income. When compared to a corporate business ownership structure, fewer after-tax funds may be available to reinvest in the partnership's business.
- Again, if operating your business through a partnership you can't take advantage of the $500,000 capital gains exemption. As noted above, to take advantage of the exemption a corporation must be used for the business ownership structure.

Corporations

A *corporation* is a legal entity separate and distinct from its owner(s) — the shareholder(s) of the corporation. A corporation is created under federal or provincial law. The income tax rules applied to federally incorporated business are identical to those that are incorporated under provincial legislation. Since a corporation has a separate existence, it owns all the assets and is responsible for all liabilities of the corporation. If a shareholder provides a creditor with a personal guarantee of a corporate liability, the shareholder's assets are exposed, but just in connection with the specific debt of the corporation. Often shareholders will be required to provide personal guarantees on corporate obligations such as bank debt, and on rental and leasing agreements for premises and equipment.

Sidestep those personal guarantees

A request for your personal guarantee is a standard request of a creditor — especially when your business is a start-up or has very little in tangible assets. Just because you are asked for the guarantee doesn't mean you always have to comply! Here are the steps in avoiding a personal guarantee:

- Get out your best negotiating skills.
- Focus your creditors on your track record.
- Highlight the successes you've had.
- Ensure your creditors know you have put a lot of money into the corporation too. (The creditors won't care about the blood, sweat, and tears you've put in — only the money.)
- Make sure your business plan contains specific, measurable, reachable, realistic goals.
- Let your creditors know that you have a network of savvy businesspeople to call on as needed — lawyers, accountants, information system specialists, corporate communication advisors, and so on.
- Promise your creditors monthly cash flow statements and accounts receivable listings.
- Perhaps pledge the receivables.
- Do anything you can to avoid a personal guarantee.

What are the other ways your creditor can secure his loan? In your mind, does the alternative security give the creditor sufficient collateral? If so, tell the creditor!

The following is taken from Richard Worzel's *From Employee to Entrepreneur* (Key Porter Books, 1989):

> Worst of all, your banker is going to ask for a personal guarantee. And here's how he is going to phrase it:
>
> "Look, if you believe in the business, you shouldn't have any problem guaranteeing it. If you don't believe it's going to succeed, then there's no way I can lend you the money."
>
> They teach that line at banker's school, so expect it.
>
> The reply is equally simple: "Of course I believe in the business. The business will carry the loan, and you've got adequate security without my guarantee. You're lending money to the business, not to me, so my guarantee doesn't enter into it.
>
> An even simpler reply is "No. I reserve my personal guarantee only for situations where there isn't any other way to secure the loan. But this loan has adequate collateral without my guarantee. So, yes, I believe in the business, but no, I'm not going to guarantee it."

Where no personal guarantees are provided, the shareholders of the corporation generally have limited their liability to their investment in the business. Our lawyer friends tell us that if a shareholder is also an officer of the corporation (officers include the president, vice-president, and secretary-treasurer) and acts in a "grossly negligent" manner, the shareholder, due to his or her role as an officer, can have some personal exposure to creditors.

Become a secured creditor of your own corporation

TIP

Even with limited liability, you still want to protect your investment in the incorporated business. Where you have put a significant amount of cash into a corporation, we recommend the following strategy to protect your investment as much as possible:

- In return for the money you have invested in the corporation, classify a minimal amount as your purchase of shares of the corporation — say, make the first $100 of your investment represent your purchase of 100 common shares of the corporation.
- Treat the remainder of your investment as a loan you've made to the corporation. This loan should be documented with a promissory note between you and the corporation. There is no requirement for you to charge interest on the loan to the corporation.
- Have your lawyer register the note under your province's personal security act.

Take advantage of the $500,000 capital gains exemption

You will now have made yourself a secured creditor of the corporation. When things turn sour, it is the secured creditors who get paid first. Unsecured creditors fight over the dregs. A big advantage of owning shares of a corporation is evident when the shares are sold. One of the purposes of our income tax rules is to offer taxpayers incentives if they spend their money in ways the government likes. The government wants to encourage all of us to invest in shares of private Canadian-owned incorporated businesses. When shareholders sell shares of these businesses, they may be eligible to claim a capital gains exemption in respect of the gain incurred on the sale. This means that all or a portion of the gain is "exempt" from regular income tax. This is the incentive the government is offering to you to make these desired investments in Canadian business. When the shares qualify, a shareholder may find that he or she can receive the first $500,000 of capital gains free of regular income tax. (There may be some alternative minimum tax to pay, but this is often refunded over the next few years. Refer to Chapter 19 for details on the alternative minimum tax.)

Only a shareholder that is an individual can claim the $500,000 capital gains exemption. If the shares of corporation A are held by corporation B and corporation B sells the shares of corporation A, no capital gains exemption is available because the "selling shareholder" is not an individual. Shares that qualify for the $500,000 capital gains exemption are referred to as Qualified Small Business Corporation Shares (QSBCS). Refer to chapters 13 and 17 for details. Like the QSBCS, certain farm property, referred to as Qualifying Farm Property, or QFD, also qualifies for the $500,000 capital gains exemption.

The first $500,000 of a capital gain on the sale of a qualifying share is free of regular income tax by virtue of the *capital gains exemption*. However, since only two-thirds of the capital gains is included in income, only two-thirds of the $500,000 capital gains exemption is actually claimed on your tax return. This two-thirds figure is referred to as the capital gains *deduction* on the tax return. The maximum capital gains deduction that can be claimed is therefore $333,333 ($500,000 × ⅔). New tax proposals announced on October 18, 2000 reduce the capital gains inclusion rate from two-thirds to one-half for sales made after October 17, 2000. Therefore, the maximum capital gains deduction for post-October 17, 2000 sales of QSBCS will be $250,000 ($500,000 × ½). You calculate your available capital gains deduction on form T657 and report it on line 254 of your tax return. (Caution: Form T657 is one of the most complicated tax forms to complete. Refer to Chapter 13, Capital Gains and Losses, and Chapter 17, The Calculation of Taxable Income, for details.)

There is the possibility that the government will remove the tax rules permitting the $500,000 capital gains exemption. If the rules are to be removed, we expect there will be some warning issued by the government prior to the effective date of the removal. This is what occurred when the $100,000 capital gains exemption was removed back in 1994. However, you can "lock" in your capital gains exemption now — without selling your shares to a third party. You sell your shares back to the corporation in consideration for new shares of the corporation — a paper shuffle, if you will. Tax geeks refer to this as "crystallizing" your $500,000 capital gains exemption.

Say you own shares of a corporation you operate, and those shares are worth $500,000. The tax cost of these shares is only the $100 you invested in the corporation on start-up. On the sale of these shares back to the corporation, you will trigger a $499,900 capital gain, but it will be sheltered from regular tax by the $500,000 capital gains exemption. (Technically, you would only claim $499,900 of your available $500,000 exemption.) The tax cost (the "adjusted cost base") of the new shares of the corporation you received on the sale of your other shares will be $500,000. Thus, when you actually sell them to a third party, only the sale proceeds in excess of $500,000 will be subject to tax.

You have increased the tax cost of your investment from $100 to $500,000 on a tax-free basis. You have "locked-in" the capital gains exemption. If the rules with respect to the capital gains exemption are changed after you do this "shuffle," you're safe! (Oops — we said "tax-free." Our editors are so picky! We should have said "free of regular tax." Alternative minimum tax may be triggered by a crystallization transaction. Beware!)

Timing is everything: When do you incorporate?

Are you currently operating your business through a sole proprietorship or a partnership? Since the $500,000 capital gains exemption is only available on the sale of shares of a corporation, you should consider converting your business to a corporation. Both a sole proprietorship and a partnership can be converted to a corporate ownership structure without you incurring any immediate income tax on the accrued capital gain of the assets of the proprietorship or partnership. You must make a tax election, and document that election by completing and filing a specific tax form with the CCRA.

The small business deduction

In addition to accessing the $500,000 capital gains exemption, a second major advantage of operating your business through a corporation is the tax savings provided by the "small business deduction." The word *deduction* here means a deduction in corporate income tax. It is the same as saying a "tax credit." Like the capital gains exemption, the small business deduction works as an incentive to become an entrepreneur — start a business, hire employees, rent a warehouse, lease a fleet of trucks, etc. These are all things the government wants you to do as it is beneficial to the Canadian economy. Also like the capital gains exemption, to take advantage of the small business deduction the business must be operated through a corporation.

The net income of a sole proprietorship or a partnership is taxed directly in the hands of the business owners — the proprietor or the partner. If you refer to Table 1-2 in Chapter 1, which summarizes the top 2000 federal/provincial/territorial tax rates, you can see that the top tax rate a business owner could pay on sole proprietorship or partnership income varies from 43.7 percent (Alberta) to 51.7 percent (Quebec). Taking Quebec as an example, on an after-tax basis the business owner is left with only 48.3 cents to put back into the business to fund operations. However, in most provinces and territories the combined federal and provincial/territorial tax rate applied to the first $200,000 of business income (non-investment income) is about 21 percent. This is referred to as the "small business deduction." The corporate tax rate on business income in excess of $200,000 is about 44 percent. The rate climbs to about 50 percent where the corporation's income is investment income. The federal government has announced its proposal to allow for a "middle" tax bracket for corporate business income between $200,000 and $300,000, beginning in 2001.

The foregoing discussions have dealt with corporate tax — not personal tax. If your business is a corporation, you are required to prepare and file a corporate tax return and pay corporate income taxes. It is the after-tax corporate funds that are available for reinvestment in the business or for the payment of dividends to shareholders or additional salary (a "bonus") to the employees. (Which in many cases will be the same individuals as the shareholders.)

Obviously, with a 21-percent tax rate on the first $200,000 of business income, 79 cents on the dollar is available for reinvestment in the business — far more than the 48.3 cents remaining in the Quebec sole proprietor's hands.

Be careful when choosing between salary versus dividends

If the operators of the corporation do not wish to reinvest the after-corporate-tax funds in the business, the funds can be paid out to the operators as a bonus (which is simply treated as additional salary) or as a dividend payment to the shareholders. Either way, the receipt will trigger *personal* income tax in the recipient's hands. We know what you are thinking. You are thinking that when faced with the choice of taking a salary or a dividend from a corporation, you should always choose the dividend because it is taxed at a lower rate. You are correct that the *personal* tax is lower. This can be confirmed by referring to Table 1-2 in Chapter 1, which summarizes 2000's top tax rates. Look at Nova Scotia. The 2000 top federal/Nova Scotia tax rate on a salary would be 48.8 percent, while a dividend would be taxed at only 32.9 percent.

However, the corporation is not entitled to deduct a dividend payment in computing its taxable income. A dividend is not considered a deductible expense incurred in the process of earning corporate income. The payment of a dividend is considered an after-corporate-tax distribution of profits — therefore, there's no tax deduction to the corporation. A salary payment is considered a deductible expense incurred to earn income of the corporation. A salary payment is deductible in computing a corporation's taxable income. A tax deduction results in a tax saving to the corporation — a dividend does not.

In summary, when looking at the dividend scenario you must aggregate the corporate and personal tax. It is this aggregate tax number you must use to compare to the personal tax on salary. In many cases, you will find the tax numbers will be almost the same. Again, this is referred to as the integration of the corporate and personal tax systems. Integration is designed to ensure business owners receive no tax savings or incur extra tax on funds taken out of a business for personal use just because they decided to use one form of business ownership over another.

Salary is "earned income," dividends are not

Salary is considered "earned income" for the purposes of making registered retirement savings plan (RRSP) contributions, while dividends are not. To be eligible to make the maximum RRSP contribution of $13,500 in 2002, an individual needs at least $75,000 in 2001 salary. This is because one of the calculations in the formula to determine your maximum RRSP contribution limit is 18 percent of your earned income: $75,000 × 18 percent equals $13,500. If you received only dividends in 2001, your 2002 RRSP contribution limit would be zero! We discuss the RRSP deduction in detail in Chapter 16. RRSPs, in connection with retirement strategies, are discussed in Chapter 28.

How would you like to pay no personal tax at all?

If you don't want to pay any personal tax, take no money out of the corporation! O.K., O.K. — we understand that you need some money to live on. But to maximize the tax deferral of your personal tax, you should minimize your withdrawals from the corporation. The period of deferral is potentially unlimited. Where a business is run through a corporate ownership structure, there is opportunity to defer tax. As we have seen, no personal tax is payable unless money is taken out by the owners (shareholders) of the corporation. The personal tax part of the overall tax rate is *deferred* until money is taken out of the corporation. A corporation offers you flexibility in determining when your personal tax liability is triggered. If personal tax rates are expected to go down, you will want to minimize the withdrawals you make from the corporation until the year when personal tax rates are the lowest.

Let's look at an example. Jack has been running a successful airport limousine service in Fredericton, New Brunswick, for a number of years, as a sole proprietorship. During 2000 he incorporated the business, and the corporation's net income, before the deduction for Jack's salary for 2000, was $100,000. Jack paid himself $60,000 in salary (his only personal income in 2000), which keeps his taxable income just under the top tax bracket. (Tax brackets and marginal tax rates are discussed in Chapter 1.) If Jack had received more salary than this, each additional dollar would have been taxed at 49.2 percent — the top 2000 marginal tax rate in New Brunswick (see Chapter 1's chart of top 2000 marginal tax rates). Jack decided he wanted to defer the personal tax on the additional $40,000 of income. He left the $40,000 in the corporation to be subject to tax at the small business rate of approximately 21 percent.

The corporation paid tax of $8,400 ($40,000 × 21 percent). This was significantly less than if Jack had taken the money out of the corporation and paid personal tax of $19,680 ($40,000 × 49.2 percent). Jack has deferred taxes of $11,280, or 28.2 percent (49.2 percent less 21 percent) of the $40,000. Once Jack decides to take the $40,000 out of the corporation, the deferral will be over and he will have to pay the personal tax.

If you decide to leave the after-corporate-tax funds in a corporation so your personal tax is deferred as long as possible, there are three tax repercussions to consider.

Consideration #1. If the funds exceed the amount needed to operate the business of the corporation, you may be tainting your access to the $500,000 capital gains exemption. For the shares of the corporation to be QSBCS *at the time of their sale,* the corporation must have at least 90 percent of the market value of its assets invested in assets used to earn business income (that is, non-investment-type assets such as trucks, machinery, computers, office equipment, and so on). Excess cash and short-term and long-term portfolio investments are not considered to be used to earn business income. Should the value of these "tainted assets" exceed 10 percent of the corporation's assets at the time you sell the shares, those shares will *not* qualify for the $500,000 capital gains exemption. It is imperative that the level of "non-business" assets of the corporation be monitored on an ongoing basis. For the 24 months prior to the sale, the tainted assets (the investment or non-business assets) of the corporation cannot exceed 50 percent of the corporation's total asset value.

Consideration #2. If you invest the excess funds, the investment income earned by the corporation will be taxed at the full corporate tax rate applied to investment income — not at the small business deduction tax rate. This tax rate may be higher than the personal marginal tax rates of the shareholders. If so, you will want to increase the shareholders' incomes so that the lower tax brackets of these shareholders are not "wasted." A shareholder's income can be increased if the corporation pays them more dividends. There is no tax saving from the small business deduction because investment income is not considered to be "earned" from operating a business. However, the first $200,000 of business income continues to qualify for the small business deduction tax rate.

Consideration #3. You are exposing high-quality assets to creditors. If this is a concern, another company can be incorporated that would serve as a holding corporation for the shares of your operating corporation. The active corporation can pay up excess funds as tax-free dividends to the holding corporation. Since the funds are not being paid to an individual, no personal tax liability arises. The funds remain in a corporation.

Corporations: The good news

A corporation offers business owners (again, known as shareholders in the corporate setting) many advantages over operating a business though a sole proprietorship or a partnership. The advantages available to you include the following:

- Your liability as an owner, is limited to your investment in the corporation plus any personal guarantees you have provided to creditors.

- The low corporate tax rate provided by the small business deduction on the first $200,000 of business income results in greater after-tax corporate cash to use in the business — for example, to pay employees, purchase a fleet of trucks, pay rent on the warehouse, and so on.
- The choice of taxation year end. Most sole proprietorship and partnerships work with a taxation year that is the same as the calendar year — December 31. A corporation is free to use any year-end it wishes provided the first taxation year-end is within a year of the incorporation. (Note — the first taxation year does not need to be 365 days — it can be anywhere from 1 day long to 365 days — 366 in a leap year!) Using a non-calendar year-end later than August 31 for a corporation can offer tax deferral on personal remuneration to the next calendar year that may have a lower personal tax rate. Any salary or bonus recorded in the financial statements of a corporation must be paid out by the 179th day after the taxation year-end to remain tax deductible to the corporation.
- Choice of personal income that can be received from the incorporated business — for example, salary or dividends.
- Timing of receipt of personal income of owners is flexible.
- Ownership can be separated from the management of the business. There can be shareholders of the corporation that do not work for the corporation. However, they can still receive funds from the corporation — not as a salary but as dividends paid on shares they own of the corporation.
- Access to the $500,000 capital gains exemption on the sale of your shares.
- If the business fails you may be able to get favourable tax treatment by claiming an allowable business investment loss (an ABIL) on your personal tax return. Refer to Chapter 16's discussion on lines 217 and 228.
- A corporation is a tool to carry out an "estate freeze," which may be part of your overall estate planning. Also, transferring assets to a corporation can reduce provincial probate fees payable on a shareholder's death. Refer to Chapter 25 for suggestions on your estate planning.

Corporations: The not-so-good news

A corporation is the most flexible business ownership structure. As detailed above it has many advantages — both tax and non-tax. With these advantages do come some disadvantages. These deal mainly with the costs involved in using a corporation — both to set it up and to maintain its existence. The disadvantages of a corporation include:

- The legal and accounting costs to set up the corporation, plus the annual costs of maintaining the corporation's minute books and preparing annual financial statements and a federal corporate tax return. (You may need a separate provincial corporate tax return if your incorporated business operates in Alberta, Ontario, or Quebec.)
- Director's liability. Shareholders of a corporation can have unlimited liability. However, the directors of the corporation can be personally liable for corporate debts such as the Goods and Services Tax, provincial sales tax, and employee payroll withholdings that have not be remitted to the CCRA, as well as environmental liabilities that may arise.
- Losses incurred by the incorporated business (say, in the start-up period) are not available to shelter the owner's personal income from tax.
- The incorporated businesses may be subject to corporate capital taxes in addition to income taxes.

Tax Planning Opportunities for Small Business Owners

So now that you know all about the three business ownership structures and the advantage and disadvantages of each let's look at the tax planning opportunities available to you as a small business owner! In this section we revisit the decision of when to incorporate, how to "split" income to leave more after-tax funds for you and your family, and the timing of purchasing and disposing of assets used in your business.

Incorporate!

As we have seen, it does not usually make sense to incorporate until the corporation is profitable. Until that time, losses can be applied against other sources of income on your personal tax return. Shortly after your business becomes profitable, you should consider incorporating it to take advantage of the small business deduction provided on the first $200,000 of business income. This will leave the corporation with greater after-tax funds to use in the business. This assumes that you desire to leave some of the after-corporate-tax cash in the corporation. As illustrated above, the advantage of the low corporate tax rate is eliminated to the extent that you withdraw funds from the corporation — by way of either a salary or a dividend. If you remove all the after-corporate-tax funds from the corporation, the tax saving provided by the small business deduction is completely eliminated. Therefore, from a tax planning point of view, incorporating your business really only makes sense under two conditions:

- The business is profitable.
- The business generates greater after-corporate-tax funds than funds you need for personal living expenses.

Split your income

Income splitting is the process of shifting or "moving" income from the hand of one family member, who pays tax at a high marginal tax rate, to another, who pays tax at a lower marginal rate. The gross income of the household remains the same, but the family's after-tax cash is greater because the tax bill has been decreased. For example, a sole proprietor could hire his or her spouse to work in the business. The spouse would earn a salary, which would be taxed personally in the spouse's hands. The spouse making the salary payment would receive a tax deduction. The spouse receiving the salary would pay tax on the amount. To reduce the family's total tax the spouse receiving the salary needs to be at a lower tax rate than the spouse that is making the payment.

Consider Ricky and Lucy's situation. Ricky is a musician in Vancouver. He earned $70,000 in 2000. Lucy does not work outside their home because she is busy raising their son, Little Ricky. Lucy earns no income. On $70,000 of income, Ricky would pay approximately $21,000 of combined federal/British Columbia income tax. (This tax is after application of the tax credits for the basic personal amount and the full spousal amount. Refer to Chapter 18 for details on these credits.) Lucy would, of course, pay no tax. Now let's change the facts. Say Ricky hired Lucy on a part-time basis to maintain his books and look after all the administration of his business. For 2000 Ricky paid Lucy $10,000. Ricky's income would drop to $60,000 because he could deduct the $10,000 paid to Lucy in calculating his business income subject to tax. On $60,000, Ricky would pay tax of about $18,000. Ricky would not be able to claim a tax credit for the spousal amount because Lucy's income would exceed $6,140. On her income of $10,000, Lucy would pay tax of only about $750. (Her tax is quite low because the first $7,231 of her $10,000 in income is not taxed due to her basic personal amount tax credit.) The total personal income tax of Ricky and Lucy would be $18,750 — down $2,250 from the $21,000 in tax Ricky would pay if he reported the entire $70,000 on his own personal tax return. The after-tax funds available to the family have increased $2,250!

Where a family member is paid a fee or salary for services provided to your business, the amount paid must be "reasonable" in the CCRA's view. In determining what is reasonable, the CCRA looks at the services rendered, the skill set needed, the time commitment, and what a non-family member would be paid in the circumstances.

In addition to paying a spouse to help you in your business and to take advantage of the tax savings of income splitting, you can also have your kids help out. Remember, each child can receive $7,231 of income in 2000 and pay no tax because of the basic personal amount tax credit. Another advantage of income splitting is to provide other family members with "earned income" to permit them to have some RRSP contribution room for the next year.

Where the business is operated through a corporation, income splitting with your spouse can be done through the payment of dividends, provided the spouse is a shareholder of the corporation. Since your spouse would be receiving dividends as a shareholder, he or she would not have to provide any services to your business. Where an individual's sole income is dividends, he or she can receive about $24,000 in dividends and pay absolutely no personal tax due to the combination of the basic personal amount credit and the dividend tax credit. Up until the end of 1999, paying dividends to minor children was a great way to take advantage of the opportunities for income splitting. However, beginning in 2000, this no longer works — minor children will now pay tax at the top marginal rate on dividends received from a private (non-public) corporation. Kids cannot even claim the basic personal credit amount to offset the tax. However, the payment of dividends to adult children still works for income splitting. Keep in mind, though, that if the adult kids are already subject to tax in the top tax bracket, the income shift will not result in any tax savings.

Where the business is incorporated, a family member can serve as one of the corporation's directors. In carrying out director's duties, the family member can receive a director's fee — another way to accomplish income splitting. Again, the fee must be reasonable in relation to the services rendered as a director. (Caution: As noted above under "Corporations: The not-so-good news," a director can be held personally responsible for certain debts of a corporation!) Refer to Chapter 24 for more details on how you can split income with your family.

Timing is everything: Asset purchases and asset disposals

As discussed in Chapter 15, on Self-Employment Income, when you purchase assets for your business (such as computers, office equipment, and machinery) you can claim capital cost allowance (CCA) or "tax depreciation" each year. The amount of depreciation you claim is expressed as a percentage. Different types of assets have different CCA, or depreciation, rates. In the year an asset is acquired, only half of the regular CCA percentage can be claimed. The "half-rate" rule was introduced many years ago as a disincentive for business owners to go out on the last day of the business's taxation year-end and purchase significant capital assets. Before the half-rate rule was introduced, some business owners could expect a significant CCA deduction on an asset that they'd only owned for, say, one day in the whole tax year.

A purchase late in your business's tax year is no longer as attractive as it was before the introduction of the half-rate rule — *but it is still attractive*. If you are planning to purchase an asset, do so before the year-end to be able to take the CCA deduction as soon as possible.

Conversely, if you are planning to dispose of a capital asset, the actual sale should be deferred until at least a day after the business's taxation year-end. This is because CCA can be claimed on all assets owned by the business on the last day of the taxation year. If you sold the asset prior to the end of the year, no CCA can be claimed.

What Expenses Are Tax Deductible?

Generally, all expenses you incur to carry on your business are tax deductible! However, let's discuss some of the not-so-obvious expenses.

Home office expenses — operating your business through a sole proprietorship or partnership

We talk in Chapter 26 about how an employee can deduct costs of maintaining a home office if that office is required by an employer. If you are operating your own business through a sole proprietorship or partnership, you will be able to deduct the cost of maintaining your home office if your workspace meets one of two tests (not both!). Under the first test, the workspace must be the chief place where your business activities are carried out. If the first test is not met, however, all is not lost. You may still qualify to deduct home office expenses if your workspace is used exclusively to carry out your business pursuits. (Note that the word *exclusively* is not used in the first test.) In addition to using the space exclusively for these activities, you must use the space on a "regular and continuous" basis for meeting customers or clients or others associated with carrying on your business. Just as there are restrictions placed on employees with home office expenses, there are restrictions here: you cannot claim home office expenses to "create or increase a loss" from your business. Any home office expenses that cannot be claimed in a year carryover for potential claim in the next year.

If you are operating your own business through a sole proprietorship or partnership, you have an advantage over an employee in terms of what type of home office expenses you can deduct. Have a look at Table 27-1 for more information. The advantage you have is that you can simply deduct more!

Table 27-1 Home Office Expense Eligibility for Income Tax Write-off

Expense	*Salaried Employee*	*Commissioned Employee*	*Self-Employed*
Utilities	Yes	Yes	Yes
Repairs and maintenance	Yes	Yes	Yes
Rent on premises	Yes	Yes	Yes
Property tax	No	Yes	Yes
Home insurance	No	Yes	Yes
Mortgage interest	No	No	Yes
Capital Cost Allowance (CCA)	No	No	Yes

The percentage of total home office expenses you can deduct is based on the size of your workspace compared to the whole house or apartment. The CCRA suggests calculating this as a percentage on a square-foot (or square-metre) basis. Someone with a 1,500-square-foot home containing a 150-square-foot office would deduct 10 percent of the applicable costs.

As noted in the chart, a self-employed individual with a home office can deduct capital cost allowance (CCA) on their home. This is not recommended, however, because it prevents the individual from claiming the principal residence exemption on the workspace portion of the home, when the home is sold. Refer to Chapter 13, Capital Gains and Losses, for details on the principal residence exemption.

Home office expenses — operating your business through a corporation

The head office of your corporation may be in your home. If you are personally incurring costs of maintaining the office, you can have the corporation reimburse you. A reimbursement of expenses is not taxable in your hands. Your corporation can claim a tax deduction for the home office expenses reimbursed to you.

What Expenses Are Partially Deductible or Not Deductible?

O.K., so you may think that every single dime you spend can be "written off." Not so fast — this is one of the most popular misconceptions that business owners have and boy, do things go crazy when they realize that everything they spend doesn't immediately get shaved off what they owe taxwise. In this section we'll help you sort through the myth and reality of deducting expenses.

Meals and entertainment expenses

Generally, only 50 percent of the cost you incur for meals and entertainment expenses is tax deductible. Entertainment is considered to include amusement and recreation. Say you purchased tickets to a Toronto Raptors game to take clients to — only 50 percent of the cost of the tickets would be tax deductible. However, there are cases when 100 percent of meals and entertainment expenses can be deducted.

- Meals and entertainment expenses provided in the ordinary course of a company's business. For example, a restaurant can deduct 100% of food costs incurred to provide dining services;
- Costs incurred as part of fund-raising events for a registered charity;
- Amounts reimbursed in full by a third party. For example, any meal and entertainment costs specifically billed to a customer or client are fully deductible if disclosed on your invoice, but the customer or client is only entitled to deduct 50% of the bill on his return;
- Any meals and entertainment expenses included as a taxable benefit to an employee;
- Costs incurred on behalf of all a business's employees. Christmas parties, staff member recognition get-togethers, and office summer barbeques are examples. This exemption to the 50 percent rule only applies to six such events held each calendar year.

Club dues and fees

Dues (initiation or annual) or fees paid to a club providing sporting (for example, your golf club and/or yacht club), recreational, or dining facilities are not tax deductible — even if they are incurred to assist in the development or expansion of your business. However, business-related meals and entertainment costs incurred at these locations can be deducted subject to the 50-percent limitation noted above. As discussed in Chapter 26, Tax Breaks for Employees, an employer can make dues and fee payments to a club on behalf of an employee. Provided the employee's attendance at the club is expected to benefit the employer — that is, generate more business — the employee is *not* considered to have received a taxable benefit. But the employer still does not get a tax deduction.

Prepaid expenses

Some costs of operating your business are paid before the goods or services are provided. For example, look at the insurance you have on your business. Insurance premiums are usually paid once a year, and it's rare that your "insurance year" is identical to your business's taxation year. You probably will find that when you prepare the cheque for the insurance premium, you are paying for future insurance coverage. Assume your business has a taxation year-end of December 31, 2000. On August 31, 2000, you received a bill for insurance your business has on its premises. The bill was for $500 and it related to the insurance year of September 1, 1999 to August 31, 2000. You paid the bill right away. Of the $500 paid for insurance, only $167 could be deducted in 2000. This is because only four months' (September to December) coverage falls into the year 2000 ($500 multiplied 4/12 = $167). You'd deduct the remaining undeducted amount of $333, the prepaid portion, in 2001 — the year to which this portion of the insurance premium relates.

Life insurance premiums

Life insurance premiums are considered a personal expense and are therefore not tax deductible. But wait, there is an exception to this rule. Where a lender has required a borrower to take out life insurance as collateral for a loan, all or a portion of the life insurance premium is tax deductible. If the life insurance is a term policy, the full premium is tax deductible provided the face amount of the policy does not exceed the lender's requirements. If the insurance is a universal or whole life policy, only the portion of the premium representing the true cost of the insurance is tax deductible. You cannot deduct for tax purposes the portion of the premium representing the savings component or "side fund" of the insurance.

Automobile expenses

The tax deduction available for automobile expenses is restricted in two ways:

- The income tax rules limit the tax deduction that can be claimed for kilometre allowances paid to employees. The maximum that can be deducted in 2000 is 37 cents for the first 5,000 kilometres driven by each employee, and 31 cents thereafter. Due to harsher weather conditions, the three territories' rates are 41 and 35 cents.

  If an employer pays more than these amounts, the additional amount is not tax deductible.

- There are maximum amounts that can be used in claiming CCA, lease costs, and interest in respect of car loans.

  For cars purchased or leased in 1997, 1998, 1999, and 2000, the maximum amounts that can be claimed are summarized in Table 27-2 below. Any amount paid in excess of these amounts is not tax deductible. These restrictions were introduced way back in 1987 to stop significant tax write-offs claimed on expensive cars.

Table 27-2 Summary of Restrictions on Tax Deduction for Automobiles

	2000	*1999/98*	*1997*
Maximum cost for CCA purposes	27,000	26,000	25,000
Maximum monthly lease payment	700	650	550
Maximum monthly interest cost	250	250	250

Note

The government reviews these limits annually and announces any changes prior to the end of the year, so taxpayers are aware of the rules in advance of the year in which they apply. The rates are set and released through press release by the Department of Finance Canada. Copies of press releases are available on the department's Web site at `www.fin.gc.ca/access/nr_se.html`. All limits are before sales tax. The limits are actually slightly higher when GST, HST, provincial, and territorial sales taxes are added in.

Advertising in non-Canadian publications

Amounts paid for advertising in foreign print or electronic media will not be deductible where the advertising is primarily targeting a Canadian market. The reason for this is that the taxman is not going to let a Canadian company have a tax deduction when the revenue is going to media in a foreign country. The taxman would rather have Canadian media earn the revenue (and, of course, pay the tax).

There is nothing to prevent you taking a deduction for advertising in a foreign media publication when the intended market audience is outside Canada.

Chapter 28

Strategies for Retirement

In This Chapter

- Using up unused contribution room today
- Choosing a self-directed RRSP or RRIF
- Making the right choice about the year to claim your RRSP deduction
- Avoiding RRSP withdrawals whenever possible

Don't read the title of this chapter and decide that you're too young to start thinking about retirement. Here's a piece of very valuable advice — you're never too young to start planning your future. After all, how many of you start thinking about the weekend on Monday morning! Well, just think of retirement as one long weekend. This chapter discusses registered retirement savings plans (RRSPs) and registered retirement income funds (RRIFs), as well as the importance of contributing funds to your RRSP now — and keeping them there.

Making the Most of Your RRSP

Let's start with the basics. A *registered retirement savings plan* (RRSP) is simply a plan registered with the CCRA that is designed to encourage you to help save for your retirement. Basically you agree to put a portion of your salary or self-employment income away, and in return the government gives you an immediate tax deduction. You won't face tax on any contributions until you withdraw the money from the plan.

But wait, there's a catch. The Department of Finance won't let you put as much money into your RRSP as you want each year. They set contribution limits that are based on your *earned income.* The concept of earned income was defined back in Chapter 16, but as a refresher, it most includes employment income, rental income (less losses), self-employment income (less losses), royalties, alimony, maintenance and taxable child support received, and disability pension income received under CPP/QPP.

Earned income does not include interest, dividends, capital gains, pension benefits, retiring allowances, severance pay, death benefits, scholarships or bursaries.

The maximum amount that can be contributed to an RRSP in any given year is set as the lesser of 18 percent of earned income of the previous year, and a limit set by the Department of Finance. Currently the limit for 2000 is $13,500. This means that a taxpayer who made $75,000 of earned income in 1999 could make the maximum contribution of $13,500.

We've defined the maximum amount of money that a person can put into an RRSP each year. But suppose there aren't enough funds available to make the contribution — is that contribution room lost forever? Thankfully no. Any unused contribution room can be carried forward and used in a future year. Which brings us to an important point. Did you know that Canadians have a combined unused RRSP contribution room of $176.4 billion? In fact, some individuals have unused contributions in excess of $30,000. Why is it so important to get money into your RRSP today? First, it provides you with a tax deferral. An RRSP contribution made today provides you with an immediate tax deduction, therefore reducing your taxable income. You won't pay tax on these funds until they're taken out, so you're effectively pushing your tax bill to a future year.

Kaitlyn decides she needs to use up some of her excess contribution room and makes a $2,000 contribution to her RRSP. If her marginal tax rate is 50 percent, she'll save $1,000 in tax that she otherwise would have paid. If she leaves this money in her RRSP for 40 years and withdraws it when her marginal rate is still 50 percent, she'll pay $1,000 in tax at that time. What has she saved? Well, paying $1,000 some 40 years from now is the same as taking $46 today and investing it to earn 8 percent. In 40 years, she'll have the $1,000 needed to pay her bill. By deferring the tax, she has effectively reduced her tax bill to $46!

Another advantage of contributing to your RRSP today is tax-free growth. You see, any income you earn inside your RRSP is not subject to tax until the money is taken out. So, regardless of how large your investment grows, you won't pay tax until the future. Since you're not paying tax on the growth, you're left with more money at the end of each year to compound inside your RRSP.

Suppose you make a $100 contribution each month to your RRSP. You earn about 9 percent on these funds. If you leave the money for 30 years, you'll have $183,000 when you retire. Compare this to contributing $100 each month *outside* your RRSP. Assuming your effective tax rate is 40 percent, you'll have only $89,600 when you retire. How's that for proof of the benefit of tax-free compounding.

Borrowing to contribute

For some, it makes sense to borrow money to make a *catch-up contribution* to an RRSP. A "catch-up" contribution is a large contribution made in one year to use up some, if not all, of your carryforward room. Why? With interest rates still relatively low, it's less costly to borrow than it used to be. As well, taxpayers continue to put off making this larger-than-life contribution, assuming that they will be able to carryforward this room indefinitely. While it's true that the rules currently allow for an indefinite carryforward, there's no guarantee that the rule will be around forever. Why risk the Department of Finance imposing restrictions on the limit and leaving you holding the bag?

Assume Dave wants to borrow $15,000 to make an RRSP contribution this year. He borrows this at a rate of 8 percent over three years, and puts the money into investments that earn approximately 9 percent annually. By making the RRSP contribution, he will enjoy a $7,500 tax refund, assuming his marginal tax rate is 50 percent. If he applies the refund toward the loan, and pays off the remaining portion over three years, he will be out of pocket approximately $8,500. By this time, however, his RRSP contribution will have grown to be worth more than $19,400 — that's a return of well over 100 percent in three years.

Obviously, borrowing doesn't make sense for everyone. You should consider the interest rate on the loan, the rate of return that's being earned inside the RRSP, and the amount of time that will likely lapse before you'll withdraw the funds. If the interest rate on the loan is too high, or you're planning on withdrawing the funds in a few years, borrowing probably doesn't make sense for you.

Beware of using up all your unused contribution room in the same year. The deduction may put you into a lower tax bracket, which will, in effect, reduce your tax savings. Where possible, apply your RRSP contribution to your highest marginal rate of tax.

Starting a Preauthorized Contribution (PAC) Plan

One method of ensuring that you get money into your RRSP is to set up a preauthorized contribution (PAC) plan. A PAC plan authorizes a bank or investment company to withdraw funds from your account and place them in your RRSP. These types of plans work well for people who find it hard to make a large one-time contribution at the end of the year. They also work for people who need the discipline to save money — as the saying goes, "You can't spend what you don't have." Since the money is withdrawn automatically, after a while you'll hardly miss it at all.

Given the rapid fluctuations in the market these days that create such uncertainty, a PAC plan is a good idea: it actually reduces your exposure to changing markets. Some investors try to time their sales and purchases to benefit from the highs and lows of the market — often unsuccessfully. A PAC plan helps eliminate this guesswork because preauthorized contributions let you take advantage of dollar-cost averaging, a strategy that averages out the market's highs and lows over time.

Visit your local bank or investment broker to set up a preauthorized contribution plan today. The sooner you do so, the more money you'll have for your future.

Assessing employer-direct RRSP contributions

There is an alternative to preauthorized contribution plans that works much the same way — only better. It's called employer-direct RRSP contributions. The concept is this: Your employer sends a portion of your compensation directly to your RRSP. The benefit is that since the payment is not made to you, the income taxes normally withheld on this payment are avoided. This provides you with almost twice as much money to make a contribution. From a practical point of view, the tax results are as follows:

- Your employer makes a contribution to your RRSP. The amount contributed cannot exceed your contribution room available.
- You avoid income tax withholdings.
- Your employer's contributed amount will appear with any other income on your T4 slip.
- You are entitled to a deduction for the full amount contributed to the RRSP.
- You won't expect a refund, since income tax withholdings were avoided from the start.

Let's look at the example of Sylvia. Suppose she's in the top marginal tax bracket, and pays tax at 50 percent. She's about to receive a $5,000 bonus from her employer. If she's paid this bonus directly, her employer will withhold tax and pay her just $2,500. This leaves her only $2,500 available to make an RRSP contribution. Instead, Sylvia arranges with her employer to have the funds deposited directly into her RRSP. By doing so, she avoids the withholding, and she's able to contribute the full $5,000 to her RRSP. If you're entitled to bonuses, take advantage of this option. It can result in significant tax savings.

Normally, RRSP contributions result in a tax refund in April. However, if your employer makes these contributions directly, you won't receive a refund because you've avoided tax withholdings from the start.

The CCRA has stated that each employer-direct RRSP contribution should be under $10,000; otherwise, the employer is required to withhold income tax.

Considering making an over-contribution in the year you turn 69

The tax rules require you to wind up your RRSP by December 31 in the year you turn 69. A common problem is that many people have earned income in the year they turn 69, yet the resulting contribution room isn't available until the next year — when they're 70. By this time, the RRSP has been wound up. There is a strategy that prevents this future contribution room from going to waste. It's called the Seniors' Over-Contribution. Instead of wasting the contribution room that results from earned income in the year the RRSP is wound up, an additional contribution should be made that year. The contribution should be made as late in the year as possible — December is the best. Provided you've already maximized your RRSP contributions to date, an additional contribution of $13,500 will result in an over-contribution.

The CCRA charges a penalty of 1 percent per month on over-contributions in excess of $2,000. This means that an over-contribution of $13,500 made in December will attract a penalty of $115. (Calculated as $13,500 less the allowable over-contribution of $2,000, times 1 percent.) Come January 1 of the year after you turn 69, you'll be entitled to RRSP contribution room based on your earned income of the previous year. Therefore, your excess contribution will be used up, and the penalty will stop accruing.

So how will this benefit you? Well, assuming your marginal tax rate is 50 percent, a contribution of $13,500 will save you $6,750 of tax — a saving well worth the $115 penalty! In addition, you'll reap the benefits of tax-free compounding.

Ask your employer to make monthly or biweekly contributions from your paycheque. You'll avoid the withholding tax, and at the same time reap all the benefits offered by a preauthorized contribution plan.

Make a contribution in kind

If you've already borrowed to the hilt, and your piggy bank is empty, don't give up hope. There's still another way for you to make an RRSP contribution. You see, there's nothing that says contributions have to be made with cash. Instead of contributing cash, you can contribute other qualifying assets. This is called a *contribution in kind*. And no, your old hockey card collection or Elvis lamp won't cut it. Qualifying assets are as follows:

- Guaranteed investment certificates (GICs)
- Shares listed on a Canadian or foreign stock exchange
- Mutual funds
- Corporate bonds, or other debt obligations
- Shares of certain private corporations
- Government-guaranteed debt obligations
- Mortgages secured by real property in Canada
- Certain annuities
- Certain life insurance policies
- Certain rights and warrants.

It may be difficult to make an in-kind contribution if your RRSP is not self-administered. Most administrators will only accept cash.

In-kind contributions are entitled to the same tax treatment as cash contributions. The amount of the contribution is measured by the fair market value of the asset on the day the contribution is made.

When you contribute an asset in kind to your RRSP, you're deemed to have disposed of the asset for proceeds equal to the fair market value on the date the contribution is made. This may result in a taxable capital gain if the asset has appreciated in value. If the asset has declined in value, don't try claiming the capital loss — the CCRA will deny it.

Your capital loss will be denied if you contribute assets that have declined in value. Instead, you should sell the asset for a loss and contribute the cash. This way you can claim both the capital loss and the RRSP contribution.

Choosing a Self-directed RRSP or RRIF

Nowhere does it state that you must hold your RRSP assets with a financial institution, mutual fund company, or life insurance company. Instead, you can set up your own self-directed RRSP. To do this, you must first establish your own trust with a trust company. After that, you can invest in whatever eligible investments appeal to you.

Not all assets qualify to be held in an RRSP. Unless you're familiar with the rules surrounding which assets are eligible, you should avoid setting up a self-directed RRSP. Unsophisticated investors beware: There are severe penalties for holding non-qualifying assets! There are several advantages to setting up a self-directed RRSP.

The sky's the limit

You can hold any RRSP-eligible investments inside a self-directed RRSP. You're not limited to specific investments, as you would be if you purchased from a financial institution or mutual fund company. Everything is available to you, all in one place. This becomes more important if you decide to adjust your holdings, or move from riskier investments to more conservative ones.

Organized system

A self-directed RRSP eliminates the need for you to hold a variety of investments in a variety of accounts. This means less paper. Come December 31, you won't be bombarded with statements from every investment company. As well, you'll be able to see clearly how each investment is performing because all the information is contained in one place. No more keeping track of which company holds what investments.

Diversification

More than ever, Canadian investors are recognizing the need to invest in the global market. After all, Canada represents just 3 percent of the world market. There are restrictions, however, on how much foreign content you can hold in your RRSP. In 2000, no more than 25 percent of the cost base of your property may be held in foreign investments. In 2001, this limit rises to 30 percent. This restriction applies to each account, not to your total RRSP holdings. Here's where people who don't have a self-directed RRSP may run into some problems.

Suppose that in 2000 Bill held his RRSPs with two different financial institutions. In one account he holds only Canadian securities with a cost base of $90,000. In the other he holds only foreign securities with a cost base of $30,000. In total, his foreign content is 25 percent. There is a problem, however, since the foreign content limits apply to individual accounts. You see, the account where he holds only foreign property will be subject to penalties because that account is 100-percent foreign. If he held all his investments in a self-directed RRSP account, he'd avoid the penalties.

The administration fees for a self-directed RRSP are often higher than those of other plans — generally more than $100 annually. You should wait until you've accumulated more than $20,000 in retirement assets before you set up a self-directed plan. Paying $100 per year on a $20,000 account means sacrificing only 0.5 percent of your return, which is reasonable.

Deciding When to Claim Your RRSP Contribution

Anyone who has earned income can make a contribution to an RRSP. Now, we've already mentioned the importance of getting the money into your RRSP as soon as possible — but what about the deduction? Did you know that you could make a contribution to your RRSP and delay taking the deduction? If you answered no, you're not alone. Many people don't understand the importance of claiming the RRSP deduction in the proper year.

Take Megan, for example. She worked as a camp counselor last summer and made $3,000 dollars. This year she worked part-time, and also had a summer job. Her total income for 2000 was $6,500. Since she's heard so much about RRSPs, she's decided to make a $500 contribution. Her $500 contribution would allow her to reduce her taxable income by $500. But does this make sense? Even without the RRSP deduction, her tax liability would be nil because her income is below the personal exemption of $7,231. Claiming the deduction would not save her any tax.

Does this mean that Megan should have waited to make an RRSP contribution? No. Even though the deduction doesn't save her tax this year, she can carry it forward to another year and use it to offset her income when she's in a higher tax bracket. Making an RRSP contribution early gives her the best of both worlds — early tax-free growth now, and a deduction at a higher marginal tax rate later!

Never use an RRSP deduction to reduce your income below the basic personal amount. If you think your taxable income is going to increase significantly from one year to the next, you should defer your RRSP deduction to the next year. This way, your marginal rate is higher and you save more tax.

For example, suppose your current annual salary is $50,000. You're starting a new job next year and you'll be making $70,000. You've made a $5,000 RRSP contribution during this year. If you take the deduction this year, you'll save approximately $1,800 of tax (assuming a 36-percent tax rate). However, if you wait until next year when your income is higher (and your tax rate is 50 percent), you'll save almost $2,500 in tax!

Avoiding RRSP Withdrawals

As a child, didn't you hate those piggy banks that you put your pennies into but couldn't get them back again? The people who designed those banks did so to make sure kids thought long and hard before smashing the bank to get their money out. Either that, or they had a sick sense of humour! Someone should develop a similar system for making RRSP withdrawals. It's understandable that unforeseen circumstances come up and the money is needed. However, some people use their RRSP account as a current bank account instead of a savings account. Those are the people we want to address in this section.

Understanding the impact of making early withdrawals

Before you take money out of your RRSP prior to retirement, you should stop and think about the consequences. Not only is your RRSP withdrawal going to leave you with a tax bill, but you'll also be giving up the growth that would have occurred had you left your assets in place. And this adds up fast. Here's proof.

Let's consider what happens if you make a $10,000 withdrawal from your RRSP. First of all, you'll pay tax on this amount, and depending on your marginal tax rate, the bill may be as high as $5,000. But that's not the worst of it. If your RRSP money grows at a rate of 8 percent, and you do not make a withdrawal, 30 years from now you'll have $100,600 more in retirement savings than if you made a withdrawal now. Even a withdrawal as small as $5,000 will deprive you of $50,300 of future growth!

If you make an RRSP contribution and decide later that you need to take the money out, the taxman isn't going to give you back any RRSP contribution room. Once you've made the contribution, the room is gone forever — even if you take it out again the very next day!

Table 28-1 Cost of Making Early Withdrawals

	Amount of Withdrawals		
Years to Retirement	***$5,000***	***$10,000***	***$20,000***
10 years	$10,795	$23,305	$50,313
20 years	$21,589	$46,609	$100,626
30 years	$43,178	$93,219	$201,253

Making withdrawals in no or low-income periods

There's no doubt that there'll be times in your life when you find you're strapped for cash, and need to dip into your RRSP assets. Maybe you're starting a family, or setting up your own business. Whatever the reason, there are ways to make your withdrawals more tax efficient. The best time to take money out of your RRSP is when you have little or no other sources of income. And in most cases, these are the times when you need your RRSP savings the most. You see, in 2000 every Canadian resident is entitled to receive the first $7,231 of income tax-free. (This amount will vary from year to year with inflation rates.) This means that you're able to withdraw up to $7,231 from your RRSP without paying any tax. Even if your income is more than this, you'll pay only about 26-percent tax on income up to $30,004. Quite often, you'll pay less tax on these withdrawals than you would have if you had taken the money out during retirement.

You will be charged withholding tax on withdrawals from your RRSP. The rates of withholding are 10 percent on withdrawals of $5,000 or less, 20 percent on withdrawals of $5,001 to $15,000, and 30 percent on withdrawals over $15,000. In Quebec, the withholding rates are 25 percent, 33 percent, and 38 percent, respectively.

The full amount of the withdrawal is included in your income for the year the money is taken out. In most cases, the tax withheld will not be enough to cover the entire tax liability, so you'll have to make up the difference when you file your tax return in April. That said, you can't forget about the growth you give up by making an early withdrawal. Although you may pay less tax now, you're giving up far more in future retirement assets. If at all possible, it's always best to keep RRSPs for retirement.

When to withdraw assets from an RRIF

There comes a point in time when you can't avoid making withdrawals from your retirement assets. Most often, RRSPs are converted to RRIFs at age 69. The tax law says you must take a minimum amount out of your RRIF each year and include this amount in your income.

There are some ways to keep a few extra dollars inside the plan each year and avoid the tax hit. Here are three rules of thumb:

- **Base your withdrawals on the age of your spouse.** If your spouse is younger, the required withdrawals will be lower, deferring tax longer.
- **Delay your first withdrawal.** You're not required to begin making withdrawals until the year after the RRIF is set up. This means that if you establish the plan in 2000, you can defer your first withdrawal until December 31, 2001. If you leave the assets in the plan longer, you'll maximize the growth.
- **Make minimum withdrawals.** You should withdraw no more than the required amount per year, if possible. This defers tax and allows the assets to grow.

Chapter 29

Using Investments to Manage Your Taxes

In This Chapter

- Understanding what income your investments earn — and how they are taxed
- Flow-through shares
- Real estate investment trusts and royalty trusts
- Labour-sponsored funds
- Exempt life insurance
- Film limited partnerships
- Art donation schemes

At least once a week we hear people say, "My taxes are too high. What can I do to reduce them?" Although we don't have the magical solution that will make your tax bill disappear altogether, there are some things you can do to reduce the amount you pay each year to the taxman. For example, are your investments tax efficient? We know this may sound like an oxymoron. After all, how can taxes be efficient? But there is a way to invest your money without paying more tax than you have to. Simply speaking, the tax efficiency of an investment is measured by the amount of tax that the investor must pay annually as a result of owning the investment. Holding a tax-efficient investment will result in as little as possible ending up in the hands of the tax collector. This chapter focuses on ways your investments can help make your tax bill manageable.

What Is Investment Earning and How Is It Taxed?

The amount of tax you pay depends on the type of income your investment is earning — whether it's interest, dividends, or capital gains. As a refresher, interest is simply compensation paid for the use of money belonging to someone else. You'd commonly earn interest on investments such as bonds, GICs, and term deposits. Dividends are after-tax profits paid out by a corporation to its shareowners. Capital gains result when you sell capital property at a profit. Unfortunately, the *Income Tax Act* does not define what capital property is. Whether a transaction is capital in nature really depends on what the owner intended to do with the property. You may want to refer back to Chapter 13 for more details on capital transactions. Interest income is the least tax efficient because it is taxed at the investor's highest marginal tax rate. Investments that earn primarily interest income include money market investments, bonds, and fixed-income investments.

Dividend income sits in the middle of the tax-efficiency scale. Since dividends from Canadian corporations qualify for the dividend tax credit, they are taxed at a lower rate than is interest. If you're looking to generate dividend income, you may want to invest in equities that pay dividends annually.

Capital gains are the most tax efficient, since they are only taxable when *realized* (that is, when your shares are sold, or, if you invest in mutual funds, when the securities in the fund are sold). Further, capital gains triggered after February 27, 2000 are just two-thirds taxable, thanks to the 2000 federal budget. (The mini-budget tabled on October 18, 2000 proposed to reduce the capital gains rate to 50 percent. However, whether or not this reduced rate is adopted depends on the outcome of the federal election on November 27, 2000.) The bottom line is that capital gains are subject to a lower rate of tax than interest and dividends. If you're looking for potential capital gains, equities are your best bet.

Capital gains are taxed more efficiently than dividends only if you're already in the top marginal tax bracket (that is, you earn more than $60,009). If you're in a lower tax bracket, you are still better off earning dividends due to the availability of the dividend tax credit. After all, assuming you have no other income, you can earn approximately $25,000 in dividends tax-free!

Table 29-1 shows the after-tax amount that you would have if you earned $100 in the various types of income. These rates assume you're in the top marginal tax bracket for the year 2000 in Ontario, but are indicative of what you'll find across Canada. We've also assumed a two-thirds capital gains inclusion rate for the entire year.

Table 29-1 Cash in Your Pocket after Earning $100 of Income

	Interest	*Dividends*	*Capital Gains*
Income	$100	$100	$100
Tax	$47.90	$32.30	$31.90
After tax	$52.10	$67.70	$68.10

If you're in a lower tax bracket, dividends are taxed more efficiently than capital gains. However, investing in equity investments allows you to defer the tax hit, since you'll only face tax when you sell your securities. The benefit of pushing the tax bill to the future may outweigh the additional tax you'll pay on the capital gains.

Know your objectives before choosing your investments. Although capital gains are the most tax-efficient form of income, equity investments are also generally more risky than other types of investments. If you are risk-adverse and require a safe means of income, fixed income or term deposits may better suit your objectives.

Flow-Through Shares

Flow-through shares are issued to investors by resource corporations to finance exploration and development programs in Canada. Resource corporations typically include those in the oil, gas, and mining industries. The companies that issue flow-through shares need cash — not tax deductions — to finance their activities. Therefore, in exchange for the investor's financing, the corporation renounces certain tax deductions and flows (hence the name) them through to the investor.

Canadian resource companies are able to renounce certain deductions and flow them through to the investor instead, so that the investor can claim the deduction. Normally these types of expenses are Canadian exploration expenses, which are 100-percent deductible by the investor, and Canadian development expenses, which are 30-percent deductible on a declining balance basis.

The investor can then use these deductions to offset other forms of income. Generally, the investor is entitled to a deduction for Canadian exploration expense incurred, equal to the amount paid for the shares — or close to it.

Not only can the corporation renounce certain expenses incurred during the year, but it can also renounce expenses that it expects to incur the next year. This means that a company issuing flow-through shares in 2000 is able to renounce eligible expenses incurred in 2000, as well as those it expects to incur in 2001.

Investors who invest in flow-through shares can expect a large deduction in the year that the investment is made — probably about 90 percent of the investment. The remainder of the deductions can be expected the next year or the year after.

Now, you may be thinking, *This sounds great, I make an investment and reduce my tax bill.* Although that's essentially true, keep in mind that all investments have a cost base that is used to determine the capital gain when the investment is sold. In the case of flow-through shares, the cost base is nil. Those of you who are not yet asleep will realize that this means a guaranteed capital gain equal to the proceeds when you sell your flow-through shares. But remember, by making this investment you've managed to reduce current taxes and defer them until the future when the shares are sold. Flow-through shares are great for using up capital losses you may have incurred in the past, since they guarantee a way to use up some or all of the loss.

The income deduction that comes with flow-through shares provides a great planning opportunity. If you know your income is going to be much higher in a given year, you may consider flow-through shares to reduce your income and your tax bill. Your income may be higher if you make RRSP or RRIF withdrawals, you receive a bonus, or you've realized capital gains. Flow-through shares also provide additional deductions once you've maximized your RRSPs.

Now that we've learned what flow-through shares are, let's talk about who should invest in them. As with most investments, these aren't for everyone because they are higher risk. The value of the investment fluctuates as resource prices rise and fall.

However, as Table 29-2 shows, even if you sell your investment for the same price you paid for it, you can achieve a 17-percent return on your investment. Obviously, this return will decrease should you sell your investment at a loss.

This isn't to say that you should stay away from them, just that you should avoid holding more than 10 percent of your portfolio in flow-through shares. Be sure to speak to your financial advisor to find out if these are right for you.

Table 29-2	Rate of Return from Flow-Through Shares
Purchase price of investment	($100,000)
Tax savings from deductions[1]	$50,000
Proceeds from sale of investment	$100,000
Tax on capital gain from sale[2]	($33,333)
Return on investment	$16,667
Percentage return on investment	16.67 percent

Notes

1. Tax savings equals $10,000 × 50 percent.
2. Tax on capital gain equals $100,000 × ⅔ × 50 percent tax rate.

These calculations assume that the taxpayer's marginal tax rate is 50 percent.

Real Estate Investment Trusts and Royalty Trusts

Let's talk now about real estate. For many readers, real estate is probably their largest investment. After all, if you consider the value of your house in relation to your other investments, we're sure that real estate takes up a large chunk of your overall portfolio.

For those of you who want to hold more real estate in your total portfolio, keep reading. We'll talk first about Real Estate Investment Trusts.

Real Estate Investment Trusts (REITs)

The idea of a REIT first came to Canada in the mid-1980s, after it proved so popular with our friends south of the border. Basically, a *Real Estate Investment Trust (REIT)* works like a closed-end mutual fund, meaning that the number of investors is restricted. Each investor owns units in the trust, which in turn owns and manages a portfolio of commercial real estate. Each year the trust earns rental income (and sometimes capital gains), which is taxed in the unit holder's hands. The actual net cash income produced by the trust is distributed to the unit holders.

At this point, the most common question asked is, "So what?" Well, here's the thing. REITs are popular because the trust is entitled to deduct capital cost allowance (CCA), which, as you've already learned, is the tax word for *depreciation.* Now, as you also know, depreciation is not a real cash expense. So putting the two together, the trust's income, which is taxed to the unit holder, is less than the cash that the unit holder actually receives. Get it? The cost base of the investment to the unit holder is then reduced by the amount of CCA claimed, so that when the investment is sold, a capital gain is created. Let's look at an example.

Julie invested $5,000 in an REIT. This means that the cost base of her investment is also $5,000. In 2000, the REIT distributed $500 in cash profits. However, the REIT also claimed $500 CCA on her portion of the units. The result? Julie's tax bill is nil, while she still has the $500 in cash. The $500 is then deducted from her cost base, giving her a new cost of $4,500. Suppose that in September 2000 Julie sells her investment for $5,000, which is the fair market value at that time. She will then report a capital gain of $500 ($5,000 less $4,500 cost base), which is just two-thirds taxable.

Did you catch all that? From the example above, you can see two advantages of an REIT. Not only does it allow you the potential to defer tax until the investment is sold, but also it can allow you to convert income that is normally 100-percent taxable (such as rental income), to capital gains, which are only two-thirds taxable.

The example above assumed the trust took CCA equal to the income earned during the year. This is not always the case. CCA may not always offset your entire income, but it will offset a large portion. As well, there is always the risk that you will sell your investment for less than your purchase price. Our example assumed the fair market value was equal to the purchase price to help illustrate how an REIT can convert rental income to capital gains. Losses incurred by an REIT cannot be allocated out to the unit holders.

REITs are an easy way for investors who do not have the funds to purchase real property and enter the world of real estate.

Should everyone go out and buy REITs? Of course not. As we've said before, these types of investments aren't for everyone. They do bring with them some risks. For example, as interest rates rise, the value of REITs will fall because fixed-income investments become more attractive to investors. As well, there is the risk that the properties held by the trust will not continue to do well, and will begin to operate at a loss. This can occur if real estate prices fall, in which case rents charged will also fall.

A REIT may be ideal for investors who have capital losses available, since these investments have a high chance of generating a capital gain.

Royalty trusts

Like an REIT, a royalty trust provides the taxpayer with the opportunity to defer tax until a future year, and to convert income that would otherwise be 100-percent taxable into capital gains. A royalty trust works like this — corporation purchases interest in certain oil and gas or mining properties. These properties are not in the exploration stages, which means that reserves have already been found. As the corporation makes money, it pays its earnings to a royalty trust. The investor owns units in this trust, and as the trust receives money from the company, it distributes the earnings to the investor.

In addition, the company also passes along certain deductions to the royalty trust that may shelter from tax all or a portion of the investor's share of the distribution. For example, the company may deduct capital cost allowance and Canadian oil and gas property expenses (COGPE), based on the original amount of the investment.

Suppose Michael bought units in a royalty trust for $1,000. During the year, the corporation earned $200, which was passed to Michael through the trust as a royalty. The corporation also claimed $200 in CCA and COGPE, so the taxable portion to Michael was nil. Like an REIT, the cost base of his investment is reduced by $200 to $800. If Michael turned around and sold his units for $1,000, he would be required to report a $200 capital gain.

See how Michael was not only able to defer the tax on his royalty payment, but also was able to convert the royalty, which is normally 100-percent taxable, to a capital gain, which is only two-thirds taxable.

Speak to your broker to determine whether a royalty trust is a good investment option for you.

Labour-Sponsored Funds

The government wants to promote investments in small and medium-size Canadian businesses. And there's no better way to encourage investors to direct their money to these businesses than by offering tax relief. Both the provincial and federal governments offer fairly generous tax credits to investors who invest in labour-sponsored venture capital corporations (or LSVCC, for short). You'll be entitled to a federal credit equal to 15 percent of your investment and a provincial credit equal to, in most provinces, another 15 percent. (Bad news for readers in Alberta, New Brunswick, and Newfoundland — you won't receive any provincial credits.) This means that in most provinces you may be eligible for a tax credit of 30 percent of your investment. However, there is a cap of $1,500 on the total credits you'll be eligible for. A $5,000 investment will provide you with the maximum credit of $1,500. Since you'll only receive credits on the first $5,000 contributed, make sure you don't contribute more than this amount in one year. Make any additional investment the following year so you can get the 30-percent credit. Although investments in LSVCC offer significant tax savings, they are a higher risk investment. Be sure to talk to your investment advisor to determine if this type of investment is appropriate for you.

If you buy a labour-sponsored investment after March 6, 1999, you'll have to keep these units invested, without selling them, for eight years from the date of purchase. If you cash them in early, you'll have to repay the generous tax credits to the taxman!

Labour-sponsored investments are also RRSP-eligible. This means you can hold LSVCC units inside your RRSP.

Exempt Life Insurance

Life insurance is a hot topic in the tax world these days. It is being used not only for the more traditional purposes, such as covering a tax liability and death, and providing a source of income for heirs, but also for investment purposes. Now, we're sure that most of you (that is, those of you who weren't scared off by this topic) are probably thinking, *How can insurance be used as an investment tool?* Well, there are lots of uses for insurance in investments these days. Some are quite complicated, but in this section we'll talk about one simple idea. Before we dive into the way life insurance is used today, it's important to understand the two most common types of life insurance: temporary insurance and permanent insurance.

Temporary or term life insurance

As the name suggests, this type of insurance is temporary in nature. That means that it has a fixed termination date. It has no cash value — just a death benefit. Because these policies only pay on death, they are considered the simplest form of life insurance protection. Generally, people buy this form of insurance so that they are covered for a specific period of time, such as when their children are young or while their mortgage is outstanding. The premiums for this type of insurance are lower than for any other form.

Most people who have life insurance or belong to a group life insurance plan have term insurance.

Permanent life insurance

This type of insurance provides protection for an individual's entire life, and typically has level premiums throughout the contract. The most common form of permanent insurance today is the *universal life policy*. This product has become a popular vehicle for combining life insurance with savings or investments. Universal life is a combination of term insurance and a side investment fund. Generally speaking, you as the policyholder will select a level of coverage under the term insurance. This decision establishes the minimum level of premiums you will need to pay. (As you get older and cost more to insure, this minimum level of premium will increase.)

For example, suppose you want $100,000 of insurance and your monthly cost (or premiums) for this is $50 a month. You can pay any amount of premium per month that you want, as long as it meets the minimum payment of $50. Why would you want to pay more than this? Well, if you decide to pay $55 a month, every month the extra $5 will go into a separate account called the side investment fund. The side investment fund works a lot like your RRSP. Although you don't get a deduction for the amounts you put into this fund, the investments inside grow tax-free. This means that you won't face a tax bill until the funds are withdrawn or the policy is surrendered.

Any death benefits, including amounts paid on death from the side fund, are received tax-free by the beneficiary.

Using insurance for investment purposes

If you have read this far and understood the concepts of permanent insurance, this section should be a snap. If a life insurance policy remains within the tax law's definition of an "exempt" policy (and most policies do meet this test), all investments within the exempt policy accumulate on a tax-sheltered basis. That is, the policyholder experiences no tax liability.

This is good news for people who have maxed-out their RRSP contributions, yet still have cash left over that they don't need for day-to-day expenses. A universal life policy gives the policyholder the opportunity to over-fund the plan (by paying more than the minimum premium required) and watch the excess amount grow on a tax-sheltered basis. Most universal life policies have a decent selection of investments to choose from — often including debt investments, guaranteed investment accounts, equity investments, and index-linked accounts — which means that the investment component of the policy could grow at a respectable rate.

Before you go and put all your excess cash into a universal life policy so that the investment can grow tax-free, be aware of the limits. Unlimited tax-sheltered growth sounds too good to be true — and it is. Our tax law places a ceiling on the amount that can be in the investment account. The maximum amount will change with the age of the owner and the size of the policy. As with everything else, there is a penalty for holding too much investment in your side fund.

This type of strategy isn't for everyone. Since you will have to pay premiums for insurance, you must weigh these costs against the benefits of tax-free growth. Generally, it makes sense for individuals holding investments in excess of $500,000 who have already maxed-out their RRSP contributions.

Film Limited Partnerships

Various tax shelters have been unearthed recently and are promoted as a way to defer tax. Tax shelters all basically work the same way. The investor is able to claim a tax deduction equal to a portion of, or in some cases the entire amount of, the investment in a short period of time. This effectively reduces current income, thereby reducing the current tax bill.

Although tax shelters appear to be a great idea, the taxman does not think very favourably of the majority of them. As we've said before, if it's too good to be true, it probably is. Be sure to speak to a tax professional before you make your final decision.

When you invest in a film limited partnership, that partnership buys shares in production partnerships that provide money and services to various film studios and film and television companies who have agreed to have their movie or television show filmed primarily in Canada. Film shelters have become very popular in the past couple of years due to the fact that many film limited partnerships are getting advance tax rulings from the CCRA. Although having an advance tax ruling does not guarantee that your investment is safe from the taxman, it does mean your risk of reassessment is reduced.

A number of rules introduced in 1997 severely reduced the benefits of the film tax shelters that were available at that time. One rule in particular was the "matchable expenditure" rule. Prior to this rule coming into effect, limited partnerships could incur expenses and pass some deductions to the investors, even if the partnership had not incurred any income. As a result, the investor could claim a deduction without having to include any income, thereby deferring tax. The matchable expenditure rule effectively reduces the expenses of the limited partnership to the extent that it has receipts included in income to which the matchable expenditures relate.

Various promoters are still offering interests in film limited partnerships. These limited partnerships are set up in such a way that they are able to bypass many of the new rules introduced to curb film limited partnerships. The details of how these partnerships work are complex, and are beyond the scope of this book (that is, we could tell you, but we would probably bore you to death). If you feel that you would benefit from an investment in a film limited partnership, be sure to visit your tax professional with the offering document in hand. Your tax pro will let you know if it is designed in such a way as to escape any negative tax effects under the revised CCRA rules.

The Once-Popular Art Donation Scheme

The CCRA has recently become interested in art. No, it is not giving up on tax to become an agency of art connoisseurs, but it has recently shut down a very popular tax-savings scheme called "art flipping." Before we go into how the CCRA slammed the door in the faces of many taxpayers, let's talk about what these clever taxpayers were up to. Personal-use property, as you learned from Chapter 13, is property used primarily for personal use or enjoyment by an individual. It includes a taxpayer's print, etching, drawing, painting, sculpture, or other similar work of art.

When personal-use property is disposed of, the adjusted cost base and proceeds of disposition are deemed to be at least $1,000. This means that if you sell personal property for less than $1,000, there is no gain to report. Essentially this rule helps to eliminate the burden of calculating gains every time a personal asset is sold for less than $1,000. Not that personal assets are normally being sold for a profit anyhow — ever visit a garage sale? With this rule in mind, a scheme was developed involving donations of art to charities. It worked like this. Basically, the promoter of the art offered investors an option to purchase a bulk order of art pieces for a price well below the fair market value. The artists agreed to sell their pieces at prices significantly below market value if a significant number of art works were purchased at the same time and if the purchaser strongly considered donating some or all of the artwork to charity. In one case, art pieces valued at approximately $28,500 could be purchased for only $8,625!

Once the artwork was purchased, the investor had to decide if he or she wanted to donate all or a portion of the art to a registered charity. If so, the promoter stated that he would be rewarded with substantial tax savings. The promoter claimed that these transactions would qualify as gifts of personal property. These paintings were then appraised for a value significantly above the purchase price (although each painting was appraised at less than $1,000), and donated to charity. Since both the purchase price and the appraised value were less than $1,000, the taxpayer was not required to report a capital gain on the disposal of the paintings to the charity. At the same time, the taxpayer claimed a donation credit for the appraised value of the paintings. The tax savings from the donation credit far exceeded the original price paid for the paintings.

Let's work through this with an example — Dave, who was very interested in saving tax (as are most people), heard of a deal that involved buying art and donating it to charity. He decided to give it a try. He purchased 50 paintings from a promoter for $5,000. The true value of these paintings was actually $15,000. The promoter told him that he was able to buy at a discount because he bought in bulk, and because he was probably donating the paintings to charity.

When Dave donated the paintings to charity, he was deemed to have sold them for their current fair market value. However, since each painting was worth less than $1,000, he didn't have to report a capital gain. He did, however, receive a donation slip from the charity for $15,000. Since he's in the top tax bracket, this donation credit saved him $7,500 in tax. Not too bad for a $5,000 investment!

Well, what Dave didn't know, and what thousands of other taxpayers didn't know, was that the CCRA was looking closely at this scheme. And it didn't pass the smell test. It looked too good to be true and it was. As a result, thousands of taxpayers are now being reassessed on their tax returns for participating in this scheme.

It appears now that the CCRA has made the final decision on art flipping. They aren't buying it — so neither should you. In fact, the 2000 federal budget introduced changes that significantly reduce the tax savings from this scheme. You see, if you bought personal-use property after February 27, 2000, as part of an arrangement in which the property is donated to charity, you will have to report a capital gain on the disposition even if the proceeds are less than $1,000 per piece of property.

The CCRA couldn't prevent taxpayers from participating in these art-flipping schemes, so rather than change the taxpayer, they changed the law. Taxpayers can no longer avoid reporting a capital gain when personal-use property is donated to charity, if the intention was to purchase the property and donate it. This tax change makes art-flipping a thing of the past.

Part VII
The Part of Tens

"Here's the tricky part: pillage is not taxed if derived out of the country. However, it is considered part of your overall plunder done locally."

In this part . . .

Well, you've made it to the end. These final few chapters are short tidbits of useful information you can read any time and any place. To be honest, these chapters are filled with information we thought you should know, but couldn't place anywhere else in the book. So here they are — on their own.

Read them over to find out the ten major tax changes that took place since 1999 that will have an impact on your return this year, the top ten ways to reduce your risk of an audit, and for all you procrastinators, the top ten last-minute filing tips.

"The nation ought to have a tax system which looks like someone designed it on purpose."

— William E. Simon

Chapter 30

Ten Ways to Reduce the Risk of an Audit

What are the two most dreaded words in the English language? For some, it's "tax audit." Chances are, if you are reading this chapter you're just putting the finishing touches on your tax return and are looking for ways to reduce your risk of getting anything other than a thank you note — called a Notice of Assessment — from the CCRA.

Well you've come to the right place. This chapter will provide you with common-sense rules to follow to reduce your chances of getting an unfriendly visit from the taxman. But before we get into all that, read the following to help reduce your anxiety.

If you happen to receive something more than just a Notice of Assessment in the mail — perhaps a request for more information — the first line of defence is to avoid breaking out in a sweat. You see, you should understand that there's a difference between an audit and a request for more information — also called a "verification procedure." The CCRA may ask to see confirmation of receipts that didn't have to be sent with your return, such as child care expenses and tuition, but that is not an audit. In fact, most individuals are never audited. They simply receive requests for additional information. Here are some helpful pointers to help you avoid becoming the CCRA's next target for an audit or review.

Audit Your Own Return

Make sure you double-check your return before you send it in. Check first for mathematical accuracy. Make your life easy and use tax software or an on-line service to ensure your numbers add up properly. Also check that you've included all relevant information, including your name, address, and SIN. Avoiding these simple mistakes is the first step in keeping the CCRA from reviewing your return more closely.

Report All Your Income

Make sure that you've reported *all* income, including interest and dividends from all accounts. If you forget something, you can be sure the taxman will eventually find it. You see, the CCRA gets a copy of the same income slips you receive, and they crosscheck them by computer to make sure everything is reported. One handy tip is to compare this year's return to last year's to ensure that you haven't missed anything.

Have a Reasonable Expectation of Profit

Be careful if you run your own business and are reporting a loss on this year's return. In order to claim these losses, you must be running your business with a reasonable expectation of profit. If not, these losses can be denied. The tax collector only flags your return the first year you report business losses, but if you continue to report losses in the next two or three years, you could be a prime candidate for an audit. Avoiding recurring losses can be as easy as reducing your largest expense over time, which, if you own your own business, is often mortgage interest. Pay down that mortgage more quickly than you might otherwise, and prepare a forecast to show the taxman when you expect to earn a profit.

File Your Tax Return

Some people argue that the only way to ensure your return doesn't get audited is simply to not file a return at all. After all, the CCRA can't audit what isn't there. To these people we say, try again. In fact, every year, the CCRA sends out countless letters to individuals requesting them to file a tax return — proof that the taxman knows who these people are. Non-filers risk not only getting caught and getting hit with interest and penalties, but also going to jail. In addition, if the CCRA has to ask you to file a return, you can bet the chances are greater that they'll take a closer look. So make sure you file every year. And if you've been a non-filer in the past, remember, it's never too late to make things right.

Be Consistent with Your Expenses

Claims for expense deductions must be reasonable, and the expenses must be incurred to earn income. This means that claiming personal expenses is not only a bad idea, it's not allowed under our tax law. Also, if you own your own business, make sure your expenses are consistent from year to year. Of course, you still must be able to support all expenses claimed, but a significant jump in travel or entertainment costs may catch the taxman's eye.

Don't Cheat

Sounds simple enough, right? Well, those of you who are tempted to cheat should be aware that the taxman has ways to track you down. The CCRA has identified the industries that have, in the past, had a higher incidence of cheaters, including construction, subcontracting, carpet installation, unregistered vehicle sales, auto repair, the independent courier business, and direct sales. If you're in one of these industries, don't be offended by our comments. You are probably aboveboard with your tax filings. But not everyone is. And so the list of industries the CCRA keeps its eye on grows longer each year.

Some of you like to voice your opinions on various Internet newsgroups — and that's fine. Some feel that taxes are unconstitutional, and feel this so strongly that they voice their opinions publicly on-line and encourage others to join in. But be aware that the CCRA may be paying attention to your on-line musings. If the taxman takes notice of your comments, you can bet that he'll check to make sure you've been filing your tax return.

Think Twice about Taking Cash under the Table

Many people think that taking cash payments for services will get them out of paying tax. What the taxman doesn't know won't hurt him, right? Don't be so sure. There is no shortage of Canadians who are willing to quietly report you for offering services on a cash basis. In one instance we're aware of, a business owner offered a customer services at a discount if the customer was willing to pay cash. Turned out that the customer worked for the CCRA. *Oops!* The business owner's tax affairs were examined, and he was eventually reassessed for underreporting revenues.

Learn from Your Mistakes

If you're caught cheating, it's almost guaranteed that the CCRA will look at that particular item again the next year. Suppose, for example, that you receive a request to substantiate your child care expenses, and find that, whether by accident or design, you've overstated your expenses. You can be sure that the CCRA will ask you to submit your receipts next time around — perhaps for the next couple of years. The moral of the story? There's absolutely no excuse for getting caught making the same mistake twice.

Don't Give the Taxman Something to Audit

Some tax returns have very little worth auditing. An employee with one T4 slip has less chance of being audited than a self-employed person with significant expenses. The CCRA likes to flag the more risky items to get more bang, so to speak, for its time spent assessing. Items such as losses from tax shelters, significant interest deductions, rental or business losses, and clergy residence deductions (believe it or not) have an increased likelihood of being flagged for an audit. These deductions may be legitimate, but if you choose to complicate your tax affairs by reporting deductions that can be higher risk, be sure you have the information necessary to back up your claim — just in case the taxman comes knocking.

Keep Your Fingers Crossed

Even if you do everything right on your return, you may get selected for an audit or receive a request for information because of plain old bad luck. Every year, the CCRA selects taxpayers at random, and uses the results of these audits or requests to determine where people make the most mistakes, and in which areas people most often cheat. So even if you've crossed all your t's and dotted your i's, you may still receive an unwelcome letter in the mail on CCRA stationery. Don't assume you've done anything wrong — just be sure you can prove that you did it right!

Chapter 31

Top Ten Tax Filing Tips

There's one thing that all Canadians can agree on: No one likes to file a tax return. Not even tax professionals — like us! But there are ways to make the "process" less painful. We've put together a list of ten tips you can use to ensure you're following the rules and to avoid mistakes where it hurts the most: your pocketbook.

Have Your Kids File a Tax Return

There's plenty of value in having a child — of any age — file a tax return if they have any earned income at all. The benefit? RRSP contribution room, of course. Taking this a step further, why not make good on that contribution room by having your child make an RRSP contribution once he or she is old enough to open an investment account. Sorry, in-trust accounts won't cut it for RRSP purposes. Though the child may make an RRSP contribution, the deduction can be saved for a future year when he or she has a higher marginal tax rate.

Deduct All Interest Possible

It's no secret that you're able to deduct interest when money has been borrowed for business or investment purposes. You'd be surprised, however, at how many tax preparers miss out on claiming certain interest costs. In particular, interest on brokerage or margin accounts and interest charged on Canada Savings Bond payroll purchase plans are often overlooked. And don't forget: Where an investment has gone sour and is no longer held by you, a portion of the interest on money borrowed to acquire that investment might still be deductible.

Remember 1994 Elections

You may recall that Canadians were allowed to make a special election in 1994 to use up the $100,000 lifetime capital gains exemption. In effect, that election simply bumped up the adjusted cost base of your properties on which the election was made. If you sold any of those properties in 2000, make sure you are using the new, higher, cost base when calculating the taxable capital gain. This will reduce the tax bill. Similarly, where an election was made on flow-through assets such as mutual funds, an "exempt capital gains balance" was created. This balance can be used, until the year 2004, to offset capital gains distributions from those funds, or gains on the sale of those funds.

Track Reinvested Distributions

Don't forget that you should add any reinvested distributions made to you, to your original adjusted cost base of the investment. It's easy to forget this — particularly if you're preparing your own tax return. Keeping track of the new adjusted cost base each year will help you avoid a double-tax problem when you finally dispose of your mutual funds.

Consider Transferring Dividends

Suppose for a minute that your spouse has earned dividends but has very little income. In this case, the dividend tax credit might be worthless to your spouse. It's possible in this situation to have the dividends reported on the tax return of the higher-income spouse — you. The benefit? You will enjoy a higher spousal tax credit because your lower-income spouse will now have less income to report. This could mean a tax saving for the family. But be sure to do the calculations first to see if you will be better off.

Claim Allowable Business Investment Losses

Let's face it, a high percentage of small businesses don't survive in the long run. Unfortunate, but true. If you own shares in or have lent money to a small business corporation, and the business has gone sour, there may be tax relief available. I'm talking about claiming an allowable business investment loss (ABIL). In many cases, your accountant may not even realize that you have made this type of investment, let alone lost money at it. An ABIL is calculated as two-thirds of the money lost by you, and can generally be deducted against any type of income — not just capital gains — although some restrictions may apply where you have claimed the capital gains exemption in the past.

Defer Deductions

One thing you will want to avoid is bringing taxable income below $7,231 in the year 2000. After all, there are no taxes to pay below this level of income. If you have discretionary deductions available, such as RRSP deductions or capital cost allowance, make the most of them by postponing them until a future year, rather than bringing your income below the taxable threshold of $7,231.

Avoid Recurring Losses

Here's the deal. If you report business or rental losses for more than two or three years, your return is going to make someone at the CCRA sit up and take notice. Revenue's computers are programmed to flag tax returns that repeatedly report losses. Ask around, and you'll no doubt meet someone who has been reassessed for this reason in the past few years. You see, the CCRA insists that you have a reasonable expectation of profit from your business or rental activities. If you don't show this expectation, don't be surprised when your losses are denied. If you're concerned about the possibility of being reassessed, make sure you've prepared forecasts showing when you expect to start making a profit, then do all you can to make the venture profitable — including paying down any mortgage that might be creating large interest deductions.

Claim All Donations on One Return

You'll enjoy greater tax savings by claiming all charitable donations on one spouse's tax return, rather than having each spouse claim some. The reason? Donations over $200 in the year offer greater tax relief. By using this strategy, you'll maximize the donations over that $200 level. Generally, we like to claim the donations on the return of the higher-income spouse, although in many cases it won't make a difference.

Claim Medical Expenses on the Lower-Income Return

You're entitled to claim medical expenses over a certain threshold. In 2000, that threshold is 3 percent of net income or $1,637, whichever is less. By claiming the expenses on the return of the lower-income spouse, you'll increase your available credit.

Chapter 32

Top Ten Tax Changes for 2000

Change is simply a part of life. And the tax law is no exception. Just when you're beginning to feel comfortable with the current tax law and feel as if you actually understand it, Finance Canada throws us a curve. Though it's usually expected that there will be some tax changes introduced in each annual federal budget, the year 2000 brought with it not only the annual federal budget, but also a mini-budget tabled in October. Of course, tax being tax, there are more than just ten changes. This chapter will highlight what we feel are the top ten differences between last year's tax outlook and this year's.

Reinstating Full Indexation

Thanks to the 2000 federal budget, every year we'll all have to remember new thresholds for tax brackets, and new values for certain tax credits. You see, prior to this budget, tax brackets, rates, and credits were indexed to changes in inflation only when the consumer price index changed by three or more percentage points in a year. As of January 1, 2000, all amounts that were partially indexed are now fully indexed annually. This includes the basic personal amount, which rises to $7,231 for 2000. As a result of the full indexation, the federal tax brackets for 2000 have also shifted. The lowest tax bracket will now include income up to $30,004, the middle tax bracket will include income between $30,005 and $60,009, and the top bracket is reserved for income in excess of $60,009.

Middle Tax Rate

The middle tax bracket was reduced for 2000 from 26 percent to 24 percent starting July 1, 2000. Due to this mid-year change, the middle tax bracket for 2000 is effectively 25 percent.

Five-percent Surtax

The 2000 federal budget reduced surtaxes by increasing the level at which the 5-percent surtax takes effect, from federal tax in excess of $12,500 to federal tax in excess of $18,500, effective July 1, 2000. This means individuals will not pay surtax until their income level exceeds approximately $85,000.

Capital Gains Inclusion Rate

The capital gains inclusion rate was reduced from three-quarters to two-thirds for all capital transactions after February 27, 2000. And to make matters just a bit more confusing, the mini-budget of October 18, 2000, reduced the inclusion rate even further to just one-half for transactions incurred after October 17. So be prepared for a bit of complexity if you have numerous capital transactions during the year.

Tax on Income System

Until 2000, provincial tax for all provinces (except Quebec) was calculated as a percentage of basic federal tax. In 2000 and 2001, the majority of provinces are moving to a tax-on-income (TONI) system, and leaving behind the old tax-on-tax system to which we had all grown accustomed. In 2000, British Columbia, Manitoba, Ontario, New Brunswick, and Nova Scotia will move to the new system. Alberta, Saskatchewan, PEI, and Newfoundland have opted to wait until 2001 to make the switch. What does this change mean for you? Not too much, except that you'll have to keep up to date on any new provincial deductions or credits to which you may be entitled. If you prepare you tax return by hand, be prepared for more manual calculations.

Family Care

As a result of the 2000 federal budget, the disability tax credit underwent a few changes. In addition, a new tax credit was introduced to help those with disabilities. First, the changes. Eligibility to receive the disability tax credit was extended to include individuals who must undergo therapy several times each week to sustain their vital functions. To qualify, these therapy sessions must total at least 14 hours per week. Examples of individuals who may now qualify for the credit include those with kidney disease who undergo dialysis, or individuals with cystic fibrosis who undergo clapping therapy to help them breathe.

In prior years, you could only transfer any unused portion of the disability tax credit to a child, spouse, parent, or grandparent. New rules now allow the credit to be transferred to a brother, sister, aunt, uncle, niece, or nephew as well. The 2000 federal budget introduced a new credit for families caring for children with severe disabilities. The maximum credit available equals $2,941, and is reduced by the amount of any child care or attendant care expenses claimed for the child in excess of $2,000. The full credit will mean an annual tax saving of $500.

Employee Stock Options

Employees of public companies who exercise stock options may no longer have to include the employment benefit in their income in the year the option is exercised. Instead, eligible employees may be entitled to defer the taxable benefit on up to $100,000 worth of options until the shares are actually sold. The $100,000 limit is based on the fair market value of the shares when the option was granted.

Foreign Property Rules

The budget increased the foreign content limit on deferred income plans (RRSPs, RRIFs) from 20 percent to 25 percent for the year 2000. This limit will be increased further to 30 percent for 2001 and subsequent years. The additional "3 for 1" bump given to investors who invest in Canadian small businesses remains at $3 for every $1 invested in a qualifying small business property, to a maximum of 45-percent foreign content (50 percent for 2001 and later years).

Donating RRSPs, RRIFs, and Life Insurance

Prior to the 2000 federal budget, individuals who wanted to donate proceeds from their RRSP, RRIF, or life insurance policy to a charity would simply leave directions in their will to donate the cash proceeds. This would ensure a donation credit in the year of death. The changes in the budget now make donating to charity easier, stating that you can now directly designate the charity as your beneficiary of your plan or policy, directly in the plan or policy documentation. If you do this, you will still be entitled to the donation credit in the year of death. Prior to the budget, the credit was not available if you directly designated the charity as your beneficiary.

Mini-Budget

The Department of Finance released a mini-budget on October 18, 2000. Although most of the changes introduced in the budget relate to the 2001 year-end, we thought we'd give you the heads-up on what you may expect to see for your return next year. One of the biggest proposed changes was in the federal tax rates and brackets. Now the Canadian tax system will see four, instead of three, tax brackets. Commencing January 1, 2001, the first and lowest tax bracket, which includes income up to $30,004, will be taxed at 16 percent. The second tax bracket, containing income between $30,005 and $60,009, will be taxed at 22 percent. The third tax bracket will contain income between $60,010 and $100,000 and will be taxed at 26 percent. Finally, the fourth tax bracket for income in excess of $100,000 will be taxed at 29 percent. Other proposed changes include an increase in the disability tax credit from $4,293 to $6,000; an increase in the caregiver amount from $2,386 to $3,500; and a doubling of the education credit from the $200 and $60 monthly amounts on which the education tax credit is calculated up to $400 and $120, respectively.

Of course, the mini-budget also resulted in many more changes, but you'll have to wait until the 2001 version of this book to get the inside story.

Appendix A

Tax Forms

Do: use the assembled tax forms in this appendix as a guide to filling out your 2000 tax return. Included here is the basic T1 General form, as well as more specialized forms that apply to some people and not others, like the T1M form for deducting moving expenses, and the T2209 form (Federal Foreign Tax Credit). We've also included all the provincial tax forms to help you calculate your provincial tax owing and credit — in whichever province you call home.

Don't: fill out these forms and send them in to Revenue Canada! You'll receive your official forms in the mail. If not, call 1-800-959-2221 or log on to the Canada Customs and Revenue Agency Web site (`www.ccra.adrc.gc.ca/formspubs`) and download them.

Note: Some of the forms you'll see here are from 1999 because the 2000 versions weren't ready at the time we went to press. Not to worry, though; the 2000 forms will be posted on the Canada Customs and Revenue Agency Web site (`www.ccra.adrc.gc.ca/formspubs`) as they become available, so keep checking. Use the 1999 forms as a guide, then fill out the official forms when the time comes. You can tell which version of the form appears by checking the year at the top of the form.

Canada Customs and Revenue Agency / Agence des douanes et du revenu du Canada

T1 GENERAL 2000

Income Tax and Benefit Return

Identification

7

Attach your personal label here. Correct any wrong information.
If you are not attaching a label, print your name and address below.

First name and initial

Last name

Address | Apt. or Unit No.

City

Province or territory | Postal code

Enter your province or territory of residence on December 31, 2000:

If you were self-employed in 2000, enter the province or territory of self-employment:

If you became or ceased to be a resident of Canada **in 2000**, give the date of:

entry — Month Day — or departure — Month Day

Enter your social insurance number if it is not on the label, or if you are not attaching a label:

Enter your date of birth: Year Month Day

Your language of correspondence:
Votre langue de correspondance : English ☐ Français ☐

If this return is for a deceased person, enter the date of death: Year Month Day

Marital status on December 31, 2000 (check the box that applies):
(see the "Marital status" section in the guide for details)

1 ☐ Married 2 ☐ Living common law 3 ☐ Widowed
4 ☐ Divorced 5 ☐ Separated 6 ☐ Single

If box 1 or 2 applies, enter your spouse's social insurance number if it is not on the label, or if you are not attaching a label:

Enter the first name of your spouse:

Check this box if your spouse was self-employed in 2000: 1 ☐

Do not use this area

Elections Canada (see the guide for details)

Do you authorize the Canada Customs and Revenue Agency to provide your name, address, and date of birth to Elections Canada to update your information on the **National Register of Electors**? .... Yes ☐ 1 No ☐ 2
Your authorization is needed each year. This information can be used for electoral purposes only.

Goods and services tax / Harmonized sales tax (GST/HST) credit application

Are you applying for the GST/HST credit? (see the guide for details) .... Yes ☐ 1 No ☐ 2

If *yes*, enter the number of children under age 19 on December 31, 2000 (if applicable) ....

If *yes*, enter your spouse's net income from line 236 of your spouse's return (if applicable) ....

Foreign income

As a Canadian resident, you have to report your income from all sources both inside and outside Canada.

Please answer the following question

Did you own or hold foreign property at any time in 2000 with a total cost of more than CAN$100,000?
(read the "Foreign income" section in the guide for details) .... 266 Yes ☐ 1 No ☐ 2
If *yes*, attach a completed Form T1135.

If you had certain dealings with a non-resident trust or corporation in 2000, see the "Foreign income" section in the guide.

Do not use this area	172					171				

2

Total income

Line	Code	Amount
Employment income (box 14 on all T4 slips)	101	
Commissions included on line 101 (box 42 on all T4 slips) 102		
Other employment income (see line 104 in the guide)	104 +	
Old Age Security pension (box 18 on the T4A(OAS) slip)	113 +	
Canada or Quebec Pension Plan benefits (box 20 on the T4A(P) slip)	114 +	
Disability benefits included on line 114 (box 16 on the T4A(P) slip) 152		
Other pensions or superannuation (see line 115 in the guide)	115 +	
Employment Insurance benefits (box 14 on the T4E slip)	119 +	
Taxable amount of dividends from taxable Canadian corporations (see line 120 in the guide)	120 +	
Interest and other investment income (attach a completed Schedule 4)	121 +	
Net partnership income: limited or non-active partners only (attach a completed Schedule 4)	122 +	
Rental income Gross 160	Net 126 +	
Taxable capital gains (attach a completed Schedule 3)	127 +	
Support payments received Total 156	Taxable amount 128 +	
RRSP income (from all T4RSP slips)	129 +	
Other income (see line 130 in the guide) Specify:	130 +	
Self-employment income (see lines 135 to 143 in the guide)		
Business income Gross 162	Net 135 +	
Professional income Gross 164	Net 137 +	
Commission income Gross 166	Net 139 +	
Farming income Gross 168	Net 141 +	
Fishing income Gross 170	Net 143 +	
Workers' compensation benefits (box 10 on the T5007 slip) 144		
Social assistance payments (see line 145 in the guide) 145 +		
Net federal supplements (box 21 on the T4A(OAS) slip) 146 +		
Add lines 144, 145, and 146 = ►	147 +	
Add lines 101, 104 to 143, and 147. This is your **total income.**	150 =	►

Net income

Line	Code	Amount
Pension adjustment (box 52 on all T4 slips and box 34 on all T4A slips) 206		
Registered pension plan deduction (box 20 on all T4 slips and box 32 on all T4A slips)	207	
RRSP deduction (see Schedule 7; attach receipts)	208 +	
Saskatchewan Pension Plan deduction (see line 209 in the guide)	209 +	
Annual union, professional, or like dues (box 44 on all T4 slips, or from receipts)	212 +	
Child care expenses (attach a completed Form T778)	214 +	
Attendant care expenses (see line 215 in the guide)	215 +	
Business investment loss (see line 217 in the guide) Gross (before) 227 Gross (after) 228	Allowable deduction 217 +	
Moving expenses (see line 219 in the guide)	219 +	
Support payments made Total 230	Allowable deduction 220 +	
Carrying charges and interest expenses (attach a completed Schedule 4)	221 +	
Exploration and development expenses (attach a completed Schedule 4)	224 +	
Other employment expenses (see line 229 in the guide)	229 +	
Cleric's residence deduction (see line 231 in the guide)	231 +	
Other deductions (see line 232 in the guide) Specify:	232 +	
Add lines 207 to 224, 229, 231, and 232.	233 = ►	–
Line 150 minus line 233 (if negative, enter "0"). This is your **net income before adjustments.**	234 =	
Social benefits repayment (if you reported income on line 113, 119, or 146, see line 235 in the guide)	235 –	
Line 234 minus line 235 (if negative, enter "0") This is your **net income.**	236 =	

Before you mail your return, make sure you have attached here all completed schedules, required information slips, receipts, and corresponding statements.

Taxable income

Enter your **net income** from line 236		236
Employee home relocation loan deduction (box 37 on all T4 slips)	248	
Stock option and shares deductions (boxes 39, 41, 98, and 99 on all T4 slips)	249 +	
Other payments deduction (if you reported income on line 147, see line 250 in the guide)	250 +	
Limited partnership losses of other years	251 +	
Non-capital losses of other years	252 +	
Net capital losses of other years	253 +	
Capital gains deduction (see line 254 in the guide)	254 +	
Northern residents deductions (attach a completed Form T2222)	255 +	
Additional deductions (see line 256 in the guide) Specify:	256 +	
Add lines 248 to 256.	257 =	▶ –
Line 236 minus line 257 (if negative, enter "0") This is your **taxable income.**		260 =

Non-refundable tax credits

Basic personal amount (see line 300 in the guide) **claim $7,231.00**		300	
Age amount (if you were born in 1935 or earlier, see line 301 in the guide)		301 +	
Spousal amount (see line 303 in the guide)			
Base amount	6,754 00		
Minus: Your spouse's net income	–		
Spousal amount (if negative, enter "0") **(maximum claim $6,140)**	=	▶ 303 +	
Equivalent-to-spouse amount (see line 305 in the guide) **(maximum claim $6,140)**		305 +	
Amount for infirm dependants age 18 or older (see line 306 in the guide)		306 +	
Canada or Quebec Pension Plan contributions			
Contributions through employment from box 16 and box 17 on all T4 slips (maximum $1,329.90)		308 +	•
Contributions payable on self-employment and other earnings (attach a completed Schedule 8)		310 +	•
Employment Insurance premiums from box 18 on all T4 slips (see line 312 in the guide)		312 +	•
Pension income amount (maximum $1,000; see line 314 in the guide)		314 +	
Caregiver amount (see line 315 in the guide)		315 +	
Disability amount (see line 316 in the guide)		316 +	
Disability amount transferred from a dependant other than your spouse		318 +	
Interest paid on your student loans (see line 319 in the guide)		319 +	
Tuition and education amounts (attach a completed Schedule 11)		323 +	
Tuition and education amounts transferred from a child (see line 324 in the guide)		324 +	
Amounts transferred from your spouse (attach a completed Schedule 2)		326 +	
Medical expenses (see line 330 in the guide; attach receipts)	330		
Minus: $1,637, or 3% of line 236, whichever is **less**	–		
Subtotal	=		
Minus: Medical expenses adjustment (see line 331 in the guide)	331 –		
Allowable portion of medical expenses (if negative, enter "0")	=	▶ 332 +	
Add lines 300, 301, 303 to 326, and 332 (if this total is more than line 260, see the note at line 338 in the guide)		335 =	
Multiply the amount on line 335 by 17% =			338
Donations and gifts: Complete Schedule 9 to calculate your tax credit for donations and gifts. Enter the amount from line 9 of Schedule 9 and attach a completed copy to your return.			349 +
Add lines 338 and 349. Use this amount to determine your federal tax on Schedule 1. These are your **total non-refundable tax credits.**			350 =

Refund or Balance owing

4

Line		Code	Amount
Federal tax: Complete Schedule 1 and enter the amount from line 11, **or** line 25, whichever applies		406	
Total federal political contributions (attach receipts)	409		
Federal political contribution tax credit (see lines 409 and 410 in the guide)	410 •		
Investment tax credit (attach a completed Form T2038(IND))	412 + •		
Labour-sponsored funds tax credit — Net cost 413 — Allowable credit	414 + •		
Add lines 410, 412, and 414.	416 =	► −	
Line 406 minus line 416 (if negative, enter "0") (if you have an amount on line 16 of Schedule 1, see Form T1206)		417 =	
Additional tax on RESP accumulated income payments (attach a completed Form T1172)		418 +	
Federal individual surtax (line 14 **or** line 32 of Schedule 1)		419 +	
Add lines 417, 418, and 419. This is your **net federal tax.**		420 =	
Canada Pension Plan contributions payable on self-employment and other earnings (from Schedule 8)		421 +	
Social benefits repayment (enter the amount from line 235)		422 +	
Provincial or territorial tax (see line 428 in the guide)		428 +	
Add lines 420 to 428. This is your **total payable.**		435 =	•

Line		Code	Amount
Total income tax deducted (from all information slips)	437 •		
Tax transfer for residents of Quebec (see line 438 in the guide)	438 − •		
Line 437 minus line 438	=	► 439	
Refundable Quebec abatement (see line 440 in the guide)		440 + •	
Canada Pension Plan overpayment (see line 448 in the guide)		448 + •	
Employment Insurance overpayment (see line 450 in the guide)		450 + •	
Refundable medical expense supplement (attach a completed Schedule 10)		452 + •	
Refund of investment tax credit (attach a completed Form T2038(IND))		454 + •	
Part XII.2 trust tax credit (box 38 on all T3 slips)		456 + •	
Employee and partner GST/HST rebate (attach a completed Form GST 370)		457 + •	
Tax paid by instalments (see line 476 in the guide)		476 + •	
Provincial or territorial credits (see line 479 in the guide)		479 + •	
Add lines 439 to 479. These are your **total credits.**		482 =	► −
Line 435 minus line 482			=

If the result is negative, you have a **refund**.
If the result is positive, you have a **balance owing**.
Enter the amount below on whichever line applies.

We do not charge or refund a difference of less than $2.

Refund 484 •

Balance owing 485 •

Amount enclosed 486 •

Attach to page 1, a **cheque** or **money order** payable to the Receiver General. Your payment is due no later than April 30, 2001.

Direct deposit – Start or change (see line 484 in the guide)

You do not have to complete this area every year. Do not complete it this year if your direct deposit information for your refund has not changed.

Refund and GST/HST credit – To start direct deposit or to change account information only, attach a "void" cheque or complete lines 460, 461, and 462.

Note: To deposit your **CCTB** payments (including certain related provincial or territorial payments) into the **same** account, also check box 463.

Branch number	Institution number	Account number	CCTB
460	461	462	463 ☐
(5 digits)	(3 digits)	(maximum 12 digits)	

I certify that the information given on this return and in any documents attached is correct, complete, and fully discloses all my income.

Sign here ____________________

It is a serious offence to make a false return.

Telephone ( ) Date

490 **For professional tax preparers only.**

Name:
Address:
Telephone: ( )

Do not use this area 487 ☐ 488 ☐ •

Privacy Act Personal Information Bank number CCRA/P-PU-005

T1-2000

Federal Tax Calculation

Schedule 1

Enter your **taxable income** from line 260 of your return ______ 1

Part 1 – Complete ONE of the following columns

Use the amount on line 1 to determine which column you have to complete.

If the amount on line 1 is:	$30,004 or less		more than $30,004, but not more than $60,009		more than $60,009	
Enter the amount from line 1 above		2		2		2
Income threshold	– 0 00	3	– 30,004 00	3	– 60,009 00	3
Line 2 minus line 3 (this amount cannot be negative)	=	4	=	4	=	4
Federal tax rate	x 17%	5	x 25%	5	x 29%	5
Multiply the amount on line 4 by the tax rate on line 5	=	6	=	6	=	6
Tax on income threshold	+ 0 00	7	+ 5,101 00	7	+ 12,602 00	7
Add lines 6 and 7	=	8	=	8	=	8
	Go to Part 2		**Go to Part 2**		**Go to Part 2**	

Part 2 – Complete ONE of the following methods

Use Method A, **or** Method B, **but not both**, to complete the rest of this schedule.

Use Method A unless any of the following items apply to your situation, in which case, use Method B. See the "Federal tax calculation" section in the guide for details.

- minimum tax
- federal dividend tax credit
- minimum tax carry-over
- split income
- overseas employment tax credit
- foreign tax credits
- federal logging tax credit
- additional investment tax credit

Method A (lines 9 through 14)

Federal tax:

Enter the amount from line 8 above		9
Total non-refundable tax credits: Enter the amount from line 350 of your return	–	10
Federal tax: Line 9 minus line 10 (if negative, enter "0") Enter this amount on line 406 of your return.	=	11

Federal individual surtax:

Base amount: $15,500	– 15,500 00	12
Line 11 minus line 12 (if negative, enter "0")	=	13
Federal individual surtax: Multiply the amount on line 13 by 5% Enter this amount on line 419 of your return.		14

See line 428 in the guide for information about how to calculate your provincial or territorial tax.

Method B (lines 15 through 32)

See the instructions on the other side to find out if you have to use this method.

Federal tax:

				Line
Enter the amount from line 8 on the other side				15
Federal tax on split income (from line 4 of Form T1206)		424	+	• 16
Add lines 15 and 16			=	17
Total non-refundable tax credits: Enter the amount from line 350 of your return		18		
Federal dividend tax credit (13.3333% of the amount on line 120 of your return)	425 +	• 19		
Overseas employment tax credit (from Form T626)	426 +	20		
Minimum tax carry-over (see line 427 in the guide)	427 +	• 21		
Add lines 18 to 21	=	►	–	22
Basic federal tax: Line 17 minus line 22 (if negative, enter "0")		429	=	23
Federal foreign tax credit: Complete the federal foreign tax credit calculation below and enter the amount from line (i) or line (ii), whichever is **less**			–	24
Federal tax: Line 23 minus line 24 (if negative, enter "0") Enter this amount on line 406 of your return.			=	25

Federal individual surtax:

				Line
Enter the total of the amounts on lines 20 and **23** above		26		
Minus: $15,500	– 15,500 00	27		
Line 26 minus line 27 (if negative, enter "0")	=	x 5% is		28
Additional federal foreign tax credit from Part 2 of Form T2209		464	–	29
Line 28 minus line 29 (if negative, enter "0")			=	30
Additional investment tax credit from Section II of Form T2038(IND)		468	–	31
Federal individual surtax: Line 30 minus line 31 (if negative, enter "0") Enter this amount on line 419 of your return.			=	32

See line 428 in the guide for information about how to calculate your provincial or territorial tax.

Federal foreign tax credit: (see lines 431 and 433 in the guide)

Make a separate calculation for each foreign country.

Non-business-income tax paid to a foreign country 431 ______ • (i)

Net foreign non-business income * 433 ______ / Net income ** ______ X Basic federal tax *** ______ = ______ (ii)

* Reduce this amount by any income from that foreign country for which you claimed a capital gains deduction, and by any income from that country that was, under a tax treaty, either exempt from tax in that country or deductible as exempt income in Canada (included on line 256). Also reduce this amount by the lesser of lines E and F on Form T626.

** Line 236 plus the amount on line 3 of Form T1206, minus the total of the amounts on lines 248, 249, 250, 253, 254, and minus any foreign income deductible as exempt income under a tax treaty or any income deductible as net employment income from a prescribed international organization (included on line 256). If the result is less than the amount on line 433, enter your **Basic federal tax***** on line (ii).

*** Line 429 plus the amount on lines 425 and 426, and minus the amount on lines 440 and 441 (Federal refundable First Nations abatement).

T1-2000

Federal Tax Calculation

Schedule 1

Enter your taxable income from line 260 of your return. However, if you are electing under section 217, enter the amount from line 260 of your return or the amount from line 16 of Schedule A, **whichever amount is greater.** ______ 1

Part 1 – Complete ONE of the following columns

Use the amount on line 1 to determine which column you have to complete.

If the amount on line 1 is:	$30,004 or less		more than $30,004, but not more than $60,009		more than $60,009	
Enter the amount from line 1 above		2		2		2
Income threshold for this column	– 0 00	3	– 30,004 00	3	– 60,009 00	3
Line 2 minus line 3 (this amount cannot be negative)	=	4	=	4	=	4
Federal tax rate	x 17%	5	x 25%	5	x 29%	5
Multiply the amount on line 4 by the tax rate on line 5	=	6	=	6	=	6
Tax on income threshold	+ 0 00	7	+ 5,101 00	7	+ 12,602 00	7
Add lines 6 and 7 Enter this amount on line 9	=	8	=	8	=	8
	Go to Part 2		**Go to Part 2**		**Go to Part 2**	

Part 2 – Complete ONE of the following methods

Use Method A, **or** Method B, **but not both**, to complete the rest of this schedule.

Use Method A unless any of the following items apply to your situation, in which case, use Method B. See the "Federal tax calculation" section in the guide for details.

- minimum tax
- federal dividend tax credit
- minimum tax carry-over
- split income
- overseas employment tax credit
- foreign tax credits
- federal logging tax credit
- additional investment tax credit

Method A (lines 9 through 14)

Federal tax:

Enter the amount from line 8 above		9
Total non-refundable tax credits: (from line 350 of your return or from Schedule B, whichever applies)	–	10
Line 9 minus line 10 (if negative, enter "0")	=	A
Section 217 tax adjustment: If you are electing under section 217, see line 445 in the guide	445 –	B
Line A minus line B.	=	C
Surtax for non-residents and deemed residents of Canada: Calculate 48% of the amount on line C	+	D
Federal tax: Add lines C and D Enter this amount on line 406 of your return.	=	11

Federal individual surtax:

Enter the amount from line C above		E
Base amount: $15,500	– 15,500 00	12
Line E minus line 12 (if negative, enter "0")	=	13
Multiply the amount on line 13 by 5%	x 5%	F
Federal individual surtax: Enter this amount on line 419 of your return.	=	14

Method B (lines 15 through 32)

See the instructions on the other side to find out if you have to use this method.

Federal tax:

Enter the amount from line 8 on the other side			15
Federal tax on split income (from line 4 of Form T1206)	424	+	• 16
Add lines 15 and 16		=	17

Total non-refundable tax credits (from line 350 of your return or from Schedule B, whichever applies)			18
Federal dividend tax credit (13.3333% of the amount on line 120 of your return)	425	+	• 19
Overseas employment tax credit (from Form T626)	426	+	20
Minimum tax carry-over (see line 427 in the guide)	427	+	21
Add lines 18 to 21		= ▶ –	22
Line 17 minus line 22 (if negative, enter "0 ")		=	G
Section 217 tax adjustment: If you are electing under section 217, see line 445 in the guide	445	–	H
Basic federal tax: Line G minus line H (if negative, enter "0")	429	=	23
Surtax for non-residents and deemed residents of Canada: Calculate 48% of the amount on line 23		+	I
Add line 23 and line I		=	J
Federal foreign tax credit: Complete the federal foreign tax credit calculation below. Enter the amount from line (i) or line (ii), whichever is **less**		–	24
Federal tax: Line J minus line 24 (if negative, enter "0") Enter this amount on line 406 of your return.		=	25

Federal individual surtax:

Enter the total of the amounts on lines 20 and **23** above		26		
Minus: $15,500	– 15,500 00	27		
Line 26 minus line 27 (if negative, enter "0")	=	x 5% is		28
Additional federal foreign tax credit from Part 2 of Form T2209			464 –	29
Line 28 minus line 29 (if negative, enter "0")			=	30
Additional investment tax credit from section II of Form T2038(IND)			468 –	31
Federal individual surtax: Line 30 minus line 31 (if negative, enter "0") Enter this amount on line 419 of your return.			=	32

Federal foreign tax credit: (see lines 431 and 433 in the guide)

Make a separate calculation for each foreign country.

Non-business-income tax paid to a foreign country 431 • (i)

Net foreign non-business income * 433 / Net income ** X The amount on line J *** = (ii)

* Reduce this amount by any income from that foreign country for which you claimed a capital gains deduction, and by any income from that country that was, under a tax treaty, either exempt from tax in that country or deductible as exempt income in Canada (included on line 256). Also reduce this amount by the lesser of lines E and F on Form T626.

** Line 236 plus the amount on line 3 of Form T1206, minus the total of the amounts on lines 248, 249, 250, 253, 254, and minus any foreign income deductible as exempt income under a tax treaty or any income deductible as net employment income from a prescribed international organization (included on line 256). If the result is less than the amount on line 433, enter (The amount on line J ***) on line (ii).

*** Line J plus the amount on lines 425 and 426, and minus the amount on lines 440 and 441 (Federal refundable First Nations abatement).

T1-2000 Amounts Transferred From Your Spouse Schedule 2

Complete this schedule to transfer from your spouse, the unused part of your spouse's age amount, pension income amount, disability amount, and tuition and education amounts.

If your spouse is not filing a 2000 return, calculate the amounts that would be on your spouse's return if your spouse were filing a return. Attach your spouse's information slips. Make sure you have checked the box on page 1 of your return to indicate your marital status, and that you have also entered your spouse's social insurance number and name.

See line 326 in the guide for more information.

Age amount (if your spouse was age 65 or older in 2000): Enter the result from the calculation on the *Worksheet** for line 301 for your spouse (maximum claim $3,531)	353		1
Pension income amount: Enter the result from the calculation on the *Worksheet** for line 314 for your spouse (maximum claim $1,000)	355	+	2
Disability amount: If your spouse is eligible for the disability amount, see line 316 in the guide	357	+	3
Tuition and education amounts transferred by your spouse: Enter an amount that is not more than the amount on line 17 of your spouse's Schedule 11	360	+	4
Add lines 1 to 4		=	5
Spouse's taxable income (line 260 of your spouse's return)			6
Enter the total of lines 300, 308, 310, and 312 of your spouse's return, and line 13 of your spouse's Schedule 11		–	7
Spouse's adjusted taxable income: Line 6 minus line 7 (if negative, enter "0")	351	= ► –	8
Amounts transferred from your spouse: Line 5 minus line 8 (if negative, enter "0") Enter this amount on line 326 of your return.		=	9

* The *Worksheet* is included with your forms.

5000-S2

T1-2000 Amounts Transferred From Your Spouse Schedule 2

Complete this schedule to transfer from your spouse, the unused part of your spouse's age amount, pension income amount, disability amount, and tuition and education amounts.

If your spouse is not filing a 2000 return, calculate the amounts that would be on your spouse's return if your spouse were filing a return. Attach your spouse's information slips. Make sure you have checked the box on page 1 of your return to indicate your marital status, and that you have also entered your spouse's social insurance number and name.

See line 326 in the guide for more information.

Age amount (if your spouse was age 65 or older in 2000): Enter the result from the calculation on the *Worksheet** for line 301 for your spouse (maximum claim $3,531)	353		1
Pension income amount: Enter the result from the calculation on the *Worksheet** for line 314 for your spouse (maximum claim $1,000)	355	+	2
Disability amount: If your spouse is eligible for the disability amount, see line 316 in the guide	357	+	3
Tuition and education amounts transferred by your spouse: Enter an amount that is not more than the amount on line 17 of your spouse's Schedule 11	360	+	4
Add lines 1 to 4		=	5
Spouse's taxable income (line 260 of your spouse's return)			6
Enter the total of lines 300, 308, 310, and 312 of your spouse's return, and line 13 of your spouse's Schedule 11		–	7
Spouse's adjusted taxable income: Line 6 minus line 7 (if negative, enter "0")	351	= ► –	8
Amounts transferred from your spouse: Line 5 minus line 8 (if negative, enter "0") Enter this amount on line 326 of your return.		=	9

* The *Worksheet* is included with your forms.

5000-S2

T1-2000

Capital Gains (or Losses) in 2000

Schedule 3

Page 1 of 4

Complete Part 1, Part 2, and/or Part 3 whichever applies before you complete Part 4. Attach all parts to your return.

Read Chapter 2 in the guide called *Capital Gains* for more information. Attach a separate sheet of paper if you need more space.

Part 1 – Dispositions BEFORE February 28, 2000 (Period 1)

Note: If you have a business investment loss, see line 217 in the General guide.	(1) Year of acquisition	(2) Proceeds of disposition	(3) Adjusted cost base	(4) Outlays and expenses (from dispositions)	(5) Gain (or loss) (column 2 minus columns 3 and 4)
1. Qualified small business corporation shares **(report mutual fund units and other shares in "3." below)**					
No. of shares / Name of corporation and class of shares					
Total 201				Gain (or loss) 202	
2. Qualified farm property					
Address or legal description					
Total 203				Gain (or loss) 204	+
Mortgage foreclosures and conditional sales repossessions – Address or legal description					
Total 210				Gain (or loss) 211	+
3. Mutual fund units and other shares including publicly traded shares					
Number / Name of fund/corporation and class of shares					
Total 216				Gain (or loss) 218	+
4. Real estate and depreciable property (do not include losses on depreciable property)					
Address or legal description					
Total 225				Gain (or loss) 226	+
5. Bonds, debentures, promissory notes, and other properties					
Face value / Maturity date / Name of issuer					
Total 238				Gain (or loss) 243	+
6. Other mortgage foreclosures and conditional sales repossessions					
Address or legal description					
Total 261				Gain (or loss) 265	+
7. Personal-use property (full description)					
				Gain only 284	+
8. Listed personal property (LPP) (full description)					
Note: You can only apply LPP losses against LPP gains.				Subtract: Unapplied LPP losses from other periods and other years	
				Net gain only 289	+

Information slips – Capital gains (or losses) (attach your T3, T5, T5013, and T4PS slips)	291	+
Capital loss from a reduction in your business investment loss	293	–
Total of all gains (or losses) in column 5 before reserves and gifts	294	=
Reserves from line 6706 of Form T2017 (if the amount is negative, show it in brackets and subtract it)	295	+
Adjusted capital gains on gifts of certain capital property (from line 7 of Form T1170)	296	+
Capital gains (or losses)	297	=
Capital gains reduction on flow-through entities (see Chapter 4 in the guide called *Capital Gains*)	298	–
Total capital gains (or losses) **before February 28, 2000**	299	=

Total of the amounts from line 296 above and line 227 of your return	–	A
Line 299 minus line A (this amount can be negative)	=	B
Total of the amounts from lines 293 and 298 above and line 3 on Form T1170 (do not show it in brackets)	+	C
Add lines B and C (this amount can be negative)	=	D
Multiply the amount on line D by 75%		E

If you do not have to complete Part 2 or Part 3, go to Part 4. Otherwise, continue.

Part 2 – Dispositions AFTER February 27, 2000, and BEFORE October 18, 2000 (Period 2)

Note: If you have a business investment loss, see line 217 in the General guide.	(1) Year of acquisition	(2) Proceeds of disposition	(3) Adjusted cost base	(4) Outlays and expenses (from dispositions)	(5) Gain (or loss) (column 2 minus columns 3 and 4)

1. Qualified small business corporation shares **(report mutual fund units and other shares in "3." below)**

No. of shares	Name of corporation and class of shares					
		Total 106			Gain (or loss) 107	

2. Qualified farm property

Address or legal description					
	Total 109			Gain (or loss) 110	+

Mortgage foreclosures and conditional sales repossessions – Address or legal description					
	Total 123			Gain (or loss) 124	+

3. Mutual fund units and other shares including publicly traded shares

Number	Name of fund/corporation and class of shares					
		Total 131			Gain (or loss) 132	+

4. Real estate and depreciable property (do not include losses on depreciable property)

Address or legal description					
	Total 136			Gain (or loss) 138	+

5. Bonds, debentures, promissory notes, and other properties

Face value	Maturity date	Name of issuer					
			Total 151			Gain (or loss) 153	+

6. Other mortgage foreclosures and conditional sales repossessions

Address or legal description					
	Total 154			Gain (or loss) 155	+

7. Personal-use property (full description)

				Gain only 158	+

8. Listed personal property (LPP) (full description)

Note: You can only apply LPP losses against LPP gains.

Subtract: Unapplied LPP losses from other periods and other years		
Net gain only	159	+
Capital gains deferral for investment in small business (see the guide called *Capital Gains*)	161	–
Farming income eligible for the capital gains deduction from the disposition of eligible capital property (see your farming income guide for details) 173		
Information slips – Capital gains (or losses) (attach your T3, T5, T5013, and T4PS slips)	174	+
Capital loss from a reduction in your business investment loss	178	–
Total of all gains (or losses) in column 5 before reserves and gifts	191	=
Reserves from line 6700 of Form T2017 (show it in brackets and subtract it)	192	+
Adjusted capital gains on gifts of certain capital property (from line 14 of Form T1170)	193	+
Capital gains (or losses)	194	=
Capital gains reduction on flow-through entities (see Chapter 4 in the guide called *Capital Gains*)	195	–
Total capital gains (or losses) **after February 27, 2000, and before October 18, 2000**	197	=

Total of the amounts from line 193 above and line 228 of your return	–	F
Line 197 minus line F (this amount can be negative)	=	G
Total of the amounts from lines 178 and 195 above and line 10 on Form T1170 (do not show it in brackets)	+	H
Add lines G and H (this amount can be negative)	=	I
Multiply the amount on line I by 66.6666%		J

If you do not have to complete Part 3, go to Part 4. Otherwise, continue.

T1-2000 **Schedule 3**

Part 3 – Dispositions AFTER October 17, 2000 (Period 3)

Note: If you have a business investment loss, see line 217 in the General guide.	(1) Year of acquisition	(2) Proceeds of disposition	(3) Adjusted cost base	(4) Outlays and expenses (from dispositions)	(5) Gain (or loss) (column 2 minus columns 3 and 4)
1. Qualified small business corporation shares **(report mutual fund units and other shares in "3." below)**					
No. of shares / Name of corporation and class of shares					
Total 5650				Gain (or loss) 5651	
2. Qualified farm property					
Address or legal description					
Total 5652				Gain (or loss) 5653	+
Mortgage foreclosures and conditional sales repossessions – Address or legal description					
Total 5654				Gain (or loss) 5655	+
3. Mutual fund units and other shares including publicly traded shares					
Number / Name of fund/corporation and class of shares					
Total 5656				Gain (or loss) 5657	+
4. Real estate and depreciable property (do not include losses on depreciable property)					
Address or legal description					
Total 5658				Gain (or loss) 5659	+
5. Bonds, debentures, promissory notes, and other properties					
Face value / Maturity date / Name of issuer					
Total 5660				Gain (or loss) 5661	+
6. Other mortgage foreclosures and conditional sales repossessions					
Address or legal description					
Total 5662				Gain (or loss) 5663	+
7. Personal-use property (full description)					
				Gain only 5664	+
8. Listed personal property (LPP) (full description)					
Note: You can only apply LPP losses against LPP gains.				Subtract: Unapplied LPP losses from other periods and other years	
				Net gain only 5665	+

Capital gains deferral for investment in small business (see the guide called *Capital Gains*)	5666	–
Information slips – Capital gains (or losses) (attach your T3, T5, T5013, and T4PS slips)	5667	+
Capital loss from a reduction in your business investment loss	5668	–
Total of all gains (or losses) in column 5 before reserves and gifts	5669	=
Reserves from line 6707 of Form T2017 (show it in brackets and subtract it)	5670	+
Adjusted capital gains on gifts of certain capital property (from line 21 of Form T1170)	5671	+
Capital gains (or losses)	5672	=
Capital gains reduction on flow-through entities (see Chapter 4 in the guide called *Capital Gains*)	5673	–
Total capital gains (or losses) **after October 17, 2000**	5674	=

Enter the amount from line C in Chart 6 in the guide called *Capital Gains* 5675			
Total of the amounts from lines 5671 and 5675 above		–	K
Line 5674 minus line K (this amount can be negative)		=	L
Total of the amounts from lines 5668 and 5673 above and line 17 on Form T1170 (do not show it in brackets)		+	M
Add lines L and M (this amount can be negative)		=	N
Multiply the amount on line N by 50%			O

Go to Part 4.

Part 4 – Taxable capital gains (or net capital loss) in 2000

SECTION I

Complete lines 1 to 9. Enter "0" on lines that do not apply to you or that you have calculated to be "0".

		Line
Amount from line D in Part 1		1
Amount from line I in Part 2	+	2
Total of lines 1 and 2	=	3
Amount from line N in Part 3	+	4
Total of lines 3 and 4	=	5
Amount from line 299 in Part 1		6
Amount from line 197 in Part 2	+	7
Amount from line 5674 in Part 3	+	8
Total of lines 6, 7, and 8	=	9

Determining your inclusion rate (the rate used to calculate your taxable capital gains or net capital loss):
Read the following instructions very carefully.
Your inclusion rate is determined by the FIRST instruction that applies to you.

- Complete Section II – if lines 1, 2, and 4 are either all gains or all losses.
  – if one of lines 1, 2, and 4 is "0" and the other two are either both gains or both losses.
- Complete Section III – if lines 1, 2, and 5 are all gains, line 4 is a loss, and none of lines 1 to 5 is "0".
  – if lines 1, 2, and 5 are all losses, line 4 is a gain, and none of lines 1 to 5 is "0".
- Complete Section IV – if lines 3 and 4 are either both gains or both losses (and neither is "0").

If Sections II, III, and IV do not apply, on line 16 below:

- Enter 66.6666% – if line 1 is "0" and lines 3 and 5 are either both gains or both losses (and neither is "0").
  – if lines 2, 3, and 5 are either all gains or all losses (and line 2 is not "0").
- Enter 75.0000% – if lines 1, 3, and 5 are either all gains or all losses (and line 5 is not "0").
- Enter 50.0000% – in all other cases.

SECTION II

Total of lines E, J, and O
Divided by: Amount from line 5 X 100 = ____ % 10
Go to line 16

SECTION III

Total of lines E and J
Divided by: Amount from line 3 X 100 = ____ % 11
Go to line 16

SECTION IV

If lines 1 and 3 are both gains (or both losses), multiply line 3 by 75%; or
if lines 2 and 3 are both gains (or both losses), multiply line 3 by 66.6666% ____ 12
Enter the amount from line O in Part 3 + ____ 13
Add lines 12 and 13 = ____ 14

Amount from line 14
Divided by: Amount from line 5 X 100 = ____ % 15
Go to line 16

Enter your inclusion rate from Section I, II, III, or IV above ____ % 16

Taxable capital gains (or net capital loss) in 2000:
Multiply the amount on line 9 by the inclusion rate you entered on line 16.
Enter the taxable capital gains on line 127 of your return.
If you have a net capital loss, see line 127 in the guide. 199 ____ 17

T1-2000

Statement of Investment Income

Schedule 4

State the names of the payers below and attach any information slips you received.
Attach a separate sheet of paper if you need more space.

I – Taxable amount of dividends from taxable Canadian corporations (see line 120 in the guide)

Specify: ______

\+

\+

Total dividends (enter on line 120 of your return) 120 =

II – Interest and other investment income (see line 121 in the guide)

Specify: ______

\+

\+

Income from foreign sources +

Total interest and other investment income (enter on line 121 of your return) 121 =

III – Net partnership income (loss) (see line 122 in the guide)

\+

Net partnership income (loss) (enter on line 122 of your return) 122 =

IV – Carrying charges and interest expenses (see line 221 in the guide)

Carrying charges (specify)

Interest expenses (specify) +

Total carrying charges and interest expenses (enter on line 221 of your return) 221 =

V – Exploration and development expenses (see line 224 in the guide) (attach T101 or T5013 slips)

(enter on line 224 of your return) 224

VI –

(enter on line 232 of your return) 232

5000-S4

T1-2000

Details of Dependant

Schedule 5

Read the guide to find out if you can claim an amount on line 305, 306, or 315 of your return. To calculate the amount of your claim, complete the applicable chart on the *Worksheet* included with your forms.

For each dependant claimed on line 305, 306, or 315, provide the details requested below. Attach this schedule to your return.

Line 305 – Equivalent-to-spouse amount

If your marital status changed in 2000, give the date of the change: Month | Day

(Make sure you have checked the box on page 1 of your return to indicate your marital status.)

Last name / First name / Address	Date of birth (Year, Month, Day)	Relationship to you	Net income in 2000	Nature of the infirmity if it applies	Amount of claim

Line 306 – Amount for infirm dependants age 18 or older *

Last name / First name / Address	Date of birth (Year, Month, Day)	Relationship to you	Net income in 2000	Nature of the infirmity	Amount of claim

Line 315 – Caregiver amount *

Last name / First name / Address	Date of birth (Year, Month, Day)	Relationship to you	Net income in 2000	Nature of the infirmity if it applies	Amount of claim

* Attach a separate sheet if you are claiming more than one dependant.

5000-S5

T1-2000 **Schedule 7**

RRSP Unused Contributions, Transfers, and HBP or LLP Activities

Only complete this schedule when **one or more** of the following situations applies:

- You will not be deducting on this return:
  - all of your unused RRSP contributions (if any) shown on your 1999 *Notice of Assessment* or *Notice of Reassessment*, or
  - all of the RRSP contributions you made from **March 1, 2000**, to **March 1, 2001**.
- You have transferred to your RRSP certain amounts you included in your income.
- You are designating contributions made to your RRSP as a 2000 repayment under the Home Buyers' Plan (HBP) or the Lifelong Learning Plan (LLP).
- You withdrew funds from your RRSP in 2000 under the LLP.

If none of these situations applies to you, enter your total RRSP contributions on line 208 of your return.

See line 208 in the guide for more information.

Unused RRSP contributions from the "Explanation of changes" area of your 1999 *Notice of Assessment* or *Notice of Reassessment*				1
Total of all RRSP contributions * made to your RRSP or your spouse's RRSP from:				
March 1, 2000, to December 31, 2000 (attach all receipts)		2		
January 1, 2001, to March 1, 2001 (attach all receipts)	+	3		
Add lines 2 and 3	245 =		▶ +	4
Total RRSP contributions: Add lines 1 and 4			=	5
Total 2000 repayments under the HBP and LLP from line 15 below			–	6
RRSP contributions available to deduct: Line 5 minus line 6			=	7
2000 deduction for:				
Contributions that are based on (and do not exceed) your 2000 RRSP deduction limit shown at the bottom of page 2 of your 1999 *Notice of Assessment* or *Notice of Reassessment*		8		
Transfers (see "Line 9 – Transfers" at line 208 in the guide)	240 +	9		
Add lines 8 and 9	=	10		
2000 RRSP deduction: Enter the amount from line 7 or line 10, whichever is **less** **Also enter this amount on line 208 of your return.**			208 –	11
Your unused RRSP contributions available to carry forward to a future year: Line 7 minus line 11			=	12

If the amount on line 12 is more than "0", we will show it on your 2000 *Notice of Assessment.*

* Include your transfers, and contributions that you are designating as a repayment under the HBP or LLP. See the guide for the list of contributions to exclude.

2000 repayments under the HBP and LLP

See "Line 6 – Repayments under the HBP and LLP" at line 208 in the guide.
Do not include any contributions or transfers that you will be including on line 8 or 9 above.

Contributions made to your RRSP from January 1, 2000, to March 1, 2001, you are designating as your:

2000 repayment under the HBP	246		13
2000 repayment under the LLP	262	+	14
Total 2000 repayments under the HBP and LLP: Add lines 13 and 14 Enter the result on line 6 above.		=	15

2000 withdrawals under the LLP

Enter the amount from box 25 of all T4RSP slips	263	16
Check this box if you want to designate your spouse as the LLP student	264 ☐	

T1-2000

Canada Pension Plan Contributions on Self-Employment and Other Earnings

Schedule 8

Complete this schedule to determine the amount of your Canada Pension Plan (CPP) contributions if:

- you reported self-employment income on lines 135 to 143 of your return;
- you reported business or professional income from a partnership on line 122 of your return; or
- you made an election on Form CPT20 to pay additional CPP contributions on other earnings.

See lines 308 and 310 in the guide for more information.

			Line
Pensionable net self-employment earnings (amounts from line 122 and lines 135 to 143 of your return)			1
Employment earnings not shown on a T4 slip on which you elect to pay additional CPP contributions (amount from line 10 of Form CPT20; attach a completed Form CPT20)	373	+	2
Add lines 1 and 2 (if the result is negative, enter "0")		=	3
Enter the amount from box 26 (or if blank, box 14) on all T4 slips (this amount already includes the amount entered on line 11 of Form CPT20, if it applies)		+	4
Total pensionable earnings (add lines 3 and 4)		=	5
Basic CPP exemption	claim $3,500	–	6
Earnings subject to contribution: Line 5 minus line 6 (if negative, enter "0") (maximum $34,100)		=	7
Multiply the amount on line 7 by 7.8% =			8
Contributions through employment (from box 16 and box 17 on all T4 slips)	x 2 =	–	9
Canada Pension Plan contributions payable on self-employment and other earnings: Line 8 minus line 9 (if negative, enter "0") Enter this amount on line 310 and on line 421 of your return.		=	10

Note: In some situations, we will prorate your CPP contributions. If this applies to you, we will calculate the correct amount and show it on your *Notice of Assessment*.

5000-S8

T1-2000

Canada Pension Plan Contributions on Self-Employment and Other Earnings

Schedule 8

Complete this schedule to determine the amount of your Canada Pension Plan (CPP) contributions if:

- you reported self-employment income on lines 135 to 143 of your return;
- you reported business or professional income from a partnership on line 122 of your return; or
- you made an election on Form CPT20 to pay additional CPP contributions on other earnings.

See lines 308 and 310 in the guide for more information.

			Line
Pensionable net self-employment earnings (amounts from line 122 and lines 135 to 143 of your return)			1
Employment earnings not shown on a T4 slip on which you elect to pay additional CPP contributions (amount from line 10 of Form CPT20; attach a completed Form CPT20)	373	+	2
Add lines 1 and 2 (if the result is negative, enter "0")		=	3
Enter the amount from box 26 (or if blank, box 14) on all T4 slips (this amount already includes the amount entered on line 11 of Form CPT20, if it applies)		+	4
Total pensionable earnings (add lines 3 and 4)		=	5
Basic CPP exemption	claim $3,500	–	6
Earnings subject to contribution: Line 5 minus line 6 (if negative, enter "0") (maximum $34,100)		=	7
Multiply the amount on line 7 by 7.8% =			8
Contributions through employment (from box 16 and box 17 on all T4 slips)	x 2 =	–	9
Canada Pension Plan contributions payable on self-employment and other earnings: Line 8 minus line 9 (if negative, enter "0") Enter this amount on line 310 and on line 421 of your return.		=	10

Note: In some situations, we will prorate your CPP contributions. If this applies to you, we will calculate the correct amount and show it on your *Notice of Assessment*.

5000-S8

T1-2000 **Schedule 8**

Quebec Pension Plan Contributions on Self-Employment and Other Earnings

Complete this schedule to determine the amount of your Quebec Pension Plan (QPP) contributions if you reported net business income on line 164 of your **provincial** return.

Also use this schedule to calculate your optional QPP contributions.

See lines 308 and 310 in the guide for more information.

Net business income (total of lines 27 and 33 of your **provincial** return; if this amount is negative, enter "0")	371		1
Income on which you wish to make optional contributions (amount from line 2 of work chart 445 of your **provincial** return)	373	+	2
Amount from line 11 of work chart 445 of your **provincial** return		+	3
Add lines 1, 2, and 3 (maximum $37,600)		=	4
Basic exemption claim $3,500		–	5
Earnings subject to contribution: Line 4 minus line 5 (if negative, enter "0")		=	6
Multiply the amount on line 6 by 7.8% =			7
Total contributions from line 98 of your **provincial** return ______ x 2 =		–	8
Quebec Pension Plan contributions on self-employment and other earnings: Line 7 minus line 8 (if negative, enter "0") Enter this amount on line 310 of your federal return.		=	9

Note: In some situations, we will prorate your QPP contributions. If this applies to you, we will calculate the correct amount and show it on your *Notice of Assessment.*

5005-S8

T1-2000 **Schedule 8**

Quebec Pension Plan Contributions on Self-Employment and Other Earnings

Complete this schedule to determine the amount of your Quebec Pension Plan (QPP) contributions if you reported net business income on line 164 of your **provincial** return.

Also use this schedule to calculate your optional QPP contributions.

See lines 308 and 310 in the guide for more information.

Net business income (total of lines 27 and 33 of your provincial return; if this amount is negative, enter "0")	371		1
Income on which you wish to make optional contributions (amount from line 2 of work chart 445 of your **provincial** return)	373	+	2
Amount from line 11 of work chart 445 of your **provincial** return		+	3
Add lines 1, 2, and 3 (maximum $37,600)		=	4
Basic exemption claim $3,500		–	5
Earnings subject to contribution: Line 4 minus line 5 (if negative, enter "0")		=	6
Multiply the amount on line 6 by 7.8% =			7
Total contributions from line 98 of your **provincial** return ______ x 2 =		–	8
Quebec Pension Plan contributions on self-employment and other earnings: Line 7 minus line 8 (if negative, enter "0") Enter this amount on line 310 of your federal return.		=	9

Note: In some situations, we will prorate your QPP contributions. If this applies to you, we will calculate the correct amount and show it on your *Notice of Assessment.*

5005-S8

T1-2000

Donations and Gifts

Schedule 9

Attach those official receipts that support your claim. Remember, you may have charitable donations shown on your T4 and T4A slips. See line 349 in the guide.

Total charitable donations and government gifts ____ 1

Enter your **net income** from line 236 of your return ____ x 75% = ____ 2

Note: If the amount on line 1 is less than the amount on line 2, enter the amount from line 1 on line 340 below and continue completing the schedule from line 340.

Gifts of depreciable property (from the calculation in the pamphlet called *Gifts and Income Tax*) 337 ____ 3

Taxable capital gains minus capital gains deduction on 2000 gifts of capital property (see the pamphlet called *Gifts and Income Tax*) 339 + ____ 4

Add lines 3 and 4 = ____ x 25% = + ____ 5

Total donations limit: Add lines 2 and 5 = ____ 6

Allowable charitable donations and government gifts (enter the amount from line 1 or line 6, whichever is **less**) 340 ____

Cultural and ecological gifts (see line 349 in the guide) 342 + ____

Add lines 340 and 342. 344 = ____

Enter $200, or the amount from line 344, whichever is **less** 345 – ____ x 17% = 346 ____ 7

Line 344 minus line 345. 347 = ____ x 29% = 348 + ____ 8

Donations and gifts: Add lines 7 and 8
Enter this amount on line 349 of your return. = ____ 9

5000-S9

T1-2000

Donations and Gifts

Schedule 9

Attach those official receipts that support your claim. Remember, you may have charitable donations shown on your T4 and T4A slips. See line 349 in the guide.

Total charitable donations and government gifts ____ 1

Enter your **net income** from line 236 of your return ____ x 75% = ____ 2

Note: If the amount on line 1 is less than the amount on line 2, enter the amount from line 1 on line 340 below and continue completing the schedule from line 340.

Gifts of depreciable property (from the calculation in the pamphlet called *Gifts and Income Tax*) 337 ____ 3

Taxable capital gains minus capital gains deduction on 2000 gifts of capital property (see the pamphlet called *Gifts and Income Tax*) 339 + ____ 4

Add lines 3 and 4 = ____ x 25% = + ____ 5

Total donations limit: Add lines 2 and 5 = ____ 6

Allowable charitable donations and government gifts (enter the amount from line 1 or line 6, whichever is **less**) 340 ____

Cultural and ecological gifts (see line 349 in the guide) 342 + ____

Add lines 340 and 342. 344 = ____

Enter $200, or the amount from line 344, whichever is **less** 345 – ____ x 17% = 346 ____ 7

Line 344 minus line 345. 347 = ____ x 29% = 348 + ____ 8

Donations and gifts: Add lines 7 and 8
Enter this amount on line 349 of your return. = ____ 9

5000-S9

T1-2000 **Refundable Medical Expense Supplement** **Schedule 10**

Complete this schedule to calculate your refundable medical expense supplement if you meet **all** of the following conditions:

- You were resident in Canada for all of 2000.
- You were age 18 or older at the end of 2000.
- The total of the following two amounts was $2,535 or more:
  - your employment income on lines 101 and 104 of your return (not including amounts from a wage-loss replacement plan) minus the amounts on lines 207, 212, 229, and 231 (if the result is negative, use "0"); and
  - your net self-employment income (not including losses) from lines 135 to 143 of your return.
- Your net family income was less than $27,804. Net family income is the total of your net income (line 236) and your spouse's net income (line 236 of your spouse's return, or the amount it would be if your spouse completed a return).

See line 452 in the guide for more information.

Allowable portion of medical expenses (from line 332 of your return)	x 25% =			1
Enter $507, or the amount from line 1, whichever is **less**				2
Your net income (from line 236 of your return)		3		
Spouse's net income (line 236 of your spouse's return) 467	+	4		
Net family income: Add lines 3 and 4	=	5		
Minus: $17,664	– 17,664 00	6		
Line 5 minus line 6 (if negative, enter "0")	=	x 5% =	–	7
Refundable medical expense supplement: Line 2 minus line 7 (if negative, enter "0") Enter this amount on line 452 of your return.			=	8

T1-2000 Tuition and Education Amounts Schedule 11

If you are a student, complete this schedule to:
- calculate your tuition and education amounts to claim on line 323 of your return; and
- determine the amount, if any, available for you to carry forward to a future year.

In either case, attach a completed copy to **your** return.

Transferring your unused 2000 amounts:
- **If you are a student**, you can use this schedule to calculate the maximum amount available for transfer. Attach this schedule to **your** return if you are filing a return. If you are not filing a return, keep it for your records.
- You can transfer your unused 2000 amounts to ONE individual, either your spouse, or your or your spouse's parent or grandparent.
- You cannot transfer your unused 2000 amounts to your or your spouse's parent or grandparent if your spouse is claiming the spousal amount (line 303) or amounts transferred from your spouse (line 326).

Make sure that the person to whom you transfer your unused 2000 amounts does not attach this schedule, or a photocopy of this schedule, to his or her return.

See line 323 in the guide for more information.

Description				Line
Unused tuition and education amounts from your 1999 *Notice of Assessment* or *Notice of Reassessment*				1
Eligible tuition fees paid for 2000		320		2
Education amount for 2000: Use Columns B and C of Forms T2202 and T2202A; count each month only once to a maximum of 12 months in total				
Enter the number of months from Column **B**	x $60 =	321 +		3
Enter the number of months from Column **C**	x $200 =	322 +		4
Total 2000 tuition and education amounts: Add lines 2, 3, and 4		=	► +	5
Total tuition and education amounts: Add lines 1 and 5			=	6
Taxable income from line 260 of your return				7
Total of lines 300 to 318 of your return	–			8
Line 7 minus line 8 (if negative, enter "0")	=			9
Unused tuition and education amounts claimed for 2000: Enter the amount from line 1 or line 9, whichever is **less**	–	►		10
Line 9 minus line 10	=			11
2000 tuition and education amounts claimed for 2000: Enter the amount from line 5 or line 11, whichever is **less**		+		12
Total tuition and education amounts claimed for 2000: Add lines 10 and 12. Enter this amount on line 323 of your return.		=	► –	13
Total unused tuition and education amounts: Line 6 minus line 13			=	14

Note: If the amount on line 14 is "0", you do not have to complete the rest of this schedule.

Description		Line
Enter $5,000, or the amount from line 5, whichever is **less**		15
Enter the amount from line 12 above	–	16
Maximum amount available for transfer: Line 15 minus line 16	=	17

If you are transferring all or a part of the amount on line 17 to another individual * :

Description		Line
Enter the amount from line 4 of your spouse's Schedule 2, **or** the amount from line 324 of your or your spouse's parent's or grandparent's return that relates to you, whichever applies	327 –	18
Your unused tuition and education amounts available to carry forward to a future year: Line 14 minus line 18	=	19

* If you are not filing a return, keep this schedule for your records. In any case, this schedule, or a photocopy of this schedule, is **not to be attached** to the other individual's return.

5000-S11

Canada Customs and Revenue Agency | Agence des douanes et du revenu du Canada

EMPLOYEE AND PARTNER GST/HST REBATE APPLICATION

- You do not qualify for this rebate if your employer is a listed financial institution (for example, a person that was at any time during the year, a bank, an investment dealer, a trust company, an insurance company, a credit union, or a corporation whose principal business is lending money).
- For details on how to complete this form, see the guides called *Employment Expenses* (for employees) and *GST/HST Rebate for Partners* (for members of a partnership).

Area A – Identification (to be completed by claimant)

Last name	First name and initials
Taxation year of claim (one year per claim)	Social insurance number
Name of employer or partnership (must be a GST/HST registrant)	Business Number of employer or partnership

Area B – Rebate calculation (to be completed by claimant)

GST rebate for eligible expenses on which you paid 7% GST

Eligible expenses other than CCA on which you paid 7% GST (from box A of Chart 1 on the back of this form, or, enter the amount of union, professional, or similar dues eligible for the GST rebate)		1	
Eligible CCA on motor vehicles, musical instruments, and aircraft for which you paid 7% GST (from box B of Chart 1 on the back of this form)		2	
Total expenses eligible for the GST rebate (line 1 plus line 2)	6485	3	
Multiply line 3 by 7/107			4

HST rebate for eligible expenses on which you paid 15% HST

Eligible expenses other than CCA on which you paid 15% HST (from box C of Chart 2 on the back of this form, or, enter the amount of union, professional, or similar dues eligible for the HST rebate)		5	
Eligible CCA on motor vehicles, musical instruments, and aircraft for which you paid 15% HST (from box D of Chart 2 on the back of this form)		6	
Total expenses eligible for the HST rebate (line 5 plus line 6)	6487	7	
Multiply line 7 by 15/115			8

Rebate for property and services brought into a participating province (i.e., Nova Scotia, New Brunswick, Newfoundland)
Do not include any expenses for which you paid 15% HST. Read Situation 5 of the applicable guide for more details.

Eligible expenses other than CCA on which you paid the provincial portion of HST separately		9	
Eligible CCA on motor vehicles, musical instruments, and aircraft for which you paid the provincial portion of HST separately		10	
Total expenses eligible for the rebate (line 9 plus line 10)	6486	11	
Multiply line 11 by 8/108			12
Employee and Partner GST/HST Rebate (add lines 4, 8, and 12) Enter the amount from line 13 on line 457 of your income tax return.			13

Area C – Declaration by claimant's employer or partnership (an authorized officer of your employer or partnership must complete this area **only** if you are claiming a rebate for any expenses included on lines 4, 8, or 12 in Area B above for which you were paid a taxable allowance, i.e., a non-reasonable allowance).

I certify that for the taxation year stated above, the claimant was paid the following allowance, which at the time it was paid, I did not consider to be reasonable for the purposes of subparagraphs 6(1)(b)(v), (vi), (vii), or (vii.1) of the *Income Tax Act*. I will not include this allowance in determining my input tax credit or rebate.

Amount received $	Reason for allowance(s) (list activities)	
Name of employer or partnership		
Signature of employer or authorized officer	Position of authorized officer	Year Month Day

Area D – Certification (to be completed by claimant)

I certify that the information in this document is, to the best of my knowledge, true, correct, and complete and that I am eligible for the Employee and Partner GST/HST Rebate for the taxation year.	Signature	Year Month Day

Personal information provided on this form is protected under the provisions of the *Privacy Act* and is kept in Personal Information Bank number RCC/P-PU-080.

Chart 1 – Eligible expenses on which you paid 7% GST

	Type of expenses	(1) Total expenses	(2) Non-eligible expenses	(3) Eligible expenses (col. 1 minus col. 2)
Expenses other than CCA	Accounting and legal fees			
	Advertising and promotion			
	Food, beverages, and entertainment			
	Lodging			
	Parking			
	Supplies			
	Other expenses (please specify)			
	Musical instrument expenses other than CCA			
	Artists' employment expenses			
	Union, professional, or similar dues			
	Motor vehicle expenses			
	Fuel			
	Maintenance and repairs			
	Insurance, licence, registration, and interest			
	Leasing			
	Other expenses (please specify)			
	Work space in home			
	Electricity, heat, and water			
	Maintenance			
	Insurance and property taxes			
	Other expenses (please specify)			
		Total eligible expenses other than CCA (Column 3) ▶		(A)
	Capital cost allowance (CCA) on motor vehicles, musical instruments, and aircraft ▶			(B)

Chart 2 – Eligible expenses on which you paid 15% HST

	Type of expenses	(1) Total expenses	(2) Non-eligible expenses	(3) Eligible expenses (col. 1 minus col. 2)
Expenses other than CCA	Accounting and legal fees			
	Advertising and promotion			
	Food, beverages, and entertainment			
	Lodging			
	Parking			
	Supplies			
	Other expenses (please specify)			
	Musical instrument expenses other than CCA			
	Artists' employment expenses			
	Union, professional, or similar dues			
	Motor vehicle expenses			
	Fuel			
	Maintenance and repairs			
	Insurance, licence, registration, and interest			
	Leasing			
	Other expenses (please specify)			
	Work space in home			
	Electricity, heat, and water			
	Maintenance			
	Insurance and property taxes			
	Other expenses (please specify)			
		Total eligible expenses other than CCA (Column 3) ▶		(C)
	Capital cost allowance (CCA) on motor vehicles, musical instruments, and aircraft ▶			(D)

Do not enter amounts in the black areas, as these expenses are not eligible for the rebate.

Printed in Canada

 Canada Customs and Revenue Agency — Agence des douanes et du revenu du Canada

FEDERAL FOREIGN TAX CREDITS

Use this form to calculate the amount you can deduct from federal tax and from the federal individual surtax for a tax year. You can claim this credit if you were resident in Canada at any time in the tax year, and you had to include, on your Canadian return, income which originated in a foreign country for which you paid non-business or business taxes to that foreign country. Attach a completed copy of this form to your return. If the total foreign taxes you paid to all foreign countries is more than $200, complete a separate form for each foreign country to which you paid taxes.

See the back for details. For more information, get Interpretation Bulletin IT- 270, *Foreign Tax Credit*, or contact your tax services office.

Part 1 – Federal foreign tax credit

Foreign non-business income

Non-business-income tax paid to a foreign country * 1

Net foreign non-business income ** ...... Divided by: Net income *** .... x Federal tax **** .... = 2

Enter the amount from line 1 or line 2, whichever is **less** .... **Federal non-business foreign tax credit** 3

Foreign business income

Business-income tax paid to a foreign country †, plus any unused foreign tax credits for that country for the seven tax years before and the three tax years immediately after this tax year 4

Net foreign business income †† .... Divided by: Net income *** .... x Basic federal tax ††† .... = 5

Federal surtax on income you earned outside Canada:
Amount from line 9 of Form T2203, *Provincial and Territorial Taxes – Multiple Jurisdictions*, or 52% of the amount from line 33 of Schedule 1. If you paid business-income tax to more than one country, enter the portion that applies to this country + 6

Add line 5 and line 6 .... = 7

Add basic federal tax ††† and the amount from line 6 ....

Enter the amount from line 3, if any .... – = 8

Enter the amount from line 4, 7, or 8, whichever is the **least** .... **Federal business foreign tax credit** 9

Add line 3 and line 9. Enter this amount on line 36 of Schedule 1 .... **Federal foreign tax credit** 10

Part 2 – Additional foreign tax credit (to be deducted from individual surtax)

Foreign non-business income

Enter the amount from line 1 11

Net foreign non-business income ** ...... Divided by: Net income *** .... x Federal tax **** plus federal individual surtax from line 47 of Schedule 1 = 12

Enter the amount from line 11 or line 12, whichever is **less** 13

Enter the amount from line 3, if any .... – 14

Line 13 minus line 14 (if negative, enter "0") .... **Additional federal non-business foreign tax credit** = 15

Foreign business income

Line 4 minus line 9 16

Net foreign business income †† .... Divided by: Net income *** .... x Basic federal tax ††† plus federal individual surtax from line 47 of Schedule 1 = 17

Federal surtax on income you earned outside Canada:
Amount from line 9 of Form T2203, *Provincial and Territorial Taxes – Multiple Jurisdictions*, or 52% of the amount from line 33 of Schedule 1. If you paid business-income tax to more than one country, enter the portion that applies to this country + 18

Add line 17 and line 18 .... = 19

Enter the amount from line 9 .... – 20

Line 19 minus line 20 (if negative, enter "0") .... = 21

Enter the federal individual surtax from line 47 of Schedule 1 ....

Enter the amount from line 15, if any .... – = 22

Enter the amount from line 16, 21, or 22, whichever is the **least** .... **Additional federal business foreign tax credit** 23

Add line 15 and line 23. Enter the result on line 48 of Schedule 1 .... **Additional federal foreign tax credit** 24

If amount E in Part 4 of Form T691, *Alternative Minimum Tax*, is more than the total of lines 10 and 24 for all your T2209 forms, you cannot claim the additional foreign tax credit. Enter "0" on line 48 of Schedule 1.

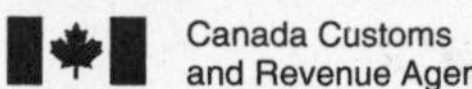

Canada Customs and Revenue Agency Agence des douanes et du revenu du Canada

PROVINCIAL FOREIGN TAX CREDIT

Use this form to calculate the foreign tax credit that you can deduct from your provincial income tax payable to your **province of residence** on December 31 of the tax year. References to a province include the Yukon, the Northwest Territories, and Nunavut.

To claim this credit, you must have been resident in a province other than Quebec on December 31 of the tax year or on the date you departed from Canada. A deceased person must have been resident in a province other than Quebec on the date of death. In addition, you must have had to include, on your Canadian return, income originating in a foreign country. The non-business taxes you paid to that foreign country must have been more than the federal non-business foreign tax credits.

Attach a completed copy of this form to your return. If the total taxes you paid to all foreign countries is more than $200, complete a separate form for each foreign country to which you paid taxes.

Non-business-income tax paid to a foreign country *			1
Federal foreign tax credit for non-business income tax:			
Enter the amount from line 3 of Form T2209 (see Note 1)		2	
Enter the amount from line 15 of Form T2209	+	3	
Add line 2 and line 3 (see Note 2)	=	▶ –	4
Excess of non-business income tax paid over the federal non-business foreign tax credits: Line 1 minus line 4 (if negative, enter "0")		=	5
Net foreign non-business income ** / Divided by: Net income ***	X Provincial tax otherwise payable ****	=	6
Enter the amount from line 5 or line 6, whichever is **less**	**Provincial foreign tax credit**		7

* **Non-business income tax paid to a foreign country** is the total income or profits taxes you paid to that country or to a political subdivision of the country for the year (excluding business income tax), minus any part of these taxes that is deductible under subsection 20(11) or deducted under subsection 20(12) of the federal *Income Tax Act*. It does not include any part of these taxes that can reasonably be attributed to amounts that:

- any other person or partnership received or is entitled to receive from the foreign country;
- relate to employment income from that country for which you claimed an overseas employment tax credit;
- relate to taxable capital gains from that country for which you or your spouse claimed a capital gains deduction;
- were deductible as exempt income under a tax treaty between Canada and that country; or
- were taxable in the foreign country because you were a citizen of that country, and relate to income from a source within Canada.

In addition, any amount of tax paid to a foreign government in excess of the amount required to be paid, according to a tax treaty, is considered a voluntary contribution and does not qualify as foreign taxes paid.

** **Net foreign non-business income** (see Note 3) is the net amount you calculate when the non-business income you earned in a foreign country exceeds the non-business losses you incurred in the same country. When you calculate the non-business income and losses, claim the allowable expenses and deductions relating to the foreign income or loss (including deductions claimed under subsections 20(11) or 20(12) of the federal *Income Tax Act*, and excluding any deduction you claimed for a dividend you received from a controlled foreign affiliate).

Reduce this amount by any income from that foreign country for which you claimed a capital gains deduction, and by any income from that country that was, under a tax treaty between Canada and that country, either deductible as exempt income in Canada, or exempt from tax in that country. Also, reduce this amount by any part of employment income from that country for which you claimed an overseas employment tax credit. If the net foreign non-business income is more than **net income**, use **net income** in the calculation.

*** **Net income** (see Note 4) is the net income you allocated to your province of residence on Form T2203, *Provincial and Territorial Taxes – Multiple Jurisdictions*, if you were not a resident of Alberta, or the amount on line 236 of your return, minus any:

- amounts deductible as an employee home relocation loan deduction (line 248 of your return);
- amounts deductible as stock option and shares deductions (line 249 of your return);
- amounts deductible as an other payments deduction (line 250 of your return);
- net capital losses of other years you claimed (line 253 of your return);
- capital gains deduction you claimed (line 254 of your return); and
- foreign income deductible as exempt income under a tax treaty, or deductible as net employment income from a prescribed international organization (included on line 256 of your return).

**** **Provincial tax otherwise payable** is the provincial tax you calculated before determining the provincial foreign tax credit. Use Form T1C or T1C-TC, whichever applies, to determine the amount of provincial tax. When you complete this calculation, determine any Ontario and Alberta tax before the provincial foreign tax credit by replacing the reference to line 33 of Schedule 1 on Form T1C (ONT.) TC or Form T1C (ALTA.) with "line 33 plus any federal dividend tax credit and overseas employment tax credit."

Note 1: Form T2209 is called *Federal Foreign Tax Credits*. If minimum tax applies and you were a resident of Ontario or Alberta, enter on line 2 the part of the special foreign tax credit you calculated on Form T691, *Alternative Minimum Tax*, that relates to non-business income taxes you paid to a foreign country.

Note 2: If you were a resident of Alberta and claimed an overseas employment tax credit, add also 144% of that amount.

Note 3: If you were a resident of Canada for part of the year, only include the income for the part of the year you were a resident of Canada.

Note 4: If you were a resident of Canada for part of the year, include the income for the part of the year you were a resident of Canada and the taxable income you earned in Canada (before deductions under paragraphs 115(1)(d) to (f) of the federal *Income Tax Act*) as reported on your Canadian return for the part of the year you were not a resident of Canada.

Canada Customs and Revenue Agency / Agence des douanes et du revenu du Canada

STATEMENT OF REAL ESTATE RENTALS

1

- For more information on how to complete this statement, see the income tax guide called *Rental Income.*

Identification

Your name	Your social insurance number ___ – ___ – ___
For the period from: Year / Month / Day to: Year / Month 1 2 / Day 3 1	Was this the final year of your rental operation? Yes ☐ No ☐
Name and address of person or firm preparing this form	Partnership identification number
	Tax shelter identification number
Business Number	Your percentage of ownership % — Industry code 7 5 1 1

Details of other co-owners and partners

Co-owner or partner's name and address	Share of net income or (loss) $	Percentage of ownership %
Co-owner or partner's name and address	Share of net income or (loss) $	Percentage of ownership %
Co-owner or partner's name and address	Share of net income or (loss) $	Percentage of ownership %
Co-owner or partner's name and address	Share of net income or (loss) $	Percentage of ownership %
Co-owner or partner's name and address	Share of net income or (loss) $	Percentage of ownership %

Income

Address of property	Number of units		Gross rents
		+	
		+	
Enter the total of your gross rents		8141	
Other related income		8230	
Gross income (enter this amount on line 160 of your income tax return)		8299	(a)

Expenses

		Total expense	Personal portion
Advertising	8521		
Insurance	8690		
Interest	8710		
Maintenance and repairs	8960		
Management and administration fees	8871		
Motor vehicle expenses (not including capital cost allowance)	9281		
Office expenses	8810		
Legal, accounting, and other professional fees	8860		
Property taxes	9180		
Salaries, wages, and benefits (including employer's contributions)	9060		
Travel	9200		
Utilities	9220		
Other expenses	9270		
Total			9949

Deductible expenses (total expenses minus personal portion)			(b)
Net income (loss) before adjustments (line a minus line b)	9369		
Co-owners – Your share of line 9369 above			(c)
Minus – Other expenses of the co-owner	9945		
Sub-total			
Plus – Recaptured capital cost allowance (see Chapter 3 for details)	9947		
Sub-total			
Minus – Terminal loss (see Chapter 3 for details)	9948		
Sub-total			
Minus – Capital cost allowance (from Area A on the back)	9936		
Net income (loss) – Enter this amount on line 9946 if you are a sole proprietor or a co-owner			(d)
Partnerships – Your share of line (d) above			
Minus – Other expenses of the partner	9943		
Your net income (loss) – Enter this amount on line 126 of your income tax return	9946		

Area A – Calculation of capital cost allowance claim

1 Class number	2 Undepreciated capital cost (UCC) at the start of the year	3 Cost of additions in the year (see Areas B and C below)	4 Proceeds of dispositions in the year (see Areas D and E below)	5 * UCC after additions and dispositions (col. 2 **plus** 3 **minus** 4)	6 Adjustment for current-year additions (1/2 x (col. 3 **minus** 4)) If negative, enter "0"	7 Base amount for capital cost allowance (col. 5 **minus** 6)	8 Rate %	9 CCA for the year (col. 7 x 8 or a lesser amount)	10 UCC at the end of the year (col. 5 **minus** 9)

Total CCA claim for the year **

* If you have a negative amount in this column, add it to income as a recapture under "Recaptured capital cost allowance" on the front of this form. If there is no property left in the class and there is a positive amount in the column, deduct the amount from income as a terminal loss under "Terminal loss" on the front of this form. For more information, read Chapter 3 of the *Rental Income* guide.

**Sole proprietors and partnerships enter the total claim on line 9936 on the front. Co-owners enter only your share of the total claim on line 9936 on the front.

Area B – Details of equipment and other property additions in the year

1 Class number	2 Property details	3 Total cost	4 Personal portion (if applicable)	5 Rental portion (Column 3 **minus** Column 4)

Total equipment and other property additions in the year 9925

Area C – Details of building additions in the year

1 Class number	2 Property details	3 Total cost	4 Personal portion (if applicable)	5 Rental portion (Column 3 **minus** Column 4)

Total building additions in the year 9927

Area D – Details of equipment and other property dispositions in the year

1 Class number	2 Property details	3 Proceeds of disposition (should not be more than the capital cost)	4 Personal portion (if applicable)	5 Rental portion (Column 3 **minus** Column 4)

Note: If you disposed of rental property in the year, see Chapter 3 in the *Rental Income* guide for information about your proceeds of disposition.

Total equipment and other property dispositions in the year 9926

Area E – Details of building dispositions in the year

1 Class number	2 Property details	3 Proceeds of disposition (should not be more than the capital cost)	4 Personal portion (if applicable)	5 Rental portion (Column 3 **minus** Column 4)

Note: If you disposed of rental property in the year, see Chapter 3 in the *Rental Income* guide for information about your proceeds of disposition.

Total building dispositions in the year 9928

Area F – Details of land additions and dispositions in the year

Total cost of all land additions in the year	9923	
Total proceeds from all land dispositions in the year	9924	

Printed in Canada

Canada Customs and Revenue Agency | Agence des douanes et du revenu du Canada

Revenue Canada | Revenu Canada

WORKSHEET FOR CALCULATING 2000 INSTALMENT PAYMENTS

Please read the instructions on the back of this worksheet before you complete this form.

Social insurance number

Calculating net tax owing by instalments

Note: The line references are from the General income tax return.

Net federal tax (line 420) .... ______ A

Old Age Security (OAS) repayment (from line 422) .... ______ B

Provincial or territorial tax (line 428) .... ______ C

First Nations tax (line 432) .... ______ D

Total payable (add lines A, B, C, and D) .... ______ ► ______ 1

Total income tax deducted (line 437)* (If you are a resident of Quebec, use line 439.) ______ E

Refundable abatement (line 440 plus line 441) .... ______ F

Refundable medical expense supplement (line 452) .... ______ G

Refund of investment tax credit (line 454) .... ______ H

Part XII.2 trust tax credit (line 456) .... ______ I

Provincial or territorial tax credits (line 479) .... ______ J

Total credits (add lines E, F, G, H, I and J) .... ______ ► ______ 2

Net tax owing by instalments (line 1 minus line 2) .... ______ 3

*If you are calculating your **1999** net tax owing, include in the amount on line E the total amount withheld from your OAS pension benefits during **1999**. If you are estimating your **2000** net tax owing, do the calculation for "line E" on the back of this worksheet.

Canada Pension Plan (CPP) contributions payable by instalments

If you reported self-employment income on lines 135 to 143 of your return or business or professional income from a partnership on line 122 of your return, complete Schedule 8, *Calculating Canada Pension Plan Contributions on Self-Employment and Other Earnings*, included with your individual tax package. Report the amount you calculated on line 10 of Schedule 8 on line 4 below. If you are estimating your 2000 CPP contributions payable, use the following figures to complete Schedule 8:

- $3,500 on line 6
- $34,100 on line 7
- 7.8% on line 8

CPP contributions payable by instalments .... ______ 4

Total amount payable by instalments

Add lines 3 and 4 .... ______ 5

Instalment amount due:

If you have to make instalment payments every three months, divide the amount on line 5 by 4 and send it by each due date. ______ 6

If your main source of income is self-employment income from farming or fishing, calculate 2/3 of the amount on line 5 and send it in one instalment payment by December 31 .... ______ 7

Note

If the amount on line 6 or 7 is more than the amount on your instalment reminders, and you pay only the amount on each of your reminders by the due date, you will not have to pay instalment interest or penalties.

Canada Customs and Revenue Agency / Agence des douanes et du revenu du Canada
Revenue Canada / Revenu Canada

REQUEST FOR LOSS CARRYBACK

- Use this form to claim a loss carryback under sections 111 and 41 of the *Income Tax Act*. Attach one completed copy of this form to your 1999 income tax return.
- Claim a loss carryforward on your return for those years following the year of the loss, within the limitations of sections 111, 41, and 80 of the *Income Tax Act*.
- Credits arising from the loss carryback adjustment(s) may be applied to outstanding taxes owing for any taxation year.
- Any late-filing penalty that applies to the return for the taxation year to which the loss is being applied will not be reduced by the loss carryback(s).
- Limited partnership losses cannot be carried back.
- The lines and guide items referred to in this form are found in the *General Income Tax and Benefit Guide*.

Full name (print)	Social insurance number
Address (print)	

Area I – Non-capital loss for carryback

Notes 1. Enter the amounts below without brackets.

2. The following amounts will reduce the income or increase the loss (as appropriate) from the source(s) to which they relate: capital cost allowance relating to investment in Canadian motion picture films (see guide item 232); deductions allowed under subsections 20(11) and 20(12) of the *Income Tax Act*; and repayments of shareholder's loans.

3. If you have an amount on line 224 of your return, deduct the amount against either your investment income or loss, or your partnership (limited or non-active) income or loss, whichever applies. Do not deduct the amount twice.

	Income		Loss	
Employment income or loss (lines 101 and 104 of your return **minus** lines 207, 212, 229, and 231)				
Investment income or loss (lines 120 and 121 of your return **minus** line 221)				
Partnership (limited or non–active partners) income / loss (from line 122 of your return)				
Rental income or loss (from line 126 of your return)				
Business income or loss (from line 135 of your return)				
Professional income or loss (from line 137 of your return)				
Commission income or loss (from line 139 of your return)				
Farming income or loss (from line 141 of your return)				
Fishing income or loss (from line 143 of your return)				
Taxable capital gains (from line 127 of your return)			Nil	
Non-taxable income (from line 147 of your return)			Nil	
Net capital losses of other years (from line 253 of your return)	Nil			
Capital gains deduction (from line 254 of your return)	Nil			
Business investment loss (from line 217 of your return)	Nil			
Employee home relocation loan deduction (from line 248 of your return)	Nil			
Stock option and shares deductions (from line 249 of your return)	Nil			
Other payments deduction (from line 250 of your return)	Nil			
Income exempt under a tax treaty (see guide item 256)	Nil			
Income from other sources (from lines 113, 114, 115, 119, 128, 129, and 130 of your return)			Nil	
Subtotal		A		B
Subtract: Amounts on lines 208, 209, 214, 215, 219, 220, 232, and 235 (except amounts in Note 2 above)				
Subtotal (if negative, enter "0")		►		C
Subtract: Line C from line B (if negative, enter "0")				D
Subtract: The lesser of line D and line H				E
Total non-capital loss for the year available for carryback (line D **minus** line E – if negative, enter "0")				F
Subtract: Non-capital loss to be applied to 1996	6625			
Non-capital loss to be applied to 1997	6626			
Non-capital loss to be applied to 1998	6627			
Subtotal		►		G
Balance of non-capital loss available for carryforward (line F **minus** line G — if negative, enter "0")		►		

Area II – Farming or fishing loss for carryback

Loss from farming or fishing

Subtract: Income from farming or fishing

Subtotal (if negative, enter "0") H

Farming or fishing loss available for carryback (enter the amount from line E) I

Subtract:			
	Farming or fishing loss to be applied to 1996	6630	
	Farming or fishing loss to be applied to 1997	6631	
	Farming or fishing loss to be applied to 1998	6632	
	Subtotal	►	J

Balance of farming or fishing loss available for carryforward (line I **minus** line J — if negative, enter "0")

Area III – Net capital loss for carryback

Notes: 1. Use this form for applying only 1999 net capital losses (see Chapter 5 of the guide called *Capital Gains* for more information).

2. You can only apply 1999 net capital losses against taxable capital gains.
3. The amount of 1999 allowable capital losses which is more than 1999 taxable capital gains is the "1999 net capital loss available for carryback" (line K).
4. Applying a net capital loss carryback will result in a reduction of the capital gains deduction, if claimed, in the year(s) of the loss application. It may also reduce capital gains deductions you claimed in subsequent years.
5. The net capital loss you apply to preceding years may affect the capital gains election you made on your 1994 income tax return.

1999 net capital loss available for carryback (see note 3 above) K

Subtract:			
	Net capital loss to be applied to 1996	6636	
	Net capital loss to be applied to 1997	6637	
	Net capital loss to be applied to 1998	6638	
	Subtotal	►	L

Balance of net capital loss available for carryforward (line K **minus** line L)

Area IV – Listed personal property loss for carryback

Amount of listed personal property losses which is more than listed personal property gains for the year available for carryback (refer to Chapter 5 of the guide called *Capital Gains*)

Subtract:			
	Listed personal property loss to be applied to 1996 listed personal property net gains	6642	
	Listed personal property loss to be applied to 1997 listed personal property net gains	6643	
	Listed personal property loss to be applied to 1998 listed personal property net gains	6644	
	Subtotal	►	

Balance of listed personal property loss available for carryforward

Area V – Restricted farm loss for carryback

Restricted farm loss for the year available for carryback (see the guide called *Farming Income* or *Farming Income and NISA)*

Subtract:			
	Restricted farm loss to be applied to 1996	6648	
	Restricted farm loss to be applied to 1997	6649	
	Restricted farm loss to be applied to 1998	6650	
	Subtotal	►	

Balance of restricted farm loss available for carryforward

I hereby certify that the information given in this form is true, correct, and complete in every respect.

(signature of individual or authorized representative)

Telephone number | Area code

Date 6655 | Year | Month | Day

Do you have a balance of tax unpaid from another tax year? ☐ Yes ☐ No

Printed in Canada

Canada Customs and Revenue Agency / Agence des douanes et du revenu du Canada

T1 ADJUSTMENT REQUEST

- Use this form to request an adjustment (a reassessment) to an individual income tax return.
- See the back of this form for information on how to complete it.
- Send the completed form to the Enquiries & Adjustments Division of your tax centre. You can find the address on the back of this form.

A Identification

Social insurance number

Adjustment request for the ______ **tax year** **(complete a separate form for each year)**

Full name: (please print your given name first, surname last)

Address: (please print)

☐ same as on the return

☐ or:

For filing ☐ DO NOT USE THIS AREA

PSN

CORLOC # ☐ Ack. ☐ St. Code

Assessor	Date	Rev.	Date

B Authorization - complete this area if a person or firm is preparing this request for you; otherwise, go to Area C.

Name and address of person or firm preparing this request: (please print)

Letter of authorization (or Form T1013, *Consent Form*) for the year under review:

was submitted previously ☐

is attached ☐

C Adjustment details

Using your copy of your tax return and your *Notice of Assessment* or *Reassessment*, list below the details of your requested change.
If you have received an assessment or reassessment notice with an amount that is different from the amount on the return, use the amount stated on the notice.
See the back of this form for information about required documentation and for examples of how to complete this area.

Line number from return or schedule	Name of line from return or schedule	Previous amount	±	Amount of change	Revised amount

Other details or explanations (attach an extra sheet if required)

D Certification

I certify that the information given on this form and on any documents attached is, to the best of my knowledge, correct and complete.

(Home) ( )

(Business) ( )

Date | Client's/Representative's signature | Telephone

T1-ADJ E (00)

You can get more copies of this form from any Canada Customs and Revenue Agency office.
(Ce formulaire existe aussi en français.)

3722

Canada

Take or send the completed form to your local tax office. You will find the address listed below.

St. John's Tax Centre
Freshwater Road/Empire Avenue
St. John's NF A1B 3Z1

Jonquière Tax Centre
2251 de la Centrale Blvd.
Jonquière QC G7S 5J1

Sudbury Tax Services
1050 Notre-Dame Ave.
Sudbury ON P3A 5C1

Surrey Tax Centre
9755 King George Highway
Surrey BC V3T 5E1

Shawinigan-Sud Tax Centre
4695 - 12th Avenue
Shawinigan-Sud QC G9N 7S6

Summerside Tax Centre
275 Pope Road
Summerside PE C1N 5Z7

Winnipeg Tax Centre
66 Stapon Road
Winnipeg MB R3C 3M2

International Tax Services Office
2204 Walkley Road
Ottawa ON K1A 1A8

HOW TO COMPLETE THE FORM

Area A: Identification

- Complete this area in full so that we know exactly who you are and what return you want us to reassess.

Area B: Authorization

- Complete this area if you are authorizing a person or firm to make this request on your behalf.
- You have to authorize us to discuss your tax matters with this person or firm by providing a signed letter or Form T1013, *Consent Form*. You do not have to provide a letter or Form T1013 if there is already one on file.
  Note: You can get Form T1013 from any Canada Customs and Revenue Agency (CCRA) office.

Area C: Adjustment details

- Please provide all details for each change you request (you do not have to show a recalculation of your taxes).
- Show any losses in brackets (e.g., self-employed business loss).
- If you are changing a line on which you already claimed an amount (see Example 1, below) and you did not previously provide the supporting documentation, you now have to provide supporting documentation for the entire revised amount.
- Supporting documentation may include receipts, schedules, or other relevant documents. Your request may be delayed if you do not provide all required information with this form.
- You can get more information about CCRA's rules and policies for reassessments in Information Circular 75-7R3, *Reassessment of a Return of Income*. You can get IC 75-7R3 from any CCRA office.
- Following are two examples of how to complete this area.

Example 1

Mary filed her 1995 return reporting the following information:
Employment income $28,600
Union dues $500

After receiving her *Notice of Assessment*, Mary received an additional T4 slip. It showed $200 in income and $20 for union dues. To request a change to her return, Mary will complete Area C as follows:

Line number from return or schedule	Name of line from return or schedule	Previous amount	+ -	Amount of change	Revised amount
101	Employment income	28,600	+	200	28,800
212	Union dues	500	+	20	520

Note: Even though Mary did not submit receipts with her tax return for the original union dues claim of $500, she must now submit those receipts along with her additional T4 slip.

Example 2

In certain situations there may not be a line number to use when requesting a change. Complete the form as shown in the following example.

John filed his 1996 return, claiming the goods and services tax (GST) credit. When he received his *Notice of Assessment*, John realized that he had not claimed the credit for his infant son, born on December 15, 1996. Since there is no line number for this claim, John will complete Area C as follows:

Line number from return or schedule	Name of line from return or schedule	Previous amount	+ -	Amount of change	Revised amount
–	GST credit - number of children	0	+	1	1

Area D: Certification

- Make sure either you or your authorized representative signs and dates the request for a change to your return.

Printed in Canada

Canada Customs and Revenue Agency / Agence des douanes et du revenu du Canada

MOVING EXPENSES DEDUCTION

Use this form to calculate your moving expenses deduction. Complete a separate form for each move. See the following pages for moving expenses information. Do not attach this form or the receipts and documents supporting your claim to your return. If you are using EFILE, show them to your EFILE service provider. In either case, or if you are using NETFILE or TELEFILE, keep them in case we ask to see them.

Who can deduct moving expenses?

You can deduct eligible moving expenses from employment or self-employment income you earn at your new location if you move and establish a new home to start a job or a business, or from award income if you move to attend courses as a full-time student at a college, university, or other institution offering post-secondary education.

Your new home must be at least 40 kilometres (by the shortest usual public route) closer to the new educational institution or place of work than your previous home was. You must establish your new home as the place where you and members of your household ordinarily reside. For example, you have established a new home if you have sold or rented (or advertised for sale or rent) your old home.

Generally, your move must be from one place in Canada to another place in Canada. See the last page for information about moves to or from Canada, or between two locations outside Canada.

Identification

Tax year ▶

Last name	
First name	Social insurance number

Details of the move

Complete address of your **old** residence

Postal code

Complete address of your **new** residence

Postal code

	Year	Month	Day
Date of move			
Date you started your new job or business, or your studies			

What was the main reason for the move? ☐ To start a job or a business **OR** ☐ To study full time

Name of employer, business, or educational institution **after** the move

Complete address

Postal code

Calculation of distance in kilometres

Distance in kilometres between your **old** home and your **new** educational institution or place of work		1
Distance in kilometres between your **new** home and your **new** educational institution or place of work	–	2
Line 1 minus line 2. **If the result is less than 40 kilometres, you cannot deduct your moving expenses.**	=	3

Statement of Expenses

		Line
Transportation and storage costs for household effects		1
Name of mover		
Travelling expenses from old residence to new residence		
Travel costs (other than accommodation and meals)	+	2
Number of household members in move		
Method of travel		
Number of kilometres		
Accommodation	+	3
Number of nights		
Meals	+	4
Number of days		
Temporary living expenses near new or old residence (maximum 15 days)		
Accommodation	+	5
Number of nights		
Meals	+	6
Number of days		
Cost of cancelling the lease for the old residence	+	7
Incidental costs related to the move (specify)	+	8
Costs to maintain your old residence when vacant (maximum $5,000)	+	9
Cost of selling old residence		
Selling price $		
Real estate commission	+	10
Legal or notarial fees	+	11
Advertising	+	12
Other selling costs (specify)	+	13
Cost of purchasing new residence		
Purchase price $		
Legal or notarial fees	+	14
Taxes paid for the registration or transfer of title (Do not include GST/HST or property taxes)	+	15
Add lines 1 to 15 **Total moving expenses**	=	16
Enter any reimbursement or allowance that is not included in your income, and that was received for moving expenses that are claimed on line 16	–	17
Line 16 minus line 17 **Net moving expenses**	=	18
If you moved to start a job or a business, enter your net income for the year from employment or self-employment in the new work location. If you moved to study full-time, enter your income for the year from scholarships, bursaries, fellowships, research grants, and prizes for achievement **Eligible income**		19
Enter the amount from line 18 or line 19, whichever is **less**. Enter the result on line 219 of your return **Allowable moving expenses**		20

If line 18 is more than line 19, you can carry forward the unused part (line 18 minus line 19) and deduct it from eligible income for the year after you move.

Canada Customs and Revenue Agency / Agence des douanes et du revenu du Canada

STATEMENT OF EMPLOYMENT EXPENSES

- The income tax guide called *Employment Expenses* has information to help you complete this statement and the schedule on the back. The chapters we refer to below are from the guide.
- Please include a copy of this form with your income tax return.

Expenses

Item			Line
Accounting and legal fees			
Advertising and promotion			
Allowable motor vehicle expenses (from line 16 below)			1
Food, beverages, and entertainment expenses (see Chapter 2 or 3, as applicable)		x 50% =	
Lodging			
Parking			
Supplies (e.g., postage, stationery, other office supplies)			
Other expenses (please specify)			
Musical instrument costs (see "Part 2" in Chapter 5)			
Capital cost allowance for musical instruments (see "Part A" on the back of this form)			
Artists' employment expenses (see "Part 1" in Chapter 5)			
Subtotal			2
Add work-space-in-the-home expenses (enter the lower amount of line 24 or 25 below)			
Total expenses (enter this amount on line 229 of your income tax return)		=	

Calculation of Allowable Motor Vehicle Expenses

Item			Line
Enter the kilometres you drove in the taxation year to earn employment income			3
Enter the total kilometres you drove in the taxation year			4
Enter the motor vehicle expenses you paid for:			
Fuel (gasoline, propane, oil)			5
Maintenance and repairs			6
Insurance			7
Licence and registration			8
Capital cost allowance (see schedule on the back)			9
Interest (see "Interest expense" in Chapter 6)			10
Leasing (see "Leasing costs" in Chapter 6)			11
Other expenses (please specify)			12
Add lines 5 to 12			13
Employment-use portion (line 3 / line 4) X line 13 =		▶	14
Enter the total of all rebates, allowances, and repayments you received that are not included in income. Do not include any repayments you used to calculate your leasing costs on line 11.			15
Allowable motor vehicle expenses (line 14 **minus** line 15)			16
Enter the amount from line 16 on line 1 in the "Expenses" area above			

Calculation of Work-Space-in-the-Home Expenses

Item			Line
Electricity, heat, and water			17
Maintenance			18
Insurance (commission employees only)			19
Property taxes (commission employees only)			20
Other expenses (please specify)			21
Add lines 17 to 21 — Subtotal			22
Subtract personal-use portion			23
Subtotal			
Add amount carried forward from previous year			
Subtotal		▶	24
Enter your employment income			
Subtract the amount from line 2 above			
Subtotal (If negative, enter "0")	=	▶	25
Work-space-in-the-home expenses available to use in **future** years (line 24 **minus** line 25; if negative, enter "0")			

CAPITAL COST ALLOWANCE SCHEDULE (DEPRECIATION) FOR EMPLOYEES

- The income tax guide called *Employment Expenses* has information to help you complete this schedule.

Part A – Class 8 and 10

1 Class no.*	2 Undepreciated capital cost at the beginning of the year	3 Cost of acquisitions during the year	4 Proceeds of disposition during the year	5 Undepreciated capital cost after acquisitions and dispositions (Col. 2 + 3 – 4)	6 Adjustments for current-year acquisitions (1/2 X (Col. 3 – 4). If negative,enter "0")	7 Base amount for capital cost allowance claim (Col. 5 – 6)	8 Rate %	9 Capital cost allowance for the year (Col. 7 X 8, or a lesser amount)	10 Undepreciated capital cost at the end of the year (Col. 5 – 9)
8							20%		
10							30%		

* Class 8 includes musical instruments.

Class 10 includes all vehicles that meet the definition of a motor vehicle, except for a passenger vehicle included in Class 10.1 (see "Part B" below).

Part B – Class 10.1

- See Chapter 7 of the *Employment Expenses* guide for details about the Class 10.1 limits.
- List each passenger vehicle on a separate line.

Date acquired	Cost of vehicle	1 Class no.	2 Undepreciated capital cost at the beginning of the year	3 Cost of acquisitions during the year	4 Proceeds of disposition during the year	5 Base amount for capital cost allowance claim**	6 Rate %	7 Capital cost allowance for the year (Col. 5 X 6, or a lesser amount)	8 Undepreciated capital cost at the end of the year (Col. 2 – 7, or Col. 3 – 7)***
		10.1					30%		
		10.1					30%		
		10.1					30%		
							TOTAL		

** a. Enter the amount from Column 2 in Column 5 if you owned the vehicle in the previous year and still owned it at the end of the current year.

b. Enter 1/2 of the amount from Column 3 in Column 5 if you bought the vehicle in the current year and still owned it at the end of the current year.

c. Enter 1/2 of the amount from Column 2 in Column 5 if you sold the vehicle in the current year and you owned the vehicle at the end of the previous year.

d. If you bought and sold a class 10.1 vehicle in the current year, enter "0" in Column 5.

*** Enter "0" in Column 8 for the year you sold or traded a class 10.1 vehicle, since the recapture and terminal loss rules do not apply.

Printed in Canada

Canada Customs and Revenue Agency / Agence des douanes et du revenu du Canada

CHILD CARE EXPENSES DEDUCTION FOR 2000

We define **child care expenses**, **eligible child**, **supporting person**, **net income**, and **earned income** on the attached information sheet. For more details, see Interpretation Bulletin IT-495, *Child Care Expenses*.

Each supporting person claiming the deduction must attach a completed Form T778 to his or her return. Do not include receipts, but keep them in case we ask to see them.

If you are the only supporting person, or you are the supporting person with the **lower net income**, complete Parts A and B.
If you are the supporting person with the **higher net income**, complete Parts A, B, and C.
If you **attended school** in 2000, read Part D to see if it applies.

Part A – Total child care expenses

List the **first and last names** and the **date of birth** of all your eligible children whether or not you had child care expenses for all of them.

Name	Year	Month	Day

First name of each child for whom payments were made	Child care expenses paid (see note)	Indicate who received the payments. Provide the **name of the child care organization** or the **name and social insurance number of the individual.**	Number of weeks for **boarding schools** or **overnight camps**
	+		
	+		
	+		
	+		
Total	=		

Note: The maximum you can claim for expenses that relate to a stay in a boarding school (other than education costs) or an overnight camp (including an overnight sports school) is **$175 per week** for an eligible child included on line 1 or line 2 in Part B, and **$100 per week** for an eligible child included on line 3.

Enter any child care expenses included above that were paid in 2000 for a child who was 18 or older ..... 6795 ______

Part B – Basic limit for child care expenses deduction

Number of eligible children:

Born in **1994 or later** for whom the disability amount cannot be claimed	____	x $7,000 =		1
Born in **2000 and earlier** for whom the disability amount can be claimed *	____	x $10,000 =	6796 +	2
Born in **1984 to 1993** (or born in 1983 and earlier with a mental or physical infirmity for whom the disability amount cannot be claimed)	____	x $4,000 =	+	3
Add lines 1 to 3			=	4
Enter your **total child care expenses** from Part A				5
Enter your **earned income**	____	x 2/3 =		6
Enter the amount from line 4, 5, or 6, whichever is **the least**				7

If you are the supporting person with the higher net income, go to Part C. Leave lines 8 and 9 blank.

Enter any child care expenses that the other supporting person with the higher net income deducted on line 214 of his or her 2000 return	–	8
Line 7 minus line 8. If you attended school in 2000 and you are the only supporting person, go to Part D. Otherwise, enter this amount on line 214 of your return .... **Your allowable deduction**	=	9

* Attach Form T2201, *Disability Tax Credit Certificate.* If this form has already been filed for the child, attach a note to your return showing the name and social insurance number of the person who filed it and the tax year for which it was filed.

(Ce formulaire existe en français.)

Canada

Part C – Are you the supporting person with the higher net income?

Complete Part C if, in 2000, the other supporting person (with the lower net income) was in a situation described below. Indicate the name, social insurance number, and the net income of the other supporting person **and** check the boxes that apply.

Name of supporting person with the lower net income ____________ Social insurance number ____________ Net income ____________

☐ **a)** The other supporting person attended school and was enrolled in a **part-time** educational program as defined in the section called "Did you or the other supporting person attend school in 2000?" on the attached information sheet.

☐ **b)** The other supporting person attended school and was enrolled in a **full-time** educational program as defined in the section called "Did you or the other supporting person attend school in 2000?" on the attached information sheet.

☐ **c)** The other supporting person was incapable of caring for children because of a mental or physical infirmity. That person must have been confined for a period of at least two weeks in 2000 to a bed or wheelchair, or as a patient in a hospital, an asylum, or other similar institution. Attach a statement from the attending physician certifying this information.

☐ **d)** The other supporting person was incapable of caring for children in 2000 because of a mental or physical infirmity. This situation is likely to continue for an indefinite period. Attach a statement from the attending physician certifying this information.

☐ **e)** The other supporting person was confined to a prison or similar institution for a period of at least two weeks in 2000.

☐ **f)** You and your spouse were, due to a breakdown in your relationship, living separate and apart at the end of 2000 and for a period of at least 90 days beginning in 2000, but you reconciled before March 2, 2001.

Number of eligible children from line 1 and line 2 (in Part B) ____	**x $175 =**		10
Number of eligible children from line 3 (in Part B) ____	**x $100 =**	+	11
Add line 10 and line 11		=	12
Multiply the amount on line 12 by the number of **full months** in 2000 that the situation in **a)** existed (other than a month that includes a week that any of the situations in **b)** to **f)** existed)			13
Multiply the amount on line 12 by the number of **full weeks** in 2000 that any of the situations in **b)** to **f)** existed		+	14
Add line 13 and line 14	6798	=	15
Enter the amount from line 7 (in Part B) or line 15, whichever is **less**. If you attended school in 2000, go to Part D. Otherwise, enter this amount on line 214 of your return	**Your allowable deduction**		16

Part D – Did you attend school in 2000?

Complete Part D if, at any time in 2000, you attended school and either of the following situations applied to you:

- You were the **only supporting person**, line 7 equals line 6 in Part B, and you were enrolled in an educational program described in the section called "Did you or the other supporting person attend school in 2000?" on the attached information sheet.
- You were the **supporting person with the higher net income**, line 7 equals line 6 in Part B, and you **and** the other supporting person were, at the same time in 2000, enrolled in an educational program described in the same section. But first, complete Part C.

Part D does not apply to the supporting person with the lower net income since the other supporting person will claim this part of the deduction for both of them.

Number of eligible children from line 1 and line 2 (in Part B) ____	**x $175 =**		17
Number of eligible children from line 3 (in Part B) ____	**x $100 =**	+	18
Add line 17 and line 18		=	19
Multiply the amount on line 19 by the number of **full months** in 2000 you (**or** the other supporting person) were in **part-time** attendance (other than a month that includes a week used in the calculation on line 21)			20
Multiply the amount on line 19 by the number of **full weeks** in 2000 you (**and** the other supporting person) were in **full-time** attendance		+	21
Add line 20 and line 21	6801	=	22
Line 4 (in Part B) minus line 9 (in Part B) or line 16 (in Part C), whichever applies to you			23
Line 5 (in Part B) minus line 9 (in Part B) or line 16 (in Part C), whichever applies to you			24
Enter your **net income** ____	$\times \frac{2}{3} =$		25
If you completed Part C: Line 15 (in Part C) minus line 6 (in Part B)			26
Enter amount from line 22, 23, 24, 25, or (if it applies) 26, whichever is the **least**			27
Enter the amount from line 9 (in Part B) or line 16 (in Part C), whichever applies to you		+	28
Add line 27 and line 28. Enter this amount on line 214 of your return	**Your allowable deduction**	=	29

Canada Customs and Revenue Agency / Agence des douanes et du revenu du Canada

ATTENDANT CARE EXPENSES

Use this form to calculate your claim for the attendant care expenses deduction.

You can claim this deduction if **all** the following conditions apply:

- you paid expenses for personal attendant care;
- you are eligible to claim the disability amount for yourself on line 316 of your return (see **Note 1**);
- the attendant was not your spouse and was 18 years or older when you made the payments; and
- no one has claimed the payments as medical expenses.

In addition, you must have paid the expenses for care in Canada (see **Note 2**) so you could:

- earn income from employment or from a business (in which you were actively involved), or carry on research or similar work for which you received a grant; or
- under proposed changes, attend a designated educational institution or a secondary school at which you were enrolled in an education program.

Do not attach this form or your receipts to your return, but keep them in case we ask to see them.

Note 1: If this is the first year you are claiming the disability amount for yourself, attach to your return a completed copy of Form T2201, *Disability Tax Credit Certificate*. If you or another person has already filed a completed Form T2201, attach a note showing the name and social insurance number of the person who filed it and the year it was filed.

Note 2: Deemed residents can claim amounts paid for care outside Canada.

Attendant care payments

Indicate who received the payments.
Give the **name and address of the organization** or the **name, address, and social insurance number of the individual.**

Name and address	Social insurance number	Amount paid
		+
		+
	Total attendant care payments	=

Enter your **total attendant care payments** 1

Enter the amount of any reimbursement or other form of assistance (other than prescribed assistance) that any person is or was entitled to get that relates to these expenses and that is not included in someone's income ... – 2

Line 1 minus line 2 .... **Attendant care payments** = 3

Attendant care expenses deduction

If you made attendant care payments so you could earn income from employment or from a business or carry on research, complete the following calculation:

Enter your **earned income** * .... x 66.6667% = 4

Enter the amount from line 3 or line 4, whichever is **less**.
Enter the amount from line 5 on line 215 of your return 5

If you made attendant care payments so you could attend a designated educational institution or a secondary school at which you were enrolled in an education program, complete the following calculation:

Enter your **net income** ** 6
Enter your **earned income** * .... – 7
Line 6 minus line 7 (if negative, enter "0") .... = 8

Enter the number of full weeks in **2000** that you attended the institution or school .... x $375 = 9

Enter the amount from line 8, line 9, or $15,000, whichever is **least** 10
Enter your **earned income** * .... + 11
Add line 10 and line 11 .... = 12
x 66.6667% 13
Multiply line 12 by 66.6667% .... = 14

Enter the amount from line 3 or line 14, whichever is **less**.
Enter the amount from line 15 on line 215 of your return 15

* Your **earned income** is the total of:

- employment income (including stock options and other employment benefits);
- self-employment income, either alone or as an active partner (excluding losses);
- the taxable part of scholarships, bursaries, fellowships, and similar awards;
- net research grants; and
- any earnings supplement received under a project sponsored by a government in Canada to encourage employment or under a project sponsored under Part II of the *Employment Insurance Act* or any similar program.

** Your **net income** is the amount you would enter on line 236 of your return if you had no claim for attendant care expenses on line 215.

Revenue Canada Revenu Canada

For departmental use

FOREIGN INCOME VERIFICATION STATEMENT

Complete and file this statement with your tax return (or, if a partnership, with your partnership information return) if at any time in the year the total cost amount of all specified foreign property you owned or held a beneficial interest in was more than $100,000.

Identification

Check (✓) a box to indicate who you are reporting for, and complete the areas that apply.

☐ individual	First name	Last name	Initial	Social insurance number
☐ corporation	Corporation's name		Business Number (BN) RC	
☐ trust	Trust's name		Account number T – –	
☐ partnership	Partnership's name		Partnership's identification number	

Reporting taxpayer's address

No. Street

Postal code

City

Province or territory

For what tax year are you filing this statement? ____ or From Year Month Day To Year Month Day

Type of Property (It is important that you see the attached instructions for details on the types of property that must be reported).	For each type of property that applies to you, indicate the total cost of the investment by checking (✓) the appropriate box					
	+ $1 Million	+ $700,000	+ $500,000	+ $300,000	+ $100,000	Less than $100,000
1. Funds held outside Canada	☐	☐	☐	☐	☐	☐
2. Shares of non-resident corporations, other than foreign affiliates	☐	☐	☐	☐	☐	☐
3. Indebtedness owed by non-residents	☐	☐	☐	☐	☐	☐
4. Interests in non-resident trusts	☐	☐	☐	☐	☐	☐
5. Real property outside Canada	☐	☐	☐	☐	☐	☐
6. Other property outside Canada	☐	☐	☐	☐	☐	☐

Where are the above investments located? (Check appropriate box(es)) United States ☐ U.K. ☐ Europe, other than U.K. ☐ Southeast Asia ☐ Caribbean ☐ Other ☐

Total income reported on your tax return in the year from the above assets $ ________ 00

Certification

I certify that the information given on this statement is, to my knowledge, correct and complete, and fully discloses the reporting taxpayer's specified foreign property and related foreign income.

Print name ____________

Sign here ____________

It is a serious offence to file a false statement.

____

Position or title

Telephone ( ) ____ Date ____

If you were paid to prepare this statement, provide the following information:

Your name ____________

Address ____________

Postal code ____________

Telephone ( ) ____________

Canada Customs and Revenue Agency / Agence des douanes et du revenu du Canada

PROVINCIAL AND TERRITORIAL TAXES FOR 1999 – MULTIPLE JURISDICTIONS

Use this form to calculate your tax (or your minimum tax supplement *) for 1999 if **either** of the following applies:

- you resided in a province or territory on December 31, 1999 (if you ceased to reside in Canada during 1999, use the last day you resided in Canada), and all or part of your business income for the year was earned and is allocable to a permanent establishment outside that province or territory, or outside Canada; **or**
- you were a non-resident throughout 1999 carrying on business in more than one province or territory.

Attach a completed copy of this form to your 1999 return.

* If you have minimum tax to pay, also attach a completed Form T691, *Alternative Minimum Tax.*

Part 1 – Allocating income and basic federal tax to various jurisdictions

Net income from line 236 of your return 1

Business income earned in the year: Add self-employment income from lines 135 to 143 of your return, and business income from a partnership from line 122 of your return (exclude losses) .... – 2

Excess income: Line 1 minus line 2 (if negative, enter "0") .... = 3

Basic federal tax from line 33 of Schedule 1 4

Enter basic federal tax from line 55 of Form T691, if you are completing that form 5

Enter the amount from line 4 or line 5, whichever is **more** 6

In column 2, allocate the amount from line 2 to each province and territory where you had a permanent establishment in 1999. Refer to Part XXVI of the *Income Tax Regulations* if you need instructions. If you are a resident of Quebec, you must allocate to Quebec any business income you earned outside Canada in the year.

In column 3, allocate to your province or territory of residence the amount from line 3, if any.

In column 4, add columns 2 and 3. If the amount from line 1 is less than the amount from line 2, determine the percentage of income allocation in column 2, and multiply the amount on line 1 by this percentage. Enter the result in column 4.

In column 5, determine the percentage for each jurisdiction based on the income you allocated in column 4.

In column 6, allocate for each jurisdiction the amount from line 6 based on the percentage calculated in column 5.

Column 1	Column 2	Column 3	Column 4	Column 5	Column 6
Jurisdiction	Allocating business income earned in the year (line 2)	Excess income (line 3)	Income allocated to jurisdiction (column 2 plus column 3)	% of income allocated to jurisdiction	Basic federal tax allocated to jurisdiction (multiply line 6 by the % in column 5)
Newfoundland					
Prince Edward Island					
Nova Scotia					
New Brunswick					
Quebec					
Ontario					
Manitoba					
Saskatchewan					
Alberta					
British Columbia					
Yukon					
Northwest Territories					
Nunavut					
Other (outside Canada)					
Totals				**100%**	

Part 2 – Federal surtax on income you earned outside Canada and refundable Quebec abatement

Federal surtax on income you earned outside Canada

Enter basic federal tax allocated to "Other" (from the chart in Part 1) 7
Federal surtax rate .... x 52% 8
Multiply line 7 by 52% .... = 9

Enter the amount from line 9 below line 33 on Schedule 1 (Method B) and write "federal surtax on income earned outside Canada". Add line 9 to the basic federal tax on line 33, and subtract line 36 from the total to arrive at federal tax on line 37.

Enter the amount from line 9 on line 56 of Form T691, if you are completing that form.

Refundable Quebec abatement

Enter basic federal tax allocated to Quebec (from the chart in Part 1) 10
Rate for the refundable Quebec abatement .... x 16.5% 11
Multiply line 10 by 16.5%, and enter the result on line 440 of your return .... = 12

Part 3 – Provincial and territorial taxes

Newfoundland

Multiply basic federal tax allocated to Newfoundland (from the chart in Part 1) by 69% .... A
Newfoundland surtax: (line A ______ minus $7,900) x 10% = ... +
Adjusted Newfoundland income tax .... =
Residents of Newfoundland: Provincial foreign tax credit, if any, from Form T2036 .... –
Newfoundland tax .... = ► 13

Prince Edward Island

Multiply basic federal tax allocated to P.E.I. (from the chart in Part 1) by 58.5% .... B
P.E.I. surtax: (line B ______ minus $5,200) x 10% = ... +
Adjusted Prince Edward Island income tax .... =
Residents of Prince Edward Island: Provincial foreign tax credit, if any, from Form T2036 .... –
Prince Edward Island tax .... = ► 14

Nova Scotia

Calculate Nova Scotia tax on Form T1C (N.S.) TC * and enter the result here 15

* Enter on line 1 of Form T1C (N.S.) TC the basic federal tax allocated to Nova Scotia from the chart in Part 1.
If you were not a resident of Nova Scotia:
Do not claim the provincial foreign tax credit on line 6 of Form T1C (N.S.) TC when you calculate Nova Scotia tax.

New Brunswick

Multiply basic federal tax allocated to New Brunswick (from the chart in Part 1) by 60% C
New Brunswick surtax: (line C ______ minus $13,500) x 8% = ... +
Adjusted New Brunswick income tax .... =
Residents of New Brunswick: Provincial foreign tax credit, if any, from Form T2036 .... –
New Brunswick tax .... = ► 16

Ontario

Multiply basic federal tax allocated to Ontario (from the chart in Part 1) by 39.5% .... D
Ontario Fair Share Health Care Levy:
(line D ______ minus $3,750.00) x 20% = ... +
(line D ______ minus $4,681.00) x 36% = ... +
Adjusted Ontario tax * .... = ► 17

* **Residents of Ontario:** Enter this amount on line 7 of Form T1C (ONT.) TC.
Use that form to complete the calculation of Ontario tax, and enter the result on line 17 above.

Part 3 – Provincial and territorial taxes (continued)

Manitoba

Calculate Manitoba tax on Form T1C (MAN.) TC * and enter the result here 18

* **If you were a resident of Manitoba:**
Enter on line 1 of Form T1C (MAN.) TC the net income allocated to Manitoba from column 4 in Part 1.
Enter on line 6 the basic federal tax allocated to Manitoba from column 6 in Part 1.

If you were not a resident of Manitoba:
Start on line 5 of Form T1C (MAN.) TC, and enter the net income allocated to Manitoba from column 4 in Part 1. Enter on line 6 the basic federal tax allocated to Manitoba from column 6 in Part 1. Do not claim the provincial foreign tax credit on line 23. After calculating the Manitoba tax reduction on Form T1C (MAN.) TC, apply the same percentage you applied for the income allocated to Manitoba from column 5, Part 1, and enter the result on line 35 of that form.

Saskatchewan

Multiply basic federal tax allocated to Saskatchewan (from the chart in Part 1) by 48%				
Saskatchewan flat tax: Multiply net income allocated to Saskatchewan (Part 1, column 4) by 2% *		+		
Basic Saskatchewan tax		=	E	
Multiply line E by 10%	=			
Reduction amount	− 150 00			
Debt reduction surtax	= ▶	+		
High income surtax: (Line E ______ minus $4,000) x 15% = ...		+		
Adjusted Saskatchewan tax **		=	▶	19

* **Residents of Saskatchewan:** Reduce net income allocated to Saskatchewan by any amount you deducted on line 250 of your return and by any foreign income exempt under a tax treaty that you included on line 256 of your return.

** **Residents of Saskatchewan:** Enter this amount on line 15 of Form T1C (SASK.).
Use that form to complete the calculation of Net Saskatchewan tax, and enter the result on line 19 above.

Alberta

Multiply basic federal tax allocated to Alberta (from the chart in Part 1) by 44%		F	
Alberta surtax: (Line F ______ minus $3,500) x 8% = ...	+	G	
Alberta flat rate tax: Multiply taxable income allocated to Alberta by 0.005 *	+		
Adjusted Alberta tax: Add the above three lines	=	H	
Enter your royalty tax rebate, if any, from line 18 on Form T79	−	I	
Alberta income tax after rebate: Line H minus line I (if negative, enter "0") **	=	▶	20

* **Taxable income allocated to Alberta:** Multiply your taxable income on line 260 of your return by the percentage you allocated to Alberta in Part 1, column 5.

** **Residents of Alberta:** Enter this amount on line 10 of Form T1C (ALTA.).
Use that form to complete the calculation of Alberta tax, and enter the result on line 20 above.

British Columbia

Calculate British Columbia tax on Form T1C (B.C.) TC * and enter the result here 21

* Enter on line 1 of Form T1C (B.C.) TC the basic federal tax allocated to British Columbia from the chart in Part 1.
If you were not a resident of British Columbia:
Do not claim the provincial foreign tax credit on line 4 of Form T1C (B.C.) TC when you calculate British Columbia tax.

Part 3 – Provincial and territorial taxes (continued)

Yukon

Multiply basic federal tax allocated to the Yukon (from the chart in Part 1) by 50% .... J

Yukon surtax: (Line J ______ minus $6,000) x 5% = ... +

Adjusted Yukon tax * .... = ▶ ______ 22

* **Residents of the Yukon:** Enter this amount on line 5 of Form T1C (YUKON).
Use that form to complete the calculation of Yukon tax, and enter the result on line 22 above.

Northwest Territories

Multiply basic federal tax allocated to the Northwest Territories (from the chart in Part 1) by 45%

Residents of the Northwest Territories: Territorial foreign tax credit, if any, from Form T2036 –

Northwest Territories tax .... = ▶ ______ 23

Nunavut

Multiply basic federal tax allocated to Nunavut (from the chart in Part 1) by 45% ....

Residents of Nunavut: Territorial foreign tax credit, if any, from Form T2036 .... –

Nunavut tax .... = ▶ ______ 24

Provincial and territorial taxes

Add lines 13 to 24. Enter this amount on line 428 of your return .... = ______ 25

Provincial and territorial credits

You do not have to be a resident of a province or territory to claim certain tax credits, as long as you otherwise qualify. For example, you could claim provincial and territorial political contribution tax credits. Just attach a completed form T1C for the applicable province or territory. You could also claim tax credits for investments you made in certain venture capital corporations. Contact us for details.

Here is a list of other credits you could claim, and the forms to complete.

Province / territory	Credits (other than political contribution tax credits)	Form
Newfoundland	Newfoundland research and development tax credit	Form T1129
New Brunswick	New Brunswick stock savings plan tax credit	Form T1C (N.B.)
Ontario	Ontario co-operative education and graduate transitions tax credits Ontario workplace child care and workplace accessibility tax credits	Form T1C (ONT.)
Manitoba	Manitoba mineral tax rebate	Form T78
Saskatchewan	Saskatchewan royalty tax rebate	Form T82
Alberta	Alberta royalty tax rebate	Form T79
British Columbia	British Columbia royalty and deemed income rebate	Form T81
	British Columbia logging tax credit (Form BCFIN 542)	Form T1C (B.C.) TC

Printed in Canada

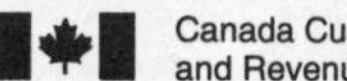

Canada Customs and Revenue Agency | Agence des douanes et du revenu du Canada

EMPLOYEE OVERPAYMENT OF 2000 CANADA PENSION PLAN CONTRIBUTIONS AND 2000 EMPLOYMENT INSURANCE PREMIUMS

Complete Part 1 to determine any overpayment of Canada Pension Plan (CPP) or Quebec Pension Plan (QPP) contributions made through employment if you had no self-employment earnings **and** you were not a resident of Quebec on December 31, 2000. If you were a resident of Quebec on December 31, 2000, and you made CPP or QPP contributions, see your Quebec provincial tax guide.

Complete Part 2 to determine any overpayment of Employment Insurance (EI) premiums.

Part 1 – Calculating your Canada Pension Plan overpayment

If any of the situations listed in the note below apply to you, prorate the total maximum amounts shown on lines 1, 2, 3, and 5 in the following calculation, using the monthly proration table on this form.

Total CPP pensionable earnings (box 26 or, if blank, box 14 of your T4 slips) .... (maximum $ 37,600) ______ 1
Basic CPP exemption .... (maximum $ 3,500) – ______ 2
Earnings subject to contribution (if negative, enter "0") .... (maximum $ 34,100) = ______ 3

Total CPP and QPP contributions deducted (from boxes 16 and 17 of your T4 slips) .... ______ 4
Required contribution: Multiply line 3 by 3.9% .... (maximum $1,329.90) – ______ 5
Line 4 minus line 5 (if negative, enter "0") .... **Canada Pension Plan overpayment** = ______ 6

If the amount from line 6 is positive, enter it on line 448 of your return.
Enter the amount from line 4 or 5, whichever is less, on line 308 of your return.

Note: If any of the following situations apply to you, use the proration table below.

- If you turned 18 in 2000, use the number of months in the year after the month you turned 18.
- If you turned 70 in 2000, use the number of months in the year up to and including the month you turned 70.
- If you received, or were entitled to receive, a Canada Pension Plan or Quebec Pension Plan retirement or disability pension for part of 2000, use the number of months in the year you did not or were not entitled to receive the pension.
- If the individual died in 2000, use the number of months in the year up to and including the month the individual died.

At the appropriate line, use the maximum amounts for the number of months that apply to your situation.

Monthly proration table for 2000

Applicable number of months	Line 1 Maximum amount of total CPP pensionable earnings	Line 2 Maximum amount of basic CPP exemption	Line 3 Maximum amount of earnings subject to contribution	Line 5 Maximum amount of required contribution
1	$ 3,133.33	$ 291.66	$ 2,841.67	$ 110.83
2	$ 6,266.66	$ 583.33	$ 5,683.34	$ 221.65
3	$ 9,400.00	$ 875.00	$ 8,525.00	$ 332.48
4	$ 12,533.33	$ 1,166.66	$ 11,366.67	$ 443.30
5	$ 15,666.66	$ 1,458.33	$ 14,208.34	$ 554.13
6	$ 18,800.00	$ 1,750.00	$ 17,050.00	$ 664.95
7	$ 21,933.33	$ 2,041.66	$ 19,891.67	$ 775.78
8	$ 25,066.66	$ 2,333.33	$ 22,733.34	$ 886.60
9	$ 28,200.00	$ 2,625.00	$ 25,575.00	$ 997.43
10	$ 31,333.33	$ 2,916.66	$ 28,416.67	$ 1,108.25
11	$ 34,466.66	$ 3,208.33	$ 31,258.34	$ 1,219.08
12	$ 37,600.00	$ 3,500.00	$ 34,100.00	$ 1,329.90

Part 2 – Calculating your Employment Insurance overpayment

Total EI insurable earnings
(box 24 or, if blank, box 14 of your T4 slips and box 16 of your T4F slips) .... (maximum $ 39,000) ______ 1

Total premiums deducted (box 18 of your T4 and T4F slips) .... ______ 2
Line 1 minus $2,000 (if negative, enter "0") .... – ______ 3
Line 2 minus line 3 (if negative, enter "0") .... = ______ 4

Total premiums deducted (box 18 of your T4 and T4F slips) .... ______ 5
Required premium: Multiply line 1 by 2.4% .... (maximum $ 936.00) – ______ 6
Line 5 minus line 6 (if negative, enter "0") .... = ______ 7

Enter the amount from line 4 or line 7, whichever is **greater** .... **Employment Insurance overpayment** ______ 8

Enter the amount from line 8 on line 450 of your return.
Enter the amount from line 3, 5, or 6, whichever is least, on line 312 of your return.

Canada Customs and Revenue Agency | Agence des douanes et du revenu du Canada

T1 GENERAL 2000

Income Tax and Benefit Return

Identification

ON 7

Attach your personal label here. Correct any wrong information.
If you are not attaching a label, print your name and address below.

First name and initial

Last name

Address | Apt. or Unit No.

City

Province or territory | Postal code

Enter your province or territory of residence on December 31, 2000:

If you were self-employed in 2000, enter the province or territory of self-employment:

If you became or ceased to be a resident of Canada **in 2000**, give the date of:

entry (Month, Day) or departure (Month, Day)

Enter your social insurance number if it is not on the label, or if you are not attaching a label:

Enter your date of birth: Year Month Day

Your language of correspondence:
Votre langue de correspondance : English ☐ Français ☐

If this return is for a deceased person, enter the date of death: Year Month Day

Marital status on December 31, 2000 (check the box that applies):
(see the "Marital status" section in the guide for details)

1 ☐ Married 2 ☐ Living common law 3 ☐ Widowed
4 ☐ Divorced 5 ☐ Separated 6 ☐ Single

If box 1 or 2 applies, enter your spouse's social insurance number if it is not on the label, or if you are not attaching a label:

Enter the first name of your spouse:

Check this box if your spouse was self-employed in 2000: 1 ☐

Do not use this area

Elections Canada (see the guide for details)

Do you authorize the Canada Customs and Revenue Agency to provide your name, address, and date of birth to Elections Canada to update your information on the **National Register of Electors**? .... Yes ☐ 1 No ☐ 2
Your authorization is needed each year. This information can be used for electoral purposes only.

Goods and services tax / Harmonized sales tax (GST/HST) credit application

Are you applying for the GST/HST credit? (see the guide for details) .... Yes ☐ 1 No ☐ 2

If *yes*, enter the number of children under age 19 on December 31, 2000 (if applicable) ....

If *yes*, enter your spouse's net income from line 236 of your spouse's return (if applicable) ....

Foreign income

As a Canadian resident, you have to report your income from all sources both inside and outside Canada.

Please answer the following question

Did you own or hold foreign property at any time in 2000 with a total cost of more than CAN$100,000?
(read the "Foreign income" section in the guide for details) .... 266 Yes ☐ 1 No ☐ 2
If *yes*, attach a completed Form T1135.

If you had certain dealings with a non-resident trust or corporation in 2000, see the "Foreign income" section in the guide.

Do not use this area 172 171

5006-R

Total income

Employment income (box 14 on all T4 slips) 101
Commissions included on line 101 (box 42 on all T4 slips) 102
Other employment income (see line 104 in the guide) 104+
Old Age Security pension (box 18 on the T4A(OAS) slip) 113+
Canada or Quebec Pension Plan benefits (box 20 on the T4A(P) slip) 114+
Disability benefits included on line 114 (box 16 on the T4A(P) slip) 152
Other pensions or superannuation (see line 115 in the guide) 115+
Employment Insurance benefits (box 14 on the T4E slip) 119+
Taxable amount of dividends from taxable Canadian corporations (see line 120 in the guide) 120+
Interest and other investment income (attach a completed Schedule 4) 121+
Net partnership income: limited or non-active partners only (attach a completed Schedule 4) 122+
Rental income Gross 160 Net 126+
Taxable capital gains (attach a completed Schedule 3) 127+
Support payments received Total 156 Taxable amount 128+
RRSP income (from all T4RSP slips) 129+
Other income (see line 130 in the guide) Specify: 130+
Self-employment income (see lines 135 to 143 in the guide)
Business income Gross 162 Net 135+
Professional income Gross 164 Net 137+
Commission income Gross 166 Net 139+
Farming income Gross 168 Net 141+
Fishing income Gross 170 Net 143+

Workers' compensation benefits (box 10 on the T5007 slip) 144
Social assistance payments (see line 145 in the guide) 145+
Net federal supplements (box 21 on the T4A(OAS) slip) 146+
Add lines 144, 145, and 146 = ▶ 147+
Add lines 101, 104 to 143, and 147
This is your **total income.** 150= ▶

Net income

Pension adjustment
(box 52 on all T4 slips and box 34 on all T4A slips) 206
Registered pension plan deduction (box 20 on all T4 slips and box 32 on all T4A slips) 207
RRSP deduction (see Schedule 7; attach receipts) 208+
Saskatchewan Pension Plan deduction (see line 209 in the guide) 209+
Annual union, professional, or like dues (box 44 on all T4 slips, or from receipts) 212+
Child care expenses (attach a completed Form T778) 214+
Attendant care expenses (see line 215 in the guide) 215+
Business investment loss (see line 217 in the guide)
Gross (before) 227 Gross (after) 228 Allowable deduction 217+
Moving expenses (see line 219 in the guide) 219+
Support payments made Total 230 Allowable deduction 220+
Carrying charges and interest expenses (attach a completed Schedule 4) 221+
Exploration and development expenses (attach a completed Schedule 4) 224+
Other employment expenses (see line 229 in the guide) 229+
Cleric's residence deduction (see line 231 in the guide) 231+
Other deductions (see line 232 in the guide) Specify: 232+
Add lines 207 to 224, 229, 231, and 232. 233= ▶ –
Line 150 minus line 233 (if negative, enter "0"). This is your **net income before adjustments.** 234=

Social benefits repayment (if you reported income on line 113, 119, or 146, see line 235 in the guide) 235–
Line 234 minus line 235 (if negative, enter "0")
This is your **net income.** 236=

Before you mail your return, make sure you have attached here all completed schedules, required information slips, receipts, and corresponding statements.

Taxable income

	Line		
Enter your **net income** from line 236	236		
Employee home relocation loan deduction (box 37 on all T4 slips)	248		
Stock option and shares deductions (boxes 39, 41, 98, and 99 on all T4 slips)	249 +		
Other payments deduction (if you reported income on line 147, see line 250 in the guide)	250 +		
Limited partnership losses of other years	251 +		
Non-capital losses of other years	252 +		
Net capital losses of other years	253 +		
Capital gains deduction (see line 254 in the guide)	254 +		
Northern residents deductions (attach a completed Form T2222)	255 +		
Additional deductions (see line 256 in the guide) Specify:	256 +		
Add lines 248 to 256.	257 =	▶	–
Line 236 minus line 257 (if negative, enter "0") This is your **taxable income.**	260 =		

Non-refundable tax credits

	Line		
Basic personal amount (see line 300 in the guide) **claim $7,231.00**	300		
Age amount (if you were born in 1935 or earlier, see line 301 in the guide)	301 +		
Spousal amount (see line 303 in the guide)			
Base amount		6,754 00	
Minus: Your spouse's net income		–	
Spousal amount (if negative, enter "0") **(maximum claim $6,140)** =	▶ 303 +		
Equivalent-to-spouse amount (see line 305 in the guide) **(maximum claim $6,140)**	305 +		
Amount for infirm dependants age 18 or older (see line 306 in the guide)	306 +		
Canada or Quebec Pension Plan contributions			
Contributions through employment from box 16 and box 17 on all T4 slips (maximum $1,329.90)	308 +		•
Contributions payable on self-employment and other earnings (attach a completed Schedule 8)	310 +		•
Employment Insurance premiums from box 18 on all T4 slips (see line 312 in the guide)	312 +		•
Pension income amount (maximum $1,000; see line 314 in the guide)	314 +		
Caregiver amount (see line 315 in the guide)	315 +		
Disability amount (see line 316 in the guide)	316 +		
Disability amount transferred from a dependant other than your spouse	318 +		
Interest paid on your student loans (see line 319 in the guide)	319 +		
Tuition and education amounts (attach a completed Schedule 11)	323 +		
Tuition and education amounts transferred from a child (see line 324 in the guide)	324 +		
Amounts transferred from your spouse (attach a completed Schedule 2)	326 +		
Medical expenses (see line 330 in the guide; attach receipts)	330		
Minus: $1,637, or 3% of line 236, whichever is **less**	–		
Subtotal	=		
Minus: Medical expenses adjustment (see line 331 in the guide)	331 –		
Allowable portion of medical expenses (if negative, enter "0") =	▶ 332 +		
Add lines 300, 301, 303 to 326, and 332 (if this total is more than line 260, see the note at line 338 in the guide)	335 =		
Multiply the amount on line 335 by 17% =	338		
Donations and gifts: Complete Schedule 9 to calculate your tax credit for donations and gifts. Enter the amount from line 9 of Schedule 9 and attach a completed copy to your return.	349 +		
Add lines 338 and 349. Use this amount to determine your federal tax on Schedule 1. These are your **total non-refundable tax credits.**	350 =		

Refund or Balance owing

4

Federal tax: Complete Schedule 1 and enter the amount from line 11, **or** line 25, whichever applies			406
Total federal political contributions (attach receipts)	409		
Federal political contribution tax credit (see lines 409 and 410 in the guide)		410 •	
Investment tax credit (attach a completed Form T2038(IND))		412 + •	
Labour-sponsored funds tax credit	Net cost 413	Allowable credit 414 + •	
Add lines 410, 412, and 414.		416 =	▶ –
Line 406 minus line 416 (if negative, enter "0") (if you have an amount on line 16 of Schedule 1, see Form T1206)			417 =
Additional tax on RESP accumulated income payments (attach a completed Form T1172)			418 +
Federal individual surtax (line 14 **or** line 32 of Schedule 1)			419 +
Add lines 417, 418, and 419. This is your **net federal tax.**			420 =
Canada Pension Plan contributions payable on self-employment and other earnings (from Schedule 8)			421 +
Social benefits repayment (enter the amount from line 235)			422 +
Provincial or territorial tax (see line 428 in the guide)			428 +
Add lines 420 to 428 This is your **total payable.**			435 = •
Total income tax deducted (from all information slips)		437 •	
Refundable Quebec abatement (see line 440 in the guide)		440 + •	
Canada Pension Plan overpayment (see line 448 in the guide)		448 + •	
Employment Insurance overpayment (see line 450 in the guide)		450 + •	
Refundable medical expense supplement (attach a completed Schedule 10)		452 + •	
Refund of investment tax credit (attach a completed Form T2038(IND))		454 + •	
Part XII.2 trust tax credit (box 38 on all T3 slips)		456 + •	
Employee and partner GST/HST rebate (attach a completed Form GST 370)		457 + •	
Tax paid by instalments (see line 476 in the guide)		476 + •	
Provincial or territorial credits (see line 479 in the guide)		479 + •	
Add lines 437 to 479 These are your **total credits.**		482 =	▶ –
Line 435 minus line 482			=

If the result is negative, you have a **refund**.
If the result is positive, you have a **balance owing**.
Enter the amount below on whichever line applies.

We do not charge or refund a difference of less than $2.

Refund 484 •

Balance owing 485 •

Amount enclosed 486 •

Attach to page 1, a **cheque** or **money order** payable to the Receiver General. Your payment is due no later than April 30, 2001.

Direct deposit – Start or change (see line 484 in the guide)

You do not have to complete this area every year. Do not complete it this year if your direct deposit information for your refund has not changed.

Refund and GST/HST credit – To start direct deposit or to change account information only, attach a "void" cheque or complete lines 460, 461, and 462.

Note: To deposit your **CCTB** payments (including certain related provincial or territorial payments) into the **same** account, also check box 463.

Branch number	Institution number	Account number	CCTB
460	461	462	463 ☐
(5 digits)	(3 digits)	(maximum 12 digits)	

Ontario Opportunities Fund

You can help reduce Ontario's debt by completing this area to donate some or all of your 2000 refund to the Ontario Opportunities Fund. Please see the provincial pages for details.

Amount from line 484 above		1
Your donation to the Ontario Opportunities Fund	465 –	• 2
Net refund (line 1 minus line 2)	466 =	• 3

I certify that the information given on this return and in any documents attached is correct, complete, and fully discloses all my income.

Sign here ____________

It is a serious offence to make a false return.

Telephone ( ) Date

490 **For professional tax preparers only.**

Name:
Address:

Telephone: ( )

Do not use this area 487 ☐ 488 ☐

Privacy Act Personal Information Bank number CCRA/P-PU-005

Canada Customs and Revenue Agency — Agence des douanes et du revenu du Canada

T1 GENERAL 2000

Income Tax and Benefit Return

YT 7

Identification

Attach your personal label here. Correct any wrong information.
If you are not attaching a label, print your name and address below.

First name and initial

Last name

Address — Apt. or Unit No.

City

Province or territory — Postal code

Enter your social insurance number if it is not on the label, or if you are not attaching a label:

Enter your date of birth: Year Month Day

Your language of correspondence: / Votre langue de correspondance : English ☐ Français ☐

If this return is for a deceased person, enter the date of death: Year Month Day

Marital status on December 31, 2000 (check the box that applies):
(see the "Marital status" section in the guide for details)

1 ☐ Married 2 ☐ Living common law 3 ☐ Widowed
4 ☐ Divorced 5 ☐ Separated 6 ☐ Single

If box 1 or 2 applies, enter your spouse's social insurance number if it is not on the label, or if you are not attaching a label:

Enter the first name of your spouse:

Check this box if your spouse was self-employed in 2000: 1 ☐

Do not use this area

Enter your province or territory of residence on December 31, 2000:

If you were self-employed in 2000, enter the province or territory of self-employment:

If you became or ceased to be a resident of Canada **in 2000**, give the date of:

entry Month Day — or departure Month Day

Yukon First Nation information (see Form YT432 for details)

Complete the following if you lived on settlement land of an agreeing Yukon First Nation on December 31, 2000.

Name of First Nation: ____________ Identification number:

Elections Canada (see the guide for details)

Do you authorize the Canada Customs and Revenue Agency to provide your name, address, and date of birth to Elections Canada to update your information on the **National Register of Electors**? .... Yes ☐ 1 No ☐ 2

Your authorization is needed each year. This information can be used for electoral purposes only.

Goods and services tax / Harmonized sales tax (GST/HST) credit application

Are you applying for the GST/HST credit? (see the guide for details) .... Yes ☐ 1 No ☐ 2

If *yes,* enter the number of children under age 19 on December 31, 2000 (if applicable) ....

If *yes,* enter your spouse's net income from line 236 of your spouse's return (if applicable) ....

Foreign income

As a Canadian resident, you have to report your income from all sources both inside and outside Canada.

Please answer the following question

Did you own or hold foreign property at any time in 2000 with a total cost of more than CAN$100,000?
(read the "Foreign income" section in the guide for details) .... 266 Yes ☐ 1 No ☐ 2

If *yes,* attach a completed Form T1135.

If you had certain dealings with a non-resident trust or corporation in 2000, see the "Foreign income" section in the guide.

Do not use this area 172 171

5011-R

Total income

Description	Line	Amount	Line	Amount
Employment income (box 14 on all T4 slips)			101	
Commissions included on line 101 (box 42 on all T4 slips)	102			
Other employment income (see line 104 in the guide)			104+	
Old Age Security pension (box 18 on the T4A(OAS) slip)			113+	
Canada or Quebec Pension Plan benefits (box 20 on the T4A(P) slip)			114+	
Disability benefits included on line 114 (box 16 on the T4A(P) slip)	152			
Other pensions or superannuation (see line 115 in the guide)			115+	
Employment Insurance benefits (box 14 on the T4E slip)			119+	
Taxable amount of dividends from taxable Canadian corporations (see line 120 in the guide)			120+	
Interest and other investment income (attach a completed Schedule 4)			121+	
Net partnership income: limited or non-active partners only (attach a completed Schedule 4)			122+	
Rental income	Gross 160		Net 126+	
Taxable capital gains (attach a completed Schedule 3)			127+	
Support payments received	Total 156		Taxable amount 128+	
RRSP income (from all T4RSP slips)			129+	
Other income (see line 130 in the guide) Specify:			130+	
Self-employment income (see lines 135 to 143 in the guide)				
Business income	Gross 162		Net 135+	
Professional income	Gross 164		Net 137+	
Commission income	Gross 166		Net 139+	
Farming income	Gross 168		Net 141+	
Fishing income	Gross 170		Net 143+	
Workers' compensation benefits (box 10 on the T5007 slip)	144			
Social assistance payments (see line 145 in the guide)	145+			
Net federal supplements (box 21 on the T4A(OAS) slip)	146+			
Add lines 144, 145, and 146	=		▶ 147+	
Add lines 101, 104 to 143, and 147 This is your **total income.**			150=	▶

Net income

Description	Line	Amount	Line	Amount
Pension adjustment (box 52 on all T4 slips and box 34 on all T4A slips)	206			
Registered pension plan deduction (box 20 on all T4 slips and box 32 on all T4A slips)			207	
RRSP deduction (see Schedule 7; attach receipts)			208+	
Saskatchewan Pension Plan deduction (see line 209 in the guide)			209+	
Annual union, professional, or like dues (box 44 on all T4 slips, or from receipts)			212+	
Child care expenses (attach a completed Form T778)			214+	
Attendant care expenses (see line 215 in the guide)			215+	
Business investment loss (see line 217 in the guide) Gross (before) 227	Gross (after) 228		Allowable deduction 217+	
Moving expenses (see line 219 in the guide)			219+	
Support payments made	Total 230		Allowable deduction 220+	
Carrying charges and interest expenses (attach a completed Schedule 4)			221+	
Exploration and development expenses (attach a completed Schedule 4)			224+	
Other employment expenses (see line 229 in the guide)			229+	
Cleric's residence deduction (see line 231 in the guide)			231+	
Other deductions (see line 232 in the guide) Specify:			232+	
Add lines 207 to 224, 229, 231, and 232.			233=	▶ –
Line 150 minus line 233 (if negative, enter "0"). This is your **net income before adjustments.**				234=
Social benefits repayment (if you reported income on line 113, 119, or 146, see line 235 in the guide)				235– •
Line 234 minus line 235 (if negative, enter "0") This is your **net income.**				236=

Before you mail your return, make sure you have attached here all completed schedules, required information slips, receipts, and corresponding statements.

Taxable income

Enter your **net income** from line 236		236
Employee home relocation loan deduction (box 37 on all T4 slips)	248	
Stock option and shares deductions (boxes 39, 41, 98, and 99 on all T4 slips)	249 +	
Other payments deduction (if you reported income on line 147, see line 250 in the guide)	250 +	
Limited partnership losses of other years	251 +	
Non-capital losses of other years	252 +	
Net capital losses of other years	253 +	
Capital gains deduction (see line 254 in the guide)	254 +	
Northern residents deductions (attach a completed Form T2222)	255 +	
Additional deductions (see line 256 in the guide) Specify:	256 +	
Add lines 248 to 256.	257 =	▶ –
Line 236 minus line 257 (if negative, enter "0") This is your **taxable income.**		260 =

Non-refundable tax credits

Basic personal amount (see line 300 in the guide)	**claim $7,231.00**	300
Age amount (if you were born in 1935 or earlier, see line 301 in the guide)		301 +
Spousal amount (see line 303 in the guide)		
Base amount	6,754 00	
Minus: Your spouse's net income	–	
Spousal amount (if negative, enter "0") **(maximum claim $6,140)**	=	▶ 303 +
Equivalent-to-spouse amount (see line 305 in the guide)	**(maximum claim $6,140)**	305 +
Amount for infirm dependants age 18 or older (see line 306 in the guide)		306 +
Canada or Quebec Pension Plan contributions		
Contributions through employment from box 16 and box 17 on all T4 slips (maximum $1,329.90)		308 + •
Contributions payable on self-employment and other earnings (attach a completed Schedule 8)		310 + •
Employment Insurance premiums from box 18 on all T4 slips (see line 312 in the guide)		312 + •
Pension income amount (maximum $1,000; see line 314 in the guide)		314 +
Caregiver amount (see line 315 in the guide)		315 +
Disability amount (see line 316 in the guide)		316 +
Disability amount transferred from a dependant other than your spouse		318 +
Interest paid on your student loans (see line 319 in the guide)		319 +
Tuition and education amounts (attach a completed Schedule 11)		323 +
Tuition and education amounts transferred from a child (see line 324 in the guide)		324 +
Amounts transferred from your spouse (attach a completed Schedule 2)		326 +
Medical expenses (see line 330 in the guide; attach receipts)	330	
Minus: $1,637, or 3% of line 236, whichever is **less**	–	
Subtotal	=	
Minus: Medical expenses adjustment (see line 331 in the guide)	331 –	
Allowable portion of medical expenses (if negative, enter "0")	=	▶ 332 +
Add lines 300, 301, 303 to 326, and 332 (if this total is more than line 260, see the note at line 338 in the guide)		335 =

Multiply the amount on line 335 by 17% =	338
Donations and gifts: Complete Schedule 9 to calculate your tax credit for donations and gifts. Enter the amount from line 9 of Schedule 9 and attach a completed copy to your return.	349 +
Add lines 338 and 349. Use this amount to determine your federal tax on Schedule 1. These are your **total non-refundable tax credits.**	350 =

Refund or Balance owing

Description	Line	Amount
Federal tax: Complete Schedule 1 and enter the amount from line 11, **or** line 25, whichever applies	406	
Total federal political contributions (attach receipts)	409	
Federal political contribution tax credit (see lines 409 and 410 in the guide)	410	•
Investment tax credit (attach a completed Form T2038(IND))	412 +	•
Labour-sponsored funds tax credit Net cost 413 Allowable credit	414 +	•
Add lines 410, 412, and 414.	416 =	► –
Line 406 minus line 416 (if negative, enter "0") (if you have an amount on line 16 of Schedule 1, see Form T1206)	417 =	
Additional tax on RESP accumulated income payments (attach a completed Form T1172)	418 +	
Federal individual surtax (line 14 **or** line 32 of Schedule 1)	419 +	
Add lines 417, 418, and 419. This is your **net federal tax.**	420 =	
Canada Pension Plan contributions payable on self-employment and other earnings (from Schedule 8)	421 +	
Social benefits repayment (enter the amount from line 235)	422 +	
Provincial or territorial tax (see line 428 in the guide)	428 +	
Yukon First Nations tax (attach a completed Form YT432)	432 +	
Add lines 420 to 432 This is your **total payable.**	435 =	•

Description	Line	Amount
Total income tax deducted (from all information slips)	437	•
Refundable Quebec abatement (see line 440 in the guide)	440 +	•
Federal refundable First Nations abatement (attach a completed Form YT432)	441 +	•
Canada Pension Plan overpayment (see line 448 in the guide)	448 +	•
Employment Insurance overpayment (see line 450 in the guide)	450 +	•
Refundable medical expense supplement (attach a completed Schedule 10)	452 +	•
Refund of investment tax credit (attach a completed Form T2038(IND))	454 +	•
Part XII.2 trust tax credit (box 38 on all T3 slips)	456 +	•
Employee and partner GST/HST rebate (attach a completed Form GST 370)	457 +	•
Tax paid by instalments (see line 476 in the guide)	476 +	•
Provincial or territorial credits (see line 479 in the guide)	479 +	•
Add lines 437 to 479 These are your **total credits.**	482 =	► –
Line 435 minus line 482		=

If the result is negative, you have a **refund**.
If the result is positive, you have a **balance owing**.
Enter the amount below on whichever line applies.

We do not charge or refund a difference of less than $2.

Refund 484 •

Balance owing 485 •

Amount enclosed 486 •

Attach to page 1, a **cheque** or **money order** payable to the Receiver General. Your payment is due no later than April 30, 2001.

Direct deposit – Start or change (see line 484 in the guide)

You do not have to complete this area every year. Do not complete it this year if your direct deposit information for your refund has not changed.

Refund and GST/HST credit – To start direct deposit or to change account information only, attach a "void" cheque or complete lines 460, 461, and 462.

Note: To deposit your **CCTB** payments (including certain related provincial or territorial payments) into the **same** account, also check box 463.

Branch number	Institution number	Account number	CCTB
460	461	462	463 ☐
(5 digits)	(3 digits)	(maximum 12 digits)	

I certify that the information given on this return and in any documents attached is correct, complete, and fully discloses all my income.

Sign here

It is a serious offence to make a false return.

Telephone ( ) Date

490 **For professional tax preparers only.**

Name:
Address:
Telephone: ( )

Do not use this area 487 488

Privacy Act Personal Information Bank number CCRA/P-PU-005

Canada Customs and Revenue Agency / Agence des douanes et du revenu du Canada

T1 GENERAL 2000

Income Tax and Benefit Return for Non-Residents and Deemed Residents of Canada

Identification

9

Attach your personal label here. Correct any wrong information.
If you are not attaching a label, print your name and address below.

First name and initial

Last name

Address — Apt. or Unit No.

City

Province or territory — Postal code

Enter your province or territory of residence on December 31, 2000:

If you were self-employed in 2000, enter the province or territory of self-employment:

If you became or ceased to be a resident of Canada **in 2000**, give the date of: entry (Month, Day) or departure (Month, Day)

Enter your social insurance number if it is not on the label, or if you are not attaching a label:

Enter your date of birth: Year Month Day

Your language of correspondence: / Votre langue de correspondance : English ☐ Français ☐

If this return is for a deceased person, enter the date of death: Year Month Day

Marital status on December 31, 2000 (check the box that applies):
(see the "Marital status" section in the guide for details)

1 ☐ Married 2 ☐ Living common law 3 ☐ Widowed
4 ☐ Divorced 5 ☐ Separated 6 ☐ Single

If box 1 or 2 applies, enter your spouse's social insurance number if it is not on the label, or if you are not attaching a label:

Enter the first name of your spouse:

Check this box if your spouse was self-employed in 2000: 1 ☐

Do not use this area

Elections Canada (see the guide for details)

Do you authorize the Canada Customs and Revenue Agency to provide your name, address, and date of birth to Elections Canada to update your information on the **National Register of Electors**? .... Yes ☐ 1 No ☐ 2
Your authorization is needed each year. This information can be used for electoral purposes only.

Goods and services tax / Harmonized sales tax (GST/HST) credit application

Are you applying for the GST/HST credit? (see the guide for details) .... Yes ☐ 1 No ☐ 2

If *yes*, enter the number of children under age 19 on December 31, 2000 (if applicable) ....

If *yes*, enter your spouse's net income from line 236 of your spouse's return (if applicable) ....

Foreign income

As a deemed resident of Canada, you have to report your income from all sources both inside and outside Canada.

If you are a deemed resident of Canada, please answer the following question

Did you own or hold foreign property at any time in 2000 with a total cost of more than CAN$100,000?
(read the "Foreign income" section in the guide for details).................................. 266 Yes ☐ 1 No ☐ 2
If *yes*, attach a completed Form T1135.

If you had certain dealings with a non-resident trust or corporation in 2000, see the "Foreign income" section in the guide.

Do not use this area	172					171				

5013-R

Total income

Description			Line	Amount
Employment income (box 14 on all T4 slips)			101	
Commissions included on line 101 (box 42 on all T4 slips)	102			
Other employment income (see line 104 in the guide)			104 +	
Old Age Security pension (box 18 on the T4A(OAS) slip)			113 +	
Canada or Quebec Pension Plan benefits (box 20 on the T4A(P) slip)			114 +	
Disability benefits included on line 114 (box 16 on the T4A(P) slip)	152			
Other pensions or superannuation (see line 115 in the guide)			115 +	
Employment Insurance benefits (box 14 on the T4E slip)			119 +	
Taxable amount of dividends from taxable Canadian corporations (see line 120 in the guide)			120 +	
Interest and other investment income (attach a completed Schedule 4)			121 +	
Net partnership income: limited or non-active partners only (attach a completed Schedule 4)			122 +	
Rental income	Gross 160		Net 126 +	
Taxable capital gains (attach a completed Schedule 3)			127 +	
Support payments received	Total 156		Taxable amount 128 +	
RRSP income (from all T4RSP slips)			129 +	
Other income (see line 130 in the guide) Specify:			130 +	
Self-employment income (see lines 135 to 143 in the guide)				
Business income	Gross 162		Net 135 +	
Professional income	Gross 164		Net 137 +	
Commission income	Gross 166		Net 139 +	
Farming income	Gross 168		Net 141 +	
Fishing income	Gross 170		Net 143 +	
Workers' compensation benefits (box 10 on the T5007 slip)	144			
Social assistance payments (see line 145 in the guide)	145 +			
Net federal supplements (box 21 on the T4A(OAS) slip)	146 +			
Add lines 144, 145, and 146	=	▶	147 +	
Add lines 101, 104 to 143, and 147 This is your **total income.**			150 =	▶

Net income

Description			Line	Amount	
Pension adjustment (box 52 on all T4 slips and box 34 on all T4A slips)	206				
Registered pension plan deduction (box 20 on all T4 slips and box 32 on all T4A slips)			207		
RRSP deduction (see Schedule 7; attach receipts)			208 +		
Saskatchewan Pension Plan deduction (see line 209 in the guide)			209 +		
Annual union, professional, or like dues (box 44 on all T4 slips, or from receipts)			212 +		
Child care expenses (attach a completed Form T778)			214 +		
Attendant care expenses (see line 215 in the guide)			215 +		
Business investment loss (see line 217 in the guide)	Gross (before) 227	Gross (after) 228	Allowable deduction 217 +		
Moving expenses (see line 219 in the guide)			219 +		
Support payments made	Total 230		Allowable deduction 220 +		
Carrying charges and interest expenses (attach a completed Schedule 4)			221 +		
Exploration and development expenses (attach a completed Schedule 4)			224 +		
Other employment expenses (see line 229 in the guide)			229 +		
Cleric's residence deduction (see line 231 in the guide)			231 +		
Other deductions (see line 232 in the guide) Specify:			232 +		
Add lines 207 to 224, 229, 231, and 232.			233 =	▶	–
Line 150 minus line 233 (if negative, enter "0"). This is your **net income before adjustments.**				234	=
Social benefits repayment (if you reported income on line 113, 119, or 146, see line 235 in the guide)				235	–
Line 234 minus line 235 (if negative, enter "0") This is your **net income.**				236	=

Before you mail your return, make sure you have attached here all completed schedules, required information slips, receipts, and corresponding statements.

Taxable income

Enter your **net income** from line 236			236
Employee home relocation loan deduction (box 37 on all T4 slips)	248		
Stock option and shares deductions (box 39 and box 41 on all T4 slips)	249 +		
Other payments deduction (if you reported income on line 147, see line 250 in the guide)	250 +		
Limited partnership losses of other years	251 +		
Non-capital losses of other years	252 +		
Net capital losses of other years	253 +		
Capital gains deduction (see line 254 in the guide)	254 +		
Northern residents deductions (attach a completed Form T2222)	255 +		
Additional deductions (see line 256 in the guide) Specify:	256 +		
Add lines 248 to 256.	257 =		► –
Line 236 minus line 257 (if negative, enter "0") This is your **taxable income.**			260 =

Non-refundable tax credits

Basic personal amount (see line 300 in the guide)	**claim $7,231.00**	300	
Age amount (if you were born in 1935 or earlier, see line 301 in the guide)		301 +	
Spousal amount (see line 303 in the guide)			
Base amount	6,754 00		
Minus: Your spouse's net world income	–		
Spousal amount (if negative, enter "0") **(maximum claim $6,140)**	=	► 303 +	
Equivalent-to-spouse amount (see line 305 in the guide)	**(maximum claim $6,140)**	305 +	
Amount for infirm dependants age 18 or older (see line 306 in the guide)		306 +	
Canada or Quebec Pension Plan contributions			
Contributions through employment from box 16 and box 17 on all T4 slips (maximum $1,329.90)		308 +	•
Contributions payable on self-employment and other earnings (attach a completed Schedule 8)		310 +	•
Employment Insurance premiums from box 18 on all T4 slips (see line 312 in the guide)		312 +	•
Pension income amount (maximum $1,000; see line 314 in the guide)		314 +	
Caregiver amount (see line 315 in the guide)		315 +	
Disability amount (see line 316 in the guide)		316 +	
Disability amount transferred from a dependant other than your spouse		318 +	
Interest paid on your student loans (see line 319 in the guide)		319 +	
Tuition and education amounts (attach a completed Schedule 11)		323 +	
Tuition and education amounts transferred from a child (see line 324 in the guide)		324 +	
Amounts transferred from your spouse (attach a completed Schedule 2)		326 +	
Medical expenses (see line 330 in the guide; attach receipts)	330		
Minus: $1,637, or 3% of line 236, whichever is **less**	–		
Subtotal	=		
Minus: Medical expenses adjustment (see line 331 in the guide)	331 –		
Allowable portion of medical expenses (if negative, enter "0")	=	► 332 +	
Add lines 300, 301, 303 to 326, and 332 (if this total is more than line 260, see the note at line 338 in the guide)		335 =	

Multiply the amount on line 335 by 17% =	338
Donations and gifts: Complete Schedule 9 to calculate your tax credit for donations and gifts. Enter the amount from line 9 of Schedule 9 and attach a completed copy to your return.	349 +
Add lines 338 and 349. These are your **total non-refundable tax credits.**	350 =

If you are a deemed resident, use the amount on line 350 to determine your federal tax on Schedule 1.

If you are a non-resident, complete Schedule A and Schedule B to determine the allowable amount to enter on Schedule 1.

Refund or Balance owing

Federal tax: Complete Schedule 1 and enter the amount from line 11, **or** line 25, whichever applies 406

Total federal political contributions (attach receipts) **409**

Federal political contribution tax credit (see lines 409 and 410 in the guide) **410** •

Investment tax credit (attach a completed Form T2038(IND)) **412** + •

Labour-sponsored funds tax credit Net cost **413** Allowable credit **414** + •

Add lines 410, 412, and 414. 416 = ▶ –

Line 406 minus line 416 (if negative, enter "0") (if you have an amount on line 20 of Schedule 1, see Form T1206) 417 =

Additional tax on RESP accumulated income payments (attach a completed Form T1172) 418 +

Federal individual surtax (line 14 **or** line 32 of Schedule 1) 419 +

Add lines 417, 418, and 419. This is your **net federal tax.** 420 =

Canada Pension Plan contributions payable on self-employment and other earnings (from Schedule 8) 421 +

Social benefits repayment (enter the amount from line 235) 422 +

Provincial or territorial tax (see line 428 in the guide) 428 +

Add lines 420 to 428

This is your **total payable.** 435 = •

Total income tax deducted (from all information slips) **437** •

Tax transfer for residents of Quebec (see line 438 in the guide) **438** – •

Line 437 minus line 438 = ▶ 439 =

Refundable Quebec abatement (see line 440 in the guide) **440** + •

Canada Pension Plan overpayment (see line 448 in the guide) **448** + •

Employment Insurance overpayment (see line 450 in the guide) **450** + •

Refundable medical expense supplement (attach a completed Schedule 10) **452** + •

Refund of investment tax credit (attach a completed Form T2038(IND)) **454** + •

Part XII.2 trust tax credit (box 38 on all T3 slips) **456** + •

Employee and partner GST/HST rebate (attach a completed Form GST 370) **457** + •

Tax paid by instalments (see line 476 in the guide) **476** + •

Add lines 439 to 476

These are your **total credits.** 482 = ▶ –

Line 435 minus line 482 =

If the result is negative, you have a **refund**.
If the result is positive, you have a **balance owing**.
Enter the amount below on whichever line applies.

We do not charge or refund a difference of less than $2.

Refund 484 •

Balance owing 485 •

Amount enclosed 486 •

Attach to page 1, a **cheque** or **money order** payable to the Receiver General. Your payment is due no later than April 30, 2001.

Direct deposit – Start or change (see line 484 in the guide)

You do not have to complete this area every year. Do not complete it this year if your direct deposit information for your refund has not changed.

Refund and GST/HST credit – To start direct deposit to a financial institution in Canada, or to change account information only, attach a "void" cheque or complete lines 460, 461, and 462.

Note: To deposit your **CCTB** payments (including certain related provincial or territorial payments) into the **same** account, also check box 463.

Branch number	Institution number	Account number	CCTB
460	461	462	463 ☐
(5 digits)	(3 digits)	(maximum 12 digits)	

I certify that the information given on this return and in any documents attached is correct, complete, and fully discloses all my income.

Sign here

It is a serious offence to make a false return.

Telephone ( ) Date

490 For professional tax preparers only.

Name:
Address:

Telephone: ( )

Do not use this area **487** **488**

Privacy Act Personal Information Bank number CCRA/P-PU-005

T1-2000

Worksheet

Use these charts to do some of the calculations you may need to complete your *T1 General Income Tax and Benefit Return for Non-Residents and Deemed Residents of Canada*.

You can find more information about these charts in your guide.

Keep this worksheet for your records. **Do not attach it to the return you send us.**

Line 235 – Social benefits repayment

Amount from line 113 of your return			1
Amount from line 146 of your return	+		2
Add lines 1 and 2	=		3
Old Age Security benefits you paid back in 2000 and deducted on line 232	–		4
Line 3 minus line 4 (if negative, enter "0")	=		5
Amount from line 234 of your return			6
EI benefits repayment from line 10 of Chart 1 or line 14 of Chart 2 on your T4E slip (if any)	–		7
Line 6 minus line 7	=		8
Base amount	–	53,960 00	9
Line 8 minus line 9 (if negative, enter "0")	=		10
Multiply the amount on line 10 by 15%			11
Enter the amount from line 5 or line 11, whichever is **less**			12
Enter the amount from line 7 above (if any)	+		13
Add lines 12 and 13. Enter this amount on lines 235 and 422 of your return.	=		14

Line 301 – Age amount

Maximum claim				3,531 00	1
Your net world income (as defined at line 301 in the guide)			2		
Base amount	–	26,284 00	3		
Line 2 minus line 3 (if negative, enter "0")	=		4		
Multiply the amount on line 4 by 15%				–	5
Line 1 minus line 5 (if negative, enter "0") Enter this amount on line 301 of your return.				=	6

Line 305 – Equivalent-to-spouse amount

Base amount		6,754 00	1
Dependant's net world income (as defined at line 305 in the guide)	–		2
Line 1 minus line 2	=		3

Enter on line 305 of your return, $6,140 or the amount on line 3, whichever is **less**.

Complete Schedule 5 to provide details for this dependant.

Line 306 – Amount for infirm dependants age 18 or older

If your dependant's net world income for 2000 (as defined at line 306 in the guide) was $7,231 or more, you cannot make a claim.

Base amount		7,231 00	1
Dependant's net world income	–		2
Line 1 minus line 2; if it is more than $2,386, enter $2,386	=		3
If you claimed this dependant on line 305 of your return, enter the amount claimed	–		4
Allowable amount for this dependant: Line 3 minus line 4 (if negative, enter "0")	=		5

Complete this calculation for each dependant.

Enter on line 306 of your return, the total amount claimed for all dependants.

Complete Schedule 5 to provide details for each dependant.

Line 314 – Pension income amount

Amount from line 115 of your return					1
Annuity payments from line 129 of your return (box 16 of your T4RSP slip) only if you were age 65 or older on December 31, 2000, or you received the payments because of the death of your spouse				+	2
Add lines 1 and 2				=	3
Foreign pension income included on line 115 and deducted on line 256			4		
Income from a U.S. individual retirement account included on line 115	+		5		
Add lines 4 and 5	=		▶	–	6
Line 3 minus line 6				=	7

Enter on line 314 of your return, $1,000 or the amount on line 7, whichever is **less**.

Line 315 – Caregiver amount

If your dependant's net world income for 2000 (as defined at line 315 in the guide) was $14,047 or more, you cannot make a claim.

Base amount		14,047 00	1
Dependant's net world income	–		2
Line 1 minus line 2; if it is more than $2,386, enter $2,386	=		3
If you claimed this dependant on line 305 of your return, enter the amount claimed	–		4
Allowable amount for this dependant: Line 3 minus line 4 (if negative, enter "0")	=		5

Complete this calculation for each dependant.

Enter on line 315 of your return, the total amount claimed for all dependants.

Complete Schedule 5 to provide details for each dependant.

Line 316 – Disability amount (calculation if you were under age 18 on December 31, 2000)

Maximum supplement				2,941 00	1
Total child care and attendant care expenses claimed for you by anyone			2		
Base amount	–	2,000 00	3		
Line 2 minus line 3 (if negative, enter "0")	=		▶ –		4
Line 1 minus line 4 (if negative, enter "0")			=		5

Enter on line 316 of your return, $4,293 **plus** the amount on line 5 (maximum claim $7,234) unless this chart is being completed for the chart for line 318.

Line 318 – Disability amount transferred from a dependant other than your spouse

Base amount		4,293 00	1
If the dependant was under age 18 on December 31, 2000, enter the amount from line 5 of the chart for line 316 for the dependant	+		2
Add lines 1 and 2	=		3
Total of amounts your dependant can claim on lines 300 to 315 of the dependant's return	+		4
Add lines 3 and 4	=		5
Dependant's taxable income from line 260 of the dependant's return	–		6
Line 5 minus line 6 (if negative, enter "0")	=		7

If your dependant was **age 18 or older** on December 31, 2000, enter on line 318 of your return, the amount on line 1 or line 7, whichever is **less**.

If your dependant was **under age 18** on December 31, 2000, enter on line 318 of your return, the amount on line 3 or line 7, whichever is **less**.

Line 410 – Federal political contribution tax credit

For total federal contributions of $200 or less:

Total contributions			x 75% =		1

Enter the amount from line 1 on line 410 of your return.

For total federal contributions of more than $200 but not more than $550:

Total contributions			2			
Credit on the first	–	200 00	3	is	150 00	4
Credit on the rest is (line 2 minus line 3)	=			x 50% = +		5
Add lines 4 and 5 Enter this amount on line 410 of your return.				=		6

For total federal contributions of more than $550:

Total contributions			7			
Credit on the first	–	550 00	8	is	325 00	9
Credit on the rest (line 7 minus line 8)	=			x 33.33% = +		10
Add lines 9 and 10 Enter on line 410 of your return, $500 or the amount on line 11, whichever is **less**.				=		11

Instalments

See the "Should you be paying your taxes by instalments?" section in the guide for details.

Total payable from line 435 of your return (**not including** the amount on line 421)					1
Total credits from line 482 of your return			2		
Total of amounts on lines 448, 450, 457, and 476 of your return	–		3		
Line 2 minus line 3	=		▶ –		4
Line 1 minus line 4			=		5

You may have to pay your 2001 taxes by instalments if the amount on line 5 for 2001 as well as that amount for either 2000 or 1999 is more than $2,000 ($1,200 if you have to file a return for the Province of Quebec).

T1-2000

Worksheet

Use these charts to do some of the calculations you may need to complete your *T1 General Income Tax and Benefit Return.*
You can find more information about these charts in your guide.
Keep this worksheet for your records. **Do not attach it to the return you send us.**

Line 235 – Social benefits repayment

Amount from line 113 of your return			1
Amount from line 146 of your return	+		2
Add lines 1 and 2	=		3
Old Age Security benefits you paid back in 2000 and deducted on line 232	–		4
Line 3 minus line 4 (if negative, enter "0")	=		5
Amount from line 234 of your return			6
EI benefits repayment from line 10 of Chart 1 or line 14 of Chart 2 on your T4E slip (if any)	–		7
Line 6 minus line 7	=		8
Base amount	–	53,960 00	9
Line 8 minus line 9 (if negative, enter "0")	=		10
Multiply the amount on line 10 by 15%			11
Enter the amount from line 5 or line 11, whichever is **less**			12
Enter the amount from line 7 above (if any)	+		13
Add lines 12 and 13. Enter this amount on lines 235 and 422 of your return.	=		14

Line 301 – Age amount

Maximum claim				3,531 00	1
Your net income from line 236 of your return			2		
Base amount	–	26,284 00	3		
Line 2 minus line 3 (if negative, enter "0")	=		4		
Multiply the amount on line 4 by 15%				–	5
Line 1 minus line 5 (if negative, enter "0") Enter this amount on line 301 of your return.				=	6

Line 305 – Equivalent-to-spouse amount

Base amount		6,754 00	1
Dependant's net income	–		2
Line 1 minus line 2	=		3

Enter on line 305 of your return, $6,140 or the amount on line 3, whichever is **less**.

Complete Schedule 5 to provide details for this dependant.

Line 306 – Amount for infirm dependants age 18 or older

If your dependant's net income for 2000 was $7,231 or more, you cannot make a claim.

Base amount		7,231 00	1
Dependant's net income	–		2
Line 1 minus line 2; if it is more than $2,386, enter $2,386	=		3
If you claimed this dependant on line 305 of your return, enter the amount claimed	–		4
Allowable amount for this dependant: Line 3 minus line 4 (if negative, enter "0")	=		5

Complete this calculation for each dependant.

Enter on line 306 of your return, the total amount claimed for all dependants.

Complete Schedule 5 to provide details for each dependant.

Line 314 – Pension income amount

Amount from line 115 of your return					1
Annuity payments from line 129 of your return (box 16 of your T4RSP slip) only if you were age 65 or older on December 31, 2000, or you received the payments because of the death of your spouse				+	2
Add lines 1 and 2				=	3
Foreign pension income included on line 115 and deducted on line 256			4		
Income from a U.S. individual retirement account included on line 115	+		5		
Add lines 4 and 5	=		▶	–	6
Line 3 minus line 6				=	7

Enter on line 314 of your return, $1,000 or the amount on line 7, whichever is **less**.

Line 315 – Caregiver amount

If your dependant's net income for 2000 was $14,047 or more, you cannot make a claim.

Base amount		14,047 00	1
Dependant's net income	–		2
Line 1 minus line 2; if it is more than $2,386, enter $2,386	=		3
If you claimed this dependant on line 305 of your return, enter the amount claimed	–		4
Allowable amount for this dependant: Line 3 minus line 4 (if negative, enter "0")	=		5

Complete this calculation for each dependant.

Enter on line 315 of your return, the total amount claimed for all dependants.

Complete Schedule 5 to provide details for each dependant.

Line 316 – Disability amount (calculation if you were under age 18 on December 31, 2000)

Maximum supplement				2,941 00	1
Total child care and attendant care expenses claimed for you by anyone			2		
Base amount	–	2,000 00	3		
Line 2 minus line 3 (if negative, enter "0")	=		▶ –		4
Line 1 minus line 4 (if negative, enter "0")			=		5

Enter on line 316 of your return, $4,293 **plus** the amount on line 5 (maximum claim $7,234) unless this chart is being completed for the chart for line 318.

Line 318 – Disability amount transferred from a dependant other than your spouse

Base amount		4,293 00	1
If the dependant was under age 18 on December 31, 2000, enter the amount from line 5 of the chart for line 316 for the dependant	+		2
Add lines 1 and 2	=		3
Total of amounts your dependant can claim on lines 300 to 315 of the dependant's return	+		4
Add lines 3 and 4	=		5
Dependant's taxable income from line 260 of the dependant's return	–		6
Line 5 minus line 6 (if negative, enter "0")	=		7

If your dependant was **age 18 or older** on December 31, 2000, enter on line 318 of your return, the amount on line 1 or line 7, whichever is **less**.

If your dependant was **under age 18** on December 31, 2000, enter on line 318 of your return, the amount on line 3 or line 7, whichever is **less**.

Line 410 – Federal political contribution tax credit

For total federal contributions of $200 or less:

Total contributions			x 75% =		1

Enter the amount from line 1 on line 410 of your return.

For total federal contributions of more than $200 but not more than $550:

Total contributions			2			
Credit on the first	–	200 00	3	is	150 00	4
Credit on the rest is (line 2 minus line 3)	=			x 50% =	+	5
Add lines 4 and 5 Enter this amount on line 410 of your return.				=		6

For total federal contributions of more than $550:

Total contributions			7			
Credit on the first	–	550 00	8	is	325 00	9
Credit on the rest (line 7 minus line 8)	=			x 33.33% =	+	10
Add lines 9 and 10 Enter on line 410 of your return, $500 or the amount on line 11, whichever is **less**.				=		11

Instalments

See the "Should you be paying your taxes by instalments?" section in the guide for details.

Total payable from line 435 of your return (**not including** the amount on line 421)					1
Total credits from line 482 of your return			2		
Total of amounts on lines 448, 450, 457, and 476 of your return	–		3		
Line 2 minus line 3	=		▶ –		4
Line 1 minus line 4			=		5

You may have to pay your 2001 taxes by instalments if the amount on line 5 for 2001 as well as that amount for either 2000 or 1999 is more than $2,000 ($1,200 if you live in Quebec).

BC 479
T1 General – 2000

British Columbia Credits

Complete the calculations that apply to you and attach a copy of this form to your return. For details, see the section called "Completing Your British Columbia Forms" in this booklet.

Sales tax credit (for low-income families and individuals)

If you had a spouse on December 31, 2000, you and your spouse have to decide who will claim this credit, since **only one of you** can claim the credit for both of you.

Income for the sales tax credit

			Line
Enter your net income from line 236 of your return			1
Enter your spouse's net income from line 236 of your spouse's return	6030	+	2
Net family income: Add lines 1 and 2		=	3
If you had a spouse on December 31, 2000, enter $18,000. Otherwise enter $15,000.		–	4
Line 3 minus line 4 (if negative, enter "0")	**Income for the sales tax credit**	=	5

			Line
Basic sales tax credit	claim $50 6033		6
Additional credit for your spouse	claim $50 6035	+	7
Add lines 6 and 7		=	8
Amount from line 5 ______ × 2% =		–	9
Line 8 minus line 9 (if negative, enter "0")	**Sales tax credit**	=	10

British Columbia venture capital tax credit

				Line
Enter your venture capital tax credit from Form VCC10	6049			• 11
Enter your unused venture capital tax credit from previous years	+			12
Add lines 11 and 12 (maximum $60,000)	=	▶	+	13

British Columbia mining exploration tax credit

			Line
Enter your mining exploration tax credit from Form T88	6051	+	• 14
Add lines 10, 13, and 14. Enter the result on line 479 of your return.	**British Columbia credits**	=	15

5010-TC

BC 428
T1 General – 2000

British Columbia Tax

Complete this form and attach a copy of it to your return.
For details, see the section called "Completing Your British Columbia Forms" in this booklet.

Step 1 – British Columbia tax on taxable income

Enter your **taxable income** from line 260 of your return ______ 1

Use the amount on line 1 to determine which **ONE** of the following columns you have to complete.

	If line 1 is **$30,004** or less		If line 1 is more than **$30,004**, but not more than **$60,009**		If line 1 is more than **$60,009**	
Enter the amount from line 1 in the applicable column		2		2		2
Income threshold	– 0 00	3	– 30,004 00	3	– 60,009 00	3
Line 2 minus line 3 (cannot be negative)	=	4	=	4	=	4
Provincial tax rate	× 8.4%	5	× 12.4%	5	× 14.35%	5
Multiply line 4 by line 5	=	6	=	6	=	6
Tax on income threshold	+ 0 00	7	+ 2,520 00	7	+ 6,241 00	7
Add lines 6 and 7	=	8	=	8	=	8
	Go to Step 2		Go to Step 2		Go to Step 2	

Step 2 – British Columbia non-refundable tax credits

Enter the amount from line 335 of your return		× 8.4% =		9
Amounts from Schedule 9, *Donations and Gifts*				
Enter the amount from line 345 of Schedule 9		× 8.4% =	+	10
Enter the amount from line 347 of Schedule 9		× 14.35% =	+	11
Add lines 9, 10, and 11		**British Columbia non-refundable tax credits** 6150	=	12

Go to Step 3

Step 3 – British Columbia tax

Enter the amount from line 8					13
British Columbia tax on split income, if applicable, from Form T1206			6151	+	• 14
Add lines 13 and 14				=	15
British Columbia non-refundable tax credits from line 12				–	16
Line 15 minus line 16 (if negative, enter "0")				=	17
B.C. dividend tax credit:					
Amount from line 120 of your return	× 6.6% =	6152 +	• 18		
B.C. overseas employment tax credit:					
Amount from line 426 on Schedule 1	× 49.5% =	6153 +	• 19		
B.C. minimum tax carry-over:					
Amount from line 427 on Schedule 1	× 49.5% =	6154 +	• 20		
Add lines 18, 19, and 20		=	▶	–	21
Line 17 minus line 21 (if negative, enter "0")				=	22
B.C. additional tax for minimum tax purposes, if applicable, from Form T1219				+	23
Add lines 22 and 23				=	24
Enter the provincial foreign tax credit, if applicable from Form T2036				–	25
Line 24 minus line 25				=	26

Continue on the back

Enter the amount from line 26 on the front of this form			26

British Columbia surtax

(Line 26 ___ minus $5,300) × 30% (if negative, enter "0")				27
(Line 26 ___ minus $8,660) × 15% (if negative, enter "0")		+		28
Add lines 27 and 28		=		29
British Columbia surtax reduction:				
Dependent spouse reduction claim $50			30	
Spousal equivalent reduction claim $50 6023	+		31	
Dependant reduction				
Number of dependants 6025 ___ × $50 =	+		32	
Add lines 30, 31, and 32	=	►	–	33
Line 29 minus line 33 (if negative, enter "0") **British Columbia surtax**		=	► +	34
Add lines 26 and 34			=	35

Go to Step 4

Step 4 – British Columbia tax adjustments

British Columbia supplementary credits

Basic credit claim $25.20				36
Spousal credit (if you claimed an amount on line 303 of your return) claim $25.20 6028	+			• 37
Spousal equivalent credit (if you claimed an amount on line 305 of your return) claim $25.20 6029	+			• 38
Add lines 36, 37, and 38	=	►	–	39
Line 35 minus line 39 (if negative, enter "0")			=	40

British Columbia logging tax credit

Enter the provincial logging tax credit, if any, from Form BCFIN 542	–	41
Line 40 minus line 41 (if negative, enter "0")	=	42

British Columbia political contribution tax credit

Enter British Columbia political contributions made in 2000	6040		43
The credit you calculated on page 2 in "Completing Your British Columbia Forms" (max. $500)		–	44
Line 42 minus line 44 (if negative, enter "0")		=	45

British Columbia employee investment tax credits

Enter your employee share ownership plan tax credit from Form ESOP 20	6045			• 46
Enter your employee venture capital tax credit from Form EVCC 30	6047 +			• 47
Add lines 46 and 47 (maximum $2,000)	=	►	–	48
Line 45 minus line 48 (if negative, enter "0") Enter this amount on line 428 of your return. **British Columbia tax**			=	49

Alberta Tax and Credit

AB 428
T1 General – 2000

Complete this form and attach a copy of it to your return. For details, see the back of the form.

Alberta tax

			Line
If you used **Method A** of Schedule 1, enter the amount from line 11 of that schedule If you used **Method B** of Schedule 1, enter the amount from line 23 of that schedule			1
Alberta income tax rate		× 44%	2
Basic Alberta income tax: Multiply line 1 by 44%		=	3
Alberta flat rate tax:			
Enter your taxable income from line 260 of your return		4	
Flat tax rate	× 0.005	5	
Multiply line 4 by 0.005	=	► +	6
Adjusted Alberta income tax: Add lines 3 and 6		=	7
Enter your royalty tax rebate, if any, you calculated on Form T79		–	8
Line 7 minus line 8 (if negative, enter "0")		=	9

Alberta selective tax reduction

If line 9 is $860 or more, enter "0" on line 15 and continue on line 16.
If line 9 is less than $860, complete the following calculation.

			Line
Basic claim		430 00	10
Enter the amount from line 9			11
Applicable rate	× 50%		12
Multiply line 11 by 50%	►	–	13
Line 10 minus line 13 (if negative, enter "0")		=	14

		Line
Enter the amount from line 9 or line 14, whichever is **less**	–	15
Line 9 minus line 15 (if negative, enter "0")	=	16
Enter the provincial foreign tax credit, if any, you calculated on Form T2036	–	17
Line 16 minus line 17. Enter the result on line 428 of your return. **Alberta tax**	=	18

Alberta political contribution tax credit

		Line
Enter the Alberta political contributions made in 2000	6003	19
Enter the credit you calculated on the back of this form (maximum $750)		20
Enter your Alberta tax from line 18		21
Enter the amount from line 20 or line 21, whichever is **less**. Enter this amount on line 479 of your return. **Alberta political contribution tax credit**		22

Government of Saskatchewan

Saskatchewan Income Tax

SK 428
T1 General – 2000

Complete this form and attach a copy of it to your return. For details, see the back of the form.

Adjusted net income

Enter net income from line 236 of your return		1
Enter the amount you claimed on line 250 of your return	–	2
Line 1 minus line 2 (if negative, enter "0")	=	3
Enter the amount you claimed on line 256 of your return for foreign income exempt under a tax treaty 6054	–	4
Line 3 minus line 4 (if negative, enter "0") **Adjusted net income**	=	5

Saskatchewan tax

If you used **Method A** of Schedule 1, enter the amount from line 11 of that schedule. If you used **Method B** of Schedule 1, enter the amount from line 23 of that schedule.		6
Saskatchewan tax rate	× 48%	7
Saskatchewan tax: Multiply line 6 by 48%	=	8
Saskatchewan flat tax: Amount from line 5 ______ × 1.5% =	+	9
Basic Saskatchewan tax: Add line 8 and line 9	=	10
Debt reduction surtax: (Amount from line 10 ______ × 10%) minus $150 (if negative, enter "0")	+	11
High income surtax: (Amount from line 10 ______ minus $4,000) × 15% (if negative, enter "0")	+	12
Adjusted Saskatchewan tax: Add lines 10, 11, and 12	=	13

Saskatchewan tax reduction (see the back for more details)

If line 5 is $40,000 or more, enter "0" on line 25 and continue on line 26.
If line 5 is less than $40,000, complete the following calculation.

If you had a spouse on December 31, 2000, only the spouse with the **higher net income** is eligible to claim the child tax reduction (line 17).

Sales tax reduction			200 00	14	
Spousal tax reduction	claim $300		+	15	
Spousal equivalent tax reduction	claim $300 6023		+	16	
Child tax reduction Number of children born in 1983 or later 6099 ____ × $250 =	(maximum $1,000)		+	17	
Senior citizens tax reduction (if born in 1935 or earlier)	claim $200		+	18	
Add lines 14 to 18			=	19	
Enter your adjusted net income from line 5		20			
Base amount	– 10,000 00	21			
Line 20 minus line 21 (if negative, enter "0")	=	22			
Applicable rate	× 5%	23			
Multiply line 22 by 5%	=	▶	–	24	
Line 19 minus line 24 (if negative, enter "0") **Saskatchewan tax reduction**			=	▶	– 25
Reduced Saskatchewan tax: Line 13 minus line 25 (if negative, enter "0")					= 26
Enter the provincial foreign tax credit, if any, you calculated on Form T2036					– 27
Line 26 minus line 27					= 28

Saskatchewan labour-sponsored venture capital tax credit

For investments in venture capital corporations that are registered in Saskatchewan: Enter your tax credit from Form T2C (SASK.) (maximum $1,000)		29	
For investments in venture capital corporations that are registered federally only: Enter your tax credit from Form T2C (SASK.) (maximum $525)	+	30	
Add lines 29 and 30 (maximum $1,000) **Saskatchewan labour-sponsored venture capital tax credit** 6374	=	▶ ●	– 31
Line 28 minus line 31 (if negative, enter "0")			= 32

Saskatchewan post-secondary graduate tax credit

Enter $350 if a certificate relating to this credit has been issued in your name for 2000 6376	–	33
Line 32 minus line 33 (if negative, enter "0") Enter the result on line 428 of your return. **Saskatchewan tax**	=	34

Manitoba

Manitoba Credits

MB 479
T1 General – 2000

Complete this form and attach a copy of it to your return if you were a resident of Manitoba at the end of the year.
For details about these credits, see the section called "Completing Your Manitoba Forms" in this booklet.

Enter your net income from line 236 of your return			1
Enter your spouse's net income from line 236 of your spouse's return	6030	+	2
Add lines 1 and 2	**Net family income for calculating credits**	=	3

At the end of the year, did you and your spouse occupy separate principal residences for medical reasons? 6089

If *yes*, **leave line 2 blank**, and enter the address of your spouse in the area beside box 6089.

Personal tax credit

Basic credit			190 00	4
Age credit for self (65 or older at the end of the year)	claim $110		+	5
Basic credit for spouse	claim $190	6		
Age credit for spouse (65 or older at the end of the year)	claim $110	+ 7		
Disability credit for spouse	claim $110	+ 8		
Add lines 6, 7, and 8	6090	=	► +	9
Equivalent-to-spouse credit	claim $190		+	10
Disability credit for self or for a dependant other than spouse — Number of disability claims	6095	x $110 =	+	11
Credit for disabled dependants born in 1982 or earlier — Number of disability claims	6097	x $60 =	+	12
Credit for dependent children born in 1982 or later — Number of children	6099	x $25 =	+	13
Add the amounts on lines 4, 5, and 9 to 13	Total credits	6105	=	14
Amount on line 3		x 1% =	–	15
Line 14 minus line 15 (if negative, enter "0")	**Personal tax credit**		=	16

Property tax credit

Total rent paid in Manitoba for 2000	6110	x 20% =		17
Net property tax paid in Manitoba for 2000		6112	+	18
Resident homeowners tax assistance received (if not received, enter "0")		6114	+	19
Add lines 17, 18, and 19		6116	=	20
Base amount			– 250 00	21
Occupancy cost: Line 20 minus line 21 (if negative, enter "0")			=	22
Basic credit: If you were **under age 65** at the end of the year, enter **$600**; If you were **65 or older** at the end of the year, enter **$700**	►	23		
Amount on line 3	x 1% =	– 24		
Line 23 minus line 24 (if the result is less than $325, enter $325)		=	►	25
Enter the amount from line 22 or 25, whichever is **less**				26
Enter the amount of Resident homeowners tax assistance received (from line 19)			–	27
Line 26 minus line 27 (if negative, enter "0").	**Property tax credit**		=	28

Continue on the back. Be sure to complete the "Declaration for the property tax credit" chart.

5007-TC

School tax credit for homeowners

Complete lines 29 to 34 only if you were a **homeowner** of at least 55 years of age at the end of the year and your net family income (line 3) is less than $23,800. Otherwise, enter "0" on line 34 and continue on line 35.

If line 3 is less than $15,100, enter $175 on line 29. If it is between $15,100 and $23,800, see the table on page 8 in the section called "Completing Your Manitoba Forms." 6120 ______ 29

School tax paid in Manitoba for 2000 6122 ______ minus $160 = ______ 30

Occupancy cost: Enter the amount from line 22 ______ 31
Enter the amount from line 26 – ______ 32
Line 31 minus line 32 (if negative, enter "0") = ______ ► ______ 33

Enter the amount from line 29, 30, or 33, whichever is **less**. **School tax credit** 6124 ______ 34

Enter the property tax credit from line 28 ______ 35
Enter the school tax credit from line 34 + ______ 36
Add lines 35 and 36 = ______ ► ______ 37
Shelter allowance program benefits received 6126 – ______ 38

Line 37 minus line 38 (if negative, enter "0") **Net property and school tax credits** = ______ 39

Add lines 16 and 39 ______ 40

If you or your spouse received provincial or municipal **social assistance** in 2000, enter the number shown in box 14 of your T5007 slip or that of your spouse, whichever is **less**. Otherwise, leave this line blank. 6130 x ______ • 41
If you have entered a number on line 41, multiply line 40 by line 41.
If not, enter the amount from line 40. = ______ 42

Learning tax credit

Enter the amount from line 5 on Schedule 11 or $10,000, whichever is **less** ______ 43
Enter the part of your unused current-year tuition and education amounts transferred to another individual (amount from line 18 of Schedule 11) – ______ 44
Line 43 minus line 44 6135 = ______ 45
Enter the total of the tuition and education amounts transferred from your children or grandchildren (line 324 of your return), and from your spouse (amount from line 360 of your Schedule 2) 6137 + ______ 46
Add lines 45 and 46 = ______ 47
Tax credit factor x 7% 48
Multiply line 47 by 7% **Learning tax credit** = ______ ► + ______ 49

Add lines 42 and 49. Enter this amount on line 479 of your return. **Manitoba credits** = ______ 50

If you do not complete the following, your property tax credit claim may be disallowed.

Declaration for the property tax credit (If you need more space, attach a separate sheet of paper)

By signing my return, I declare the following information about my principal residence(s) in Manitoba during 2000:

Address	# of months resident in 2000	Rent and/or property tax paid in 2000	Name of any individual(s) who shared accommodation with you*	Name of landlord or municipality to whom payment was made	Roll number

***NOTE:** The *Manitoba Income Tax Act* allows **only one property tax credit per residence**. If you shared accommodation with one or more individuals (other than your spouse and/or dependent children), only one of you can claim a property tax credit for that residence for the time you were sharing.

Manitoba

MB 428

T1 General – 2000

Manitoba Tax

Complete this form and attach a copy of it to your return.
For details, see the section called "Completing Your Manitoba Forms" in this booklet.

Step 1 – Manitoba tax on taxable income

Enter your **taxable income** from line 260 of your return ______ 1

Use the amount on line 1 to determine which **ONE** of the following columns you have to complete.

	If line 1 is **$29,590** or less		If line 1 is more than **$29,590**, but not more than **$59,180**		If line 1 is more than **$59,180**	
Enter the amount from line 1 in the applicable column		2		2		2
Income threshold	– 0 00	3	– 29,590 00	3	– 59,180 00	3
Line 2 minus line 3 (cannot be negative)	=	4	=	4	=	4
Provincial tax rate	× 8%	5	× 12.22%	5	× 13.63%	5
Multiply line 4 by line 5	=	6	=	6	=	6
Tax on income threshold	+ 0 00	7	+ 2,367 00	7	+ 5,983 00	7
Add lines 6 and 7 **Tax on taxable income**	=	8	=	8	=	8
	Go to Step 2		**Go to Step 2**		**Go to Step 2**	

Step 2 – Manitoba non-refundable tax credits

Enter the amount from line 335 of your return		× 8% =		9
Amounts from Schedule 9, *Donations and Gifts*				
Enter the amount from line 345 of Schedule 9		× 8% =	+	10
Enter the amount from line 347 of Schedule 9		× 13.63% =	+	11
Add lines 9, 10, and 11		**Manitoba non-refundable tax credits** 6150	=	12

Go to Step 3

Step 3 – Manitoba adjusted net income

Enter the amount from line 236 of your return			13
Enter the amount from line 250 of your return		–	14
Line 13 minus line 14 (if negative, enter "0")		=	15
Enter the amount you claimed on line 256 of your return for foreign income exempt under a tax treaty	6054	–	16
Line 15 minus line 16 (if negative, enter "0")	**Manitoba adjusted net income**	=	17

Go to Step 4
(if line 17 is $30,000 or less, go directly to **Step 5**)

Step 4 – Manitoba surtax

Enter the amount from line 17			× 2% =			18
Basic credit				600 00	19	
Basic credit for dependent spouse	claim $100			+	20	
Equivalent-to-spouse credit	claim $100			+	21	
Age credit for self	claim $50			+	22	
Age credit for spouse	claim $50	6057		+	23	
Disability credit for spouse	claim $50	6058		+	24	
Disability credit for self or for dependants other than spouse — Number of disability claims		6059	× $50 =	+	25	
Credit for disabled dependants born in 1982 or earlier — Number of disabled dependants		6060	× $40 =	+	26	
Credit for dependent children born in 1982 or later (**Complete the chart on the back**) — Number of dependent children		6062	× $25 =	+	27	
Add lines 19 through 27				=	►	– 28
Line 18 minus line 28 (if negative, enter "0")			**Manitoba surtax**			= 29

Go to Step 5

Step 5 – Manitoba tax

Description	Code	Amount	Line
Enter your Manitoba tax on taxable income from line 8			30
Manitoba tax on net income: Amount from line 17 × 2% =		+	31
Enter your Manitoba surtax, if any, from line 29		+	32
Enter your Manitoba tax on split income, if applicable, from Form T1206	6151	+	• 33
Add lines 30 through 33		=	34
Enter your Manitoba non-refundable tax credits from line 12			35
Manitoba dividend tax credit: Amount from line 120 of your return × 6.27% =	6152	+	• 36
Manitoba overseas employment tax credit Amount from line 426 on Schedule 1 × 47% =	6153	+	• 37
Manitoba minimum tax carry-over: Amount from line 427 on Schedule 1 × 50% =	6154	+	• 38
Add lines 35 through 38		= ► –	39
Line 34 minus line 39 (if negative, enter "0")		=	40

Manitoba tax reduction (see page 2 in the section called "Completing your Manitoba Forms")

Description	Code	Amount	Line
Basic credit		430 00	41
Basic credit for dependent spouse claim $370		+	42
Equivalent-to-spouse credit claim $370		+	43
Age credit for self claim $270		+	44
Age credit for spouse claim $270	6070	+	45
Disability credit for spouse claim $270	6071	+	46
Disability credit for self or for a dependant other than spouse Number of disability claims [6072] × $270 =	6072	+	47
Credit for disabled dependants born in 1982 or earlier Number of disabled dependants [6074] × $250 =	6074	+	48
Credit for dependent children born in 1982 or later **(Complete the chart below)** Number of dependent children [6076] × $250 =	6076	+	49
Add lines 41 through 49		=	50
Enter the amount from line 31		–	51
Line 50 minus line 51 (if negative, enter "0") **Manitoba tax reduction**		= ► –	52
Line 40 minus line 52		=	53
Manitoba additional tax for minimum tax purposes, if applicable, from Form T1219		+	54
Add lines 53 and 54		=	55
Enter the Manitoba political contributions made in 2000	6140		56
Political contribution tax credit: Enter the credit you calculated on page 3 in the section called "Completing your Manitoba Forms" in this booklet (maximum $500)		–	57
Line 55 minus line 57 (if negative, enter "0")		=	58
Labour-sponsored funds tax credit from Form T2C (MAN.) (maximum $750)	6080		• 59
Equity tax credit from Form T2ETC (MAN.) (maximum $1,500)	6081	+	• 60
Add lines 59 and 60		= ► –	61
Line 58 minus line 61 (if negative, enter "0")		=	62
Enter the provincial foreign tax credit, if applicable, from Form T2036		–	63
Line 62 minus line 63 (if negative, enter "0"). Enter the result on line 428 of your return. **Manitoba tax**		=	64

Details of dependent children born in 1982 or later

Complete this chart if you claimed an amount on line 27 or line 49 of this form, or on line 13 of Form MB479, *Manitoba Credits*. If you need more space, attach a separate sheet of paper.

Child's name	Relationship to you	Child's date of birth Year	Month	Day	Social insurance number (if available)

ON 428
T1 General – 2000

Ontario

Ontario Tax

Complete this form and attach a copy of it to your return.
For details, see the section called "Completing Your Ontario Forms" in this booklet.

Step 1 – Ontario tax on taxable income

Enter your **taxable income** from line 260 of your return ______ 1

Use the amount on line 1 to determine which **ONE** of the following columns you have to complete.

	If line 1 is **$30,004** or less		If line 1 is more than **$30,004**, but not more than **$60,009**		If line 1 is more than **$60,009**	
Enter the amount from line 1 in the applicable column		2		2		2
Income threshold	– 0 00	3	– 30,004 00	3	– 60,009 00	3
Line 2 minus line 3 (cannot be negative)	=	4	=	4	=	4
Provincial tax rate	× 6.37%	5	× 9.62%	5	× 11.16%	5
Multiply line 4 by line 5	=	6	=	6	=	6
Tax on income threshold	+ 0 00	7	+ 1,911 00	7	+ 4,798 00	7
Add lines 6 and 7 **Tax on taxable income**	=	8	=	8	=	8
	Go to Step 2		Go to Step 2		Go to Step 2	

Step 2 – Ontario non-refundable tax credits

Enter the amount from line 335 of your return		× 6.37% =		9
Amounts from Schedule 9, *Donations and Gifts*				
Enter the amount from line 345 of Schedule 9		× 6.37% =	+	10
Enter the amount from line 347 of Schedule 9		× 11.16% =	+	11
Add lines 9, 10, and 11		**Ontario non-refundable tax credits** 6150	=	12

Go to Step 3

Step 3 – Ontario tax

Enter your Ontario tax on taxable income from line 8				13
Enter your Ontario tax on split income, if applicable, from Form T1206		6151	+	• 14
Add lines 13 and 14			=	15
Enter your Ontario non-refundable tax credits from line 12			–	16
Line 15 minus line 16 (if negative, enter "0")			=	17

Ontario dividend tax credit Amount from line 120 on your return		× 5.13% =	6152 +	• 18		
Ontario overseas employment tax credit: Amount from line 426 on Schedule 1		× 38.5% =	6153 +	• 19		
Ontario minimum tax carry-over: Amount from line 427 on Schedule 1		× 37.5% =	6154 +	• 20		
Add lines 18, 19, and 20			=	▶	–	21
Line 17 minus line 21 (if negative, enter "0")					=	22
Ontario additional tax for minimum tax purposes, if applicable, from Form T1219					+	23
Add lines 22 and 23					=	24
Ontario surtax						
(Line 24		minus $3,561) × 20% (if negative, enter "0")		25		
(Line 24		minus $4,468) × 36% (if negative, enter "0")	+	26		
Add lines 25 and 26			=	▶	+	27
Add lines 24 and 27					=	28
Enter the Ontario foreign tax credit, if applicable, from Form T2036					–	29
Line 28 minus line 29					=	30

Go to Step 4 on the back

Step 4 – Ontario tax reduction

Enter the amount from line 30 on the front of this form ____ 30

Basic reduction 156|00 31

If you had a spouse on December 31, 2000, **only** the spouse with the **higher net income** can claim the deductions on lines 32 and 33. The term "spouse" is defined on page 11 in the *General Income Tax and Benefit Guide*.

Reduction for dependent children born in 1982 or later
Number of dependent children **6269** ____ × $317 = + ____ 32

Reduction for disabled or infirm dependants
Number of disabled or infirm dependants **6097** ____ × $317 = + ____ 33

Add lines 31, 32, and 33 = ____ 34

If line 34 is equal to or more than line 30, no Ontario tax is payable. Enter "0" on line 38.

Enter the amount from line 34 ____ × 2 = ____ 35

Enter the amount from line 30 – ____ 36

Line 35 minus line 36 (if negative, enter "0") **Ontario tax reduction** = ____ ► – ____ 37

Line 30 minus line 37 (if negative, enter "0"). = ____ 38

If you are claiming Ontario investment and employee ownership tax credits, go to Step 5. Otherwise, enter the amount from line 38 on line 428 of your return.

Step 5 – Ontario investment and employee ownership (OIEO) tax credits

Labour-sponsored investment fund tax credit:

Cost of shares from OIEO(LSIF) certificate(s) ____ × 15% (maximum $750) **6275** ____ • 39

Employee ownership tax credit:

Credit amount from OIEO(EO) certificate(s) (max $4,150) **6280** ____ • 40

Unused employee ownership tax credits from previous years + ____ 41

Add lines 40 and 41 = ____ ► + ____ 42

Add lines 39 and 42 **OIEO tax credits** = ____ ► – ____ 43

Line 38 minus line 43 (if negative, enter "0").
Enter the result on line 428 of your return. **Ontario tax** = ____ 44

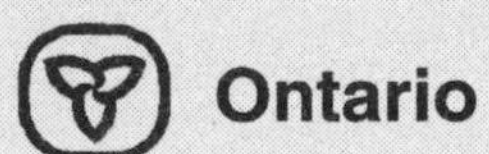

Ontario Credits

ON 479
T1 General – 2000

Attach a completed copy of this form to your return to claim your Ontario credits. **Please note that the instructions on lines 8 and 16 are different depending on your age on December 31, 2000.**

For details, see the section called "Completing Your Ontario Forms" in this booklet.

If you have a spouse, special rules may apply. See page 2 in "Completing Your Ontario Forms" for details. See also the "Involuntary separation" section below.

Enter your net income from line 236 of your return			1
Enter your spouse's net income from line 236 of your spouse's return	6030	+	2
Add lines 1 and 2	**Income for Ontario credits**	=	3

Involuntary separation
If, on December 31, 2000, you and your spouse occupied separate principal residences for medical, educational, or business reasons, **leave line 2 blank** and enter your spouse's address in the area beside box 6089. 6089

Ontario property and sales tax credits

Property tax credit

Rent paid in Ontario in 2000	6110	× 20% =		4
Property tax paid in Ontario in 2000		6112	+	5
College residence		claim $25 6114	+	6
Add lines 4, 5, and 6		**Occupancy cost** 6116	=	7

If under age 65: Enter the amount from line 7 or $250, whichever is **less**
If age 65 or older: Enter the amount from line 7 or $500, whichever is **less** ▶ 8

Amount from line 7		× 10% =	+	9
Add lines 8 and 9. Complete the **Declaration for the property tax credit** box below.		**Property tax credit**	=	10

Sales tax credit

Basic sales tax credit		claim $100 6033			11
Additional credit for spouse		claim $100 6035	+		12
Number of dependent children born in 1982 or later	6099	× $50 =	+		13
Add lines 11, 12, and 13		**Sales tax credit**	=	▶ +	14
Add lines 10 and 14				=	15

If under age 65: (Line 3 minus $4,000) × 2% (if negative, enter "0")
If age 65 or older: (Line 3 minus $22,000) × 4% (if negative, enter "0") ▶ – 16

Line 15 minus line 16 (if negative, enter "0") = 17

Enter the amount from line 17 or $1,000, whichever is **less**.
Enter the amount from line 18 on line 479 of your return unless you are claiming other Ontario tax credits on the back of this form. **Ontario property and sales tax credits** 18

Declaration for the property tax credit (If you need more space, attach a separate sheet of paper.)

I declare the following information about my principal residences in Ontario during 2000:

Address	Number of months resident in 2000	Rent paid in 2000	Property tax paid in 2000	Name of landlord or municipality to whom payment was made

5006-TC

Enter your Ontario property and sales tax credits from line 18 on the front of this form 18

Ontario political contribution tax credit

Ontario political contributions made in 2000 6310 19

Credit calculated on page 4 of "Completing Your Ontario Forms" (maximum $1,000) **Ontario political contribution tax credit** + 20

Ontario home ownership savings plan (OHOSP) tax credit

OHOSP qualifying income:
If you lived with your spouse on December 31, 2000, or you claimed an equivalent-to-spouse amount on line 305 of your return, enter one-half of the amount from line 3. Otherwise, enter the amount from line 3. 6315 21

Enter contributions to your plan in 2000 (maximum $2,000) 6236 22

Enter contributions to your spouse's plan in 2000 (maximum $2,000) 6237 + 23

Total contributions: Add lines 22 and 23 = 24

Look up the amount from line 21 in the table on page 7 of "Completing Your Ontario Forms" and enter the tax credit factor here x 25

Multiply line 24 by the factor on line 25 **OHOSP tax credit** = ▶ + 26

Add lines 18, 20, and 26. **If you are claiming Ontario tax credits for self-employed individuals, complete the next section. Otherwise, enter the amount from line 27 on line 479 of your return.** = 27

ONTARIO TAX CREDITS FOR SELF - EMPLOYED INDIVIDUALS

For details, see page 5 in "Completing Your Ontario Forms"

Number of eligible work placements your business or partnership is claiming under the Ontario co-operative education tax credit program 6325

Number of eligible post-secondary graduates your business or partnership hired under the Ontario graduate transitions tax credit program 6328

Number of eligible individuals with a disability your business or partnership incurred an expense for under the Ontario workplace accessibility tax credit program 6329

Are you claiming one or more of these tax credits as a member of a partnership? 6326 1 ☐ Yes 2 ☐ No

If *yes*, enter the first nine digits of your Business Number. 6327

Ontario co-operative education tax credit
Credit calculated on page 6 of "Completing Your Ontario Forms" (maximum $1,000 per qualifying workplacement) 6320 + •28

Ontario graduate transitions tax credit
Credit calculated on page 6 of "Completing Your Ontario Forms" (maximum $4,000 per qualifying workplacement) 6321 + •29

Ontario workplace child care tax credit
Qualifying expenditures 6332 × 5% = + 30

Ontario workplace accessibility tax credit
Eligible expenditures 6334 × 15% = + 31

Ontario educational technology tax credit
Eligible donations and price discounts 6330 × 5% = + 32

Add lines 27 to 32. Enter the result on line 479 of your return. **Ontario credits** = 33

New Nouveau Brunswick

NB 428
T1 General – 2000

New Brunswick Tax

Complete this form and attach a copy of it to your return.
For details, see the section called "Completing Your New Brunswick Forms" in this booklet.

Step 1 – New Brunswick tax on taxable income

Enter your **taxable income** from line 260 of your return ______ 1

Use the amount on line 1 to determine which **ONE** of the following columns you have to complete.

	If line 1 is **$29,590** or less		If line 1 is more than **$29,590**, but not more than **$59,180**		If line 1 is more than **$59,180**	
Enter the amount from line 1 in the applicable column		2		2		2
Income threshold	– 0 00	3	– 29,590 00	3	– 59,180 00	3
Line 2 minus line 3 (cannot be negative)	=	4	=	4	=	4
Provincial tax rate	× 9.94%	5	× 15.21%	5	× 16.96%	5
Multiply line 4 by line 5	=	6	=	6	=	6
Tax on income threshold	+ 0 00	7	+ 2,941 00	7	+ 7,442 00	7
Add lines 6 and 7 **Tax on taxable income**	=	8	=	8	=	8
	Go to Step 2		**Go to Step 2**		**Go to Step 2**	

Step 2 – New Brunswick non-refundable tax credits

Enter the amount from line 335 of your return		× 9.94% =		9
Amounts from Schedule 9, *Donations and Gifts*				
Enter the amount from line 345 of Schedule 9		× 9.94% =	+	10
Enter the amount from line 347 of Schedule 9		× 16.96% =	+	11
Add lines 9, 10, and 11		**New Brunswick non-refundable tax credits** 6150	=	12
			Go to Step 3	

Step 3 – New Brunswick tax

Enter the amount from line 8					13
New Brunswick tax on split income, if applicable, from Form T1206				6151 +	• 14
Add lines 13 and 14				=	15
Enter your New Brunswick non-refundable tax credits from line 12				–	16
Line 15 minus line 16 (if negative, enter "0")				=	17
N.B. dividend tax credit: Amount from line 120 of your return		× 7.8% =	6152 +	• 18	
N.B. overseas employment tax credit Amount from line 426 on Schedule 1		× 58.5% =	6153 +	• 19	
N.B. minimum tax carry-over: Amount from line 427 on Schedule 1		× 58.5% =	6154 +	• 20	
Add lines 18, 19, and 20			=	► –	21
Line 17 minus line 21 (if negative, enter "0")				=	22
N.B. surtax: (Amount from line 22		minus $13,500) × 8% (if negative, enter "0")		+	23
Add lines 22 and 23				=	24
Enter the provincial foreign tax credit, if applicable, from Form T2036				–	25
Line 24 minus line 25. Enter the result on line 428 of your return.			**New Brunswick tax**	=	26

5004-C

New Nouveau Brunswick

NB 479
T1 General – 2000

New Brunswick Credits

Complete the calculations that apply to you and attach a copy of this form to your return.
For details, see the section called "Completing your New Brunswick Forms" in this booklet.

Political contribution tax credit

Enter New Brunswick political contributions made in 2000	6155		1
The credit you calculated in "Completing Your New Brunswick Forms" (max. $500)			2
Enter your New Brunswick tax from line 428 of your return			3
Enter the amount from line 2 or 3, whichever is **less**	**Political contribution tax credit**		4

Stock savings plan tax credit

Enter your stock savings plan tax credit from Certificate NB-SSP-1	6162		• 5
Enter your unused New Brunswick stock savings plan tax credit from previous years		+	6
Add lines 5 and 6		=	7
Enter your New Brunswick tax from line 428 of your return			8
Enter your political contribution tax credit from line 4		–	9
Line 8 minus line 9		=	10
Enter the amount from line 7 or 10, whichever is **less**	**Stock savings plan tax credit**	+	11
Add lines 4 and 11		=	12

Labour-sponsored venture capital fund tax credit

Labour-sponsored venture capital fund tax credit from Certificate NB-LSVC-1 (maximum $750)	6167		• 13
Enter your New Brunswick tax from line 428 of your return			14
Enter the amount from line 12		–	15
Line 14 minus line 15		=	16
Enter the amount from line 13 or 16, whichever is **less**	**Labour-sponsored venture capital fund tax credit**	+	17
Add lines 12 and 17. Enter the result on line 479 of your return.	**New Brunswick credits**	=	18

5004-TC

Nova Scotia Credits

NS 479
T1 General – 2000

Complete the calculations that apply to you and attach a copy of this form to your return.
For details, see the section called "Completing Your Nova Scotia Forms" in this booklet.

Political contribution and labour-sponsored venture-capital tax credits

Political contribution tax credit

Enter the Nova Scotia political contributions made in 2000 **6210** ______ 1

Enter the credit you calculated in the chart on page 2 of "Completing Your Nova Scotia Forms" (maximum $500) ______ 2

Labour-sponsored venture-capital tax credit

Cost of shares from Form NSLSV ______ x 15% = (max. $525) **6238** + ______ • 3

Add line 2 and line 3 = ______ 4

Enter your Nova Scotia tax from line 428 of your return ______ 5

Enter the amount from line 4 or line 5, whichever is **less**.

Political contribution and labour-sponsored venture-capital tax credits ______ 6

If you are claiming the Nova Scotia equity tax credit or home ownership savings plan tax credit, complete the back of this form. Otherwise, enter the amount from line 6 on line 479 of your return.

5003-TC

NOVA SCOTIA

Nova Scotia Credits

NS 479
T1 General – 2000

Complete the calculations that apply to you and attach a copy of this form to your return.
For details, see the section called "Completing Your Nova Scotia Forms" in this booklet.

Political contribution and labour-sponsored venture-capital tax credits

Political contribution tax credit

Enter the Nova Scotia political contributions made in 2000 6210 ______ 1

Enter the credit you calculated in the chart on page 2 of "Completing Your Nova Scotia Forms" (maximum $500) ______ 2

Labour-sponsored venture-capital tax credit

Cost of shares from Form NSLSV ______ x 15% = (max. $525) 6238 + ______ • 3

Add line 2 and line 3 = ______ 4

Enter your Nova Scotia tax from line 428 of your return ______ 5

Enter the amount from line 4 or line 5, whichever is less.

Political contribution and labour-sponsored venture-capital tax credits ______ 6

If you are claiming the Nova Scotia equity tax credit or home ownership savings plan tax credit, complete the back of this form. Otherwise, enter the amount from line 6 on line 479 of your return.

5003-TC

Enter the amount from line 6 on the front of this form 6

Equity tax credit

Enter your equity tax credit from Form NSETC-1	6220		• 7
Enter your unused Nova Scotia equity tax credit from previous years		+	8
Add lines 7 and 8		=	9
Enter your Nova Scotia tax from line 428 of your return			10
Enter the amount from line 6		–	11
Line 10 minus line 11		=	12
Enter the amount from line 9 or line 12, whichever is **less** (maximum $9,000)	**Equity tax credit**	+	13

Request for carryback of unused equity tax credit

Enter the amount you want to carry back to **1999**	6225	•
Enter the amount you want to carry back to **1998**	6226	•
Enter the amount you want to carry back to **1997**	6227	•

Nova Scotia home ownership savings plan (NSHOSP) tax credit

	You		Your spouse		
Net income from line 236 of the return		+	6030	=	14
Contributions to NSHOSP	You		Your spouse		
In 2000					
In the first 60 days of 2001	6233 +		6234 +		
Total (max. $2,000 per person)	6236 =	+	6237 =	=	15
Credit rate: Enter the amount from the table in "Completing Your Nova Scotia Forms"				× %	16
Multiply line 15 by line 16			**NSHOSP tax credit**	= ► +	17
Add lines 6, 13, and 17. Enter the result on line 479 of your return.			**Nova Scotia credits**	=	18

Enter the amount from line 6 on the front of this form 6

Equity tax credit

Enter your equity tax credit from Form NSETC-1	6220		• 7
Enter your unused Nova Scotia equity tax credit from previous years		+	8
Add lines 7 and 8		=	9
Enter your Nova Scotia tax from line 428 of your return			10
Enter the amount from line 6		–	11
Line 10 minus line 11		=	12
Enter the amount from line 9 or line 12, whichever is **less** (maximum $9,000)	**Equity tax credit**	+	13

Request for carryback of unused equity tax credit

Enter the amount you want to carry back to **1999**	6225	•
Enter the amount you want to carry back to **1998**	6226	•
Enter the amount you want to carry back to **1997**	6227	•

Nova Scotia home ownership savings plan (NSHOSP) tax credit

	You		Your spouse		
Net income from line 236 of the return		+	6030	=	14
Contributions to NSHOSP	You		Your spouse		
In 2000					
In the first 60 days of 2001	6233 +		6234 +		
Total (max. $2,000 per person)	6236 =	+	6237 =	=	15
Credit rate: Enter the amount from the table in "Completing Your Nova Scotia Forms"				× %	16
Multiply line 15 by line 16			**NSHOSP tax credit**	= ► +	17
Add lines 6, 13, and 17. Enter the result on line 479 of your return.			**Nova Scotia credits**	=	18

Nova Scotia Tax

NS 428
T1 General – 2000

Complete this form and attach a copy of it to your return.
For details, see the section called "Completing Your Nova Scotia Forms" in this booklet.

Step 1 – Nova Scotia tax on taxable income

Enter your **taxable income** from line 260 of your return ______ 1

Use the amount on line 1 to determine which **ONE** of the following columns you have to complete.

	If line 1 is **$29,590** or less		If line 1 is more than **$29,590**, but not more than **$59,180**		If line 1 is more than **$59,180**	
Enter the amount from line 1 in the applicable column		2		2		2
Income threshold	– 0 00	3	– 29,590 00	3	– 59,180 00	3
Line 2 minus line 3 (cannot be negative)	=	4	=	4	=	4
Provincial tax rate	× 9.77%	5	× 14.95%	5	× 16.67%	5
Multiply line 4 by line 5	=	6	=	6	=	6
Tax on income threshold	+ 0 00	7	+ 2,891 00	7	+ 7,315 00	7
Add lines 6 and 7 **Tax on taxable income**	=	8	=	8	=	8
	Go to Step 2		**Go to Step 2**		**Go to Step 2**	

Step 2 – Nova Scotia non-refundable tax credits

Enter the amount from line 335 of your return ______ × 9.77% = ______ 9

Amounts from Schedule 9, *Donations and Gifts*

Enter the amount from line 345 of Schedule 9 ______ × 9.77% = + ______ 10

Enter the amount from line 347 of Schedule 9 ______ × 16.67% = + ______ 11

Add lines 9, 10, and 11 **Nova Scotia non-refundable tax credits** 6150 = ______ 12

Go to Step 3

Step 3 – Nova Scotia tax

Enter your Nova Scotia tax on taxable income from line 8			13
Nova Scotia tax on split income, if applicable, from Form T1206	6151	+	• 14
Add lines 13 and 14		=	15
Enter your Nova Scotia non-refundable tax credits from line 12		–	16
Line 15 minus line 16 (if negative, enter "0")		=	17

Nova Scotia dividend tax credit:
Amount from line 120 of your return ______ × 7.7% = 6152 + ______ • 18

Nova Scotia overseas employment tax credit
Amount from line 426 on Schedule 1 ______ × 57.5% = 6153 + ______ • 19

Nova Scotia minimum tax carry-over:
Amount from line 427 on Schedule 1 ______ × 57.5% = 6154 + ______ • 20

Add lines 18, 19, and 20 = ______ ► – ______ 21

Line 17 minus line 21 (if negative, enter "0")	=	22
Nova Scotia additional tax for minimum tax purposes, if applicable, from Form T1219	+	23
Add lines 22 and 23	=	24
Nova Scotia surtax: (Amount from line 24 ______ minus $10,000) x 10% (if negative, enter "0")	+	25
Add lines 24 and 25	=	26
Enter the provincial foreign tax credit, if applicable, from Form T2036	–	27
Line 26 minus line 27	=	28

Go to Step 4 on the back

5003-C

Step 4 – Nova Scotia low-income tax reduction

Enter the amount from line 28 on the front of this form ______ 28

If you had a spouse on December 31, 2000, you and your spouse have to decide who will claim the tax reduction, as **only one of you** can make the claim for your family.

Description				Line
Basic reduction	claim $300 6195			29
Reduction for spouse	claim $300 6197	+		30
Reduction for equivalent-to-spouse	claim $300 6199	+		31
Reduction for dependent children born in 1982 or later: Number of dependent children 6099	x $165 =	+		32
Add lines 29 through 32		=		33

Description			Line
Enter your net income from line 236 of your return			34
Enter your spouse's net income (from line 236 of your spouse's return) 6205	+		35
Net family income: Add lines 34 and 35	=		36
Base amount	–	15,000 00	37
Line 36 minus line 37 (if negative, enter "0")	=		38
Applicable rate	x	5%	39
Multiply line 38 by 5%	=	► –	40

Line 33 minus line 40 (if negative, enter "0").
Nova Scotia low-income tax reduction = ______ ► – ______ 41

Line 28 minus line 41 (if negative, enter "0").
Enter this amount on line 428 of your return. **Nova Scotia tax** = ______ 42

Prince Edward Island

Prince Edward Island Tax and Credit

PE 428
T1 General – 2000

Complete this form and attach a copy of it to your return. See the back of the form for more information.

Prince Edward Island tax

Description	Code	Amount	Line
If you used **Method A** of Schedule 1, enter the amount from line 11 of that schedule If you used **Method B** of Schedule 1, enter the amount from line 23 of that schedule			1
Prince Edward Island income tax rate		x 57.5%	2
Basic Prince Edward Island income tax: Multiply line 1 by 57.5%		=	3
Prince Edward Island surtax: (Amount from line 3 ______ minus $5,200) x 10% (if negative, enter "0")		+	4
Adjusted Prince Edward Island income tax: Add line 3 and line 4		=	5
Enter the provincial foreign tax credit, if applicable, you calculated on Form T2036		–	6
Line 5 minus line 6		=	7
Amount of unused low-income tax reduction available from your spouse's Form PE428, if applicable	6342	–	8
Line 7 minus line 8 (if negative, enter "0")		=	9

If you are claiming an amount on line 8, the amount on line 9 is your Prince Edward Island tax. Enter this amount on line 428 of your return.

Prince Edward Island low-income tax reduction

If you had a spouse on December 31, 2000, you and your spouse must decide which one of you will claim this tax reduction for your family. However, any unused amount can be claimed by the other spouse.

Description	Code	Amount	Line	Amount	Line
Basic reduction — claim $250	6339		10		
Reduction for spouse — claim $250	6340	+	11		
Reduction for equivalent-to-spouse — claim $250	6341	+	12		
Reduction for dependent children born in 1982 or later Number of dependent children 6099 ______ x $200 =		+	13		
Add lines 10 to 13		=	►		14
Enter your net income from line 236 of your return			15		
Enter your spouse's net income from line 236 of your spouse's return	6030	+	16		
Net family income: Add line 15 and line 16		=	17		
Base amount		– 15,000 00	18		
Line 17 minus line 18 (if negative, enter "0")		=	19		
Applicable rate		x 5%	20		
Multiply line 19 by 5%		=	►	–	21
Line 14 minus line 21 (if negative, enter "0") **Prince Edward Island low-income tax reduction**				=	22
Enter the amount from line 7					23
Enter your Prince Edward Island low-income tax reduction from line 22				–	24
Line 23 minus line 24 (if negative, enter "0"). Enter the result on line 428 of your return. **Prince Edward Island tax**				=	25

Amount of unused low-income tax reduction that can be claimed by your spouse

Description	Amount	Line
Enter the amount from line 24		26
Enter the amount from line 23	–	27
Line 26 minus line 27 (if negative, enter "0") **Unused amount**	=	28

Prince Edward Island political contribution tax credit

Description	Code	Amount	Line	Amount	Line
Prince Edward Island political contributions made in 2000	6338		29		
Enter the credit you calculated on the back of this form (maximum $500)			30		
Enter your Prince Edward Island tax from line 428 of your return			31		
Enter the amount from line 30 or line 31, whichever is **less**. Enter this amount on line 479 of your return. **Prince Edward Island political contribution tax credit**					32

5002-C

Newfoundland Tax and Credits

NF 428
T1 General – 2000

Complete this form and attach a copy of it to your return. For details, see the back of the form.

Newfoundland tax

If you used **Method A** of Schedule 1, enter the amount from line 11 of that schedule. If you used **Method B** of Schedule 1, enter the amount from line 23 of that schedule.			1
Newfoundland income tax rate		x 62%	2
Basic Newfoundland income tax: Multiply line 1 by 62%		=	3
Newfoundland surtax			
(Line 3 ______ minus $250) x 6% (if negative, enter "0")	4		
(Line 3 ______ minus $7,050) x 10% (if negative, enter "0")	+ 5		
Add line 4 and line 5	= ►	+	6
Adjusted Newfoundland income tax: Add line 3 and line 6		=	7
Enter the provincial foreign tax credit, if any, you calculated on Form T2036		–	8
Line 7 minus line 8. Enter the result on line 428 of your return. **Newfoundland tax**		=	9

Newfoundland credits

Political contribution tax credit

Newfoundland political contributions made in 2000	6175	10	
Enter the credit you calculated on the back of this form (maximum $500)		11	
Enter your Newfoundland tax from line 9		12	
Enter the amount from line 11 or line 12, whichever is **less** **Political contribution tax credit**			13

Equity tax credit

Enter amount of credit from tax credit certificate NFETC-1	6177	• 14	
Enter your Newfoundland tax from line 9		15	
Enter your political contribution tax credit from line 13	–	16	
Line 15 minus line 16	=	17	
Enter the amount from line 14 or line 17, whichever is **less** **Equity tax credit**		+	18
Add line 13 and line 18. Enter the result on line 479 of your return. **Newfoundland credits**		=	19

5001-C

Yukon

Yukon Tax

YT 428
T1 General – 2000

Complete this form and attach a copy of it to your return. For details, see the back of the form.

If you used **Method A** of Schedule 1, enter the amount from line 11 of that schedule. If you used **Method B** of Schedule 1, enter the amount from line 23 of that schedule.			1
Yukon income tax rate		x 49%	2
Basic Yukon tax: Multiply line 1 by 49%		=	3
Yukon surtax: (Amount from line 3 ______ minus $6,000) x 5% (if negative, enter "0")		+	4
Adjusted Yukon tax: Add line 3 and line 4.		=	5
Enter the territorial foreign tax credit, if any, you calculated on Form T2036		–	6
Line 5 minus line 6		=	7

Yukon low income family tax credit

If your net income (line 236 of your return) is $25,000 or more, enter "0" on line 16.
If your net income is less than $25,000, complete the following calculation.
If you had a spouse on December 31, 2000, only the spouse with the **higher net income** can claim this credit.

Basic credit			Claim $300 **6384**		8
Net income from line 236 of your return		9			
Base amount	– 15,000 00	10			
Line 9 minus line 10 (if negative, enter "0")	=	11			
Applicable rate	x 3%	12			
Multiply line 11 by 3%	=	▶	–		13
Line 8 minus line 13 (if negative, enter "0")			=		14
Amount from line 7	x 80% =				15
Enter the amount from line 14 or 15, whichever is **less**.			**Yukon low income family tax credit**	–	16
Line 7 minus line 16 (if negative, enter "0"). Enter the result on line 428 of your return.			**Yukon tax**	=	17

5011-C

Yukon

Yukon Tax

YT 428
T1 General – 2000

Complete this form and attach a copy of it to your return. For details, see the back of the form.

If you used Method A of Schedule 1, enter the amount from line 11 of that schedule.
If you used Method B of Schedule 1, enter the amount from line 23 of that schedule. 1
Yukon income tax rate × 49% 2
Basic Yukon tax: Multiply line 1 by 49% = 3
Yukon surtax: (Amount from line 3 minus $6,000) × 5% (if negative, enter "0") + 4
Adjusted Yukon tax: Add line 3 and line 4. = 5
Enter the territorial foreign tax credit, if any, you calculated on Form T2036 – 6
Line 5 minus line 6 = 7

Yukon low income family tax credit
If your net income (line 236 of your return) is $25,000 or more, enter "0" on line 16.
If your net income is less than $25,000, complete the following calculation.
If you had a spouse on December 31, 2000, only the spouse with the higher net income can claim this credit.

Basic credit Claim $300 6384 8
Net income from line 236 of your return 9
Base amount – 15,000 00 10
Line 9 minus line 10 (if negative, enter "0") = 11
Applicable rate × 3% 12
Multiply line 11 by 3% = ▶ – 13
Line 8 minus line 13 (if negative, enter "0") = 14
Amount from line 7 × 80% = 15
Enter the amount from line 14 or 15, whichever is less. Yukon low income family tax credit – 16
Line 7 minus line 16 (if negative, enter "0"). Enter the result on line 428 of your return. Yukon tax = 17

5011-C

Yukon

YT 479
T1 General – 2000

Yukon Credits

Complete the calculations that apply to you and attach a copy of this form to your return. For details, see the back of the form.

Yukon political contribution tax credit

Yukon political contributions made in 2000	6385		1
Enter the credit you calculated on the back of this form (maximum $500)			2
Yukon tax from line 428 of your return			3
Enter the amount from line 2 or 3, whichever is **less.** **Yukon political contribution tax credit**			4

Other Yukon tax credits

Small business investment tax credit (Certificate YSBITC-1)	6387		• 5
Unused small business investment tax credit from previous years		+	6
Add lines 5 and 6		=	7
Yukon tax from line 428 of your return			8
Amount from line 4		–	9
Line 8 minus line 9		=	10
Enter the amount from line 7 or line 10 whichever is **less.** (maximum $25,000) **Small business investment tax credit**		+	11

Request for carryback of unused small business investment tax credit
(See the chart on the back)
Enter the amount you want to carry back to **1999** 6380 •

Labour-sponsored venture capital corporation tax credit from the tax credit certificate (Maximum $1,250)	6383		• 12
Yukon tax from line 428 of your return			13
Enter the total of lines 4 and 11		–	14
Line 13 minus line 14		=	15
Enter the amount from line 12 or line 15, whichever is **less** **Labour-sponsored venture capital corporation tax credit**		+	16
Mineral exploration tax credit from Form T1199 **Mineral exploration tax credit**	6388	+	• 17
Add lines 11, 16, and 17 **Other Yukon tax credits**		= ▶ +	18

Yukon First Nations income tax credit

Enter the amount from line 8 of Form YT432 **Yukon First Nations income tax credit**	6386	+	• 19
Add lines 4, 18, and 19. Enter the result on line 479 of your return. **Yukon credits**		=	20

Yukon First Nations Tax

YT 432
T1 General – 2000

Did you live on one of the following Yukon First Nation settlement lands at the end of the year?

First Nation name	Identification number	First Nation name	Identification number
Champagne and Aishihik	11002	Teslin Tlingit	11011
Little Salmon/Carmacks	11006	Tr'ondëk Hwëch'in	11012
Nacho Nyak Dun	11007	Vuntut Gwitchin	11013
Selkirk	11009		

If *yes*, enter the First Nation name and Identification number in the "Yukon First Nation Information" area on page 1 of your return. If you have federal or Yukon tax payable, attach a completed copy of this form, Form YT428, *Yukon Tax*, and Form YT479, *Yukon Credits*, to your return. See the back for details.

Federal refundable First Nations abatement

Enter the amount from line 1 of Form YT428			1
Federal abatement rate	x 75%		2
Multiply line 1 by 75%. Enter the result on line 441 of your return.	=	▶	3

Yukon First Nations income tax credit

Enter the amount from line 17 of Form YT428			4
Enter the amount from line 18 of Form YT479	–		5
Line 4 minus line 5 (if negative, enter "0")	=		6
Yukon income tax credit rate	x 95%		7
Multiply line 6 by 95%. Enter the result on line 19 of Form YT479	=	▶ +	8
Add line 3 and line 8. Enter the result on line 432 of your return.	**Yukon First Nations tax**	=	9

5011-C1

Yukon First Nations Tax

YT 432
T1 General – 2000

Did you live on one of the following Yukon First Nation settlement lands at the end of the year?

First Nation name	Identification number	First Nation name	Identification number
Champagne and Aishihik	11002	Teslin Tlingit	11011
Little Salmon/Carmacks	11006	Tr'ondëk Hwëch'in	11012
Nacho Nyak Dun	11007	Vuntut Gwitchin	11013
Selkirk	11009		

If *yes*, enter the First Nation name and Identification number in the "Yukon First Nation Information" area on page 1 of your return. If you have federal or Yukon tax payable, attach a completed copy of this form, Form YT428, *Yukon Tax*, and Form YT479, *Yukon Credits*, to your return. See the back for details.

Federal refundable First Nations abatement

Enter the amount from line 1 of Form YT428			1
Federal abatement rate	x 75%		2
Multiply line 1 by 75%. Enter the result on line 441 of your return.	=	▶	3

Yukon First Nations income tax credit

Enter the amount from line 17 of Form YT428			4
Enter the amount from line 18 of Form YT479	–		5
Line 4 minus line 5 (if negative, enter "0")	=		6
Yukon income tax credit rate	x 95%		7
Multiply line 6 by 95%. Enter the result on line 19 of Form YT479	=	▶ +	8
Add line 3 and line 8. Enter the result on line 432 of your return.	**Yukon First Nations tax**	=	9

5011-C1

Northwest Territories Tax and Credits

NT 428
T1 General – 2000

Complete this form and attach a copy of it to your return. For details, see the back of this form and the sheet called *About Northwest Territories Credits.*

Northwest Territories tax

Description		Amount	Line
If you used **Method A** of Schedule 1, enter the amount from line 11 of that schedule. If you used **Method B** of Schedule 1, enter the amount from line 23 of that schedule.			1
Northwest Territories income tax rate		x 45%	2
Basic Northwest Territories tax: Multiply line 1 by 45%		=	3
Enter the territorial foreign tax credit, if any, you calculated on Form T2036		–	4
Line 3 minus line 4. Enter the result on line 428 of your return	**Northwest Territories tax**	=	5

Northwest Territories tax credits

Cost-of-living tax credit

Description		Amount	Line
Enter your net income from line 236 of your return			6
Enter the amount you claimed on line 250 of your return		–	7
Line 6 minus line 7 (if negative, enter "0")		=	8
Enter the amount you claimed on line 256 of your return for foreign income exempt under a tax treaty	6054	–	9
Line 8 minus line 9 (if negative, enter "0")	**Adjusted net income**	=	10
Enter the credit you calculated on the back of this form (maximum $645)	**Cost-of-living tax credit** 6250		11

Political contribution tax credit

Description		Amount	Line
Northwest Territories political contributions made in 2000	6255		12
Enter the credit you calculated on the back of this form (maximum $500).			13
Enter your Northwest Territories tax from line 5			14
Enter the amount from line 13 or line 14, whichever is **less**	**Political contribution tax credit**	+	15

Risk capital investment tax credits

Labour-sponsored venture capital corporation tax credit

Description	Code	Amount			Result	Line
Cost of shares from Form T2C(NWT) (maximum $100,000)	6241		A			
Enter the amount from line A or $5,000, whichever is **less**		–	B	x 15% =		16
Line A minus line B		=	C	x 30% =	+	17

Employee venture capital corporation, Community endorsed venture capital corporation, and Territorial business corporation direct investment tax credits

Description	Code	Amount		Result	Line
Cost of shares from Form T2C(NWT) (maximum $100,000)	6243		x 30% =	+	18
Add lines 16 to 18				=	19
Annual limit: $30,000 **minus** (amount from line 16			) =		20
Enter the amount from line 19, or 20, whichever is **less**					21
Unused risk capital investment tax credit from previous years				+	22
Add lines 21 and line 22				=	23
Enter your Northwest Territories tax from line 5					24
Enter your political contribution tax credit from line 15				–	25
Line 24 minus line 25				=	26

Description		Amount	Line
Enter the amount from line 20, 23, or 26, whichever is **less**	**Risk capital investment tax credits**	+	27
Add lines 11, 15, and 27. Enter the result on line 479 of your return.	**Northwest Territories credits**	=	28

Request for carryback of unused risk capital investment tax credits

Description	Code	Amount	
Enter the amount you want to carry back to **1999** (see the chart on the "About NWT Credits")	6244		•
Enter the amount you want to carry back to **1998** (see the chart on the "About NWT Credits")	6245		•

ᓄᓇᕗᑦ
NUNAVUT

Nunavut Tax and Credits

NU 428
T1 General – 2000

Complete this form and attach a copy of it to your return. For details, see the back of this form and the sheet called *About Nunavut Credits.*

Nunavut tax

			Line
If you used **Method A** of Schedule 1, enter the amount from line 11 of that schedule. If you used **Method B** of Schedule 1, enter the amount from line 23 of that schedule.			1
Nunavut income tax rate		x 45%	2
Basic Nunavut tax: Multiply line 1 by 45%		=	3
Enter the territorial foreign tax credit, if any, you calculated on Form T2036		–	4
Line 3 minus line 4. Enter the result on line 428 of your return.	**Nunavut tax**	=	5

Nunavut credits

Cost-of-living tax credit

			Line
Enter your net income from line 236 of your return			6
Enter the amount you claimed on line 250 of your return		–	7
Line 6 minus line 7 (if negative, enter "0")		=	8
Enter the amount you claimed on line 256 of your return for foreign income exempt under a tax treaty	6054	–	9
Line 8 minus line 9 (if negative, enter "0")	**Adjusted net income**	=	10
Enter the credit you calculated on the back of this form (maximum $645)	**Cost-of-living tax credit** 6390		11

Political contribution tax credit

			Line
Nunavut political contributions made in 2000	6391		12
Enter the credit you calculated on the back of this form (maximum $500)			13
Enter your Nunavut tax from line 5			14
Enter the amount from line 13 or line 14, whichever is **less**	**Political contribution tax credit**	+	15

Risk capital investment tax credits

Labour-sponsored venture capital corporation tax credit

						Line
Cost of shares from Form T2C(NWT) (maximum $100,000)	6393		A			
Enter the amount from line A or $5,000, whichever is **less.**		–	B	x 15%	=	16
Line A minus line B		=	C	x 30%	= +	17

Employee venture capital corporation, Community endorsed venture capital corporation, and territorial business corporation direct investment tax credits

				Line
Cost of shares from Form T2C(NWT) (maximum $100,000)	6395	x 30%	= +	18
Add lines 16 to 18			=	19
Annual limit: $30,000 **minus** (amount from line 16)			=	20
Enter the amount from line 19, or 20, whichever is **less**				21
Unused risk capital investment tax credit from previous years			+	22
Add lines 21 and line 22			=	23
Enter your Nunavut tax from line 5				24
Enter your political contribution tax credit from line 15			–	25
Line 24 minus line 25			=	26
Enter the amount from line 20, 23, or 26, whichever is **less**	**Risk capital investment tax credits**		+	27
Add lines 11, 15, and 27. Enter the result on line 479 of your return.	**Nunavut credits**		=	28

Request for carryback of unused risk capital investment tax credits

Enter the amount you want to carry back to **1999** (see the chart on the *About Nunavut Credits* Sheet)	6396	•
Enter the amount you want to carry back to **1998** (see the chart on the *About Nunavut Credits* Sheet)	6397	•

2001 SASKATCHEWAN PERSONAL TAX CREDITS RETURN

TD1SK

Do I have to complete this form?

Complete this SaskatchewanTD1 form if you completed a federal Form TD1, *2001 Personal Tax Credits Return*, and you are:

- an employee working in Saskatchewan; or
- a pensioner residing in Saskatchewan.

If you complete this form, be sure to sign and date it on the back page and give it to your employer or payer with your federal TD1 form. Your employer or payer will use both forms to determine the amount of your payroll tax deductions.

Last name	First name and initial(s)	Date of birth (YYYY/MM/DD)	Employee number
Address including postal code		**For non-residents only** – Country of permanent residence	Social insurance number

1. Basic personal amount – Every person employed in Saskatchewan and every pensioner residing in Saskatchewan can claim this amount. If you will have more than one employer in 2001, see the section called "Income from other employers or payers" on the back. **$8,000**

2a. Age amount – If you will be 65 or older on December 31, 2001, and your net income from all sources will be $26,941 or less, enter $3,619. If your net income will be between $26,941 and $51,068 and you want to calculate a partial claim, get the *Worksheet for the 2001 Saskatchewan Personal Tax Credits Return* (TD1SK-WS) and complete the appropriate section.

2b. Senior supplement amount – Every senior who resides in Saskatchewan can claim the senior supplement amount. If you will be 65 or older on December 31, 2001, enter $500, regardless of your estimated net income.

3. Pension income amount – If you will receive regular pension payments from a pension plan or fund (excluding Canada or Quebec Pension Plans (CPP/QPP), Old Age Security and guaranteed income supplements), enter $1,000 or your estimated annual pension income, whichever is less.

4a. Tuition and education amounts (full-time) – If you are a student enrolled full-time at a university, college, or educational institution certified by Human Resources Development Canada, enter the total of the tuition fees you will pay, if more than $100 per institution, plus $200 for each month that you will be enrolled full-time.

4b. Tuition and education amounts (part-time) – If you are a student enrolled part-time at a university, college, or educational institution certified by Human Resources Development Canada, enter the total of the tuition fees you will pay, if more than $100 per institution, plus $60 for each month that you will be enrolled part-time.

5. Disability amount – If you will claim the disability amount on your income tax return by using Form T2201, *Disability Tax Credit Certificate*, enter $4,400.

6. Spousal amount – If you are supporting your spouse or common-law partner who lives with you, and his or her net income for the year will be $800 or less, enter $8,000. If his or her net income for the year will be between $800 and $8,800 and you want to calculate a partial claim, get the *Worksheet for the 2001 Saskatchewan Personal Tax Credits Return* (TD1SK-WS) and complete the appropriate section.

7. Equivalent-to-spouse amount – If you do not have a spouse or common-law partner and support a dependent relative who lives with you, and his or her net income for the year will be $800 or less, enter $8,000. If his or her net income for the year will be between $800 and $8,800 and you want to calculate a partial claim, get the *Worksheet for the 2001 Saskatchewan Personal Tax Credits Return* (TD1SK-WS) and complete the appropriate section.

8. Child amount – If you are supporting children who will be under 18 on December 31, 2001, enter $1,500 for each child, regardless of the child's estimated net income. You cannot claim an amount for a child claimed on line 7.

9. Caregiver amount – If you are taking care of a person who lives with you, whose net income for the year will be $11,953 or less, and who is **either** your or your spouse's or common-law partner's:

- parent or grandparent age 65 or older, **or**
- relative age 18 or older who is dependent on you because of an infirmity,

enter $2,446. If the dependant's net income for the year will be between $11,953 and $14,399 and you want to calculate a partial claim, get the *Worksheet for the 2001 Saskatchewan Personal Tax Credits Return* (TD1SK-WS) and complete the appropriate section.

10. Amount for infirm dependant age 18 or older – If you are supporting an infirm dependant age 18 or older who is your or your spouse's or common-law partner's relative, who lives in Canada, and his or her net income for the year will be $4,966 or less, enter $2,446. You cannot claim an amount for a dependant claimed on line 9. If the dependant's net income for the year will be between $4,966 and $7,412 and you want to calculate a partial claim, get the *Worksheet for the 2001 Saskatchewan Personal Tax Credits Return* (TD1SK-WS) and complete the appropriate section.

11a. Amounts transferred from your spouse or common-law partner – If your spouse or common-law partner will not use all of his or her age amount, pension income amount, tuition and education amounts (maximum $5,000), or disability amount on his or her income tax return, enter the unused part.

11b. Amounts transferred from your dependant – If your dependant will not use all of his or her tuition and education amounts (maximum $5,000) or disability amount on his or her income tax return, enter the unused part.

12. TOTAL CLAIM AMOUNT – Add lines 1 through line 11b. Your employer or payer will use your claim amount to determine the amount of your provincial payroll tax deductions. **$**

Form continues on the back ——

Forms and publications

You can get the forms and publications mentioned on this form from the Internet at **www.ccra-adrc.gc.ca** or by calling 1-800-959-2221.

Why is there a Saskatchewan TD1 form?

Saskatchewan has adopted a new method of calculating personal income tax. This new method is called "Tax on Income." With this method, your provincial income tax will no longer be a percentage of federal income tax. You will calculate your provincial income tax directly on your taxable income, according to Saskatchewan's own tax rates and brackets, as well as Saskatchewan's own non-refundable tax credits. Similarly, your employer or the payer of your pension will now calculate the provincial tax to deduct from your pay or pension cheque using the "Tax on income" method.

Your employer or payer uses the personal tax credit amounts you claim on your TD1 form to calculate your payroll tax deductions. With the former "Tax on tax" method, there was only a federal TD1 form. With "Tax on income", there is also a Saskatchewan TD1 form because Saskatchewan established its own values for many of the personal tax credit amounts.

Income from other employers or payers

Your earnings may not be subject to payroll tax deductions if your employment income from all employers for the year will be less than your total claim amount.

Will your total employment income for the year be less than your total claim amount on line 12 on the front page? Yes ☐ No ☐

If you have more than one employer or payer and you have already claimed personal tax credit amounts on another Form TD1SK for 2001, you can choose not to claim them again. By doing this, you may not have to pay as much tax when you file your income tax return. To choose this option, enter "0" on line 12 on the front page and do not complete lines 2 to 11.

Certification

I certify that the information given in this return is, to the best of my knowledge, correct and complete.

Signature ______________________ Date ____________

It is a serious offence to make a false return.

Printed in Canada

WORKSHEET FOR THE 2001 SASKATCHEWAN PERSONAL TAX CREDITS RETURN

TD1SK-WS

Complete this worksheet if you want to calculate partial claims for your Form TD1SK, *2001 Saskatchewan Personal Tax Credits Return*, for the following:

- Age amount
- Spousal amount
- Equivalent-to-spouse amount
- Caregiver amount
- Amount for infirm dependant age 18 or older

Do not give your completed worksheet to your employer or payer. Keep it for your records.

Line 2a of your TD1SK form – Age amount

If you will be 65 or older on December 31, 2001, and your estimated net income from all sources for the year will be between $26,941 and $51,068, calculate your allowable amount as follows:

Maximum age amount			$3,619	1
Your estimated net income for the year		2		
Base amount	$26,941	3		
Line 2 minus line 3	=	4		
Multiply the amount on line 4 by 15%	X 15% =	→	–	5
Line 1 minus line 5. Enter this amount on line 2a of your TD1SK form.			=	

Line 6 of your TD1SK form – Spousal amount

If your spouse's or common-law partner's estimated net income for the year (including the income earned before and during the marriage or common-law relationship) will be between $800 and $8,800, calculate your allowable amount as follows:

Base amount	$8,800	1
Your spouse's or common-law partner's estimated net income for the year	–	2
Line 1 minus line 2. Enter this amount on line 6 of your TD1SK form.	=	

Line 7 of your TD1SK form – Equivalent-to-spouse amount

If your dependant's estimated net income for the year will be between $800 and $8,800, calculate your allowable amount as follows:

Base amount	$8,800	1
Your dependant's estimated net income for the year	–	2
Line 1 minus line 2. Enter this amount on line 7 of your TD1SK form.	=	

Line 9 of your TD1SK form – Caregiver amount

If your dependant's estimated net income for the year will be between $11,953 and $14,399, calculate your allowable amount as follows:

Base amount	$14,399	1
Your dependant's estimated net income for the year	–	2
Line 1 minus line 2 (maximum $2,446)	=	3
Minus: the equivalent-to-spouse amount claimed on line 7 of your TD1SK form for this person	–	4
Line 3 minus line 4. Enter this amount on line 9 of your TD1SK form.	=	

Line 10 of your TD1SK form – Amount for infirm dependant age 18 or older

You cannot claim this amount for a dependant for whom you claimed the caregiver amount on line 9 of your TD1SK form.

If your infirm dependant's estimated net income for the year will be between $4,966 and $7,412, calculate your allowable amount as follows:

Base amount	$7,412	1
Your infirm dependant's estimated net income for the year	–	2
Line 1 minus line 2 (maximum $2,446)	=	3
Minus: the equivalent-to-spouse amount claimed on line 7 of your TD1SK form for this person	–	4
Line 3 minus line 4. Enter this amount on line 10 of your TD1SK form.	=	

(Ce formulaire existe en français.)

MANITOBA MINERAL TAX REBATE

Use this form if you are an individual who paid mineral taxes to the Province of Manitoba, and you earned resource profits in Manitoba for which you deducted a resource allowance.

- **Mineral taxes** are taxes assessed, levied, and paid under the Manitoba *Oil and Gas Production Tax Act*.
- **Resource allowance** is defined in paragraph 20(1)(*v.1*) of the federal *Income Tax Act*.
- **Resource profits** is defined in Part XII of the federal *Income Tax Regulations*.

Attach to your return a completed copy of this form and any documents that prove you paid Manitoba mineral taxes.
Also, send a completed copy of this form and the documents to the Manitoba Tax Assistance Office, Room 309, Norquay Building, 401 York Avenue, Winnipeg MB R3C 0P8.

Name (print)	Social insurance number
Address	
	Tax year ▶

Revised taxable income for tax rebate purposes

Taxable income from line 260 of your return .... ______ 1

Resource allowance allocated to Manitoba:

Resource allowance claimed .... ______ 2

Percentage of resource profits earned in Manitoba .... x ______ % 3

Multiply line 2 by the percentage on line 3 .... = ______ ▶ + ______ 4

Add line 1 and line 4 .... = ______ 5

Mineral taxes paid to Manitoba for the year .... – ______ 6

Line 5 minus line 6 .... **Revised taxable income for tax rebate purposes** = ______ 7

Manitoba tax payable

Calculate the Manitoba tax you would pay on your taxable income before the rebate calculation (line 1) .... ______ 8

Calculate the Manitoba tax you would pay on the revised taxable income for tax rebate purposes (line 7) .... ______ 9

Enter on line 428 of your return the amount from line 8 or line 9, whichever is **less**.

Certification

I certify that the information given on this form is correct and complete.

Signature ______________________ Date ______________

ALBERTA ROYALTY TAX REBATE (INDIVIDUALS)

Use this form if you are an individual who had attributed Canadian royalty income in the tax year and had either a permanent establishment in Alberta **or** were resident in Alberta on the last day of the year. **Attributed Canadian royalty income** is defined in paragraph 11(1)(*a*) and subsection 11(1.2) of the Alberta *Income Tax Act*.

Attach a completed copy of this form to your return.

Tax year ▶

Tax rebate calculation

Attributed Canadian royalty income carried forward from the year ______		1
Attributed Canadian royalty income for the year (if negative, enter "0")	+	2
Total attributed Canadian royalty income: Add line 1 and line 2	=	3
Percentage of resource income allocated to Alberta, if applicable	x %	4
Attributed Canadian royalty income allocated to Alberta: Multiply line 3 by the percentage on line 4	=	5
Adjusted Alberta income tax: (line 8 of Form T1C(ALTA.) or line H of Form T2203, *Provincial and Territorial Taxes – Multiple Jurisdictions*)		6

Royalty tax rebate available:

Alberta income tax rate X $\frac{\text{Basic federal tax *}}{\text{Taxable income *}}$ X line 5 = ... 7

Alberta surtax:
(line 4 of Form T1C(ALTA.) or line G of Form T2203) 8

Basic Alberta income tax: (line 3 of Form T1C(ALTA.) or line F of Form T2203)			9
Enter the amount from line 7	–		10
Line 9 minus line 10	=		11
	–	3,500 00	12
Line 11 minus line 12	=		13
Multiply line 13 by 8% and enter the result here	–		14
Line 8 minus line 14 (if negative, enter "0")	=	▶ +	15
Multiply line 5 by 0.005 and enter the result here		+	16
Total rebate available: Add lines 7, 15, and 16		= ▶	17

Enter the amount from line 6 or line 17, whichever is **less**.
Enter this amount on line 9 of Form T1C(ALTA.) or line I of Form T2203 .... **Alberta royalty tax rebate** 18

Attributed Canadian royalty income carried forward

Enter the amount from line 7		19
Basic Alberta income tax: (line 3 of Form T1C(ALTA.) or line F of Form T2203)	–	20
Line 19 minus line 20 (if negative, enter "0")	=	21

Attributed Canadian royalty income carried forward to the year 20___:

$$\frac{\text{Line 21}}{\text{Alberta income tax rate X}\left(\frac{\text{Basic federal tax *}}{\text{Taxable income *}}\right)\text{X line 4}} = \text{............} \quad 22$$

If no basic federal tax is payable, the attributed Canadian royalty income carried forward is the amount on line 3.

* If you are subject to minimum tax, change "Basic federal tax" and "Taxable income" in the calculations on line 7 and line 22 to read:

$\frac{\text{Minimum amount}}{\text{Net adjusted taxable income}}$ (line 46 of Form T691, *Alternative Minimum Tax*) / (line 37 of Form T691, *Alternative Minimum Tax*)

Certification

I certify that the information given on this form is correct and complete.

Signature ______________________ Date ____________

BRITISH COLUMBIA ROYALTY AND DEEMED INCOME REBATE (INDIVIDUALS)

Use this form if you are an individual subject to British Columbia income tax, and your income is affected by paragraph 12(1)(*o*), 12(1)(*z.5*), 18(1)(*m*), or 20(1)(*v.1*), or by subsection 69(6) or 69(7) of the federal *Income Tax Act*. Attach a completed copy of this form to your return.

Taxable income for the current tax year calculated without reference to paragraph 12(1)(*o*), 12(1)(*z.5*), 18(1)(*m*)*, or 20(1)(*v.1*), or to subsection 69(6) or 69(7) of the federal *Income Tax Act* ** .... ______ 1

* Calculate taxable income as if paragraph 18(1)(*m*) permits only a deduction for amounts paid or payable under the *Mining Tax Act*, *Mineral Tax Act*, or any other prescribed act, or for a royalty for 1976 under the *Mineral Royalties Act*.

** Calculate the portion of income from natural gas produced in British Columbia that was not sold to the British Columbia Petroleum Corporation without reference to paragraph 20(1)(*v.1*).

British Columbia tax that would be payable if you were not claiming this rebate .... ______ 2

British Columbia tax that would be payable if you were not claiming this rebate and you used the amount on line 1 to determine your basic federal tax .... – ______ 3

British Columbia royalty and deemed income rebate/addition to British Columbia tax payable: Line 2 minus line 3 (if negative, show this amount in brackets) .... = ______ 4

If the amount on line 4 is positive, deduct it from the "Adjusted British Columbia income tax" on line 5 of Form T1C(B.C.)TC, *British Columbia Tax*.

If the amount on line 4 is negative, adjust the "Adjusted British Columbia income tax" on line 5 of Form T1C(B.C.)TC, *British Columbia Tax*, by adding the amount from line 4 above as a positive value (without the brackets).

Certification

I certify that the information given on this form is correct and complete.

Signature ______________________ Date ______________

T81(IND.) (99) (Français au verso) 0680 Canada
Printed in Canada

BRITISH COLUMBIA

BRITISH COLUMBIA ROYALTY AND DEEMED INCOME REBATE (INDIVIDUALS)

Use this form if you are an individual subject to British Columbia income tax, and your income is affected by paragraph 12(1)(*o*), 12(1)(*z.5*), 18(1)(*m*), or 20(1)(*v.1*), or by subsection 69(6) or 69(7) of the federal *Income Tax Act*. Attach a completed copy of this form to your return.

Taxable income for the current tax year calculated without reference to paragraph 12(1)(*o*), 12(1)(*z.5*), 18(1)(*m*)*, or 20(1)(*v.1*), or to subsection 69(6) or 69(7) of the federal *Income Tax Act* ** .... ______ 1

* Calculate taxable income as if paragraph 18(1)(*m*) permits only a deduction for amounts paid or payable under the *Mining Tax Act*, *Mineral Tax Act*, or any other prescribed act, or for a royalty for 1976 under the *Mineral Royalties Act*.

** Calculate the portion of income from natural gas produced in British Columbia that was not sold to the British Columbia Petroleum Corporation without reference to paragraph 20(1)(*v.1*).

British Columbia tax that would be payable if you were not claiming this rebate .... ______ 2

British Columbia tax that would be payable if you were not claiming this rebate and you used the amount on line 1 to determine your basic federal tax .... – ______ 3

British Columbia royalty and deemed income rebate/addition to British Columbia tax payable: Line 2 minus line 3 (if negative, show this amount in brackets) .... = ______ 4

If the amount on line 4 is positive, deduct it from the "Adjusted British Columbia income tax" on line 5 of Form T1C(B.C.)TC, *British Columbia Tax*.

If the amount on line 4 is negative, adjust the "Adjusted British Columbia income tax" on line 5 of Form T1C(B.C.)TC, *British Columbia Tax*, by adding the amount from line 4 above as a positive value (without the brackets).

Certification

I certify that the information given on this form is correct and complete.

Signature ______________________ Date ______________

T81(IND.) (99) (Français au verso) 0680 Canada
Printed in Canada

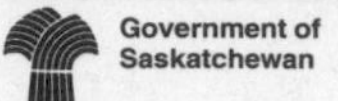

SASKATCHEWAN ROYALTY TAX REBATE

Use this form if you are an individual who had attributed Canadian royalties and taxes in the tax year, and you were:

- resident in Saskatchewan on the last day of the tax year; or
- not resident in Saskatchewan on the last day of the tax year but had taxable income earned in Saskatchewan in accordance with Part XXVI of the *Income Tax Regulations.*

If you are completing a return for a corporation, use Schedule 400 of the T2 return.

Attach a completed copy of this form to your return and send a completed copy to the Government of Saskatchewan, Department of Finance, 9th floor, 2350 Albert Street, Regina SK S4P 4A6.

Sections and paragraphs referred to in this form are sections and paragraphs of the federal *Income Tax Act* unless otherwise specified.

Name (print)	Social insurance number
Address (print)	Tax year ▶

Attributed Canadian royalties and taxes

Attributed Canadian royalties and taxes as a result of transactions with Saskatchewan		1
Attributed Canadian royalties and taxes as a result of transactions with territories or other provinces	+	2
Attributed Canadian royalties and taxes under clause 2(1)(*a*) of *The Saskatchewan Royalty Tax Rebate Regulations:* Add line 1 and line 2	=	3

Depletion adjustment factor

Complete this calculation if you are claiming **earned depletion** under section 65 on your return for the tax year.

Resource profits under Part XII of the *Income Tax Regulations*		4
Attributed Canadian royalties and taxes from line 3	–	5
Line 4 minus line 5 (can be a positive or negative amount)	=	6
Resource allowance deduction under paragraph 20(1)(*v.1*)	+	7
Add line 6 and line 7 (if negative, enter "0")	=	8
Depletion allowance deducted under section 65		9
Line 8 ________ x 25%	–	10
Depletion adjustment factor: Line 9 minus line 10 (can be a positive or negative amount)	=	11
Saskatchewan depletion adjustment carryforward at the end of the preceding tax year	+	12
Saskatchewan depletion adjustment carryforward for the tax year: Add line 11 and line 12 (if negative, enter "0")	=	13

Tax rebate

Attributed Canadian royalties and taxes from line 3		14
Resource allowance deduction from line 7	–	15
Line 14 minus line 15	=	16
Depletion adjustment: If line 11 is positive or zero, enter the amount from line 11, and subtract line 17 from line 16. If line 11 is negative, enter (line 11 x –1.0) **or** line 12, whichever is **less**, and add line 16 and line 17.	±	17
Adjusted attributed Canadian royalties and taxes: See the instruction on line 17 (if negative, enter "0")	=	18
Percentage of income earned allocated to Saskatchewan under Part XXVI of the *Income Tax Regulations*: * Income earned in the tax year in Saskatchewan / Income for the year x 100	x %	19
Adjusted attributed Canadian royalties and taxes allocated to Saskatchewan: Line 18 x line 19	=	20
Federal adjusted basic tax rate (see the calculation below)	x %	21
Federal basic tax on adjusted Canadian royalties and taxes allocated to Saskatchewan: Line 20 x line 21	=	22
Available credit for tax year: Line 22 ________ x Saskatchewan income tax rate		23
Royalty tax rebate carryforward at the end of the preceding tax year	+	24
Royalty tax rebate: Add line 23 and line 24	=	25
Net Saskatchewan tax payable as on your T1C (SASK.) **before** deducting Saskatchewan royalty tax rebate		26
Saskatchewan royalty tax rebate: Enter line 25 or line 26, whichever is **less**	–	27
Net Saskatchewan tax payable after rebate: Line 26 minus line 27. Enter the result on line 428 of your return	=	28
Royalty tax rebate carryforward at end of tax year: Line 25 ________ minus line 27 ________	=	29

* When an individual has no income for the year, see section 7 (*a*) of *The Saskatchewan Royalty Tax Rebate Regulations.*

Federal adjusted basic tax rate

Enter your taxable income from line 260 of your return		30
Adjusted attributed Canadian royalties and taxes from line 18	–	31
Revised taxable income: Line 30 minus line 31 (if negative, enter "0")	=	32

On line 21, enter the marginal federal tax rate for the revised taxable income (line 32) for the applicable year.

Certification

I certify that the information given on this form is correct and complete.

Signature ______________________ Date ______________

T82 (99)
Printed in Canada

(Français au verso)

1162

Canada

ALBERTA STOCK SAVINGS PLAN TAX CREDIT

Use this form if you are an individual who resided in Alberta on the last day of a tax year and you had an unused stock savings plan tax credit to carry forward to that tax year. On this form, we will refer to the year you indicate below as **this year**. **Last year** is the year just before the applicable tax year, and **next year** is the year right after.

Attach a completed copy of this form to your return. Keep a copy for your records.

Tax year ▶

Unused Alberta stock savings plan tax credit from last year:
If **this year** is 1992, use the amount from line F of the 1991 Form T89.
If **this year** is after 1992, use the amount from line 6 of last year's Form T89 1

Alberta tax from line 428 of your return for this year 2
Alberta political contribution tax credit for this year from Form T1C (ALTA.) .... – 3
Line 2 minus line 3 (if negative, enter "0") .... = 4
Alberta stock savings plan tax credit for this year (line 1 or line 4, whichever is **less**):
If **this year** is 1996 or after, include this amount on line 479 of your return.
If **this year** is 1995 or before, include this amount on line 480 of your return .... – 5

Unused Alberta stock savings plan tax credit to carry forward to next year: Line 1 minus line 5 .... = 6

Certification

I certify that the information given on this form is correct and complete.

Signature ____________________ Date ____________

Alberta

ALBERTA STOCK SAVINGS PLAN TAX CREDIT

Use this form if you are an individual who resided in Alberta on the last day of a tax year and you had an unused stock savings plan tax credit to carry forward to that tax year. On this form, we will refer to the year you indicate below as **this year**. **Last year** is the year just before the applicable tax year, and **next year** is the year right after.

Attach a completed copy of this form to your return. Keep a copy for your records.

Tax year ▶

Unused Alberta stock savings plan tax credit from last year:
If **this year** is 1992, use the amount from line F of the 1991 Form T89.
If **this year** is after 1992, use the amount from line 6 of last year's Form T89 1

Alberta tax from line 428 of your return for this year 2
Alberta political contribution tax credit for this year from Form T1C (ALTA.) .... – 3
Line 2 minus line 3 (if negative, enter "0") .... = 4
Alberta stock savings plan tax credit for this year (line 1 or line 4, whichever is **less**):
If **this year** is 1996 or after, include this amount on line 479 of your return.
If **this year** is 1995 or before, include this amount on line 480 of your return .... – 5

Unused Alberta stock savings plan tax credit to carry forward to next year: Line 1 minus line 5 .... = 6

Certification

I certify that the information given on this form is correct and complete.

Signature ____________________ Date ____________

T89 (99)
Printed in Canada
(Français au verso) 2313 Canada

Canada Customs and Revenue Agency / Agence des douanes et du revenu du Canada

ALTERNATIVE MINIMUM TAX

Use this form to calculate your 1999 federal tax payable under Alternative Minimum Tax.
If you are completing a return for a trust, use Schedule 12 of the T3 return.

Complete parts 1, 2, and 8 if you do not have to pay minimum tax in 1999 and you are applying a minimum tax carryover from previous years against your 1999 tax payable. Alternative Minimum Tax does not apply to a person who died in 1999, or to returns filed under subsection 70(2) or 150(4), or under paragraph 104(23)(*d*) or 128(2)(*e*) of the *Income Tax Act*.

Attach a completed copy of this form to your 1999 return.
If you have to pay tax to more than one jurisdiction, also attach a completed Form T2203, *Provincial and Territorial Taxes - Multiple Jurisdictions.*

Part 1 – Adjusted taxable income and minimum amount (See page 2 of this form for the explanatory notes.)

Taxable income from line 260 of your return, or the amount that you would have entered at line 260 if the instruction "if negative, enter '0'" on lines 236 and 260 was replaced with the instruction "if negative, enter the result in brackets" ...... ______ 1

Film property (Note 1)

Capital cost allowance (CCA) and carrying charges claimed on certified film property acquired before March 1996 (usually included on lines 221 and 232 of your return) .... ______ 2

Net income from film property before CCA and related carrying charges (if negative, enter "0") **(Note 2)** .... – ______ 3

Line 2 minus line 3 (if negative, enter "0") .... 6782 = ______ ► + ______ 4

Rental and leasing property (Note 1)

Capital cost allowance (CCA) and carrying charges claimed on rental and leasing property (included on line 126 of your return) .... ______ 5

Net income from rental and leasing property before CCA and related carrying charges (if negative, enter "0") **(Note 2)** .... – ______ 6

Line 5 minus line 6 (if negative, enter "0") .... 6783 = ______ ► + ______ 7

Tax shelters, limited partnerships, and non-active partners

Losses from partnerships of which you are a limited or non-active partner (line 122 of your return), or partnerships that are tax shelters **(Note 3)** .... ______ 8

Amounts deductible in respect of properties that are tax shelters **(Note 4)** .... + ______ 9

Carrying charges relating to the acquisition of an interest in a partnership of which you are a limited or non-active partner, or that owns a rental or leasing property or a film property (included on line 221 of your return) **(Note 5)** .... + ______ 10

Add lines 8, 9, and 10 .... 6784 = ______ ► + ______ 11

Resource property and flow-through shares

Total of all resource expenditures, depletion allowances, and carrying charges related to resource property and flow-through shares (included on lines 221, 224, and 232 of your return) ______ 12

Income from production of petroleum, gas, and minerals, (including royalties) before carrying charges, resource expenditures, and depletion allowances included on line 12 (if negative, enter "0") .. ______ 13

Income from dispositions of foreign resource properties, and recovery of exploration and development expenses (if negative, enter "0") .... + ______ 14

Add line 13 and line 14 .... = ______ ► – ______ 15

Line 12 minus line 15 (if negative, enter "0") .... 6786 = ______ ► + ______ 16

Non-taxable portion of capital gains reported in the year

Total capital gains from line 197 of Schedule 3 (do not include a reserve from any year before 1986) ... ______ 17

Capital gains arising from mortgage foreclosures and conditional sales repossessions from lines 124 and 155 of Schedule 3 ...... ______ 18

Portion of total capital gains included on line 17 that is exempt from Canadian tax under a tax treaty .... 6788 + ______ 19

Adjusted capital gains on gifts of certain capital property from line 193 of Schedule 3 .... + ______ 20

Capital gains from donations not included on line 20 .... 6789 + ______ 21

Add lines 18 to 21 .... = ______ ► – ______ 22

Line 17 minus line 22 .... = ______ 23

Amount from line 23 .... ______ x 25% = ... + ______ 24

Add lines 1, 4, 7, 11, 16, and 24 .... = ______ 25

Do not use this area 6790

Part 1 – Adjusted taxable income and minimum amount (continued)

Amount from line 25 from page 1 of this form			25
Employee home relocation loan deduction from line 248 of your return		26	
Stock option and shares deductions from line 249 of your return	+	27	
Portion of limited partnership losses, restricted farm losses, farm losses, and non-capital losses applied in 1999 from any CCA, and carrying charges claimed on MURBs, rental and leasing property, certified feature films, and certified productions, and the portion of these losses related to resource expenditures and depletion allowances (included on lines 251 and 252 of your return) **(Note 6)**	+	28	
Add lines 26 to 28 **(Note 7)**	=	► +	29
Add line 25 and line 29		=	30
Amount from line 120 of your return ______ x 20% =		31	
Amount from line 217 of your return ______ x 33.3333% =	+	32	
Net non-deducted capital losses from line 111 in Part 9 **(Note 8)**	+	33	
Add lines 31 to 33	=	► –	34
Line 30 minus line 34 (if negative, enter "0")	**Adjusted taxable income**	=	35
Basic exemption		– 40,000 00	36
Line 35 minus $40,000 (if negative, enter "0")	**Net adjusted taxable income**	=	37

If line 37 is "0", you are not subject to minimum tax.
Attach a copy of this form to your return, and complete Schedule 1 and your return as usual.

Enter the amount from line 37				38
Federal tax rate			x 17%	39
Gross minimum amount: Multiply line 38 by 17%			=	40
Total non-refundable tax credits from line 350 of your return		41		
Enter the total of lines 314, 318, 324, and 326 of your return	42			
Federal tax rate	x 17% 43			
Multiply line 42 by 17%	=	► – 44		
Line 41 minus line 44		=	► –	45
Line 40 minus line 45 (if negative, enter "0")		**Minimum amount**	=	46

If line 46 is "0", you are not subject to minimum tax.
Attach a copy of this form to your return, and complete Schedule 1 and your return as usual.

Note 1
If you are a member of a partnership, include your share of the income and deductions for the partnership's fiscal period ending in 1999. Do not include any amounts that you have to include on lines 8 to 10 of this form.

Note 2
For film property and rental and leasing property, first add income from these investments (before CCA and/or carrying charges, if applicable) and net taxable capital gains, if any, from dispositions of such investments. Then subtract losses from these investments (before CCA and/or carrying charges, if applicable). If the result is negative, enter "0".

Note 3
If you are a limited or non-active partner of a partnership, or if your interest in the partnership is one that needs or has obtained an identification number under section 237.1 of the Act, include your share of the net losses of the partnership from each source (allowable capital losses, business losses, and property losses) that exceeds the amount allowed under paragraph 127.52(1)(*c.1*) of the Act.

Generally, the allowable amount should correspond with the net taxable capital gains that were attributed to you by the partnership or that you have realized on the disposition of your interest in the partnership.

Note 4
Also include all other amounts deducted for property for which an identification number is needed or has been obtained under section 237.1 of the Act; for example, carrying charges relating to the acquisition of the property. Include amounts from Form T5004 that you reported on your return.

Note 5
Enter on this line carrying charges relating to the acquisition of an interest in a partnership of which you were a limited or non-active partner, or in a partnership that owns a rental or leasing property or a film property. Include only carrying charges that exceed your share of the partnership's income.

Note 6
Calculate the limited partnership losses, restricted farm losses, farm losses, and non-capital losses for other years from CCA and carrying charges, using the rules in effect for that particular year.

Note 7
If you elect under section 40 of the *Income Tax Application Rules*, add the elected income to the total on line 29.

Note 8
If you have unapplied capital losses from other years, complete Part 9 and enter the net non-deducted capital losses on line 33. This applies even if you have not claimed any net capital losses of other years on line 253 of your return.

Part 2 – Basic federal tax for the year

Complete Schedule 1 using **Method B** and stop at line 28. Enter the amount from line 28 of that schedule here				47
Total non-refundable tax credits from line 350 of your return		48		
Overseas employment tax credit from Form T626	+	49		
Dividend tax credit from line 120 of your return ______ x 13.3333%	+	50		
Add lines 48 to 50	=	▶	–	51
Tax payable before minimum tax carryover: Line 47 minus line 51			=	52
Minimum tax carryover applied in 1999 from line 87 in Part 8			–	53
Line 52 minus line 53 **Basic federal tax**			=	54

Basic federal tax from line 54 ______ **A** Minimum amount from line 46 ______ **B**

Enter amount A or amount B, whichever is **more (Note 9)** **Basic federal tax for the year** ______ 55

Part 3 – Net federal tax payable

Federal surtax on income you earned outside Canada: Enter the amount from line 9 of Form T2203 or multiply the amount from line 55 by 52%			+	56
Add lines 54 and 56			=	57
Federal foreign tax credit from Part 1 of Form T2209		58		
Federal logging tax credit	+	59		
Add line 58 and line 59	=	▶	–	60
Line 57 minus line 60 (if negative, enter "0") **Federal tax**			=	61
Federal political contribution tax credit from line 410 of your return		62		
Investment tax credit from line 412 of your return	+	63		
Labour-sponsored funds tax credit from line 414 of your return	+	64		
Add lines 62 to 64	=	▶	–	65
Line 61 minus line 65 (if negative, enter "0")			=	66

Part 4 – Special foreign tax credit

(Terms identified by the symbols * and † are defined in Form T2209.)

(i) Foreign business income (total business income earned in the foreign country minus allowable expenses and deductions relating to the foreign income)			
Foreign non-business income (on which non-business-income tax was paid to a foreign country *)	+		
Total foreign income	=		
Federal tax rate	x	17%	
Foreign income limit for special foreign tax credit	=		C
(ii) Total non-business-income tax paid to a foreign country * ______ x 66.6667% =			
Total business-income tax paid to a foreign country †	+		
Foreign taxes paid for special foreign tax credit	=		D
Enter amount C or amount D, whichever is **less**			E
Enter amount E, or the amount from line 58 above, whichever is **more** **Special foreign tax credit**			67

Part 5 – Obligation to pay minimum tax

Minimum amount from line 46				68
Special foreign tax credit from line 67			–	69
Net minimum tax payable: Line 68 minus line 69 (if negative, enter "0")			=	70
Enter the amount from line 66		71		
Federal surtax on income you earned outside Canada from line 56	–	72		
Regular tax payable: Line 71 minus line 72 (if negative, enter "0")	=	▶	–	73
Line 70 minus line 73 (if negative, enter "0")			=	74

If the amount on line 74 is positive, complete Parts 6 and 7.

If line 74 is "0", you are not subject to minimum tax. Attach a copy of this form to your return. Complete Schedule 1 and your return as usual. (Note 9)

Note 9: Whether or not you have minimum tax to pay, use the amount on line 55 as basic federal tax (instead of line 33 of Schedule 1) when you calculate the refundable Quebec abatement and provincial or territorial tax on Form T1C or Form T1C-TC, if applicable.
If you have to pay tax to more than one jurisdiction, enter this amount on line 5 of Form T2203.

Part 6 – Federal tax payable (under Alternative Minimum Tax)

Net minimum tax payable from line 70 75

Federal surtax on income you earned outside Canada from line 56 .... + 76

Add lines 75 and 76. Enter this amount on line 417 of your return .... = 77

Use line 55 as basic federal tax (instead of line 33 of Schedule 1) when you calculate the federal individual surtax on Schedule 1.

Part 7 – Additional taxes paid for minimum tax carryover

(Terms identified by the symbols * and † are defined in Form T2209.)

Minimum amount from line 46 78

Basic federal tax from line 54 79

Special foreign tax credit from line 67 .... F

Federal foreign tax credit from line 58 .... – G

Line F minus line G .... = H

Line H x (Foreign taxes paid for special foreign tax credit (line D in Part 4)) / (Foreign taxes paid (non-business-income tax paid to a foreign country * plus business-income tax paid to a foreign country †)) = + 80

Add lines 79 and 80 .... = ▶ – 81

Line 78 minus line 81 (if negative, enter "0") .... **Additional taxes paid for minimum tax carryover** = 82

Part 8 – Applying a minimum tax carryover from previous years against 1999 tax payable

Minimum tax carryover from previous years (1992 to 1998) 83

Tax payable before minimum tax carryover from line 52 84

Minimum amount from line 46 .... – 85

Maximum carryover that can be applied in 1999 (if negative, enter "0") .... = 86

Minimum tax carryover applied in 1999:
Claim an amount that is not more than line 83 or 86, whichever is **less**, and enter it on line 31 of Schedule 1 .... – 87

Balance of minimum tax carryover available for subsequent years, if any: Line 83 minus line 87 .... = 88

Additional 1999 taxes for carryover to subsequent years from line 82 .... + 89

Add lines 88 and 89 .... = 90

Additional 1992 taxes not applied .... – 91

Total minimum tax carryover available for 2000: Line 90 minus line 91 .... = 92

Part 9 – Net non-deducted capital losses (Complete this part only if you have unapplied capital losses from other years)

Amount from line 23 93

Capital gains deduction from line 254 of your return **(Note 10)** .... – 94

Capital gains available for capital losses of other years: Line 93 minus line 94 .... = 95

Pre-1988 unapplied net capital losses .... x 2 = 96

1988 and 1989 unapplied net capital losses .... x 3/2 = + 97

1990 through 1998 unapplied net capital losses .... x 4/3 = + 98

Add lines 96 to 98 **(Note 11)** .... = ▶ 99

Adjusted capital losses of other years applied against total capital gains:
Enter the amount from line 95 or line 99, whichever is **less** 100

Unapplied net capital loss incurred before May 23, 1985 (if none, enter "0" on line 108) 101

Capital gains deductions claimed:

In 1990 through 1998 .... x 2/3 = 102

In 1988 and 1989 .... x 3/4 = + 103

Before 1988 .... + 104

Add lines 102 to 104 .... = ▶ – 105

Pre-1986 capital loss balance for 1999: Line 101 minus line 105 (if negative, enter "0") .... = 106

Line 99 minus line 100 (if negative, enter "0") .... x 1/2 = 107

Enter the amount from line 106, line 107, or $2,000, whichever is **least** .... + 108

Adjusted capital losses: Add lines 100 and 108 .... = 109

Net capital losses of other years from line 253 of your return .... – 110

Line 109 minus line 110. Enter this amount on line 33 .... **Net non-deducted capital losses** = 111

Note 10: Do not include the part of the capital gains deduction that relates to the disposition of eligible capital property which is qualified farm property.

Note 11: Exclude the non-deducted portion of capital losses from mortgage foreclosures and conditional sales repossessions.
For post-1994 net capital losses, the first paragraph under Note 3 on page 2 also applies here.

Printed in Canada

Canada Customs and Revenue Agency / Agence des douanes et du revenu du Canada

CALCULATING YOUR DEDUCTION FOR REFUND OF UNDEDUCTED RRSP CONTRIBUTIONS

- You can use this form if you are claiming a deduction for undeducted (also called "unused") registered retirement savings plan (RRSP) contributions that you or your spouse received in a year from an RRSP, or from a registered retirement income fund (RRIF) to which RRSP property was transferred.
- Attach a completed copy of this form and any appropriate T4RSP and T4RIF slips to your income tax return for the year in which the unused contributions were received or considered received.
- **Do not** use this form to claim a deduction for unused RRSP contributions received if those contributions arose because of an excess lump-sum transfer from a registered pension plan. Instead, use Form T1043, *Deduction for Excess Registered Pension Plan Transfers You Withdrew From Your RRSP or RRIF.*

Area 1 – Calculating your unused RRSP contributions

Enter the year in which you made the unused RRSP contributions. ________

1. Enter the total RRSP contributions you made in the year to any of your or your spouse's RRSPs. **Do not** include direct transfers of lump sums from registered pension plans, deferred profit-sharing plans, RRIFs, the Saskatchewan Pension Plan, or other RRSPs if you do not have to report such transfers on your income tax return. ________ 1
2. Enter the part of the line 1 amount that you deducted or will deduct from your income for the previous year. You had to have contributed this amount in the first 60 days of the year. ________ 2
3. Enter the part of the line 1 amount (other than the amount entered on line 2) that you deducted or will deduct from your income for the year. + ________ 3
4. Enter the part of the line 1 amount (other than the amounts entered on lines 2 and 3) that you expect to deduct or have deducted for a future year. + ________ 4
5. **Add** lines 2, 3, and 4. = ________ ► – ________ 5
6. Line 1 **minus** line 5: This amount is your **unused RRSP contributions for the year.** = ________ 6

Area 2 – Calculating the unused RRSP contributions received

Enter the year you received the unused RRSP contributions. ________

7. Enter the amount of unused RRSP contributions you received in the year from the plan as a refund of those contributions. This amount is shown in box 20 on the T4RSP slip, based on an approved Form T3012A you submitted to the plan issuer. Report this amount on line 129 of your income tax return. ________ 7
8. Enter the amount of unused RRSP contributions you received in the year as a withdrawal from an unmatured plan or as a commutation payment from a matured plan. This amount is shown in box 22 on the T4RSP slip. Report this amount on line 129 of your income tax return. **Do not** enter any amount you designated as a qualifying withdrawal on Form T1006, *Designating an RRSP Withdrawal as a Qualifying Withdrawal.* + ________ 8
9. Enter the amount of unused RRSP contributions you received in the year from a RRIF to which they were transferred as shown in box 24 on your T4RIF slip. Report this amount on line 130 of your return. + ________ 9
10. If you are including an amount in your income for an unused RRSP or RRIF amount that your spouse received, enter the amount you are reporting as income (the amount is shown on Form T2205, *Calculating Amounts From a Spousal RRSP or RRIF to Include in Income for* __, that you may have completed). On your income tax return, report the unused RRSP amount on line 129 and the unused RRIF amount on line 130. + ________ 10
11. **Add** lines 7, 8, 9, and 10: This amount is the total unused RRSP contributions received in the year. = ________ 11

Area 3 – Deducting an amount for your unused RRSP contributions received in the year

To qualify to deduct this amount on line 232 of your return, you have to meet the conditions explained below.

12. Enter the amount from line 6 or the amount from line 11, **whichever is less.** If you received unused RRSP contributions that were made in more than one year, read the note below. ________ 12

Deduction for unused contributions you made after 1990 that are withdrawn

For unused RRSP contributions you made in a calendar year after 1990, you can withdraw the unused contributions and claim a deduction at line 232 of your return to offset the amount included in your income, **or** you can leave them in the plan and carry them forward to deduct for a future year. To claim a deduction at line 232 of your return, you have to meet all of the following conditions.

- You or your spouse must receive the unused contributions:
  - in the year you contributed them or in the following year; or
  - in the year we sent you a *Notice of Assessment* or *Notice of Reassessment* for the year you contributed them, or in the following year.
- You have not designated the withdrawal of the unused RRSP contribution as a qualifying withdrawal so that you could have your past-service pension adjustment certified. If you want to know about qualifying withdrawals, see "Past-service pension adjustments (PSPAs)" in Chapter 6 of the income tax guide called *RRSPs and Other Registered Plans for Retirement.*
- It has to be reasonable for us to consider that:
  - you expected to fully deduct the RRSP contributions for the year you paid them or for the previous year; or
  - you did not make the unused RRSP contributions intending to withdraw them and deduct an offsetting amount.

Note

If you received unused RRSP contributions that were made in more than one year, you have to adapt the calculation in Area 1. Do a separate calculation for each year in which unused contributions were made, then total the amounts from line 6. Finally, report this total on line 6 of the most recent form T746 and complete Areas 2 and 3 on that form.

If you made, or we consider you to have made, RRSP contributions in a calendar year after 1990 which you could not deduct for the year or for the previous year, you may have to pay a tax on those unused contributions. If you have to pay the tax, you have to send us a completed T1-OVP, _ *Individual Income Tax Return for RRSP Excess Contributions.* For more details, see the section called "Unused RRSP contributions" in Chapter 2 of the income tax guide called *RRSPs and Other Registered Plans for Retirement* and the T1-OVP. You can get these two publications from any tax services office. Amounts withdrawn or repaid under the Home Buyers' Plan (HBP) or Lifelong Learning Plan (LLP) do not generally increase or reduce the RRSP contributions that are subject to tax.

If we allow the deduction for the unused RRSP contributions you or your spouse received, we do not consider such contributions to be RRSP contributions, and you cannot deduct them for any year. Do not enter this amount on Schedule 7, *RRSP Unused Contributions, Transfers, and HBP or LLP Activities.* If, in a previous year, you included these contributions on Schedule 7, ask for an adjustment to your income tax return for that year. The adjustment will reduce your unused contributions available to carry forward to a future year.

Canada Customs and Revenue Agency | Agence des douanes et du revenu du Canada

Revenue Canada | Revenu Canada

CALCULATION OF CUMULATIVE NET INVESTMENT LOSS (CNIL) TO DECEMBER 31, 1999

Use this form if you had any **investment income** or **investment expenses** for 1999.
Your CNIL reduces the amount of your cumulative gains limit for the year and may affect the allowable amount of your capital gains deduction.
Even if you are not claiming a capital gains deduction in 1999, you should still complete this form if you had any investment income or expenses in 1999.
Because the balance in your CNIL account is a cumulative total, you may need this information in a future year. Keep one copy for your records and attach the other copy to your return.
If you need more information, contact your tax services office.

Note
If you have capital gains other than from the disposition of qualified farm property or qualified small business corporation shares in 1999, you should start by completing Chart A on the back of this form to determine if you have additional investment income to include when you calculate your CNIL.

Part 1 – Investment expenses claimed on your 1999 return

Carrying charges and interest expenses (from line 221)			1
Net rental losses (from line 126 or related schedules or statements)		+	2
Limited or non-active partnership losses (from line 122) other than allowable capital losses		+	3
Limited partnership losses of other years after 1985 (from line 251)		+	4
50% of exploration and development expenses (from line 224)		+	5
Any other investment expenses claimed in 1999 to earn property income (see the list of other investment expenses below)	6808	+	6
Additional investment expenses: If you did not complete Chart A on the back of this form, enter "0." Otherwise, enter the **lesser** of line 17 in Chart A, or the amount you claimed on line 253 of your return		+	7
Total investment expenses claimed in 1999 (total of lines 1 to 7)		= ▶	A

Part 2 – Investment income reported on your 1999 return

Investment income (from lines 120 and 121)			8
Net rental income, including recaptured capital cost allowance (from line 126)		+	9
Net income from limited or non-active partnership (from line 122) other than taxable capital gains		+	10
Any other property income reported in 1999 (see the list of other property income below), including annuity payments taxable under paragraph 56(1)(d) or 56(1)(d.1) **minus** the capital portion deducted under paragraph 60(a)	6810	+	11
50% of income from the recovery of exploration and development expenses (from line 130)	6811	+	12
Additional investment income: If you did not complete Chart A on the back of this form, enter "0." Otherwise, enter the amount from line 17 in Chart A		+	13
Total investment income reported in 1999 (total of lines 8 to 13)		= ▶	B

Other investment expenses

Include: • repayments of inducements • repayments of refund interest • the uncollectible portion of proceeds from dispositions of depreciable property (except passenger vehicles that cost more than $26,000) • sale of agreement for sale or mortgage included in proceeds of disposition in a previous year under subsection 20(5) • foreign non-business tax under subsections 20(11) and 20(12) • life insurance premiums deducted from property income • capital cost allowance claimed on certified films and videotapes • farming losses claimed by a non-active partner or a limited partner

Do not include: • expenses incurred to earn business income • repayment of shareholders' loans deducted under paragraph 20(1)(j) • interest paid on money borrowed to: i) buy an income-averaging annuity contract; ii) pay a premium under a registered retirement savings plan; iii) make a contribution to a registered pension plan; or iv) make a contribution to a deferred profit-sharing plan

Other property income

Include: • amounts from insurance proceeds for the recapture of capital cost allowance (other than amounts already included on line 9) • home insulation or energy conversion grants under paragraph 12(1)(u) • payments received as an inducement or reimbursement • income from the appropriation of property to a shareholder • farming income reported by a non-active or a limited partner • other income from a trust • allowable capital losses included in partnership losses of other years after 1985 • amounts withdrawn from Net Income Stabilization Account (NISA) Fund No. 2

Do not include: • income amounts that relate to business income • payments received from an income-averaging annuity contract • payments received from an annuity contract bought under a deferred profit-sharing plan • shareholders' loans included in income under subsection 15(2)

Do not use this area
6813

Part 3 – Cumulative net investment loss (CNIL)

Total investment expenses claimed in 1999 (from line A in Part 1) 14

Total investment expenses claimed in previous years (after 1987): Enter the amount from line 16 in Part 3 of Form T936 for 1998. If you did not complete Form T936 for 1998, see note 1 below .... + 15

Cumulative investment expenses (total of lines 14 and 15) .... = ▶ 16

Total investment income reported in 1999 (from line B in Part 2) 17

Total investment income reported in previous years (after 1987): Enter the amount from line 19 in Part 3 of Form T936 for 1998. If you did not complete Form T936 for 1998, see note 2 below .... + 18

Cumulative investment income (total of lines 17 and 18) .... = ▶ – 19

Cumulative net investment loss (CNIL) to December 31, 1999 (line 16 **minus** line 19; if negative, enter "0") .... = C

If you are claiming a capital gains deduction on your 1999 return, enter the amount from line C on line 24 of Form T657.

Notes

1. To calculate your **total investment expenses from previous years**, complete Part 1 of Form T936 for each year from 1988 to 1998 in which you had investment expenses (do not complete line 7 for 1988 to 1991). Add the amounts from line A and enter the total on line 15 of Form T936 for 1999.
2. To calculate your **total investment income from previous years**, complete Part 2 of Form T936 for each year from 1988 to 1998 in which you had investment income (do not complete line 13 for 1988 to 1991). Add the amounts from line B and enter the total on line 18 of Form T936 for 1999.

Chart A

Enter the amount from line 199 of Schedule 3 (if negative, show it in brackets) 1

Enter the amount from line 173 of Schedule 3 .... + 2

Line 1 **plus** line 2 (if negative, enter "0"). If the amount on this line is zero, do not complete lines 4 to 16, and enter "0" on line 17 .... = 3

Enter the amount from line 1 above (if negative, enter "0") 4

Enter the total of the amounts from lines 107, 110, and 124 of Schedule 3 (if negative, show it in brackets) 5

If you reported an amount on line 192 of Schedule 3, enter the total of the amounts from lines 6683 and 6690 on Form T2017. Otherwise, enter the amount from line 5 on line 7 .... + 6

Line 5 **plus** line 6 (if negative, enter "0") .... = 7

Enter 3/4 of line 7 .... – 8

Line 4 **minus** line 8 (if negative, enter "0"). If the amount on this line is zero, do not complete lines 10 to 16, and enter "0" on line 17 .... = 9

Total net non-eligible taxable capital gains (line 3 or line 9, **whichever is less**). If the amount on this line includes an amount from a T3 slip, complete lines 11 to 15 below. Otherwise, enter "0" on line 16 10

Enter the amount from box 21 of all 1999 T3 slips 11

Enter the amount from box 30 of all 1999 T3 slips .... – 12

Line 11 **minus** line 12 .... = 13

Enter the portion, if any, of the amount from line 195 of Schedule 3, used to reduce the gain on line 13 .... – 14

Line 13 **minus** line 14 .... = 15

Enter 3/4 of line 15 .... – 16

Additional investment income (line 10 **minus** line 16; if negative, enter "0") .... = 17

Printed in Canada

Canada Customs and Revenue Agency / Agence des douanes et du revenu du Canada

Revenue Canada / Revenu Canada

INFORMATION RETURN IN RESPECT OF TRANSFERS OR LOANS TO A NON-RESIDENT TRUST

Do not use this area

- Complete this form if you or your controlled foreign affiliate has transferred or loaned property to a specified foreign trust or a non-resident corporation controlled by the trust.
- Give all amounts in Canadian dollars.
- You have to file a separate return for each non-resident trust.
- Attach a separate sheet if you need more space.

Part I – Identification

Section 1 – Reporting taxpayer

Tick a box to indicate who you are reporting for, and complete the areas that apply.

☐ individual	First name	Last name	Initial	Social insurance number
☐ corporation	Corporation's name		Business number	R C
☐ trust	Trust's name			Account number T – –

Reporting taxpayer's address

No. Street

Postal code

City

Province or territory

Section 2 – Reporting period

Is this the first year that you have filed this return for this trust? Yes ☐ No ☐

If *no*, does the reporting period for this year begin and end on the same dates as last year? Yes ☐ No ☐

If *no*, why has the reporting period changed? ______

To which reporting period does this return apply?

From Day Month Year To Day Month Year

Section 3 – Non-resident trust information

Name of trust	Trustee(s)		
	Name	Address	Telephone ( )
	Name	Address	Telephone ( )
	Name	Address	Telephone ( )

Trust's country of residence at the end of the reporting period	Under the laws of which country is the trust governed?

Person with whom a trustee has to consult before the trustee can exercise any discretionary powers

Name: ______ Address: ______

Persons who have any powers relating to the trust, including:

- the power to change the governing law or situs of the trust;
- the power to veto distributions of capital or income; and
- the power to remove existing trustees and appoint new ones.

Name: ______ Address: ______

Name: ______ Address: ______

Attach the following documents to this return:

- If this is the first year, attach a copy of the trust documents, including terms of the trust, memorandum of wishes, and any change to the original trust documents.
- If this form was filed before, attach a copy of any trust documents that have been changed or created since the previous reporting period.
- If the trust prepares financial statements, attach a copy of the financial statements for the reporting period.

If the original documents are not written in English or French, they must be translated into English or French if requested by Canada Customs and Revenue Agency.

Section 4 – Settlor(s) of the trust

Name	Address

Section 5 – Specified beneficiaries of the trust

Name	Address

Part II – Transactions

Section 1 – Reporting requirements

Was a transfer or loan to the trust that gave rise to an obligation to file this return made before 1991? Yes ☐ No ☐

If *yes*, indicate the first year there was a transfer or loan 19 ____

- Report only transactions that occurred after 1990 in Sections 2 and 3 below.
- In Sections 2 and 3 below, include only transactions that were not reported on other T1141 forms.

Section 2 – Transfers and loans before the end of the reporting period to the trust and each non-resident corporation that the trust controlled

Name and address of transferor or creditor	Description of property transferred or loaned	Year of transfer or loan	Amount
			00
			00
			00
		Total 11	00

Section 3 – Distributions before the end of the reporting period from the trust

Name and address of recipient	Description of property distributed	Year of distribution	Amount
			00
			00
			00
		Total 21	00

Section 4 – Non-arm's-length persons indebted to the trust at the end of the reporting period

Name and address of non-arm's length person	Description of indebtedness	Amount
		00
		00
		00
	Total 31	00

Section 5 – Persons to whom the trust or a non-resident corporation that the trust controlled is indebted at the end of the reporting period

Name and address of person	Description of indebtedness	Amount
		00
		00
		00
	Total 41	00

Section 6 – Disclosure

Is any information requested on this return not available? Yes ☐ No ☐

If *yes*, please specify the information and the reason it is not available. Also, indicate the steps taken in attempting to obtain the information.

Certification

I certify that the information given on this return and in any documents attached is, to my knowledge, correct and complete, except as disclosed in Section 6.	Person or firm paid to prepare this return.
Print name	Name
Sign here	Address
It is a serious offence to file a false return.	
Position or title	Postal code
Telephone ( ) Date	Telephone ( )

Printed in Canada

Revenue Canada / Revenu Canada

INFORMATION RETURN IN RESPECT OF DISTRIBUTIONS FROM AND INDEBTEDNESS TO A NON-RESIDENT TRUST

For departmental use

NOTE: The first filing deadline has been extended from April 30, 1997 to April 30, 1998.

- You have to file a separate return for each non-resident trust.
- Give all amounts in Canadian dollars.
- Attach a separate sheet, if you need more space.
- If you are reporting for a partnership, read all references to year or tax year as fiscal period and all references to taxpayer as partnership.

Part I – Identification

Tick a box to indicate who you are reporting for, and complete the areas that apply.

☐ individual	First name	Last name	Initial	Social insurance number
☐ corporation	Corporation's name			Business Number (BN) RC
☐ trust	Trust's name			Account number T – –
☐ partnership	Partnership's name			Partnership's identification number

Reporting taxpayer's address

No. Street

City — Province or territory — Postal code

For what tax year are you filing this return?

199 ____ **or** From Day Month Year To Day Month Year

Part II – Identification of Non-resident Trust and Trustee

Name of trust	Trustee(s)	
	Name	Address
	Name	Address
	Name	Address

Part III – Distributions from the Non-resident Trust

Complete this part if the reporting taxpayer has received funds or property from a non-resident trust at any time in the tax year.

Funds	Property other than funds		Nature of receipt for Canadian income tax purposes (tick appropriate box)	
Amount	Description	Estimated fair market value when received	Income	Capital
00		00	☐	☐
00		00	☐	☐
00		00	☐	☐
00		00	☐	☐
11 00 **Total**	**Total**	12 00		

Part IV – Indebtedness to the Non-resident Trust

Complete this part if the reporting taxpayer was indebted to a non-resident trust at any time in the tax year.

Date debt incurred	Principal amount	Unpaid principal amount at end of year	Unpaid interest at end of year	Interest rate (per annum)	Was interest actually paid on the debt in the year (*yes/no*)?
	00	00	00		
	00	00	00		
	00	00	00		
	00	00	00		
Total	21 00	22 00	23 00		

Certification

I certify that the information given on this return and in any documents attached is, to my knowledge, correct and complete, and fully discloses all distributions received from and indebtedness to the non-resident trust.

Print name ____________________

Sign here ____________________

It is a serious offence to file a false return.

____
Position or title

Telephone ( ) ____________ Date ____________

If you were paid to prepare this return, provide the following information:

Your name ____________________

Address ____________________

Postal code ____________________

Telephone ( ) ____________________

Printed in Canada

Canada Customs and Revenue Agency Agence des douanes et du revenu du Canada

NORTHERN RESIDENTS DEDUCTIONS – 2000

Use this form to calculate your northern residents deductions if you lived in a prescribed northern zone or in a prescribed intermediate zone for at least six consecutive months beginning or ending in 2000.

Read the attached information sheet for details on claiming these deductions.

Attach to your 2000 income tax return one completed copy of this form.

Step 1 – List your places of residence

Under "Zone **A** or **B**," enter "**A**" if your place of residence was in a prescribed northern zone. Enter "**B**" if it was in a prescribed intermediate zone. If you claimed these deductions in 1999 and you have not moved, see your 1999 Form T2222 for your zone.

Under "Place of residence," enter the location of the place where you live. (This may be different from your mailing address.)

Under "Period of residence," be sure to enter the earliest date you lived at each place for a continuous period.

Zone A or B	Place of residence	Province or territory	Period of residence (see **Note** below)						Number of days in 2000 that you lived in a prescribed zone	
			From			To			Northern zone (Zone A)	Intermediate zone (Zone B)
			Year	Month	Day	Year	Month	Day		
									+	+
								Total	= 1	= 2

Attach a separate sheet of paper if you need more space.

Note: Print below, the names and addresses of all persons who lived with you in 2000 during the period(s) indicated above. Include boarders and anyone who house-sat during your absence. Do not include any dependent household members (including your spouse) whose net income in 2000 was less than $7,231.

Name: Address:	Name: Address:
Name: Address:	Name: Address:

Attach a separate sheet of paper if you need more space.

Step 2 – List your trips

Under column 1, enter "**A**" if your trip started from a prescribed northern zone. Enter "**B**" if it started from a prescribed intermediate zone.

Enter the **lowest** amount from columns 3, 4, or 5 in the appropriate column below.

Column 1 Origin of trip		**Column 2** Purpose of trip	**Column 3** Employment benefit	**Column 4** Travel expenses	**Column 5** Lowest return airfare	**Column 6** Enter the amount here if you wrote "**A**" in Column 1	**Column 7** Enter the amount here if you wrote "**B**" in Column 1
Trip 1							
Trip 2						+	+
					Total	= 3	= 4

Attach a separate sheet of paper if you need more space.

See reverse

T2222 E (00) (Ce formulaire existe en français.) Canada

Step 3 – Calculate your residency deduction

Zone A – Residents of prescribed northern zones

Basic residency amount: Enter the number of days from line 1 in Step 1, or enter only the number of days you are claiming .... ______ x $7.50 = ______ 5

Additional residency amount: Enter the number of days that qualify for the additional residency amount .... ______ x $7.50 = + ______ 6

Add lines 5 and 6 .... 6749 = ______ 7

Enter the amount from box 31 of your T4 slip, or from the footnotes area of your T4A slip, as a **non-taxable** benefit for board and lodging at a special work site in a prescribed northern zone .... 6757 – ______ 8

Line 7 minus line 8 (if negative, enter "0") .... = ______ ▶ ______ 9

Zone B – Residents of prescribed intermediate zones

Basic residency amount: Enter the number of days from line 2 in Step 1, or enter only the number of days you are claiming .... ______ x $3.75 = ______ 10

Additional residency amount: Enter the number of days that qualify for the additional residency amount .... ______ x $3.75 = + ______ 11

Add lines 10 and 11 .... 6752 = ______ 12

Enter the amount from box 31 of your T4 slip, or from the footnotes area of your T4A slip, as a non-taxable benefit for board and lodging at a special work site in a prescribed intermediate zone .... 6759 – ______ 13

Line 12 minus line 13 (if negative, enter "0") .... = ______ ▶ + ______ 14

Add lines 9 and 14 .... = ______ 15

Enter your net income from line 236 of your return ... ______ x 20% = ______ 16

Residency deduction: Enter the amount from line 15 or line 16, whichever is **less** .... ______ 17

Step 4 – Calculate your travel deduction

Enter the amount from line 3 in Step 2 .... 6754 ______ 18

Enter the amount from line 4 in Step 2 .... 6756 ______ x 50% = + ______ 19

Travel deduction: Add lines 18 and 19 .... = ______ ▶ + ______ 20

Step 5 – Calculate your northern residents deductions

Northern residents deductions: Add lines 17 and 20
Enter this amount on line 255 of your return .... = ______ 21

Printed in Canada

T1-2000

Allowable Amount of Non-Refundable Tax Credits

Schedule B

Complete Box A if you were a non-resident of Canada for all of 2000.

Complete Box B if you were a non-resident of Canada for all of 2000 and you are electing under section 217 of the *Income Tax Act*.

Box A – Non-residents

Enter the amount from line 236 of your return / Enter the amount from line 14 of Schedule A ______ x 100 = ______% **A**

If line **A** is **90% or more,** your allowable amount of non-refundable tax credits is the amount on line 350 of your return.

If line **A** is **less than 90%,** your allowable amount of non-refundable tax credits is 17% of the amounts on lines 316, 319, and 323 (other than the education amount) **plus** the amount on line 349 of your return.

Enter your allowable amount on line 10 or line 18, whichever applies, on Schedule 1, *Federal Tax Calculation.*

Box B – Non-residents electing under section 217

Enter the amount from line 236 of your return / Enter the amount from line 14 of Schedule A ______ x 100 = ______% **A**

If line **A** is **90% or more,** your allowable amount of non-refundable tax credits is the amount on line 350 of your return.

If line **A** is **less than 90%,** your allowable amount of non-refundable tax credits is **the lesser of:**

- the amount on line 350 of your return . . . . = ______

or

- the amount of your income eligible for the section 217 election ______ x 17% = ______
  (see page 49 in the guide for the list of eligible income)

Enter your allowable amount on line 10 or line 18, whichever applies, on Schedule 1, *Federal Tax Calculation.*

5013-SB

Cut along this line

T1-2000

Allowable Amount of Non-Refundable Tax Credits

Schedule B

Complete Box A if you were a non-resident of Canada for all of 2000.

Complete Box B if you were a non-resident of Canada for all of 2000 and you are electing under section 217 of the *Income Tax Act*.

Box A – Non-residents

Enter the amount from line 236 of your return / Enter the amount from line 14 of Schedule A ______ x 100 = ______% **A**

If line **A** is **90% or more,** your allowable amount of non-refundable tax credits is the amount on line 350 of your return.

If line **A** is **less than 90%,** your allowable amount of non-refundable tax credits is 17% of the amounts on lines 316, 319, and 323 (other than the education amount) **plus** the amount on line 349 of your return.

Enter your allowable amount on line 10 or line 18, whichever applies, on Schedule 1, *Federal Tax Calculation.*

Box B – Non-residents electing under section 217

Enter the amount from line 236 of your return / Enter the amount from line 14 of Schedule A ______ x 100 = ______% **A**

If line **A** is **90% or more,** your allowable amount of non-refundable tax credits is the amount on line 350 of your return.

If line **A** is **less than 90%,** your allowable amount of non-refundable tax credits is **the lesser of:**

- the amount on line 350 of your return . . . . = ______

or

- the amount of your income eligible for the section 217 election ______ x 17% = ______
  (see page 49 in the guide for the list of eligible income)

Enter your allowable amount on line 10 or line 18, whichever applies, on Schedule 1, *Federal Tax Calculation.*

5013-SB

T1-2000

Statement of World Income

Schedule A

Complete this schedule and **attach it** to your return if you:

- were a non-resident of Canada for all of 2000; **or**
- were a non-resident of Canada for all of 2000 and you are electing under section 217 of the *Income Tax Act*.

Be sure to report all income in Canadian dollars. If you need more space, attach a separate sheet of paper.

Income from Canadian sources

Enter the amount from line 236 on your return		1			
Net interest and other investment income	+	2			
Net rental income	+	3			
Other Canadian-source income. Specify:	+	4			
Add lines 1 to 4	=		▶		5

Income from sources outside Canada

Net employment income		6			
Net pension income	+	7			
Net interest and other investment income	+	8			
Taxable capital gains	+	9			
Net rental income	+	10			
Net self-employment income	+	11			
Other foreign-source income. Specify:	+	12			
Add lines 6 to 12	=		▶	+	13
Add lines 5 and 13. **This is your net world income.**			167	=	14
Enter the deductions claimed on lines 248 to 256 of your return that **only** apply to your Canadian-source employment and business income and taxable capital gains from disposing of taxable Canadian property.				–	15
Line 14 minus line 15 (if negative, enter "0"). **This is your net world income after adjustments.**			169	=	16

5013-SA

Cut along this line

T1-2000

Statement of World Income

Schedule A

Complete this schedule and **attach it** to your return if you:

- were a non-resident of Canada for all of 2000; **or**
- were a non-resident of Canada for all of 2000 and you are electing under section 217 of the *Income Tax Act*.

Be sure to report all income in Canadian dollars. If you need more space, attach a separate sheet of paper.

Income from Canadian sources

Enter the amount from line 236 on your return		1			
Net interest and other investment income	+	2			
Net rental income	+	3			
Other Canadian-source income. Specify:	+	4			
Add lines 1 to 4	=		▶		5

Income from sources outside Canada

Net employment income		6			
Net pension income	+	7			
Net interest and other investment income	+	8			
Taxable capital gains	+	9			
Net rental income	+	10			
Net self-employment income	+	11			
Other foreign-source income. Specify:	+	12			
Add lines 6 to 12	=		▶	+	13
Add lines 5 and 13. **This is your net world income.**			167	=	14
Enter the deductions claimed on lines 248 to 256 of your return that **only** apply to your Canadian-source employment and business income and taxable capital gains from disposing of taxable Canadian property.				–	15
Line 14 minus line 15 (if negative, enter "0"). **This is your net world income after adjustments.**			169	=	16

5013-SA

Canada Customs and Revenue Agency / Agence des douanes et du revenu du Canada

OVERSEAS EMPLOYMENT TAX CREDIT CALENDAR YEAR ______

Step I – Must be fully completed by the employer (print or type)

Employer certification

I, ______________________________ (authorized officer), certify that ______________________________ (employee's full name),

social insurance number ______________________________, was employed by* ______________________________ (employer's full name)

throughout a **period of more than 6 consecutive months** (the **"qualifying period"**) that began before the end of the calendar year and included any part thereof. **

The employer has met the requirements of subsection 122.3(2) of the *Income Tax Act* as a specified employer and is one of the following (check one):

☐ a person (including a corporation) resident in Canada;

☐ a partnership in which persons resident in Canada or corporations controlled by persons resident in Canada own interests which exceed 10% of the fair market value of all interests in the partnership; or

☐ a corporation that is a foreign affiliate of a person resident in Canada.

The employee, during that qualifying period extending from [Y | M | D] to [Y | M | D]:

(1) was employed, **other than** for performing services under international development assistance program of the **Canadian International Development Agency (CIDA);**
and

(2) throughout that period performed **all or substantially all (90% or more)** of the duties of employment **outside Canada** in connection with a contract under which the employer carried on a business outside Canada conducting one of the following activities outlined in clause 122.3(1)(b)(i) (A),(B), or (C) of the *Income Tax Act* (check one):

☐ the exploration for or exploitation of petroleum, natural gas, minerals, or other similar resources;

☐ any construction, installation, or agricultural or engineering activity; or

☐ an activity performed under contract with the United Nations; (For 1994 and subsequent calendar years only)

or

☐ for the purpose of obtaining, on behalf of the employer, a contract to undertake any of the above activities.

Please provide details

Country where activities are performed	Name of the project
Description of the project	

If a waiver on withholding had been requested with respect to this credit, please provide the name of the tax services office where the waiver request was processed:

Tax services office

The employer also undertakes to provide to the Canada Customs and Revenue Agency, on request, any necessary information to substantiate the accuracy of the information on this form.

Date	Signature of authorized officer	Employer's business account number	( ) Telephone number

Notes: * Employment income will **not** qualify for this tax deduction for 1997, and subsequent taxation years, **if all of the following conditions are met:**

- the employer:
  - carries on a business of providing services;

  and
  - does not employ throughout the year more than 5 full-time employees,
- the individual either:
  - does not deal at arm's length with the employer, or is a "specified shareholder" of the employer (i.e.: generally, an individual who owns directly or indirectly not less than 10% of any class of shares of the employer);

  or where the employer is a partnership,
  - does not deal at arm's length with a member of the partnership, or is a specified shareholder of a member of the partnership,
- **and,** the individual, but for the existence of the employer,
  - would be reasonably be regarded as an employee of another person or partnership that is not a specified employer (e.g.: foreign corporation).

** If the qualifying period extends over more than one calendar year, you must complete this form for each of the years.

Step II – Calculation of employment income

1. Number of days in the qualifying period referred to in Step I that are in this calendar year and during which you were resident in Canada .... 6770 ______ A
2. Gross salary, wages, and other remuneration for the period referred to in A .... $ ______ B
3. Deduct: Employment deductions related to amount B:
4. Sales expenses .... $ ______
5. Travelling expenses........ ______
6. Annual union or professional dues........ ______
7. RPP contributions........ ______
8. Other deductions (please specify)........ ______
9. **Total**........ $ ______ ► $ ______ C

10. Net salary, wages, and remuneration for the period referred to in A (amount B minus amount C) .... 6772 $ ______ D

Note: You should apportion employment deductions partly related to the period referred to in A in the same ratio as the number of days relates to 365.

Step III – Calculation of credit limits

11. Enter the number of days in A above ______ X $80,000 divided by 365 .... = $ ______ E
12. Enter the amount in D above $______ X 80% .... = $ ______ F
13. Net income for the year (line 236 of T1 return) .... $ ______
14. Add: Forward-averaging withdrawal (Form T581) included in calculating taxable income (for 1997 and prior tax years) .... ______

Notes: If the amount on line 5 of Form T581 is positive, enter the amount from line 6 of that form on line 14 above. If the amount on line 5 of Form T581 is negative, enter any positive amount from line 7 of that form on line 14 above. If line 7 of Form T581 is also negative, enter nil on line 14 above.

15. Subtotal (lines 13 and 14) .... $ ______
16. Deduct: Any deduction for net capital losses of other years (line 253 of T1 return) .... $ ______
17. Amounts for shares deductible under paragraph 110(1)(*d.2*) or 110(1)(*d.3*) .... ______
18. Employee home relocation loan deductible under paragraph 110(1)(*j*) .... ______
19. Capital gains deduction (line 254 of T1 return)........ ______
20. Payments of income deductible under paragraph 110(1)(*f*) .... ______
21. **Total** of line 15 minus lines 16 to 20 .... $ ______ ► $ ______ G

Step IV – Calculation of basic federal tax (you must report the calculated amount on Schedule 1, *Federal Tax Calculation*)

22. Enter taxable income (line 260 of T1 return) .... $ ______
23. On the first ______ the tax is ...... ______
24. On the remaining ______ tax at ____ % is ______
25. **Total** (lines 23 and 24) .... $ ______
26. Add: Tax adjustments (see line 423 of guide) .... ______
27. **Total** (lines 25 and 26) .... ______ ► $ ______
28. Subtract: Total of non-refundable tax credits (line 350 of T1 return)........ ______
29. **Total** .... $ ______ H
30. Subtract: Overseas employment tax credit (note c) (amount I from step V below) .... ______
31. **Total** .... $ ______
32. Subtract: Federal dividend tax credit (see line 425 of guide) .... ______
33. **Total** .... $ ______ ► $ ______
34. Subtract: Minimum tax carry-over (see line 427 of guide) .... ______
35. Basic federal tax (enter this amount on line 429 on Schedule 1 of T1 return)........ $ ______ ► $ ______

Notes: a) A foreign tax paid on income subject to an overseas employment tax credit must be excluded in calculating any foreign tax credit to which you may be entitled.

b) If you are otherwise entitled to a foreign tax credit, the amount on line 30 must be added to the federal tax plus any dividend tax credit in the multiplier (on Schedule 1) of the foreign tax credit calculation.

c) The amount on line 30 must be added to basic federal tax for purposes of calculating lines 38, 39 and 42 of the individual surtax calculation (on Schedule 1).

d) A claim for the overseas employment tax credit may result in the application of minimum tax. You should also complete Form T691, *Alternative Minimum Tax*, to determine if minimum tax is payable.

Step V – Calculation of overseas employment tax credit

36. Enter the lesser of E and F $ ______ X amount H $ ______ divided by amount G $ ______ .... 6774 $ ______ • I

GOVERNMENT OF NEWFOUNDLAND AND LABRADOR

NEWFOUNDLAND RESEARCH AND DEVELOPMENT TAX CREDIT (INDIVIDUALS)

Use this form to calculate your Newfoundland research and development (R&D) tax credit.
If you are completing a return for a corporation, use Schedule 301 of the T2 return.

You may qualify if your business had a permanent establishment in Newfoundland in the year, and you made eligible expenditures for scientific research and experimental development carried out in Newfoundland in the year.

The credit is available for 1996 and subsequent tax years, and is equal to 15% of **eligible expenditures** as defined under subsection 127(9) of the federal *Income Tax Act*. It is applied against your total payable on line 435 of your return, and any remaining balance is refunded.

Provide details of your expenditures on a separate sheet of paper.
Attach it and a completed copy of this form to your return.

Tax year ▶

Eligible expenditures

Enter your total eligible expenditures for R&D in the tax year .... ______ 1

Calculation of credit

Enter the amount from line 1 .... ______ x 15% = ...			______	2
Credit allocated from a partnership	______	3		
Credit allocated from a trust	+ ______	4		
Add line 3 and line 4	= ______	▶	+ ______	5
Add line 2 and line 5. Include this amount on line 479 of your return .... **Total credit**			= ______	6

GOVERNMENT OF NEWFOUNDLAND AND LABRADOR

NEWFOUNDLAND RESEARCH AND DEVELOPMENT TAX CREDIT (INDIVIDUALS)

Use this form to calculate your Newfoundland research and development (R&D) tax credit.
If you are completing a return for a corporation, use Schedule 301 of the T2 return.

You may qualify if your business had a permanent establishment in Newfoundland in the year, and you made eligible expenditures for scientific research and experimental development carried out in Newfoundland in the year.

The credit is available for 1996 and subsequent tax years, and is equal to 15% of **eligible expenditures** as defined under subsection 127(9) of the federal *Income Tax Act*. It is applied against your total payable on line 435 of your return, and any remaining balance is refunded.

Provide details of your expenditures on a separate sheet of paper.
Attach it and a completed copy of this form to your return.

Tax year ▶

Eligible expenditures

Enter your total eligible expenditures for R&D in the tax year .... ______ 1

Calculation of credit

Enter the amount from line 1 .... ______ x 15% = ... ______ 2
Credit allocated from a partnership .... ______ 3
Credit allocated from a trust .... + ______ 4
Add line 3 and line 4 .... = ______ ▶ + ______ 5
Add line 2 and line 5.
Include this amount on line 479 of your return .... Total credit = ______ 6

T1129 (99)
Printed in Canada
(Français au verso)
3729
Canada

Canada Customs and Revenue Agency / Agence des douanes et du revenu du Canada

STATEMENT OF BUSINESS ACTIVITIES

2

- For more information on how to complete this statement, see the income tax guide called *Business and Professional Income.*

Identification

Your name	Your social insurance number ___ – ___ – ___
From: Year Month Day To: Year Month Day	Was 1999 your last year of business? Yes ☐ No ☐
Business name	Main product or service
Business address	Industry code (see the appendix in the *Business and Professional Income* guide)
City, town, or municipality, and province / Postal code	Partnership identification number
Name and address of person or firm preparing this form	Tax shelter identification number
Business number	Your percentage of the partnership %

Income

	Code			
Sales, commissions, or fees				a
Minus – Goods and services tax/harmonized sales tax (GST/HST) and provincial sales tax (if included in sales above)				
– Returns, allowances, and discounts (if included in sales above)				
Total of the above two lines			▶	b
Net sales, commissions, or fees (line a minus line b)	8000			
Reserves deducted last year	8290			
Other income	8230			
Gross income (total of the above three lines) – Enter on the appropriate line of your income tax return	8299			c

Calculation of cost of goods sold (enter business part only)

	Code		
Opening inventory (include raw materials, goods in process, and finished goods)	8300		
Purchases during the year (net of returns, allowances, and discounts)	8320		
Subcontracts	8360		
Direct wage costs	8340		
Other costs	8450		
Total of the above five lines			
Minus – Closing inventory (include raw materials, goods in process, and finished goods)	8500		
Cost of goods sold	8518	▶	d
Gross profit (line c minus line d)	8519		e

Expenses (enter business part only)

	Code		
Advertising	8521		
Bad debts	8590		
Business tax, fees, licences, dues, memberships, and subscriptions	8760		
Delivery, freight, and express	9275		
Fuel costs (except for motor vehicles)	9224		
Insurance	8690		
Interest	8710		
Maintenance and repairs	8960		
Management and administration fees	8871		
Meals and entertainment (allowable part only)	8523		
Motor vehicle expenses (not including capital cost allowance)	9281		
Office expenses	8810		
Supplies	8811		
Legal, accounting, and other professional fees	8860		
Property taxes	9180		
Rent	8910		
Salaries, wages, and benefits (including employer's contributions)	9060		
Travel	9200		
Telephone and utilities	9220		
Other expenses	9270		
Subtotal			
Allowance on eligible capital property	9935		
Capital cost allowance (from Area A on page 3 of this form)	9936		
Total business expenses (total of the above three lines)	9368	▶	f
Net income (loss) before adjustments (line e minus line f)	9369		

Net income (loss) before adjustments (from line 9369 on page 1 of this form)			g
Your share of line g above			h
Minus – Other amounts deductible from your share of net partnership income (loss) from the chart below	9943		i
Net income (loss) after adjustments (line h minus line i)			j
Minus – Business-use-of-home expenses (from the chart below)	9945		
Your net income (loss) line j minus line 9945 (enter on the appropriate line of your income tax return)	9946		

Other amounts deductible from your share of net partnership income (loss)

Claim expenses you incurred that were not included in the partnership statement of income and expenses, and for which the partnership did not reimburse you.

Total (enter this amount on line i above)	

Calculation of business-use-of-home expenses

Heat		
Electricity		
Insurance		
Maintenance		
Mortgage interest		
Property taxes		
Other expenses		
Subtotal		
Minus – Personal use part		
Subtotal		
Plus – Amount carried forward from previous year		
Subtotal		1
Minus – Net income (loss) after adjustments (from line j above) – If negative, enter "0"		2
Business-use-of-home expenses available to carry forward (line 1 minus line 2) – If negative, enter "0"		
Allowable claim (the lesser of amounts 1 or 2 above) – Enter this amount on line 9945 above		

Details of other partners

Partner's name and address	Share of net income or (loss)	Percentage of partnership
	$	%
	$	%
	$	%
	$	%

Details of equity

Total business liabilities	9931	
Drawings in 1999	9932	
Capital contributions in 1999	9933	

Area A – Calculation of capital cost allowance claim

1 Class number	2 Undepreciated capital cost (UCC) at the start of the year	3 Cost of additions in the year (see Areas B and C below)	4 Proceeds of dispositions in the year (see Areas D and E below)	5 * UCC after additions and dispositions (col. 2 **plus** 3 **minus** 4)	6 Adjustment for current year additions (1/2 x (col. 3 **minus** 4)) If negative, enter "0"	7 Base amount for capital cost allowance (col. 5 **minus** 6)	8 Rate %	9 CCA for the year (col. 7 x 8 or an adjusted amount)	10 UCC at the end of the year (col. 5 **minus** 9)

Total CCA claim for the year (enter this amount, minus any personal part, on line 9936 on page 1 of this form)

* If you have a negative amount in this column, add it to income as a recapture on line 8230, "Other income," on page 1 of this form. If no property is left in the class and there is a positive amount in the column, deduct the amount from income as a terminal loss on line 9270, "Other expenses," on page 1 of this form. Recapture and terminal loss do not apply to a Class 10.1 property. For more information, read Chapter 4 of the *Business and Professional Income* guide.

Area B – Details of equipment additions in the year

1 Class number	2 Property details	3 Total cost	4 Personal part (if applicable)	5 Business part (column 3 **minus** column 4)

Total equipment additions in the year 9925

Area C – Details of building additions in the year

1 Class number	2 Property details	3 Total cost	4 Personal part (if applicable)	5 Business part (column 3 **minus** column 4)

Total building additions in the year 9927

Area D – Details of equipment dispositions in the year

1 Class number	2 Property details	3 Proceeds of disposition (should not be more than the capital cost)	4 Personal part (if applicable)	5 Business part (column 3 **minus** column 4)

Note: If you disposed of property from your business in the year, see Chapter 4 in the *Business and Professional Income* guide for information about your proceeds of disposition.

Total equipment dispositions in the year 9926

Area E – Details of building dispositions in the year

1 Class number	2 Property details	3 Proceeds of disposition (should not be more than the capital cost)	4 Personal part (if applicable)	5 Business part (column 3 **minus** column 4)

Note: If you disposed of property from your business in the year, see Chapter 4 in the *Business and Professional Income* guide for information about your proceeds of disposition.

Total building dispositions in the year 9928

Area F – Details of land additions and dispositions in the year

Total cost of all land additions in the year	9923	
Total proceeds from all land dispositions in the year	9924	

Note: You cannot claim capital cost allowance on land.

Printed in Canada

Canada Customs and Revenue Agency / Agence des douanes et du revenu du Canada

STATEMENT OF FARMING ACTIVITIES

• For information on how to complete this statement, see the guide called *Farming Income.*

Identification

5

Name	Social insurance number
For the period from: Year Month Day to: Year Month Day	Was 1999 your final year of farming? Yes ☐ No ☐
Farm name	Acres owned
Farm address	Acres farmed
Township or municipality and province	Postal code
Accounting method Cash ☐ Accrual ☐ — Main product or service	Industry code (see Chapter 2 of the *Farming Income* guide)
Name and address of person or firm preparing this form	Partnership identification number
Business Number	Your percentage of the partnership %

Income

Item	Code	Amount
Wheat		
Oats		
Barley		
Mixed grains		
Corn		
Canola		
Flaxseed		
Soya beans		
Other grains and oilseeds		
Total grains and oilseeds	9370	▶
Fruit	9421	
Potatoes	9422	
Vegetables (excluding potatoes)	9423	
Tobacco	9424	
Other crops	9420	
Greenhouse and nursery products	9425	
Forage crops or seeds	9426	
Livestock sold		
- Cattle	9471	
- Swine	9472	
- Poultry	9473	
- Sheep and lambs	9474	
- Other animal specialties	9470	
Milk and cream (excluding dairy subsidies)	9476	
Eggs	9477	
Other commodities	9520	
Program payments		
- Dairy subsidies	9541	
- Crop insurance	9542	
- Other payments	9540	
Rebates	9570	
Custom or contract work, and machine rentals	9601	
Insurance proceeds	9604	
Patronage dividends	9605	
Other income (Specify)		
	9600	
Gross income – total of lines 9370 to 9600 (enter on line 168 of your income tax return)	9659	

2

	Code			
Gross income (from line 9659 on page 1)				a
Expenses (enter business portion only)				
Containers and twine	9661			
Fertilizers and lime	9662			
Pesticides (herbicides, insecticides, fungicides)	9663			
Seeds and plants	9664			
Feed, supplements, straw, and bedding	9711			
Livestock purchased	9712			
Veterinary fees, medicine, and breeding fees	9713			
Machinery expenses				
- Repairs, licences, and insurance	9760			
- Gasoline, diesel fuel, and oil	9764			
Building and fence repairs	9795			
Clearing, levelling, and draining land	9796			
Crop insurance, GRIP, and stabilization premiums	9797			
Custom or contract work, and machinery rental	9798			
Electricity	9799			
Heating fuel	9802			
Insurance program overpayment recapture	9803			
Other insurance	9804			
Interest	9805			
Office expenses	9808			
Legal and accounting fees	9809			
Property taxes	9810			
Rent (land, buildings, and pasture)	9811			
Salaries, wages, and benefits (including employer's contributions)	9814			
Motor vehicle expenses (not including capital cost allowance)	9819			
Small tools	9820			
Mandatory inventory adjustment included in 1998	9937			
Optional inventory adjustment included in 1998	9938			
Other expenses				
Total other expenses	9790	►		
Subtotal of all expenses				
Allowance on eligible capital property	9935			
Capital cost allowance (from Area E on page 3)	9936			
Total farm expenses (total of the above three lines)	9898		►	b
Net income (loss) before adjustments (line a minus line b)	9899			
Optional inventory adjustment included in 1999	9941			
Mandatory inventory adjustment included in 1999	9942			
Total of the above three lines				c
Your share of the amount on line c				d
Minus – Other amounts deductible from your share of net partnership income (loss) from the chart on page 4	9943			e
Net income (loss) after adjustments (line d minus line e)				f
Minus – Business-use-of-home expenses (from the chart on page 4)	9945			
Your net income (loss) (line f minus line 9945)	9946			

Area A – Details of equipment additions in the year

1 Class number	2 Property details	3 Total cost	4 Personal portion (if applicable)	5 Business portion (column 3 minus column 4)

Total equipment additions in the year 9925

Area B – Details of building additions in the year

1 Class number	2 Property details	3 Total cost	4 Personal portion (if applicable)	5 Business portion (col .3 minus col. 4)
			Total building additions in the year 9927	

Area C – Details of equipment dispositions in the year

1 Class number	2 Property details	3 Proceeds of disposition (should not be more than the capital cost)	4 Personal portion (if applicable)	5 Business portion (column 3 minus column 4)
			Total equipment dispositions in the year 9926	

Note: If you disposed of property from your farming business in the year, see Chapter 3 of the *Farming Income Guide* for information about your proceeds of disposition.

Area D – Details of building dispositions in the year

1 Class number	2 Property details	3 Proceeds of disposition (should not be more than the capital cost)	4 Personal portion (if applicable)	5 Business portion (column 3 minus column 4)
			Total building dispositions in the year 9928	

Note: If you disposed of property from your farming business in the year, see Chapter 3 in the *Farming Income Guide* for information about your proceeds of disposition.

Area E – Calculation of capital cost allowance (CCA)

Part XI properties (acquired after 1971)

1 Class number	2 Undepreciated capital cost (UCC) at the start of the year	3 Cost of additions in the year (see Area A on page 2 and Area B above)	4 Proceeds of dispositions in the year (see Areas C and D above)	5 * UCC after additions and dispositions (col. 2 plus col. 3 minus col. 4)	6 Adjustment for current- year additions (1/2 x (col. 3 minus col. 4) – if negative, enter "0")	7 Base amount for CCA (col. 5 minus col. 6)	8 Rate (%)	9 CCA for the year (col. 7 x col. 8 or an adjusted amount)	10 UCC at the end of the year (col. 5 minus col. 9)

* If you have a negative amount in this column, add it to income as a recapture on line 9600 "Other income" on page 1 of this form. If there is no property left in the class and there is a positive amount in the column, deduct the amount from income as a terminal loss on line 9790 "Total other expenses" on page 2 of this form. Recapture and terminal loss do not apply to a Class 10.1 property. For more information, see Chapter 3 of the *Farming Income* guide.

Total CCA on Part XI properties ▶ ______ (i)

Part XVII properties (acquired before 1972)

1 Year acquired	2 Kind of property	3 Month of disposition	4 Cost (business portion)	5 Rate (%)	6 Allowance for this year	7 Total allowance for this and previous years

Enter the total of lines (i) and (ii) on line 9936 on page 2 of this form. **Total CCA on Part XVII properties** ▶ ______ (ii)

Area F – Details of land additions and dispositions in the year

Note: You cannot claim capital cost allowance on land. See Chapter 3 in the *Farming Income Guide* for more information.

Total cost of all land additions in the year	9923	
Total proceeds from all land dispositions in the year	9924	

Area G – Details of quota additions and dispositions in the year

Note: Quotas are eligible capital property. See Chapter 4 in the *Farming Income Guide* for more information about this kind of property.

Total cost of all quota additions in the year	9929	
Total proceeds from all quota dispositions in the year	9930	

Other amounts deductible from your share of net partnership income (loss)

Claim expenses you incurred that you did not include in the partnership statement of income and expenses, and for which the partnership did not reimburse you.

Total (enter this amount on line e on page 2 of this form)

Calculation of business-use-of-home expenses

Heat		
Electricity		
Insurance		
Maintenance		
Mortgage interest		
Property taxes		
Other expenses		
Subtotal		
Minus – Personal use portion		
Subtotal		
Plus – Amount carried forward from previous year		
Subtotal		1
Minus – Net income (loss) after adjustments from line f on page 2 of this form (if negative, enter "0")		2
Business-use-of-home expenses available for carryforward (line 1 minus line 2) – if negative, enter "0"		
Allowable claim (the lower of amounts 1 or 2 above) – enter this amount on line 9945 on page 2 of this form		

Details of equity

Total business liabilities	9931	
Drawings in 1999	9932	
Capital contributions in 1999	9933	

Details of other partners

Partner's name and address	Share of net income or (loss) $	Percentage of partnership %
Partner's name and address	Share of net income or (loss) $	Percentage of partnership %
Partner's name and address	Share of net income or (loss) $	Percentage of partnership %
Partner's name and address	Share of net income or (loss) $	Percentage of partnership %

Printed in Canada

Canada Customs and Revenue Agency / Agence des douanes et du revenu du Canada

STATEMENT OF FISHING ACTIVITIES

- For more information on how to complete this statement, see the guide called *Fishing Income.*

4

Identification

Your name

Your social insurance number

For the period from: Year Month Day to: Year Month Day

Was 1999 your final year of fishing? Yes ☐ No ☐

Boat name

Main species

CFV licence #

Industry code (see Chapter 2)

Name and address of person or firm preparing this form

Partnership identification number

Tax shelter identification number

Business Number

Your percentage of the partnership %

Income

Item	Code	Amount	Line
Fish products			
Other marine products			
Grants, credits, and rebates			
Subsidies			
Compensation for loss of fishing income or property			
Other income			
Sharesperson income – List name of fishing boat and captain:			
Gross income (total of the above lines, enter this amount on line 170 of your income tax return)	8299		a

Expenses (enter business portion only)

Item	Code	Amount
Bait, ice, salt	9138	
Crew shares	9062	
Fuel costs (except for motor vehicles)	9224	
Gear	9136	
Insurance	8690	
Interest	8710	
Food	8523	
Licences	8760	
Motor vehicle expenses (not including capital cost allowance)	9281	
Office expenses	8810	
Nets and traps	9137	
Legal, accounting, and other professional fees	8860	
Salaries, wages, and benefits (including employer's contributions)	9060	
Repairs – Fishing boat		
– Engine		
– Electrical equipment		
Total of the above three lines		
Minus – Insurance recovery		
Your cost	8963	▶
Other expenses	9270	
Subtotal		
Capital cost allowance (from Area A on page 2 of this form)	9936	
Allowance on eligible capital property	9935	
Total expenses (total of the above three lines)	9368	▶ b

Item	Code	Amount	Line
Net income (loss) before adjustments (line a minus line b)	9369		
Your share of line 9369 above			c
Minus – Other amounts deductible from your share of net partnership income (loss) from the chart on page 2 of this form	9943		d
Net income (loss) after adjustments (line c minus line d)			e
Minus – Business-use-of-home expenses (from the chart on page 2 of this form)	9945		
Your net income (loss) line e minus line 9945 (enter on line 143 of your income tax return)	9946		

Other amounts deductible from your share of net partnership income (loss)

Claim expenses you incurred that were not included in the partnership statement of income and expenses, and for which the partnership did not reimburse you.

Total (enter this amount on line d on page 1 of this form)

Calculating business-use-of-home expenses

Heat
Electricity
Insurance
Maintenance
Mortgage interest
Property taxes
Other expenses

Subtotal

Minus – Personal use portion

Subtotal

Plus – Amount carried forward from previous year

Subtotal 1

Minus – Net income (loss) after adjustments from line e on page 1 of this form (if negative, enter "0") 2

Business-use-of-home expenses available to carry forward (line 1 minus line 2), if negative, enter "0"

Allowable claim (the lower of amounts 1 or 2 above) enter this amount on line 9945 on page 1 of this form

Details of equity

Total business liabilities	9931	
Drawings in 1999	9932	
Capital contributions in 1999	9933	

Area A – Calculating capital cost allowance claim

Part XI properties (acquired after 1971)

1 Class number	2 Undepreciated capital cost (UCC) at the start of the year	3 Cost of additions in the year (see Areas B and C on page 3)	4 Proceeds of dispositions in the year (see Areas D and E on page 3)	5 UCC * after additions and dispositions (col. 2 **plus** 3 **minus** 4)	6 Adjustment for current year additions (1/2 x (col. 3 **minus** 4)) If negative, enter "0"	7 Base amount for capital cost allowance (col. 5 minus 6)	8 Rate %	9 CCA for the year (col. 7 x 8 or an adjusted amount)	10 UCC at the end of the year (col. 5 **minus** 9)
							Total CCA on Part XI properties ▶		i

* If you have a negative amount in this column, add it to income as a recapture under "Other income" on the appropriate line on page 1 of this form. If there is no property left in the class and there is a positive amount in the column, deduct the amount from income as a terminal loss on line 9270 "Other expenses" on page 1 of this form. Recapture and terminal loss do not apply to a Class 10.1 property. For more information, read Chapter 3.

Part XVII properties (acquired before 1972)

1 Year acquired	2 Kind of property	3 Month of disposition	4 Cost (business portion)	5 Rate %	6 Allowance for this year	7 Total allowance for this and previous years
			Total CCA on Part XVII properties ▶			ii

Enter the total of lines i and ii on line 9936 on page 1 of this form.

Area B – Details of equipment additions in the year

1 Class number	2 Property details	3 Total cost	4 Personal portion (if applicable)	5 Business portion (Column 3 **minus** Column 4)
			Total equipment additions in the year 9925	

Area C – Details of building additions in the year

1 Class number	2 Property details	3 Total cost	4 Personal portion (if applicable)	5 Business portion (Column 3 **minus** Column 4)
			Total building additions in the year 9927	

Area D – Details of equipment dispositions in the year

1 Class number	2 Property details	3 Proceeds of disposition (should not be more than the capital cost)	4 Personal portion (if applicable)	5 Business portion (Column 3 **minus** Column 4)
			Total equipment dispositions in the year 9926	

Note: If you disposed of property from your fishing business in the year, see Chapter 3 for information about your proceeds of disposition.

Area E – Details of building dispositions in the year

1 Class number	2 Property details	3 Proceeds of disposition (should not be more than the capital cost)	4 Personal portion (if applicable)	5 Business portion (Column 3 **minus** Column 4)
			Total building dispositions in the year 9928	

Note: If you disposed of property from your fishing business in the year, see Chapter 3 for information about your proceeds of disposition.

Area F – Details of land additions and dispositions in the year

Total cost of all land additions in the year	9923	
Total proceeds from all land dispositions in the year	9924	

Note: You cannot claim capital cost allowance on land.

Details of other partners

Partner's name and address	Share of net income or (loss)	Percentage of partnership
	$	%
	$	%
	$	%
	$	%

Printed in Canada

Canada Customs and Revenue Agency — Agence des douanes et du revenu du Canada

STATEMENT OF TRUST INCOME ALLOCATIONS AND DESIGNATIONS
ÉTAT DES REVENUS DE FIDUCIE (RÉPARTITIONS ET ATTRIBUTIONS) — **T3**

Trust year ending / Fin d'année de la fiducie							
Year / Année	If the recipient identification number is not shown, or if it is incorrect, contact the issuer of this slip. Si le numéro d'identification du bénéficiaire n'est pas indiqué, ou s'il est erroné, communiquez avec l'émetteur de ce feuillet.	12 Recipient identification number / Numéro d'identification du bénéficiare		14 Account number / Numéro de compte — T		16 Report code / Code de genre de feuillet	18 Beneficiary code / Code du bénéficiaire
Month / Mois	21 Capital gains / Gains en capital	22 Lump-sum pension benefits / Prestations de pension forfaitaires	23 Actual amount of dividends / Montant réel des dividendes	24 Foreign business income / Revenu étranger tiré d'une entreprise	25 Foreign non-business income / Revenu étranger non tiré d'une entreprise	26 Other income / Autres revenus	
	30 Capital gains eligible for deduction / Gains en capital admissibles pour déduction	31 Qualifying pension income / Revenu de pension admissible	32 Taxable amount of dividends / Montant imposable des dividendes	33 Foreign business income tax paid / Impôt étranger payé sur un revenu tiré d'une entreprise	34 Foreign non-business income tax paid / Impôt étranger payé sur un revenu non tiré d'une entreprise	35 Eligible death benefits / Prestations consécutives au décès admissibles	36 Miscellaneous / Divers
	37 Insurance segregated fund capital losses / Pertes en capital sur les fonds réservés d'assureur	38 Part XII.2 tax credit / Crédit d'impôt de la partie XII.2	39 Federal dividend tax credit / Crédit d'impôt fédéral pour dividendes	Investment tax credit – Crédit d'impôt à l'investissement: 40 Investment cost or expenditures / Investissement ou dépenses	41 Tax credit / Crédit d'impôt	45 Other credits / Autres crédits	

Recipient: Last name first, and full address – Bénéficiaire : Nom de famille, prénom et adresse

Footnotes – Notes

Name of trust / Nom de la fiducie

T3 (00) 0179

Return with T3 Summary
Retournez avec le formulaire T3 *Sommaire* **1**

For information in English see back of copy 2
Pour des renseignements en français, lisez le verso de la copie 3 **2**

For information in English see back of copy 2
Pour des renseignements en français, lisez le verso de la copie 3 **3**

For trustee
Pour le fiduciaire **4**

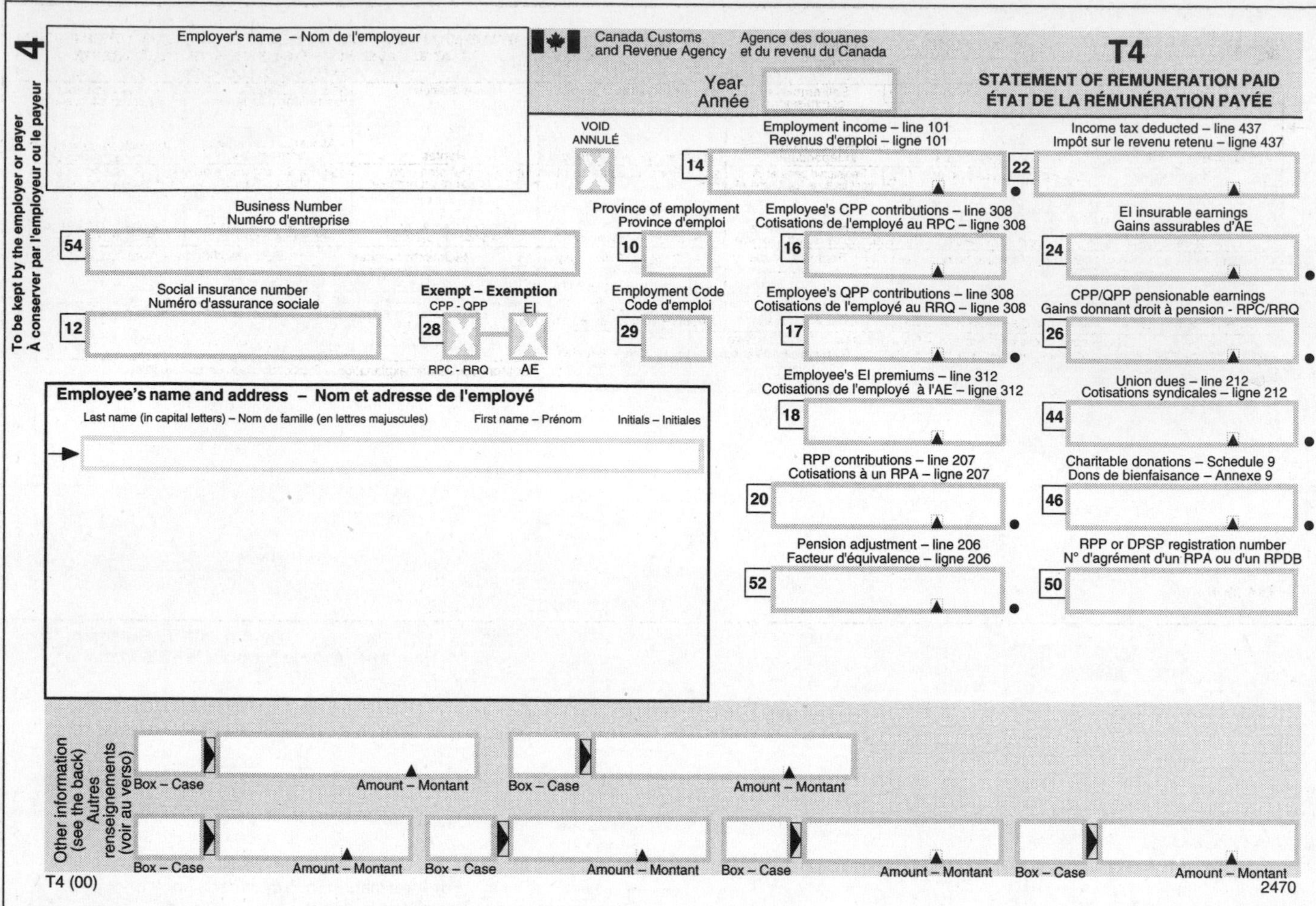

4

To be kept by the employer or payer
À conserver par l'employeur ou le payeur

Employer's name – Nom de l'employeur

Canada Customs and Revenue Agency
Agence des douanes et du revenu du Canada

Year
Année

T4
STATEMENT OF REMUNERATION PAID
ÉTAT DE LA RÉMUNÉRATION PAYÉE

VOID
ANNULÉ

Employment income – line 101
Revenus d'emploi – ligne 101
14

Income tax deducted – line 437
Impôt sur le revenu retenu – ligne 437
22

Business Number
Numéro d'entreprise
54

Province of employment
Province d'emploi
10

Employee's CPP contributions – line 308
Cotisations de l'employé au RPC – ligne 308
16

EI insurable earnings
Gains assurables d'AE
24

Social insurance number
Numéro d'assurance sociale
12

Exempt – Exemption
CPP - QPP
EI
28
RPC - RRQ
AE

Employment Code
Code d'emploi
29

Employee's QPP contributions – line 308
Cotisations de l'employé au RRQ – ligne 308
17

CPP/QPP pensionable earnings
Gains donnant droit à pension - RPC/RRQ
26

Employee's name and address – Nom et adresse de l'employé
Last name (in capital letters) – Nom de famille (en lettres majuscules)
First name – Prénom
Initials – Initiales

Employee's EI premiums – line 312
Cotisations de l'employé à l'AE – ligne 312
18

Union dues – line 212
Cotisations syndicales – ligne 212
44

RPP contributions – line 207
Cotisations à un RPA – ligne 207
20

Charitable donations – Schedule 9
Dons de bienfaisance – Annexe 9
46

Pension adjustment – line 206
Facteur d'équivalence – ligne 206
52

RPP or DPSP registration number
N° d'agrément d'un RPA ou d'un RPDB
50

Other information (see the back)
Autres renseignements (voir au verso)

Box – Case | Amount – Montant | Box – Case | Amount – Montant

Box – Case | Amount – Montant | Box – Case | Amount – Montant | Box – Case | Amount – Montant | Box – Case | Amount – Montant

T4 (00)
2470

Canada Customs and Revenue Agency — Agence des douanes et du revenu du Canada

Year / Année

T4A

STATEMENT OF PENSION, RETIREMENT, ANNUITY, AND OTHER INCOME
ÉTAT DE REVENU DE PENSION, DE RETRAITE, DE RENTE OU D'AUTRES SOURCES

Box	English	French
16	Pension or superannuation	Prestations de retraite ou autres pensions
18	Lump-sum payments	Paiements forfaitaires
20	Self-employed commissions	Commissions d'un travail indépendant
22	Income tax deducted	Impôt sur le revenu retenu
24	Annuities	Rentes
26	Eligible retiring allowances	Allocations de retraite admissibles
27	Non-eligible retiring allowances	Allocations de retraite non admissibles
28	Other income	Autres revenus
30	Patronage allocations	Répartitions selon l'apport commercial
32	Registered pension plan contributions (past service)	Cotisations à un régime de pension agréé (services passés)
34	Pension adjustment	Facteur d'équivalence
36	Pension plan registration number	Numéro d'agrément du régime de pension
40	RESP accumulated income payments	Paiements de revenu accumulé d'un REEE
42	RESP educational assistance payments	Paiements d'aide aux études d'un REEE
46	Charitable donations	Dons de bienfaisance
12	Social insurance number	Numéro d'assurance sociale
38	Footnote codes	Codes de notes
39	Government use only	Réservé au gouvernement
14	Recipient's number	Numéro du bénéficiaire
61	Business Number	Numéro d'entreprise

Employer's or payer's name – Nom de l'employeur ou du payeur

Recipient's name and address – Nom et adresse du bénéficiaire

Last name (in capital letters) – Nom de famille (en lettres majuscules) First name – Prénom Initials – Initiales

Footnote codes and explanation – Explication des codes de notes

T4A (00)

Revenue Canada / Revenu Canada

T4A(OAS)

STATEMENT OF OLD AGE SECURITY
RELEVÉ DE LA SÉCURITÉ DE LA VIEILLESSE

Year / Année	18 Taxable pension paid / Versement de pension imposable	19 Gross pension paid / Versement brut de pension	20 Overpayment recovered / Paiement en trop recouvré	21 Net supplements paid / Versement net des suppléments	22 Income tax deducted / Impôt sur le revenu retenu	23 Quebec income tax deducted / Impôt sur le revenu du Québec retenu

Issued by: Human Resources Development Canada, Income Security Programs
Émis par : Développement des ressources humaines Canada, Programmes de la sécurité du revenu

12 Social insurance number / Numéro d'assurance sociale

13 Old Age Security number / Numéro de la sécurité de la vieillesse

T4A (OAS) (99)
PO137 B (1998/06/23)

Please see explanation on the back.
Lisez les explications au verso.

COPY/COPIE 1

Canada

Canada Customs and Revenue Agency / Agence des douanes et du revenu du Canada

STATEMENT OF EMPLOYMENT INSURANCE BENEFITS
ÉTAT DES PRESTATIONS D'ASSURANCE-EMPLOI

T4E Q

Year / Année	Report code / Code du feuillet	7 Repayment rate / Taux de remboursement	14 Total benefits paid / Prestations totales versées	15 Regular and other benefits paid / Prestations régulières et autres prestations versées	16 Special benefits paid / Prestations spéciales versées	17 Employment benefits & support measures paid / Prestations d'emploi et mesures de soutien versées	18 Tax exempt benefits / Prestations exemptes d'impôt
	22 Federal income tax deducted / Impôt fédéral sur le revenu retenu	23 Quebec income tax deducted / Impôt du Québec sur le revenu retenu	24 Non-resident tax deducted / Impôt des non-résidents retenu	12 Social insurance number / Numéro d'assurance sociale	**Repayment of an overpayment → Remboursement d'un paiement en trop**	30 Total / Total	
					26 Paid to issuer / Payé à l'émetteur	27 Reversal of federal tax deducted / Annulation de l'impôt fédéral retenu	

You may have to repay all or part of the benefits shown in boxes 15 and 16 if the amount on line 234 of your return is more than $39,000. See line 235 in your tax guide for details.

Vous pourriez devoir rembourser la totalité ou une partie des prestations indiquées aux cases 15 et 16 si le montant à la ligne 234 de votre déclaration dépasse 39 000 $. Lisez votre guide d'impôt à la ligne 235 pour plus de précisions.

Issued by
Émis par

Attach this copy to your federal return
Joignez cette copie à votre déclaration fédérale **2**

T4E (99)

Canada Customs and Revenue Agency / Agence des douanes et du revenu du Canada

STATEMENT OF INCOME FROM A REGISTERED RETIREMENT INCOME FUND
ÉTAT DU REVENU PROVENANT D'UN FONDS ENREGISTRÉ DE REVENU DE RETRAITE

T4RIF

Year / Année

16 Taxable amounts / Montants imposables

Amounts deemed received by the annuitant / Montants réputés reçus par le rentier: 18 Deceased / Personne décédée; 20 Deregistration / Annulation de l'enregistrement

22 Other income or deductions / Autres revenus ou déductions

24 Excess amount / Excédent

26 Spousal / Conjoint

28 Income tax deducted / Impôt sur le revenu retenu

30 Year / Année, Month / Mois, Day / Jour

Contributor spouse – Conjoint cotisant

32 Social insurance number * / Numéro d'assurance sociale *

34 Name (last name, first name) / Nom (nom de famille, prénom)

* If your social insurance number is not shown, see the back of this slip.
Si votre numéro d'assurance sociale n'est pas indiqué, lisez le verso de ce feuillet.

Recipient's name and address – Nom et adresse du bénéficiaire

Last name (capital letters) / Nom de famille (lettres majuscules) — First name / Prénom — Initials / Initiales

12 Social insurance number * / Numéro d'assurance sociale *

14 Contract number / Numéro de contrat

60 Name of payer (carrier) of fund / Nom du payeur (émetteur) du fonds

61 Business Number / Numéro d'entreprise

36 Tax-paid amount / Montant libéré d'impôt

Return with the T4RIF Summary
Retournez avec le T4RIF *Sommaire* **1**

T4RIF (99) 1321

Canada Customs and Revenue Agency / Agence des douanes et du revenu du Canada

STATEMENT OF INCOME FROM A REGISTERED RETIREMENT INCOME FUND
ÉTAT DU REVENU PROVENANT D'UN FONDS ENREGISTRÉ DE REVENU DE RETRAITE

T4RIF

Year / Année

16 Taxable amounts / Montants imposables

Amounts deemed received by the annuitant / Montants réputés reçus par le rentier: 18 Deceased / Personne décédée; 20 Deregistration / Annulation de l'enregistrement

22 Other income or deductions / Autres revenus ou déductions

24 Excess amount / Excédent

26 Spousal / Conjoint

28 Income tax deducted / Impôt sur le revenu retenu

30 Year / Année, Month / Mois, Day / Jour

Contributor spouse – Conjoint cotisant

32 Social insurance number * / Numéro d'assurance sociale *

34 Name (last name, first name) / Nom (nom de famille, prénom)

* If your social insurance number is not shown, see the back of this slip.
Si votre numéro d'assurance sociale n'est pas indiqué, lisez le verso de ce feuillet.

Recipient's name and address – Nom et adresse du bénéficiaire

Last name (capital letters) / Nom de famille (lettres majuscules) — First name / Prénom — Initials / Initiales

12 Social insurance number * / Numéro d'assurance sociale *

14 Contract number / Numéro de contrat

60 Name of payer (carrier) of fund / Nom du payeur (émetteur) du fonds

36 Tax-paid amount / Montant libéré d'impôt

For information in English, see the back of copy 2
Pour des renseignements en français, lisez le verso de la copie 3 **2**

T4RIF (99) 1321

Canada Customs and Revenue Agency / Agence des douanes et du revenu du Canada

STATEMENT OF RRSP INCOME
ÉTAT DU REVENU PROVENANT D'UN REER

T4RSP

Year / Année	16 Annuity payments / Paiements de rente	18 Refund of premiums to spouse / Remboursement de primes au conjoint	20 Refund of excess contributions / Remboursement des cotisations excédentaires	22 Withdrawal and commutation payments / Retrait et paiements de conversion	25 LLP withdrawal / Retrait REEP	26 Amounts deemed received on deregistration / Montants réputés reçus lors de l'annulation de l'enregistrement
	28 Other income or deductions / Autres revenus ou déductions	30 Income tax deducted / Impôt sur le revenu retenu	34 Amounts deemed received on death / Montants réputés reçus au décès	24 Contributor spouse / Conjoint cotisant — Yes / Oui ☐ No / Non ☐		36 Social insurance number * / Numéro d'assurance sociale *

38 Contributor Spouse (last name, first name) – Conjoint cotisant (nom de famille, prénom)

Recipient's name and address – Nom et adresse du bénéficiaire

Last name (capital letters) / Nom de famille (lettres majuscules) — First name / Prénom — Initials / Initiales

* If your social insurance number is not shown, see the back of this slip.
Si votre numéro d'assurance sociale n'est pas indiqué, lisez le verso de ce feuillet.

12 Social insurance number * / Numéro d'assurance sociale *	14 Contract number / Numéro de contrat
60 Name of payer (issuer) of plan – Nom du payeur (émetteur) du régime	
61 Business Number / Numéro d'entreprise	40 Tax-paid amount / Montant libéré d'impôt

T4RSP (00)

Return with the T4RSP Summary
Retournez avec le T4RSP Sommaire **1**

Canada Customs and Revenue Agency / Agence des douanes et du revenu du Canada

STATEMENT OF RRSP INCOME
ÉTAT DU REVENU PROVENANT D'UN REER

T4RSP

Year / Année	16 Annuity payments / Paiements de rente	18 Refund of premiums to spouse / Remboursement de primes au conjoint	20 Refund of excess contributions / Remboursement des cotisations excédentaires	22 Withdrawal and commutation payments / Retrait et paiements de conversion	25 LLP withdrawal / Retrait REEP	26 Amounts deemed received on deregistration / Montants réputés reçus lors de l'annulation de l'enregistrement
	28 Other income or deductions / Autres revenus ou déductions	30 Income tax deducted / Impôt sur le revenu retenu	34 Amounts deemed received on death / Montants réputés reçus au décès	24 Contributor spouse / Conjoint cotisant — Yes / Oui ☐ No / Non ☐		36 Social insurance number * / Numéro d'assurance sociale *

38 Contributor Spouse (last name, first name) – Conjoint cotisant (nom de famille, prénom)

Recipient's name and address – Nom et adresse du bénéficiaire

Last name (capital letters) / Nom de famille (lettres majuscules) — First name / Prénom — Initials / Initiales

* If your social insurance number is not shown, see the back of this slip.
Si votre numéro d'assurance sociale n'est pas indiqué, lisez le verso de ce feuillet.

12 Social insurance number * / Numéro d'assurance sociale *	14 Contract number / Numéro de contrat
60 Name of payer (issuer) of plan – Nom du payeur (émetteur) du régime	
	40 Tax-paid amount / Montant libéré d'impôt

T4RSP (00)

For information in English, see the back of copy 2
Pour des renseignements en français, lisez le verso de la copie 3 **2**

Canada Customs and Revenue Agency — Agence des douanes et du revenu du Canada

Year / Année

T5

STATEMENT OF INVESTMENT INCOME
ÉTAT DES REVENUS DE PLACEMENTS

Dividends from Canadian corporations – Dividendes de sociétés canadiennes

Box	Description
10	Actual amount of dividends / Montant réel des dividendes
11	Taxable amount of dividends / Montant imposable des dividendes
12	Federal dividend tax credit / Crédit d'impôt fédéral pour dividendes
13	Interest from Canadian sources / Intérêts de source canadienne
14	Other income from Canadian sources / Autres revenus de source canadienne
15	Foreign income / Revenus étrangers
16	Foreign tax paid / Impôt étranger payé
17	Royalties from Canadian sources / Redevances de source canadienne
18	Capital gains dividends - Period 3 / Dividendes sur gains en capital - Période 3
19	Accrued income: Annuities / Revenus accumulés : Rentes
40	Capital gains dividends - Period 1 / Dividendes sur gains en capital - Période 1
41	Capital gains dividends - Period 2 / Dividendes sur gains en capital - Période 2
	VOID X ANNULÉ
20	Amount eligible for resource allowance deduction / Montant donnant droit à la déduction relative aux ressources
21	Report code / Code du feuillet
22	Recipient identification number / Numéro d'identification du bénéficiaire
23	Recipient type / Type de bénéficiaire

Recipient's name (last name first) and address - Nom et prenom et adresse du bénéficiaire

Payer's name and address – Nom et adresse du payeur

Currency and identification codes
Codes de devise et d'identification

Box	Description
27	Foreign currency / Devises étrangères
28	Transit – Succursale
29	Recipient account / Numéro de compte du bénéficiaire

Return with T5 Summary
À retourner avec le T5 *Sommaire* 1

T5 (00) 0761

Canada Customs and Revenue Agency / Agence des douanes et du revenu du Canada
Revenue Canada / Revenu Canada

STATEMENT OF PARTNERSHIP INCOME
ÉTAT DES REVENUS D'UNE SOCIÉTÉ DE PERSONNES

T5013

Fiscal period end / Exercice se terminant le: Year / Année — Month / Mois

01 Partnership's filer identification number: H A — Numéro d'identification de la société de personnes

02 Tax shelter identification number: T S — Numéro d'inscription de l'abri fiscal

04 Partnership code — Code du genre de société de personnes

05 Business code — Code du genre d'activité

06 Tax shelter's principal business activity and code — Principale activité commerciale de l'abri fiscal et code

07 Country code — Code du pays

08 Member code — Code de l'associé

09 Number of partnership units held — Nombre d'unités détenues de la société de personnes

10 Partner's share (%) of partnership income (loss) — Part (%) de l'associé dans les revenus (pertes) de la société de personnes

11 Recipient code — Code du bénéficiaire

12 Recipient's identification number — Numéro d'identification du bénéficiaire

Partner's name (last name first) – Nom et prénom de l'associé

Address – Adresse de l'associé

Postal code – Code postal

Partnership's name and address – Raison sociale et adresse de la société de personnes

Section 1 – Partnership information – Renseignements sur une société de personnes

18 Canadian and foreign net business income (loss) — Revenu net (perte nette) d'entreprise canadien et étranger	19 Foreign net business income (loss) — Revenu net (perte nette) d'entreprise étranger	20 Canadian and foreign net rental income (loss) — Revenu net (perte nette) de location canadien et étranger	21 Foreign net rental income (loss) — Revenu net (perte nette) de location étranger	22 Capital cost allowance — Déduction pour amortissement	23 Capital gains (losses) — Gains (pertes) en capital	24 Capital gains reserve — Réserve relative aux gains en capital
25 Actual amount of dividends from corporations resident in Canada — Montant réel des dividendes de sociétés résidant au Canada	26 Interest from Canadian sources — Intérêts de source canadienne	27 Foreign dividend and interest income — Revenu étranger en dividendes et en intérêts	28 Business investment loss — Perte au titre d'un placement d'entreprise	29 Partnership's total gross income — Revenu brut total de la société de personnes	30 Carrying charges — Frais financiers	31 Limited partnership loss available for carryforward — Perte comme commanditaire disponible à reporter
32 Income tax deducted — Impôt sur le revenu retenu	33 Foreign tax paid — Impôt étranger payé	34 Charitable donations and government gifts — Dons de bienfaisance et dons au gouvernement	35 Cultural and ecological gifts — Dons de biens culturels ou écosensibles	36 Federal political contributions — Contributions politiques fédérales	37 Provincial political contributions — Contributions politiques provinciales	38 Investment tax credit — Crédit d'impôt à l'investissement
39 Canadian exploration expenses — Frais d'exploration au Canada	40 Canadian development expenses — Frais d'aménagement au Canada	41 Canadian oil and gas property expense — Frais à l'égard de biens canadiens relatifs au pétrole et au gaz	42 Foreign exploration and development expenses — Frais d'exploration et d'aménagement à l'étranger	43 Recapture of earned depletion — Récupération de la déduction pour épuisement gagnée	44 Amount eligible for resource allowance deduction — Montant donnant droit à la déduction relative aux ressources	45 Limited partner's at-risk amount — Fraction à risques de la participation du commanditaire

Section 2 applies only if the partnership is a tax shelter. Remplissez la section 2 seulement si la société de personnes est un abri fiscal.

Section 2 – Tax shelter information – Renseignements sur un abri fiscal

53 Number of units acquired — Nombre d'unités acquises	54 Cost per unit — Coût par unité	55 Total cost of units — Coût total des unités	56 Limited-recourse amounts — Montant à recours limité	57 At-risk adjustment — Montant de rajustement à risque	58 Other indirect reductions — Autres réductions indirectes

Note: **The identification number issued for this tax shelter shall be included in any income tax return filed by the investor. Issuance of the identification number is for administrative purposes only and does not in any way confirm the entitlement of an investor to claim any tax benefits associated with the tax shelter.**

Remarque : **Le numéro d'inscription attribué à cet abri fiscal doit figurer dans toute déclaration d'impôt sur le revenu produite par l'investisseur. L'attribution de ce numéro n'est qu'une formalité administrative et ne confirme aucunement le droit de l'investisseur aux avantages fiscaux découlant de cet abri fiscal.**

Section 3 applies only if the partnership invested in flow-through shares of a principal-business corporation. Remplissez la section 3 seulement si la société de personnes a fait des placements dans des actions accréditives d'une entreprise principale.

Section 3 – Allocation of renounced resource expenses, reduction of amounts previously renounced, and amount of assistance – Répartition des frais de ressources renoncés, réduction de montants déjà renoncés et montant d'aide

	130 Renunciation / Renonciation	132 Adjustment / Correction	134 Assistance / Aide	136 Total
60 Canadian exploration expense / Frais d'exploration au Canada				
61 Canadian development expense / Frais d'aménagement au Canada				

Details – Détails

Privacy Act personal information bank number RCT/P-PU-005
Loi sur la protection des renseignements personnels, Fichier de renseignements personnels numéro RCT/P-PU-005

T5013 (99) 2794

For tax centre / Pour le centre fiscal **1**

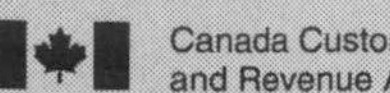

Canada Customs and Revenue Agency / Agence des douanes et du revenu du Canada

DISABILITY TAX CREDIT CERTIFICATE

This form will allow a person, or someone (including a spouse) who supports that person, to apply for the disability amount.

What is the disability amount?

This is a non-refundable tax credit that you can use to reduce the amount of income tax you have to pay. You can transfer to your spouse or to another supporting person the part of the disability amount you do not need to use to reduce your federal income tax to zero.

Supplement

Under proposed changes, starting for 2000, a person who was under 18 at the end of the year and who qualifies for the disability amount can claim an additional amount, or transfer the unused amount to a spouse or to another supporting person. However, child care expenses and attendant care expenses anyone claimed for the person may reduce the claim.

Who can claim the disability amount?

You may be able to claim the disability amount if a **qualified person** certifies **either** of the following:

- You are blind all or almost all the time, even with the use of corrective lenses or medication, and the impairment is **prolonged**.
- You have a severe mental or physical impairment which causes you to be **markedly restricted** in any of the **basic activities of daily living**, and the impairment is **prolonged**.

Life-sustaining therapy

You may also be able to claim the disability amount if you need life-sustaining therapy to support a vital function such as "clapping" therapy to help in breathing, or kidney dialysis to filter your blood. Under proposed changes, starting for 2000, you may qualify if a medical doctor certifies that you need, and dedicate time specifically for, this therapy—at least three times per week, to an average of at least 14 hours per week. The need for this therapy must have lasted, or be expected to last, for a continuous period of at least 12 months. Life-sustaining therapy does not include implanted devices, such as a pacemaker, or special programs of diet, exercise, hygiene, or medication.

Not all people with disabilities can claim the disability amount. **If you receive Canada or Quebec Pension Plan disability benefits, workers' compensation benefits, or other types of disability or insurance benefits, it does not necessarily mean you can claim the disability amount.** These programs are based on other criteria, such as an individual's inability to work.

Definitions

Qualified person

Qualified persons are medical doctors, optometrists, audiologists, occupational therapists, psychologists, and, under proposed changes, after October 17, 2000, speech-language pathologists.

What impairments can they certify?	
Medical doctors	all
Optometrists	seeing
Audiologists	hearing
Occupational therapists	walking, feeding, and dressing
Psychologists	perceiving, thinking, and remembering
Speech-language pathologists	speaking

Prolonged

An impairment is prolonged if it has lasted, or is expected to last, for a continuous period of at least 12 months.

Basic activities of daily living

These are:

- walking
- speaking
- perceiving, thinking, and remembering
- hearing
- feeding and dressing
- eliminating bodily waste

Basic activities of daily living do not include general activities such as working, housekeeping, or social or recreational activities.

Markedly restricted

You may be markedly restricted if, all or almost all the time, you are unable (or it takes you an extremely long time) to perform a basic activity of daily living, even with therapy (other than life-sustaining therapy) and the use of appropriate devices and medication.

When do we need Form T2201?

If you are making a new application for this amount, you have to file a completed Form T2201, *Disability Tax Credit Certificate*. If you have already qualified, do not file another form unless your previous period of approval has ended or we ask you to send in a new form. You must also advise us if your circumstances change. For example, if we advised you in 1997 that your claim would need to be re-evaluated for the 2000 tax year, you will need to file a new Form T2201 with your 2000 return. However, there is no need to file another Form T2201 if you will not be claiming the disability amount for 2000 and future years.

Part A – To be completed by the applicant or his or her representative

If you meet the conditions outlined on the previous page, complete Part A of this form. Then, take the form to a qualified person who can complete and certify Part B.

Attach the completed Form T2201 to your return or, if you have already filed your return, send it to your tax centre.

We will accept a photocopy only if the qualified person's signature is an original.

Be sure to keep a copy for your records.

We will review your claim **before** we assess your return. Providing incomplete or incorrect information may delay the processing of your return and any disability amount to which you may be entitled. We may ask our medical advisors to review your claim to determine if you meet the eligibility criteria, and they may contact you or the qualified person for more information.

Any fees that a qualified person may charge to complete Part B, or to provide us with additional information, are your responsibility. These fees are not covered by the Canada Customs and Revenue Agency or by provincial medicare plans.

6730 The person with the disability is:

1. ☐ Me
2. ☐ My spouse
3. ☐ Other (indicate relationship) ____________

Information about the person with the disability

Name and address

____

____

____

Date of birth (Year / Month / Day)	Social insurance number	Maiden name
6732	6734	

Information about the person claiming the disability amount (if different from above)

Name	Social insurance number

Give the **name**, **address**, and **telephone number** of any qualified person (defined on the previous page) who knows about the individual's impairment. If you need more space, attach a separate sheet of paper.

____

____

Authorization

As the person with the disability or an authorized representative, I authorize any qualified person having medical records to disclose the information contained in those records to the Canada Customs and Revenue Agency for the purpose of determining if the person with the disability meets the eligibility requirements for the disability amount.

Sign here ____________ Telephone ____________ Date ____________

6744 ☐ **DO NOT USE THIS AREA**

Part B – To be completed by a qualified person who is familiar with the patient's impairment

Be sure to review the eligibility requirements on page 1.

Eligibility for the disability amount is based on the functional impairment of your patient, and not on the medical diagnosis.

Your patient **does not** qualify if he or she receives therapy (other than life-sustaining therapy), uses appropriate devices, or takes medication that removes a marked restriction in a basic activity of daily living.

Your patient is responsible for any fees you may charge to complete this form. These fees are not covered by the Canada Customs and Revenue Agency or by provincial medicare plans.

Claims for children

If the child is blind or needs life-sustaining therapy to support a vital function, complete Part B as you would for an adult.

For impairments affecting a basic activity of daily living for a child from birth to three years of age, assess the child's developmental progress in relation to the normal range of development. Basic activities of daily living for a child up to the age of three are normally performed with the help of a parent or legal guardian. However, if the impairment is obvious or medically proven, an assessment can be done at an early age. After the age of three, assess how the impairment affects the child's ability to perform the basic activities of daily living.

Patient's name ____________________

Answer the following questions as they apply to your patient's impairment.

■ Can your patient see?

Answer **no** only if, all or almost all the time, even with corrective lenses or medication, your patient cannot see; that is, visual acuity in both eyes with proper refractive lenses is 20/200 (6/60) or less with the Snellen Chart or an equivalent, or when the greatest diameter of the field of vision in both eyes is less than 20 degrees .... **yes** ☐ **no** ☐ 1

What is your patient's visual acuity after correction? Right eye: ____ Left eye: ____
What is your patient's visual field? (if possible in degrees) Right eye: ____ Left eye: ____

■ Can your patient walk?

Answer **no** only if, all or almost all the time, even with therapy, medication, or a device, your patient cannot walk 50 metres on level ground, or he or she takes an inordinate amount of time to do so .... **yes** ☐ **no** ☐ 2

If you answered **no** and your patient is confined to a bed or a wheelchair, how many hours per day (excluding sleeping hours) does this apply? .... ____

■ Can your patient speak?

Answer **no** only if, all or almost all the time, even with therapy, medication, or a device, your patient cannot speak so as to be understood in a quiet setting, or he or she takes an inordinate amount of time to do so (exclude language differences) .... **yes** ☐ **no** ☐ 3

■ Can your patient perceive, think, and remember?

Answer **no** only if, all or almost all the time, even with therapy, medication, or a device, your patient cannot perceive, think, and remember. For example, answer **no** if he or she cannot manage or initiate personal care without constant supervision .... **yes** ☐ **no** ☐ 4

■ Can your patient hear?

Answer **no** only if, all or almost all the time, even with therapy, medication, or a device, your patient cannot hear (without lip reading) so as to understand a spoken conversation in a quiet setting (exclude language differences) .... **yes** ☐ **no** ☐ 6

■ Can your patient feed or dress himself or herself?

Answer **no** only if, all or almost all the time, even with therapy, medication, or a device, your patient cannot feed or dress himself or herself, or he or she takes an inordinate amount of time to do so ....
Feeding **yes** ☐ **no** ☐ 7
Dressing **yes** ☐ **no** ☐ 7

■ Can your patient personally manage bowel and bladder functions?

Answer **no** only if, all or almost all the time, even with therapy, medication, or a device, your patient cannot personally manage bowel or bladder functions, or he or she takes an inordinate amount of time to do so. For example, answer **no** if your patient needs help from another person on a daily basis to care for his/her ostomy .... **yes** ☐ **no** ☐ 8

DO NOT USE THIS AREA 6742 BADLs 1 ☐ 2 ☐ 3 ☐ 4 ☐ 6 ☐ 7 ☐ 8 ☐ Life-sustaining therapy 9 ☐

Part B (continued)

Life-sustaining therapy (starting for 2000)

If your patient needs life-sustaining therapy to support a vital function (see page 1), he or she may qualify for the disability amount, even if the therapy has alleviated the condition. Your patient must specifically dedicate the time needed for this therapy—at least three times per week, to an average of at least 14 hours per week (**do not** include time needed for travel, medical appointments, or to recuperate after therapy).

Does your patient meet these conditions for life-sustaining therapy? ...... **yes** ☐ 9 **no** ☐

If **yes**, please specify the type of therapy: ____________

Duration

Has your patient's blindness, marked restriction in a basic activity of daily living, or need for life-sustaining therapy (as outlined above) lasted, or is it expected to last, for a continuous period of at least 12 months? .... **yes** ☐ **no** ☐

If **yes**, give the date your patient became blind or markedly restricted, or the life-sustaining therapy began .... 6738 Year ☐ Month ☐

Is the impairment likely to improve sufficiently such that the patient may no longer be blind, markedly restricted in a basic activity of daily living, or need life-sustaining therapy (as outlined above)?

If **yes**, give the year the blindness, marked restriction, or need for life-sustaining therapy ceased, or is expected to cease .... 6740 Year ☐

If **no**, check this box .... ☐

Diagnosis

State the medical diagnosis related to the impairment and describe the restriction and devices used. **Please print.** Attach any other information or documents that may be relevant to your patient's impairment.

Certification

As a **qualified person**, I certify that to the best of my knowledge the information given in Part B is correct and complete.

Sign here ____________

Print your name ____________

Telephone number ____________

Fax number ____________

Date ____________

Address

Check whichever of the following applies to you:

☐ Medical doctor ☐ Optometrist ☐ Audiologist ☐ Occupational therapist ☐ Psychologist ☐ Speech-language pathologist

Printed in Canada

Canada Customs and Revenue Agency — Agence des douanes et du revenu du Canada

STATEMENT OF PROFESSIONAL ACTIVITIES

- For more information on how to complete this statement, see the income tax guide called *Business and Professional Income.*

3

Identification

Your name	Your social insurance number
From: Year Month Day To: Year Month Day	Was 1999 the last year of your professional business? Yes ☐ No ☐
Business name	Main product or service
Business address	Industry code (see the appendix in the *Business and Professional Income* guide)
City, town or municipality, and province	Postal code
Name and address of person or firm preparing this form	Partnership identification number
	Tax shelter identification number
Business Number	Your percentage of the partnership %

Income

Professional fees (includes work-in-progress)			a
Minus – Goods and services tax/harmonized sales tax (GST/HST) and provincial sales tax (if included in fees above)			
– Work-in-progress, end of the year (election to exclude WIP, see Chapter 2 of the guide)			
Total of the above two lines		▶	b
Subtotal (line a minus line b)			
Plus – Work-in-progress, beginning of the year (election to exclude WIP, see Chapter 2 of the guide)			
Adjusted professional fees (total of the above two lines)	8000		
Reserves deducted last year	8290		
Other income	8230		
Gross income (total of the above three lines) – Enter on line 164 of your income tax return	8299		c

Expenses (enter business part only)

Advertising	8521		
Bad debts	8590		
Business tax, fees, licences, dues, memberships, and subscriptions	8760		
Delivery, freight, and express	9275		
Fuel costs (except for motor vehicles)	9224		
Insurance	8690		
Interest	8710		
Maintenance and repairs	8960		
Management and administration fees	8871		
Meals and entertainment (allowable part only)	8523		
Motor vehicle expenses (not including capital cost allowance)	9281		
Office expenses	8810		
Supplies	8811		
Legal, accounting, and other professional fees	8860		
Property taxes	9180		
Rent	8910		
Salaries, wages, and benefits (including employer's contributions)	9060		
Travel	9200		
Telephone and utilities	9220		
Other expenses	9270		
Subtotal			
Allowance on eligible capital property	9935		
Capital cost allowance (from Area A on page 3 of this form)	9936		
Total expenses (total of the above three lines)	9368	▶	d
Net income (loss) before adjustments (line c minus line d)	9369		
Your share of line 9369 above			e
Minus – Other amounts deductible from your share of net partnership income (loss) from the chart on page 2 of this form	9943		f
Net income (loss) after adjustments (line e minus line f)			g
Minus – Business-use-of-home expenses (from the chart on page 2 of this form)	9945		
Subtotal			h
Plus – Net amount to be reported for your reserve for 1971 accounts receivable (from the chart on page 2 of this form)	8236		i
Your net income (loss) line h plus line i (enter on line 137 of your income tax return)	9946		

Other amounts deductible from your share of net partnership income (loss)

Claim expenses you incurred that were not included in the partnership statement of income and expenses, and for which the partnership did not reimburse you.

Total (enter this amount on line f on page 1 of this form)	

Calculation of business-use-of-home expenses

Heat		
Electricity		
Insurance		
Maintenance		
Mortgage interest		
Property taxes		
Other expenses		
Subtotal		
Minus – Personal use part		
Subtotal		
Plus – Amount carried forward from previous year		
Subtotal		1
Minus – Net income (loss) after adjustments (from line g on page 1 of this form) – If negative, enter "0"		2
Business-use-of-home expenses available to carry forward (line 1 minus line 2) – If negative, enter "0"		
Allowable claim (the lesser of amounts 1 or 2 above) – Enter this amount on line 9945 on page 1 of this form		

Reserve for 1971 accounts receivable (for professionals in practice before 1972 only)

Enter your 1998 reserve for 1971 receivables.	
Minus – Your 1999 reserve for 1971 receivables	
Your net amount to be reported for 1971 receivables (enter this amount on line i on page 1 of this form)	

Details of other partners

Partner's name and address	Share of net income or (loss) $	Percentage of partnership %
Partner's name and address	Share of net income or (loss) $	Percentage of partnership %
Partner's name and address	Share of net income or (loss) $	Percentage of partnership %
Partner's name and address	Share of net income or (loss) $	Percentage of partnership %

Details of equity

Total business liabilities	9931	
Drawings in 1999	9932	
Capital contributions in 1999	9933	

Area A – Calculation of capital cost allowance claim

1 Class number	2 Undepreciated capital cost (UCC) at the start of the year	3 Cost of additions in the year (see Areas B and C below)	4 Proceeds of dispositions in the year (see Areas D and E below)	5 * UCC after additions and dispositions (col. 2 **plus** 3 **minus** 4)	6 Adjustment for current year additions (1/2 x (col. 3 **minus** 4)) If negative, enter "0"	7 Base amount for capital cost allowance (col. 5 **minus** 6)	8 Rate %	9 CCA for the year (col. 7 x 8 or an adjusted amount)	10 UCC at the end of the year (col. 5 **minus** 9)

Total CCA claim for the year (enter this amount, minus any personal part, on line 9936 on page 1 of this form)

* If you have a negative amount in this column, add it to income as a recapture on line 8230, "Other income," on page 1 of this form. If no property is left in the class and there is a positive amount in the column, deduct the amount from income as a terminal loss on line 9270 , "Other expenses," on page 1 of this form. Recapture and terminal loss do not apply to a Class 10.1 property. For more information, read Chapter 4 of the *Business and Professional Income* guide.

Area B – Details of equipment additions in the year

1 Class number	2 Property details	3 Total cost	4 Personal part (if applicable)	5 Business part (column 3 **minus** column 4)

Total equipment additions in the year 9925

Area C – Details of building additions in the year

1 Class number	2 Property details	3 Total cost	4 Personal part (if applicable)	5 Business part (column 3 **minus** column 4)

Total building additions in the year 9927

Area D – Details of equipment dispositions in the year

1 Class number	2 Property details	3 Proceeds of disposition (should not be more than the capital cost)	4 Personal part (if applicable)	5 Business part (column 3 **minus** column 4)

Note: If you disposed of property from your professional business in the year, see Chapter 4 in the *Business and Professional Income* guide for information about your proceeds of disposition.

Total equipment dispositions in the year 9926

Area E – Details of building dispositions in the year

1 Class number	2 Property details	3 Proceeds of disposition (should not be more than the capital cost)	4 Personal part (if applicable)	5 Business part (column 3 **minus** column 4)

Note: If you disposed of property from your professional business in the year, see Chapter 4 in the *Business and Professional Income* guide for information about your proceeds of disposition.

Total building dispositions in the year 9928

Area F – Details of land additions and dispositions in the year

Total cost of all land additions in the year	9923	
Total proceeds from all land dispositions in the year	9924	

Note: You cannot claim capital cost allowance on land.

Canada Customs and Revenue Agency | Agence des douanes et du revenu du Canada

INFORMATION RETURN RELATING TO FOREIGN AFFILIATES THAT ARE NOT CONTROLLED FOREIGN AFFILIATES

Do not use this area

- A separate return must be filed for each foreign affiliate.
- Do not file a return for "dormant" or "inactive" foreign affiliates. Refer to the attached instructions for the definition of dormant or inactive foreign affiliates.
- References on this return to the foreign affiliate or the affiliate refer to the foreign affiliate in respect of which the reporting taxpayer is filing this return.
- If you are reporting on a partnership, references to year or taxation year should be read as fiscal period and references to taxpayer should be read as partnership.
- If you need more space to report information, you can use attachments.
- Unless otherwise noted, all amounts should be in Canadian dollars.

Part I – Reporting Taxpayer Information

Tick a box to indicate who you are reporting for, and complete the areas that apply.

☐ individual	First name	Last name	Initial	Social insurance number
☐ corporation	Corporation's name			Business Number RC
☐ trust	Trust's name			Account number T – –
☐ partnership	Partnership's name			Partnership's identification number

Reporting taxpayer's address

No. Street

City Province or territory Postal code

For what taxation year are you filing this return? ☐ **or** from Year Month Day to Year Month Day

Is this the first time that the reporting taxpayer has filed form T1134 for this foreign affiliate? Yes ☐ No ☐

Total number of T1134's filed by the reporting taxpayer for this taxation year. ☐

Part II – Foreign Affiliate Information

Section 1 – General information

A. Identification of foreign affiliate

Name	Address of head office

Identification number (optional) (see filing instructions) N C – (country code) – (assigned number)

Year in which the corporation became a foreign affiliate of the taxpayer Year

Did the corporation cease to be a foreign affiliate of the reporting taxpayer in the year? Yes ☐

Specify the principal activities of the foreign affiliate. (Enter the appropriate standard industrial code(s) from the list in the instructions.)
Standard industrial code(s): 1 2 3 4

Specify the countries or jurisdictions in which the foreign affiliate carries on a business or other income earning activity. (Enter the appropriate country code(s) from the list in the instructions.) Country code(s): 1 2 3 4

Specify the countries or jurisdictions in which the foreign affiliate carries on business through a permanent establishment. (Enter the appropriate country code(s) from the list in the instructions.) Country code(s): 1 2 3 4

Country or jurisdiction of residence of the foreign affiliate. (Enter the appropriate country code from the list in the instructions.)
Country code:

(Ce formulaire existe en français.) 3772

Canada

B. Capital stock of foreign affiliate

(i) Description of shares of the foreign affiliate's capital stock owned by the reporting taxpayer	Number and book cost of shares – End of year – No.	Cost
		00
		00
		00
		00
		00
	Total	00

(ii) Description of shares of the foreign affiliate's capital stock owned by a controlled foreign affiliate of the reporting taxpayer or other person related to the reporting taxpayer	Number and book cost of shares – End of year – No.	Cost – Canadian $ (if available)	Cost – Foreign currency*	Currency code
		00	00	
		00	00	
		00	00	
		00	00	
		00	00	
	Total	00	00	

C. Other information

(i) What was the reporting taxpayer's equity percentage in the foreign affiliate at the beginning of the reporting taxpayer's taxation year? ______ %

(ii) What was the reporting taxpayer's equity percentage in the foreign affiliate at the end of the reporting taxpayer's taxation year? ______ %

(iii) If the Act were read without paragraph 95(2.2)(a), would the reporting taxpayer have a qualifying interest in the foreign affiliate:

(a) at the beginning of the reporting taxpayer's taxation year? Yes ☐ No ☐

(b) at the end of the reporting taxpayer's taxation year? Yes ☐ No ☐

(iv) Was the foreign affiliate indebted to the reporting taxpayer at any time during the reporting taxpayer's taxation year? Yes ☐ No ☐

(v) If *yes*, specify the gross amount of debt the affiliate owed to the reporting taxpayer at the end of the reporting taxpayer's taxation year: ______ 00

Section 2 – Financial information of the foreign affiliate

For each taxation year of the foreign affiliate ending in the reporting taxpayer's taxation year, provide the following information in respect of the affiliate:

- unconsolidated financial statements or, if unavailable, the financial information that is available to you as a shareholder — Attached (tick) Yes ☐ No ☐

	Canadian $ (if available)	Foreign Currency*
• accounting net income before tax	00	00
• income or profits tax paid or payable on income	00	00

- country to which income or profits tax was paid or payable (Enter appropriate country code(s) from the list in the instructions.) 1 ☐☐☐ 2 ☐☐☐ 3 ☐☐☐ 4 ☐☐☐
- currency code ☐☐☐

*If financial information is reported in a foreign currency, provide the appropriate currency code from the list in the instructions.

Section 3 – Surplus accounts

1. Did the reporting taxpayer, at any time in the taxation year, receive a dividend on a share of the capital stock of the foreign affiliate for which an amount is deductible from the income of the reporting taxpayer under subsection 91(5) or section 113 of the Act?

   Yes ☐ No ☐ If *yes*, provide amount of dividend. ______ 00

   If *yes*, and the reporting taxpayer is a corporation, the reporting taxpayer must provide summary calculations of the exempt surplus, exempt deficit, taxable surplus, taxable deficit, and underlying foreign tax of the foreign affiliate at the end of the affiliate's last taxation year ending in the reporting taxpayer's taxation year in support of the dividend deduction claimed. Documentation supporting these calculations need not be filed but should be retained as it may be requested for examination. Surplus calculations should be made in the calculating currency under *Regulation* 5907(6).

   From what surplus account was the dividend paid? Exempt ☐ Taxable ☐ Pre-acquisition ☐

2. Was a subsection 93(1) election made or will such an election be made for the disposition of shares of the foreign affiliate in the year? Yes ☐ No ☐

   If *yes*, provide the actual or estimated amount elected on. ______ 00

Section 4 – Disclosure

Is any information requested in this return not available? Yes ☐ No ☐

If *yes*, please specify the information and the reason it is not available. Also indicate the steps taken in attempting to obtain the information.

Certification

I certify that the information given on this return and in any documents attached is, to my knowledge, correct and complete, except as disclosed in Section 4.	Person or firm paid to prepare this return:
Print name	Name
Sign here	Address
It is a serious offence to file a false return.	
Position or title	Postal code
Telephone ( ) Date	Telephone ( )

Printed in Canada

Canada Customs and Revenue Agency / Agence des douanes et du revenu du Canada

INFORMATION RETURN RELATING TO CONTROLLED FOREIGN AFFILIATES

Do not use this area

- A separate return must be filed for each controlled foreign affiliate (including a non-resident non-discretionary trust deemed to be a controlled foreign affiliate under paragraph 94(1)(d) of the *Income Tax Act).*
- Do not file a return for "dormant" or "inactive" foreign affiliates. Refer to the attached instructions for the definition of dormant or inactive foreign affiliates.
- References on this return to the foreign affiliate or the affiliate refer to the foreign affiliate in respect of which the reporting taxpayer is filing this return.
- If you are reporting on a partnership, references to year or taxation year should be read as fiscal period and references to taxpayer should be read as partnership.
- If you need more space to report information, you can use attachments.
- Unless otherwise noted, all amounts should be in Canadian dollars.

Part I – Identification

Section 1 – Reporting taxpayer information

Tick a box to indicate who you are reporting for, and complete the areas that apply.

☐ individual	First name	Last name	Initial	Social insurance number
☐ corporation	Corporation's name			Business Number RC
☐ trust	Trust's name			Account number T – –
☐ partnership	Partnership's name			Partnership's identification number

Reporting taxpayer's address

No. Street

Postal code

City

Province or territory

For what taxation year are you filing this return? [Year] or from [Year Month Day] to [Year Month Day]

Is this the first time that the reporting taxpayer has filed form T1134 for this foreign affiliate? Yes ☐ No ☐

Total number of T1134's filed by the reporting taxpayer for this taxation year.

Section 2 – Group structure – Attach a separate page with the following information

- List the name and country of residence of each corporation (other than another foreign affiliate of the reporting taxpayer) that is related to the reporting taxpayer and that has an equity percentage (as defined in subsection 95(4) of the Act) in the foreign affiliate.
- If the reporting taxpayer is a partnership, list the name and address of each member of the partnership.
- List the name and country of residence of each other foreign affiliate of the reporting taxpayer that has an equity percentage in the foreign affiliate.
- List the name and country of residence of each other controlled foreign affiliate of the reporting taxpayer in which the foreign affiliate has an equity percentage and of each non-controlled foreign affiliate of the reporting taxpayer in which the foreign affiliate has a direct equity percentage.
- List the name and address of each partnership of which the foreign affiliate is a member.

Note: You can satisfy the above requirements by submitting a group organizational chart that includes the requested information. You only have to file one organizational chart for a group of persons that are related to each other.

Identify the reporting taxpayer filing the organizational chart for the related group. | Name

Part II – Foreign Affiliate Information

Section 1 – General information

A. Identification of foreign affiliate

Name	Address of head office

Identification number (optional) (see filing instructions) C – [ ] [ ] [ ] (country code) – [ ] [ ] [ ] [ ] [ ] (assigned number)

Year in which the corporation or trust became a foreign affiliate of the taxpayer — Year	Did the corporation or trust cease to be a foreign affiliate of the reporting taxpayer in the year? Yes ☐

Specify the principal activities of the foreign affiliate. (Enter the appropriate standard industrial code(s) from the list in the instructions.)

Standard industrial code(s): 1 [ ] 2 [ ] 3 [ ] 4 [ ]

Specify the countries or jurisdictions in which the foreign affiliate carries on a business or other income earning activity. (Enter the appropriate country code(s) from the list in the instructions.) Country code(s): 1 ☐☐☐ 2 ☐☐☐ 3 ☐☐☐ 4 ☐☐☐

Specify the countries or jurisdictions in which the foreign affiliate carries on business through a permanent establishment. (Enter the appropriate country code(s) from the list in the instructions.) Country code(s): 1 ☐☐☐ 2 ☐☐☐ 3 ☐☐☐ 4 ☐☐☐

Country or jurisdiction of residence of the foreign affiliate. (Enter the appropriate country code from the list in the instructions.)
Country code: ☐☐☐

B. Capital stock of foreign affiliate (including a paragraph 94(1)(d) trust)

(i) Description of shares of the foreign affiliate's capital stock owned by the reporting taxpayer	Number and book cost of shares End of year	
	No.	Cost
		00
		00
		00
		00
		00
	Total	00

(ii) Description of shares of the foreign affiliate's capital stock owned by a controlled foreign affiliate of the reporting taxpayer or other person related to the reporting taxpayer	Number and book cost of shares End of year			
	No.	Cost Canadian $ (if available)	Cost Foreign currency*	Currency code
		00	00	
		00	00	
		00	00	
		00	00	
		00	00	
	Total	00	00	

C. Other information

(i) What was the reporting taxpayer's equity percentage in the foreign affiliate at the beginning of the reporting taxpayer's taxation year? ______ %

(ii) What was the reporting taxpayer's equity percentage in the foreign affiliate at the end of the reporting taxpayer's taxation year? ______ %

(iii) If the Act were read without paragraph 95(2.2)(a), would the reporting taxpayer have a qualifying interest in the foreign affiliate:

(a) at the beginning of the reporting taxpayer's taxation year? Yes ☐ No ☐

(b) at the end of the reporting taxpayer's taxation year? Yes ☐ No ☐

(iv) Was the foreign affiliate indebted to the reporting taxpayer at any time during the reporting taxpayer's taxation year? Yes ☐ No ☐

(v) If *yes*, specify the gross amount of debt the affiliate owed to the reporting taxpayer at the end of the reporting taxpayer's taxation year: ______ 00

Section 2 – Financial information of the foreign affiliate (including a paragraph 94(1)(d) trust)

For each tax year of the foreign affiliate ending in the reporting taxpayer's taxation year, provide the following information in respect of the affiliate:

- unconsolidated financial statements or, if unavailable, the financial information that is available to you as a shareholder — Attached (tick) Yes ☐ No ☐

	Canadian $ (if available)	Foreign Currency*
• accounting net income before tax	00	00
• income or profits tax paid or payable on income	00	00

- country to which income or profits tax was paid or payable (Enter appropriate country code(s) from the list in the instructions.) 1 ☐☐☐ 2 ☐☐☐ 3 ☐☐☐ 4 ☐☐☐
- currency code ☐☐☐

*If financial information is reported in a foreign currency, provide the appropriate currency code from the list in the instructions.

Section 3 – Surplus accounts

1. Did the reporting taxpayer, at any time in the taxation year, receive a dividend on a share of the capital stock of the foreign affiliate for which an amount is deductible from the income of the reporting taxpayer under subsection 91(5) or section 113 of the Act?

   Yes ☐ No ☐ If *yes*, provide amount of dividend. ______ 00

   If *yes*, and the reporting taxpayer is a corporation, the reporting taxpayer must provide summary calculations of the exempt surplus, exempt deficit, taxable surplus, taxable deficit, and underlying foreign tax of the foreign affiliate at the end of the affiliate's last taxation year ending in the reporting taxpayer's taxation year in support of the dividend deduction claimed. Documentation supporting these calculations need not be filed but should be retained as it may be requested for examination. Surplus calculations should be made in the calculating currency under *Regulation* 5907(6).

   From what surplus account was the dividend paid? Exempt ☐ Taxable ☐ Pre-acquisition ☐

2. Was a subsection 93(1) election made or will such an election be made for the disposition of shares of the foreign affiliate in the year?

   Yes ☐ No ☐ If *yes*, provide the actual or estimated amount elected on. ______ 00

3. At any time in the taxation year of the reporting taxpayer, was the reporting taxpayer or any foreign affiliate of the reporting taxpayer involved in a corporate or other organization, reorganization, amalgamation, merger, winding-up, liquidation, dissolution, division, or an issuance, redemption, or cancellation of share capital or a similar transaction in a manner that affected the exempt surplus, exempt deficit, taxable surplus, taxable deficit, or underlying foreign tax of the affiliate for the reporting taxpayer?

   Yes ☐ No ☐

4. At any time in the taxation year of the reporting taxpayer, did the reporting taxpayer or another foreign affiliate of the reporting taxpayer acquire or dispose of a share of the capital stock of the foreign affiliate?

   Yes ☐ No ☐ If the answer to either question 3 or 4 is *yes*, provide a summary description of each transaction or event.

Part III – Nature of Income

Section 1 – Employees per business

How many full-time employees or employee equivalents (as described in subparagraph (b)(ii) of the **investment business** definition in subsection 95(1) of the Act) on a business by business basis, did the foreign affiliate employ throughout each taxation year of the affiliate ending in the reporting taxpayer's taxation year?
(Enter the appropriate standard industrial code(s) from the list in the instructions and tick the appropriate box or boxes.)

Business	Number of full-time employees or employee equivalents		
	Less than 6	Between 6 and 15	More than 15
1 ☐☐☐☐	☐	☐	☐
2 ☐☐☐☐	☐	☐	☐
3 ☐☐☐☐	☐	☐	☐
4 ☐☐☐☐	☐	☐	☐

Section 2 – Composition of revenue

Give the amount of the foreign affiliate's gross revenue from a business or property for each of the affiliate's taxation years ending in the reporting taxpayer's taxation year, derived from each of the following sources. (Tick appropriate box or boxes.)

Source	Foreign affiliate's gross revenue				
(i) Interest	less than $25,000 ☐	$25,000 to $100,000 ☐	$100,000 to $500,000 ☐	$500,000 to $1 million ☐	more than $1 million ☐
(ii) Dividends	less than $25,000 ☐	$25,000 to $100,000 ☐	$100,000 to $500,000 ☐	$500,000 to $1 million ☐	more than $1 million ☐
(iii) Royalties	less than $25,000 ☐	$25,000 to $100,000 ☐	$100,000 to $500,000 ☐	$500,000 to $1 million ☐	more than $1 million ☐
(iv) Rental and leasing activities	less than $25,000 ☐	$25,000 to $100,000 ☐	$100,000 to $500,000 ☐	$500,000 to $1 million ☐	more than $1 million ☐
(v) Loans or lending activities	less than $25,000 ☐	$25,000 to $100,000 ☐	$100,000 to $500,000 ☐	$500,000 to $1 million ☐	more than $1 million ☐
(vi) Insurance or reinsurance of risks	less than $25,000 ☐	$25,000 to $100,000 ☐	$100,000 to $500,000 ☐	$500,000 to $1 million ☐	more than $1 million ☐
(vii) Factoring of trade accounts receivable	less than $25,000 ☐	$25,000 to $100,000 ☐	$100,000 to $500,000 ☐	$500,000 to $1 million ☐	more than $1 million ☐
(viii) Disposition of investment property	less than $25,000 ☐	$25,000 to $100,000 ☐	$100,000 to $500,000 ☐	$500,000 to $1 million ☐	more than $1 million ☐

Section 3 – Foreign accrual property income (FAPI)

(i) Did the foreign affiliate earn FAPI in any taxation year of the affiliate that ended in the reporting taxpayer's taxation year?	Yes ☐	No ☐
(ii) If *yes*, give the reporting taxpayer's total participating percentage for the foreign affiliate for that year		______%

Also, give the amount of FAPI the affiliate earned that year in respect of each of the following:	Amount
(iii) FAPI that is income from property under subsection 95(1) of the Act	00
(iv) FAPI from the sale of property under paragraph 95(2)(a.1) of the Act	00
(v) FAPI from the insurance or reinsurance of risks under paragraph 95(2)(a.2) of the Act	00
(vi) FAPI from indebtedness and lease obligations under paragraph 95(2)(a.3) of the Act	00
(vii) FAPI from indebtedness and lease obligations under paragraph 95(2)(a.4) of the Act	00
(viii) FAPI from providing services under paragraph 95(2)(b) of the Act	00
(ix) FAPI from the disposition of capital property	00
(x) FAPI under the description of paragraph (c) in the definition of FAPI in subsection 95(1) of the Act	00
Total FAPI	00

Section 4 – Capital gains and losses

A. Excluded property

Did the foreign affiliate dispose of a share in another foreign affiliate that was excluded property or an interest in a partnership that was excluded property in a taxation year of the affiliate that ended in the reporting taxpayer's taxation year?

Yes ☐ No ☐

B. Property that is not excluded property

Did the foreign affiliate dispose of capital property that was not excluded property in a taxation year of the affiliate that ended in the reporting taxpayer's taxation year?

Yes ☐ No ☐

Section 5 – Income included in income from an active business

A. Was income of the foreign affiliate that would otherwise have been included in its income from property included in its income from an active business:

• because of subparagraph 95(2)(a)(i) of the Act?	Yes ☐	No ☐
• because of subparagraph 95(2)(a)(ii) of the Act?	Yes ☐	No ☐
• because of subparagraph 95(2)(a)(iii) of the Act?	Yes ☐	No ☐
• because of subparagraph 95(2)(a)(iv) of the Act?	Yes ☐	No ☐
• because of the type of business carried on and the number of persons employed by the foreign affiliate in the business pursuant to paragraphs (a) and (b) of the definition of investment business in subsection 95(1) of the Act?	Yes ☐	No ☐
• because of paragraph 95(2)(l) of the Act?	Yes ☐	No ☐

B. Was income of the foreign affiliate that would otherwise have been included in its income from a business other than an active business included in its income from an active business:

• because of the 90% test in paragraphs 95(2)(a.1) through (a.4) of the Act?	Yes ☐	No ☐
• because of subsection 95(2.3) of the Act?	Yes ☐	No ☐
• because of subsection 95(2.4) of the Act?	Yes ☐	No ☐

Section 6 – Disclosure

Is any information requested in this return not available? Yes ☐ No ☐

If *yes*, please specify the information and the reason it is not available. Also indicate the steps taken in attempting to obtain the information.

Certification

I certify that the information given on this return and in any documents attached is, to my knowledge, correct and complete, except as disclosed in Section 6.

Print name ______________________

Sign here ______________________

It is a serious offence to file a false return.

____

Position or title

Telephone ( ) __________ Date __________

Person or firm paid to prepare this return:

Name ______________________

Address ______________________

Postal code ______________________

Telephone ( ) ______________________

Printed in Canada

Index

• A •

absolute discharge, 53
academic awards, 175, 176
accelerated write-off, 129
accordian file, 56
accountants, 78, 79
accounting
  farming income, 203
  self-employment, 180–81
  software packages, 186–187
accrual method (accounting), 180–181
additional deductions (line 256)
  employment with intl. org., 257
  income exempt under tax treaty, 256–257
  vow of perpetual poverty, 257
additional information, CCRA request for, 327–328, 421. *See also* Notice of Assessment
additional NR4 slip, 37
additional T5013 slip, 31
additional tax on RESP accumulated income payments (line 418), 280–281
adjusted base cost (ABC), calculation of, 164–165
adjustment requests, 328
advanced tax rulings, 63, 71–72
advertising in non-Canadian publications, 399
after-corporate tax funds, 391–392
after-tax rate of return, 16
age credit (line 301), 260
aircraft, use of employer's, 100
Alberta
  probate fees, 356
  sales tax, 369
  tax credit, 26
  tax rates, 15, 286
  tax system, 291–292, 430
alimony and separation allowance, 132
allowable business investment loss (ABIL), 226, 426
allowable capital losses, 165–166, 248. *See also* net capital loss
allowable charitable donations, 271–272
allowance, paid to working [minor or adult] child, 349
allowance, retiring, 174–175, 177
allowance, severance, 17, 212, 220–221, 366
allowances, reasonable (non-taxable benefit), 102
alternative minimum taxes (AMT), 53, 276–277
amending
  NR4 slips, 36
  returns, 328–339
  T4A-NR4 summaries/slips, 38
  T5013 slips, 31
amortization, assets, to calculate CCA, 129
amounts transferred from spouse (line 326), 84, 269
annuities, 118, 146, 153
  charitable, 362
Anti-Poverty Fund, 301
appeals, 324–25, 340–41
application for fairness, 341
approximation, rule of. *See* Cohan rule
armed forces, pensions, 119
art, capital gains/losses, 22, 160
art donations, 416–17
art flipping, 416–17
Arthur Andersen, 78
artists, 377–378
"Assessments Beyond the 3-Year Limit" (IT-241), 326
assessment date, 322
at-risk amount, limited partner, 122
attendant care expenses, 225–226
attributed rule, income splitting, 345–346
audit
  and e-filing, 80, 327
  and recordkeeping, 59, 421
  selection of returns for, 334
  tax advisors and, 79
  types of, 334–336
  ways to reduce risk of, 336–340, 421–431
authentication of expenses. *See* recordkeeping
automobile expenses—employee, 57, 370–371
  car owned, 371–372
  reconstructing, 60
  restrictions, 373–374, 398–399
automobile expenses—self-employed, 188–190
  maximum amounts deductible, 190
  restrictions of, 189–90, 198–200
automobile standby charge, 100
awards
  academic, 175, 176
  due to employment, 101

• B •

baby boomers child tax credit, 25
bad debts, 157
balance owing, 330
 interest on, 331
bank statements, 56
bankruptcy, discharge from, 53, 93
bankruptcy returns, 51–52
 bankruptcy straddles calendar year-end, 93
 post-bankruptcy, 51, 52, 53, 92
 pre-bankruptcy, 91–92
 trustee return, 53, 93
basic personal credits, 259
beneficiary
 charity designated, 431
 child, minor (trust), 151
 infant, 151
 preferred election, 150–151
benefit audits, 335
benefits, non-taxable, 102–103, 365–366
benefits, taxable, 99–102
betterment, concept of, 128
board & lodging, northern zone, 254. *See also* meals and lodging
boats, 22
bonds, 22
 capital gains/losses, 157, 158
 stripped, 153, 158
bookkeeping, self-employed, 186–188. *See also* recordkeeping
books. *See* recordkeeping
books, rare, capital gains/losses, 160
borrowing for RRSP, 402–403
British Columbia
 probate fees, 356
 tax credits, 26, 290–291
 tax rates, 15
 tax system, new legislation, 430
Bulleting IT-241 ("Assessments Beyond the 3-year Limit"), 326
bulletins, tax, 63
bursaries, 175, 176. *See also* academic awards; scholarships
business income, self-employment, 183, 384
business investment loss (BIL)
 deduction for, 226
 restrictions in calculating deductible portion of, 227
 rules in calculating deductible portion of, 226
business loss. *See* non-captial loss; loss carryover
business number (BN), 184
business ownership structure, 383–384
 corporations, 388–393
 partnerships, 386–387
 sole proprietorships, 384–386
business partnerships, 29–33, 386–387
business records, re-creating, 60
business trips, 101

• C •

calculating adjusted base cost, 164–165
calculating allowable capital losses, 165–166
calculating amounts from spousal RRSP/RRIF, 136
calculating
 capital cost allowance, 129–30, 193–200, 372
 capital gains/losses, 164–166
 capital gains reserve, 171
 capital gains, taxable, 165
 CPP/QPP contributions, 263
 CPP reduction, 113
 deductible home office costs, 375–376
 effective tax rate, 15–16
 federal tax, 275–83
 GST/HST rebate, 380–81
 marginal tax rate, 16
 medical expenses claim, 271
 net capital losses, 249
 net income, 211–218
 non-capital losses, 247
 OAS repayment, 110
 partnership income, 32
 RRSP contribution limit, 217–218
 taxable income, 239–57
 undepreciated capital cost, 196
Canada Child Tax Benefit, 25, 49
Canada Customs and Revenue Agency (CCRA), 10, 63–64
 administration, 321–332
 contacting by phone, 76–77
 dealing with, 333–42
 new agency structure, 334
 TIPS service, 76
 TSOs, 66, 76
 Web site, 76
Canada Elections Act, 311
Canada Pension Plan (CPP), 27, 112. *See also* Quebec Pension Plan (QPP)
 additional contributions to, 263
 amount entitled to, 111–12, 113
 applying for, 114
 calculating contributions, 263
 child-rearing dropout provision, 113
 children's benefit, 115, 116
 compared with QPP, 112
 death benefits, 177
 increasing, 114
 lump sum, 112

other benefits offered by, 114–116
overpayment, 117, 282
and reciprocal social security agreements, 113
reduction in, 65, 113
repayment, 236
reporting on return, 112
and self-employment, 84, 281
splitting income, 116–117, 347–348
when to start taking, 114
Canadian currency, reporting in, 58. *See also* currency fluctuations
Canada Savings Bonds, 146–147, 425
Canada Student Financial Assistance Act, 266
Canada Student Loans Act, 266
Canada-U.S. tax treaty, 68
Canadian cities, travel benefits deduction, 256
Canadian-controlled private corporations (CCPC), 242
Canadian development expenses (CDE), 233
Canadian exploration expenses (CEE), 233
Canadian oil and gas property expenses (COGPE), 233, 413
Canadian Institute of Chartered Accountants, 79
Canadian residency, 17–21
Canadian source income, 20–21, 139–41
Canadian Tax Letter, 75
cancelled cheques, 56, 57
cancelled NR4 slips, 37
cancelled T4A-NR summaries/slips, 38
cancelled T5013 slips, 31
CCA (capital cost allowance) classes, 129, 130. *See also* capital cost allowance
capital assets, sale of (self-employed), 196
capital cost
defined, 194
undepreciated (UCC), 196
capital cost allowance, 127
calculating, 129–30, 193–200
car, employee expense, 371–372
classes and rates, 194–195, 372
combining classes to calculate, 130
half-rate rule, 195, 395
recapture of and terminal loss rules, 162
separate classes, 130
capital cost allowance—self-employment, 192–193, 397
calculating, 193–1194, 195
capital cost, 194
eligibility to claim, 193
impact on short taxation year, 195
undepreciated capital cost, 196
capital dividends, 143
capital gains/losses, 410
calculating, 164–166
currency fluctuations, 131
debentures, 22, 157
and final tax return, 51
new tax legislation, 131, 338
on rental properties, 123–124, 131
Schedule 3, 84
tax rates, prov./terr., 15
versus ordinary income, 155–156
capital gains balance, exempt, 425
capital gains deduction, 10, 39, 249–250, 386
CNIL (cumulative net investment loss), 252
corporations, 389
qualified farm property, 251–252
qualified small business corp. shares, 250
capital gains exemption
corporations, 389
lifetime, 170
capital gains inclusion rates, 249, 389 429
capital gains reserve, 22, 170–171
capital loss. *See also* loss carryovers
available for use, 355, 384–385
business investment loss, 226
capital property
bonds, debentures, promissory notes, 157–158
conditional sale repossessions, 158–159
defined, 22
depreciable property, 161
eligible, 163
foreign currencies, 161
listed personal property, 160–161
mortgage foreclosures, 158–159
mutual fund units and shares, 157
personal-use property, 159–160
real estate, 156
recapture of CCA and terminal losses, 162
stripped bonds, 158
T-bills, 158
capital vs. current expenditures, real property, 127–128
car. *See also* automobile expenses
company, 100
owned rather than leased, 371–372
caregiver amount (line 315), 264–265
carryback, non-capital loss, 28, 51
carryforward, deductions and credits, 27
carrying charges, undeveloped land, 124–125
cash method, accounting, 181
cash, offering services for, 422
cash register receipts, 55
Certified Financial Planners, 79. *See also* tax advisors and preparers
Certified General Accountants (CGAs), 78. *See also* tax advisors and preparers
charitable annuity, 362
charitable donations. *See* donations
charitable receipts, 57

charitable remainder trust (CRT), 361–362
charitable tax credit, 10
charity, designated beneficiary, 431
Chartered Accountants (CA), 78.
  See also tax advisors and preparers
cheques, cancelled, 56, 57
child. *See also* dependants
  beneficiary, trust, 151
  and CPP, 133, 115, 116
  filing tax return, 425
  and GST/HST credit, 25
  and investing child tax benefit, 349
  tuition and education amounts transferred from, 269
  leaving RRSP/RRIF to, 359
  lending money to, 347, 349
  paying allowance to, 349
  paying dividends to, 395
  paying a salary to, 348
  and residency status, 18
  RRSP contribution, 425
  transfers to, 346
child care expenses, 9, 103, 222–224, 366
  documenting, 57
child-rearing dropout provision, CPP, 113
child support
  deductibility of legal fees, 235–236
  new rules, 132, 230–231
  received from U.S. residents, 257
child tax benefit (CCTB), 25
  amount available, 316–317
  applying for, 315–316
  eligibility, 315, 318
  investing in child's name, 349
cities (Canadian), travel benefits deduction, 256
Citizenship and Immigration Canada, 47
civil pensions, 119
Civilian War Pensions and Allowances Act, 119
clawbacks, 23
  employment insurance, 121–122, 238, 282
  Old Age Security, 109, 237, 282
cleric's residence deduction, 235, 378–379
clipped coupons, 153
club dues/fees, 100, 398
Cohan rule, 60–61
coins, 22, 160
collection actions, 324
collection letter, non-resident tax, 37–38
commercial income (self-employment), 184
commission income, 184, 369–370, 384, 387. *See also* business income
common-law partners, 260
commuted value, 120
company cars, 100
company, foreign-owned, 142
compounded interest, 144
computerized recordkeeping, 56–57
computerized tax preparation, 74–75
concept of integration, 140
conditional discharge (bankruptcy), 53, 93
conditional sales repossession, 22, 158–159
contests, employee-related, 101
contractor, independent, 98
contracts, formal written, 55
contribution in kind, 215, 404–405
contribution limits, RRSPs, 216–218, 219, 401
contribution room, RRSP, 26–27
CoolTax, 75
co-ownership, rental property, 123. *See also* partnerships
corporate tax, 390–391
corporations. *See also* qualified small business corporation shares
  advantages, 392–393
  Canadian-controlled, 242
  capital gains deduction, 389
  capital gains exemption, 389–390
  home office expenses, 397
  and income splitting, 395
  personal guarantees, 388–389
  and personal tax, 391–392
  salary vs. dividends, 391
  secured creditors, 389
  small business deduction, 390–391
  timing incorporation, 390
corporations, foreign, income paid to, 35
cottage, 22, 126, 168
counselling
  employer-paid, 366
  personal, 102, 366
country of residence, new, 18
coupons, clipped, 153
CPP/QPP premiums (lines 308–310), 262–263. *See also* Canada Pension Plan; Quebec Pension Plan
credit card receipts, 55, 57
credit carryforward, 27
creditor, secured (corporation), 389–390
Criminal Code, 11
corporate shareholders, 139–41
criminal prosecutions, 332, 342. *See also* audits; tax evasion
cultural property, gift, 272, 416–417
cumulative net investment loss (CNIL), 170, 252, 339
currency
  fluctuations, 131, 161

foreign exchange gains/losses, 131, 157
current expenditures, capital versus, 127–128

• D •

date-of-death return. *See* final tax return
death. *See also* deceased person, returns for
armed services member, pension, 119
and CPP benefits, 115–116, 117
deemed disposition on, 50, 356
shareholder, 393
tax-friendly assets, 355–356
tax implications of, 254–56
death—minimizing taxes. *See also* estate planning
donating to charity after death, 360–362
giving assets away, 357
leaving assets to spouse, 357–359
leaving RRSP/RRIF to dependent child, 359
making final RRSP contribution, 360
setting up testamentary trust, 362–363
death—publications
"Guidelines for Cancellation and Waiver of Interest and Penalties," 89
"Income of Deceased Persons," 89
"Testamentary Spousal Trusts," 91
death benefits, 103, 115, 177, 355, 366, 414
debentures, capital gains/losses, 22, 157
debt forgiveness, 99, 148. *See also* bankruptcy
discharge from debt obligation, 144
debts, bad, 157
deceased person, returns for, 49–51, 66
balance owing, 330
filing final return, 88–89
prior period return, 88
return for income from testamentary trust, 90
return for partner or proprietor, 90
return for rights and things, 89
trust income tax and information return, 90–91
withdrawal from spousal RRSP, 136
Declaration of Taxpayer's Rights, 64, 342
declining balance (CCA class), 129, 193
exceptions to, 198
deductible expenses, self-employment, 187–192
deductible expenses, small business, 396–397
deduction for annual union, professional, or like dues (line 212), 221
deduction for carrying charges and interest expense for investments (line 232), 232
deduction for cleric's residence (line 231), 235
deduction for exploration and development expenses (line 224), 232–234
deduction for support payments (lines 220 and 230), 30–231
deductions,
deferring, 426
employees, 367
ordering of, 239–240
other payments, 244
overstated, 339
stock options/shares, 242
deemed acquisition rules, 48
deemed disposition, 163
new legislation, 45, 46
deemed residents, 19
TI General, 85
deferred compensation/pension plans, 366
deferred profit sharing plan (DPSP), 212, 366
deferring deductions, 426
deferring (departure) tax, 45
deficient instalment payments, penalty, 71
delivery slips, 56
Deloitte and Touche, 75, 78
Department of Finance, 64, 333
Web site, 75
Department of Indian Affairs, 43
departure tax, 17, 44–46
dependants
caregiver amount, 264–265
claims made by more than one person, 265
details of (Schedule 5), 84
disability amount, transferred from, 266
equivalent-to-spouse credit, 261
infirm, credit, 261–262
medical expense adjustment, 271
minor, tax credit. *See* Child Tax Benefit
deposit slips, 56
depreciable property, 161. *See also* capital cost allowance
depreciation, declining balance method, 193, 198
desk audits, 327, 335
details of dependants (Schedule 5), 84
direct deposit, refund, 330
director, family member, 395
director's fee, 104, 395
director's liability, 393
disabled, capital expenditures to assist, 128
disability benefits
amount transferred from dependant other than spouse, 266
Canada Pension Plan, 115
Workers' Compensation, 138
disability tax credit, 10, 265
new legislation, 430, 431
discharge from bankruptcy, 53
discounts, merchandise, 103, 366

disposition, 163
disputes, CCRA/taxpayer. *See* Objections, dealing with
dividends
  Canadian source, 139–141
  compared to wages, 141
  defined, 139
  foreign, 141–142
  new legislation, 395
  non-taxable, 143–144
  paying to children, 395
  received by spouse, 143
  sole income, 395
  stock, 141
  tax credit, 277, 409, 426
  tax rates, prov./terr., 15
  transferring, 426
  U.S. salry, 391
divorce. *See also* spousal support
  and child care expenditures, 224
  and CPP benefits, 117
  and legal fees, deductibility, 236
  and withdrawal from spousal RRSP, 136
documentation. *See* recordkeeping
donations, 10
  allowable, and govt. gifts, 271–272
  after death, 360–362
  art, 416–417
  claiming on return, 427
  cultural and ecological gifts, 272
  to foreign university, 272
  publicly traded securities, 157, 158, 272, 361
  RRSP, RRIF, life insurance, 431
  to U.S. charities, 272
donations and gifts (line 349), 271–72
double taxation, 19
due dates, returns. *See* filing deadlines
dues, 221
duplicate NR4 slips, 37
duplicate T5013 slips, 31
dying intestate, 49. *See also* death; estate planning

• E •

early retirement, 113, 120, 213
earned income
  and child care expenses, 223
  concept of, 401
  RRSP contribution, 216–217, 401
  salary vs. dividends, 391
ecological gifts, 272
education amounts (Schedule 11), 84
education costs, employer-paid, 103, 366
education tax credits, 9, 267–268
  new legislation, 431
effective tax rate, calculating, 15–16
e-filing, 79–80
  and requests for additional information, 327
EI clawback, 121–122, 238, 282
EI premiums, 122
Electing under Section 216, 21
election for child support payments, 133
Elections Canada, 31
elections, late-filed, 329
electronic filing
  e-filing, 79–80
  net filing, 81
  tele-filing, 81
eligible allowances, 174
eligible capital property (ECP), 193, 200
  capital gains/losses, 163
emigrating (from Canada), tax implications of, 44–47
employee debt, forgiveness of, 99
"Employee or Self-Employed" (Tax Guide), 99
employee
  automobile expenses, 370–374
  government, abroad, 20
  home relocation loans, 240–241
  non-taxable benefits, 365–366
  personal tax credit return, 67
  stock options, new legislation, 430
  vs. self-employed, factors determining, 97–99
  tax breaks for, 365–381
  tax deductions, 367
  in transportation industry, 376
employer
  contributions to pension plans, 102, 366
  contributions to RRSPs, 403–404
  death benefits, 103, 115, 177, 355, 366
  education paid by, 103
  foreign, pension plan, 118
  gifts from, 101
  loans from, 99, 365–366
  moving expenses paid by, 229
  reimbursements paid by, 366
  using aircraft of, 100
employment credit, 278–279
employment expenses
  deductions, 234
  earning salary vs. commissions, 369–70
  special circumstances, 376–379
employment income
  defined, 98
  employee vs. self-employed, 97–99
  non-taxable benefits, 102–103
  other employment income, 103–104
  taxable benefits, 99–102

employment insurance benefits (EI), 23, 121–122
clawback, 121–122, 238, 282
overpayment, 27, 263–64, 282
repayment, 236
employment insurance, periodic, 100
employment, loss of, 104
employment-related training, 103
employment-specific training, 103
employment status, determining, 97–99
employment, with international organization, 257
entertainment expenses, 188, 397
envelopes, recordkeeping, 56
equity investments, 410
equivalent-to-spouse credit, 261
Ernst & Young, 75, 78
errors
amending a return, 328–329
in partnership information return, 31, 32
initial processing, 339–340
estate, defined, 49
estate freeze, 393
estate planning, 50, 353–63
estate taxes, 49–51
exchange rates, foreign, 58
executor, 49, 50, 104
exempt life insurance contribution, 153
exemption
capital gains balance, 425
lifetime, capital gains, 170
expenses, authentication of. *See* recordkeeping
expenses, automobile, 370–374
expenses, deductible (self-employed), 187–192
expenses, exploration and development, 10, 232–234
expenses, GST-rebate eligible, 379
expenses, GST-rebate non-eligible, 380
expenses, home office, 190–192, 374–376
expenses, partially deductible/ not deductible (small business), 397–399
expenses, reimbursement of, 366
exploration and development expenses, 10, 232–234, 413
flow-through shares, 410–411

• F •

factual Canadian resident, 17–19
failure to file, 21–22, 31. *See also* non-filer audits
failure to report income, 332
failure to provide complete information, penalty, 332
failure to file information returns, penalty, 332
failure (repeated) to report income, penalty, 332
fairness, application for, 341
false statements, 41, 332
farm property, qualified, 169, 251–252
farming income, 184, 202–203, 384
accounting method, 203
losses, 204–206
statement of farming activities, 203–204
Federal Court of Appeal, 340
federal dividend tax credit, 277
federal political contributions tax credit, 10, 279
federal surtax, 15, 281, 429
federal tax, calculating, 275–283
Federal Tax Calculator (Schedule 1), 84
federal tax rates, 276
fees
accountants, 78
advance tax rulings, 71
legal, 120, 126, 235–236, 367
tax professionals, 78
field audits, 336
file folders, for recordkeeping, 56
filing deadlines
arm's-length transactions with non-resident, 40
emigrating from Canada, 46
final tax return, 50, 66
and missing information slips/receipts, 58
N4R, 35
newcomers to Canada, 48
non-resident deductions, 37
non-resident receiving rent from real property, 36
partnership information returns, 31
post-bankruptcy return, 92
pre-bankruptcy return, 91
prior period return (deceased), 88
refund for non-resident tax withheld, 38
T1 General, 65–66
T4A-NR, 38
testamentary trust return, 90
trustee's return, 53
filing requirements
leaving Canada, 46–47
newcomers to Canada, 48–49
at time of death, 50–51
fillable forms, on-line, 82
film limited partnerships, 415–416
final tax return, 50–51, 66, 88
deceased not self-employed, 88
deceased self-employed, 89
tax payment due date, 68
transferring assets to spouse, 359
"financially dependent," 359
First Nations tax credit, 85, 307. *See also* Status Indians
fishing income, 184, 206–207, 384

five-percent surtax, 15, 281, 429
flow-through shares, 410–411
fluctuations, currency (capital gains/losses), 131, 161
food and lodging, non-taxable benefit, 102
foreclosures, 22, 158–159
foreign charities, donations to, 272
foreign company
  ownership of, 142
  Part XIII tax, 35
foreign content rules
  new legislation, 430
  RRSPs, 405–406
foreign currency
  fluctuations (capital gains/losses), 161
  and reporting, 58, 178
foreign dividends, 141–142, 277
foreign exchange gains/losses, 131, 157
foreign exchange rates, 58
Foreign Income Verification Statement, 142
foreign media, advertising in, 399
foreign-owned investment properties, 142, 338
foreign pensions, 118–119, 257
  tax treatment of, by country, 119
foreign rental income, 130–131
foreign source income, 178
  interest on, 147
  reporting, 20–21, 34–39, 58, 312–313
  verification statement, 142
foreign tax credits, 19, 147, 152, 236
  federal, 277–278
  provincial, 289
foreign trusts, 142
foreign university, donations to, 272
forgiveness, employee debt, 99
formal written contracts, 55
form CPT-1 (Request for a Ruling as to the Status of a Worker under the Canada Pension Plan or Employment Insurance Act), 99
form CPT20 (Election to Pay Canada Pension Plan Contributions), 263
form GST370 (Employee and Partner GST/HST Rebate Application), 368, 379, 380
form ISP-1000 (applying for CPP), 114
form ISP-1003 (Estimate Request for Canada Pension Plan Retirement Pension), 113
form ISP-1640 (CPP child-rearing dropout provision), 113
form ISP-3000 (applying for OAS), 107
form IT-210 (Income of a Deceased Person), 88
form NR4 slip, 34, 35
form NR4 summary, 34, 35
  changes to, 37
form NR5 (Application by a Non-Resident of Canada for a Reduction in the Amount of Non-resident Tax Required to be Withheld), 36
form NR6 (Undertaking to File an Income Tax Return by a Non-Resident Receiving Rent from Real Property), 36
form NR7–R (Application for Refund of Non-resident Tax Withheld), 38
form NR75 (Non-resident Tax Remitter Registration Form), 37
form NR76 (Non-resident Tax Statement of Account), 37
form NR81 (Non-resident Notice of Assessment), 37
form NR82 (Non-resident Notice of Reassessment), 37
form NR83 (Non-resident Collection Letter), 37
form RC66 (Canada Child Tax Benefit), 25
form RC96 (Lifelong Learning Plan), 220
form TD-1 (Employee's Personal Tax Credit Return), 67
form TD-3 (withholdings increased), 67
form TLA7 (Appealing to the Tax Court), 341
form TL2 (Claim for Meals and Lodging Expenses), 376
form TP.1–D-V (tax return, Quebec), 13
form T1A (Request for Loss Carry Back), 28, 385
form T1 General
  due dates. *See* filing deadlines
  versions of, 84–85
  where to send, 66
form T1 General for Non-residents and Deemed Residents, 19
form T1–M (Moving Expenses Deduction), 229
form T1S-A (Pensioners), 86–87
form T1S-B (Wage and Salary Earners), 87
form T1S-C (Tax Credit), 87
form T1S-D (Native Canadians), 87
form T1–ADJ (Adjustment Request), 328
form T1C (Yukon) AG (Yukon First Nations Tax), 307
form T1–DD (Request for Direct Deposit of Refund), 330
form T1 Special, 80, 85, 86
  eligibility criteria, 86
form T3 return, 49, 51
form T3 slips, 58
form T3 trust income tax and information returns, 90–91
form T4s, 25
form T4A (OAS) information slip, 107
form T4A-NR Supplementary, 34, 38
form T4A-NR Summary, 34, 38
form T4RSP information slip, 25, 106, 108

form T5 slip, 146
form T4A (OAS) slip, 108, 110, 111
form T451E (Notice of Assessment), 321–322
form T4RIF, 137
form T4RSP (Withdrawals from Unmatured RRSPs), 134
form T5 slips, 58
form T7B-RF (Instalment Remittance Form), 71
form T7DR (Instalment Remittance Form), 71
form T106 Summary (Non-arm's length Transactions with Non-residents), 40
  when to file, 40–41
  where to file, 41
form T106 Supplementary, 40
form T116 (person emigrating from Canada), 46, 47
form T183 (authorization to e-file), 80
form T222 (Northern Residents Deduction—2000), 253
form T626 (Overseas Employment Tax Credit), 278
form T652 (Revocation of Waiver), 327
form T691 (Alternative Minimum Tax), 277
form T746 (Calculating Your Deduction for Refund of Undeducted RRSP Contribution), 135, 236
form T776 (Statement of Real Estate Rentals), 124
form T776 (Other Related Income), 124
form T777 (Statement of Employment Expenses), 368
form T929 (Attendant Care Expenses), 225
form T1013 (consent to contact CCRA), 77
form T1033WS (Worksheet for Calculating Instalment Payments), 70
form T1036 (Home Buyer's Plan Request to Withdraw Funds from an RRSP), 220
form T1134 (business has foreign affiliates), 39
form T1135 (Foreign Income Verification Statement), 142, 312, 313, 338
form T1141 (Transfers and Loans to Foreign Trusts), 39, 338
form T1142 (transfer or lending money to non-resident trust), 39
form T1157 (Election for Child Support Payments), 133
Form T1161 (emigrating from Canada), 46, 47
form T1170 (Capital Gains on Gifts of Certain Capital Property), 157, 158
form T1171 (Tax Withholding Waiver on Accumulating Income Payments from RESPs), 151
form T2029 (Waivers), 326–327
form T2032 (Statement of Farming Activities), 203–204
form T2032 (Statement of Professional Activities), 201, 384
form T2036 (Provincial Foreign Tax Credit), 278, 289
form T2038 (Investment Tax Credit), 280
form T2042 (Statement of Farming Activities), 184, 384
form T2091 (designating property as principal residence), 167
form T2121 (Statement of Fishing Activities), 184, 206–207, 384
form T2124 (Statement of Business Activities), 183, 184–186, 384
form T2200 (travel expenses), 84
form T2201 (Disability Tax Credit Certificate), 225, 265, 266
form T2202 (Education Amount Certificate), 267, 268, 269
form T2202A (Tuition and Education Amount Certificate), 267, 268, 269
form T2203 (Provincial and Territorial Taxes for 2000—Multiple Jurisdictions), 288–289
form T2204 (Employee Overpayment of 2000 Canada Pension Plan Contributions and 2000 Employment Insurance Premiums), 262, 263
form T2205 (Calculating Amounts from a Spousal RRSP or RRIF to Include in Income), 136
form T3012A (Tax Reduction Waiver on Refund of Your Undeducted RRSP Contribution), 135
form T5007 (Statement of Benefits), 244
form T5007 (Workers' Compensation), 138
form T5008 slip (Statement of Securities Transactions), 158
form T5013 (Partnership Information Return) 245, 387
form T5013, Summary
  changes to, 32
  how to complete, 33
  where to submit, 32
form T5013 Supplementary, 30, 32
  dealing with errors on, 31
  where to submit, 32
forms
  on-line fillable, 82
  prov./terr. tax credits, 26
  short. *See* special returns
  where to get, 81–82
France, pensions from, 119
frequent flyer programs, 101
full indexation, 429

• G •

gas industry, 10, 232–234, 410–414
General Anti-Avoidance Rule (GAAR), 342
General Division hearings, 341
general partnerships, 386
Germany, pensions from, 119
Gifts. *See also* donations
 allowable (govt.), 271–272
 from employer, 101
 in kind, 360–361
GIS program, 108
giving up Canadian residency, 17, 18. *See also* Non-residents
Goods and Services Tax. *See* GST
government employees, abroad, 20
government, gifts to, 271–272
grants, research, 104, 175, 176–177
gross negligence, penalty, 332
grossed-up dividends, 140–141
group pension plans, 102
group term life insurance, 101
GST, 25, 181–182
 eligibility to register, 183
GST/HST credit, 25, 49, 87, 108
 amount available, 314
 calculating, 315
 eligibility, 313–314
GST rebate, 283
 application (employment expenses), 368
 calculating, 380–381
 eligibility for, 379
 expenses that qualify, 379
 expenses that do not qualify, 380
 prior year, 104
guarantee, personal, 388–389
Guaranteed Income Supplement (GIS), 108, 109
"Guidelines for Accepting Late, Amended or Revoked Elections" (IC 92–1), 329, 341
"Guidelines for the Cancellation and Waiver of Interest and Penalties" (IC 92–2), 89
"Guidelines for Refunds Beyond the Normal Three-Year Period" (IC 92–3), 328, 329, 341

• H •

"half-rate" rule, 195, 395
Halifax disaster pension, 119
Harmonized Sales Tax (HST), 25, 181–183, 369. *See also* GST/HSST credit
health services plans, private, 102
Home Buyer's Plan (HBP), 23, 93, 134, 136, 219–220
home loans, 149
home office expenses
 calculating deductible costs, 191–192, 375–376
 deductible, 191, 374–375
 eligibility, 374, 396–397
 restrictions on deductions, 374
home relocation loans, 149, 240–241, 365–366
housing, rent-free/low-rent, 101
Human Resources Centre of Canada, 48
Human Resources Development Canada (HRDC), 65, 105–106, 236

• I •

identical properties, 164
indexed debt obligations, 146
immigrants, 47–49
imprisonment, 31
incentive awards, 101
income
 annuities, 153
 of beneficiaries (trust), 150–151
 capital gains vs. ordinary, 155–156
 dividends, 395
 EI benefits, 121–122
 employment-related, 97–104
 exempt, tax treaty, 256–257
 interest, 144–145
 investment, 139–153, 338
 not subject of withholdings, 68
 partnerships, 32, 122–123
 pension, 105–120
 from property, 232. *See also* capital gains/losses; capital property
 net, calculating, 211–238
 rental, 123–131, 338
 self-employment, 179–207
 taxable, calculating, 239–257
 of a trust, 150–51
 types, 20–21, 174–178
 underreporting, 337–339, 422
"Income of a Deceased Person" (IT-212), 89
income maintenance insurance plan, 104
income security programs, 106. *See also* Canada Pension Plan; Guaranteed Income Supplement; Old Age Security; Quebec Pension Plan; Spouse's Allowance; Widowed Spouse Allowance
income splitting
 attribution rules, 345–346
 small business, 394–395
income splitting—tips
 contribute to RESP, 350
 contribute to spousal RRSP, 350
 higher-income spouse pays

household expenses, 349
invest child tax benefit in child's name, 349
lend money/investments to family member, 347
pay allowance to working child, 349
pay salary/wages to family, 348
split tax on CPP payments, 347–348
transfer money for business purposes, 348–349
Income Tax Act, 11
income tax preparers. *See* tax advisors and preparers
incorporating. *See also* corporations
sole proprietorship, 385
timing of, 390
independent contractor, 98
Indian (term), 43
Indian Act, 43
Indian band (term), 43
ineligible allowance, 175
infants, beneficiary (trust), 151
infirm dependants credit, 261–262
Informal Division hearings, 340
Information Bulletin IT-305 ("Testamentary Spousal Trusts"), 91
Information Bulletin IT-434 ("Rental of Real Property by Individuals"), 123
Information Circulars, 63
Information Circular 70–6R3 ("Advanced Tax Rulings"), 71
Information Circular IC 92–1 ("Guidelines for Accepting Late, Amended or Revoked Elections"), 329, 341
Information Circular 92–2 ("Guidelines for the Cancellation and Waiver of Interest and Penalties"), 89
Information Circular 92–3 ("Guidelines For Refunds Beyond the Normal Three-Year Period"), 328, 329
Information Circular IC73–10R3 ("Tax Evasion"), 342
information returns
emigrating from Canada, 46
failure to file, penalties, 332
non-arm's length transactions with non-residents, 40–41
non-residents, 34–39
partnership information return, 29–33
transfer pricing, 39
initial processing errors, 339–340
in-kind contributions, 215, 404–405
instalment payments, 331
calculating, 69–70
interest and penalties, 70–71
and refunds, 25
insurance
donating, 431
employment. *See* employment insurance
life. *See* life insurance
periodic employment, 288
using for investment, 415
intangible assets, 200
integrated tax system, 140–141
integration, concept of, 140
interest
on balance due, 331
borrowing to invest, 10
deductions, 232, 425
foreign source income, 147
instalment payments, 70–71
loans from employer, 99, 148
nondeductible, 331
reassessment, 322
on refunds, 330
student loans, 9, 266–267
tax rates, prov./terr, 15
waiving, 332
interest income, 44, 409, 410
how to report, 144
methods of reporting, 145
types of, 144
interest-offset policy, 70
international organization, employment with, 257
International Tax Services (CCRA), 19
Internet
charges, 369, 370, 375
net-filing, 81
on-line tax protests, 422
tax tips on, 75
Interpretation Bulletins (ITs), 63, 76, 82
Interpretive Bulletin IT-212 ("Income of Deceased Persons"), 89
inter vivos trust, 150
intestate, 49
inventory adjustment rules, farming, 203–204
investment clubs, 30
investment income, 139–53, 338
deductions, 232
how it is taxed, 409–410
underreporting, 338
investment, special reporting methods, 145–147
investment, statement of (Schedule 4), 84
investment tax credit, 279–80
investments acquired at discount, 146
IRS (Internal Revenue Service), 334

Italy
pensions from, 119
withholding tax rate, 36
ITs. *See* Interpretation Bulletins

• J •

jewelry, 22, 160
joint and several liability, 386
joint ownership with right of survivorship, 357
jurisdictions, multiple, tax calculation, 288–289

• K •

KPMG, 75, 78

• L •

labour-sponsored funds, 280, 413–414
labour-sponsored venture capital corporation (LSVCC), 153, 280, 413
land, undeveloped, tax treatment, 124–126
landed immigrant, child tax benefit, 25
landed immigrant status, 47
late-filed elections, 329
late-filing penalty, 331
final tax return, 89
no SIN number, 65
non-resident tax, 38
partnership information return, 31
late instalment payments, interest on, 70
lease restriction rules, 373, 399
leased car, 371–372
leasehold improvements, 198
leaving Canada, tax implications, 44–47
legal awards, 177
legal fees, deductions, 120, 126, 235–236, 367
lending money to family member, 347, 349. *See also* income splitting
liability, director's, 393
liability insurance, 384
liability, partnerships, 386
life insurance, 146
donating to charity, 361, 431
proceeds, exempt, 153, 355, 415
and small business, 398
types, 414
Lifelong Learning Plan (LLP), 23, 134, 136, 220
lifetime capital gains exemption, 170, 425
limited and non-active partnership income, 122–123
limited partnership, film, 415–416
limited partnership losses, 245–246
limited liability partnerships (LLPs), 386
limited partnerships (LPs), 386
underreporting income, 338
line 113: Old Age Security, 105
line 114: income from CPP and QPP, 105, 111–117
line 115: other pensions and superannuation, 105, 117–119
line 119: EI benefits, 121–122
line 120: dividends, 139–144
line 122: limited and non-active partnerships income, 122–123
line 126: rental income, 123–131
line 128: support payments
line 129: RRSP and RRIF income, 133–38
line 130: other income, 174–178
line 135: business income, 384, 487
lines 137 and 164: professional income, 184, 384, 387
lines 139 and 166: commision income, 184, 384, 387
lines 141 and 168: farming income, 202–206, 384, 387
lines 143 and 170: fishing income, 206–207, 384, 387
line 144: workers' compensation, 138
line 145: social assistance, 138
line 206: pension adjustment, 212–213
line 207: Registered Pension Plan deduction, 213–214, 367
line 208: RRSP deduction, 214–221, 367
line 209: Saskatchewan Pension Plan deduction, 221
line 212: deduction for annual union, profession, or like dues, 221, 367
line 214: deduction for child care expenses, 222–224, 367
line 215: attendant care expenses, 225–226, 367
line 217 and 226: deduction for a business investment loss, 226
line 219: deduction for moving expenses, 227–229, 367
lines 220 and 230: reduction for support payments, 230–231
line 221: deduction for carrying charges and interest expense for investments, 232
line 224: deduction for exploration and development expenses, 232–234
line 229: deduction for employment expenses, 234
line 231: deduction for cleric's residence, 235
line 232: other deductions, 235–236, 367
line 234: net income before adjustments, 236
line 235: social benefits repayment (OAS and EI clawbacks), 237–238
line 248: employee home relocation loans, 240–241

line 249: stock option and shares deduction, 241–244
line 250: other payment deductions, 244
lines 251 to 253: loss carryovers, 244–245, 385
line 254: capital gains deduction, 249–250, 386, 389
line 255: northern residence deductions, 253–256
line 256: additional deductions, 256
line 300: basic personal credit
line 301: age amount, 260
line 303: spousal amount, 260
line 305: equivalent-to-spouse amount, 261
line 306: amount for infirm dependants, 261–262
lines 308 to 310: CPP/QPP premiums, 262–263
line 312: EI premiums, 263–264
line 314: pension income amount, 264
line 315: caregiver amount, 264–265
line 316: disability amount for yourself, 265
line 318: disability amount transferred from a dependant other than your spouse, 266
line 319: student loan interest, 266–267
line 323: tuition and education amounts for yourself, 267–68
line 324: tuition and education amounts transferred from child, 269
line 326: amounts transferred from your spouse, 269
line 349: donations and gifts, 271–272
lines 309 and 410: federal political (contributions) tax credit, 279
line 412: investment tax credit, 279–280
lines 413 and 414: labour-sponsored funds tax credit, 280
line 418: additional tax on RESP accumulated income payments, 280–281
line 419: federal surtax
line 421: CPP contributions on self-employment earnings, 281
line 422: social benefits repayment, 282
line 425: federal dividend tax credit, 277
line 428: provincial and territorial taxes and credits, 285–309
line 429: overseas employment credit, 278–79
lines 431 and 433: federal foreign tax credit, 277–78
line 448: CPP overpayment, 282
line 448: EI overpayment, 282
line 452: medical expense supplement
line 457: GST rebate, 283
line 9941: optional inventory adjustment, 204
line 9942: mandatory inventory adjustment, 203–204
listed personal property (LPP), 160–161
loans
  from employers, 99, 365–366
  home, 149
  home relocation, 149, 240–241, 366
  RRSP, 402–403
  shareholder and employee, 147–149
  student, 9, 176, 266–267
locked-in RRSP, 120
loss carryback, 28
loss carryovers, 244–245, 384–385
  limited partnership losses, 245–246
  net capital losses, 248–249
  non-capital losses, 246–248
lost documentation, 37, 57
lottery winnings, 68
low-rent housing, 101

• M •

Mandatory Inventory Adjustment (MIA), 203–204
Manitoba
  probate fees, 356
  tax credits, 26, 294–295
  tax rates, 15, 287
  tax system, 293–294, 430
manuscripts, rare, 160
marginal tax rate
  calculating, 16
  top, 6
matchable expenditure rule, 45
mature RRSP, withdrawals, 134
meals and lodging, 188, 368, 376, 397
media, advertising in, 399
medical expense credit, 10, 283
  Quebec, 300–302
medical expenses, 269
  adjustment, 271
  allowable, 270
  calculating claim, 271
  claim on lower-income return, 427
  credit, 10, 283
Medical Expenses Supplement, Refundable, 84
merchandise discounts, 103, 366
Merchant v. The Queen, 61
Microsoft Money, 57
middle tax bracket, 431, 429
military pensions, 119
mini-budget (Oct. 2000), 431
mining industry, 10, 232–234, 410–414
Ministère du Revenu du Québec, 12
minor dependants, tax credit. *See* Child Tax Benefit
missing information, reconstructing business records, 60

receipts, 59
tax records, 59–60
mistakes. *See* errors
mixed annuity, 118
mortgage foreclosures, 22, 158–59
moving expenses, 27. *See also* home relocation loans; relocation expenses
claiming on return, 229
coming to or leaving Canada, 229
eligibility, 228
employer-paid/reimbursed, 229, 366
when you can deduct, 227
multiple jurisdictions, tax calculation, 288–289
musicians, 377
mutual funds, 22, 152
capital gain/loss, 157
identical properties, 164
MYOB, 187

• N •

National Child Benefit Supplement (NCBS), 317
National Register of Electors, 311
National Training Act, 175
Native Canadians
Status Indians, 43–44, 87
TIS-D return, 87
Yukon First Nations tax, 85
Nazi persecution, compensation pensions, 119
net capital losses, 248–249
net-file, 81
net income, calculating, 211–238
Net Income Before Adjustments (line 234), 236
net income, partnerships/partners, 32
net worth assessment, 21–22, 337
New Brunswick
Harmonized Sales Tax, 369
probate fees, 356
tax credits, 26
tax rates, 287
tax system, 303–304, 430
newcomers to Canada, 47–49
Newfoundland
Harmonized Sales Tax, 369
probate fees, 356
tax credits, 26
tax rates, 15, 286
tax system, 303, 430
no tax payable, return. *See* form T1S-C
non-active partners, 122–123
non-capital losses, 28, 246–248, 384–385
non-deductible interest, 331
non-filers, 21
audits, 335, 339, 422
non-integrated tax system, 140
non-qualifying RRIFs, 137
non-refundable tax credits, 84, 259–272
Manitoba, 294
non-residents, 20–21
deductions
how to remit, 37
lost remittance form, 37
when to remit, 37, 39
earning money in Canada, 339
OAS recipients, 106
overseas employment credit, 278–279
personal credit, 259
transactions with, returns, 34–39, 40, 68
non-resident tax
late-remitting
collection letter, 37–38
penalty, 38
notice of assessment/reassessment, 37–38
Part XIII tax, 34–35, 36
reduction in, 36
T1 General, 85
non-tax returns, 29–41
non-taxable benefits, 102–14
employees, 365–366
non-taxable dividends, 143–144
non-taxable pension income, 119
northern residence deduction, 10, 253
residency deduction, 253–254
travel benefit deductions, 255–256
Northwest Territories
tax credits, 26, 307–308
tax rates, 15, 286
tax system, 307
Notice of Assessment, 321–322
Notice of Objection, 340
Notice of Reassessment, 322, 336
Nova Scotia
Harmonized Sales Tax, 369
probate fees, 356
tax credit, 26
tax rates, 15, 287
tax system, 304–305, 430
Nunavut
probate fees, 356
tax credits, 26, 308–309
tax rates, 15, 286

• O •

OAS. *See* Old Age Security
Objection, Notice of appeals, 324–325
when to file, 323
objections, dealing with, 323–325

office examinations, 335
officer of corporation, 389
offset (interest) mechanism, 70
oil industry, 10, 232–234, 410–411
Old Age Security, 23
  applying for, 107
  clawback, 109–110, 237, 282
  eligibility criteria, 106–107
  non-resident recipients, 106
  overpayment, 111
  repayment, 109–110, 236
  reporting on tax return, 110–111
  taxation of, 109
on-line "fillable" forms, 82
Ontario
  calculating taxes, 295–297
  ordering of deductions, 239–240
  probate fees, 356
  surtax, 296
  tax credits, 26, 297–298
  tax rates, 15, 286–286
  tax reductions, 297
  tax system, 13, 430
operating benefit (company car), 100
optional inventory adjustment (OIA), (line 9941), 204
overcontributions, RRSP, 218–219, 236
  withdrawals of, 135
  year turn 69, benefits of, 404
overpayment, CPP/QPP, 117, 262
overseas employment credit, 278–279
overstated deductions, 339
ownership, foreign company, 142

• P •

parking costs, 366, 370
Part XIII tax
  defined, 34
  incorrectly withheld, 38
  rates of, 35–36
  types of income paid to non-residents, 34–35
part-year residents, 19–20
partially deductible/non-deductible expenses, small business, 397–399
partner or proprietor (deceased), return, 90
Partnership Identification Number (PIN), 30
partnership
  deductible home office expenses, 396–397
  income, 29
    calculating, 32
    limited and non-active, 122–123
partnership information return
  due dates, 31
  eligibility, 30
  errors on, 31
  exemptions, 30
  failure to file, 31
  late filing, 31
  PIN number, 30
  tips, 30
partnerships, 386–387
  advantages of, 387
  disadvantages of, 387
  and GST/HST rebate, 380
  tax implications of, 387
  types of, 386
partnerships, film, 415–416
partnerships, limited
  losses, 245–246
  underreporting income, 338
paying salary/wages to family members, 348
payroll costs (self-employed), 187
payroll taxes, 27
penalties, 331–332
  cancellation. *See* "Guidelines for the Cancellation and Waiver of Interest and Penalties"
  departure tax, 44
  final tax return, 89
  instalment payments, 70–71
  partnership income return, 31
  foreign return, 38, 39, 338
  non-resident tax, 38
  T106, 41
  tax evasion, 332, 342
Pension Act, 119
pension adjustment (PA), 212–213
pension adjustment reversal (PAR), 212–213
pension credit, 120
pension income. *See also* income security programs
  amount (line 314), 264
  foreign, 118–119
  non-taxable, 119
  transferring, 120
  types of, 118
  what is not, 105
pension plans. *See also* specific plans
  employer contribution to, 366
  group, 102
pensioners, return. *See* form TIS-A
periodic employment insurance, 100
permanent establishment, 288
permanent life insurance, 414
perpetual poverty, vow of, 257
Personal Amount Supplement (Schedule 13), 84

personal counseling, 102
personal credits, basic, 259
personal guarantees, 388–389
personal property
 listed (LPP), capital gains/losses, 160–161
 Status Indian, 43–44
 types of income covered in, 43–44
personal tax, deferring, 391–392
personal tax returns. *See* form T1
personal-use property, disposition of, 22, 59–60, 416–417
political tax credit (federal), 10, 279
post-bankruptcy return, 51, 52, 53, 92
"Pre-1972 Capital Surplus on Hand" account, 143
preauthorized contribution plan (PAC), 403
pre-bankruptcy return, 51, 52, 91–92
preferred beneficiary election, 150–151
prepaid expenses, small business, 398
prepaid taxes (self-employed), 188
preparation (tax) software, 74–75
"Preparing Returns for Deceased Persons," 88
preparing your own return, 73
 help from CCRA, 75–77
 tax tips Web sites, 75
 software, 74–75
 TIPS service, 76
 using computer, 74–75
prescribed annuity, 118
PricewaterhouseCoopers, 75, 78
Prince Edward Island
 probate fees, 356
 tax credits, 26
 tax rates, 15
 tax system, 13, 286, 305, 430
principal residence
 exemption, 355, 397
 and leaving Canada, 18
 renting out, 18
 sale of, 166
prior period return (deceased person), 88
private health services plans (PHSP), 102
prize, field of endeavour, 175, 176
probate fees, 356
processing errors, 339–340
professional dues, 221
professional income
 form T2032, 201
 reporting, 201
 self-employment, 184, 201–202, 384
 work-in-progress, 201–202
profit, reasonable expectation of, 123–124, 421–422, 426
profit-sharing plans, 100
progressive tax rate system, 14
promissory notes, capital gains/losses, 22, 157
properties, identical, 164
property
 capital vs. current expenditures, 127–128
 deemed disposition rules, 45
 depreciable, 22, 161
 disposition of, criteria, 163
 eligible capital, 163
 farm, qualified, 169
 foreign-owned investment, 142
 personal-use, capital gains/losses, 159–160
 rental income from, non-resident receiving, 36
 repairs to, 127, 128
 repossession of, 158–159
 sale of principal residence, 166–168
 sale of qualified small business shares, 168–169
 transferred to spouse, 345, 346, 358–359
protestors (tax), 422
provincial foreign tax credits, 289
provincial/territorial
 probate fees, 356
 sales tax, 369, 381
 tax credits, 25–26, 289–309
 tax rates, 15, 285–289
 tax system, 12–13, 63
 top marginal tax rates, 6
public company shares, 242
publications, tax, 63, 82
publicly traded companies, donations of shares, 157, 158, 272, 361
purchase invoices, 55

• Q •

Qualified farm property (QFP), 169, 251, 339, 357, 389
qualified small business corporation shares (QSBC), 168–169, 250, 339, 355
qualifying RRIFs, 137
Quebec
 dividend tax credit, 141
 medical expense credit, 300–302
 probate fees, 356
 tax rates, 15, 287
 tax system. *See* Quebec tax system
 withholding rates on RRSP Withdrawals, 407
Quebec Pension Plan (QPP)
 amounts, 111–112
 calculating contribution, 263
 death benefits, 177
 lump sum, 113
 overpayment, 117, 282

repayment, 236
reporting on return, 113
self-employment, 84
Quebec prescription drug insurance plan, 301
Quebec tax system, 13–14, 69, 299, 303
difference between federal Return and Quebec return, 299–300
medical expenses credits, 300–301
non-refundable credits, 302
refundable credits, 302
questions, to ask tax professional, 78–79
QuickTax, 74
QuickBooks, 57, 187
Quicken, 57

• R •

raises, tax implications of, 16
rare books, capital gains/losses, 22, 160
real estate. *See* property
Real Estate Investment Trusts (REITs), 412–413
reasonable expectation of profit, 123–124, 131, 421–422, 426
reassessment
notice of, 322, 325
outside 3-year limit, 325–326
and reporting recurrent losses, 426
recapture adjustments (CCA claims), 130, 162
and self-employment, 198–198
receipts, missing, 58, 59
reciprocal social security agreements, 113
reciprocal tax agreements. *See* tax treaties
reconstructing missing records
business records, 60
receipts, 59
tax records, 59–60
record-keeping
importance of, 55, 337
setting up system, 56
special situations, 57
tips, 57
records
approximation, rule of, 60–61
automobile expenses, 371
employment expense claims, 368
computerized, 56–57
damaged, 59–60
e-filing, 81
length of time to keep, 57–58
missing information, 58–59
reconstructing, 59–60
rental properties, 126
self-employment, 186–187
source documents, 55–56
reduction for employment expenses (line 229), 234
refugees, 25, 47
Refundable Medical Expenses Supplement (Schedule 10), 84
Refunds
beyond 3-year period, 328–329
direct deposit of, 330
and e-filing, 80
excess or incorrectly withheld Part XIII tax, 38
interest on, 330
and non-capital loss, 28
and tax preparation companies, 77
registered charity, 57
Registered Education Savings Plan (RESP), 64
distribution from, 151–152
Registered Pension Plan (RPP), 212
employer contributions to, 366
transferring pension amounts to, 120
registered pension plan deduction (line 207), 213–214
Registered Retirement Income Fund. *See* RRIF
Registered Retirement Savings Plan (RRSP) deduction (line 208), 214–221
regular interest, 144
reimbursements and awards, 101, 366
religious orders
cleric's residence, 235, 378–379
vow of perpetual poverty, 257
relocation expenses, 101 *See also* home relocation loans; moving expenses
rent-free housing, 101
rental expenses, classification of, 128
rental income, 21, 36, 44
capital cost allowance, 128–129
capital vs. current expenditures, 127–128
reasonable expectation of profit, 123–124
and REIT, 412
restrictions on rental losses, 131
types of, 124
underreporting, 338
undeveloped land, 124–127
rental property
principal residence, 18, 127
records, 127
"Rental of Real Property by Individuals" (IT-434), 123
repairs to real property, 127, 128

repayment, OAS. *See* Old Age Security, clawback repayment, social benefits, 237–238. *See also* clawbacks
Replacing T4A-NR summary/slips, 38
repossessions, property, 158–159
Request for Additional Information, 327, 421
research grants, 104, 175, 176–177
reserve, capital gains, 170–171
reserves, Status Indians, 43, 44
residence
  cleric's, 235, 378–379
  rental from, 127
residency, Canadian
  deemed residents, 19
  factors determining, 17–19
  giving up, 17, 18, 44–47
  government employees abroad, 20
  non-residents, 20–21
  part-year, 259
residency, northern, deductions, 253–256
resource corporations, 410. *See also* exploration and development
RESPs
  additional tax on, 280–281
  and income splitting, 350
  summary, 351
restricted farm losses, 203, 205
retirement compensation arrangements (RCA), 366
retiring allowance
  eligible allowance, 174–175
  ineligible allowance, 175
  legal awards, 177
  reporting, 174–175
  transferring to RRSP, 220–221, 366
  what is not, 175
returns. *See* non-tax returns; tax returns
Revenue Canada. *See* Canada Customs and Revenue Agency
revocation of waiver, 327
rights, taxpayer's, 64
rights or things return, 50, 89
royalties, 104, 153
royalty trusts, 413
RRIFs, 133, 134
  donating to charity, 431
  foreign content limit, 430
  leaving to dependant child, 359
  self-directed, 405–406
  withdrawals from, 136–138, 408
RRSPs. *See also* Home Buyer's Plan; Lifelong Learning Plan
  advantages of, 9, 16, 27, 401–402
  borrowing to contribute to, 402
  catch-up contribution, 402
  child's contribution, 425
  claiming contributions, 406
  contribution in kind, 215, 404–405
  contribution limits, 216–218, 401
  converting to annuity or RRIF, 134
  deduction, 214–221
  definition, 214
  and dividends, 141
  donating to charity, 431
  eligible investments, 215–216
  and emigrating from Canada, 46
  employer-direct contributions, 403–404
  foreign content, 405–406, 430
  labour-sponsored investments, 414
  leaving to dependant child, 359
  locked-in, 120
  maximizing contribution, 26–27
  and newcomers to Canada, 49
  overcontributions, 218–219, 236, 404
  pre-authorized contribution plan, 403
  salary required for maximum contribution, 391
  self-directed, 215, 405–406
  setting up, 215
  spousal. *See* spousal RRPS
  tax savings provided by, 214–215
  transferring retiring allowances to, 120, 174–175, 220–221
RRSPs—withdrawals, 133–138, 406–408
  of overcontributions, 135
  under HBP or LLP, 23–24
  from unmatured RRSP, 134
  of unused contribution, 135, 401–402
rule of approximation. *See* Cohan rule
rulings, advanced tax, 71–72
Rulings and Interpretations directorate (Ottawa), 71

salaried employees, deductions, 369–370
salary earners return. *See* T1S-B return
salary vs. dividends, 391
salary/wages paid to family member(s), 348
sale of capital assets, self-employed, 196
sale of principal residence, 166–168
sales invoices, 55
sales tax, prov./terr., 369. *See also* GST; GST/HST rebate; Harmonized Sales Tax
same-sex partners, 260
Saskatchewan
  probate fees, 356
  tax credits, 293

tax rates, 15, 286
tax system, 292–293, 430
Saskatchewan Pension Plan Deduction, 221
Schedule 1: Federal Tax Calculation, 84, 275–283
Schedule 3: Capital Gains and Losses, 84, 156
Schedule 4: Statement of Investment Income, 84, 122
Schedules, T1 General (13 schedules), 84
scholarships, 175, 176
shareholders, corporate, 139–141
scoring return, 337–340
Section 87, Indian Act, 43
Section 153(1.1), Income Tax Act, 67
secured creditor, corporation, 389–390
securities, donating, 272. *See also* shares
self-directed RRSPs, 215, 405–406
self-employed vs. employed, factors determining, 97–99
self-employment. *See also* small business
accounting methods, 180–81
capital cost allowance, 192–198, 397
choosing year-end, 180
CPP/QPP contributions, 262, 281
EI premiums, 122
final tax return, 89
and GST, 181–183
and minimizing taxes, 180
and multiple jurisdictions, 288
paying salary/wages to family member(s), 348, 394–395
record-keeping, 186–187
tax implications of, 179–207
self-employment—income
business income, 183
deductible expenses, 187–192
eligible capital property, 200
farming and fishing income, 184, 202–206
form T2124, 183, 184–186
professional income, 184, 201–202
reporting, 183–192
underreporting, 337
seniors, income security programs. *See* income security programs
seniors, receiving pension income. *See* form T1S-A
severance allowance, 17, 212, 366
transferrring to RRSP, 220–221
shareholder and employee loans, 147–149
shareholders, 388, 392
shares, 10, 22. *See also* stock option and share deductions
calculating adjusted cost base, 164–165
capital gains/losses, 157
donating, 157, 158, 272
public company, 242, 272
qualified small business corporation, 168–169, 250
short forms. *See* special returns
signing bonuses, 104, 365
Simply Accounting, 187
SIN number. *See* social insurance number
small business—expenses *See also* self-employment
partially deductible/not deductible, 397–399
tax deductible, 396–397
small business—ownership structure
corporations, 388–393
partnerships, 386–387
sole proprietorships, 384–386
small business—tax planning tips
income splitting, 394–395
incorporating, 394
timing purchase/disposal, assets, 395–396
small business corporation (SBC), 226
small business deduction, 390–391
small business shares, qualified, 168–169
social assistance payments (line 145), 138, 244
social benefits repayment (OAS and EI clawbacks) (line 235), 237–238, 282
social insurance number, 48, 64
for child, 349
filing return without, 65
getting a number, 65
social security income, U.S., 118
software
small business bookkeeping, 186–187
tax preparation, 74–75, 81
tracking expenses, 56–57
sole proprietorships, 384–386
advantages of, 385
deductible home office expenses, 396–397
disadvantages of, 385–386
Spain
pensions from, 119
withholding tax rate, 36
special care expenses, 225–226
special clothing, 366
special projects, 340
special returns, 85–87
non-residents, 21
special taxation situations
bankruptcy, 51–53
death, 49–51
leaving Canada, 44–47
newcomers to Canada, 47–49
Status Indians, 43–44
special work site, deductions, 254

specialists, tax preparation. *See* tax advisors and preparers
specific purpose payments (support payments), 132–133
split CPP payments, 347–348
spousal credit (line 303), 260
spousal rollover rules, 358–359
spousal RRSPs, 219
contributing to, after death, 360
income splitting, 350
withdrawals from, 136
spousal support, 132, 230, 235–236
spousal trusts, 50, 358
spouse
death benefits, 177
dividends received by, claiming, 143
higher-income, 345, 347, 349
leaves Canada, 18
leaving assets to, 50, 357–359
paying a salary to, 348
same-sex, 260
sharing CPP with, 116–117
surviving, benefit, 115
transfers to, 346
travelling expenses, 101
tuition and education amounts transferred from, 269
Spouse's Allowance, 108. *See also* Widowed Spouse's Allowance
taxation of, 109
stamps (listed personal property), 160
Status Indians, 43–44, 87
stock dividends, 141
stock options, employee, 430
stock split, 141
stock options and share deductions, 241
Canadian-controlled private corporations, 242
public company shares, 242
stock option deductions, 242–244
straight line (CCA class), 129
stripped bonds, 146, 153, 158
student loans, 9, 176, 266–267
students, withdrawals from RESPs, 351
superannuation (defined), 117
supplementary unemployment benefit plan, 104
support payments
deductions, 230–231
new rules, 132
old rules, 132
specific purpose payments, 132–33
supporting persons living apart, and child care expenses, 224
Supreme Court of Canada, 341
surtax, federal, 15, 281, 429
surviving spouse's pension, 115. *See also* widowed spouse's allowance
survivor benefits, CPP, 115

• T •

tax advisors and preparers
accountants, 78
audits, 79
competence, 78, 79
finding, 78
preparers, 77
questions to ask, 78
tax avoidance, 342
tax brackets
federal, 6, 14
full indexation, 429
new legislation, 429, 431
tax breaks, 365–381
tax centres, 66
tax court, 340–341
tax credits. *See* specific credits
tax credits, non-refundable, 84, 259–272
tax credits, prov./terr., 25–26
tax deductions. *See* deductions
tax evasion, 11, 342, 422–423
penalty, 332
tax filing tips, 425–427
tax forms, sources for, 81–82. *See under* forms
Tax information, organizing. *See* record-keeping
Tax Information Phone Service (TIPS), 76
tax, interpretation. *See* Technical Interpretations
tax laws
administration and enforcement, 10–11, 63–64
new, 429–431
purposes of, 9–10
tax-on-income system (TONI), 13, 430
tax-on-tax systems, 12–13
tax planning tips
estate planning, 353–363
income splitting, 345–351
investments, 410–416
retirement strategies, 401–408
small business, 383–399
tax breaks for employees, 365–381
tax preparation
preparing your own return, 73–77
professionals. *See* tax preparers
software, 74–75, 81
tax preparation companies, 77
tax preparers
finding, 78
hiring, 77

hiring accountant, 78
questions to ask, 78–79
tax protestors, 422
tax publications, 63, 82
taxable benefits, 99–102
taxable capital gains, calculating, 165
TaxQuest, 75
tax rates. *See also* effective tax rate; marginal tax rate
federal, 14, 276
prov./terr., 15, 285–287
tax records, missing/damaged, reconstructing, 59–60
tax reduction, non-resident, 36, 38
tax refunds. *See* refunds
tax returns. *See also* non-tax returns
adjustments to, 328–329
bankruptcy, 91–93
deceased persons. *See* final tax return
e-filing, 79–80
failure to file, 21–22, 31, 50–51, 66, 88–89
scoring, 337–340
self-assessment, 11–12
special, 85–87
types, 83–93
who must file, 22–28
tax rulings, advanced, 71–72
tax schedules. *See* schedules
Tax Services Offices (TSOs), 66, 76
tax system—Canada, 9–12
concept of integration, 140
management/administration of. *See* Canada Customs and Revenue Agency
new legislation, 430
non-integrated, 140
provincial/territorial, 12–13
purposes of, 9–10
tax treaties, 19, 36, 68, 119, 256–57
taxable income, calculating, 239–257
taxation guides, 63
taxpayer's rights, 64, 342
TaxWiz, 74
taxation rules, 17–21
T-bills. *See* Treasury bills
Technical Interpretatins, 63, 71
tele-filing, 80–81
temporary life insurance, 414
temporary site, work at, 102
term life insurance, 414
terminal loss adjustment, 130
terminal loss, recapture of, 162
terminal tax return. *See* final tax return
termination payments, 104, 174
territories, tax rates. *See* provincial/territorial tax system
"Testamentary Spousal Trust" (IT-305), 91
testamentary trust, 49, 90, 150, 362–363
third-party, payments to, 132–133, 231
timing
incorporation, 390
purchases/disposal, assets, 394–395
TIPS, 76
training courses, 103, 366
transfer pricing, 39
transfers to adult child, 346
transfers for business purposes, 348–349
transfers to foreign trusts, 338
transfers, income-producing property, 345–346
transfers to minor children, 346
transfers to spouse, 346
transfers of tuition/education amount to another person, 268
transport-industry employees, 376
travel benefits deduction
designated cities, 256
northern residency, 255–256
travel expenses
reasonable allowances, 102
and rental properties, 126
spouse's, 101
travel to/from job, 102, 366
Treasury bills, 158
treaty countries, 36
trustee (bankruptcy), 52, 53, 93
trusts
foreign, 142
income of, 150
real estate investment, 412–413
spousals, 358
taxation of, 150–151
testamentary, 49, 150, 362–363
why use, 150
tuition, 9, 27, 84, 267–268, 269

• U •

Undepreciated capital cost (UCC), 196
Undeducted contributions, RRSP withdrawals, 135
underground economy, 340, 422
underreporting income, 337–39, 422
undeveloped land, tax treatment, 124–126
uniforms, 366
union dues, 221
unique tax treatment. *See* special taxation situations

United Kingdom
  pensions from, 119
  withholding tax rate, 36
United Nations, employment with, 257
universal life policy, 414, 415
university, foreign, donations to, 272
unmatured RRSPs, withdrawals from, 134
unused contribution room, RRSP, 401–402
U.S.-Canada tax treaty, 68
U.S. charities, donations to, 272
U.S. child support payments, 257
U.S. residents, money from Canadian RRSPs, 46
U.S. social security income, 118, 257

• V •

verification audits, 327, 335, 421
veterans pensions, 119
voluntary disclosures, 339, 341–342
vow of perpetual poverty, 257

• W •

wage earners, return. *See* TIS-B
wages, compared to dividends, 141
waivers, 326
War Veterans Act, 119
WaterStreet Group Inc., 75
widowed spouse's allowance, 108–109
will
  donating through, 360
  importance of having, 354
  setting up testamentary trust, 362, 363
withholding tax, 20, 21
  how amount determined, 67
  income not subject to, 68
  increasing amounts, 67
  reducing amount at source, 67
  transactions with non-residents, 34–39, 68
withholding tax rates, treaty countries, 36
work-in-progress (WIP), 201–202
work site, special, deductions, 254
workers' compensation, 138, 244
working abroad, government employee, 20
working child, allowance paid to, 349

• Y •

year-end
  corporations, 393
  self-employed, 180, 393
Yukon
  probate fees, 356
  T1 General, 85
  tax credits, 26, 306–307
  tax rates, 286
  tax system, 306
Yukon First Nations, 85